MW00805061

Leadership the Wesleyan Way

An Anthology for Shaping Leaders in Wesleyan Thought and Practice

Leadership in the Wesleyan Way

An Anthology for Shaping Leaders in Wesleyan Thought and Practice

Aaron Perry and Bryan Easley,
Editors

EMETH PRESS
www.emethpress.com

Leadership in the Wesleyan Way, An Anthology for Shaping Leaders in Wesleyan Thought and Practice

Copyright © 2016 Aaron Perry, Bryan Easley
Printed in the United States of America on acid-free paper

All rights reserved. No part of this book may be reproduced, or stored in a retrieval system or transmitted in any form or by any means, electronic, mechanical, photocopying, recording, scanning or otherwise, except as permitted by the 1976 United States Copyright Act, or with the prior written permission of Emeth Press. Requests for permission should be addressed to: Emeth Press, P. O. Box 23961, Lexington, KY 40523-3961. http://www.emethpress.com.

'

Library of Congress Cataloging-in-Publication Data

Names: Perry, Aaron Jenkins, editor. | Easley, Bryan R., editor.
Title: Leadership the Wesleyan way : an anthology for shaping leaders in
   Wesleyan thought and practice / Aaron Perry and Bryan Easley, editors.
Description: Lexington, Kentucky : Emeth Press, [2016]
Identifiers: LCCN 2016024654 | ISBN 9781609471026 (alk. paper)
Subjects: LCSH: Christian leadership--Methodist Church. | Methodist
   Church--Doctrines. | Wesley, John, 1703-1791.
Classification: LCC BX8349.L43 L43 2016 | DDC 253/.37--dc23
LC record available at https://lccn.loc.gov/2016024654

Interior design and cover by Bryan Easley
Front cover photo of Shanghai by kalafoto

Endorsements

"What is John Wesley's legacy for leaders of today? A common thread running through the diverse chapters of the Anthology gives us an answer. Wesleyan leadership is distinguished by the dynamic of the Holy Spirit to keep believing, being, and doing in balance and by the discipline of the faith community for its developmental process. With this unifying perspective for passion and compassion, responsibility and accountability, personal and social holiness, the Anthology multiplies in value as a resource for understanding our Wesleyan distinctive. Existing leaders will be reaffirmed in their calling and emerging leaders will be recruited to the ranks of those called Wesleyans."

David L. McKenna, Retired President of Asbury Theological Seminary, Seattle Pacific University, and Spring Arbor University

"A comprehensive, readable book, yet with excellent research, on shaping leaders both in thought and practice from a Wesleyan perspective. This is a book that has lasting impact reaching beyond the church. Leadership the Wesleyan Way is a culture-changing book on leadership that transcends the business model to a theological foundation. The many voices in this anthology blend to a beautiful harmony of Kingdom missional focus for the 21st century."

Jo Anne Lyon, former General Superintendent, The Wesleyan Church; interim Vice President, Wesley Seminary at Indiana Wesleyan University

"This substantive volume captures insights on a variety of topics and from a breadth of scholars, some familiar and others new. While the explicitness of the connection may vary, the "Wesleyan Way" permeates the pages. My first temptation was to skim the table of contents and read only those chapters that appealed to me. I disciplined myself to read them all, and am glad I did — some of the richest 'ahas' were found in unexpected places."

Wayne Schmidt, General Superintendent of The Wesleyan Church

"Drs. Aaron Perry and Bryan Easley have assembled an all-star cast of contributors who offer a wealth of insight into leadership from a Wesleyan perspective. Much like turning the facets of a diamond slowly in the sunlight, there are brilliant and fresh perspectives in every chapter. I am glad to recommend this book to leaders and Wesleyans everywhere."

Mark Gorveatte, author of *Lead Like Wesley* and Indiana Central District Superintendent for The Wesleyan Church.

"Leadership the Wesleyan Way *invites readers to think about a distinctive Wesleyan style of leadership through the writings of 30 leaders drawn from across the full range of the Wesleyan tradition. The anthology's uniting principle is that Wesleyan leadership, whether in theory or practice, is grounded in deep and faithful Christian discipleship. The varied essays draw on the rich resources of theology, Biblical studies, and leadership theory. Whether a beginner or veteran in the area of leadership, this collection will not only challenge the reader, but provide an extensive list of bibliographic resources for further exploration. We should be grateful to Aaron Perry and Bryan Easley whose efforts have made this available to leaders both inside and outside the Wesleyan tradition.*"

Shirley Mullen, President, Houghton College

"*Aaron and Bryan have done a great service for Wesleyans by collecting chapters that illuminate how leadership can be carried out in the Wesleyan spirit. They include well-known writers and ministry practitioners in a variety of fields across the North American Wesleyan tradition, and give the reader keen insights into the practice and teaching of leadership.*"

Sharon Drury, Faculty Emerita in Org Leadership, Indiana Wesleyan University

"*This book should have existed years ago. In a way, Aaron Perry, Bryan Easley, and colleagues make clear, it did: for the broader Wesleyan family has always brought distinctive gifts to the practice of Christian leadership. We just didn't call it that. After Christendom we have no time for the implicit. These essays boldly and beautifully show that we Wesleyans have gifts for the broader church and world. Perhaps God is not done with our revival yet.*"

Jason Byassee, Butler Chair in Homiletics and Biblical Hermeneutics, Vancouver School of Theology, British Columbia

Contents

ORIENTATION: WESLEYAN LEADERSHIP IN THE POSTMODERN WORLD

1   Leadership the Wesleyan Way 15
    Aaron Perry

2   What Makes Leadership Wesleyan?... 27
    Lovett H. Weems, Jr.

3   Wesleyan Leadership in a Postmodern Context 33
    Rob Muthiah

4   The Potential of Wesleyan Leadership: A Reformed Perspective 45
    Richard Mouw

BIBLICAL & THEOLOGICAL REFLECTIONS

5   A Theology of Leadership for Wesleyans.. 57
    Christopher Bounds

6   Old Testament Models for Leading the Wesleyan Way........................ 71
    Jerome Van Kuiken

7   New Testament Perspectives on Leadership...................................... 83
    Abson Prédestin Joseph

8   The Cartography of Kingdom Leadership: Charting a New Course 93
    David F. Smith

9   Holiness, Power, and Mission 107
    Matthew I. Ayars

10 Women in Ministry: The "Problem Texts" 119
    Ken Schenck

11 The Leader as Shepherd 131
    Jennifer Ellison

12 A Wesleyan Sacramental Spirituality of Leadership 141
    Robert Moore-Jumonville

HISTORICAL PERSPECTIVES

13 John Wesley's Practical Divinity..163
    William Willimon

14 The Leadership of John Wesley 177
    Daniel L. Burnett

15 The Leadership of Francis Asbury 189
    Bryan R. Easley

16 Wesleyan Pragmatism in Leadership 207
    Thomas Tumblin

17 A Wesleyan Critique of Political Leadership......................................217
    Charles Gutenson

18 Institutional Thinking and Living in the Wesleyan Tradition 225
    L. Gregory Jones and Laceye C. Warner

LEADERSHIP THEORY AND PRINCIPLES

19 Authentic & Ethical Leadership 241
    Tim Beuthin

20 Transformational Leadership..255
    Priscilla Hammond

21 Contingency Theory 267
    Aaron Perry

22 Shared Leadership and Expert Followers 279
    Bryan R. Easley

23 Leading Well Under Pressure...291
    Rob McKenna and Amy Nagley

24 Gender and Organizational Leadership 303
    Aaron Perry

25 Adaptive Wesleyan Spiritual Leadership 317
    Bryan Sims

LEADERSHIP IN MINISTRY

26 Rethinking Servant Leadership 333
    Kevin Mannoia

27 Leading in an Urban Context..341
    Richard L. Gray

28 Leading Ministry Teams and Small Groups..355
    Daryl Smith

29 Leadership through Preaching..365
    Lenny Luchetti

30 Ethical Leadership and Gifts..377
    Aaron Perry and Eric R. Hallett

31 Clergywomen and Ministry Leadership 383
    Beth K. Armstrong

32 Challenge of Board Leadership 401
    Brian S. Simmons

Preface

Leadership continues to be a topic of interest. Yet, Wesleyans are not necessarily known for leadership reflections. The Wesleyan movement, however, embodies various practices and values that are relevant for leadership in today's world. As Wesleyans, we have a unique voice and history out of which we can significantly contribute to both the study and practice of effective and wise leadership. This contribution is broader than just the boundaries of our own historical tradition. Leaders from all traditions, not just Wesleyans, can benefit from the unique focus and passion for active discipleship, spiritual vitality, and community life rooted in the Triune God that characterizes the Wesleyan movement.

This anthology aims to consider leadership from a Wesleyan perspective that integrates rich theological and biblical reflection, historical assessment, and contemporary theory, practice, and application. The following chapters — from a variety of Wesleyan scholars and practitioners — offer reflections from biblical studies and theology, address contemporary challenges of leadership including chapters on change, organizational complexity, women in ministry, and multi-ethnic contexts, and explore leadership practices and principles found in Wesleyan history. Our contributors examine the current context of leadership, the foundations of Wesleyan leadership through biblical and historical lenses, engage with various leadership theories, address contemporary leadership challenges, and offer useful, practical wisdom for engaging such leadership in the world that is.

The book is intended for adult learners, pastors, and ministerial students. We believe this type of anthology can fill a gap in the wider Wesleyan world of leadership thinking. We want the book to entice current and emerging leaders to further reading, action, and personal growth. Our goal is to help practitioners think and thinkers practice in the richness of life in the Spirit. It is our hope that this volume will expose you to meaningful leadership theory, encourage you to tackle leadership challenges, and convince you, as we are convinced, that the time is right for Wesleyans to emerge as leaders.

Dr. Aaron Perry, Marion, Indiana; Ontario, Canada
Dr. Bryan Easley, Tulsa, Oklahoma

Contributors

Armstrong, Beth K. (PhD). Leadership development consultant and adjunct faculty member, Central Christian College of Kansas.

Ayars, Matt. (PhD candidate). Completing PhD dissertation in Old Testament at St. John's College of Nottingham (UK). President of Emmaus Biblical Seminary in northern Haiti; author, *Salvation in Fresh Perspective* and *Holy is a Four Letter Word*.

Beuthin, Tim. (PhD). Professor in the Department of Leadership Studies, Indiana Wesleyan University.

Bounds, Christopher. (PhD). Professor of Wesleyan Studies and Gardner Professor for Promotion and Holiness, Asbury University.

Burnett, Daniel L. (DMin). Pastor of Olde Towne Community Church, Ridgeland, Mississippi; author, *In the Shadow of Aldersgate.*

Easley, Bryan R. (PhD). Co-editor. Dean of Online Education & faculty member, Oklahoma Wesleyan University; adjunct professor, Nazarene Bible College.

Ellison, Jennifer. (ThM). Associate Outreach Pastor, All Shores Wesleyan Church in Spring Lake, Michigan; adjunct online instructor for Western Seminary.

Gray, Richard L. (PhD). Professor of Leadership and Christian Ministries, Asbury Theological Seminar; Author, *Beneath the Lode of the Cross, The Personal Spiritual Development Analysis Guide*, and a series of children's books featuring Evangel the Smallest Angel.

Gutenson, Charles (Chuck). (PhD*)*. Church consultant and former COO, Sojourners.

Hallett, Eric R. (DMin). Lead Pastor of Centennial Road Church, Brockville, Ontario. Ministry training faculty, FLAME program of The Wesleyan Church.

Hammond, Priscilla. (PhD). Adjunct professor of business, Southern Wesleyan University and Oklahoma Wesleyan University; Teaches ministerial preparation courses as an ordained minister of The Wesleyan Church.

Jones, L. Gregory. (PhD). Williams Professor of Theology and Christian Ministry, Duke Divinity School; Executive Director, A Foundation for Theological Education.

Joseph, Abson. (PhD*)*. Associate Professor of New Testament and Ancient Languages, Indiana Wesleyan University School of Theology and Ministry.

Luchetti, Lenny. (DMin). Associate Professor of Proclamation and Christian Ministries, Wesley Seminary at Indiana Wesleyan University.

Mannoia, Kevin. (PhD). Chaplain and Professor of Ministry at Azusa Pacific University, as well as Founder and Chair of the Wesleyan Holiness Consortium.

McKenna, Rob. (PhD). Chair of the Department of Industrial-Organizational Psychology, Seattle Pacific University; Executive Director of the Center for Leadership Research & Development.

Moore-Jumonville, Robert. (PhD). Professor of Christian Spirituality, Spring Arbor University; Pastor of Pope United Methodist Church.

Mouw, Richard. (PhD). Professor of Faith and Public Life, Fuller Theological Seminary.

Muthiah, Robert. (PhD). Professor of Practical Theology, Azusa Pacific Seminary at Azusa Pacific University.

Nagley, Amy. Completing PhD in Industrial-Organizational Psychology at Seattle Pacific University with research, teaching, and consulting experience in holistic well-being and engagement.

Perry, Aaron. (PhD). Co-editor. Assistant Professor of Pastoral Care, Wesley Seminary at Indiana Wesleyan University.

Schenck, Ken. (PhD). Professor of New Testament and Ancient Languages, Indiana Wesleyan University.

Simmons, Brian S. (EdD). Associate Provost of Online Studies, Columbia International University.

Smith, Daryl. (EdD). Associate Professor of Mentored Ministry and Christian Leadership, Asbury Theological Seminary-Florida Dunnam campus; Team leader of The Orlando Fellowship, an incarnational, missional community.

Smith, David. (PhD). Academic Dean, Wesley Seminary at Indiana Wesleyan University.

Sims, Bryan. (PhD). Associate Professor of Leadership and Lay Equipping, Director of Center for Lay Mobilization & Lifelong Learning, Asbury Theological Seminary; Leadership & Organizational Change Coach at Spiritual Leadership, Inc.

Tumblin, Thomas F. (PhD). Associate Vice President for Global Initiatives and Professor of Leadership, Asbury Theological Seminary.

Van Kuiken, Jerome. (PhD). Associate Professor of Ministry and Christian Thought, Oklahoma Wesleyan University.

Warner, Laceye C. (PhD). Associate Professor of the Practice of Evangelism and Methodist Studies, Duke Divinity School.

Weems, Jr., Lovett H. (DMin). Distinguished Professor of Church Leadership and Director of the Lewis Center for Church Leadership, Wesley Theological Seminary.

Willimon, William H. (STD). Professor of the Practice of Christian Ministry, Duke Divinity School; retired United Methodist Bishop and author.

Part 1

ORIENTATION: WESLEYAN LEADERSHIP IN THE POSTMODERN WORLD

1

Leadership the Wesleyan Way

Aaron Perry

Leadership involves goals, relationships, and processes. Leaders must observe, interpret, and act. Each of these components are necessary and must be done in order. While it is easy to not theologically about them, Wesleyan theology and history presents a fruitful dialogue between the components, formation, and practice of leadership that lets us practice it rightly. The time is right for Wesleyan leadership — marked by Commonality, Conflict, Conversation, Cultural Creation, and Charity — to emerge as a culture-changing redemptive force in both church and society.

JENNY WAS SHORTER than most, but of stronger will than all. Our class president, Jenny was willing to risk stepping out from her peers to lead. On one such occasion, she provided the first peer-to-peer leadership lesson I can remember learning. Sitting with excited soon-to-be graduates discussing our senior trip, I heard the announcement that we would be selling raffle tickets as a fundraiser. But there was a problem: I didn't sell raffle tickets (gasp!) because that, in my pietistic tradition, was a form of gambling. I knew that buying 3 tickets for 99 cents was going to lead the purchaser down a troubled path. An anonymous voice in the gallery objected to this decreed organized gambling and the raffle champion quickly provided an out: If anyone didn't want to sell raffle tickets, they didn't have to. It was then that Jenny showed leadership. While her legs barely reached to the floor as she sat at the stage's edge, her voice carried to the back of the room. "No! We're all going on our senior trip, so we're all going to sell raffle tickets." Many nodded and agreed. Peer leadership was happening all around me, but it was not happening within me. My first lesson in peer-to-peer leadership was also my first lesson in peer-to-peer followership. Sitting in that auditorium, I took a principled stand: Not only would I not sell raffle tickets, but I would not go on my senior trip.

I have reflected on this story multiple times through my own leadership responsibilities. What I have reconsidered and seen displayed numerous times is that there is a dance between the leaders and followers. Sometimes the way dances is not the way the other partner wants to dance. It is awkward, difficult, and ultimately futile. But sometimes there is a match and the dance is a beautiful expression of teamwork, cooperation, and unity. I was not willing to dance with Jenny, but could the dance have been changed just enough that I would have joined in without radically changing her rhythm and style?

The dance of leadership and followership is not limited to relational dynamics and personalities. It is cultural, economic, philosophical, and even spiritual. When various factors combine and the context is right for a kind of leadership, then followers give permission and affirmation in an expression of community, productivity, and purpose. Every generation provides such a context.

I am convinced that the 21st century is a century primed for Wesleyan leadership. I could develop different lines of evidence from statistics and stories to show this opinion is true, but I prefer for this conviction to develop intuitively in you as Wesleyan leadership is fleshed out through this book. John Maxwell speaks of the Law of Intuition.[1] Leaders have ways of reading the world from within. There are promptings that leaders have not only because the prompting is *true*, but because the prompting is *good*. The sense I have that Wesleyan leadership is primed for this era and this era is primed for Wesleyan leadership is not simply because it is truly happening, but because it *should* happen. It is a *good thing* to happen. I do not simply want you to share the opinion that Wesleyan leadership is emerging, but to share the conviction that Wesleyan leadership must emerge. In what follows, I will introduce you to several key ideas for this conviction to develop, including leadership, discipleship, and Wesleyan leadership. Hopefully, these ideas will clarify, encourage, and inspire you to participate in this leadership dance in a uniquely Wesleyan way.

What is Leadership?

"Leadership is an art," said leadership guru Max DePree. Rather than a specific set of formulaic steps, leadership is a "weaving of relationships."[2] For Wesley, the weaving of relationships in societies, classes, and especially the bands was both the means of discipleship and the source of leadership. The societies, classes, and bands were different groups that Wesley helped to set up as contexts of discipleship. The societies were essentially local churches, made up of men and women, who were taught in structured ways. The gatherings included singing, prayer, and Scripture. Classes were groups of 10-12 of men and women where leaders were role models, although not people above any kind of fault. These groups sought to encourage members and inquire into the spiritual life of people. The bands were same-sex groups, smaller than classes, which delved more deeply into the Christian life. Each of these settings provided a different kind and set of relationships. In leadership, the weaving of relationships is not simply for relationship, however. Leadership is also way of helping others come to understand and agree about what needs to be done, and of making individual and group efforts to those ends possible.[3]

We can summarize leadership with three words: *goals, relationships,* and *processes*. Leadership is achieving goals through relationships by processes. The work of leadership—agreement, commitment, and cooperation from multiple parties—is complex. Sounds simple enough, but if you have ever worked to get two people to agree on something, then you know it isn't that simple, after all. If you have never had trouble getting people to agree, then take a family vacation with more than one family! Even if there is agreement about *what* to do, *how* it should be done can be another hurdle. Leadership complexity grows exponentially because many decisions and tasks involve not just two people, but two (or more) groups, and even multiple organizations.

There can be teams (relationships) and processes, but without goals there is no intention or aim. This is like a sports team that prepares for every game, but does not care to win a championship. There can be processes and goals that are accomplished, but without teams the basic component of leadership—relationships—is missing. There are two forms that leadership without teams takes. First, a person can accomplish a lot on their own, but they are not considered a leader without influencing others in what is accomplished. Second, a person may implement processes and coordinate people who are not a team. This kind of accomplishment can look like leadership, but it is closer to slavery. Finally, there may be healthy group dynam-

---

"We can summarize leadership with three words: goals, relationships, and processes. Leadership is achieving goals through relationships by processes"

---

ics and impressive accomplishments, but without processes more could be accomplished. Process is part of leadership because processes help goals get achieved faster, smarter, and easier.

We can summarize the leader's responsibility with another three words: *observe, interpret,* and *apply*. Max DePree said that the first act of leadership is to define reality.[4] Leaders must learn to observe the present world. This involves a full range of senses. Leaders listen to the hopes, complaints, concerns, fears, and aims of other people. Listening helps leaders grasp reality through the cultural language embedded both in one's own culture and cultures leaders encounter.[5] Leaders observe so that they may see what others do not see. No leader occupies a perfect vantage point from which the whole world can be seen at once, so consistent and creative observation is absolutely necessary.

Yet leaders are not simply data hounds.[6] Leaders do not simply observe; leaders must also interpret. Leaders are sense-makers. Leaders must understand what they are hearing, seeing, and sensing. Suppose a community has an undeniable lack of educational opportunities and facilities. What does this mean? Does it mean that education is not valued? Does it mean that other goods are more urgent? Does it mean that an opportunity for education is present? Suppose a mentor observes a disheveled client. What does this mean? Does it mean they have been working out of order? Does it mean they are having interpersonal relationship challenges? Does it mean they are lazy or got up too late? When DePree says that leaders must define reality, it means there is both observation and interpretation.

Finally, leaders must act. Leaders do not simply gather data (observe) and figure out what it means (interpret). Leaders must act in response to reality. Theologically, this is because the Kingdom of God is not fully present. Leaders must act because there is an emerging future that God prefers.

Learning Leadership

How do relationships, goals, and processes all interact? Multiple leadership theories abound that seek to explain *why* one person can get another person to do, think, or feel something. Theories such as the Great Man theory can focus on the heroic status of the leader. Some people are just great and they are the ones who can prompt another's action. A variety of trait theories look at leader attributes (e.g., height, hair color, or education). Behavioral theories focus on what leaders actually do, such as visioning, listening, serving, coordinating, or empathizing. Situational or contingency theories consider differences in contexts or situations as an explanation of how leadership works. Theories of leadership such as spiritual leadership, authentic leadership, servant leadership also examine relationships. Do people follow because it is mutually beneficial or because the leader can improve the follower's talent? Think back to the people you followed. Why did you follow them? You likely followed for different reasons with different people at different times.

In the face of this complexity, we also hear simple summaries such as the axiom popularized by Ken Blanchard, and then John Maxwell, that leadership is influence.[7] After all, without influence, there is no leadership. Because leadership is influence, it means that anyone can grow in leadership. Regardless of whether one is tall or short, more naturally a talker or a listener, or always sees the best in others, people can learn how to lead better because people can learn to influence others through skills, attitudes, and behaviors.

Faith traditions influence leadership, too, because they influence the way leaders see the world, how they interpret the world, and what actions they believe are necessary. I am a Christian of the Wesleyan tradition. I have learned to live a certain way because I have been influenced by the leadership of John Wesley, Anglican priest of the 18th century, who still influences the leadership of the movement that bears his name. The remainder of this book provides a variety of perspectives on the nature and value of a Wesleyan perspective on leadership. Let me begin this discussion.

Discipleship as Leadership

There's a way to lead like a Wesleyan and it isn't about being first or going in front. It's about following. It's about discipleship. Early in the development of the Methodists, the Holy Club—the small group of Wesley's friends, including his brother Charles, that focused on personal growth in holiness—would visit the sick, imprisoned, and elderly.[8] The leaders of the Wesleyan movement were concerned with a *method* of being disciples, discipleship, and a disciple-making structure.[9] From this, the movement soon was referred to as the "Methodists." The Wesleyan movement was concerned about making disciples before it was concerned about making leaders.

Leadership as discipleship is not unique to John Wesley, however. The broader Christian faith makes clear that leadership is primarily about followership because Christian faith is about following Jesus. In other words, Christianity's leader is already established. The Gospels of Matthew, Mark, and Luke all record Jesus' challenge to his disciples' contemporary leadership models. Rather than behaving like lords, Jesus says his followers should be servants. Luke (22:7-30) captures these words in the midst of communion and betrayal. Mark (10:35-45) places the paradigm shift just after a bold request for authority and power from James and John. Matthew (20:20-28) uses the same story as Mark, but provides even more detail: The request comes through the men's mother! Each story challenges the typical expectation of lordship and leadership by pointing to Jesus himself. Any efforts to lead in the Christian faith must be grounded in the desire to serve, to offer more than received, to give for the sake of others. Leadership *for* Jesus only happens by following *after* Jesus.

The Wesleyan movement grasps this leadership posture because it is a discipleship movement. From its roots, the Wesleyan movement was filled with people who sought to submit every aspect of the Christian life in service to God. Leadership is no different. Wesleyan leadership is not primarily about tactics, strategies, or systems. It is about discipleship.

Theology of Leadership

A disciple's approach to leadership is different from a non-disciple's approach to leadership. At first glance, theology and leadership can be two subjects that do not connect. But when leadership is primarily discipleship, then it is not simply concerned with relationships, goals, and processes, but *right* goals, *godly* relationships, and *holy* processes.

Theologically considered, goals are right when they contribute to the reality that God desires. A goal that is not in line with God's desires is not a right goal. Right goals must be in line with the unfolding story God is telling. If a goal is not part of the unfolding story of God, then it is not a right goal and leadership in its direction is therefore ungodly leadership. Goals in Wesleyan leadership are about achieving the parts of the future that God desires.

Wesleyan leadership is also grounded in the accomplishing right goals the *way* God intends. The accomplishment of godly goals in ungodly ways is ungodly leadership. People are not to be used for the purposes of leaders. Neither are unfair practices justified if they are used to achieve good goals.

The Marks of Wesleyan Leadership

Wesleyan leadership is different from others forms of leadership because while other forms of leadership may emphasize good goals, meaningful relationships, and just processes, Wesleyan leadership keeps God at the center because it is about discipleship. With these foundations of leadership and theology in place, let me suggest five markers of Wesleyan leadership. Wesleyan leadership that emerges into the 21st century in the way and direction God desires will be marked by:

Commonality—21st century Wesleyan leadership will maintain a conviction that leaders emerge from all kinds of people.

Conflict—21st century Wesleyan leadership will exhibit wise courage to work in difficult situations, even when there is opposition.

Conversation—21st century Wesleyan leadership will continue its tradition of mutual learning and growth. Wesleyan leadership will be marked with an ability to listen, understand, speak, and dialogue. This is especially important in increasingly multi-cultural and multi-religious contexts and ever increasing social media.

Cultural Creation—21st century Wesleyan leadership will inspire and create goods that can be shared publically within and across cultures for common good.

Charity—21st century Wesleyan leadership will be rooted in love. Love is the start, the end, and the journey of leadership.

Commonality

Commonality means sharing attributes and features. Wesleyans believed that people were alike—needing God and needing to hear the Gospel message. As a result, the Wesleyan movement did not distinguish between types of people—either for discipleship or leadership.

From the beginning, Wesleyan leadership was marked by the experience of community in physical communal gatherings of various forms and sizes. Sharing in mission and relationship with other people, even ones at first glance different from each other, was reflective of God's intended harmony in salvation. Wesley learned the value of community from the Puritans and wanted to develo[could be thought of as a "sweet society."[10] Thus, the discipleship ⟨ made up of all sorts of people from all sorts of backgrounds, inclu smiths, barbers; men and women. The value for diversity is wh of leaders. Shepherds emerged *from* various group contexts ar of various ministries for many different people.[11]

This did not mean that every individual was tagged for leadership, but that there were no boundaries of background, gender, or education as to what kind of person had leadership potential. A recent speaker at a local Rotary club shared this Wesleyan lesson. After visiting a remote community of an ethnic minority, the leader confessed his surprise at finding good leadership in the small community. Many of us nodded that finding good leadership in such a remote place was surprising. Then he captured the poignancy of the moment: "Why was I surprised?" Indeed, why would any of us have been surprised? The Wesleyan movement, because it made the path of discipleship wide, also made the path to leadership wide. Leadership was potentially common to many people from many backgrounds.

Commonality helped to widen the source of good leaders and was, in part, a necessary strategy. In other words, it was not just *right* it was *wise*. Wesley was aware that leadership "demanded awareness of people and their needs."[12] Leaders were reproduced because of a conviction every person should receive support and ministry in their discipleship. For Wesley, leadership emerged *from* the people and *for* the people. Simple structures and significant mission were the convictions for common leadership.[13]

Two main groups provided leadership development. First, there were classes. These groups of 12-20 people with pastoral care, teaching, and evangelism, and were ideal contexts for leadership development.[14] Second, the bands, same-gender groups of 3-4 members, were useful for leadership development. Because bands were both for men and women, it meant that women were trained for leadership in these discipleship contexts. The simplicity but replicability of the structures meant that Wesleyan leadership was necessarily focused on training and delegating for leadership in a consistent way.[15] Thus, the conviction of commonality that led to Wesleyan leadership was not simply an ideal, but a necessity for the movement to grow and continue.

21st century Wesleyans must share these convictions. The movement is too big to control all emerging leaders. Likewise, leaders will come from every kind of person being discipled in the movement of Jesus in the Wesleyan way. The needs of leadership emerge from people and the source of leadership is from the people, too. 21st century Wesleyan leaders will eliminate barriers to leadership by empowering and convening people.

⌐nflict

Wesley didn't fear a fight. His leadership unfolded in the context of conflicts between Calvinism and Arminianism, antinomianism (lawlessness)[16], slavery (which Wesley called an "execrable villainy which is the scandal of religion, of England, and of human nature"[17]), and the American Revolution. While Wesley could be domineering in leadership style[18], on the whole Wesley's leadership, even in conflict, could be described using the theory of transformational leadership.[19] By this, I mean that Wesley inspired action, stimulated thinking, and developed other leaders to influence the shape of the future, including a vision of slavery-free England.

The 21st century has thus far been a century of theological and cultural conflict around sexuality, security versus privacy, natural resources and the environment, immigration, and, in unique ways to the Anglican, Catholic, Presbyterian denominations, ordination. National and international conflicts regarding energy, religion, and terrorism dominate the news and internet. The development and deployment of traditional, news, and social media is not only a kind of conflict onto itself, but enables greater forms of conflict. There is Wesleyan precedent for engaging in conflict. Leaders of the Wesleyan spirit will be marked with a willingness for strategic conflict.

Conversation

Conversation was a key part of early Wesleyan discipleship. The practice of confession in the Wesleyan bands allowed for accountability without condemnation.[20] The leaders who emerged from the bands and the classes were formed because they conversed in the journey of discipleship with other disciples. The language learned was formed through singing, prayer, and teaching that happened in societies. They shared daringly with each other and listened deeply to each other.

Wesley's own leadership was developed through careful conversation with himself through diaries and journals. Wesley consistently evaluated his own growth, motives, and use of time for the purpose of growing in holiness. Wesley's interaction between his feelings, his reflections, and Scripture created a sort of conversation. At one point, Wesley reflected on the fact that he would doubt the truth of Christian faith and the meaningfulness of his life in the midst of a storm. Wesley engaged in the conversation by asking the Pauline question, "Oh! Who will deliver me from this fear of death?" and by asking his journaling self, "Where he should flee" from this fear. Yet Wesley concluded by encouraging himself to continue on in the work of the Lord.[21]

Wesleyan leadership is formed through conversation. It is formed in community where there is mutual sharing and interpersonal communication. Wesleyan leaders will share conviction and skill in conversation—listening, confessing, encouraging, expressing forgiveness, and correcting. This kind of leadership is urgent given the growing interchange of ideas, values, and religions. The end of Christendom means the end of gatekeepers. Network television, the Internet, and immediate social media allow an increasingly free exchange of ideas. Wesleyan leaders must be comfortable and skilled at listening and understanding in conversation and sharing their own values and convictions through conversation. If leadership is influence, there has never been a greater time for influence through conversation.

Cultural Creation

Leaders create[22] and Wesleyan leaders create like Wesleyans. This does not necessarily mean that Wesleyans are creative in the sense of being *original*. It means that Wesleyans *create*. It means that Wesleyan leadership should make a difference by contributing to culture and the common good. Wesley faced poverty, poor working conditions, and educational challenges, and worked to remedy these ills by creating cultural goods. Wesley wrote and produced sermons, hymns, tracts, medical pamphlets, and letters to encourage, empower, and educate. These efforts as a social movement sought real social improvements through improved families and organizations,[23] decreased alcohol use, increased education in trades, and increased personal finance skills.[24] The Wesleyan movement established schools for adults, free education for the poor, Sunday Schools for children who worked during the week; challenged economic issues of (taxation for support of poor); built clinics for the poor; and argued for equal treatment of slaves to celebrate Lord's supper in worship.[25] Wesley made a difference in culture by creating goods for culture.

Creative Wesleyan leadership seeks to advance a "social mission to serve a larger good."[26] Jones refers to this as social entrepreneurship. This leadership bent adopts a social mission, serves through real opportunities, is innovative and adaptive, learns to meet people's needs, and acts with abundance in mind. The results of social entrepreneurship marked with creativity in 18th England and 19th century United States included educational institutions, hospitals, and health care organizations.[27]

For leaders willing to be sensitive to the ails and ills of the world and able to make appropriate interpretations, the Wesleyan spirit of creativity can be reinvigorating in creating cultural goods. Such a spirit of creativity and "social entrepreneurship would reinvigorate pastors, congregations and Christian leaders with a commitment to mission."[28]

Andy Crouch, who self-identifies as a Wesleyan Anglican, argues that culture is what people make *of* the world (interpretation) and what they *make* of the world itself (various goods, artifacts, practices, institutions).[29] Crouch says that cultural change does not happen strictly through critiquing culture, but through *making* culture.[30] Leadership in the Wesleyan spirit is concerned with the typical leadership actions of seeing and interpreting and then acting in a creative way.

Charity (Love)

In the context of Wesleyanism, charity (love) is concerned with sanctification, the disciple's perfection in love. Sanctification is about the disciple being empowered in the whole heart with the love of God for God and his creation.[31] Sanctification sets people free from the *power* and *nature* of sin to love so freely. The Methodist movement flowed from the inward transformation of the disciple—their conversion of heart, lived and achieved in societies and classes.[32] For Wesley, charity was a defining characteristic of leadership. Wesley's organizational leadership was defined by love not only for those inside the organization, but for those outside the organization.[33] Wesley's famous dictum, "I look upon the whole world as my parish"[34] captures this sense of love.

Earlier I gave three key words on the role of leadership: observe, interpret, apply. While love may naturally be associated with *action*, love is also about *observation* and *interpretation*. If the true observer of the world is God, who is love, then love is the appropriate manner of observation. Leaders lead by being formed in love and seeing through as people formed in love. Further, love is the best hermeneutic—the best way to make sense of what a leader sees. Love never assumes bad motives, but love also seeks wisdom. Love allows the leader to see the world as God sees it and to interpret it from the right mindset. Sanctification—the formation of the disciple in love—allows the leader to act not only with proper motivation, but with *power*.[35]

Wesleyan leadership in the 21st century must continue to be marked by love. Love must be the lens by which the world is interpreted. Love must be the pursuit of the disciple as they become like Christ. Love must be the impetus to risk leading. Love is the beginning, the end, and the journey.

Conclusion

When you look at the world around you, do you see how badly it needs leaders who will listen, fight, create, and love? The world involves conflict and has unprecedented opportunities for conversation. Will you listen and speak respectfully? The context is primed for Wesleyan leadership to emerge and, through cultural creations, to influence and shape the future in a godly way to conform, by the power of God, to God's desire. The Wesleyan way of leadership is laid out in front of those who would seek to be formed in the power of God for the love of God and neighbor. The way is laid out; the path lies ahead.

Aaron Perry, PhD, is Assistant Professor of Pastoral Care at Wesley Seminary at Indiana Wesleyan University in Marion, Indiana. He recently served as Associate Pastor at Centennial Road Church in Ontario, Canada.

Bibliography

Bentley, W. "The Formation of Christian Leaders: A Wesleyan Approach." *Koers* 75, no. 3 (2010): 558.

Bergquist, L., and A. Karr. *Church Turned Inside Out.* San Francisco, CA: Jossey-Bass, 2010.

Bounds, Christopher. "Setting Holiness Too High." April 29, 2013. Acessed Feb. 2016. http://bit.ly/1WRTEBL

Collins, Kenneth. *A Real Christian: The Life of John Wesley.* Nashville: Abingdon Press, 2010.

Crouch, Andy. *Culture Making: Recovering our Creative Calling.* Downer's Grove: Intervarsity Press, 2013.

DePree, Max. *Leadership is an Art.* New York: Doubleday, 1989.

Frabrycky, L. M., and A. Joyce. "Playing God: An Interview with Andy Crouch." *Washing Institute for Faith, Vocation, and Culture.* 2014. Accessed Jan. 2016. http://bit.ly/1X3vvJ6

Henderson, Michael. *A Model for Making Disciples.* Nappannee, IN: Evangel Publishing House, 1997.

Hucks, J. "John Wesley and the Eighteenth Century Methodist Movement: A Model for Effective Leadership". PhD dissertation, Regent University, 2013

Jones, L.G. "Bold Initiative." *Christian Century*, November 27, no. 33 (2007): 33.

Maxwell, John. *Developing the Leader Within You.* Nashville, TN: Thomas Nelson, 2005.

—. *The 21 Irrefutable Laws of Leadership.* Nashville: Thomas Nelson, 2007.

Sumner, G. "John Wesley and the Common Thread of Modern Anglican Mission." *The Living Church* 2014. Accessed Jan. 2016. http://www.livingchurch.org/wesley-and-anglican-mission.

Tennent, Timothy. "Reimagining the Gospel." timothytennant.com. April 30, 2012. http://timothytennent.com/ 2012/04/30/re-imagining-the-gospel/.

Tennant, Timothy. "Four Great Wesleyan Distinctives (Part II)." timothytennant.com. Sept. 25, 2014 http://timothytennent.com/2014/09/ 25/four-great-wesleyan-distinctives/.

Warner, "Making Disciples in the Wesleyan Tradition: Practicing the Means of Grace," *Quarterly Review: A Journal for Theological Resources on Ministry*, 23:2 (2003): 164.

Wesley, John. *The Works of Rev. John Wesley*, 3rd edition, vol. 1. London: Wesleyan Methodist Book Room, 1972. Grand Rapids: Baker, reprinted 2007.

Withrow, L. "Disciples for the Future: Small Groups and Vital Faith Development." *Quarterly Review: A Journal for Theological Resources on Ministry* 23, no. 2 (2003): 141-150.

Yukl, Gary. *Leadership in Organizations*, 5th Edition. Upper Saddle River: Prentice-Hall, 2004

Chapter 1 Notes

[1] Maxwell, *The 21 Irrefutable Laws of Leadership.*

[2] DePree, *Leadership is an Art*, 3.

[3] Yukl, *Leadership in Organizations*, 8.

[4] DePree, *Leadership*, 1.

[5] Bergquist and Karr, *Church Turned Inside Out.*

[6] DePree, *Leadership.*

[7] Maxwell, *Developing the Leader Within You*, 1.

[8] Warner, "Making Disciples in the Wesleyan Tradition," 164.

[9] Tennent, "Reimagining the Gospel"

[10] Tennent, "Four Great Wesleyan Distinctives (Part II)"

[11] Henderson, *A Model for Making Disciples*

[12] Bentley, "The Formation of Christian Leaders: A Wesleyan Approach," 558.

[13] Henderson, *Model.*

[14] Withrow, "Disciples for the Future" 141-150.

[15] Hucks, *John Wesley and the Eighteenth Century Methodist Movement.*

[16] Warner, "Making Disciples", 161-162.

[17] John Wesley, "Letter to William Wilberforce" (1791), Global Ministries: The United Methodist Church, accessed Jan 11, 2016, http://bit.ly/1U3g5ho

[18] Bentley, "Formation," 558.

[19] Hucks, *John Wesley.*

[20] Sumner, "John Wesley and the Common Thread of Modern Anglican Mission"

[21] Wesley, *Works*, Jan. 24, 1738: 74. See also Collins, *A Real Christian*, 40-42.

[22] DePree, *Leadership.*

[23] Henderson, Model.

[24] Sumner, "John Wesley and the Common Thread".

[25] Bentley, "Formation," 555.

[26] Jones, "Bold Initiative," 33.

[27] Ibid.

[28] Ibid.

[29] Frabrycky and Joyce, "Playing God: An Interview with Andy Crouch."

[30] See Crouch, *Culture Making.*

[31] Bounds, "Setting Holiness Too High."

[32] Sumner, "John Wesley and the Common Thread".

[33] Hucks, *John Wesley*

[34] Wesley, Works, June 11, 1739: 202. http://www.ccel.org/ccel/wesley/journal.vi.iii.v.html

[35] Bounds, "Setting Holiness Too High"

2
What Makes Leadership Wesleyan?

Lovett H. Weems, Jr.

Wesleyan leadership is theological, innovative, and global. John Wesley was spurred by his desire to see people come to know God in Jesus Christ. This led Wesley to be innovative, even to the point of disrupting cultural conventions and expectations. Nothing short of influencing the whole world is the Wesleyan mandate.

ONE CAN EASILY ENVISION the themes that might characterize a discussion of Wesleyan theology or Wesleyan history, but the content of a conversation on Wesleyan leadership is less obvious. Some would even question if there is such a thing as a "distinctive" Wesleyan leadership. Surely there is no unique model of leadership that emerges either from the theology or history of the Wesleyan movement. However, there are themes that give a flavor to Wesleyan leadership from which Wesleyans and others can learn. I lift up three criteria from among many more that not only characterize Wesleyan leadership but are greatly needed today: grounded in theology, disruptive innovation, and focused on the poor.

Grounded in Theology

There are many ways to understand the history of the Methodist movement. Some focus on the personalities of key leaders while others point to decisive historical events and turning points. Still others highlight polity and the impact of an itinerant "sent" ministry on early Methodism in the United States. While there are many lenses through which to understand Methodism, the dimension that gives meaning to them all is the *message* of the Wesleyan movement.

John Wesley had a passion for all humanity to come to know the love of God revealed in Jesus Christ. This was his overriding passion and paramount concern. There is no way to understand Wesley or early Methodism apart from this guiding vision. One reason he was called a "folk theologian" had to do with the passion Wesley had for a faith that connects with the actual spiritual and human needs of all people. Despite his particular education, background, and personality, Wesley connected with people very different from himself. Many previously unreached people came to know the love of Christ because of him. Theology mattered a great deal to Wesley, but not merely as an end in itself. Doctrine was a means of connecting God's love and power to people at their points of need. This Wesleyan dimension of leadership can save us from a theology that sets up shop for itself and is unrelated and unresponsive to people and their needs.

Wesley never forgot what was primary. Proclaiming the Good News revealed in Jesus Christ was the beginning, middle, and end of his entire life's work. He charged his preachers constantly, "You have nothing to do but to save souls. Therefore spend and be spent in this work."[1]

It is easy to forget what is primary and instead focus on lesser things. At a time when there is a tremendous spiritual longing among so many, too few religious leaders and churches speak to these spiritual needs. This is one reason people

> *"Effective leadership in the church begins with God's call, God's people, and a vision of God's reign"*

instead move toward such distressing alternatives. Religious leaders have left a vacuum. Generic spirituality quickly moves to fill the void, grounded in nothing more than self-centeredness.

Perhaps we have lost spiritual power today because we have cut ourselves off from our source of power that comes from the message itself. We may talk freely about the tradition of the "warmed heart," when we may have forgotten the fire that warmed it in the first place. "Why are we not more holy?" was one of the questions in the *Large Minutes* from the early years of Methodism. The answer was that people were "looking for the end, without using the means."

No faithful Christian leadership is possible apart from a lively and ongoing experience of God's presence in our lives. It is from this communion with God's Spirit that our spirits find direction, purpose, power, and resilience. In his sermon "The Circumcision of the Heart," John Wesley admonished to "have no end, no ultimate end, but God."[2] Leadership disconnected from God leaves leaders adrift.

Wesley understood that all religious leadership has a theological beginning. Effective leadership in the church begins with God's call, God's people, and a vision of God's reign. From the beginning, the focus must be theological, not personal.

Leaders lead best when they are passionately and prayerfully seeking to know and follow God's vision rather than promoting a personal agenda. If we lose the theological grounding for change, we lose our credibility and power as spiritual leaders.

Disruptive Innovation

There is much talk today about disruptive innovation. But in many ways, John Wesley and the early Methodist movement were early disrupters. In established organizations, the tendency is to focus on "sustaining innovations" that make what they do better. But the very practices that made an organization strong can become the practices keeping it from responding adequately to new challenges. For example, the emergence of discount stores was a "disruptive innovation" for department stores. What department stores did best was meet the needs of their primary constituents—upper-middle to upper-class shoppers. But they knew little about the needs of a different constituency – lower-middle to lower-class shoppers—now cultivated by a new breed of retailers. One characteristic of disruptive innovations is that they tend to serve previously underserved constituencies.

For the established churches of Wesley's time, the disruptive innovations that reached the previously unreached came from the Methodists through such practices as field preaching, class meetings, popular music, shared leadership, and preaching by laity and women. It is worthy of note that some of these practices that Wesley permitted were those about which he had some doubts, but, in the end, their fruitfulness convinced him that they served the sake of the Gospel. The same thing happened in North America with circuit riders, revivals, camp meetings, and the Sunday School Movement. This disruption changed the religious landscape in a matter of decades.

Today, denominations sharing the Wesleyan heritage tend to be the established churches in communities, often content to focus on sustaining innovation while others practice disruptive innovation. Remember that some degree of disruption is needed to reach those not currently being reached. It was not new techniques that gave growth to the Wesleyan movement; it was the passion for souls that required those innovative changes in order to reach the people—whether in the coal mines of England or on the North American frontier.

We need to assess carefully and prayerfully our mission and our current effectiveness in achieving that mission. In doing so, we may save ourselves from doing what seems right based on our past instead of doing what actually furthers God's reign in our time.

Good practices cause congregations and denominations to take hold and minister faithfully. Those same practices may not be adequate for today. The test that John Wesley might use is: "Are the things you are doing bearing fruit?" In many places today, the answer is that they are not.

Wesley understood that problems of reaching people did not stem from the people's lack of interest in God. People care deeply about the purpose of life. Humanity is desperate for release from all the bondages that enslave people today. People care deeply about precisely what is primary in the Christian message. Wesleyan passion for souls and adaptability to changing circumstances could serve us well in reaching those in need of God's redemptive love in the 21st century.

The futile tendency in the church, however, is to repeat the forms from the past long after they have lost their power. The forms of the past are preserved even as virtually everyone has forgotten the original power and values that gave rise to the forms in the first place. Wesley was "not afraid that the people called Methodists should ever cease to exist," but his fear was that "they should only exist as a dead sect, having the form of religion without the power."[3] Innovation is not for the sake of change but for the sake of preserving the power of an ancient message. The Gospel is carried in earthen vessels, and many of those containers are no longer adequate for the new wine needed for God's spirit to come alive in new times.

Community as Parish

Recently I heard the former pastor of a Congregational church in New England tell what it was like to prepare for a church's 300th anniversary celebration. This church was established in 1712. In addition to discovering that they only had two pastors in their first 104 years, he found a profound understanding of the concept of "parish" in those early years. It was clear that the church was responsible to and for the community, not only those who were participants in the congregation. That gave me a new and richer understanding of what may have been in John Wesley's mind when he said, "I look upon the world as my parish."

Leadership in the Wesleyan spirit begins precisely at that point. It begins with the needs of people and then focuses on meeting those needs through serving in the name of Christ. This involves meeting their personal spiritual and material needs. It also means contributing to the larger society as a natural outgrowth of those personal concerns. The story of the Wesleyan movement is indeed one of finding God lying between people and serving God there.

The Wesleyan movement was built around "outsiders" and the poor. Wesley's move to field preaching came not from an intellectual commitment but from an emerging practical necessity. Despite real reservations, Wesley yielded to encouragement to try field preaching for the sake of the gospel and those excluded by conventional worship. Nothing about field preaching fit who John Wesley was, except his calling as a bearer of God's good news for the poor. He adapted his more natural personal leanings for the sake of the message.

Here is a case where our Wesleyan theological and historical heritage can help. If evangelism, social issues, and theological stances have become ideological battlegrounds, then it is the poor who should bring us together. For example, two pastors in the Wesleyan tradition might have taken different theological paths along the way. Different theological streams nurtured them. They went to different theological schools. They read different theologians. Indeed, these two pastors represent archetypes of polarities in Wesleyan theological and social thought. However, if these two pastors are serving in the same community, they will encounter each other regularly. They may not see each other at the bookstore or clergy study group. But these two pastors, if they are true to the Wesleyan tradition, will bump into each other regularly among the poorest of the poor of that community.

The call for churches in the Wesleyan spirit today is to once again begin to see our communities (the "world" around us) as our parishes , and not just those who show up for weekly church events. This Wesleyan perspective is essential in the changed context the church faces today in North America. For decades, churches expected people to come to them. The first entry point for most new members was their attendance at worship. Today fewer people are initiating interest in the church, especially among the young. The physical location of the church is unlikely to be where new people first encounter the church, and the community is far more likely to be the first point of contact. We cannot expect the community to come to us. The future for churches is to find ways to take church to the community where the people are.

There is no future for the Wesleyan witness in North America apart from our ability to reach more people, younger people, and more diverse people. Just as Wesleyans moved across an expanding frontier to take the Gospel to all people, that same spirit is needed today to engage major metropolitan areas and population centers. The Wesleyan witness that saw uneducated clergy establishing numerous schools and colleges for the young must today find ways to engage emerging generations so estranged from religious life. The Wesleyan movement that in the United States could say at the time of Bishop Asbury's death that fully one-quarter of its constituents were African-American must engage the radically changing racial makeup of North America. That will take new skills and a new way of thinking. And, finally, this religious movement that began with the poor and neglected must once more reclaim its heritage of being a church for, with, and of the poor.

Conclusion

No theological tradition is so true and self-evident that new expressions are not needed for new times and new challenges. Every generation after Wesley has wrestled with the faithful appropriation of Wesley's liberating message of grace for new people, cultures, and circumstances. In this sense, the Wesleyan legacy is a living and dynamic heritage for the universal church. Claims of exclusive insights or superior practices get in the way of sharing from our Wesleyan heritage as graciously and freely as Wesley did himself.

The power of the Wesleyan tradition comes not from John Wesley as a model leader or the Methodist Way as the preferred way to order church life and discipline. Wesley was far from a perfect example, and practices of his time carry much of the historical context he faced. Wesley's enduring example is a spiritual legacy of one who spent virtually his entire lifetime on a spiritual pilgrimage to know, love, and serve God. Until his dying moments, he continued to seek growth in grace, peace of soul, communion with God, and perfection in love.

Lovett H. Weems, Jr., DMin, is Distinguished Professor of Church Leadership and Director of the Lewis Center for Church Leadership at Wesley Theological Seminary in Washington, DC.

Chapter 2 Notes

[1] John Wesley, *The Works of the Rev. John Wesley,* 3rd ed., vol. 7, edited by Thomas Jackson (London: John Mason, 1829), 310.

[2] Albert Outler, ed., *The Works of John Wesley,* vol. 1 (Nashville: Abingdon Press, 1984), 408.

[3] Rupert Davies, ed. *The Works of John Wesley,* vol. 9 (Nashville: Abingdon Press, 1989), 527.

3
Wesleyan Leadership in a Postmodern Context

Rob Muthiah

Is the world getting better or getting worse? Does the world address our emotional needs or enable us purchase whatever we might desire? Beyond the emerging monetized, therapeutic culture racing toward bliss or ruin, there are colliding cultures. These tensions mark postmodern culture. Yet the foundation and history of Wesleyan leadership can help contemporary leaders to understand the cultural climate that succumbs not to a pick-and-choose spirituality, but to a vibrant, effective, and transforming faith.

IF JOHN WESLEY WERE to time travel and drop into your church today, how would you explain to him the contours of our current cultural context? What is different in our day and age from Wesley's? The Wesleyan tradition contains a pattern of adaptability that encourages such conversations. We see this pattern in the move from preaching in churches to preaching in fields during Wesley's day, in the move from spontaneous revival services to organized tent meetings in the late 19th and early 20th centuries, and in the move during the early and mid 20th century to a more reasoned approach to faith in response to the growing emphasis on reason in the broader culture. How might this adaptability lead to new ministry approaches that effectively engage today's context?

While other chapters will address these and related questions, let's listen closely to discern the nature of today's culture itself. Deirdre Brower Latz, in her work on culture and Wesleyanism, gives us the reason for listening in this way:

For those in the Wesleyan tradition—with our profound reliance on an optimism of grace, an understanding of the way the Spirit works in, through, and beyond the church in what we know of as justifying, sanctifying, and prevenient grace; with a sacramental theology (that is, God-with-us in material, embodied ways); with an understanding of holiness as contagious, corporate, *and* personal—the attitude of relation to the culture seems clear: *we cooperate with God* [emphasis added] who is at work in and around us.

Such cooperation requires us to know as much as possible about our culture. As we come to understand more fully our cultural context, we can then draw on the historical Wesleyan ethos of adaptability for encouragement to evaluate inherited ways of embodying and communicating the gospel. This will allow us to make adjustments in light of God's present work and leading in relation to the current dynamics of today's culture. Describing some of those dynamics is the focus of this chapter. Attention to the themes addressed here provides a significant starting point for understanding the world in which our congregations exist today.

Utopia or Dystopia?

One tenet of modernity was that human reason would move society forward on an ever-improving trajectory. Advances in medicine would cure diseases. Advances in technology would make work easier. Advances in production would make goods cheaper and more available. The modern era, in spite of two world wars, operated with an overarching optimism regarding the human ability to lead to a better world.

This outlook is still very much alive today. It is captured with the phrase "cybernetic global optimism," a phrase that describes a pervasive faith in technology to usher in a better world.[1] Social media can enhance our relationships by allowing us to keep up with far-flung friends and relatives more easily. The dramatic advances in medical screenings and procedures mean that cancer can be caught at earlier stages, stents can be placed in arteries to prevent heart attacks, and people can live longer. Self-driving cars hold the promise of significantly reducing injuries and fatalities

"As we come to understand more fully our cultural context, we can then draw on the historical Wesleyan ethos of adaptability...to evaluate inherited ways of embodying and communicating the gospel.

from car accidents. On the international stage, hope is placed in new technologies like precision missiles and drones to degrade the enemy's capabilities and resolve conflicts. Of course, technologies have their downsides, but cybernetic global optimism holds onto the hope that these downsides—and the problems of humanity more generally—can be solved through technological advances. Taken to its logical end, cybernetic global optimism believes that humanity can create a utopia. This is a prevalent outlook in our culture today.

Paradoxically, a contradictory mood simultaneously exists: what we might call "postmodern disquiet."[2] This phrase points to the hopelessness and nihilism that drifts through our society. It is a mood reflected in the burgeoning genre of dystopian literature and film, represented by *The Hunger Games* and *Divergent*. Both stories are about societies in which people have little control over their own lives. In these stories, those in power construct and control competing classes of people in society. The protagonists are those few who are seeking to break out of a hopeless way of life dominated by the ruling elites and are challenging the iron-fisted control of the system.

The popularity of this dystopian genre is an indicator of postmodern disquiet, manifest in feelings of despair and being trapped in the system with no hope of escape. In our culture today, wealth has become dramatically more concentrated in the hands of a small percentage of the population even as 1 in 5 children in the United States is at risk of hunger,[3] leading to a feeling of futility among some when it comes to meeting the basic human needs of all. Many feel hopeless about catastrophic environmental changes that are wreaking havoc on food production and causing the highest rate of species extinction in millennia.[4] Cyber-insecurity is everywhere, ranging from personal identity theft to international cyber attacks on corporations and governments. This is an age marked by restless anxiety about the way things are. This postmodern disquiet contradicts and coexists with cybernetic global optimism.

Congregational leaders must pay attention to both of these themes. Faithful leadership will challenge the idea of a human-generated utopia. At the same time, faithful leadership will bring the hope of the gospel to bear in the face of dystopian despair.

Rationalistic Atheism and Spiritual Decoupage

Flowing from modernity's elevation of reason and its suspicion of experience as sources of truth and meaning, today's postmodern context is witness to a resurgent rationalistic atheism. Today's avowed atheists in general hold that all of life can be explained completely by science and reason. This perspective is reinforced by continual advances in areas such as physics, medical research, and computer technology. The assumption is that human reason will eventually lead to logical, provable explanations for everything that is. This part of our population thus sees no need to resort to the idea of a god. And based on the laws of the universe known via reason, this group is supremely confident that no god or supernatural sphere exists.

While our culture contains multiple forms of atheism, several subtypes are similar in terms of their stridency.[5] They not only hold strongly to an atheistic perspective, but also actively challenge and debate those who hold religious perspectives. Their deep disdain for religion in general is often targeted at Christianity most specifically. Other types of atheists are less strident and take more of a live-and-let-live approach which says, "This is my (un)belief system, but if you hold to something else, I don't really have a problem with that." While only a small percentage of the U.S. population identifies as atheist, we note this theme because of its strong voice and influence in our culture.[6]

Existing side by side with this resurgent rationalistic atheism is a pattern of what we might call "spiritual decoupage." In a sign that atheism has not won the day, studies show that the U.S. culture remains a highly religious one.[7] However, the nature of this religiosity has changed. Rather than subscribing to a single religious tradition, many today create for themselves a spiritual decoupage by clipping bits and pieces from self help books, quotable celebrities, Eastern religious traditions, talk show hosts, and dominant cultural values.[8] This decoupage looks different for each individual, and is an ongoing work in progress. An individual's decoupage makes no normative claims on others. In this construct, one hears of another's spiritual experiences or interpretations and nods affirmatively to validate the experience of the other, but this is done without any sense that one's own decoupage should look similar. Here we see the relativism of postmodernity shining through.

The rise of spiritual decoupage correlates to the rise of the "nones"—people who, when asked about their religious preference, state "none." Historically, most Americans identified with a religious tradition even if they were not active in that tradition. In the 1990s, a dramatic shift began to occur: among those reaching adulthood, the percentage of those who identified with no religious tradition at all began to rise dramatically.[9] The rapidity of the shift is dramatic: between 2007 and 2014, the *nones* increased from 16 percent to 23 percent of the adult population—a change of over 40 percent in just seven years.[10] Robert Putnam and David Campbell note this about the growing population of *nones*:

> The new nones are not uniformly unbelievers, and few of them claim to be atheists or agnostics. Indeed, most of them express some belief in God and even in the afterlife, and many of them say that religion is important in their lives. While the new nones are, by definition, less attached to organized religion than other Americans, they do not seem to have discarded all religious beliefs or predilections. While observers sometimes describe them as "spiritual, not religious," they themselves generally do not use that language. They reject conventional religious affiliations, while not entirely giving up their religious beliefs.[11]

The nones are spiritual decoupagers who feel no need to embrace a specific religious tradition. The coexistence of these two contradictory perspectives is crucial to recognize. Such recognition will allow pastors and congregations to choose differing ministry initiatives to best serve differing segments of the population. A one-size-fits-all approach will not do.

A Monetized Culture

Time is money. This common phrase stands as a symbol of how our whole culture has been monetized. We live in an age in which a monetary value has been assigned to nearly every aspect of life. From caring for the sick to educating our youth, everything gets translated into dollars. This is a logical outworking of modernity's rationality. Rationality insists on measurability; monetization provides a means for this measuring.

McDonald's, the fast-food chain, serves as an example and metaphor for what has unfolded in the broader culture. The fast and low-cost production of food as developed by McDonald's is predicated on efficiency. Hamburgers are machine-produced to exact specifications so that cooking and handling procedures can be precision-tuned and variance can be reduced, if not eliminated, from the system. Hamburger buns arrive in the restaurant pre-sliced to increase the speed at which they can be put into use. Workers are trained to follow precise steps for cooking French fries. Kitchens are set up to create the smoothest flow of work possible. The driving force behind these efficiencies is not worker comfort or even customer satisfaction. These matter, but only to the extent that they contribute to the fundamental issue: profit maximization. In the fast food world, time is indeed money. Efficiency is the means; economic gain is the measurable goal.

George Ritzer argues convincingly that our whole society has become McDonaldized. The means and goals of McDonald's, representative of the economic sphere more broadly, have seeped from the marketplace sphere into all other spheres of life.[12] In the education sphere, for example, the purpose of our schools and universities is framed more and more in economic terms: we should fund education because a good education system produces a better pool of future employees who will better serve economic expansion. Classic educational goals such as nurturing wisdom and forming well-rounded people interested in serving the common good become secondary. In the medical sphere, efficiency and cost are now the fundamental drivers of the conversation. Ideas to humanize the ways we care for the sick are secondary concerns. In the home sphere, we hire others to do our mundane work at $10 an hour while we work for some multiple of that rate because this is more efficient economically. The calculation does not factor in goods inherent to the work itself that cannot be monetized—identification with others who do such work, satisfaction, and character formation inherent in gardening or cleaning up after oneself that cannot be obtained when someone else is paid to do the work. American society contains this overwhelming force to monetize every aspect of life and to ignore as unimportant those dimensions of life that are difficult or impossible to equate to a dollar value.

This proves true even in the ways we relate to one other. Upon meeting someone new, one of the most common questions to ask is, "What kind of work do you do?" It is a way of assigning social status in relation to earning power. Of course those who are unemployed or not paid for their work are granted minimal social status in this system. Our views of one another are filtered through this lens of monetary value.

Pastors and other congregational leaders must pay attention to this theme and ask what it might mean for congregational formation and mission. We must wrestle with how to draw people into the life of the congregation when people are monetizing their time and their relationships. We must be aware of the temptation to monetize Christian faith as a way of making it attractive to a monetized people, whether by promoting a prosperity gospel, promising increased productivity for those who rest one day a week, or other similar moves. Within the life of the body, programming and budget decisions must be based on something bigger than a monetary cost-benefit analysis. Understanding this contour of the cultural geography is crucial if we are to lead the people of God along the path of gospel faithfulness.

A Therapeutic Culture

The language and perspectives of the psychotherapist's office have become pervasive in society in general today. We live in a therapeutic culture. At one time, when people faced personal struggles or issues, they would turn to a pastor. Today many people—both those within the church as well as those outside the church —turn to a therapist.

The goal of most therapy is personal fulfillment and the well-being of the client. The path to this goal is to look inward and to focus intently upon one's feelings. This paradigm is what Robert Bellah and his colleagues call "expressive individualism."[13] It is a paradigm that has come to characterize an approach to relationships well outside the walls of the therapist's office. Many now view marriage and friendships primarily in terms of personal fulfillment. Such a view pushes out ideas of self-sacrifice and of commitment to things greater than oneself. The focus is placed on personal satisfaction and personal benefit.

The therapeutic influence on today's culture can be seen in the way that the language of therapy has displaced the language of scripture within the church itself. Commenting on one prominent preacher, David McKenna notes, "Very seldom are the words 'sin,' 'conviction,' 'repentance,' and 'confession' heard in his sermons or read in his books. In their place are such psychological terms as 'negative past experience,' 'low self-esteem,' 'positive thinking,' and 'human potential.'"[14] Pastors must consider the results of such language substitution on Christian spiritual formation.

For pastoral counseling to be done faithfully, it is imperative that pastors and counselors pay attention to this pervasive therapeutic influence. Will Willimon says a major responsibility of pastoral counseling involves laying "our need alongside the story of the good news of Jesus Christ in such a way that both the gospel and our need are illuminated."[15] The substitution of therapeutic language for the language of the gospel makes it difficult, if not impossible, to fulfill this pastoral counseling responsibility.

Those in the Wesleyan tradition who value Wesley's model of bands and classes will want to be particularly discerning about the influence of the dominant therapeutic culture. Whereas Wesley's small groups were focused on confession and the Holy Spirit's sanctifying work, today what many congregational small groups or community groups do more closely resembles the dominant type of group therapy in which the language and content of the gospel gets forgotten. The self becomes the focus, and self-discovery the solution to life's problems.

While many of the therapist's tools may prove useful in the hands of the pastor, careful attention to the influence of therapy in our culture is essential in order handle these tools in ways that serve the life and purposes of the church. Christian leaders today must discern the ways in which a therapeutic culture undercuts Christian formation and the ways in which it might serve Christian formation.

Not a Melting Pot

The school textbooks from my youth described the United States of America as a melting pot. The idea was that people from all over the world who immigrated to the United States were being blended together into one culture that could be described as "American." However, America today is more ethnically diverse than ever. This diversity has *not* been cooked into one homogeneous culture, nor will it be anytime soon.[16] The ethnic landscape of America is wonderfully diverse. To minister within a specific ethnic context or to minister across ethnic lines requires an awareness of the unique dimensions of each setting. The importance of this can be seen by looking at three specific ethnic contexts within the church.

The Korean-American Context

Generational differences present a major challenge in the Korean-American church context. First-generation Koreans have been formed in a Confucian-influenced culture that gives great respect to those in leadership. Followers formed in that same context do not expect to have a highly collaborative role as equals in decision-making. Second generation Korean-Americans, who were born in and grew up in the United States, tend to chafe somewhat under the leadership assumptions and approaches of the older generation, in part because they have experienced educational and work settings in which they are invited into dialogue with their superiors. While having to navigate cultural-generational issues is by no means unique to the Korean-American church, the specific dynamics faced by of Korean-Americans are different from what was faced by German-Americans a hundred years ago or by Nigerian-Americans today. Knowledge of these specifics is essential to minister faithfully within this community.

The African-American Context

The African-American context provides another example. The African-American community that must deal continually with the injustice and racism of being pulled over by law enforcement for routine checks at a highly disproportionate rate has more difficulty obtaining loans even when equally qualified, and on average has access to lower-quality education. The issue of racism and the injustices it spawns are national issues and ones that all Christians have a responsibility to be aware of and to confront. At the same time, African-American pastors face the challenge of ministering daily in the midst of these issues in ways that pastors in other contexts do not. These pastors' experience within that context uniquely equips them to understand and minister to the needs of their congregants. Context matters in relation to how we minister the gospel. A move away from the melting pot metaphor will help us to take differing contexts more seriously.

The Mexican-American Context

A third example comes from the Mexican-American context. In the Mexican-American culture it is common for church leadership and family networks to have significant overlap. The pastor's father might have been the one who started the church, siblings and in-laws might be elders, nieces and nephews might compose the majority of the praise team, and the pastor's daughter might be the youth leader. While leadership books abound regarding how to lead church boards and how to navigate staff relations, literature is scarce or non-existent regarding how to do this if most of the members of the church are related to you in some way. Few authors have paid attention to this dynamic, which is a common reality for many Mexican-American pastors. In white American culture, having family in leadership raises immediate concerns about nepotism. But in the Mexican-American context, as well as in a number of other cultures, it is natural for the family network to overlap significantly with the church structure. The construct is not without its problems, but the same can be said of church structures within which no family connections exist. For those who wish to lead well in the Mexican-American context or to support those leading in that particular ethnic context, an understanding of the role and expectations of extended family is required.

The larger Wesleyan tradition has a mixed record when it comes to dealing with issues of race and ethnicity.[17] For example, while some within the tradition led the abolitionist movement, others staunchly supported slavery. Wesleyan leaders must learn from past failures in this area and build upon past successes. A growing awareness and deepening desire to understand the current diversity of our society today will set pastors up to lead faithfully in today's mosaic of race, ethnicity, and culture.

Conclusion

Wesley understood that the church by its very nature is called to engage with the culture in which it is located. In order to engage the host culture with sensitivity and appropriateness, congregational leaders must develop a deep understanding of that culture. Such understanding comes by attentive listening to the stories all around us: in the news, in movies, in novels, in advertising, on the internet, and in the lives of our people. Only by continually listening in these ways and hearing the major themes of our day will congregational leaders be able to help others see the connections between the Gospel and life as they experience it today.

The themes addressed in this chapter provide a starting point for the listening work that needs to be done. In addition to pondering these and other broad cultural characteristics, congregational leaders must also attend to the uniqueness of their local communities. While we are all affected by themes like consumerism in the broader culture, a church in urban California will face different issues from a church in rural North Dakota, and a small Korean-American church in New York will face issues different than those of an African-American mega-church in Texas.

As Wesleyan pastors and others study the broad contours of today's culture and factor them into local approaches to ministry, they will gain the insight required to continue the pattern of adaptability found in the Wesleyan tradition. It is a pattern to be embraced not for the purpose of being new and novel, but in order to effectively engage our twenty-first century context for the sake of the Gospel.

Robert Muthiah, PhD, is Professor of Practical Theology Azusa Pacific Seminary at Azusa Pacific University, Azusa, California.

Bibliography

Bellah, Robert, Richard Madsen, William Sullivan, Ann Swidler, and Steven Tipton. *Habits of the Heart: Individualism and Commitment in American Life*. New York: Harper and Row, 1985.

Ceballos, Gerardo, Paul R. Ehrlich, Anthony D. Barnosky, Andrés García, Robert M. Pringle, and Todd M. Palmer. "Accelerated Modern Human–Induced Species Losses: Entering the Sixth Mass Extinction," *Science Advances* 1:5 (2015).

Coleman-Jensen, Alisha, Matthew Rabbitt, Christian Gregory, and Anita Singh. "Household Food Security in the United States in 2014," *Economic Research Report (ERR-194)*. U.S. Department of Agriculture, Economic Research Service. September 2015.

Davis, Morris. "Methodists and Race." *The Cambridge Companion to American Methodism*. Ed. Jason E. Vickers. New York: Cambridge University Press, 2013.

Emerson, Michael and Rodney Woo. *People of the Dream: Multiracial Congregations in the United States*. Princeton: Princeton University Press, 2006.

Latz, Deirdre Brower. "Cultural Correlation: The 'Postmodern' Marks of the Church." In *Essential Church: A Wesleyan Ecclesiology*, edited by Diane Leclerc and Mark A. Maddix. Kansas City, Missouri: Beacon Hill Press, 2014.

Lipka, Michael. "A Closer Look at America's Rapidly Growing Religious 'Nones'." Pew Research Center. May 13, 2015. Accessed October 22, 2015. http://pewrsr.ch/1cUpSZ9

McKenna, David. *Wesleyan Leadership in Troubled Times: Confronting the Culture, Challenging the Church*. Kansas City: Beacon Hill Press, 2002.

Putnam, Robert & David Campbell, *American Grace: How Religion Divides and Unites Us*. New York: Simon and Schuster, 2010.

Ritzer, George. *The McDonaldization of Society*. Thousand Oaks, CA: Pine Forge Press, 2000.

Walsh, Brian and Sylvia C. Keesmaat, *Colossians Remixed: Subverting the Empire*. Downers Grove, Ill: InterVarsity Press, 2004.

Williamson, David and George A. Yancey. *There Is No God: Atheists in America*. Lanham, MD: Rowman & Littlefield Publishers, 2013.

Willimon, William H. *Pastor: The Theology and Practice of Ordained Ministry*. Nashville: Abingdon Press, 2002.

Wuthnow, Robert. *After the Baby Boomers: How Twenty- and Thirty-Somethings Are Shaping the Future of American Religion*. Princeton: Princeton University Press, 2007.

Yancey, George. "What the 'Six Types of Atheists' Mean for Christian Outreach." *Christianity Today web-only content*. August 12, 2013. Accessed October 22, 2015. http://bit.ly/1XENZ0W

Chapter 3 Notes

[1] Deirdre Latz, "Cultural Correlation," 85.

[2] Walsh and Keesmaat, *Colossians Remixed*, 26.

[3] Ibid, 21.

[4] Coleman-Jensen et al, "Household Food Security in the United States in 2014"

[5] Ceballos et al, "Accelerated Modern Human–Induced Species Losses"

[6] Yancey, "What the 'Six Types of Atheists' Mean for Christian Outreach".

[7] For a more in-depth look at atheism in the United States, see Williamson and Yancey, *There Is No God*.

[8] Putnam and Campbell, *American Grace*, 7.

[9] Wuthnow refers to this phenomenon as "spiritual tinkering." See Wuthnow, *After the Baby Boomers*, 14-15; 134-135. For a concurring perspective on this cultural characteristic, see McKenna, *Wesleyan Leadership in Troubled Times*, 45-46.

[10] Putnam & Campbell, *American Grace*, 122.

[11] Lipka, "A Closer Look at America's Rapidly Growing Religious 'Nones'".

[12] Ibid, 126.

[13] Ritzer, *The McDonaldization of Society*.

[14] Bellah et al, *Habits of the Heart*, 34-35.

[15] McKenna, *Wesleyan Leadership in Troubled Times*, 42.

[16] Willimon, *Pastor: The Theology and Practice of Ordained Ministry*, 178.

[17] For an excellent overview and critique of the melting pot metaphor and other metaphors applied to American culture, see Emerson and Woo, *People of the Dream*.

[18] For an insightful treatment of this topic, see Davis, "Methodists and Race"

4

The Potential of Wesleyan Leadership: A Reformed Perspective

Richard Mouw

Reflections from the strengths of Wesleyan piety and personal holiness and Reformed Kingdom theology can provide a unique and powerful combination for leadership. By drawing on the life and thought of Abraham Kuyper and his experience with Robert Pearsall Smith and Hannah Whitall Smith, this chapter shows personal holiness as a resource when engaging in the wider spheres of culture and how holiness is a vocation in serving the global context.

DURING THE LAST FEW DECADES of the 19th century, the Dutch Calvinist leadership of the Christian Reformed Church began to debate the question of whether they ought to be adapting more to their North American environment by making greater use of the English language. This community emigrated from the Netherlands in the 1840s, and had managed to maintain a fairly strong sense of Dutch ethnic identity. But generational change brought new challenges, not the least of which was the question of language.

As folks inclined to find an important theological principle at stake in almost any serious human disagreement, it was no surprise when many argued that changing from Dutch to English would have disastrous doctrinal consequences. The English language, the argument went, was inextricably embedded in a culture that was essentially "Methodist." As such, it was incapable of serving as the linguistic medium for capturing the truths of Reformed orthodoxy. The use of "Methodist" in this case was fairly generic, as historians who have chronicled these debates have shown.[1] The Dutch Calvinists saw themselves as a people possessing deep "principles." In their view, the religion of American evangelicalism was thoroughly pragmatic and experiential. Churches that actually identified themselves by the "Methodist" label were for them only the most obvious manifestations of the heterodox proclivities that pervaded the North American ethos.

Abraham Kuyper

Back in the Netherlands, Abraham Kuyper, one of the heroes of this American branch of Dutch Calvinism, had a more charitable assessment of Methodism. Kuyper was a "multi-tasking" champion of Reformed orthodoxy in Dutch ecclesiastical life as well as a journalist, educator, and party leader in the Dutch Parliament. (He later served as Prime Minister after the turn of the century.) A person of action, he regularly experienced emotional and physical exhaustion, which forced him to take rest leaves. On one occasion, he went to England to attend the Brighton meetings of Robert Pearsall Smith and his wife Hannah Whitehall Smith. Kuyper was very taken with their Holiness teachings, and returned to the Netherlands to take up his political leadership with a renewed sense of the importance of a personal godliness that drew more deeply on the power of the Holy Spirit.[2]

Eventually, though, Kuyper became disillusioned with the Brighton leadership, primarily because of some highly publicized sexual scandals. This disillusionment in turn occasioned some retrospective theological objections to the Holiness movement in general. He criticized their inattention to both the integrity of created reality and political concerns, but more generally he objected to what he came to see as the Arminian underpinnings of some of the teachings that had initially attracted him. But for all of that, he began to emphasize in new ways the importance of the cultivation of personal spirituality, calling, for example, for increased emphasis on piety in theological education.

What is especially interesting to me is why Kuyper was drawn in the first place to what he discovered at Brighton. What he clearly found so compelling in the Holiness teachings that he was exposed to there—at a time when he was seeking to replenish his energies and vision for public leadership—were the spiritual resources that spoke to important felt needs in his life. His testimony about Brighton, when he was still enthusiastic about his experience there, is telling in this regard:

> I felt something in my soul that I had not known before. Before I had indeed professed the Lord but kept complaining about the barren circumstances in which believers found themselves; but there [at Brighton] my soul and my life received that conviction besides—indeed saw it revealed in its full reality—that Jesus lives in my heart.[3]

Although Kuyper came to regret his initial enthusiasm for the Holiness perspective, he was convinced that he had discovered something in that perspective that had been missing in the Calvinist-colored view of his own leadership calling.

Sphere Sovereignty

Even when he was enthusiastic about the Brighton movement, Kuyper had noted its inattention to the social-political arena in which he was so involved as a public leader. In his pro-Brighton phase, though, he had not complained about that defect, since he had not come to Brighton for help in his understanding of the details of Christian public leadership. Kuyper was content with his own perspective on the issues of societal life, which was grounded in a detailed theology of culture and which he spelled out with a concern for a multiple areas of Christian leadership.

Particularly important in Kuyper's overall perspective was his teaching regarding "sphere sovereignty."[4] God had built into the very design of the creation the potential for a variety of diverse spheres of human interaction. These spheres, Kuyper argued, would eventually "differentiate" in the process of historical development. He insisted that the reason why explicit attention was not given to these spheres in the Genesis creation account was the fact that the story begins with only two human beings. But in commanding Adam and Eve to "be fruitful and multiply," God made it clear that he definitely had in mind a larger human community with a complex socio-cultural fabric: families, political life, artistic pursuits, economic activity, education, scholarship—all of these were intended by God for the overall patterns of human life. Each of these spheres are, in turn, characterized by different goals and patterns of authority, a complexity which Kuyper insisted on exploring theologically.

A personal example serves to illustrate this Kuyperian point. When I was on the faculty at Calvin College, there was a time when the administrative leadership talked quite a bit about Calvin as "a family." However, when a minor controversy broke out in the faculty and one of our colleagues failed to be granted tenure, they retreated from this rhetoric. The assembled evidence supported the no tenure decision. This person was consistently rated a very poor teacher by his students. He had not published anything of scholarly significance. He often did not show up to meetings of committees of which he was a member. When the tenure decision went against him, though, he made it clear that he had listened carefully to the speeches by Calvin's leaders: "How can you do this to me?" he asked. "This is no way to treat a longtime member of your family!"

The fact is that teaching institutions are not families. A family is bound together by kinship relationships. Only under the most extreme conditions do we "disown" a family member. But a college faculty is a performance-based endeavor. And each of those spheres differs from other arenas of interaction. The bonds that hold together a church congregation are not quite as indissoluble as a family but should be far stronger than the employees of a soccer team or a clothing store. These diverse settings are characterized by different patterns of authority—which also means different patterns of leadership.

Holiness in Other Spheres

My own impression—and this would have been obvious to Kuyper in his encounter with the Brighton movement— is that Holiness perspectives on leadership typically have not paid much attention to spheres beyond the church. Much of the leadership literature in recent years has addressed clergy and lay leadership within the context of ecclesiastical life. In contrast, it is not easy to find Wesleyan discussions of business or political or military leadership, for instance.

But it isn't simply a matter of focusing too narrowly. One can even discern frequent examples of sphere confusion in the Wesleyan understanding of ecclesial life. This is certainly the point of Gregory Schneider's critical comments about Wesleyan ecclesiology in his illuminating study of the rise of Methodism in America.[5] Schneider argues that the 19th century Methodists increasingly "domesticated" their understanding of the life and calling of the Christian community, making primary use of "the image of home: the secluded and affectionate domestic circle constrained by the self-effacing love of the mother."

In its ecclesiological self-understanding, Schneider observed, the Methodist church "housed the family of God. The outlooks and sentiments they learned as members of the spiritual family disposed them to evolve a vision of domesticity and increasingly to identify their literal families and home circles with the idea of the spiritual family."[6] As the Methodist movement grew, however, many of its functions increasingly required the skills associated with managerial expertise. It was difficult, argued Schneider, for Methodists to integrate these functions into their theological understanding of the church, since they were operating with a bifurcated view of ecclesial life: "domestic piety and bureaucratic enterprise" seemed irreconcilable.[7]

To explore Wesleyan resources for understanding the differences among spheres of interaction does not have to be applied in rigid ways. Of course, the church *is* like a family in many ways. We are indeed, in an important, particular sense, brothers and sisters in Christ. But there are also ways in which the family image can take us in wrong directions. Some members—pastors, administrators, janitors—are employees of the church, and their individual relationships with specific congregations are based on performance criteria. The strengths and weaknesses of applying familial imagery to church life should encourage us to be careful in how we apply concepts from non-ecclesial areas of human interaction to church life.

While Kuyper was aware of the inattention to these issues in the kind of Wesleyanism that he encountered at Brighton, he did find something in the Holiness movement that fed his soul in important ways. He clearly found his heart "strangely warmed" by what he experienced at Brighton. What that experience came down to for him was the recognition that a faithful Christian leadership, formed by a theology of creation, can be sustained only when it is firmly grounded in a vibrant personal spirituality nurturing the awareness that, as Kuyper put it, "Jesus lives in my heart." Kuyper had been very fond of talking about the Kingdom in all of its rich complexity. His best known proclamation points to this comprehensive vision of created reality: "There is not one square inch of the entire creation about which Jesus Christ does not cry out, 'This is mine! This belongs to me!'"[8] At Brighton, however, he saw in a new way the intimate connection between having a commitment to the Kingdom and having a living personal relationship with the King himself. Kuyper came to his encounter with Brighton already in possession of a robust understanding of multi-sphere leadership. But at Brighton he found that the Holiness movement offered him deeper resources for his personal spiritual life.

A Multi-Sphere Perspective of Leadership

I want now to reverse that direction, looking at how beginning with that vibrant personal spirituality can lead us toward a robust understanding of multi-sphere leadership. In considering this direction, I want to make it clear that I am not wanting to superimpose a specifically Reformed conception of leadership onto a specifically Wesleyan theology of personal spirituality. While I take the Kuyperian system as a model of what a robust theology of multi-sphere leadership looks like, I am genuinely interested in reflecting upon the uniquely Wesleyan resources for a theology of leadership.

Obviously, I am not raising a brand new subject here. Wesleyans certainly have not ignored the theology of leadership as such. But I am convinced that more work must be done. For one thing, as I have already observed, the leadership focus has often been primarily on ecclesial life—although the Wesleyan movement has also made considerable contributions to a Christian understanding of the call to justice, peace-making, care for creation, and the like.

I admire Wesleyanism in this regard, and have learned much from its contributions. What I would like to see, however, is more of a *multi*-sphere perspective. How can we get from the personal aspects of Wesleyan spirituality to a multi-sphere perspective that bears distinctive Wesleyan marks? And what are some of the obstacles that have kept many Wesleyans from this more expansive vision of leadership?

While my spiritual identity from my earliest years has been shaped by Reformed

> *"How, then, can we get from the personal aspects of Wesleyan spirituality to a multi-sphere perspective that bears distinctive Wesleyan marks?"*

Christianity, I have had significant engagement with Holiness life and thought along the way. In my high school years, I attended camp meetings with my Holiness friends. I spent two of my undergraduate years at a Wesleyan college, and my wife is from a family that held active leadership positions in the Holiness movement. In my scholarly career, I have had many occasions to lecture at Wesleyan campuses and consult with organizations in the Holiness movement.

When I first read the important book by Donald Dayton (my Houghton College classmate) recounting his adult discovery of a social justice and peacemaking tradition in the Holiness movement,[9] I understood well his complaints about how that tradition had remained hidden in Holiness circles for much of the twentieth century. I had directly experienced in my own spiritual pilgrimage the strong "world flight" tendencies in Holiness Christianity.

In the 1970s, however, things began to change in evangelicalism in general and in Holiness circles in particular. The 1973 Chicago Declaration of Evangelical Social Concerns signaled the emergence of a new social-political activism in the evangelical movement. This renewed interest in issues of justice and peace was not without opposition, however. In my own—and admittedly limited—contacts with some of the older generation in the Holiness movement, I heard worries that a new Wesleyan activism among younger folks would simply follow the path of the more liberal activism in mainline Methodist circles. These concerns were not unfounded. During those years I was contacted by mainline Methodist leaders who were looking for ways of enlisting evangelical "liberals"—I resented being tagged with that label— like myself for involvement in their social advocacy projects.

The obvious lesson in this from my perspective is that we must find an activism that is genuinely grounded in the biblical understanding of holiness embodied in the Wesleyan tradition. An obvious place to begin is with John Wesley's oft-quoted maxim: "The world is my parish". It has the kind of grand scope can be seen as a Holiness parallel to Kuyper's "every square inch" manifesto. To be sure, Wesley's immediate application of this confession was evangelistic: "[I]n whatever part of [the world] I am, I judge it meet, right, and my bounden duty to declare unto all that are willing to hear, the glad tidings of salvation." But he does go on rather quickly to acknowledge, using a biblical formulation, a more general duty: "As I have opportunity, doing good unto all men."[10] He then reinforces this point, observing that the teaching of God's Word "has disengaged me from all things else, that I might singly attend on this very thing, 'and go about doing good.'"[11]

Wesley provides us here with two significant claims that can be expanded for a robust leadership perspective. First, God wants us to care about the whole world as our "parish." Second, within that world we need not only to evangelize but more generally to "go about doing good." Each of these has profound implications for a developing a robust multi-sphere perspective within a Holiness framework.

Avoiding Corruption, Embracing the Cosmos

Wesley's positive portrayal of "the world" as the arena for his ministry is a crucial starting point for thinking about leadership. This is true especially in the light of the fact that many within the Holiness movement have often thought of "the world" as a hostile—even dangerous—context for cultivating a life of faithful Christian living. The condemnation of "worldliness" has been a key Holiness theme, a condemnation that, properly understood, is legitimate. We can certainly find biblical warnings against a too-friendly relationship to "the world." John's first epistle provides clear a straightforward warning in this regard: we are not to "love the world or the things in the world" (1 John 2:15). And the Savior himself issued a similar warning when he told his disciples that since they are "not of the world" they should not be surprised if "the world hates you" (John 15:19). So, the condemnations of "worldliness" have much biblical support. We must avoid at all costs the patterns of life that have become corrupted by our shared rebellion against the Living God. To love the world in this sense is to be attached to those things that are, from the perspective of Christ's kingdom, transitory and illusionary; it is to adopt the values of the sinful social order.

But there are other biblical references to "the world" that have positive connotations. Indeed, in this more positive sense God himself is a lover of the world, as is evident in that most concise of all biblical summaries of the gospel: "For God so loved the world that he gave his one and only son, that whoever believes in him shall not perish but have eternal life" (John 3:16). The Greek word here for "world" is *cosmos*, referring to the *created order*. Even though the creation is presently distorted by sin and rebellion, it is not unsalvageable. Jesus came "not to condemn the *cosmos*, but that the *cosmos* might be saved through him" (John 3:17).

God created the cosmos (world) and celebrated it as "very good" at its beginnings (Gen. 1:31). Though badly broken by human sinfulness, God reaffirmed fundamental worth of the world by sending his Son to renew it. As followers of Jesus Christ, we are sent into the sinful cosmos, not to conform to it, but to confront its rebellion. Jesus prayed to the Father on behalf of his disciples: "My prayer is not that you take them out of the world but that you protect them from the evil one" (John 17:15). Christians are called to penetrate the territory over which sin presently rules, identifying with all that is good in the *cosmos*, the good creation. Accordingly, the psalmist's proclamation of God's dominion over the good cosmos was not limited to a specific period of time: "the earth is the Lord's and the fullness thereof, the world and all who dwell therein" (Psalm 24:1).

To say that the Gospel is about God's love for "the world" in the *cosmos* sense is to recognize that the Christian message extends beyond mere concern for the individual; it has implications for the entirety of creation. To be sure, Jesus Christ did indeed come to save individual sinners. But he also came to reclaim a larger creation that has suffered because of human sinfulness. The curse of sin is cosmic in scope, affecting the whole of the world that God has made. The gospel is God's response to sin.

I will not focus here on the ways in which sin has impacted non-human physical reality: plants, animals, rivers, oceans, or the air that we breathe. My specific interest here is how sin has affected human institutions. Greed, prejudice, lust, violence— these vices have their origins in the rebellion of individuals, but they come to be woven into our institutional life, into the corporate patterns of human interaction. Institutions in turn perpetuate and reinforce these attributes in individuals. Sexual trafficking is one example. If we managed to bring every individual prostitute in a given country to Christ, we would still have to deal with the economic realities of the situation. Where will they now get access to education and job training? What about those who manage—and benefit from—the "industry" of sexual trafficking?

Recognizing the scope of "the world" in this institutional sense points us to the importance of Wesley's insistence upon "doing good" in the world that he had come to see as his parish. Like many other evangelical sub-groups, the Holiness community saw itself as culturally marginalized during most of the twentieth century. Spiritually, the primary mandate was to survive as a faithful and holy people in a larger culture that was seen as hostile to the faith. The hostility that these folks discerned is certainly still there. But Holiness churches have experienced their own clear pattern of upward mobility in recent decades. Local congregations that were located "on the wrong side of the tracks" in a given community now often have the best real estate in town. The sons and daughters of the earlier camp meetings now hold significant positions of influence in government, business, entertainment, sports, and the academy. What does it mean today for them to see their places of influence as a part of the larger "parish" in which they are called to "do good"? The answer to that important question must go beyond simply engaging in efforts at personal evangelism.

Holiness as Vocation

A Kuyperian friend who owned an insurance firm appeared on a panel with four other business leaders to talk about what it means to be a Christian leader in their working lives. Each of the other four gave strong expression to honor their Lord by finding occasions to witness to others about Christ and maintaining personal integrity in their dealings. Just before my friend spoke, the previous panelist said that each week he asked his secretary to reserve one lunch hour where he could stay in his office, "leaving the dog-eat-dog world of business, to spend time in the presence of my Lord."

My friend began by affirming this practice. "Yes, I do that too," he said. "I need it!" But then he went on to testify that he also wanted to cultivate an awareness of the presence of the Lord "while I am *not* alone in my office." He reported that the week before he had met with a newly married couple, now expecting their first child, to discuss their insurance needs. "They were asking some of the deepest questions a young couple can face," he said. "They were thinking about their basic priorities in life, about what kind of marriage they wanted to sustain, about what kind of family life wanted to nurture." And then he said this: "I sensed that my Lord was looking over my shoulder as I wrote their insurance policies. God cares about how we provide insurance to young couples!"

The same kind of thing can be said about marketing agricultural equipment, selling groceries, coaching football teams, providing medical care, and so on. God cares about these patterns of human interaction. And we have much work to do by way of equipping God's people to take leadership in these areas of service with utmost seriousness. As a theological educator, I want to insist that it isn't just a matter of teaching pastors how to be good leaders in churches. Leadership in the church must encourage these other diverse leadership callings.

What my insurance agent friend was pointing to in his own daily path of discipleship was the need for cultivating a holiness that had a direct bearing on his work. Basic to everything else was his conviction that God was looking on with a deep concern for what he was attempting to accomplish in his work. He was exercising spiritual gifts, especially the gift of discernment as he interacted with this young couple: What genuine human needs were they bringing to this session about insurance policies? What hopes and fears were at play in that conversation? How, for the Christian agent who certainly needs to think about business success, can he see his service to them as more than simply selling policies?

This Calvinist insurance agent was recognizing what Abraham Kuyper also felt when he spent time at Brighton. Public leadership in various spheres of human interaction has to be grounded in a deep and abiding sense of the Spirit's presence in our lives. Or, to say it another way, holiness has to penetrate our sense and practice of vocation, whatever it may be. The Holiness movement has much to teach us about that personal dimension of our public lives. But the specific challenge here is for that Wesleyan focus to be applied to the complex patterns of leadership flowing out of the desire to "do good" in the cosmic "parish" that Jesus Christ came to renew. The wider world of Christian leadership can learn even more from such a perspective.

Richard Mouw, PhD, is Professor of Faith and Public Life at Fuller Theological Seminary.

Bibliography

Bratt, James D. *Dutch Calvinism in Modern America: A History of a Conservative Subculture.* Grand Rapids: William B. Eerdmans Publishing, 1984.

—. *Abraham Kuyper: Modern Calvinist, Christian Democrat.* Grand Rapids: William B. Eerdmans Publishing, 2013.

Dayton, Donald W. *Discovering an Evangelical Heritage.* Harper and Row, 1976.

Kuyper, Abraham. "Sphere Sovereignty." In *Abraham Kuyper: A Centennial Reader,* ed. James D. Bratt. Grand Rapids: Wm. B. Eerdmans Publishing Co., 1998.

Schneider, Gregory. *The Way of the Cross Leads Home: The Domestication of American Methodism.* Bloomington, Ind.: Indiana University Press, 1993.

Wesley, John. *The Works of Rev. John Wesley,* 3rd edition, vol. 1. London: Wesleyan Methodist Book Room, 1972. Grand Rapids: Baker, reprinted 2007.

Zwaanstra, H. *Reformed Thought and Experience in a New World: A Study of the Christian Reformed Church and Its American Environment, 1890-1918.* Kampen: J. H. Kok, 1973.

Chapter 4 Notes

[1] See Zwaanstra, *Reformed Thought and Experience,* 31, 42-52; Bratt, *Dutch Calvinism,* 57-59.

[2] My account here of Kuyper's experience with the Holiness movement in England draws on Bratt's chapter on the subject in *Abraham Kuyper,* 87-108.

[3] Quoted in Bratt, *Abraham Kuyper,* 94.

[4] Kuyper, "Sphere Sovereignty," 463-490.

[5] Schneider, *The Way of the Cross Leads Home.*

[6] Ibid, 196.

[7] Schneider, *The Way,* 205-207

[8] Kuyper, "Sphere Sovereignty," 488.

[9] Dayton, *Discovering an Evangelical Heritage.*

[10] Wesley, *Works,* June 11, 1739: 202. See also http://www.ccel.org/ccel/wesley/journal.vi.iii.v.html

[11] Ibid.

Part 2

BIBLICAL & THEOLOGICAL REFLECTIONS

5
A Theology of Leadership for Wesleyans

Christopher Bounds

Wesleyan theology recognizes leadership as a gift given by the Holy Spirit, empowering men and women to mobilize individuals and communities toward the "new creation" inaugurated by the life, death, resurrection, and exaltation of Jesus Christ. A Wesleyan theology of leadership is defined by an optimistic conception of divine grace in, a vibrant understanding of personal formation in the image of God fueled by spiritual disciplines, and a clear vision of a redeemed society and world.

THE STUDY OF CHRISTIAN LEADERSHIPA as an academic discipline has accelerated with the dawn of a new millennium. The *Journal for Applied Christian Leadership* (2006) and the *Journal for Biblical Perspectives in Leadership* (2008) represent the type of focused attention now being given to the field. More specifically, scholars have begun to express a distinctive theology of leadership as a way to integrate practical and theoretical aspects into a meaningful Christian understanding.

Wesleyans are active participants in this burgeoning conversation, reflecting upon the unique resources they bring to the table from their distinctive theological tradition. Lovett Weems' *Leadership in the Wesleyan Spirit* provided the first serious foray into the field, followed by Richard Heitzenrater's "Take Thou Authority: Ministerial Leadership in the Wesleyan Heritage," and Randy Maddox's "Formation for Christian Leadership: Wesleyan Reflections."[1] Even graduate institutions like Asbury Theological Seminary have begun to offer degrees in leadership from a Wesleyan perspective. At this point, however, only Kenneth Carder and Laceye Warner's *Grace to Lead: Practicing Leadership in the Wesleyan Tradition* has a fully developed theology of leadership.[2]

With the advent of focused studies in Christian leadership in the Wesleyan tradition serving as a backdrop, the purpose of this chapter is to articulate a theology of leadership for Wesleyans. Because the heart of Wesleyan teaching focuses on the doctrine of salvation, its understanding of Christian leadership is integrated seamlessly into this framework. While leadership and redemption are distinguishable, they are inseparable. Christian leadership exists in service of the "new creation." Therefore, five central points of Wesleyan soteriology must be examined for their relevance in Christian leadership: the doctrine of a new creation.[3]

Leadership and the "New Creation"

Generally speaking, Wesleyans are not known for their detailed work in systematic theology. The one exception is their extensive reflection on soteriology. Individual salvation, the redemption of society, and the restoration of fallen creation drive their theology. While most Christian traditions recognize creation's ultimate salvation does not occur until Christ's second coming, they believe "first evidences" of the *eschaton* are being expressed already. Wesleyans concur, but distinguish themselves from the larger church by their "optimism" in the power of divine grace to bring about in greater ways the "new creation" in present life.

Wesleyans see leadership as a gift of the Holy Spirit given to certain women and men, enabling them to "energize, inspire, and mobilize individuals and communities" toward the "new creation."[4] Beginning with John and Charles Wesley in the British Methodist revival and Francis Asbury and Thomas Coke in the formation of American Methodism, Wesleyan history is punctuated by visionary, transformative, pragmaticin and clergy. While many of its women and men have been leaders focused in the church, others have been at the forefront in struggles for social equality and justice, in the formation of enduring missionary organizations, in the establishment of higher education institutions, in the creation of innovative businesses, in the construction of hospitals, in the service of government and politics, and in the stewardship of creation.[5] Each leader in their respective field has been used by God to contribute to a fuller realization of the "new creation" inaugurated by Christ.

Therefore, Wesleyans believe the gift of leadership must be identified in people, developed, and then employed in service of God's "new creation" in the world. John Wesley believed leaders could be identified by their "natural endowments" and tangible "fruits" in advancing the kingdom of God.[6] To their natural gifts, Wesley believed "acquired endowments" should be added through education in the Christian Scriptures, the liberal arts, logic, and through the development of problem solving and communication skills.[7] Leaders, then, must be "employed in what the angels of God have not the honor to do," to work with Jesus Christ as instruments of God's redemptive work in the world.[8]

The Optimism of Divine Grace in Leadership

Divine grace drives the Wesleyan understanding of redemption. While divine grace is undivided, "it precedes salvation as 'prevenient grace,'" continues in "justifying grace," and is brought to fruition in "sanctifying grace."[9] The scope and depth of divine grace in the world sets Wesleyan soteriology apart from other Protestant perspectives and has implications for a theology of leadership.

The Scope of Grace

A Wesleyan theology of redemption begins with God's prevenient grace, given to humanity to make salvation possible for everyone.[10] Undergirding Wesleyan hope is belief in the unlimited atonement of Christ, confident that "God wills that all be saved and come to the knowledge of the truth." This grace is the work of the Holy Spirit wooing bringing sinful humanity and the world into the experience of the "new creation."[11] While this divine work can be and is resisted, the Spirit continues to work and draw humanity and the larger world to this end.

According to Wesley, prevenient grace makes possible the recognition of general revelation, (a) enabling discernment from the natural order that there is a God who exercises power over the world; (b) giving humanity a moral conscience, helping to understand what is right and wrong, to do the "good;" and (c) preparing them for saving and sanctifying grace in Jesus Christ.[12] Prevenient grace operates on an individual and social level, hastening the first impulses of "new creation" in Christ.

Reformed theology, in contrast, emphasizes a more restrictive view of "common grace" given to all. The Holy Spirit enables humanity to overcome the more destructive elements of sin, establish an ordered society, and achieve some good in the world. However, common grace does not lead to individual or social salvation; it does not make possible participation in the "new creation." Only individuals who are predestined by God's sovereign decree are given electing grace, enabling them to participate in redemption.[13]

An optimism in the scope and fruits of divine grace greatly shapes a Wesleyan understanding of leadership. God is at work in every person, in the different levels of society, and in the created order seeking a positive response to the impinging Kingdom of God. Christian leadership collaborates with this grace. Its exercise therefore must not be confined to the church alone, but stretched to serve wherever the preventing (or prevenient) work of God is found: in the civic, social, economic, political, educational, humanitarian, and ecological spheres of life.

The Depth of Grace

God's prevenient grace seeks to draw all people and society into justifying and sanctifying grace. In justifying grace, through faith in Christ Jesus, repentant believers are pardoned from sin and restored into divine favor. The righteousness of Christ is imputed to them. Adoption into God's family takes place accompanied by its rights, privileges, and responsibilities. New birth is given, bringing them into new life, breaking the hold of sin, and demonstrating the first fruits of God's "new creation."[14]

Sanctifying grace continues what is initiated in new birth. Expressed in the most general terms, sanctification addresses the entire work of transformation in human lives by the Holy Spirit from the moment they are born again until given glorification in death. When the Spirit takes residence in Christians, he begins the process of transforming their attitudes, interests, and actions, leading to entire sanctification, whereby the Spirit liberates them to walk fully in the love of God and neighbor.[15] This sanctifying grace seeks not only their complete transformation, but the full transformation of the larger society as well, enabling the world to anticipate the "new creation " in significant ways in its social bonds and institutions.[16]

While every major Christian tradition believes in justifying and sanctifying grace, the Wesleyan tradition is distinguished by its confidence in the depth to which divine grace can renovate human life and society. Individual and social sin can be broken and the love of God and neighbor can energize every sphere of human life. From a Wesleyan perspective, therefore, Christian leadership in the world goes beyond the goal of restraining sin and evil. Rather, it seeks to cooperate with God in the transformation of the personal and social, mirroring in greater ways the "new creation" experienced fully in the eschatological age to come. A Wesleyan theology of leadership is not characterized by pessimism at the extent of sin in the world, but by the optimism in the power of God's justifying and sanctifying grace to redeem the full measure of the world.

Leadership and the Renewal of the *Imago Dei*

More specifically, the Wesleyan doctrine of "new creation" begins on the personal level. God's redemptive work centers on the restoration of the *imago dei* in humanity. John Wesley believed humanity reflects the image of God in three ways: moral, natural and political.[17] The *moral* image enables humanity to enjoy true righteousness, holiness, love, and knowledge of God through the immediacy of a relationship with God. It forms the guiding principle of humanity's disposition, thoughts, words and deeds. The *natural* image endows humanity with rationality, understanding, free will, and perfectly ordered affections.[18] The *political* image gives humanity the power to govern, whereby they exercise dominion in the created order and relate appropriately to God and humanity.[19] In the Garden of Eden, holiness, righteousness and love informed humanity's reasoning, understanding, will and affections, resulting in the wise exercise of stewardship in the created order, rightly ordered relationships with fellow humanity, and perfect love and obedience to God.

Because of Adam and Eve's fall, the moral image was destroyed in humanity, the natural and political extensively marred.[20] Wesley taught, however, that through participation in God's work of "new creation," the full moral image can be restored in life and significant progress can be made in renewal of the natural and political image.[21] This is the heart of Wesley's doctrine of Christian perfection. Ultimately, whatever is left undone in the *imago dei's* restoration culminates in glorification when the "new creation" is fully realized.[22]

While not all of Wesley's theological heirs appropriate his moral, natural and political paradigm, they describe in similar ways the divine image in humanity, its ruin through sin, and its restoration through Christian perfection in the present life and glorification in the eschatological.[23] This restoration enables believers to walk

> *"Renewal in the moral, natural, and political image is foundational to the formation of Christian leadership"*

in loving relationship and obedience to God, as well as empowered service in the love of neighbor. While there can be progress presently in rationality, understanding, and judgment, these will not be fully renewed and made perfect until glorification.[24] By divine grace, Christians are able to live a life motivated and empowered by holy love, but remain subject to mistakes, misunderstandings, and errors in judgment until final restoration.

Renewal as the Foundation

Renewal in the moral, natural, and political image is foundational to the formation of Christian leadership. From a Wesleyan perspective, no truly Christian leadership is possible apart from a genuine experience of salvation centered in a personal relationship with Jesus Christ and formation in holy love. Restoration of the moral image begins in conversion and continues progressively through sanctifying grace, moving to full reinstatement in life. This restoration forms the inward character and motivation of leaders in the holy love of God and others, empowering them to walk with integrity in the light of God's "new creation" and defining their exercise of leadership.

Sustaining and expanding moral renewal in leaders is active participation in the "means of grace." These are individual and corporate practices essential to the formation of every Christian. In the Wesleyan tradition these include the "instituted" and "prudential" disciplines. The instituted means of grace are associated with works of piety, including prayer, reading the Scriptures, sharing in Holy Communion, fasting, and Christian conferencing. The prudential means, or "works of mercy," consist of practices focused on others, embracing John Wesley's famous instructions to "do no harm," to "do good," and to "attend to all the ordinances of God."[25]

In leadership formation, moral renewal cannot be separated from the natural image. While proper motivation and character in leadership is non-negotiable, it must be united with growth in the natural: an increase in knowledge, wisdom and understanding. These exist in varying degrees from the vestiges of the natural image that remain in fallen humanity; through Holy Spirit given gifts; and from attainment through personal experience and education. A Wesleyan theology of leadership recognizes the need for gifts of wisdom and discernment, combined with education and critical reflection in the exercise of leadership. Because the natural image is never fully restored in life, humility must characterize leadership, with openness to listen from the perspective of others and to embrace constructive criticism as mistakes are made.

Finally, the Spirit's work in redeeming the *imago dei* includes the political image. From a Wesleyan perspective, the redemption of the political is indispensable to the formation of Christian leaders. No human, much less a leader, can thrive in isolation. Leaders need significant connections with other people where they can share their joys, burdens, questions, needs, gifts and spiritual life in mutually reciprocating relationships. Essential to these friendships is accountability in Christian discipleship and in the exercise of leadership. In the Wesleyan tradition, this is accomplished primarily through small groups patterned after "class meetings" in connection with active participation in the local church.

The Redemption of the Social Order

Through renewal of the *imago dei*, separation and alienation caused by sin in every sphere of human relationships is addressed. Holy love through the renewed moral image propels Christians to seek reconciliation in all social connections. The redeemed moral image, operating through the natural, drives and directs the political image. While Wesleyans recognize that the political cannot be restored completely in life, they believe significant progress can be made.[26]

The political image points to the social and relational nature of humanity. The nature of holy love makes humanity other-oriented: directed toward God and other people. Humanity is incomplete and cannot thrive without other people. Within these relationships, holiness and love develop. The impinging 'new creation' for Wesleyans provides grace to overcome human divisions caused by sin, opening people to new relationships with others, empowering reconciliation between divided parties, and supporting stable social systems necessary for human flourishing.[27]

Because of the devastation caused by humanity's first parents, Wesleyan theology takes seriously the systemic nature of sin and looks realistically at the fallen social order. However, it does not despair over such fallenness, looking instead to the possibilities of divine grace that redeems and sanctifies individuals seeking to renew society.[28] While traditional millennial terms—premillennial, postmillennial, realized millennial—are absent in Wesley's writings or sermons, he eschews any perspective that sees human history as a long downward spiral into misery. Instead, he expresses confidence in the power of the Gospel to permeate and transform the world. Wesley's postmillennial sympathies became more explicit in those who followed him: by divine grace the kingdom of God can come here "on earth, as it is in heaven" in greater degrees and power.[29]

The Wesleyan vision of a flourishing human society as an expression of the "new creation" is the goal of Christian leadership. This vision, shaped by the redeemed moral and natural image, is expressed through the political on three levels. Foundationally, it moves Christians to seek reconciliation at every level of society with people from whom they are alienated.[30] It motivates them further to serve those enslaved by social and systemic sin: feeding the hungry, clothing the naked, providing shelter for the homeless, ministering to the sick, visiting prisoners, educating the unwitting, and freeing the captives.[31] Finally, it leads them by the power of God's grace to confront and overcome the root causes of social injustice and systemic sin. Thus, political renewal empowers Christians to apply the "healing balm" of the "new creation" to both the outward symptoms as well as the inward disease of human society.[32]

While the exercise of Christian leadership may be different depending upon its context, the ultimate goal is human flourishing, mirroring in greater degrees the kingdom of God here on earth in personal, social, economic, legal, political, and educational relationships. Christian leaders use their gifts in their respective spheres of influence as a means of God's grace for the transformation of the world.

The Redemption of the Physical Order

Because of human nature's constitution, salvation necessarily includes the created order. For humanity to flourish, the physical world must be redeemed with the personal and social. John Wesley saw the "cosmic" dimensions of God's redemptive work in Christ as a continued expression of the political image of God beyond human social relationships. In contrast to any form of pesky Gnosticism infecting Christianity, a Wesleyan soteriology teaches that God does not destroy fallen creation in the *eschaton*. Because of the "goodness" of the physical world and divine love[33], God renews and perfects it. Humanity's full nature of "body and soul," the diversity of natures in the created order, and the entire universe will be redeemed from all forms of corruption and brought to their ultimate end: union with God.

In the 18th century, John Wesley inherited from his Anglican tradition a form of medieval eschatology focused on a "spiritual" heaven where, at death, Christians are immediately ushered into a transcendent reality, eternally free of the constraints of the physical world.[34] Wesley rejected this model and shifted focus. At Christ's second coming, the dead will be reunited with their bodies, now transformed and suited for their respective destinies through bodily resurrection.[35] After final judgment, the entire created order will be transformed and made incorruptible, no longer subject to disease, decay and death.[36] The "new creation" made possible through the life, death, resurrection and exaltation of Jesus Christ will be fully realized.

Wesley's theological heirs followed suit, recognizing the place of human nature and the created order in the eschatological. Like Christ's resurrection, humanity's resurrected body is identical with the one that died, although with a change in its properties; it will not be a different body, but a different form of the same body, perfectly suited for the "new creation."[37] Wesley's heirs then made the connection between humanity's bodily resurrection and the necessity of a physical world in which to live in the *eschaton*.[38] Christ's bodily resurrection anticipates the future of all created existence, when God will transform the world and be "all in all." As creation has shared in humanity's corruption and fall in the Garden, it participates in the full work of God's redemption, in the glorified and incorruptible state of resurrection.[39] Just as human salvation in Christ is "already" and "not yet," beginning in this life and culminating in the next, so creation participates in the *eschaton* even now in anticipatory ways.[40]

More specifically, like social redemption, a Wesleyan understanding of creation in God's eternal purposes is crucial in defining further the goals of Christian leadership. As physical beings made in the image of God, people do not fully flourish apart from bodily health. God created a perfect material world and human illness, disease, and decay are consequences of sin, not intrinsic to human ontology. There is a certainly measure of flourishing that can occur even in illness. However, I would maintain biblically and theologically that *full* flourishment in the *imago* Dei cannot occur without bodily health as a whole. In the end, this is a significant point of a physical resurrection to incorruptible bodies. As such, Christian leaders therefore must be concerned with humanity's physical health, recognizing its necessity for ultimate human flourishing.

On the other hand, the Wesleyan tradition recognizes that not every aspect of illness, disease, or deprivation will be fully dealt with this side of eternity, and, as Jesus noted, the poor will always be with us. Righteous and godly people deal with illness or face terminal diseases and suffering. Consequently, a corresponding concern of Christian leadership lies in helping people face these physical struggles with trust, faith, embracing a hopeful eschatological vision in which physical death and disease is fully and finally conquered.

Wesleyan theology embraces the role leadership plays in facilitating physical health as an expression of the impinging "new creation." In its theology of the physical world, just as in all other aspects, Wesleyan leadership emphasizes both the "already" and the "not yet" of the kingdom of God in the world.[41]

Christian leadership also must be concerned with the wise care and stewardship of creation. As God restores the full divine image in humanity, the work of reconciliation between humanity and creation deepens. Because humanity is a part of the created order and given stewardship over it, humanity cannot flourish while the created order languishes. The "curse" existing between humanity and the physical world because of sin is being lifted through the "new creation." Godly care of the physical world becomes increasingly possible for humanity through Christ's redemptive work.[42] Therefore, one of the overarching goals of Wesleyan leadership is the holistic care and healing of human nature in "body and soul" and all creation.

Conclusion

In summary, Wesleyan theology recognizes leadership as a Holy Spirit given gift to certain women and men, empowering them to inspire and mobilize individuals and communities toward the "new creation" inaugurated by the life, death, resurrection and exaltation of Jesus Christ. A theology of leadership for Wesleyans is defined by an optimistic conception of divine grace in the world, a vibrant understanding of personal formation in the image of God fueled by spiritual disciplines, and a clear vision of a redeemed society and world.

First, Wesleyans believe divine grace is active in every person and in all levels of human society, seeking to draw the world into the new creation. Christian leadership therefore is not strictly limited to the church and not prone to despair, but works in synergistic partnership with the Holy Spirit to experience Christ's inaugurated kingdom.

Second, for leadership to be Christian, leaders must experience extensive renewal of the *imago dei*. Most important is restoration of the moral image which begins in spiritual conversion and progresses in life, leading to entire sanctification. Renewal of the moral image is foundational for a Christian leader, sanctifying their intentions and affections, and enabling them to walk in holy love of God and neighbor.[43] While proper motivation and character in leadership is non-negotiable, it must be united with growth in the natural and political image. Christian leaders must hone their gift by accruing knowledge, wisdom and understanding through education, critical reflection and experience. The political image must be cultivated through the development of significant friendships and relationships of . Wesleyan theology recognizes Christian leaders are formed by practicing spiritual disciplines. The holistic and holy renewal in the image of God is sustained and nourished through active engagement with the "instituted" and "prudential" means of grace.

Finally, Wesleyan theology provides a clear vision of the purpose of Christian leadership—participation in the redemption of society and the created order—whether in the personal, social, economic, legal, political, educational, medical or ecological spheres of life. Wherever a Christian leader serves, the vision is one that expresses in some way the dawning of Christ's new creation. Christian leaders renewed in the image of God who exercise their gifts become a means of God's transforming grace in the lives of individual person, in human society, and in the physical world.

Christopher Bounds, PhD, is Professor of Wesleyan Studies and Gardner Professor for Promotion and Holiness at Asbury University.

Bibliography

Alexander, Neil M., ed., *The Book of Discipline of The United Methodist Church, 2008.* Nashville, TN: The United Methodist Publishing House, 2008.

Berkhof, Louis. *Systematic Theology.* Grand Rapids, MI: William. B. Eerdmans Publishing Co., 1968.

Bounds, Christopher T. "God's Ongoing Redemption of All Creation," in *Creation Care: Christian Voices on God, Humanity, and the Environment,* ed. Joseph Coleson. Indianapolis, IN: Wesleyan Publishing House, 2010. 40-57

Carder, Kenneth, and Laceye Warner. *Grace to Lead: Practicing Leadership in the Wesleyan Tradition.* Nashville, TN: General Board of Higher Education and Ministry, The United Methodist Church, 2010.

Cobb, John. *Grace and Responsibility: A Wesleyan Theology for Today.* Nashville, TN: Abingdon Press, 1995.

Collins, Kenneth J. *The Theology of John Wesley: Holy Love and the Shape of Grace.* Abingdon Press, 2007.

Fletcher, John. *The Whole Works of the Reverend John Fletcher.* London: Partridge and Oakley, 1835.

Grider, Kenneth. *A Wesleyan-Holiness Theology.* Kansas City: Beacon Hill Press of Kansas City, 1994.

Henderson, D. Michael. *John Wesley's Class Meeting: A Model for Making Disciples.* Nappanee, IN: Evangel Publishing House, 1997.

Heitzenrater, Richard. "Take Thou Authority: Ministerial Leadership in the Wesleyan Heritage." *Pulpit and Pew: Research on Pastoral Leadership.* Accessed February 2016. http://bit.ly/1Z6813v

Hills, A.M. *Fundamental Christian Theology: A Systematic Theology.* Pasadena, CA: C. J. Kinne, Pasadena College, 1931.

Hodge, Charles. *Systematic Theology, vol. II.* Grand Rapids, MI: William. B. Eerdmans Publishing Co., 1997.

Maddox, Randy. "Formation for Christian Leadership: Wesleyan Reflections." *Summary of Proceedings* (American Theological Library Association) 57 (2003):114–26

Maddox, Randy. "Nurturing the New Creation." In *Wesleyan Perspectives on the New Creation,* edited by M. Douglas Meeks (Nashville, TN: Kingswood Books, 2004).

Miley, John. *Systematic Theology.* New York: Eaton and Mains, 1894.

Oden, Thomas C. *John Wesley's Teaching: Volume 4: Ethics and Society.* Grand Rapids, MI: Zondervan, 2014.

Oden, Thomas C. *Classic Christianity: A Systematic Theology.* New York: HarperOne, 2009.

Pope, William B. *A Compendium of Christian Theology.* New York: Phillips & Hunt, 1880.

Ralston, Thomas N. *Elements of Divinity,* ed. T. O. Summers. Nashville: Cokesbury Press, 1924.

Reasoner, Vic. "The Hope of a Christian World: Wesleyan Eschatology and Cultural Transformation," *The Arminian Magazine* 25 (Spring 2007): 1-4.

Runyon, Theodore. *The New Creation: John Wesley's Theology Today.* Nashville, TN: Abingdon Press, 1998: 200-6.

Smith, Timothy L. *Revivalism and Social Reform*. Nashville, TN: Abingdon Press, 1957.

Thompson, Andrew. *The Means of Grace: Traditioned Practice in Today's World*. Franklin, TN: Seedbed Publishing, 2015.

Watson, Richard. *A Biblical and Theological Dictionary*. New York: Carlton & Porter, 1856.

Watson, Richard. *Theological Institutes*. New York: Hunt and Eaton, 1889.

Watson, Kevin. *Pursuing Social Holiness: The Band Meeting in Wesley's Thought and Popular Methodist Practice*. New York, NY: Oxford University Press, 2014.

Weems, Lovett. *Leadership in the Wesleyan Spirit*. Nashville, TN: Abingdon Press, 1999.

Wesley, John. *The Works of John Wesley*, ed. Thomas Jackson. London: Wesleyan Methodist Book Room, 1872; Reprint by Baker Book House, 1978.

—. "The Bristol Conference of May 12-15, 1746," §47-48, *Works*, 10:177-78.

Wesley, John. *Sermons*, ed. Albert C. Outler, *The Bicentennial Edition of the Works of John Wesley* (Nashville, TN: Abingdon Press, 1976.

Wiley, H. Orton. *Christian Theology*. Kansas City: Beacon Hill Press, 1943.

Chapter 5 Notes

[1] Weems, *Leadership in the Wesleyan Spirit*; Heitzenrater's "Take Thou Authority"; Maddox' "Formation for Christian Leadership: Wesleyan Reflections".

[2] Carder and Warner, *Grace to Lead*.

[3] Central to my task is the identification of certain fundamental ideas in Wesleyan theology relevant to leadership, originating in John Wesley and early Methodists and running through the history of the Wesleyan tradition. To do so, I draw upon the works of early Methodists: John Wesley, *The Works of John Wesley* (Thomas Jackson, ed.), and Outler, *Sermons, The Bicentennial Edition of the Works of John Wesley*, Fletcher, *The Whole Works of the Reverend John Fletcher*; and Watson, *Theological Institutes*, and *A Biblical and Theological Dictionary* (New York: Carlton & Porter, 1856); from the nineteenth and early twentieth centuries: Pope, *A Compendium of Christian Theology*; Miley, *Systematic Theology*; and Ralston, *Elements of Divinity*; and from the twentieth and twenty-first centuries: Hills, *Fundamental Christian Theology*; Wiley, *Christian Theology*; Grider, *A Wesleyan-Holiness Theology*; Maddox, *Responsible Grace*; and Thomas C. Oden, *Classic Christianity*.

[4] Carder and Warner, *Grace to Lead*, 27.

[5] Examples of exemplary Wesleyan women and men leaders in the Church: Phoebe Palmer and E. Stanley Jones; in causes of social inequity and justice: Luther Lee and Jo Anne Lyon; in forming enduring mission agencies: Charles and Lettie Cowman; in establishing institutions of higher education: Iva Durham Vennard and Henry Clay Morrison; in innovative businesses: Stanley Tam and S.S. Kresge; and in politics: Elizabeth Dole and William McKinley.

[6] Wesley, "An Address to Clergy," *Works*, 10: 481-82.

[7] Ibid, 482-86.

[8] Wesley, "The Bristol Conference of May 12-15, 1746," §47-48, *Works*, 10:177-78.

[9] Alexander, *The Book of Discipline*, 46.

[10] Kenneth J. Collins accurately describes Wesley's doctrine of prevenient grace in *The Theology of John Wesley*. See also Wesley, 'Predestination Calmly Considered', *Works*, vol. 10: 229, 'A Dialogue between a Predestinarian and a Friend', *Works*, 10: 392; Watson, *A Theological Dictionary*, 217; Pope, *Compendium of Christian Theology*, 2: 365-66; Ralston, *Elements of Divinity*, 329-44; Wiley, *Christian Theology*, 2: 344-57; Grider, *A Wesleyan-Holiness Theology*, 351-55.

[11] Watson, *A Theological Dictionary*, 51-56; Pope, *Compendium of Christian Theology*, 2: 292-97; Ralston, *Elements of Divinity*, 262-77; Wiley, *Christian Theology*, II: 295-97; Grider, *A Wesleyan-Holiness Theology*, 334-35.

[12] Collins, *The Theology of John Wesley*, 14-15, 73-82; Watson, *A Theological Dictionary*, 217; Pope, *Compendium of Christian Theology*, 2: 365-66; Ralston, *Elements of Divinity*, 329-44; Wiley, *Christian Theology*, II: 344-57; Grider, *A Wesleyan-Holiness Theology*, 351-55.

[13] Berkhof, *Systematic Theology*, 432-46; Hodge, *Systematic Theology*, II:654-675.

[14] Wesley, Sermon 1, "Salvation by Faith," §II.2-7, *Works*, 1:121-25; Sermon 5, "Justification by Faith," §II.5, *Works*, 1:189-90; Watson, *A Theological Dictionary*, 297-302; Pope, *Christian Compendium*, II: 404-17; Ralston, *Elements of Divinity*, 355-73; Maddox, *Responsible Grace*, 166-76.

[15] John Wesley, Sermon 43, "The Scripture Way of Salvation," §III.4-13, *Works*, 2:164-67; Sermon 14, "The Repentance of Believers," §I.1-III.4, *Works*, 1:335-52; Watson, *A Theological Dictionary*, 490-91; Pope, *Christian Compendium*, III: 35-44; Ralston, *Elements of Divinity*, 444-72; Wiley, *Christian Theology*, 2: 471-76; Maddox, *Responsible Grace*, 177-79.

[16] John Wesley, Sermon 40, "Christian Perfection," §I.1-II.30, *Works*, 2:100-21; Sermon 76, "On Perfection," §I.1-III.12, *Works*, 3:72-87; Watson, *A Theological Dictionary*, 490-91; Pope, *Christian Compendium*, III: 44-61; Ralston, *Elements of Divinity*, 457-72; Wiley, *Christian Theology*, II:487-517; Grider, *A Wesleyan-Holiness Theology*, 367-420; Maddox, *Responsible Grace*, 179-89.

[17] Wesley, Sermon 45, "The New Birth," §I.1, *Works*, 2:188.

[18] Wesley, Sermon 62, "The End of Christ's Coming," § I.3-7, *Works*, 2:474-76.

[19] Wesley, "The New Birth," §I.1, *Works*, 2:188.

[20] Ibid., § I.2-3, *Works*, 2:189-90; Sermon 62, "The End of Christ's Coming," § I.10, *Works*, 2:477. Also see Wesley, Sermon 141, "The Image of God," *Works*, 4:290-300.

[21] Maddox, "Nurturing the New Creation," 29; Wesley, Sermon 77, "Spiritual Worship," §II.6, *Works*, 3:96; Sermon 62, "The End of Christ's Coming," § III.1-6, *Works*, 2:480-84; Sermon 76, "Christian Perfection," *Works*, 3:70-87; Sermon 141, "The Image of God," § III.1-3, *Works*, 4:299-300.

[22] Wesley, Sermon 76, "Christian Perfection," §I.1-3, *Works*, 3:72-74; Sermon 40, "Christian Perfection," §I.1-9, *Works*, 2:100-5.

[23] For examples of those who follow Wesley's basic paradigm, see Watson, *Theological Institutes*, II: 8-18; Pope, *Christian Compendium*, I:424-28; Wiley, *Christian Theology*, II:32-39; Maddox, *Responsible Grace*, 68-72; and Runyon, *The New Creation*, 14-19.

[24] Watson, *A Biblical Dictionary*, 439; Pope, *Christian Compendium*, 3: 450-54; Miley, *Systematic Theology*, 2: 473-75; Ralston, *Elements of Divinity*, 538-42; Hills, *Fundamental Christian Theology*, 2: 411-14; Wiley, *Christian Theology*, 3: 380-85; Oden, *Classic Christianity*, 794, 824-26, 836-39.

[25] John Wesley, "Minutes of Several Conversations," Jackson, vol. 8: 322-24.

[26] Wesley, Sermon 60, "The General Deliverance," §I.3-5, *Works*, 2:440-41; Collins, *The Theology of John Wesley.*

[27] For an excellent discussion of this issue from a larger Christian perspective, see Miroslav Volf, *A Public Faith: How Followers of Christ Should Serve the Common Good* (Grand Rapids, MI: Brazos Press, 2011).

[28] Wesley, Sermon 60, "The General Deliverance," §I.3-5, *Works*, 2:440-41; Sermon 63, "The General Spread of the Gospel," § 1-27, *Works*, 2:485-99; Pope, *Christian Compendium*, 2: 359-64; Ralston, *Elements of Divinity*, 815-48; Maddox, *Responsible Grace*, 235-47.

[29] Reasoner, "The Hope of a Christian World."

[30] Henderson, *John Wesley's Class Meeting*, 17-32; Watson, *Pursuing Social Holiness*, 39-71.

[31] Thompson, *The Means of Grace*, 111-22.

[32] Oden, *John Wesley's Teaching*, 59-178; Smith, *Revivalism*, 114-47.

[33] The basic premise here is that the material world is good simply because God created it and called in "good". That it is badly corrupted by the effects of fallen humanity does not diminish its ultimate goodness as a fundamental expression of a holy, good, and perfect Creator. The Bible makes the case from Genesis to Revelation that God will ultimately redeem, heal, and renew the material world as well as the spiritual. Both the Reformed and Wesleyan traditions ultimately agree on the eternal destiny of creation, the difference is how each views the redemption of the temporal order.

[34] Maddox, *Responsible Grace*, 231-35. Here, Maddox is reliant upon Colleen McDannell and Bernard Lang, *Heaven: A History* (New Haven, CT: Yale University Press, 1988).

[35] Benjamin Calamy, "The Resurrection of the Dead," ed. John Wesley in *The Works of John Wesley*, ed. Thomas Jackson, 7:474-85.

[36] Wesley, Sermon 64, "The New Creation," 2:500-10. See Maddox's discussion of Wesley's vision of animals in the "new creation" in *Responsible Grace*, 246-47, 253.

[37] Watson, *A Biblical Dictionary*, 822; Pope, *Compendium of Christian Theology*, 3: 406-8; Miley, *Systematic Theology*, 2:453; Ralston, *Elements of Divinity*, 408-9; Wiley, *Christian Theology*, 3:325-38; Oden, *Classic Christianity*, 794-95.

[38] Pope, *Compendium of Christian Theology*, 3:447-48; Miley, *Systematic Theology*, 2:472-73; Wiley, *Christian Theology*, 3:388; Oden, *Classic Christianity*, 820-21.

[39] Pope, *Compendium of Christian Theology*, 3:447-48; Miley, *Systematic Theology*, 2:472-73; Wiley, *Christian Theology*, 3:388; Oden, *Classic Christianity*, 820-21. See also Bounds, "God's Ongoing Redemption of All Creation."

[40] Maddox, "Nurturing the New Creation"; Runyon, *The New Creation,* 200-206.

[41] There are scientific and theological debates about human nature's constitution, whether humanity is composed of just physical matter or matter joined with a spiritual substance. Within these debates, Wesleyans recognize the fundamental unity between human nature and person-hood. There is certainly a distinction between human nature and the human person, but they are inseparably one and affect one another. Formation as persons is mediated through human nature as "embodied souls."

[42] Cobb, *Grace and Responsibility,* 52-53; Maddox, 'Nurturing the New Creation,' 43-49; Runyon, *The New Creation*, 200-7.

6
Old Testament Models for Leading the Wesleyan Way

Jerome Van Kuiken

The Old Testament presents a significant foundation for a Wesleyan approach to leadership. The main categories of leadership in the Old Testament, including prophet, priest, king, and sage (shepherd is considered elsewhere) all present leadership insights both from Scripture and as contemporary categories of cultural leaders. Far from being a facile patriarchal approach, as well, the Old Testament helps to found values of shared leadership and empowering of unexpected leaders, helpful for today's leadership discussions.

LEADERSHIP IN ANCIENT ISRAEL took a variety of forms. One much-used method of categorizing the most important forms of leadership in the Old Testament is the *munus triplex* or "threefold office " of prophet, priest, and king. Holders of each of these offices were initiated into their duties by a ceremony of anointing, so that when we confess Jesus of Nazareth as the Christ or Messiah (both of these titles mean "Anointed One"), we are identifying him as the ultimate fulfillment of these three offices. This theology of the *munus triplex* appeared in the early church and again at the Reformation, when John Calvin strongly promoted it. Calvin influenced the Church of England, which in turn influenced John Wesley.[1] In his *Explanatory Notes upon the New Testament*, Wesley writes,

> We are by nature at a distance from God, alienated from Him, and incapable of a free access to Him. Hence we want [i.e., need] a Mediator, an Intercessor; in a word, a Christ in His priestly office. This regards our state with respect to God. And with

respect to ourselves, we find a total darkness, blindness, ignorance of God, and the things of God. Now here we want Christ in His prophetic office, to enlighten our minds, and teach us the whole will of God. We find also within us a strange misrule of appetites and passions. For these we want Christ in His royal character, to reign in our hearts, and subdue all things to Himself.[2]

In spite of its pedigree, the *munus triplex* is not without critics. As Adam Johnson has noted, "The lone reference to the anointing of a prophet occurs in 1 Kgs 19:16, making for an exegetically weak connection between the name 'anointed one' and the prophetic office."[3] He continues, "The *munus triplex* offers a promising framework for integrating the Israelite theocracy into our understanding of the person and work of Christ....While this is an admirable strength, why...omit a consideration of Jesus as shepherd, wisdom and husband?"[4] Why indeed? Although none of these roles has an anointing ceremony tied to it, each is indeed a form of biblical leadership. Still, the Old Testament generally uses the language of shepherding particularly as a figure of speech for kingship, as discussed elsewhere in the present volume.[5] Familial terms are likewise used metaphorically for those in other offices, especially the royal one.[6] In the case of wisdom, things are a bit different. Sages ("wise ones") in Israel and the rest of the ancient Near East were a distinct class from kings, priests, and prophets. Like these other offices, wisdom, too, served the theocracy and had its own special literature.[7] Ben Witherington has called attention to the ways in which Jesus fulfills this wisdom tradition just as he does the other three theocratic offices.[8] Hence this chapter will expand the usual *munus triplex* to a *munus quadruplex* and look for leadership insights from the Old Testament models of king, priest, prophet, and sage.

Understanding the Four Offices

Before looking at Old Testament history and contemporary relevance of the four offices, we need a clear idea of what ancient Near Eastern people meant by these terms. The ancient significance of kings, priests, prophets, and sages can be fairly unfamiliar to readers raised in a democratized, secularized culture. In the context of contemporary Western civilization, monarchs (even in nations in which they are allowed to remain as figureheads) have been usurped functionally by elected politicians. The cosmic meaning-making ceremonies of priests are now the domain of entertainers (such as artists and athletes), with cinemas, sports stadiums, and concert stages as the latter-day sanctuaries of public worship.[9] The prophetic mantle has passed to the press and social media in terms of documenting and interpreting current events, exposing corruption, "speaking truth to power," and even foretelling the future by means of manifestos, op-eds, weather forecasts, and astrology columns.[10] The sages have evolved into scientists, whether those such as psychologists, political scientists, and anthropologists who study human nature or others like paleontologists, climatologists, and cosmologists who study nature more generally.

In the world of the Old Testament, kings were primarily commanders-in-chief charged with fighting foreign armies. For this reason, they were male; women were not typically warriors in the ancient world (Greek legends of Amazons are the exception which proves the rule). Kings were also expected to uphold domestic justice by making and enforcing laws. They had religious responsibilities as well: building or maintaining temples and setting a good example of piety for their subjects to follow. At times in the ancient Near East, kings doubled as priests. Lastly, kingship was hereditary, being passed down through a dynastic line in order to ensure the peaceful, orderly transition of administration.

Besides the monarchy, the priesthood represented a second foundational institution in ancient Near Eastern societies. Everyone in these societies believed in the gods, and since the gods governed the cosmos and had at their disposal such ills as diseases, natural disasters, madness, and infertility of people, animals, and land, keeping them happy was a matter of life-and-death importance. Priests served as the bureaucracy for managing relations between people and their deities. What kept the gods placated was public worship and especially blood sacrifice (usually of animals, although human—particularly child—sacrifice was sometimes practiced). Shrines and temples were the worship centers where sacrifices regularly took place and where the gods were thought to dwell bodily in the form of idols. These worship centers required staffing by priests who had mastered the complex rituals involved in properly honoring deity. As the gods came in both sexes, so too did their priests.

Priesthood under Old Testament regulations stood apart from standard ancient Near Eastern priesthood at several points. Worship was to be offered only to a single, all-sovereign God who could not be imaged by an idol; there was to be only one sanctuary (first the portable Tabernacle, later the immobile Temple in Jerusalem); priests were exclusively male, although women could act in a very limited supporting role (Exodus 38:8; 1 Sam. 2:22); priests were also exclusively from one tribe (Levi) and family (Aaron's), and kings from other tribes were never permitted to usurp priestly duties.5[11] Despite these significant differences, Israel's priests paralleled those of pagan nations in serving as mediators between the divine and human realms: they represented the people to God by offering sacrifices, incense, and prayer in order to atone for the people's sins and express the people's praise and thanks; and they represented God to the people by pronouncing pardon and blessing in God's name and instructing them in God's will. Although in the quote at this chapter's start Wesley assigns the task to "teach us the whole will of God" to the prophetic office, in Scripture the priests had the duty to teach God's law[12] and to use the enigmatic "Urim and Thummim" to give God's answer to specific inquiries.[13]

Kings employed sages and prophets as court advisers, although there were also members of both groups who functioned independently of official funding and control. Both sages and prophets could be male or female. Sages were simply persons recognized for their wisdom; across the ancient Near East, though, there were schools for training sages.[14] While sages drew on a tradition of keen observation of life in order to give counsel, prophets were considered to be the mouthpieces of the gods, relaying divine messages to human beings. These messages might predict the future or comment on the present or the past. Prophets could use a variety of means to receive divine revelations: some biblical examples include pagan prophets' divination (Num. 23:1) and ecstatic dancing and self-harm (1 Kgs. 18:26–29), as well as Elisha's use of music (2 Kgs. 3:15). Israel's prophets also chronicled the nation's history.[15] As did the priests, so also the prophets and sages of the Old Testament operated within the parameters of the moral monotheism encoded in the Law of Moses. We turn now to the development and interaction of the priestly, prophetic, sapiential (wisdom), and royal roles across the pages of Israel's Scriptures.

An Old Testament History of the Four Offices[16]

The Old Testament's opening chapter portrays God as creating humankind in the divine image (Gen. 1:26–27). In the ancient Near East, kings and priests—but not ordinary people—were considered to be "in the image" of the gods. The Bible begins, then, with a radically democratized, inclusive vision of priesthood and kingship: humans in general, not just an elite few, are in the image of the one true God and carry regal, priestly dignity and responsibility.[17] Given that later Israelite kingship and priesthood were limited to males (queens were royal consorts, not rulers in their own right),[18] it is especially striking that Gen. 1:27 presents females as well as males as made in God's image.

Later chapters of Genesis describe a much less egalitarian world: there are rulers ranging from Pharaoh, lord of ancient superpower Egypt, down to the petty kinglets of individual Canaanite cities like Sodom. Egypt has a priestly caste (Gen. 41:45; 47:22) and sages in Pharaoh's court (Gen. 41:8), among whom Joseph rises to near-royal authority due to his God-given wisdom. In Canaan, we meet at least one king who is also a priest: Melchizedek of Salem (Gen. 14:18). The patriarchs Abraham, Isaac, and Jacob are prophets[19] and function as priests for their extended families by building altars, offering sacrifices, and interceding for others—especially when Abraham prays for divine mercy on Sodom (Gen. 18:16–33). Abraham also fulfills one of the chief functions of later Israelite kings by leading his people into battle against foreign foes (Gen. 14:14–16).

Prophet & Priest

The era of the exodus from Egypt witnesses the birth of Israelite theocracy under the leadership of the prophets Moses and Miriam and the priest Aaron. Moses is the prophet *par excellence*, setting an unmatched standard for intimacy with God and miraculous deeds.[20] Yet he also exercises the roles of the other three offices: Like a sage, he teaches precepts to make Israel a "wise and understanding people"

(Deut. 4:5–6).[21] Brought up in the Egyptian royal household, Moses acts as *de facto* monarch of his people, performing the duties commonly expected of an ancient Near Eastern king: he judges their disputes, hands down laws, summons Israel to arms, and establishes a sanctuary and a priesthood. Moses himself conducts the priestly functions of altar-building, sacrifice, and consecration of people[22], as well as intercession.[23]

Yet he is not possessive of his privileges. The hereditary priestly line which he establishes is not his own but his brother Aaron's (and this despite Aaron's role in the idolatrous Golden Calf incident). He delegates judicial duties to Israel's elders.[24] When these elders temporarily receive the gift of prophecy, he sighs, "I wish that all the Lord's people were prophets and that the Lord would put his Spirit on them!" (Num. 11:29) He hopes that Israel as a whole will become wise in the ways of the Lord so that surrounding nations will be drawn to the witness of its wisdom (Deut. 4:6). He communicates God's intention for all Israel—not just Aaron's descendants—to be "a kingdom of priests and a holy nation" (Exo. 19:6) mediating knowledge of the one true God to the world (Exod. 34:10). This democratizing vision of priestly holiness receives general expression in the Holiness Code, in which all Israelites are called to be holy as God is holy by avoiding ritually unclean animals (that is, non-kosher food) and idolatry and by maintaining justice (including towards resident foreigners) and sexual purity (Lev. 19–20, esp. 19:2; 20:7–8, 22–26). More specific expressions of this democratizing impulse are the laws about vows, whereby any person, animal, or property may be devoted to God (Lev. 27), and especially the Nazirite vow, by which any man or woman from any tribe and family may voluntarily imitate some of the same standards of holiness as those which were mandatory for the exclusively male, exclusively Aaronic high priests (compare Num. 6:1–21 with Lev. 10:8–9; 21:5, 10–11).

Judges

Between the death of Moses and the birth of the monarchy under Saul, the administration of Israel comes mainly from an irregular series of leaders: Joshua and the so-called judges. In fact, the only "judges" recorded as exercising judicial functions are the prophet Deborah (Judg. 4:4–5), the priest Eli (1 Sam. 4:18), and the prophet-priest Samuel and his sons (1 Sam. 7:15–8:3). During this period, the nation of Israel consists of a collection of largely independent tribes that band together under a charismatic figure just long enough to gain a foothold in Canaan (under Joshua) and then again and again to throw off the foreign forces that keep oppressing them as God's punishments for Israel's repeated tumbles into idolatry. The instability of no strong central government and no fixed line of leadership succession leaves Israel vulnerable not only to external threats but also to infighting. Repeatedly we see civil wars or rumors of them among the tribes.[25] The author of Judges brackets the final story, in which brother tribes nearly wipe out the tribe of Benjamin, with the terse explanation, "In those days Israel had no king" (Judg. 19:1; 21:25).

Also during this era, sagecraft is scarce (see Judg. 8:21; ch. 9; 14:12–18)[26] and, with the exemplary exceptions of Deborah and Samuel, prophets are in short supply: "In those days the word of the Lord was rare" (1 Sam. 3:1; cf. 2:27–36). The most stable of the four offices is the hereditary priesthood, but near the end of the judges' era, abuse of priestly power and military defeat result in the deaths of the high priest Eli and his sons and the brief captivity of the Ark of the Covenant (1 Sam. 2:12–6:21), as well as the destruction of God's sanctuary, which was then located at Shiloh (Ps. 78:59–64; Jer. 7:12–14; 26:6).

Kings

The craving for stable security prompts the Israelites to demand that their last judge, Samuel, institute kingship. This was not a new idea. The judge Gideon had been urged to start a monarchic dynasty, but he had refused on theological grounds: only God was king of Israel (Judg. 8:22–23). Samuel takes Gideon's view on the matter, but at God's direction anoints Saul as king, all the while warning the people that kingship brings loss of personal liberty and that it cannot substitute for obedience to God (1 Sam. 8–12). Over the next few centuries, Israel's experience of monarchy is mixed. Under its second and third kings, David and Solomon, Israel achieves a golden age of national unity, security, and prosperity. God rewards David's whole-hearted devotion with the promise of an everlasting dynasty (1 Chr. 17). David displays his piety by reorganizing the priesthood and its worship, as well as preparing for the building of a temple (1 Chr. 22:1–29:9). He humbly takes counsel from priests (1 Sam. 22:9–10; 23:9–12; 30:7–8), wise women and men (1 Sam. 25:18–35; 2 Sam. 14:1–21; 16:23), and prophets (2 Sam. 7:1–17; 12:1–15; 24:11--14). His son Solomon builds God's temple and gains an international reputation as the greatest sage of his day, inspiring the writing of the Old Testament's Wisdom Literature.

As recorded in the books of Kings and Chronicles, later rulers from David's line are at their best when they imitate him by heeding the prophets, maintaining the temple, and reforming national worship in the face of ever-encroaching idolatry. The dark side of the monarchy, though, shows when rulers promote idolatry and injustice. Due to these sins, Solomon's kingdom splits apart after his death, with a series of idolatrous kings reigning over the northern tribes while David's dynasty endures in Judah. God sends prophet after prophet to both kingdoms, but eventually both fall to Mesopotamian empires as punishment for false worship and oppression of the weak. Writing in the last days of the Kingdom of Judah, the priestly prophet Jeremiah bemoans the foolish sages, false prophets, godless priests, and lawless kings, all of whom expect God to save them from destruction even as they break God's covenant (e.g., Jer. 8:1–11; chs. 23, 28–29, 34). Yet he pledges God's commitment to restore and multiply the kingly line of David and the priestly line of Levi (Jer. 33:14–22).

Israel's kingdoms fall; God's temple is razed; the people are exiled from their homeland for seven decades before a small minority return and rebuild the temple under the auspices of their foreign overlords. Yet even in exile, God raises up the prophet Ezekiel; the sage and prophet Daniel; and Queen Esther and her cousin Mordecai, whose ancestry recalls King Saul's and whose story reverses the disobedience that cost Saul his kingship.[27] Those who return from exile find that the lineages of the royal and priestly lines have been preserved (1 Chr. 2, 3, 6). Among their leaders are priestly sage Ezra, David's descendant Zerubbabel, the high priest Joshua, and the prophets Haggai, Zechariah, and Malachi. Haggai foresees glory for the temple and royal honor for Zerubbabel (Hag. 2:7–9, 23). Zechariah crowns Joshua the high priest, symbolizing a union of priestly and kingly roles (Zech. 6:9–14). He also predicts that Israel's king will ride in on a donkey to make peace (Zech. 9:9) and that prophecy will cease (Zech. 13:2–6). Malachi reaffirms God's universal kingship (Mal. 1:14) and foretells that God will purify the priests (Mal. 3:1–4) and send the prophet Elijah before coming in judgment (Mal. 4:5–6). In the roughly four centuries between Malachi, the last of the Old Testament's prophets, and the advent of Jesus, we find sages like Jesus the son of Sirach and the author of The Wisdom of Solomon (both of whose writings are included in the Apocrypha), as well as the union of temple and palace in the Maccabees, descendants of Aaron who win Israel's independence and serve as both kings and high priests. One of the Maccabean dynasty, John Hyrcanus, is even considered to be a prophet as well as priest-king.[28] In the end, though, the Roman Empire conquers Israel, and the stage is set for the New Testament fulfillment of the fourfold office.

Learning as Wesleyans from the Four Offices

Rooted in Divine Purpose

The Old Testament contributes several perspectives to a "Wesleyan way" of leadership. First, leadership is a necessity, rooted in God's creative purpose. The postmodern climate promotes a deep suspicion, even hostility, toward the notions of power and authority bound up with leadership. But the Bible's vision of the world has no place for any "holy anarchy" even before the original invasion of sin or after its overcoming in the New Creation. Humanity is meant to be the benevolent rulers and sages who steward God's world (Ps. 8) in keeping with the divine Wisdom through whom it was made (Prov. 8) so that it becomes all that it was intended to be. We are called to exercise a prophetic, priestly role in "voicing creation's praise"[29] and interceding on its behalf before God while also blessing it and expressing the divine will for it on God's behalf.[30]

Democratization of Ministry

Second, as pioneered by the Gen. 1 creation story, a democratizing impulse surfaces from time to time in the Old Testament. Even under Israelite patriarchy, in which women lose full access to the priestly and royal functions implied in their creation in the *imago Dei*, they still may be Nazirites, judges like Deborah, prophets like Huldah (2 Kgs. 22:12–20), and sages like the wise woman of Abel Beth-Maacah (2 Sam. 20:14–22). Even in a status-conscious ancient Near Eastern context, leaders may arise from unlikely conditions: Joseph is by turns a slave and a prisoner before becoming second-in-command of Egypt; Moses (Exod. 4:10) and Jeremiah (Jer. 1:6) lack competence in public speaking; Gideon (Judg. 6:15) and Saul (1 Sam. 9:21) express shock that God would choose them despite their lowly lineages; David is the youngest of eight sons (1 Sam. 16:10–11); Miriam and Esther are the daughters of a subject people under mighty empires. Even with the surrounding nations steeped in paganism and hostility toward Israel, the Old Testament dares to foretell that these nations and their rulers will serve Israel's God[31] and that he will pour out his Spirit on all people, so that young and old, male and female alike will be prophets (Joel 2:28–29). This democratizing biblical theme grounds much historic Wesleyan practice, from Wesley's commissioning lay preachers and opposing slavery to The Wesleyan Church's ordaining women and recognizing former mission fields as equal General Conferences. The democratizing principle means that leaders in the church may come from any background; but it also means that, as Methodist theologian Tom Greggs has stressed, the church *as a whole* acts in a spiritual leadership role towards the world by praying for it and evangelizing it.[32]

Accountability of Leaders

Third, the offices of leadership, like every other aspect of the created order, have been warped by the Fall. The paradox of leadership outside of Eden is that while leadership becomes all the more necessary for the sake of restraining sinful disorder, leadership itself becomes part of the problem. Without leadership, evil flourishes; with leadership, evil may flourish even more. Democratization prevents the absolute power that, so the saying goes, corrupts absolutely; but a democracy of the depraved can produce dangerous gridlock or deadly mob rule, thus setting the conditions for the rise of despotism. The Old Testament proves this paradox at length. Leading the Wesleyan way means seeking and offering accountability to fight the perennial twin temptations of leadership: worship of power (idolatry) and abuse of power (injustice).[33] Regular reflection on the Old Testament history of leadership provides one means of holding ourselves and others accountable. We may likewise learn from the separation of powers and system of checks and balances that we see both in the biblical division of kingship from priesthood and in the whistleblowing roles of prophets and sages. Neither the sacredness of an office nor the godliness of a past administrative record nor God's covenant to bless their future ever exempted any Old Testament leader from the possibility and punishing of moral failure—just ask Moses, excluded from the Promised Land for presumptuously striking a rock (Num. 20:1–13), or David, who brought disaster on his kingdom as a result of adultery and murder (2 Sam. 11–20) and a census that smacked of self-reliance (2 Sam. 24).

Leadership of the Holy Spirit

Fourth, the Old Testament points ahead to a Leader in whom priesthood and king-ship (Ps. 110) unite with prophecy and sagecraft (Isa. 11:1 – 5; 42:1 – 7) absolutely yet incorruptibly. Here we build on the thought from Wesley with which we began this chapter: Jesus Christ is the Lord and King who vanquishes every power of evil (whether in our world or in our hearts) and ushers in God's peaceable kingdom through servanthood rather than self-will. He is the pure and holy Priest who rec-onciles God and humanity because he *is* both truly God and truly human. He is the Prophet and the very Word of the Lord made flesh to reveal to us the heart of God. He is the one "in whom are hidden all the treasures of wisdom and knowledge"

> *"Christians lead on the model of the fourfold office as they speak the truth…like prophets, worship God and pray for others like priests, do justice and protect the needy like kings, and live wisely…like sages"*

(Col. 2:3) so that we may learn from him how to live in light of our Creator's design. Despite their failings, the Old Testament uses Moses as the benchmark for all later prophets and David as the model for monarchs, but the gospel calls us to a Leader who not only sets an example but also achieves for us what we never could. We do not simply imitate or learn from him; we worship him, live in him as he lives in us, and draw from him the divine power that we need for Christian living.[34] The same Spirit who enabled the judges and kings to govern and the prophets to prophesy can fulfill the ancient promise to make our hearts new through and through, sanc-tifying us from our idols to serve the living God in full devotion.[35]

Not a Socio-political Model

Finally, in light of the new covenant established by Jesus, we must note what the Old Testament does *not* teach us about leadership: it does not give us a timeless model of political theocracy which we are to impose upon one's own country or the globe. In the mid-twentieth century, Old Testament scholar John Bright traced the theme of the Kingdom of God across Scripture and ended with a caution to the church of his day: do not confuse the cultural-political Christendom that is crumbling around you with the Kingdom of God! The church expresses God's present reign by bearing patient, hopeful witness to God's future, perfected reign despite the current clash of regimes.[36] Bright's warning is all the more relevant in today's post-Christendom West and religiously violent world. Christians lead on the model of the fourfold office as they speak the truth (especially the truth of the gospel) like prophets, worship God and pray for others like priests, do justice and protect the needy like kings, and live wisely in the culture like sages.[37] In this way, they will do the most worthwhile form of leading: they will lead the world toward Christ.

Jerome Van Kuiken, PhD, is Associate Professor of Ministry and Christian Thought at Oklahoma Wesleyan University.

Bibliography

Bright, John. *The Kingdom of God: The Biblical Concept and Its Meaning for the Church.* Nashville: Abingdon, 1953.

Flick, Stephen A. "John William Fletcher, Vicar of Madeley: A Pastoral Theology". PhD dissertation. Drew University, 1994

Greggs, Tom. "The Priesthood of No Believer: On the Priesthood of Christ and his Church." *International Journal of Systematic Theology* 17, no. 4 (2015): 374–98.

Johnson, Adam J. "The Servant Lord: A Word of Caution Regarding the *munus triplex* in Karl Barth's Theology and the Church Today," *Scottish Journal of Theology* 65, no. 2 (2012), 160 n. 2

Josephus. *Antiquities of the Jews* 13.10.7

Middleton, J. Richard. *The Liberating Image: The* Imago Dei *in Genesis 1.* Grand Rapids: Brazos, 2005.

Oswalt, John N. *Called to be Holy: A Biblical Perspective.* Nappanee, IN: Evangel, 1999.

Overland, P. B. "Wisdom," in Bill T. Arnold and H. G. M. Williamson, eds., *Dictionary of the Old Testament Historical Books.* Downers Grove, IL: InterVarsity, 2005.

Rainey, David. "John Wesley's Doctrine of Salvation in Relation to His Doctrine of God." PhD thesis, London: King's College, University of London, 2006, 41.

van der Leeuw, Gerardus. *Sacred and Profane Beauty: The Holy in Art,* trans. David E. Green. New York: Holt, Rinehart & Winston, 1963.

Witherington III, Ben. *Jesus the Sage: The Pilgrimage of Wisdom.* Minneapolis: Augsburg Fortress, 1994.

Woods, Jr., Robert H., and Kevin Healey. *Prophetic Critique and Popular Media: A Theoretical Foundations and Practical Applications.* New York: Peter Lang, 2013.

Chapter 6 Notes

[1] Rainey, "John Wesley's Doctrine of Salvation in Relation to His Doctrine of God"), 41. See John Calvin, *Institutes of the Christian Religion* 2.15 for his position and its precedents in the early church.

[2] Note on Matt. 1:16 in John Wesley, *Explanatory Notes upon the New Testament* (London: Epworth Press, repr. 1948), 16.

[3] Johnson, "The Servant Lord: A Word of Caution Regarding the *munus triplex* in Karl Barth's Theology and the Church Today". He goes on to note that Ps. 45 and Isa. 61:1 have been used to support a special anointing to the prophetic office.

[4] Ibid., 170 n. 28.

[5] See Jennifer Ellison, "Shepherding with Integrity of Heart and Skilled Hands," Chapter 9 of this anthology.

[6] e.g., 2 Sam. 7:12–16; 2 Kgs. 2:12; 13:14; Ps. 2; Isa. 9:6

[7] Overland, "Wisdom," 984–89.

[8] Witherington, *Jesus the Sage: The Pilgrimage of Wisdom.*

[9] In ancient times, the arts were tightly interwoven with religion. See van der Leeuw, *Sacred and Profane Beauty.*

[10] Woods and Healey, *Prophetic Critique and Popular Media*

[11] see 1 Sam. 13:6–14; 2 Chr. 26:16–21

[12] Leviticus 10:11; 2 Chronicles 17:7–9; Malachi 2:4–7

[13] e.g., Exo. 28:30; Num. 27:21; 1 Sam. 23:1–13

[14] Overland, "Wisdom," *DOTHB*, 985.

[15] 1 Chr. 29:29; 2 Chr. 26:22; 32:32

[16] In what follows, I employ a canonical-theological reading of the Old Testament rather than a historical-critical reconstruction of the history and sources behind its present form.

[17] Middleton, *The Liberating Image*, chs. 1–5, esp. ch. 3.

[18] K. M. Heim, "Kings and Kingship," *DOTHB*, 610.

[19] Genesis 20:7; 27:39–40; ch. 49; cf. Psalms 105:15, in which the patriarchs are called both "prophets" and "anointed ones"

[20] Numbers 12:5–8; Deuteronomy 34:10–12

[21] All Scripture quotes NIV.

[22] Exodus 19:4; 24:4–8; Leviticus 8

[23] e.g., Exodus 32:30–32; Numbers 14:13–19

[24] Exod. 18:13–26; Num. 11:11–17, 24–30

[25] Josh. 22; Judg. 8:1–3; 12:1–6; chs. 19–21

[26] Overland, "Wisdom," *DOTHB*, 985–86.

[27] For this reading of the book of Esther, see Karen H. Jobes, *The NIV Application Commentary: Esther* (Grand Rapids: Zondervan, 1999).

[28] Josephus, *Antiquities of the Jews* 13.10.7.

[29] I take this line from Jeremy S. Begbie's thought-provoking *Voicing Creation's Praise: Towards a Theology of the Arts* (London: T&T Clark, 2000).

[30] For a concentrated discussion of "the human priesthood of creation," see Colin E. Gunton, *Christ and Creation* (Milton Keynes, UK: Paternoster, 1992), 119–27. Cf. Randy L. Maddox, "John Wesley's Precedent for Theological Engagement with the Natural Sciences" and Marc Otto and Michael Lodahl, "Mystery and Humility in John Wesley's Narrative Ecology," both in *Wesleyan Theological Journal* 44, no. 1 (2009): 23–54 and 118–40, respectively.

[31] Ps. 47:8–9; Isa. 19:18–25; 66:19–23; Zeph. 3:9–10

[32] Greggs, "The Priesthood of No Believer".

[33] On Wesley's development of accountability groups, see D. Michael Henderson, *John Wesley's Class Meeting: A Model for Making Disciples* (Nappanee, IN: Evangel, 1997. For a practical guide to the contemporary application of accountability, see Matt Friedeman, *The Accountability Connection* (Wheaton, IL: Victor, 1992).

[34] On the implications of Christ's priestly office for Christian worship, see briefly Alan J. Torrance, "Reclaiming the Continuing Priesthood of Christ: Implications and Challenges," in Oliver D. Crisp and Fred Sanders, eds., *Christology, Ancient and Modern: Explorations in Constructive Dogmatics* (Grand Rapids: Zondervan, 2013), 184–204, or, more expansively, James B. Torrance, *Worship, Community and the Triune God of Grace* (Downers Grove: InterVarsity, 1996).

[35] Oswalt, *Called to be Holy*, ch. 5.

[36] Bright, T*he Kingdom of God*, chs. 8–9.

[37] I draw this sketch of the fourfold office in part from Flick, "John William Fletcher, Vicar of Madeley," who uses the *munus triplex* to organize the various aspects of the parish ministry of Wesley's early Methodist colleague John Fletcher.

7

New Testament Perspectives on Leadership

Abson Prédestin Joseph

The New Testament describes the role and function of leadership using terms such as *diakonos* (servant), *episkopos* (overseer), and *poimēn* (shepherd). Each of these terms is characterized by the posture of "leading from below" and reflects the attitude and example of Jesus Christ. To lead from below is to exemplify for others a life of holiness and humility guided by a genuine pursuit of perfection, a suitably Wesleyan practice.

A NEW TESTAMENT MODEL for leading the Wesleyan way finds its clearest expressions in the life of Jesus himself as exemplified in the life of his followers. The present chapter uses Peter's exhortation to the elders in as a starting point because this text contains in a nutshell the characteristics that one needs to embody in order to lead in a manner that is pleasing to God:

> To the elders among you, I appeal as a fellow elder and a witness of Christ's sufferings who also will share in the glory to be revealed: Be shepherds of God's flock that is under your care, watching over them--not because you must, but because you are willing, as God wants you to be; not pursuing dishonest gain, but eager to serve; not lording it over those entrusted to you, but being examples to the flock. And when the Chief Shepherd appears, you will receive the crown of glory that will never fade away. 1 Peter 5:1-4

Leading from below[1] is self-sacrificing, self-effacing, self-giving, and exemplary leadership that is patterned after the life of Jesus Christ and takes seriously his teaching to serve those one is called to lead. This chapter provides an overview of the language associated with the notion of leadership in New Testament. The concept of "leading from below" permeates the way New Testament authors discuss the concept of leadership and provides a helpful model for leading the Wesleyan Way.

The Language of Leadership in the New Testament

A survey of the several key words associated with the discussions on leadership can begin to paint a picture of the appropriate model(s) of leadership that can be appropriated in a Wesleyan context. Our treatment will focus on *diakoneō* (to serve) and its derivatives *diakonia* (service), and *diākonos* (servant, deacon); *epīskopos* (overseer) and other related terms *episkēptomai* (to look upon, look after, to visit), *episkopēo* (to watch over); *poimēn* (shepherd).[2]

Diākonos: The Leader as Servant

Before the term *diākonos* came to be associated with a particular office, this word group was used more broadly in the context of service rendered to another person.[3] In its original sense, it is connected to the idea of serving tables, providing or caring for someone, or serving in a general sense (often in a servile manner). In Hellenistic culture, serving another person was often viewed as something menial and undesirable.[4] Yet, one of the primary characteristics of this term is its close connection with the concept of love. *Diakonēo* is used at times to convey service of love rendered to another.[5]

In the New Testament, the term carries a wide range of meaning. For example, service in the context of preparing, providing, and/or serving a meal is attested in the service Peter's mother-in-law rendered to Jesus and his disciples after she was healed from her fever (Matt. 8:15; Mark 1:31; Luke 4:39). It is also present in the case of Martha's hospitality toward Jesus (Luke 10:40; John 12:2). It conveys the general idea of caring for someone's needs;[6] though, providing food might be part of the background of Matt 4:11 and Mark 1:13 given the fact that Jesus was fasting prior to that time.

In Acts 6:1-2, the context of "serving tables" is present but the focus there seems to be on the supervision of the distribution of food.[7] It is even possible that the issue at stake involves more than food distribution based on the Acts narrative (cf. Acts 5:4-37). The community members were sharing everything and the apostles supervised the collection and distribution of resources.[8] This narrative presents us with an instance of the community selecting and appointing a group of people for the work which later will be associated with the office of the diaconate.

In the text, a strong contrast is made between serving tables and the service of the word [preaching] (Acts 6:2). However, the narrative goes on to highlight Stephen's activities not in connection with the meal supervision, but the signs and wonders he performs as well as his wisdom and the Spirit-filled manner with which he speaks. It can be said that Stephen's service to the word, the work of proclamation, is what led to his subsequent martyrdom (Acts 6:11-8:1). The reader also encounters Philip in a similar context of Spirit-filled preaching and performing signs and wonders (Acts 8:4-8, 26-40). It is even suggested that the activities of Stephen and Philip as narrated by Luke might be characteristic of the entire group.[9]

It is worthy to note a similar ambivalence in the case of Barnabas and Saul. Acts 13:1 lists Barnabas and Saul among the preachers and teachers of that congregation, yet they are also involved in the collection and transfer of resources. The latter is pictured speaking boldly in the name of Jesus [preaching] (Acts 9:26-30). Yet they are described as bearers of the gifts (financial and other resources) the church of Antioch sent to the church in Judea (Acts 11:27-30). Their *service* was the act of ensuring that the goods collected by the church of Antioch reached those in Judea who were in need (Acts 12:25).

If indeed the office of the diaconate finds its earliest expression in Acts,[10] it is clear that the work of those appointed to that office was not limited to the supervision or/and distribution of resources. In the same way, there is evidence that those who occupy other offices (e.g., prophets, teachers, apostles) also perform duties that on the surface seem to be related specifically to "serving tables" broadly understood.[11] Also important to our discussion are the qualifications of those chosen for such roles and the process of their selection. These leaders were chosen from within the community, by the community, and for the community they would serve. They were filled with the Holy Spirit and were trustworthy.

Paul's use of this word group is multi-faceted and covers a wide range of meanings. The language of *diākonos* as a particular office [deacons] is attested in Rom. 16:1; Phil. 1:1; and 1 Tim 3:8, 12. In Romans and Philippians, Paul mentions the offices in passing as part of a greeting and salutation. However, in his letter to Timothy, the focus in more the office itself. There, Paul does not offer details relating to the duties of such office, but instead focuses on the qualifications for serving in such capacity. He uses the term to also refer to himself and his colleagues vis-à-vis their engagement in the work of the Gospel; e.g., ministers/servants of Christ[12], of God[13]; of the Gospel (Eph. 3:7); of the church (Col. 1:25); of righteousness (2 Cor. 11:15), of the new covenant (2 Cor. 3:6). This same plurality is observed in the way Paul uses *diakonīa*; e.g., ministry/service that involves Paul's work, that of his colleagues, and in some instances the service of the entire community.[14] *Diakonīa* also is used to refer to the help, and financial contribution offered to those in need.[15]

The New Testament's treatment of the group word *diakonēo, diakonīa, diākonos* provides few details of the duties of deacons where the specific office is concerned. However, there is a clear indication that this concept presents a close connection between preaching the Gospel, the work of ministry as a whole, and the provision of resources for those in need. Therefore, discussion on leadership that stems from this concept needs to take into serious consideration the nuances that are present. From this standpoint, leading from below is the kind of leadership that does not see a bifurcation between serving the Word and serving tables broadly understood. It is holistic in providing theological formation and transformation while equally concerned with providing financial and other resources for those who are in need. It is leadership that arises from among the community and that understands its plight because the leader has lived among the people and shared their experience. Leading from below is leadership that embodies the Gospel and boldly lives it out in a way that challenges others to do the same.

Jesus' countercultural statements about how this concept should be understood are very significant. Jesus exhorts his followers to pattern their lives after his by seeking to serve others rather than being served. For, he came not to be served, but to serve others and offer up his life on their behalf (Matt. 20:38; Mark 10:45). This challenged the status quo where each person sought self-validation through status-enhancing roles and activities, where service was considered a menial task, and serving others was not an ideal that was sought after. Jesus took the posture of a servant among his disciples and provided a tangible example of how and why they too must serve others.[16] He provided a new definition for greatness and for leadership.[17] Those who want to lead must lead from below.

Epīskopos: The Leader as Overseer

In its original context, *epīskopos* is used to identify an onlooker, a patron, a watcher, or a protector.[18] In Greek literature, for example, it is used to refer to the gods in their capacity to provide protection to humans and to act as witnesses of covenant between individuals. This designation is also associated with human beings as watchers and protectors of others.[19] For example, it is applied to ship captains who oversee the cargo or to people who tutor children.[20] The use of this term as a title for local and state officials is attested as well.[21] One encounters a similar understanding of the term in the OT where the term is used in the LXX to translate the Hebrew *'el* [God] (Job 20:29). Similarly, the term is used to as a designation for people who hold a particular office which imbues them with authority.[22]

The word occurs only five times in the New Testament. The occurrences in Acts and the Pauline letters refer to individuals, while the occurrence in 1 Peter describes Jesus' role as protector of the suffering audience. In Acts, the term is found in the context of Paul's farewell to the Ephesian leaders. There the duties of overseeing are closely connected with the idea of protection. Overseers are to protect themselves and the flock God has placed under their care from the impending attack of the detractors (wolves) that will come in after Paul's departure. Already here, one identifies a close connection with this concept and that of shepherding. The merging of these two concepts is also prominent in 1 Peter.

In Paul's letters to Timothy and Titus, Paul's focus is on the qualities and qualifications of the overseers (1 Tim. 3:1-7; Titus 1:7-9). Overseers are called to display a life of holiness. They should be faithful to their spouse and aspire for perfection (be blameless). They should be honest and show humility.[23] They should also demonstrate the ability to oversee their own household before being trusted with oversight of the household of God. It should be noted, the qualifications that Paul provides are not only for the overseers. The same is required of the deacons (1 Tim. 3:8-12). These leaders are called to be examples to the flock. Therefore, these are qualities that every member of the community should aspire to possess.

The description of Jesus' response to suffering in 1 Peter serves as an example for overseers and the audience to follow. When he faced suffering and humiliation Jesus did not retaliate, but entrusted his life to God. In addition, the author's depiction of Christ as the overseer of their lives set Jesus as the one in whom the audience should put their trust when they face a similar predicament. As Christ maintained a right attitude when he suffered, so the audience is expected to display a life of righteousness when facing suffering. As he entrusted his life to the Father, so is the audience called to entrust their lives to him, their shepherd and overseer. As he suffered on behalf of the audience, so are the overseers expected to be ready and willing to protect those whom God has placed under their care. The author will pick up the metaphor of the shepherd again in 1 Pet. 5:2 and combine it with the verbal idea of *episkopēo* [to watch over] and the concept of *presbuteros* [elder], to drive home the meaning of implications of Jesus' example for those in leadership roles.

In sum, the author of 1 Peter is rehearsing Jesus' demonstration of what it means to lead from below. The guardian of our lives once found himself in a vulnerable situation where he suffered humiliation. His experience not only allows him to serve as our example, it also empowers him to empathize with our suffering and our plight. While having power at his disposal, he refrains from using it but chose put his trust in God in order to experience his deliverance and vindication.[24] Further, leading from below is expressed in Paul's emphasis on humility and the requirement for overseers to control their own household. Overseeing rightly understood is leading from below because in order to protect the flock, one needs to be willing to sacrifice self for the sake of the community. It is leading from below because overseers need to be willing to operate from within a place of vulnerability and weakness in order to learn to empathize with those they lead. It is leading from below because overseers need to refrain from using power that is at their disposal but instead put their trust in God in order to experience his deliverance and vindication.

Several related terms are also attested which contribute to our understanding of this concept. For example, *episkēptomai*—to look upon, or to look after; to inspect or examine with one's eyes; to visit and go see someone—sometimes conveys care and concerned for the needy in view of providing a solution to their situation. This is a kind of attitude, a habit of the heart that Jesus describes as a key characteristic that determines whether or not one will share in the kingdom in the eschaton. "I was hungry and you gave me food to eat. I was thirsty and you gave me a drink. I was a stranger and you welcomed me. I was naked and you gave me clothes to wear. I was sick and you took care of me. I was in prison and you visited me".[25] The same idea is rehearsed by James when he defines true religion, that which is pleasing to God in terms of visiting/caring for widows and orphans in their distress (James 1:27). A rapprochement between *episkĕptomai* and *diakonĕo* is attested in Acts 6:1-3, where there is an intersection between the service and the selection of those who would oversee the response to the plight of the Hellenistic widows.

Further, Stephen uses the same language of *visiting* with its implications to describe what Moses' actions toward the Israelites (Acts 7:23). More importantly this language is used earlier in Luke-Acts to describe what God does on behalf of his people (Luke 1:68, 78; 7:16). By visiting his people, Yahweh brings hope and deliverance from affliction and oppression.

Other closely related terms are the noun *episkopē* and the verb *episkopēo. Episkopē* is attested four times in the New Testament. It is used twice in the context of the office/role of the overseer (Acts 1:20; 1 Tim. 3:1). The other two instances refer to the eschatological reality of a day of reckoning.[26] Finally the verb is found twice in

"The call to lead is to the call to shape the community's theological transformation"

the New Testament. In Hebrews 12:15, it is used in a context of watchfulness for the sake of living a life of holiness and peacemaking as a prerequisite to encounter God.[27] In 1 Peter 5:2, the author urges other *presbuteroi* to watch over the flock in view of the coming of Chief Shepherd. So, four out of the six occurrences of *episkopē* and *episkopēo* carry some eschatological undertone.

A more holistic picture of leadership emerges as one takes the larger word group of *epĭskopos* into consideration. The work of overseeing involves paying close attention to the plight of marginalized and the outcasts in the community and caring for their needs. It requires those in power to be willing to visit with the lowly and join them where they are in view of improving their situation, instilling hope, and bringing freedom. The eschatological theme connected with the concept serves to remind overseers of the accountability with which they serve. Overseers do not serve themselves. Rather, they watch over their lives and their flocks in humility and holiness. They are responsible to ensure that the community is ready on the day of visitation, when the guardian of their lives appears.

Poimēn: The Leaders as Shepherd

The term *poimĕn*—shepherd—and the metaphor of shepherding (*poimainō*) is used throughout the LXX to describe Yahweh's care of Israel. Yahweh is Israel's shepherd who provides, guides, and protects his people.[28] A similar picture of portrayed in the Prophets.[29] The concept is also used to speak of God's choice of David as king over Israel (Ps. 78:71-72).[30] In an oracle that foresees the restoration of Israel, an indictment is laid out against the shepherds that failed in their duties to care, provide, and protect Yahweh's flock. God promises to take care of Israel himself and to raise the kind of shepherds who will tend his flock adequately (Jer. 23:1-4).

In the Gospel according to Matthew, the evangelist draws on Mic.5:2 and 2 Sam. 5:2 to frame the birth of Jesus as the fulfillment of prophecy that God will one day raise a shepherd, like David, who will tend his people (Matt. 2:1-12).[31] Jesus appropriates this image and applies it to his own life. He contrasts his loving, self-sacrificing care for his sheep to the disengaged, disinterested, and selfish approach of mercenaries. He is the good shepherd who willingly lays down his life for his sheep. He protects and cares for them. As the good shepherd, he possesses intimate knowledge of his sheep and they know him and obey his voice (John 10:11-16). He later mandates one of his disciples, Peter, to do the same: "Take care of my sheep" (John 21:16).

The image of shepherding as a model for leading the church community is not broadly attested, but this does not diminish its significance and the implications it carries. One gets a glimpse of shepherding as an office in Eph. 4:11. There the concept is listed along with apostles, prophets, evangelists, and teachers as part of the gifts the Spirit has bestowed on members of the body.

As mentioned above, during his farewell address to the leaders in Ephesus, Paul brings together the concepts of shepherding and overseeing to bring home to the leaders the nature of their responsibilities (Acts 20:28-29). In 1 Peter, the author urges the *presbuteroi* to shepherd the flock in their midst in a way that follows the OT characteristics and Jesus' description and of a good shepherd (1 Pet. 5:2). The shepherds were called to serve not only by following Christ's example, but also by being aware of their dependence and accountability toward him. He is the great Shepherd of the sheep (Heb. 13:10); the Shepherd and Overseer of their lives (1 Pet 2:25); and the Chief Shepherd (1 Pet 5:4).

Shepherding may be the strongest indication that leadership properly understood should be done from below. It involves self-sacrifice, self-denial, and the recognition that one serves at the behest of another, the Chief Shepherd of the sheep. As in the case of serving and overseeing, shepherding done properly follows the example of Christ. It is carried out with the awareness that the flock place under one's care is God's flock. Therefore, one is accountable to God himself for the manner one leads his people.

Conclusion

A careful study of the language of leadership in the New Testament reveals that to lead effectively is to follow Christ's example. In his teachings and through his actions, Jesus Christ demonstrated that the appropriate way to lead is from below. Jesus proclaimed that he came to serve, and demonstrated tangibly what he meant by washing the feet of his disciples. He claimed to be the good shepherd and willingly offered himself up to endure the shame and humiliation of death by crucifix-ion for the sake of the flock God entrusted to him. The meaning of these acts were not lost on his followers. They sought to embody Jesus way of leading and shep-herding and echoed this counter-cultural re-definition of greatness and leadership in their proclamation of the Gospel and in their own lives.

The call to lead is to the call to shape the community's theological transforma-tion. It is a call to serve the widow, the orphan, and the stranger. The call to lead is a call to visit the afflicted, to do life with the outcasts, to empathize with the needy by learning their plight through shared experience. The call to lead is the call to embody the qualities of the good shepherd who protects, provides, and guides the flock in holiness and humility.

The call to lead is honorable. Yet, to lead like Christ is to lead from below. To lead from below is to be willing to exemplify for others a life of holiness and humil-ity guided by a genuine pursuit of perfection. To lead from below is to share in the sufferings of Christ. To lead from below is to live with the awareness that the flock under our care belongs to God. This model of leadership could be easily adopted as the Wesleyan Way of leadership because these are practices and habits of the heart that Wesleyans are or should be practicing.

Abson Joseph, PhD, is Associate Professor of New Testament and Ancient Languages at Indiana Wesleyan University School of Theology and Ministry.

Bibliography

Bock, Darrell L. *Acts.* Baker Exegetical Commentary of the New Testament. Grand Rapids: Baker, 2007.

Bruce, F. F. *The Book of Acts.* The New International Commentary on the New Testament. Grand Rapids: Eerdmans, 1988.

Cockerill, Gareth Lee. *The Epistle to the Hebrews.* The New International Commentary on the New Testament. Grand Rapids: Eerdmans, 2012.

France, R. T. *The Gospel of Matthew.* The New International Commentary on the New Testament. Grand Rapids: Eerdmans, 2007.

Goodrich, John K. "Overseers as Stewards and the Qualifications for Leadership in the Pastoral Epistles." Pages 77-97. *Zeitschrift für die Neutestamentliche Wissenschaft* 104. 2013.

Jeremias, Joachim. "poimēn." *TDNT* 6:485-502.

Joseph, Abson Prédestin. *A Narratological Reading of 1 Peter.* Library of New Testament Studies 440. London, T&T Clark, 2012.

Kittel, Gerhard, and Gerhard Friedrich, eds. *Theological Dictionary of the New Testament.* Translated by Geoffrey W. Bromiley. 10 vols. Grand Rapids: Eerdmans, 1964-1976.

Koenig, John. "Hierarchy Transfigured: Perspectives on Leadership in the New Testament." *Word & World* 23.1, Winter (1993): 26-33.

Pugh, Ben. "Subverted Hierarchies: Towards a Biblical Theology of Leadership." *The Journal of European Pentecostal Association* 33.2 (2013): 25-42.

Silva, Moisés, ed. *New International Dictionary of New Testament Theology and Exegesis.* Second Edition. 4 vols. Grand Rapids: Zondervan, 2014.

Tidball, Derek. "Leaders as Servants: A Resolution of the Tension." Pages 31-47. *Evangelical Review of Theology* 36:1. 2012.

Chapter 7 Notes

[1] Ben Pugh uses similar language in his discussion on a biblical theology of leadership. See also Pugh, "Subverted Hierarchies: Towards a Biblical Theology of Leadership," 25-42, and Tidball, "Leaders as Servants: A Resolution of the Tension," 31-47.

[2] The scope of the chapter does not allow us to treat all the terms associated with the concept of leadership in the NT. One key concept omitted here is presbuteros (presbyter/elder). It is an office imbued with authority to lead and guide the community in critical times (e.g., Acts 14:23; 15:2-6, 22-23; 20:17). They are called to lead an exemplary life (1 Tim 5:17; Tit. 1:5-7); and care for the community (Jas. 5:14; 1 Pet. 5:1). They are not given a separate treatment in this chapter because there seems to some overlap between the offices of the elders and overseers (cf. Tit. 1:5, 8; 1 Pet. 5:2); and because the qualifications, roles, and expectations of how to lead the community are similar with the other offices discussed. Using 1 Pet. 5 as a starting point, it can be argued that serving, overseeing, and shepherding are all roles associated with the office of the presbuteros. Therefore, in treating these concepts, one gets a glimpse of that is expected on an elder. This notwithstanding, care will be taken to highlight instances where the office of the presbuteros come into focus during our treatment of the other concepts.

[3] Herman W. Beyer, "Diakonēo, diakonía, diākonos," TDNT, 2:81-92.

[4] Beyer, "Diakonēo," 82; Moisés Silva, "Diakonēo, diakonīa, diākonos," NIDNTTE, 1:701-707.

[5] Beyer, "Diakonēo," 81.

[6] e.g., Matt. 4:11; 25:44; 27:55; Mark 1:13; 15:41; 2 Tim 1:18; Philem. 1:13; 1 Pet. 4:10-11

[7] Ibid, 84.

[8] Koenig, "Hierarchy Transfigured, 26-33. So also Bruce, *The Book of Acts*, 119-122.

[9] Bock, *Acts*, 261.

[10] The word *diākonos* is not used in Acts 6 and the seven are not called thus. However, the concept is present as attested by the use of *diakonēo* and *diakonīa*.

[11] cf. Rom. 15:25; 15:3; 2 Cor. 8:19-21

[12] see 2 Cor. 11:23; Col. 1:7; 1 Tim. 4:6; cf. Eph. 6:21

[13] see Rom. 13:4; 2 Cor. 6:4; 1 Thess. 3:2

[14] Rom. 11:13; 12:7; 1 Cor. 12:5; 16:15; 2 Cor. 4:1; 6:3; Eph. 4:12; 2 Tim 4:5

[15] Rom. 15:31; 2 Cor. 8:4; 9:1, 12-13

[16] Luke 22:25-27; John 12:25-26; cf. John 13:12-17

[17] Matt. 20:25-26; 23:11; Mark 9:35; 10:43

[18] Herman W. Beyer, "Epīskopos," TDNT 2:608-622.

[19] Beyer, "Epīskopos," TDNT 2:609-11. Moisés Silva, "Epīskopos," NIDNTTE 2:248-252.

[20] Silva, "Epīskopos," NIDNTTE 2:249.

[21] Beyer, "Epīskopos," TDNT 2:611-614.

[22] e.g., Num. 31:14; Judg. 9:28; 2 Chron. 34:12, 17; Neh. 11:9, 14, 22

[23] See Goodrich, "Overseers as Stewards and the Qualifications for Leadership," 77-97.

[24] See Joseph, *A Narratological Reading of 1 Peter*, 148-171.

[25] Matt. 25:35-36, CEV; cf. Matt. 25:41-43

[26] Cf. Isa. 10:3. See further, at the time of visitation (e.g., Jer. 6:15; 10:15; Wis. 3:7); at the hour of visitation (Sir. 18:20).

[27] See Cockerill, *The Epistle to the Hebrews*, 635-639.

[28] Ps. 23:1-4; 28:9; 79:13; 80:1-3

[29] Isa. 40:11; Jer. 23:2; 31:10; 50:19

[30] Moisés Silva, "poimēn," NIDNTTE 4:81-87; Joachim Jeremias, "poimēn," TDNT 6:485-502.

[31] France, *The Gospel of Matthew*, 71-73.

8

The Cartography of Kingdom Leadership: Charting a New Course

David F. Smith

Rather than taking its cues from the contemporary "script," Wesleyan leadership must go back to Christ. Because Wesley was a man of Scripture, a leadership approach in his movement must engage the text of Scripture and the Lord Wesley sought to follow. Wesleyan leadership, then, will engage Scripture deeply and reform its leadership assumptions and practices in its light. From the Gospel of Mark, these leadership practices include repentance, following, and listening.

ON A RECENT CARIBBEAN CRUISE, my wife, Angie, and I were about to disembark for a visit to the island of Cozumel. I had been studying the map guest services had provided in our stateroom that morning. Because I have a wonderful internal compass, the map mainly served to set my bearings for the day. As we neared the ship's exit, I realized I had left the map in our room, so I picked up another copy from the steward's supply in the hallway and we proceeded into the city. The map that I picked up was exactly the same color and essentially the same design as my original map of Cozumel. Unbeknownst to me, the new map I had just grabbed was for the island of Puerto Rico.

Once we arrived in the shopping center of the city, my carefully calculated turns consistently took us in the wrong direction. I was disoriented and could not determine why. I kept turning in the right direction according to my internalized map yet we were ending up in the wrong place. Worst of all, I was misleading Angie. Why? The map in my hand did not reflect the reality of the place I was attempting to navigate. My internal compass that rarely fails me was calibrated according to faulty coordinates I had acquired from this map. I was lost, yet at the same time determined I knew where I was. I was certain I was making the correct turns, and I would have if only I had been working from the correct map. I was allowing my leadership decisions to be made based upon faulty orientation and mismatched internal and external information.

Kingdom Cartography

This is the story of every Christian leader who has a life-mission set by the wrong internal "true north." The leader's internal coordinates must be properly (re)calibrated to Jesus' missional map. Moreover, the leader must also read carefully to integrate the Christ-centered map legend[1] which reveals how the map is to be understood. Yet we do not begin with a blank "leadership" map. An oft-quoted axiom maintains that "ministry rises or falls on leadership."[2] We all assume this to be true without question. But what presuppositions stand behind this idea? What do we mean by *Christian* leadership? What model is already in play? Before delving into chapters on biblical perspectives and theology of leadership, let's focus on Jesus, allowing our initial bearings to be recalibrated by him.

This kind of calibration is the profound nature of the introduction to the Gospel of Mark. Mark is a lesson in Kingdom-cartography: map-making for Christian discipleship. While the entire book is shaped as a journey narrative in which Jesus reveals his person and divine mission, the introduction can provide re-orientation and re-calibration for Wesleyan leaders.

Listen to Jesus' opening map coordinates in 1:14-15: "After John was put in prison, Jesus went into Galilee, proclaiming the good news of God. 'The time has

"we must recalibrate our compasses to the new coordinates found in the Kingdom of God"

come,' he said. 'The kingdom of God has come near. Repent and believe the good news!'" Jesus' first words in the Second Gospel declare to the readers that we must recalibrate our compasses to the new coordinates found in the Kingdom of God. If we do not, we will suffer the life-consequences of thinking we are in one place— whether first century Palestine under the leadership of Caesar and his sphere of influence or twenty-first century North America under the leadership of parliaments, senates, presidents, and Prime Ministers—when in fact Jesus says we live in the Kingdom of God under his divine reign. I will present an analysis of the introduction to Mark before providing more practical reflections on leadership for Wesleyans in the Jesus way.

Kingdom Coordinates

Let's focus on the very first verse of Mark's introduction, starting with the three-fold modifiers, to triangulate the Kingdom map coordinates. Mark 1:1 begins: The Beginning (1) of the gospel (2) about Jesus Christ, (3) the Son of God.

It might be fair to say that this is Mark's introduction to the introduction. This sentence sets the agenda as a counter-cultural way forward. Let me explain with several brief contextualized word studies.

Coordinate #1 - Gospel: Good News about Caesar of Jesus?

First, what does Mark mean as he employs the term "gospel"? It should be understood that this word is not invented by Mark or even by the post-Pentecost Christian movement. Rather, in Jesus' day, it was almost exclusively attributed to Caesar and the ongoing Good News that emanated from Rome. If an heir to the Imperial throne was born, a "gospel" was sent throughout the land that national stability was a reality. When Roman legions won battles over the enemies of the empire, heralds from every town square proclaimed a "gospel" the contents of which could be summarized, "The usurpers have been put down and Caesar still stands supreme." Simply, "gospel," according to the cultural lexicon of Jesus' day, was ascribed to Rome and her world of influence and power.

In a sense, the greatest evangelist in world history to date was Alexander the Great, who converted the entire Mediterranean world to the Greek "gospel "— Greek culture and worldview. The Romans continued and improved this conversion-by-power model, taking it to unimaginable heights. *Pax Romana* always came at a high human cost. Adam's mandate to "tend the garden" (Gen. 2:15) was turned upside down as Caesar dominated creation and its creatures by brute force. In reclaiming the word 'gospel' by following Jesus in a cruciform life, the early Christians were courageously reclaiming true leadership.

Coordinate #2 - Christ/Messiah

The second modifier to the noun "beginning" is "of Jesus Christ." We could take this as his name, which would be partially correct. But that would only be true if we viewed the book (and the title messiah/Christ) from a post-crucifixion, post-resurrection scenario. Rather, in Mark's Gospel, the term messiah is rarely utilized (8:29; 9:41; 12:35; 13:21; 14:61; 15:32) and almost never with divine overtones. Conversely, when the term messiah and all its cultural nuances are attributed to Jesus, either by followers or persecutors, Jesus corrects their earthly misunderstanding with his own title of preference, "Son of Man." For instance, when Peter declares, "You are the Christ," Jesus firmly commands the disciples not to share *their* seemingly misinformed messianic view (8:29-30). Rather, he begins "to teach them that the *Son of Man* will suffer many things…" (8:31). While Peter's mental lexicon for the title messiah means "a human agent of God who will cast out the Roman oppressors who have defiled the land," the Jesus-way of the messiah will incorporate physical suffering and social shame. The Markan readers are being called to follow a new model of leadership. Jesus' way of leadership will not harness power as its source but will instead include suffering.

Further, Peter's excited blurt, "You are the Christ," reveals his expectation that Jesus will rise up as the chosen one (anointed) of YHWH who will cleanse the land of all her pagan rulers and re-institute the "kingdom of David." But Jesus rebukes Peter with the words, "Get behind me Satan, for you are seeing things from a human point of view, not from God's" (8:33). Jesus' unwavering stand is that a Kingdom without a cross at its center is satanic in its perspective. Even though the "cross-agenda" is only first introduced here, at the midpoint of the Gospel, its shadow is cast over all future conversations and teachings of Jesus. Rejecting a cross-centered Kingdom is rejecting Jesus himself. A Kingdom-agenda without suffering, shame, and death has origins in a world in direct opposition to the "way" being described in Mark 1.

It must be understood that there is a clear epistemological dilemma that undergirds humanity in the Gospel of Mark, even among those closest to Jesus. Their perception of Jesus as the Anointed One coupled with the religious expectations of the messianic future that will flow out of his person and mission is based upon a non-cruciform reality. For Jesus' followers, suffering and death are the epitome of failure. Simply, their perceptions are confined to Jesus ushering in a new Davidic dynasty. No other reality is conceivable.

Today for us the same can be said regarding modern leadership theory. It is far too common to see engrained in our cultural leadership DNA the exercise of power and authority. Jesus' model is humble and patient when it comes to those under him. They would have freely acquiesced to him if he used power. It was the ancient cultural expectation. Thus, their surprise (and ours) is that leadership in the Jesus-way comprises a desire "to serve and not to be served" (10:45).

Coordinate #3 – Son of God: Caesar or Jesus?

The final modifier to Gospel's first noun, beginning, is "of Son of God." Much like the meaning behind the term "gospel" and "messiah," the culture of Jesus' day often attributed the title "son of God" as an Imperial title. Augustus, referred to his deified father Julius Caesar as *son of god* (via the Latin phrase *divi filius*). This was also true of Augustus' adopted son, Tiberius. Thus, religious culture as defined through the Imperial cult ascribed "son of God" to the ruling Caesar during Jesus' day.

Seemingly as an act of imperial defiance, Mark appropriates this modifier as the crucial title for Jesus throughout his Gospel. We hear it in 1:1. It's quickly followed up with an even higher authority through the affirming voice of the Father in 1:11,

"You are my beloved Son, in you I am well pleased." Moreover, in the first third of Mark, when the demons are confronted by Jesus, they shout his name aloud, "Jesus, son of the Most High God" (5:7).[3] Interestingly, the spiritual world recognizes and must submit to Jesus as the Son of God, but no human uses the term—until the strategic moment when the High Priest places "Messiah" and "Son of the Blessed" into his lone accusatory question (14:61).[4] Yet the High Priest does not believe this to be true and his reaction can be housed in one word, "blasphemy." Sadly, earth's religious leader rejects what heaven knows to be a spiritual reality.

As the plot pushes forward to the cross, we find the climactic moment not in Jesus' death[5] but rather in the eyewitness testimony of a Roman soldier who directly participates in Jesus' crucifixion. The first time Mark connects Jesus' sonship to a human voice, and it comes from the lips of a Roman centurion at the cross, "Truly this man was the son of God." Mark seems to be pushing us in an uncomfortable direction; no one can fully grasp the divine reality of Jesus without participating in his public shame and physical death on a cross. The human epistemological dilemma (i.e., being blind and deaf to God's revelation) can only be overcome by the recalibration of our spiritual compasses through the cross.

This is the beginning of salvation, the opening of our spiritual eyes to see and experience God's in-breaking Kingdom." We do not become followers of Jesus by employing the means of Rome (power and dominance) to defeat our enemies. Employing a humanly constructed means results in human ends—an empty and destructive self-fulfilling prophecy. Rather, the Jesus way calls for a complete reversal of the human power structures and reception of God's new calibration.

Coordinate #4 – Beginning or Rule?

Let's end this series of word modifiers with a closing thought on the principal noun itself: "beginning." Almost every good student of this passage translates it within the semantic domain of "begin," with "first things," "onset," "starting," even "origins" as our only options. However, Robert Guelich, wrestling with the same word in its larger context says it this way: "The meaning of *'archa'* ultimately depends on the meaning of the qualifying phrase, "the gospel of Jesus Messiah, Son of God," and the relationship of 1:1 to what follows.[6] As Guelich points out, the content of the modifiers should be determinative in the meaning of the noun. Thus, the context of Mark's introduction should also play a significant factor in the creation of Mark's word meanings. Let's examine the modifiers Mark uses to re-examine the meaning of 'archa' and whether 'beginning' is the best meaning.

As seen above, two of the modifiers, "gospel" and "son of god," could easily be found in Greco-Roman literature attributed to Caesar. Yet, Mark is unapologetically appropriating them to Jesus. The third modifier of "messiah" will also be redefined throughout the second gospel. Its normative meaning in Jesus' day usually refers to a man who will defeat the enemies of Israel and reestablish the throne of David. This Hebrew view of God "putting all things right" arises during the Intertestamental period (400 years before Jesus) is correct in principle but not in specificity. The "messiah" will indeed redeem Israel and inaugurate a new era in world history, but Jesus will not allow this eschatological event to be defined within humanity's myopic definition of "messiah." Rather, the first words out of Jesus' mouth in Mark's Gospel are these: "The time promised by God has come at last. The Kingdom of God is near. Repent and believe the Gospel" (1:15). This is a not so subtle critique of the Israelite culture and her religious cult who have defined "messiah" in a self-limiting manner, as the redeemer of *our* land for the removal of *our* shame in the here and now. Jesus is declaring a Gospel that is cosmic is scope for *all* people at *all* times.

Thus, the Kingdom of God language that flows repeatedly from Jesus' lips will force us to redefine every word of our religious lexicon, starting with Mark's opening word, "beginning." The standard definition is "origin or beginning." On one's first encounter with the text, reading or the more normal first century "oral storytelling event," this would be the normal first choice. Yet, after several meetings with the Markan Jesus, readers or hearers will come to know there is nothing normal (or even safe) about Jesus. The plot of the book is establishing a new sense of loyalty to a whole new value system. As the story reaches its climax in the Passion Narrative, Kingship becomes the primary topic. Pilate asks, "Are you the King of the Jews?" (15:2), to which Jesus gives the somewhat cryptic answer, "You have said so."[7] This could be quite an unsatisfying answer for the reader, unless we understand it as a call for Pilate (and for us!) to decide which king and kingdom to pledge our loyalty. Subsequently, Pilate acts as Jesus' sole advocate in the trial scene, trying unsuccessfully to get Jesus released. Again and again the term "King of the Jews" is thrown into the conversation. As the soldiers take Jesus away to be mocked in a pre-crucifixion ritual of shame and beating, he is once again revealed in his regal status. The soldiers meant to present him as the court jester, but we readers see and hear this as royal announcement. Next, we see the placard (Latin *titulus* from John 19:19) placed on the cross as it reads, "The King of the Jews." One could almost hear the trumpets sounding a royal processional. Finally, the climax of the book is located not in Jesus' death but rather in the declaration of Roman Kingship housed in the confession of the centurion, "Surely this man was the son of God." This is not a pagan declaring Jesus as divine but rather a Roman verbally exchanging loyalty from a living Caesar to a dead Jew. He has chosen a new leader to follow.

This Christ-event would create such an epistemological dilemma for readers and listeners that upon their next encounter with Mark's Gospel, they will have to reevaluate their definition of every word and interpretation of each pericope. For our purposes, if we are witnessing the ushering in of a new era in the person of King Jesus, then the word "beginning" may have a dual meaning. The traditional meaning of the word, "begin," is now supplemented by a secondary meaning, "rule".[8] Thus, if Mark is indeed a Kingdom-minded book about Heaven's call upon humanity to reorient herself under a new royal leader with a new mission and an entirely different means to fulfilling that end, then the word "begin" might be a bit reductionist and safe to convey the whole truth of Gospel of Jesus. Mark 1:1, as defined by the rest of the gospel's 16 chapters should be read as a declaration, "The rule of the Gospel of Jesus Christ, Son of God."

Kingdom Practices

From these new coordinates, we can employ several key leadership practices.

Repent

With this emerging "Kingdom-reality now overshadowing the current cultural way of life, recalibration begins with repentance. "Repent" is the first vocal call by Jesus for humanity as found in Mark 1:14-15.

> After John was put in prison, Jesus went into Galilee, proclaiming the good news of God. "The time has come," he said. "The kingdom of God has come near. Repent and believe the good news!"

Though this is a well-known appeal in the evangelical church, it's quite an unusual word in Mark. It occurs only twice, here in 1:15 and again in 6:12, where Mark describes the disciples' action as they go out two-by-two to mimic Jesus' ministry, saying, "And they went out and preached that people should repent." Old Testament history is replete with the appeal for Israel to "repent" and return to her love for God and his way. Yet "repent" may not most accurately describe the core of Mark's journey narrative. Rather than employing a "turning" metaphor, Mark describes Jesus' call with the word "follow."[9] Jesus is the *embodied* compass. He does not *point* us in the right direction nor give us a new compass heading and send us on our way. He says, "Get behind me" (1:7, 17; 8:33, 34). He leads the way. Immediately the disciples follow. First, Peter and Andrew; then James and John. And in so doing, Jesus and the disciples will travel together experiencing the new Kingdom. He is our recalibration.

The obedience of the disciples is explicit, yet their motive is left unstated. Why do they follow? They say "yes" to Jesus without hesitation but the surprise will come when they realize where he is going (Jerusalem) and what he intends to do once he arrives (die shamefully on the cross). We know this is a foregone conclusion, but when the disciples come to understand him and his mission fully, they will not continue to follow, fulfilling Jesus' later prophecy, "You will all fall away" (14:27, 50).

Thus, what does Mark say about the shaping of a leader to follow after Jesus? Recalibration to the Jesus-way is a consistent requirement. *Repentance is not a one-time event.* Leaders in the way of Jesus are repentant leaders.

Follow

"Following" is a Markan concept used pervasively throughout his Gospel to describe Christian leadership. The unexpected nature of the story of Jesus—his gospel, his leadership, his rule—must create a different set of expectations. Let's trace the theme of "following" through Mark and see how it opens unexpected opportunities and places.

The "way" is a subtle yet quite suitable means of describing the overall movement in the Second Gospel—from Jesus' initial call to come follow right up to the climactic Cross event. It might be said that the word "way" occurs both overtly and covertly; one straightforward and the other functioning more like a riddle to be unlocked. There is no passivity in kingdom reading; we must be attentive and alert. So, let's proceed accordingly.

In the opening verses (1:2 and in 1:3) Mark defines the term the "Way of Lord" from Isaiah's point of view: "Behold, I send My messenger before Your face, Who will prepare Your *way* The voice of one crying in the wilderness, 'Make ready the *way* of the Lord, Make His paths straight'" (Mk. 1:2-3 NAS; italics inserted).

Mark uses the word "way" fourteen more times to describe Jesus' journey that eventually climaxes in Jerusalem. Sometimes it is translated as the neutral word "road," as if Mark is simply describing the physical path on which Jesus is walking (see 4:4, 14, 8:3). However, Mark's quotation of Isaiah in 1:2-3 sets the tone that "way" is more a pilgrimage of faith that began long before Jesus' arrival in the baptismal waters of the Jordan River.[10] From that mid-point of Mark (8:27ff), Jesus "sets his face toward Jerusalem" (phrase borrowed from Luke 9:51) and "way" should never again be understood as a mere map coordinate ("road"). Once the "way of messianic suffering" has been revealed to the disciples (and to us) in 8:31, conflict between Jesus and his followers gradually escalates. [11] Jesus may be leading the discipleship processional but the disciples are not only out of touch with his true mission; they openly oppose him. They are going to the same place, but his map and theirs have different legends.[12]

The map-legend symbol through which to properly read Jesus' map is a divinely appointed cross while the disciples interpret their map as if the legend key is a human throne. This sets them on an inevitable collision course. Jesus envisions and acts upon one reality, the nearing Kingdom. Jesus' magnetic north points to Golgotha and the cross, while the disciples' pseudo-gospel-map is calibrated on the re-establishment of the Davidic throne resulting from a military coup over Rome. In Mark, the cross is the map legend which unlocks the "mystery of the Kingdom of God" (4:11) and the nature of Jesus' divine mission. Without the Cross as their true reference point, the disciples are destined to "fall away" when Jesus makes that final turn on the "way" to Jerusalem.

For Christian leaders, then and now, you see only what your internal compass allows you to see. Simply, appearances in life can be very deceiving. Let's use Mark's introduction to see a few unexpected marks of leading in Jesus' way. In rapid-fire succession, Mark's opening scenes reveal three surprises. The Greek is unmistakable; John appeared (1:4), Jesus appeared (1:9), and the voice from heaven appeared (1:11).[13]

John Appeared: Forgiveness in Unexpected Places

First, John sets the stage. The Isaianic prophecy of 1:2-3 is immediately fulfilled in John the Baptist. He is most assuredly the one "preparing the way in the wilderness." Furthermore, John is calling people out of Jerusalem to be baptized for the forgiveness of sins. There are very important cultural implications for this act that cannot be fully unpacked here, but note that in the first century Jewish world, forgiveness was offered and received in the temple in Jerusalem. Nowhere else.

Forgiveness was ritually exchanged by the Jewish cult practices documented in the Torah. Yet the introduction of Mark tells us that there was a massive recalibration at work. All of Jerusalem and all of Judea went out to the wilderness to find John and the forgiveness he was offering. The implications are subtle but clear. In Jesus' day, Jewish people were declared ceremonially forgiven by priests at the temple through their sacrifices, yet the scope of their exodus from Jerusalem, the place of temple cult, to the wilderness reveals they wanted more. It appears that being forgiven by ritual is not the same as being transformed by the long awaited Holy Spirit that John promises (1:8).[14] Suffice it to say that in Mark's day, transactional forgiveness will no longer satisfy when transformation of heart is available in the age of the Spirit.

Modern Christian liberalism has run the same course as the emptiness of its theological promises was abandoned in droves for the hunger of an evangelical faith experience. The same might be said for the pan-Wesleyan movement as we respond to the resurgence of the New Calvinists. The focus on five-point Calvinist theology leaves New Calvinism open to the charge of "transactional pardon" without any substantive hope for imparted righteousness. Being called a son or daughter of God is not the same as actually being a child of the King. People are hungry and poised for an interpretation and application of the Word that leads them into a deeply transformational experience of the Spirit.

The implications of this passage on Christian leadership are undeniable. One cannot give to others what one does not personally possess. Moreover, they cannot lead in a direction ("way") they do not know even exists on the map of spiritual possibility. There is nothing more practical for leaders than biblical theology housed in the narrative of Jesus "way."

The second cultural insight arising from John the Baptist's introductory passage (1:4-8) surrounds the "baptism" he is offering. In the first century, no Jewish person was baptized as an entrance into faith. Jewish children were "born into the faith." The clearest historic reference marker we have of people practicing a ritual similar to Christian baptism prior to Jesus is a water immersion/purification that pagan proselytes underwent as they were converting to Judaism. This gives a profound fresh sense to John's work. Jewish people in mass were coming out to receive what John was offering. A fresh start was implicit, as was the inherent spiritual inadequacies of the Jewish faith. Furthermore, Mark is telling us, "If you like what John makes available, just wait for Jesus and the baptism of the Holy Spirit." Christian leaders must appropriate all the Kingdom resources Jesus makes available. Tried and true leadership principles that arise from the business realm cannot supplant the innovative strategies that the Spirit gives rise to as the Kingdom descends in our midst. Leading like Jesus should never mimic Wall Street or a Harvard MBA.

Jesus Appeared: The Holy Spirit in Unexpected Ways

Then Jesus appears in the wilderness. Without any words from Jesus directly and with minimal narrative explanation, Jesus is baptized by John. As Jesus was coming out of the water, the heavens are "torn open" and the Holy Spirit comes down "into Him." Mark is revealing this as the eschatological moment that changes all human history. What John promised as an eventual reality for humans ("He will baptize in the Holy Spirit" 1:8) has now been initiated in Jesus as the first "Spirit-filled man." Mark is carefully crafting his theology of the Spirit. In 1:8-12, the Spirit is mentioned three times as the One who will empower Jesus' earthly ministry.

Interestingly, even though the term Holy Spirit disappears from the language of the remainder of Mark's Gospel, it is the Holy Spirit who enables Jesus to act in perfect accord with the Kingdom agenda.[15] Thus, this event narratively alerts Mark's readers that Jesus' internal compass is attuned by the divine Spirit rather than any culturally confining script which will soon be shown to be the driving force for humanity (8:33). Jesus may have the outward appearance of every other person in the story but everyone also recognizes he obeys a different set of marching orders.

Christian leaders must refrain from leading predominantly out of their positional authority. Utilizing a title on a business card to implement an agenda rarely results in harmonious results. Nor should Christian leaders rely exclusively on their academic training for decisions. Rather, with those human resources as a starting point, leaders must pursue wisdom that comes from the wellspring of the Spirit's presence.

The Father's Voice Appears: Unexpected Validation

The final "appearance" comes from the Heavenly voice, "You are my beloved son. In you I am well-pleased." Before Jesus has spoken any words and before he has done any signs and wonders, the divine pleasure of God emanates from heaven. It should be pointed out that the words echo Psalm 2:7 and Isaiah 42:1. The Isaiah passage begins the "Suffering Servant" motif in the second half of Isaiah, forewarning Mark's readers of Jesus' developing role in the narrative to follow. Additionally, Psalm 2 has a most interesting ritual history in the nation of Israel as a coronation Psalm read over Hebrew kings as they were crowned. Thus, while the people only see Jesus bowing in humility as he receives John's baptism, the Father in Heaven is simultaneously crowning him as the ruling King. As leaders, especially Christian leaders we must be cautious of the affirmations we seek. Do we seek out the affirmation of our immediate superiors, subtly positioning ourselves to be seen as their clones? Or do we use the Jesus "way" of ruling; knowing who we are as *his*, results in humbling and raising up others into their new position and responsibility.

Finally, we must be careful as leaders not to be too critical that our "followers" do not advance at the pace we desire. Sadly, Jesus' disciples see and act on a different set of expectations than his. Their understandings are limited to the cultural and religious realities of their confining world. There are two competing compass settings in the Gospel of Mark: the "way of Caesar" and the "way of the Jesus." In contemporary terms, the way of Caesar involves people adhering to the basic value system constructed by culture (Rom 12:1-2): let's call it the script of culture. With this in mind, Mark's prologue poses this question, "What factors determine the calibration of your inner compass: the *script of culture* (and its various modern-day Caesars) or the *Scripture of the Kingdom* (Jesus and the Holy Spirit)?"[16] Leaders must pay attention to the greater narrative of God's work in human experience. Effective, godly leaders act out of an orientation and compass that has been thoroughly recalibrated by Christ, his commitment to the Father's divine agenda, and the wisdom made know by the indwelling Holy Spirit.

Listen

Finally, let me suggest a key leadership practice that (1) reveals Jesus' submission to the "Cross/Kingdom" agenda; and (2) suggests how all future generations might appropriate Mark's lessons to become faithful followers and cross-bearers themselves: *Listen*. Yes, the word "listen" is the Markan key to fully grasping Kingdom cartography and Jesus' call to follow—then and now.

In 1:11, the voice from heaven declares over Jesus both his divine Sonship and imminent kingship. Then, Jesus acts upon this spoken reality. His first mission is to obey the compelling Spirit immediately by going into the wilderness and overcoming the temptations of the evil one.[17] Jesus will not be swayed by any voice other than his Father's, no matter how alluring.[18] This temptation is not to be seen as a singular event. The call for Jesus to reconfigure his agenda along different lines happens again and again. Later in the first chapter, when the disciples find Jesus alone and praying, they inform him of his earthy popularity: "Everyone is seeking you!" (1:37). Mark's narrative reveals that their desire is for Jesus to meet their physical needs.[19] Empowered by his habitual prayers with the Father, Jesus replies, "Let us go somewhere else to the towns nearby, in order that I may preach there also; *for that is what I came out for*" (Mk. 1:38 NAS). It's vital to recognize that Mark does not imply any moral wrongness to their request for the miraculous. Rather, there is a higher value to which Jesus has conformed his life. Simply, Mark portrays Jesus' life to be "call-based" as his decisions flow from the voice of the Father and the Spirit, rather than as a "needs-based" ministry which eventually exhausts any and all who enter in.[20] Jesus listened—continuously taking his direction from God.

This foundation of life will become vital as we witness Jesus' faulty-followers in the chapters ahead. Again and again, Jesus speaks out of his call as he reveals his mission yet the disciples do not have the ability to comprehend his words because they are not able to listen for their internal compasses are focused in the wrong direction. Jesus describes humanity's lack of perception with the sensory metaphors:

> "Why do you discuss the fact that you have no bread? Do you not yet see or understand? Do you have a hardened heart? Having eyes, do you not see? And having ears, do you not hear? (Mk. 8:17-18 NAS)

His Kingdom-agenda seems to be both overlooked and even worse, outright rejected.

Moreover, Jesus' paradigmatic parable about Kingdom realities in Mark 4 is bracketed with two commands. It begins with the word "*listen*" and then closes with this warning, "*He who has ears to hear, let him hear.*" The kingdom revelation as being manifest in and through Jesus must be heard and obeyed. Mark is describing the disciples as living under a false narrative while refusing to re-calibrate their lives according to Jesus' words.

This is most clearly stated in the Transfiguration narrative. First, Jesus is revealed as a foretaste of the resurrection life, when "Jesus' appearance is transfigured and his clothes became dazzling white, far whiter than any bleach could ever make them" (9:3). Next, clouds come down on the mountain with a Sinai-like force. Finally, the voice from heaven speaks directly to Peter, James, and John, saying, "This is my beloved Son. Listen to Him." The kingdom is not seen by unwittingly following in the same direction as Jesus but rather in adopting the mind of Jesus.[21] Listening and obeying thus becomes the means by which the minds of the disciples and all future generations can and will be transformed.

It is in the shaping of the Christian imagination that one can see what Jesus sees, even though one's senses may call these conclusions into question. Christian leadership may begin by becoming informed about the Jesus "way" and his direction. But its true destination for the leader and his/her followers is to be fully transformed so his kingdom compass settings become internalized.

Conclusion

Thus, the Gospel of Mark can be understood as a lesson in Kingdom Cartography; coordinate setting with Jesus as the captain. Mark will fully unpack the new Gospel Positioning System that places Jerusalem, not Rome, at the center of the map. All perceptions of the world flow from this new starting point. Everyone, from Jesus' first century disciples to us, must recalibrate their definition of the "way" based upon this new revelation, with all points leading to the events which transpire in Jerusalem.

But our destination cannot be found at Herod's palace, and not at Caiaphas' home, not at the conferring of the Sanhedrin, not even at the worshipping temple. Rather, as we gather at Golgotha and listen to the voice of Jesus, his cross will become our new compass heading upon which we set our eyes, which models for us what it means to lead in the Jesus "way."

David Smith, PhD, is Academic Dean of Wesley Seminary at Indiana Wesleyan University, Marion, Indiana.

Chapter 8 Notes

[1] The map legend is a small box or table on the map image that explains what those symbols means. This might include icons or even mileage scale. This will be carefully explained later in the chapter.

[2] I have not footnoted this quote intentionally, for its pervasive use places it in the realm of common knowledge.

[3] See also summary of demons "whenever those possessed by evil spirits caught sight of him, the spirits would throw themselves to the ground in front of him shrieking, 'You are the son of God'" (3:11). Also, the first miracle in Mark is an exorcism in the synagogue where the evil spirit recognizes Jesus with this similar name, "Why are you interfering with us Jesus of Nazareth? Have you come to destroy us? I know who you are-the Holy one of God?"

[4] It should be noted that in the Sanhedrin trial (14:53-65), the ones who bring false testimony against Jesus have ample time to plan out their testimony. They could rehearse their lies as needed. But ironically, many false witnesses are twice said to contradict one another. As the story unfolds, the reader should be cheering, "Jesus, just remain silent and they will have to release you!" But when the High Priest comes to Jesus with the paradigmatic question, "Are you the Christ the Son of the Blessed One" Jesus immediately breaks his trial silence with the eschatologically loaded response, "I AM" (*ego eimi*) + the quote from Daniel 7. Thus, humanity fails to convict Jesus in her courtroom mockery (humanity's shame) while Jesus is found guilty by His own testimony (heaven's honor). For the first time since the opening verse of 1:1; Messiah and Son of God are carefully re-connected.

[5] Jesus' death is rhetorically underplayed by these words, "and Jesus breathed out" (15:37).

[6] R. A. Guelich, R. A. *Mark 1–8:26*, Vol. 34A (Dallas: Word, 1998), 38.

[7] Grk., ὁ δὲ ἀποκριθεὶς αὐτῷ λέγει Σὺ λέγεις. Here, Σὺ λέγεις *(su legei)* is in the present active indicative, so a literal rendering would be: "you say it" (cf. Mounce's Reverse-Interlinear). The NRSV is the closest to the original. The NIV renders it as "Yes, it is as you say." Similarly, the NASB reads: "It is as you say". The ESV renders it as "You have said so."

[8] see also Ephesians 1:21 and Romans 8:38

[9] The Greek word "follow" occurs 18 times. The prepositional phrase "get behind me" is used an additional 4 times.

[10] This *sensus plenior* definition of the kingdom trajectory term "way" is used almost without exception following Peter's confession "on the way" in Mark 8. *Sensus Plenior* is Latin for "fuller meaning." This is often ascribed to the prophetic material in the Old Testament as it relates to Jesus' fulfillment in the New Testament. See Mark 8:27; 9:33-34; 10:17, 32, 46, 52; 11:8; 12:14. Following Jesus' arrival in Jerusalem the word stops; for He has reached His destination and now employed the way of life as He is shamed and killed.

[11] We should keep in mind that Jesus' passion prediction comes into direct conflict with the disciples' three times in Mark (Thinking like God vs. Thinking like men):

      1. Jesus 8:31-32a   Disciples 8:32b
      2. Jesus 9:30-31   Disciples 9:32-34
      3. Jesus 1032-34   Disciples 10:35-45

[12] Now the legend on a map is usually found in a small box and it serves to describe all unknown or unique symbols used. It's the key to unlocking how the map actually operates in the hands of the reader.

[13] Each "appearance" scene begins with the same Greek word, "*egeneto*" almost as an introductory marker. The English translations can miss this reading clue.

[14] Readers of Mark must also keep in mind there are numerous Old Testament passages that promise a similar Holy Spirit event; especially Ezekiel 36:25-37 which employs baptismal language and the promise of forgiveness and cleansing of the Land

[15] The only time the Holy Spirit is discussed as present with Jesus' followers is in the Eschatological discourse of Mark 13. It is during post-death post-resurrection persecution that the Holy Spirit will empower believers; just as He does with Jesus now.

[16] The best monograph on the subject of leadership in the way of Jesus is by Eugene Peterson, *The Jesus Way: A Conversation on the Ways that Jesus is The Way* (Eerdmans: Grand Rapids, MI, 2007). The first half of the book describes the Jesus way, based upon multiple biblical models. The second half depicts the other options, as found in the persons of Herod, Caiaphas, and Josephus.

[17] Though Mark does not explicitly state that Jesus triumphs over Satan as Matthew and Luke do; the result is implicit that the "stronger man" has won (3:23-27).

[18] I am "tempted" to explore the three specific temptation described in Matthew and Luke. But summarily, each of the temptations offered to Jesus by Satan do become his as the narrative unfolds. But they only happen in God's timing as Jesus submits to the divine agenda not the instant gratification offered by Satan.

[19] By the end of the chapter (1:45) we discover that Jesus' miracle-centered popularity is actually undermining His Kingdom calling. "As a result large crowds surrounded Jesus and He could not publically enter a town anywhere. He had to stay out in the secluded places, but people from everywhere kept coming to him."

[20] Mark 14:3-9 one of the most poignant revelations of Jesus' identity, as the unnamed woman comes to anoint Jesus with "very costly pure nard." The disciples value system tells them this is a waste, for they could have sold it and given it to the poor. Yet Jesus forcefully declares their observation wrong-headed. "The poor you will always have with you. But you will not always have me."

[21] See N.T. Wright, *The Paul Debate* (Baylor University Press, 2015), 1. Wright summaries his Pauline emphasis, suggesting this about "knowing the name or having the mind" of Jesus.

9
Holiness, Power, and Mission

Matthew I. Ayars

The book of Isaiah presents a radical view of leadership. Rather than affirming brute strength and power, Isaiah presents powerlessness and weakness that is rooted in the trust of God as true leadership. As a result, categories such as servanthood, holiness, kingdom oriented power, and mission are offered for their leadership value in light of Isaiah. Leaders are to model this Christ-like, upended kind of leadership as a contemporary expression of faith in God.

THE BOOK OF ISAIAH turns the human concept of power on its head. As a result of his unique vision experience recorded in chapter 6, the prophet works within a different framework in thinking about the convergence of power, leadership (the Messiah), redemption, and the kingdom of God. Throughout Isaiah's ministry, he proclaimed with undying persistence that the leadership of the Messiah would be different than that of the corrupted monarchs and kingdoms of the world. Isaiah's message reinforces the contrast between human and holy power. Human power, as represented in the kings of Assyria and Babylon, is characterized by military might, aggression, oppression, violence, cruelty, and coercion. In contrast, holy power paradoxically takes the form of weakness and innocence, characterized by love, mercy, physical infirmity or deprivation, humility, and submission.

Ultimately, Isaiah shows us two significant leadership truths regarding the Messiah. First, as the model for leadership, the Messiah is holy *in character*. Second, the Messiah's *strategy* for effective leadership is also to be holy (set apart). In the messianic leadership model, leadership effectiveness is found in the paradoxical tension of strength through weakness, influence through innocence, and effectiveness through obedience. In his description of the Servant of Yahweh as the center-piece of God's world renewal plan, Isaiah illustrates what it looks like when power converges with holiness. Through Isaiah, we rediscover the biblical foundations for a model of holy leadership that stands in stark contrast to secular models rooted in a non-biblical worldview.

Isaiah's Theological Framework: Power and Holiness

Power and holiness are the two attributes of God most heavily present in the impressive theological manifesto that is the book of Isaiah. These two themes converge to form the central point of reference for a comprehensive view of the prophet's theology. This is particularly important for Isaiah because the book as a whole has no shortage of theological motifs. One of the factors contributing to Isaiah's reputation as the "Prince of the Prophets"[1] is the book's vast and multidimensional theology. Major theological themes woven throughout the book include: (1) servanthood, (2) redemption, (3) human sin, (4) judgment, and (4) hope. Each theme is developed against the backdrop of the *power and holiness* of Yahweh, the Holy One of Israel.[2] Redemption, according to Isaiah, can *only* be understood in light of the power and holiness of Yahweh.

A strong case can be made that the preeminent agenda of Isaiah is to *redefine power*. It is not merely enough to propose the sovereignty of Yahweh; the prophet goes further than this. He attests that power in the context of *Kingdom ethics* is not only different than profane human power, but also diametrically opposed to it to the point of paradox. Kingdom ethics define power in terms of weakness, influence in terms of innocence, and greatness in terms of servanthood.

These dimensions come into focus as Isaiah prophesies that the hope of Israel's future lies in the *leadership of the coming Messiah* who will be endowed with power from heaven to lead a holy nation of priests.[3] Not only will Israel be set apart as the covenant people of Yahweh, but the *kind of power* the Messiah will wield will be unlike power as we know it. This is a kingdom that is set apart (holy), ruled by a king who is set apart (holy) who wields a sort of power that is set apart (holy). The entire model for power in leadership is centered on Jesus who will redefine altogether what it means to be a person of authority and influence.

Holiness, Ontology, and Vocation

Our thinking about holiness is typically framed within concepts like cleanliness and purity from sin-guilt, godly character, and a circumcised heart. In other words, we normally think about holiness in terms of our character, or *ontology*. We use the "to be" verb to describe holiness: "people *are* holy." Paralleling this, however, is the holiness of vocation; that is, the holiness of what we *do*. For the ancients, being and action (more precisely, "function") were inseparable. Being is only activated when something (or someone) is given a function. Speaking to this, John Walton writes,

> In the ancient world something came into existence when it was separated out as a distinct entity, given a function, and given a name. For purposes of discussion I will label this approach to ontology as "function-oriented." This is in stark contrast to modern ontology, which is much more interested in what might be called the structure or substance of something along with its properties. In modern popular thinking (as opposed to technical philosophical discussion), the existence of the world is perceived in physical, material terms.... In the ancient Near East, something did not necessarily exist just because it happened to occupy space.[4]

Walton goes on to say, "If ontology in the ancient world is function-oriented, then to create something (i.e., bring it into existence) would mean to give it a function or a role within an ordered cosmos."[5] What does this say about holiness and vocation? From the perspective of the ancients, one cannot *be* holy until one *does* *holy*. Ontological holiness (arguably even "positional holiness") is inseparable from obedience to the commission of God. They are not the same, but they are two sides to the same coin.

This comes to the front in Isaiah's vision of seeing Yahweh as a king.[6] The kingship of Yahweh is wrapped up in his being "seated on a throne, high and lifted up,"[7] with the train of his robe filling the temple. This description attests to the fact that this is no ordinary king; this is the *most powerful king*. This king is without parallel

---

*"leadership effectiveness is found in the paradoxical
tension of strength through weakness, influence through
innocence, and effectiveness through obedience"*

---

in his authority and faithful governance. At the same time, the text speaks to the unparalleled *holiness of the King Yahweh*. The holiness of this king is evidenced in the calling out of the seraphim, "Holy! Holy! Holy!"[8] But how does this holiness link up with ontology-as-function as Walton understands it? *Yahweh is holy in his governance as king*. His holiness is activated through his vocation.

This is fleshed out further when we look at the governing responsibilities of the Messiah. The Messiah is the ultimate image of holiness. But the Messiah also rules his kingly office with *power* and authority (Romans 1:4).[9] As a result, power and authority become essential parts of holiness in any dialogue about Christian (and especially Wesleyan) leadership. To remove the question of the use of power from this conversation, as is often the case with well-intended models and theories regarding servant or authentic leadership, is to lay aside one of the most significant messages regarding the nature and work of the Messiah as the redeemer of the world and the model for leadership in the kingdom.

Ancient Assyria, Human Power, and the Messiah

The message of Isaiah comes against the backdrop of the Assyrian expansion (Isaiah 1–39) of the eighth century BC and the Babylonian Exile (Isaiah 40–66) of the sixth century BC. The historical setting further attests to the prophet's agenda to explain what happens to power when mixed with holiness. The imperial growth of Assyria and the Babylonian destruction of the temple called Yahweh's power into question. Does Yahweh have the power to protect his people from the violent and aggressive Tiglath-Pileser III? What about Nebuchadnezzar of Babylon?

Does the fact that the covenant people end up living in an unclean land and cohabitating with pagan people mean that the Holy One of Israel no longer sits on his throne? These are precisely the questions the prophet is answering. It was time for God's people to understand that the manifestation of his power is *foolish* within a secular framework. His power is weakness. His influence and effectiveness are solely the result of his innocence. His power is a paradox. We see this with great clarity in Isaiah 7:14.

Emmanuel: A Newborn Image of Holy Power

Isaiah 7:14 is a famous passage because of the New Testament's application of the text to the birth of Jesus as the Jewish Messiah. From a New Testament perspective, this is certainly appropriate. However, how did this passage function in its original eighth century BC Judean context? As Assyria grew stronger, the smaller nations of the ancient Near East created alliances in order to fortify themselves against the growing Assyrian superpower. One of these alliances included Syria and Israel, who, in order to boost their chances of victory over Assyria, sent a threatening invitation to Ahaz, king of Judah, to join them in their efforts to thwart Assyrian expansion. This put Ahaz in a tough spot. Would his future be more secure by joining their coalition or should he side with Assyria? Either way, it meant going to battle. No matter how Ahaz measured it, things were going to turn out badly.

This is the context in Isaiah 7 when Isaiah goes to Ahaz and says, "Be careful, be quiet, do not fear, and do not let your heart be faint because of these two smoldering stumps of firebrands, at the fierce anger of Rezin and Syria and the son of Remalia" (Isaiah 7:4). In other words, God commands Ahaz not to fear regardless of his circumstances. Through Isaiah, Yahweh is calling Ahaz to trust him. This dynamic of trust as the foundation for *holy power and leadership* is essential and comes to the front in Isaiah 52:13–53:12.

In order to secure God's promise, Isaiah offers Ahaz a sign. From Ahaz's perspective, a reasonable sign for God's protection against human violence and imperial growth would have been something such as a sword from heaven or legions of angels; perhaps even a promise of the Holy Spirit endowing Judean soldiers with divine might and battle-skill. We read in Isaiah 7:14, however, that this isn't at all the sort of sign that God gives Ahaz. What sign does the prophet offer? *A helpless baby!* What in all of creation is less threatening than a human baby?! Isaiah might as well have said, "Ahaz, don't fear! God is with you and will protect you! You will know this because he's giving you a box of kittens!" Rather than a symbol of might, God gives Ahaz a symbol of human frailty, physical weakness, and human innocence to remind him that his powerful presence is in their midst.

God was making an astounding claim through his prophet Isaiah: that in an innocent, helpless human baby, God has more power than all the armies of men. God's power does not look like or work like human power. The way that he works in the world to accomplish his will is not like the way that humanity works in the world. He is not violent, harsh, coercing or forceful. With God, power is not *primarily* measured by the sharpness of his sword, the numbers of his chariots, or the brutality of his armies. This is the first paradox of holy power in Isaiah: God's power is in weakness, innocence, and servanthood. In particular, Isaiah's message announces, "Deliverance will come, not through alliances or military might, but through divine intervention, by a God who keeps promises."[10]

Servanthood and the Messiah

The contrast between holy power and human power is most deeply fleshed out in the so-called "Servant Songs" found in Isaiah 40–55.[11] As previously mentioned, Isaiah is especially interested in the coming Messiah, who, according to Isaiah, will rule as the king of Israel in the likeness of David (Isaiah 11:1–4a). Certainly, this Messiah will be powerful and able to protect God's people from their enemies. This Messiah will also be able to establish and reign over a global Jewish empire. After all, if Israel's patron deity is the only sovereign Creator, then he should claim his authority and rule over not only Israel and the Promised Land, but over *all people* and *the whole cosmos*. This Messiah is the *epitome* of power. In the conventional sense of military might and physical strength, he also embodies kingly leadership.

But from the revelation of identity of this great and powerful Messiah the second interesting paradox of leadership emerges: this mighty Messiah-king is a *servant*, a *slave*. In this Kingdom, it is the slave who is crowned king. It is the *submissive one* who wields royal authority. It is the one who emptiness himself of all self-interest, the one who trusts and obeys Yahweh to the point of death, even death on a cross (Philippians 2), who stands as the supreme example of divine authority.

This point rushes to the front of Isaiah's message in the fourth and final Servant Song in 52:13–53:12. Here, the poem describes for us in detail the source of the servant king's power.[12] The song itself starts right out with "Behold, my servant shall act wisely; he shall be *high and lifted up*, and shall be *exalted*" (Isaiah 52:13, ESV, italics original). The first discovery that the reader encounters is the paradoxical juxtaposition of the terms "servant" and "high and lifted up." These two do not go together! What makes a servant a servant is the fact that he is powerless to do his or her own will; someone else dictates their activities, actions, and behaviors. A person without the *right* to exert his or her own will is lowly. To have power means being able to do what you want or having the authority and competence to exercise one's own will. A servant is the opposite of power, characterized instead by weakness and lowliness. The phrase that the "servant" will be "high and lifted up" is oxymoronic.

This point is accentuated all the more when we consider the Hebrew phrase which is translated "high and lifted up" in the ESV. This is the same phrase found in Isaiah 6:1, which reads: "In the year that King Uzziah died I saw the Lord sitting upon a throne, *high and lifted up*" (italics original). What is odd about this is that the same phrase that is used to describe the all-powerful, all sovereign Yahweh is also used to describe the one who

> grew up before him like a young plant, and like a root out of dry ground; he had no form or majesty that we should look at him, and no beauty that we should desire him. He was despised and rejected by men; a man of sorrows, and acquainted with grief; and as the one from whom men hide their faces he was despised, and we esteemed him not… he was oppressed and he was afflicted, yet he opened not his mouth; like a lamb that is led to the slaughter, and like a sheep that before his shearers is silent, he opened not his mouth. (Isaiah 53:2–3, 7)

It just does not fit. How does this work? This submissive one who gives up his life, the innocent one: is this the one who has power? Who is exalted? The one whose power can be compared to the *Cosmos King* in chapter 6?

This Suffering Servant Song is a clear attestation that the unmatched power of the Messiah is wrapped up in obedience, weakness, and innocence. This is the holy vocation of the Messiah. The passage also indicates that the humility and obedience of the Servant are key to redemption. Functioning within the context of the book at large, the servant of Yahweh epitomizes the nature of human influence and power as intended by the transcendent Creator. Running counter to the typical human understanding of power, the prophet teaches that human value is inseparable from a submissive and intimate relationship with Yahweh. Yahweh is the one who is able to work powerfully in history.

Furthermore, Yahweh is able to use even the injustice and corrupt behavior of fallen humanity to redeem the world.[13] His redemption, however, comes to humanity through his faithful and obedient one who is faithful until death. Those who fully entrust themselves to Yahweh will be exalted and they will be exalted because of their trust and obedience.

The criteria for exaltation in the kingdom of God contrasts the world's criteria. Human power was characterized by military might, coercion and dominance in a time of Assyrian aggression, the rise of the Babylonian empire, rebellions, and political alliances. Throughout the entirety of his ministry, Isaiah speaks out against this paradigm for leadership because it is at such odds with the nature of the Holy One of Israel. The Suffering Servant depicts a leader whose influence is not earned through might, political manipulation, or strategic alliances. Rather, his effectiveness in carrying out the will of the Creator in the creation is through *weakness, innocence,* and *submission* to Yahweh. It is the one whom others would not even think to look upon that the Holy One of Israel uses powerfully for his purposes in the world.[14]

The servant of Yahweh knows his Lord enough to trust that he is capable of redeeming any and all human behavior—even acts of injustice. In response to the loyalty of the servant, Yahweh is able to redeem human acts of injustice fully, thereby demonstrating exactly what he is capable of accomplishing. The servant merits exaltation based on two things: (1) humble faithfulness and trust in Yahweh and (2) offering himself as the instrument for redemption of his enemies.

The Life of Jesus, the Servant King

The life of Jesus falls right in line with this. God's greatest, most powerful redemptive act in human history is manifest through the submissive act of Jesus as the Messiah. The Messiah demonstrates his greatest power through his own weakness and submission. This submission resulted in the fulfillment of God's world renewal plan, the fulfillment of the mission of God, and simultaneously the great witness to the holy love of God.

This dynamic is especially present in the proper interpretation of Jesus' words, "*Eli, Eli, lema sabachthani*" (Matt 27:46). Many New Testament readers miss the fact that Jesus is citing Psalm 22:1 when he says this. When we read all of Psalm 22, the parallels between the circumstances poetically described by Psalmist (David) and Jesus on the cross are staggering. The major difference is that in Psalm 22, David uses figurative speech whereas for Jesus it is literal (see Table 1).

Psalm 22 is ultimately a Trust Psalm.[15] The thrust of this psalm is that even though the psalmist suffers, he will trust in Yahweh. *This is the heart of holiness and the core of saving faith and biblical leadership.* Jesus, by quoting Psalm 22, declares that even though his submission and obedience to Yahweh has landed him in excruciating pain on the cross, he still trusts in his Father.

This theme runs parallel to Isaiah's song of the Suffering Servant (Is 52:13–53:12). The Suffering Servant, by being obedient, weak, and submissive, ends up being the means through which God's redemptive work is manifest for the covenant people of God. There is an even stronger statement of faith in Isaiah 50:4–9:

> The LORD GOD has given me the tongue of those who are taught, that I may know how to sustain with a word him who is weary. Morning by morning he awakens; he awakens my ear to hear as those who are taught. The Lord God has opened my ear, and I was not rebellious; I turned not backward. I gave my back to those who strike, and my cheeks to those who pull out the beard; I hid not my face from disgrace and spitting.

David in Psalm 22	Jesus in the Crucifixion Narrative
But I am a worm and not a man, scorned by mankind and despised by the people. All who see me mock me; they make mouths at me; they wag their heads; "He trusts in the LORD; let him deliver him; let him rescue him for he delights in him!" (22:6–8)	And they stripped him and put a scarlet robe on him, and twisting together a crown of thorns, they put it on his head and put a reed in his right hand...they mocked him, saying 'Hail, the King of the Jews!' And they spit on him and took the reed and struck him on the head... and led him away to crucify him (Matt 27:27–31).
	And those who passed by derided him... "You who would destroy the temple and rebuilt it in three say, save yourself! If you are the Son of God, come down from the cross." So also the chief priests, with the scribes and the elders, mocked him, saying, "He saved others; he cannot save himself. He is the King of Israel; let him come down not from the cross, and we will believe in him. He trusts in God; let God deliver him now, if he desires him. (Matt 27:39–43)
I am poured out like water, and all my bones are out of join; my heart is like wax; it is melted within my breast; my strength is dried up like a potsherd, and my tongue sticks to my jaws; (22:14–15)	After this, knowing that all was now finished, said (to fulfill the Scripture), "I thirst." (John 19:28).
For dogs encompass me; a company of evildoers encircles me; they have pierced my hands and feet. (22:16)	And they crucified him... (Matt 27:35)
...they divide my garments among them, and for my clothing the cast lots. (22:18)	And when they had crucified him, they divided his garments among them by casting lots. (Matt 27:35)

Table 1 - Poetic parallels of Jesus and David

This also runs parallel to what Paul says in Philippians 2:5–8:

> Have this mind among yourselves, which is yours in Christ Jesus, who, though he was in the form of God, did not count equality with God a thing to be grasped, but emptied himself, by taking the form of a servant, being born in the likeness of men. And being found in human form, he humbled himself by becoming obedient to the point of death, even death on a cross.

Here, as in Isaiah 52:13–53:12, Paul highlights the perfect obedience of Jesus that goes hand-in-hand with submissiveness and the emptying of power for effective leadership. Christ's redemptive work is effective because of his complete obedience and weakness. Thus, salvation and holiness as both heart posture and vocation go hand-in-hand; they are two sides of the same coin.

What is the solution for a rebellious people with egos that have run amok? Submission, weakness, obedience, and, ultimately, love. This is biblical leadership. Through weakness, submission, humility, and obedience, the power of God comes to life in the world through his human agents for the cause of his redemptive purposes.

Leadership Lessons

We can draw the following leadership lessons based on the interpretation of Isaiah's recapitulation of power as demonstrated through the messianic model for leadership:

Holiness is not only ontological, but also vocational.

The call to holiness in the Scriptures is not only about having a purified heart. That is certainly a central part of it, but it is not the end. The purpose of God's purifying work in the lives of his people is to commission them as agents of redemption in his world renewal plan (see Isaiah 6). It is the holy function in ministry that goes hand-in-hand with purity of heart.

Leaders are to be holy and use a holy model for leadership.

One cannot have a holy heart without a holy method. In the same way that God desires to transform and heal the human heart completely, he also desires to transform our way of thinking about how we relate to other people. This means approaching people through the cross—with forgiveness and grace as the central point of reference for all human exchange. Through his purifying work in our lives we become a vessel through which God can channel his presence into a broken world *via* the Holy Spirit in the lives in his leaders. Through the purified heart God can make us effective in operating within a model of leadership that is pure. Not only this, but God can also use the day-to-day activities of engaging in ministry as the *means through which* he brings deep-level healing.

Power that is holy is framed within kingdom ethics.

The definition of power is the capacity to exercise one's own will. In a non-Christian setting, one's will is oriented around the wellbeing of the self. In a Christian setting, one's will is oriented around the desire for the wellbeing for *others*. This means that power is still used in both settings to accomplish one's will; the difference is the orientation of that will. Is it calibrated for the selfish desires, or for the wellbeing of others?

Holiness is inseparable from the mission to the world.

The cross is the symbol of redemption as well as God's holy, self-giving love for the world. When we look at the cross we see the heart of God. At the same time, the cross also symbolizes the fulfillment of God's mission to the world. This means that the holy love of God is inseparable from mission. It is his love that is to compel the church into full engagement with God's world renewal plan. Holiness and mission are inseparable. This point links up directly to the previous conclusion that *holy power is framed within kingdom ethics* in the sense that *others* are the central point of reference for all Christian behavior. In other words, being *others-focused* is only ever the result of the love of Christ shed abroad in the hearts of his followers.

Holy power through self-giving love engenders trust of others.

The biblical concept of power through weakness means first and foremost that the leader's influence is a *natural result* of earned trust and love. The leader does not have to *force* his or her will or vision upon constituents. Instead, the leader's persistent posture of self-giving love creates faithful and zealous followers. When others are the central point of reference for all human behavior, allegiance and trust become the primary dimensions for corporate operation. People follow people they trust. Furthermore, they trust because they are convinced that the leader's primary concern is the best interest of the follower. Allegiance is not forced, but comes naturally. A forced will is not power at all. No human manipulation is needed to force desired outcomes; no human conniving is needed when the leader trusts that God directs the outcomes of events.

Conclusion

Power in weakness means that influence and execution is never the result of manipulation or human tactics. The holy leader waits on God's timing, strategy, plan, and insight. God is involved in the details. This means that the anxiety that comes with the leader's "how" concerns are eliminated because the leader trusts that Christ directs the outcomes of events. It is *his* plan, not our own, which again means that human *force or coercion* is eliminated from the equation.

When leaders wield their positional or influential power out of a posture of weakness, self-giving love, and humble waiting on God, joy rather than fear becomes the ultimate incentive for followers. This kind of holy power at work in godly leaders produces life, vitality, hope, freedom, and, ultimately, points people to God as the true leader. In this paradoxical use of power, biblical leadership presents a radically different alternative to the world's view and use of power in leadership.

Matt Ayars, PhD (candidate), is the President of Emmaus Biblical Seminary in northern Haiti and author of Salvation in Fresh Perspective *and* Holy is a Four Letter Word.

Bibliography

Ayars, Matthew. *Salvation in Fresh Perspective: Covenant, Cross, and Kingdom.* Eugene: Wipf and Stock, 2015.

Goldingay, John. *The Message of Isaiah 40–55: A Literary-Theological Commentary.* New York: T & T Clark, 2005.

Motyer, J. Alec. *Isaiah: An Introduction and Commentary.* Tyndale Old Testament Commentaries. Downers Grove: InterVarsity, 1999.

Oswalt, John. *Isaiah.* The NIV Application Commentary. Grand Rapids: Zondervan, 2003, 17.

—. *The Book of Isaiah, Chapters 40–55.* New International Commentary on the Old Testament. Grand Rapids: Eerdmans, 1998.

Tucker, Gene M. *The Book of Isaiah 1–39: Introduction, Commentary, and Reflections.* The New Interpreter's Bible, vol. 6. Nashville: Abingdon, 2001.

Walton, John. *Ancient Near Eastern Thought and the Old Testament: Introducing the Conceptual World of the Hebrew Bible.* Grand Rapids: Baker Academic, 2006.

Chapter 9 Notes

Some content in this chapter is borrowed with permission from my *Salvation in Fresh Perspective: Covenant, Cross, and Kingdom.*

[1] Oswalt, *Isaiah*, 17.

[2] The title "Holy One of Israel" is unique title for Israel's Patron Deity. The title appears 32 times in the Old Testament at large; 26 of those are in Isaiah.

[3] Isaiah is also known as "Prince of the Prophets" because his messianic prophecies are unequaled in quantity among the writing prophets.

[4] Walton, *Ancient Near Eastern Thought and the Old Testament*, 180.

[5] Ibid, 181.

[6] In actuality, there are two kings in Isaiah 6: Uzziah, who is dead, and Yahweh, who is very much alive.

[7] This Hebrew phrase "high and lifted up" we will treat in further detail in just a moment.

[8] In Hebrew, superlatives are expressed by the three-part repetition of adjectives.

[9] On the power and authority of the Messiah in the NT, see Matt 7:28–29, 8:27, 9:6, 10:1; Luke 4:32, 5:1; John 10:18, 16:33; Acts 5:31; Rom 1:4; Col 1:16, 2:5; Heb 1:3, 2:14.

[10] Tucker, *The Book of Isaiah 1–39*, 112.

[11] Isaiah 42:1–9; 49:1–13; 50:4–9; 52:13–53:12.

[12] There is intense debate over the identity of the Messiah. For details, see John Oswalt, "Excurses: Select Bibliography on the Servant and the Servant Songs," *The Book of Isaiah: Chapters 40–66*, 113–114.

[13] This is the theological thrust of the Joseph story that comes to a culmination in Genesis 50:19–20.

[14] See Isaiah 40:1–44:23.

[15] For a detailed discussion on a form critical approach to interpreting the psalms see Hermann Gunkel, *Introduction to the Psalms: The Genres of Religious Lyric of Israel* (Mercer: University Press, 1998).

10
Women in Ministry: The "Problem Texts"

Ken Schenck

Two verses in the New Testament seem to forbid women in official leadership in the church: 1 Timothy 2:12 and 1 Corinthians 14:33-34. This chapter argues that rather than interpreting the rest of Scripture in their light, that the best hermeneutic is to read these two verses in light of the whole Bible. Because the whole Bible is much clearer on the role of women in leadership, giving examples in both the Old and New Testaments, and the trajectory of Scripture is to overcome a patriarchal approach to leadership is consistent, these two verses should be analyzed critically.

DEBATES OVER WOMEN IN MINISTRY often focus on the interpretation of one or two verses in the New Testament. Given the inherent polyvalence of texts, it is no wonder that 1 Timothy 2:12 has failed to settle the issue. The setting of 1 Timothy itself is a matter of debate, making it difficult to place the verse in a concrete context. It is difficult to apply a verse with certainty when we are uncertain about its precise original connotations. Beyond this "clobber verse" lie more fundamental hermeneutical questions about biblical theology. For example, is the application of Scripture more or less the direct application of passages to today or is the appropriation of Scripture more of a "whole Bible," canonical task?

Since this book aims particularly to serve Wesleyan leadership contexts, some answers to these questions seem more appropriate than others. For example, the interpretive method of Wesley in his approach to Scripture was far more holistic and canonical than atomistic.[1] Wesley lived before the rise of historical consciousness in the late 19th century. For that reason, we must consider him "pre-modern" in his approach to the biblical texts. By this, I mean that he jumps from Scripture to Scripture, making connections primarily on a literary level, without a deep sense of the historical particularity of each passage. This approach, which is similar to the approach of most Christians throughout history, is by its very nature a "whole Bible" approach, for the meaning of any one text exists in a network of interconnected meanings.[2]

My own branch of the Wesleyan tradition, The Wesleyan Church, claims abolitionism in the 19th century as part of its roots. The abolitionists, in their biblical interpretations, were opposed to the more atomistic methods of the Princeton Calvinists, who looked more to individual proof texts in their arguments in favor of slavery.[3] By contrast, the Wesleyan Methodist abolitionist took a principled approach to the biblical text and, accordingly, found the practice of slavery in the South to come up wanting, even though others could marshal verses and individual passages to give surface support to their position.[4]

Ironically, the New Testament case in favor of slavery is much stronger than the New Testament case against women in ministry. It is my contention in this chapter that there is not a single verse in the entire Bible that can be used to prohibit women from leadership roles and ministry roles in the church today. There is a set of texts that assume the husband is the default leader of the home. However, leadership in the home is a distinct issue from leadership in the church. Since Christ is the head of the husband, if God wishes to call a woman to ministry, the husband had better yield to the higher authority.

My claim in the pages that follow is that the few passages that are often used against women in ministry are in fact not against women ministry at all but have to do with relationships within the household. I also wish to show that the trajectory of Scripture is toward women in ministry. I aim to show that women in ministry and leadership roles are actually indicative of the age of the Holy Spirit, where in Christ "there is not male and female" (Gal. 3:28).

The Age of the Spirit

The Spirit of God is certainly present in the Old Testament. Bezalel, the artist who helps construct the tabernacle in Exodus, is filled by the LORD with the Spirit of God (Ex. 31:3). Some of the judges of Israel have the Spirit of the LORD come on them, especially to do specific tasks and purposes (e.g., Judg. 3:10; 11:29; 14:19). The Spirit of the LORD comes on David (1 Sam. 16:13) and on the servant of the LORD in Isaiah 61:1. In these instances, the Spirit comes upon specific, very important individuals with very important roles to play in the story of Israel.

By contrast, the Spirit comes upon *all* believers on the day of Pentecost in Acts 2. This is a remarkable shift in the story of humanity! Whereas before Pentecost, the Spirit primarily comes on special individuals, now the Holy Spirit comes upon all who believe. Peter tells the crowd that this remarkable event on the Day of Pentecost is the fulfillment of Joel 2:28-32: "I will pour out my Spirit on all people. Your sons and daughters will prophesy" (Acts 2:17-21). Of course! We would expect the Spirit to come upon all human individuals the same, for in the spiritual realm, distinctions in embodiment make no difference. Paul expresses this same principle in Galatians 3:2: In Christ Jesus "there is no longer Jew or Greek, there is no longer slave or free, there is no longer male and female; for all of you are one in Christ Jesus."[5]

It seems difficult now to argue theologically that our bodies in some way distinguish the spiritual *insight* or *value* of a person. Since both male and female have equal access to God and his Spirit, our first guess would be that there is now no distinction in wisdom or leadership potential between the genders. In so much of history, men could pretend that women were not as intelligent or insightful as themselves. Men might fool themselves into thinking that women did not have the natural potential for leadership. However, the modern age has made it impossible to make such claims without making oneself look ignorant. Some individual men are better leaders than some individual women, and some individual women are better leaders than some individual men. Nevertheless, there is no "always" that connects gender with leadership. In the end, the question of who has the most insight or leadership ability has nothing to do with gender; only with the specific individuals in question.

Women Leaders in the New Testament

It is therefore no surprise that we find women involved in the ministry of the early church. The book of Acts in particular seems to feature this aspect of early Christianity. We have already mentioned Acts 2:17. In Acts 16, when we reach the city of Philippi, a woman named Lydia, an apparently successful merchant in Greece and Asia Minor, is highlighted. It is difficult to tell whether she is married or not, but her entire household is baptized under her influence and Paul uses her house as his base in the city. A woman thus takes the lead in providing a church for the believers at Philippi.

The most prominent woman in Acts, of course, is Priscilla. She and her husband Aquila were Jews who had lived in Rome but were expelled by the Emperor Claudius when he put Jewish Christians out of the city in AD 49. She and her husband meet up with Paul in Corinth not long after he himself has arrived. They minister with him there until they all leave for Ephesus around the year AD 51. Then when Paul returns to Ephesus in the last part of Acts 18, they are key partners with him in his ministry for several years at Ephesus.

It is at this point that Apollos enters the story of Acts. He is an Alexandrian Jew who believes in the message of John the Baptist, but he does not yet know about Jesus. Priscilla and Aquila invite him to their home and explain the way of God more accurately to him (Acts 18:26). What is interesting, especially for the ancient world, is the fact that her name is mentioned first. In our day, we might mention the wife first in a husband-wife pair if we knew the wife better than the husband or if she was the more dominant of the pair. However, in the ancient world, which was overwhelmingly male-dominated, the mention of her first is very striking indeed. Of the three times she and her husband are mentioned in Acts, twice she is mentioned first (Acts 18:18, 26). Similarly, of the three times the couple are mentioned in the Pauline letters, twice she is mentioned first (Rom. 16:3; 2 Tim. 4:19). So two-thirds of the times the couple is mentioned in the New Testament, she is mentioned first. In the first century, this order is very striking and suggests that, at least in Christian matters, she was the dominant player. She is the first one who came to mind when Paul and the author of Acts spoke of this couple in relation to the Christian mission.

Beyond Lydia and Priscilla, there are other women mentioned in the Pauline writings. There is Phoebe in Romans 16:1, whom Paul mentions as a deacon of the church at Cenchreae, one of the port villages of Corinth. The Greek word here is *diakonos*, the same word used for all the male deacons of the early church. It is not "deaconess." There is no feminine ending on the word. It is exactly the same word as used for any early Christian deacon (e.g., Phil. 1:1), and it should be taken as such. Indeed, Romans 16:1 is Paul's recommendation of her for ministry at Rome (or, on a different theory, perhaps Ephesus).

The mention of Junia in Romans 16:7 is also noteworthy. Paul mentions her and her husband as individuals who had been prisoners with him at some point, perhaps at Ephesus. He says that they were believers before he was and, at the very least, indicates that they were known to the apostles. The Greek, however, reads that they are prominent "among the apostles" (woodenly, "in" the apostles).[6] Many wonder if Paul is in fact indicating that both of them were apostles, two individuals who had seen the risen Christ and been tasked by him with testifying to the resurrection. Paul's emphasis on the earliness of their faith would fit with this interpretation, and you could argue that this approach is the most natural reading of the Greek preposition *en*.[7]

Euodia and Syntyche are said to be two of Paul's co-workers at Philippi (Phil. 4:3). He places them right alongside a man, Clement, as people who have labored with him in the gospel. Nothing about this context suggests that they only worked with women or children. Paul never makes such distinctions in any of his writings. He mentions female leaders alongside male leaders without making clear any particular difference they have in type or nature of their work. It is only if you come to these texts with prior assumptions about what is or is not possible that you will conclude any differentiation of mission or role.

The bottom line here is that, both in theory and in practice, women seem to have played significant roles in the ministry of the early church. Acts 2:17 predicted that women would prophesy in the new age, just as men would. We are not surprised to hear of Lydia and Priscilla playing leading roles in the early church. We are not surprised to find that Philip the evangelist had four daughters who were prophetesses (Acts 21:8-9), and we should assume that they prophesied both to men and women. We are not surprised to hear of Phoebe, Junia, Euodia, and Syntyche in Paul's letters. This is exactly what we *should* expect in an age of the Spirit, where bodies and external qualifiers cease to be significant when it comes to spiritual activities.[8]

"That Time" and "All Time"

Because this chapter is meant specifically to address the problem texts, we cannot spend too much time on the broader question of the Bible's patriarchalism. It is my contention that the question of a husband's headship in the home is a distinct issue from women in leadership and ministry. We do not have to answer the first question to answer the second. Nevertheless, any treatment of this issue that *only* looks at the two problem texts—1 Corinthians 14:34-35 and 1 Timothy 2:12-15—is bound to be skewed from the very beginning. Their exceptional character needs to be seen before they are addressed. Similarly, we should also have a strong sense of how well they reflect the broader culture of the ancient world from the start. There is nothing of their basic import that is distinctively Christian.[9] The vilest pagan from the ancient world would have had no problem what they were saying.

A hermeneutical challenge that always faces us when we read the Bible contextually is to distinguish those aspects that are intrinsic to the biblical setting and cultural situation from those that transcend that immediate historical context. As a general principle, the places where the biblical text challenges the predominant social or theological assumptions of the day are more likely to transcend the immediate circumstances. In contrast, when the text conforms to or does not challenge

"It then becomes incumbent on those who oppose women in ministry to be careful not to quench the Spirit"

those assumptions, it is more likely to apply only to that contextual setting. This dynamic is particularly significant when it comes to the patriarchalism of the biblical worlds that privileged male dominance. It seems reasonable to see points where the biblical texts *contrast* with this underlying patriarchalism as more universal in significance than those texts that conform to such cultural assumptions.

No one should doubt that the subordination of women was the default state of women in the ANE. In this light, individuals such as Deborah (Judg. 4:4) and Huldah (2 Kings 22:14) stand out as highly exceptional in the Old Testament. What is especially significant about them for our purposes is that they demonstrate that the normal role of women in Israel *was not an absolute*. The general norm was male leadership, but there were exceptional circumstances. In itself, this is instructive for the debate over women in leadership today.

There was never an absolute prohibition on women having leadership or spiritual roles in the Old Testament. It was simply that such public leadership was not the social norm. Today, this fact suggests that those who disagree with women in leadership and ministry should treat the issue as a case-by-case situation rather than an absolute prohibition. Indeed, given that God regularly meets his people where they are, we might predict that he would call more women to lead and minister in a context that emphasizes equality between men and women. It then becomes incumbent on those who oppose women in ministry to be careful not to quench the Spirit. It would be bad indeed, as Gamaliel suggested (Acts 5:29), to find oneself fighting God!

Challenging the Culture

The Day of Pentecost opened the doors to more and more female prophets in the Church. A fact that seemed to cause conflict in the early church just as it still does today. The default culture was male-oriented and male-dominated. Paul might proclaim in Galatians 3:28 that "in Christ there is not male and female," but it caused problems at Corinth when wives began to pray and prophesy in public worship. The trajectory of the kingdom, the equal playing field of the Spirit, came into conflict with the patriarchal culture of Paul's day.

Paul walks a fine line in 1 Corinthians 11. On the one hand, he assumes that women and the wives of the church will pray and prophesy in worship. On the other, he does not want to undermine the stability of the husband-wife relationship. How can the wives of the church exercise the spiritual gifts that God has granted them in an age of the Spirit without undermining the homes of those within the church? Paul's answer is the veil. If the wives will cover their heads when they pray and prophesy, then they will remain in proper relationship with their husbands (1 Cor. 11:10). The fact that most Christian women today do not wear veils indicates that we do not take his solution here as trans-situational.[10]

Once again, the husband-headship issue is distinct from the question of women in leadership over men in general. Deborah and Huldah were both married but that fact played no role whatsoever in their leadership within Israel. Aquila was apparently not intimidated by the fact that his wife was his co-partner in ministry or that she took the lead in some cases. After all, which is more important for a husband, to dominate his wife or to submit to the LORD? If the LORD calls a woman to lead or minister, then the husband had better submit to his LORD rather than be offended at his wife's calling! There should be no conflict between a husband who is secure in his masculinity and a wife that God calls to lead.

The Clobber Verses

So we finally reach the "clobber verses" most often used to argue that women cannot lead men. These are of course 1 Corinthians 14:34-35 and 1 Timothy 2:12-15. It is my contention that neither of these passages are about women in ministry or general leadership. The first is about disruptive speech in worship; the second is still about the husband-wife relationship, not general leadership. Accordingly, we are left without a single verse in the Bible that prohibits women in ministry or leadership roles while having several positive examples of female leadership in Israel and the church. We are left with principled verses that suggest it should happen in an age of the Spirit. As we have said, the only verse that even sounds like it prohibits female leadership is 1 Timothy 2:12.

1 Corinthians 14

In the case of 1 Corinthians 14:33-34, we have seen above that Paul *assumes* that women, indeed wives, will pray and prophesy in the worship assembly (1 Cor. 11:5). His instruction on head coverings is meant to maintain a balance between their relationship to their husbands and their spiritual activity in the presence of other men who are not their husbands. When we come to 1 Corinthians 14:33-34, we are puzzled. Paul has already assumed that women will speak in the assembly. Why now would he prohibit them? It sounds like a contradiction.

The answer is quick at hand. The context is disorder in public worship. Paul is trying to rein in the chaotic worship scene with people speaking in tongues and prophesying over one another. His answer is that each should speak one at a time (1 Cor. 14:27), and that those who speak in tongues should only speak if there is someone to interpret (14:28). Order is seen in the parallel of two or three prophets (14:29) and two or three tongues speakers (14:27), and finally made explicit: "For God is not a God of disorder but of peace" (14:33).

This is the context in which we find 1 Corinthians 14:34-35. When 14:35 instructs wives to ask their own husbands at home, we get a sense that the primary concern in these verses is disruption, wives who are asking questions of the husbands *of other women*. We probably should not translate 14:34 to say "women" but "wives," making a better reading, "*Wives* should remain silent in the churches." The likely issue here is that of wives in relation to their husbands, not women in general in relation to men in general. We might also ask whether Paul had specific wives in mind. For example, if you were to ask, "What about Priscilla?" would Paul respond, "Of course not. I'm talking about Erastus' wife"?

Of course there is yet another possibility, which I think is most likely of all.[11] Although 1 Corinthians 14:34-35 appear in all known manuscripts, they do not appear in the same place in all known manuscripts. In several manuscripts considered part of the "Western" tradition, these two verses appear after verse 40 at the end of the chapter. This displacement might indicate that these verses were not part of the original text but something first written in the margin. A number of other factors speak in favor of this conclusion.

The first is the fact that the passage reads more smoothly without the verses. "God is not a God of disorder but of peace—as in all the churches of God—or did the word of God originate with you? Or are you the only people it has reached?" The instruction to wives comes out of nowhere and returns to nowhere just as quickly. Similarly, the point of view changes from "you" in 14:33 to "they" in 14:34 and 35 and then back to "you" again in 14:36.

Another subtle shift is that Paul now addresses churc*es*, plural. Whereas in 1 Corinthians 1:1, Paul is writing to the church, singular, at Corinth, in 14:13 he is writing to churc*es*. This shift leads suggests a later addition because instruction to churches does not fit the initial context of 1 Corinthians because only one church is listening. The reader who does not read in context is prone to miss this significant shift, thinking Paul wrote the text for all time rather than to a specific church.

Two other observations suggest that these verses are a foreign body. One is the reference to the Jewish Law: "they must be in submission, as the law says." It is uncharacteristic of Paul to consider Gentiles to be under the law. Finally, although if they are original we have to understand 14:34-35 in relation to disruptive speech, this interpretation still leaves some tension between a statement like, "it is disgraceful for a woman to speak in church" and the praying and prophesying of 1 Corinthians 11. It simply does not sound like the same person, and there are no textual issues of this sort in 1 Corinthians 11.

1 Timothy 2

After all the passages in the Bible are considered, we are left with only one verse in the entire Bible that might potentially prohibit women from teaching men: 1 Timothy 2:12. We should never base our theology on one verse. This is especially true in relation to a text as obscure as this. If this seems like a focal verse, it is only because it is the center of our contemporary debates. On its own terms, it is a better candidate for an "unclear" one that needs to be processed in the light of more fundamental principles. For example, what does it mean to say that women have come to be in transgression because of the sin of Eve but will be saved through childbearing (1 Tim. 2:14-15)? Are not women saved through the blood of Jesus Christ?! Is it not the person that sins that will die, not his or her descendants (Ezek. 18:4)?[12]

In a sense, to think that we have to come up with an explanation for this verse is to set off on the wrong foot from the very start. It creates a situation where the burden of proof is on the person who does not take this verse at modern face value. Women in ministry is presumed until proven otherwise. However, from a canonical perspective, *this verse* is the puzzling one. It is inappropriate hermeneutically, especially from a Wesleyan perspective, to think that we have to account for every last verse in order to formulate a biblical theology on an issue. Biblical theology is a canonical task. One that must find its center in the whole of Scripture. On this topic, equal access of both male and female to the Spirit is the central principle, and we are left puzzled at any text that seems not to play that principle out thoroughly.

Indeed, 1 Timothy as a whole is unique enough in comparison to Paul's other writings that the majority of biblical scholars do not think Paul himself wrote it.[13] Evangelicals are hesitant to take that position, and I will not take it here either. But the fact that a significant majority of scholars for over a century have concluded against Pauline authorship highlights the fact that 1 Timothy is unique within the Pauline corpus. As an example, Paul prefers celibacy and encourages widows not to remarry in 1 Corinthians 7 (7:8-9, 39-40), but in 1 Timothy he prefers marriage and insists that widows under sixty remarry (1 Tim. 4:3; 5:9-14). So also in the case of 1 Timothy 2:12, we should recognize that these verses are strikingly unique within the Pauline corpus. Paul does not talk this sternly toward women in this way in any other place in his writings, with the possible exception of 1 Corinthians 14:34-35.

For this reason, scholars have hypothesized more than one contextual explanation for the heightened rhetoric. I will not land on one. It is enough to show that these verses are so strange that many scholars have tried their hands at an explanation. N. T. Wright and others have turned to the Temple of Artemis in Ephesus for an explanation.[14] In a city where the dominant religious force was a temple with only female priestesses, Paul is seen as pushing back against this cultural force. I am intrigued with the intersection in 1 and 2 Timothy between language relating to widows and language relating to false teachers. Were wealthy widows (e.g., 2 Tim. 3:6; 1 Tim. 5:13) in some way serving as catalysts for false teachers (1 Tim. 6:3-10)?

When a passage is this unique and subject to so many different interpretations by scholars, one thing is certain: It is not a passage on which you should base your theology in relation to some topic. I will only make one interpretive claim. I believe that Paul once again has wives and husbands in view. The Greek word *gyne* can mean a woman in general, but when it is in such proximity to *anēr*, it most likely means "wife."[15] By and large, women were not independent agents. The cultural expectation was that they would be married and live under the authority and protection of a husband. So when you have a text such as this one about the relationship between a woman and a man, it is overwhelmingly likely that we are talking about the relationship between a wife and a husband.

The mention of Adam and Eve strongly supports this conclusion, as does the mention of childbirth. Paul is thus speaking of a *wife* learning in quietness and of her not teaching or usurping the authority of her husband. He is not speaking generally of women in relation to men. Adam has the primary authority as the "first-born" of sorts, and Eve the wife showed that she was gullible by being deceived.

The shame of Eve's gullibility has remained over wives to the present, although it is removed through childbearing. Whether this line of thinking is what 1 Timothy had in mind or not, it does seem likely that wives and husbands are in view.

Again, what a strange set of thoughts in the New Testament. Theologically, has not Christ definitively removed the stain of all sin from all individuals in Christ, both male and female? Certainly women in the ancient world had much less access to education than men did, but we could not say today that women are less educated. It simply is not true today that in any given situation, a wife is going to be more easily deceived than her husband. We are not surprised that so many scholars have sought some explanation for these statements in the context of 1 Timothy and Ephesus.

We often do not realize how our perspective can get out of focus. Like a facial feature at which we cannot stop staring, an unusual verse can capture our attention and our perspective can get out of whack. In the same way, the 1 Timothy 2 passage is quite bizarre when you put it up against the way in which Acts and Paul's earlier writings open up the door for women to work for the gospel in ways astounding for the time. Yet for some reason, some elements in the church cannot see those other passages, they are so focused on this one verse.

Surely there was something going on in the context of 1 Timothy in order to produce such harsh-sounding instruction to wives. Surely when we hear, "I do not allow a wife to teach," we should suspect that there were some wives at Ephesus who were serving as catalysts for false teaching. And surely when we hear, "I do not allow a wife to dominate her husband," we should suspect that there were such women at Ephesus who were lording it over their husbands. As Howard Marshall has said, Paul doesn't tell the husbands to dominate their wives either![16] The Spirit of Jesus and Paul push us to sense a strangeness to this passage, and the diversity of interpretations suggest the same. This is an "unclear" verse.

Conclusion

Two options are set before us. One of them is a path that sees Scripture on a trajectory toward the full equality of women and the full participation of women in ministry and leadership. In Christ, there is not male and female. In the kingdom of God there will be no subordination of wives to husbands. In the Spirit, your sons and daughters will prophesy. The other path focuses on one or two quite strange verses and implies that the patriarchal world of the Bible was part of God's eternal plan for all history.

We have argued for the first path. Far from God's eternal plan, the subordination of wives is either a product of the Fall or an accommodation to worldly culture. Either way, husband-headship is a distinct issue from women in leadership. In the

Old Testament, we find notable exceptions to the prevailing culture, and we find them on the highest levels of authority. In the New Testament, we find that women often participated in the mission and leadership of the church, with no mention of them being sequestered with other women or children. In this light, we must see 1 Timothy 2:12 as the puzzle, the unclear verse, not ground zero on this issue.

Ken Schenck, PhD, is Professor of New Testament and Ancient Languages at Indiana Wesleyan University.

Bibliography

Dayton, Donald W. *Discovering an Evangelical Heritage.* Grand Rapids: Baker Academic, 1988.

France, R. T. *Women in the Church's Ministry: A Test Case for Biblical Hermeneutics.* Carlisle: Paternoster, 1995.

Marshall, I. Howard. *Beyond the Bible: Moving from Scripture to Theology.* Grand Rapids: Baker Academic, 2004.

Noll, Mark. *The Civil War as a Theological Crisis.* Chapel Hill: University of North Carolina, 2006.

Watson, David F. "Scripture as Canon." In *Wesley, Wesleyans, and Reading Bible as Scripture,* J. B. Green and D. F. Watson, eds. Waco: Baylor University, 2012.

Webb, William J. *Slaves, Women, and Homosexuals: Exploring the Hermeneutics of Cultural Analysis.* Downers Grove, IL: InterVarsity, 2001.

Wright, N. T. *Paul for Everyone: The Pastoral Letters: 1 and 2 Timothy, and Titus.* Louisville: Westminster John Knox, 2003.

Chapter 10 Notes

[1] Watson, "Scripture as Canon," 161-176.

[2] Hans Frei has been particularly insightful here. See *The Eclipse of Biblical Narrative: A Study in Eighteenth and Nineteenth Century Hermeneutics* (New Haven, CT: Yale University, 1974), 1-50.

[3] Noll, *The Civil War as a Theological Crisis,* esp. 31-50.

[4] Dayton, *Discovering an Evangelical Heritage.*

[5] Paul's wording here is fascinating. He says, "neither-nor" when it comes to the first two pairs: "neither Jew nor Greek, neither slave nor free." However, he says, "not male and female" when he gets to the third pair. Is it possible that he is alluding to Genesis 1:27, where it is said, "male and female he made them"? Is Paul boldly suggesting that the distinction between male and female in creation is in some way undone in the new birth?

[6] Romans 16:7 reads: εἰσιν ἐπίσημοι ἐν τοῖς ἀποστόλοις

[7] In keeping with the theological tendencies of the ESV, this grammatical possibility is obliterated by a translation apparently meant to hide it entirely from view: they are said to be "well-known to the apostles."

[8] For the idea of a "redemptive trajectory" in history, see France, *Women in the Church's Ministry.*

[9] An interesting book to explore in relation to this issue is Webb, *Slaves, Women, and Homosexuals,* 241-44.

10 I would argue that the household structure is not trans-situational either. Space forbids interaction with Aristotle's Politics (1.12), but he demonstrates how much husband headship was a part of the culture of the day.

[11] This position is also taken by Gordon Fee, *The First Epistle to the Corinthians,* rev. ed. (Grand Rapids: Eerdmans, 2014), 780-92 and Richard Hays, *First Corinthians: A Bible Commentary for Teaching and Preaching* (Nashville: Abingdon, 2011), 245-49.

[12] As a key theological claim here, Paul does not think that we die directly as a consequence of Adam's sin. We die because we sin *like* Adam did (Rom. 6:12).

[13] Pseudonymity was the practice of writing under the authority of an important figure from the past in order to speak or convey their voice to a later time or situation. We have numerous instances of pseudonymity in Judaism at the time of the New Testament, suggesting that it was a well-known practice in certain circles. Although most evangelicals have historically opposed the idea that such writings are in the New Testament, some scholars have argued that the practice did not intrinsically have to involve deception. See Paul J. Achtemeier, Joel B. Green, and Marianne Thompson, *Introducing the New Testament: Its Literature and Theology* (Grand Rapids: Eerdmans, 2001), e.g., 562.

[14] Wright, *Paul for Everyone,* 25-26.

[15] διδάσκειν δὲ γυναικὶ οὐκ ἐπιτρέπω, οὐδὲ αὐθεντεῖν ἀνδρός, ἀλλ᾽ εἶναι ἐν ἡσυχίᾳ. Ἀδὰμ γὰρ πρῶτος ἐπλάσθη, εἶτα Εὕα· καὶ Ἀδὰμ οὐκ ἠπατήθη, ἡ δὲ γυνὴ ἐξαπατηθεῖσα ἐν παραβάσει γέγονεν. σωθήσεται δὲ διὰ τῆς τεκνογονίας, ἐὰν μείνωσιν ἐν πίστει καὶ ἀγάπη καὶ ἁγιασμῷ μετὰ σωφροσύνης.

[16] See his exploration of this passage hermeneutically in Marshall, *Beyond the Bible,* 33-40.

11
The Leader as Shepherd
Jennifer Ellison

While the Old Testament presents numerous pictures for leadership, shepherding may stand out from the rest. The vocation of shepherding is not unique to the Israelites and so the metaphor can be used to discuss ongoing pictures of leadership—both styles to emulate and to avoid—as both the positive and negative pictures of shepherding leadership have much to teach contemporary leaders.

EVERYTHING RISES AND FALLS on leadership. Nowhere is this more evident than with the people of Israel during the time of the kings. Repeatedly in the Old Testament, the people of Israel's hearts wandered from worshiping the one true God. Good leaders would rein the people in when they had strayed, restoring true worship and calling them to holy living. Bad leaders did the opposite, encouraging worship of false gods and leading the people in all kinds of religious and moral offenses. Psalm 78 describes this tendency to stray and ends with the description of the kind of leader necessary to help the people live lives that honored God. The people would go where God wanted them to go when there was a skilled leader with integrity of heart.

Psalm 78 aimed to motivate the people of Israel to teach their children to follow God's statutes so "they would put their trust in God" (v. 7), rather than being "like their ancestors—a stubborn and rebellious generation, whose hearts were not loyal to God" (v. 8). The psalmist shows the foolishness of Israel's forefathers as they were unable or unwilling to trust the God who had delivered them from slavery, providing for and protecting them as he brought them to the Promised Land (vv. 9-55). After rebelling against God in the Promised Land, God allowed their enemies to have victory over them (vv. 56-64) until, as the poet says, "[T]he Lord awoke as from sleep, as a warrior wakes from the stupor of wine. He beat back his enemies; he put them to everlasting shame " (vv. 65-66).

The culmination of God's faithfulness is expressed at the end of this psalm by the appointment of a *shepherd* whom God selected to lead and care for his people. "He chose David his servant and took him from the sheep pens; from tending the sheep he brought him to be the shepherd of his people Jacob, of Israel his inheritance" (vv. 70-71). The psalm ends by honoring David, saying, "And David shepherded them with integrity of heart; with skillful hands he led them" (v. 72). David is admired as a good king because he shepherded his people well, leading with *integrity of heart* and with *skillful hands*. The end of Psalm 78 summarizes what the Old Testament teaches regarding good leadership: Leaders are shepherds.

Shepherding in the Old Testament

Shepherding is a common metaphor used to describe leaders and leadership in the Old Testament.[1] Undoubtedly the metaphor of a shepherd readily illustrated leadership because the Israelites were surrounded by sheep and shepherds, with shepherding examples in their history. Abraham, Isaac, and Jacob were semi-nomadic pastoralists, primarily supporting their families by raising flocks. To care for the flocks well they traveled to find pasture, water, and peaceful land in which to live.

Jacob's family settled in the land of Goshen where they raised livestock and grew into a great nation. Shepherding continued to be part of the culture and economy of Israel throughout the Old Testament even as they settled and took up farming.[2] There are several examples of the shepherding metaphor during different eras in Israel's history. First, at the end of his life, Moses prayed that God would provide a shepherd to lead the people after he died, saying, "May the Lord, the God who gives breath to all living things, appoint someone over this community to go out and come in before them, one who will lead them out and bring them in, so the Lord's people will not be like sheep without a shepherd" (Num. 27:15-17). Later we learn that the answer to this prayer was Joshua who faithfully established the people in the Promised Land. When the people of Israel came together to anoint David as king they reminded him of what the Lord had said to him previously, "You will shepherd my people Israel, and you will become their ruler" (2 Samuel 5:2). Jeremiah the prophet saw himself as a shepherd (Jeremiah 17:16). As we will explore more fully below, Ezekiel 34 condemns Israel's leaders in a series of woes, using the shepherd metaphor to illustrate their leadership failures.

The shepherd metaphor is not unique to the people of Israel. Many Mesopotamian gods are described as shepherds who maintained social order through their rule which was marked with power, justice and mercy as they protected and provided generously for their people.[3] Further, Mesopotamian rulers were often described as having been shepherded by the gods and, in turn, as shepherds to the people in their kingdom.[4] In the preamble to the Hammurabi code, perhaps the most famous extra-biblical law code in the Ancient Near East, Hammurabi refers to himself as a "beneficent shepherd whose scepter is righteousness."[5]

More likely to be surrounded by concrete and people rather than pastures and sheep, contemporary readers need to understand the role of a farmer during the time the Old Testament was formed. Even 21st century country dwellers and farmers will understand the role much differently from a resident of the Levant four thousand years ago. At that time, the average family would need a flock of 25-60 sheep to provide the milk, wool and meat needed for their family. Any number over that could be used to generate additional income for the family. Large flocks of goats and sheep were often cared for in open pastureland. A good shepherd could care for up to 500 sheep at one time but would need others to facilitate collecting milk and wool and to provide general care of the flock. When many shepherds were employed flocks could grow to thousands.[6] Shepherds could get to know their sheep individually and know details of each animal's birth, history, eating habits, and other peculiarities.[7]

Shepherds were responsible to lead, protect, and care for their flocks and were able to benefit from all of the goods a sheep's body provided. Sheep were valuable for a number of reasons. They provided milk for making curds and butter, fat for soap and candles, wool for clothing, and meat for meals. Sheep were among the most common animals used for sacrifices and were sought after for this purpose. Sheep could also provide fertilizer for fields. Skins could be used for wine and water containers, clothing, rugs and all kinds of coverings. Sheepskin can be made into parchment and their bones could be used to make a variety of tools.[8]

Caring for sheep meant that a shepherd was often isolated and vulnerable. The shepherd's life might be threatened by the elements, wild animals, and raiders. Despite the value that shepherds added to family and national economies, shepherding was not a well-respected occupation. Yet it is this humble and difficult profession that God uses as a metaphor to instruct the leaders of his people.

Forming the Heart of a Shepherd

In spite of all the power and authority that Israel's leaders had, the Bible is clear that they were not the ultimate authority. They were responsible to God for how they shepherded God's people; they were actually under-shepherds, leading under the authority of God. David was keenly aware of this reality when he wrote Psalm 23. He knew that his primary relationship was with God who shepherded him and formed his heart. Being shepherded and shaped by God was the basis from which David served and shepherded *his* people. In Psalm 23, we can learn from David's example what it means to be shepherded well and from God's example what it means to shepherd well. God provides for his sheep and blesses them, even in, or especially in, the presence of their enemies. In this psalm, David paints the picture of a good Shepherd who cares for the practical and emotional needs of his sheep. This Shepherd provides food, water, and rest for his flock. He protects his sheep from those who wish to harm them and comforts them in danger. David shows us that the presence of enemies does not diminish the power or provision of the Good Shepherd.

A leader who thrives under God's shepherding is able to shepherd others from this place of health and security established by God. But the duties of shepherding can challenge the freedom of being shepherded. I often feel like I am too busy to be shepherded. As I sit writing this on a Sunday night after a full day of ministry, I am distracted by all that is in the coming week. I know that slowing down and being

"A leader who thrives under God's shepherding is able to shepherd others"

shepherded is critical for my soul to thrive—even survive. I also know that in the short term it is easier to keep going. I am thankful that my church pays me to take one day off a month and spend the day alone with God. I call these soul care days. I need these days because they remind me *how much* care my soul needs and how important it is to allow myself to be shepherded on continual basis.

When I neglect God's shepherding, I find myself more irritable. I relapse into patterns of overcommitment, neglecting my family for my work. I am more susceptible to lies from the enemy and discouragement. I drink more caffeine, eat more sugar, and sleep less. When I take the time to allow myself to be shepherded, I am reminded that I am not God—that I am not responsible for outcomes, only obedience. I work hard but I cease striving. I prioritize my family better and have more joy. I tend to eat and sleep better. I wake up with prayers of gratitude. Everyone has unique indicators of a well- (or poorly-) shepherded soul. What are your soul-care indicators? What does your soul exhibit when you are being shepherded? What does it exhibit when you are not?

Saul and David

When we allow God to shepherd us, he will form in us a heart that pleases him. The Old Testament makes it clear that leadership pleasing to God begins with a heart that pleases God. In the lives of Saul and David, the first two kings of Israel, we see a contrast between two men, one whose heart is seeking after God, one whose heart is not. Both men sin but, when confronted, respond very differently and their destinies are subsequently shaped.

Consider the story of Saul. In 1 Samuel 13, the stage is set for the anticipated battle at Gilgal between the Israelites, led by King Saul, and the Philistines who had assembled against them. Seeing the size of the Philistine army—"three thousand chariots, six thousand charioteers, and soldiers as numerous as the sand on the seashore" (v. 5)—the Israelites became afraid and began to scatter and hide. Saul remained at Gilgal waiting for the prophet Samuel to arrive at the appointed time. When Samuel did not arrive, Saul took matters into his own hands and offered the burnt offerings and fellowship offerings. As he finished making the offerings, Samuel arrived. What followed was an unpleasant exchange.

> "What have you done?" asked Samuel. Saul replied, "When I saw that the men were scattering, and that you did not come at the set time, and that the Philistines were assembling at Mikmash, I thought, 'Now the Philistines will come down against me at Gilgal, and I have not sought the Lord's favor.' So I felt compelled to offer the burnt offering."
>
> "You have done a foolish thing," Samuel said. "You have not kept the command the Lord your God gave you; if you had, he would have established your kingdom over Israel for all time. But now your kingdom will not endure; the Lord has sought out a man after his own heart and appointed him ruler of his people, because you have not kept the Lord's command." (1 Samuel 13: 11-14)

The text is unclear as to whether by offering the sacrifice Saul was usurping a prophetic or priestly function. But Saul *clearly violated a command*, a disobedience which revealed Saul was not a man after God's heart. As a result, God was displeased with him and vowed to take Saul's kingdom from him for all time. Instead, the kingdom would be passed to another man to rule. Saul seems to accept Samuel's words with no protest and proceeds to Gibeah where he continues to prepare for battle.

David, Saul's eventual successor, is described as a man after God's own heart. I have often struggled with this descriptor of David. For much of his life, David seems to be making choices in line with the things God values. He spends time in worship, he defends God's honor against the giant Goliath, and he refuses to kill Saul, despite Saul's attempts on David's life. But after he becomes king, he sees Bathsheba bathing on the roof, sleeps with her, finds out she is pregnant, and murders her husband so he can marry her to cover up the illegitimate pregnancy. By comparison, David's sin of taking and sleeping with a married woman then murdering her husband to cover up his sin seems much greater than Saul's sin of violating a command by offering a sacrifice. It seems that David's heart has wandered far from God's but God does not reject him or his kingdom. Why not?

When confronted by the prophet Nathan, David simply responds, "I have sinned against the Lord" (2 Samuel 12:13). There is no justification and no excuse. He owns his sin. Psalm 51 records David's reaction to the confrontation in more detail. The first four verses read:

> Have mercy on me, O God, according to your unfailing love;
> according to your great compassion blot out my transgressions.
> Wash away all my iniquity and cleanse me from my sin.

For I know my transgressions, and my sin is always before me.
Against you, you only, have I sinned and done what is evil in your sight;
so you are right in your verdict and justified when you judge.

Saul and David respond very differently when confronted with their sin. Saul offered excuses. David acknowledged and repented of his sin. Their hearts are revealed not only by the choices they made but how they respond when confronted. God does not require perfection; he requires us to seek after his heart. This means that we respond to his commands with obedience, and, when we fail to do this, we respond to his rebuke with repentance. David is a helpful example of what it looks like to lead with integrity of heart, even after living through catastrophic moral failure.

Because it is so easy to stray and the consequences impact not only ourselves but those around us including our families and our flocks, we cannot overemphasize the point. We lead by example. If we expect those under our leadership to submit to being shepherded, we need to submit to shepherding. If we want to shepherd well, we need to learn from our experience with the Good Shepherd.

A Good Shepherd

When Jesus claims the title of Good Shepherd (John 10:14), it is in contrast to the failed shepherds of Ezekiel 34, which details the shepherd's responsibility to his sheep. In this passage we learn a lot about what a good shepherd does by seeing what bad shepherds are condemned for not doing. Ezekiel 34:2-5 reads,

> Woe to you shepherds of Israel who only take care of yourselves! Should not shepherds take care of the flock? You eat the curds, clothe yourselves with the wool and slaughter the choice animals, but you do not take care of the flock. You have not strengthened the weak or healed the sick or bound up the injured. You have not brought back the strays or searched for the lost. You have ruled them harshly and brutally. So they were scattered because there was no shepherd, and when they were scattered they became food for all the wild animals. (Ezekiel 34: 2-5)

From this account, we see that good shepherds benefit from the flock while taking care of their flock. We learn that good shepherds strengthen the weak, heal the sick, and bind up the injured. Good shepherds bring back the stray and seek the lost. They lead with kindness and gentleness. Good shepherds prevent sheep from scattering and being attacked by wild animals.

Benefit and Care

Good shepherds benefit from the flock while taking care of their flock. After a pastoral internship and before attending seminary, I was offered a job at INJOY and worked with the Seminar Operations Team. My manager that year was a man named Brad. He was an excellent example of someone who looked out for his people rather than himself. Brad understood that one of the primary functions of his job was to make his team, his flock, successful. He served us well so we could perform well. He never asked us to sacrifice for him and he often sacrificed for us. He would fight to protect our time or avoid useless policies, he fed us well when we worked late and cared about the details of our personal and professional lives. Brad's care and concern for us was exceedingly evident and, as a result, we were more than willing to sacrifice for him, and for the team, when it was necessary. It was never about Brad or his ego; it was about his team and the task at hand. As a result, Brad reaped the benefits of a well-functioning team. Brad was a good shepherd who cared for his flock.

Strengthen and Heal

Good shepherds strengthen the weak, heal the sick, and bind the injured. This aspect of leadership is countercultural for most of us. Leaders are typically encouraged to focus on the top performers in their organization. They are encouraged to spend time investing in people who will multiply their efforts. The weak, the sick, and the injured are often ignored or let go. However, a good shepherd both invests in other leaders and cares for the wounded.

Seek the Lost

Good shepherds bring back the strays and seek the lost. This verse addresses those who physically separated from the flock and those who strayed from their relationship with God. In both scenarios, a leader seeks the lost and brings back the strays. When Lot was kidnapped by raiders, Abraham pursued him and brought him back (Genesis 14). When David's family, and the families of his men were kidnapped, he pursued them and brought them back (1 Samuel 30). When Josiah and Hezekiah each became king, they both destroyed the high places and cleansed the temple. They pursued their people and gave them opportunities to come back to the Lord and to make a covenant with him. It takes time to pursue the lost. There is always a risk that they will not be able to return or unwilling to return. But a good shepherd pursues them anyway.

Kindness and Gentleness

Good shepherds lead with kindness and gentleness. When Rehoboam, Solomon's son, was stepping into his role as king, the whole assembly of Israel sought him out and said, "Your father put a heavy yoke on us, but now lighten the harsh labor and the heavy yoke he put on us, and we will serve you" (1 Kings 12:4). Rehoboam, in turn, sought advice from the elders who served Solomon. The elders suggested that he win the people's favor by lightening their load. But Rehoboam did not like that counsel and listened only to people who told him what he wanted to hear. His response to the people was harsh: "My father made your yoke heavy; I will make it even heavier. My father scourged you with whips; I will scourge you with scorpions" (1 Kings 12:14). The people rebelled and he lost half of his kingdom. A good leader should be both strong and gentle, firm and kind.

Protect and Defend

Good shepherds prevent sheep from scattering and being attacked by wild animals. David protected his father's flocks of sheep from lions and bears (1 Samuel 17:34). He protected his Yahweh's sheep of Israel from the Philistines and others who sought to destroy the Israelites. When military leaders are killed or captured, their troops often scatter. When David killed Goliath, the Philistines fled (1 Samuel 17:51). When King Zedekiah was captured, his troops scattered (2 Kings 25:5). People often become distracted, lose vision, get stuck, and get lost without leaders. There are many times that I have seen a leader of a small group let their group know they will not be able to attend the group's next meeting only to have the whole group respond by choosing not to meet at all; without their leader, they scatter. Leaders prevent the sheep from scattering by giving them vision and direction and encouraging them along the way.

Conclusion

Old Testament leaders were called to be shepherds of people before they are called to be accomplishers of tasks. The metaphor of shepherd is carried into the New Testament and informs how we are to lead today. As we invest in our people—caring for them, strengthening the weak, healing the sick, binding the injured, seeking the strays, bringing back the lost, leading with kindness and gentleness, preventing the sheep from scattering, and protecting them from predators—we will benefit from our relationships with them and from the goods they produce because they do not exist to serve the leader, but the leader to serve them.

Old Testament leaders show us that to lead God's people well we must first follow God well. We need to allow God to shepherd us both so our souls are cared for (enabling us to shepherd from a place of health) and so we can learn how to shepherd others by following the example we experience. It can be difficult for leaders to slow down or stop long enough to allow ourselves to be led by streams of quiet waters but it is critical for the long-term health and endurance of our leadership and our relationships.

We do not need perfect character or perfect skills, but both character and skills are important and should be intentionally developed. A wise missionary once told me that "the best time to prepare a ship is before the storm." Her encouragement was to begin forming my character and developing my skills intentionally before I realized I needed them and before they were tested. Whether you are in a period of waiting or in the thick of the storm, you have the opportunity to evaluate and improve your leadership. Listen to where God is challenging you. Is he asking you to slow down and submit to being shepherded? Is he showing you your strengths and weakness as a shepherd? Is he calling you to develop integrity? Or calling you to develop your leadership skills? Follow where he leads so that, at the end of the day, others will be able to say of you: "And (fill in your name) shepherded them with integrity of heart; with skillful hands s/he led them."

Jennifer Ellison, ThM, is Associate Outreach Pastor at All Shores Wesleyan Church in Spring Lake, Michigan, and online adjunct instructor at Western Seminary in Portland, OR.

Chapter 11 Notes

[1] See, for example, Numbers 27:15-17; 2 Samuel 5:2, Psalm 23, Jeremiah 17:16, and Ezekiel 34 which will be explored below.

[2] Shepherding and farming are mentioned throughout Israel's history. Once settled, the Israelites raised crops including but not limited to wheat, grapes, figs, and olives in addition to continuing to raise flocks. In Judges 6, before Gideon is found threshing wheat in a winepress, the text mentions that invaders trampled on crops and destroyed flocks and cattle. Saul's chief shepherd is mentioned in 1 Samuel 21:7 near the beginning of the monarchy. Both King Hezekiah and the people giving a tithe of their crops and flocks. In Jeremiah 8:13, toward the end of the monarchy, God threatens to destroy the Israelite's crops naming several different kinds of crops.

[3] Timothy Laniak, *Shepherds after My Own Heart: Pastoral Traditions and Leadership in the Bible* (Downers Grove: IVP Academic, 2006), 61

[4] Ibid.

[5] James B. Pritchard, *Ancient Near Eastern Texts Relating to the Old Testament* (Princeton University Press, 1969), 177.

[6] Laniak, *Shepherds,* 51

[7] Ibid, 57

[8] Ibid, 53.

12

A Wesleyan Sacramental Spirituality of Leadership

Robert Moore-Jumonville

This chapter presents two phases in the life of the leader. The first half involves the building of a life, making decisions that impact the rest of life, including marriage, skill building, and vocation. The second half is marked by a reversal where one begins to invest in the world. The Wesleyan tradition can form and sustain leaders in both phases as a Wesleyan view of mission and kingdom may suitably engage the desire for meaning and purpose in the first half of life. When linked with ecclesial communities and rich sacramental theology, leaders can be sustained in the second half of life, as well.

NIKOS KAZANTZAKIS GREW UP in a religiously schizophrenic household, raised by an atheist father and a pious Greek Orthodox mother. As a young college man, he embarked on a pilgrimage to the Mount Athos monastery situated high on a Greek peninsula. There he sought guidance from Father Makarios, a wise, old monk. He recounted a conversation that went something like this:

> Nikos: "So, Father, you are alone here, and you wrestle with the devil?"
> Makarios: "No. The devil and I have fought for years. I've grown old and so has he. We have made our peace."
> Nikos: "Oh, then your solitude must be pleasant."
> Makarios: "No, for now I wrestle with God."
> Nikos (with some surprise): "You wrestle with God and you hope to win!"
> Makarios: "No, when you wrestle with God, you hope to lose."[1]

The Two Stages of Spiritual Formation

Kazantzakis's story signifies two stages of the typical spiritual formation journey—perhaps also two stages of personal leadership development. During the first half we build our life: forging our identity through struggle, mapping our theological worldview, discovering our vocation, forming life-long relational commitments. We wrestle with the devil during this first stage: fighting to bring our affections—our passions and desires—under the control of spiritual disciplines. Each of us must develop certain proficiencies in life—certain life skills. Often we pursue goals and dreams at this stage like an athlete in training. Like Jacob, we grasp after birthright, blessing, our life's calling, and a spouse. Like the Prodigal, we have to leave home to find home. Like Wesley, we form Holy Clubs to tame our passions and eventually sail to Georgia in an effort to save our souls.

In the second half of life, we fill the container we have built and then gradually learn to let go of life. We wrestle with God, learning the meaning of detachment, of living a life of sanctification as we give ourselves away in love to God and neighbor, and as we prepare for death. Along with other mystics, John of the Cross teaches that we do not enter this second stage of life happily on our own.[2] "What about our legacy?", we may ask selfishly. Dying to self is not something we set out to do; it's normally something done to us. Moving into this stage successfully often requires facing something impeding our progress, such as failures, as when Jacob stood alone and silent at the brook—wrestling with his past crimes, with Esau, with himself, and with God (Gen. 32:22-32). Wesley, in similar fashion, faced his failures in Georgia.[3] In this phase, our temptations now revolve less around prodigal pleasures and more around facing the melancholy and anger of the Elder Brother within us.[4]

In the first half of life, we mostly try to manipulate our spiritual destiny. Like the disciples who cannot fathom the meaning of a crucified Messiah prior to the resurrection, we fasten our own belts, pursue ministry, and go wherever we wish. In the second half of life, God asks us to embrace a more radical faith, where someone else will fasten a belt around us and take us where we do not wish to go.[5] To counter Western culture's individualism, a distinct, robust Wesleyan approach to spiritual formation must be taken. Therefore, this essay will attempt to weave Wesleyan resources available to form young leaders spiritually while emphasizing life-long sanctification, imparted holiness, and salvation as healing that which was fractured in the Fall[6]—all through the means of grace mediated through the church.

Wesleyan Spiritual Formation

Wesley's own religious biography in some ways represents the "two halves" of spirituality. Divided by the Aldersgate experience, we can identify a shift between before and after.[7] Thus, Wesleyan spiritual formation should seek to create disciples and leaders capable of navigating both halves.

In the past, Wesleyan institutions (churches and schools) often have engaged young people well with "first-half issues."[8] Thus, on the one hand, Wesleyan theology stands particularly endowed to lead young people along foundational paths of formation—that of wrestling with the devil. On the other hand, holiness theology—especially when filtered through modern North American culture—has sometimes tended to stress conversion and revival, thus enabling young adults to imbibe an individualistic and self-centered version of Christian formation that leaves them ill prepared to negotiate deeper spiritual maturation later in life.[9]

Wesleyan spiritual formation is ecclesial formation. Wesleyans will help disciples face the second half of life by connecting everyone to the church early on in life. Any form of spirituality that remains disengaged from congregational life and practice (Wesley's "means of grace" which were originally configured communally) may actually hinder persons from maturing spiritually in the second half of life. Frank Whaling correctly affirms that Wesley's "main concern was for spirituality itself, for knowing God in the heart by faith, for practicing the presence of God, for seeking after perfect love."[10] And although Wesley assumed an ecclesial context for this formation, we can easily identify modern tendencies that undermine the role of the church and community in spirituality. After all, we live in an age where "Spiritual but not Religious" rings as a serious slogan.[11]

Wesleyan spirituality must be lived out in communities in an increasingly individualistic and materialistic culture Wesleyan spirituality as an essentially ecclesial theology ought not to be primarily academic, but practical. As leaders in the Wesleyan tradition, we have available the vital theological and intellectual resources to practice this sort of practical, communal spirituality. Too often, unfortunately, we have allowed the culture to squeeze us into its mold and the result for many of us is a demystification of spirituality that turns Eucharistic wine into water.

Foundational Formation

The initial phase of spirituality, in which Wesleyans have often excelled, we will call foundational formation. Emerging adults overflow with grand hopes and dreams, but also often with great turmoil, bearing deep emotional and spiritual wounds. As we consider the main contours of emerging adult experience and the various spiritual challenges faced by this age group we also notice the unique resources Wesleyan theology offers. Ronald Rolheiser expresses well the restlessness of young adults:

[This stage] hits us with a tumult and violence that overthrows our childhood and sends us out, restless, sexually driven, full of grandiose dreams, but confused and insecure, in search of a new home, one that we build for ourselves. And this is a time of much longing and searching: searching for an identity, searching for acceptance, searching for a circle of friends, searching for intimacy, searching for someone to marry, searching for a vocation, searching for a career, searching for the right place to live, searching for financial security, and searching for something to give us substance and meaning—in a word, searching for a home.[12]

The litany Rolheiser presents here sounds familiar. His list provides classic themes targeted in universities and churches: forming identity, discerning vocation, cultivating responsible relationships, and living the examined life. These sorts of topics lie at the root of the Wesleyan Christian agenda as we encourage young people to develop a biblical-theological worldview. Drawing on the spiritual tools of Wesleyan holiness, our institutions call individuals to repentance and personal responsibility,[13] instructing them in Wesleyan biblical literacy,[14] urging vocation as holy calling beyond mere occupation,[15] and fostering relationships grounded in love of God and neighbor rather than in self-interest.[16] Wesley's "means of grace" offer spiritual nourishment and armor as young adults wrestle with the devil.[17]

The ample resources within the Wesleyan tradition for the spiritual formation of leaders must be given a viable shape. But where shall we begin? One option, with all the churning desire bursting from the emerging adult population, is to begin with what Rolheiser calls "holy longing."[18] This approach seeks to capitalize on the young person's openness to mission trips, inner city work with the homeless, and noble causes for justice and compassion. Young adults typically dream of changing the world, they possess boundless energy, and true piety produces fruit evidenced through action. Thus, emerging adults often consider social action as an invigorating path to formation.[19] This approach is in line with Wesley's emphasis that there is no private religion, that "Christianity is essentially a social religion, and to turn it into a solitary one is to destroy it."[20] However, in Wesley's theology, love of God comes first and neighbor love only flows from it.[21] Further, works of social justice not rooted in love of God can easily turn into self-justification, pride, or bitterness.

Contemplative Formation

A second starting point, then, must be considered. Compassion needs grounding in contemplation, in what Wesley practiced as a life of prayer.[22] Therefore, the contours of Wesleyan spiritual formation for emerging adult leaders should begin with surrender to God and adoption as daughters and sons into his familial Kingdom, which means repentance and conversion as pardon of sins. While a person who has already experienced God's saving grace may find it natural to rush headlong into social action, a better place to continue the process of spiritual formation with young people who are already overly stimulated is with silence and solitude.[23] Wesley urged his followers to notice their condition, to open their eyes: "Repent, that is, know yourselves…. Awake, then, thou that sleepest…. The eyes of thine understanding are darkened, so that they cannot discern God or the things of God."[24] Spiritual discernment rests at the heart of all Christian leadership and discernment requires inner silence. Although contemplative prayer needs to be taught gradually, nevertheless, seasoned practitioners can ease young leaders into the practice of deeper prayer over time by raising questions of personal desire and passion—what

Wesley termed "the affections."

To some extent, Rolheiser's profile of young people as restless, searching, full of longing and passion, yet also struggling with fear and anxiety, has always been the case for post-adolescents. Consider, for instance, Augustine's autobiographical description in Confessions of his youthful angst and restlessness. Or remember his call for the Christian to rightly order his or her loves: "He is a man who has an ordinate love: he neither loves what should not be loved nor fails to love what should be loved."[25] To order our loves rightly during our twenties will likely save us from much suffering later in life. This ordering of desires lies at the heart of the biblical wisdom tradition and the spiritual disciplines—and it's something never outgrown.

Yet the two aspects of contemplation and desire need not be separated. The process of spiritual formation might begin, then, for a young person by reflecting on Jesus' simple queries: "What are you looking for?" or "What do you want me to do for you?"[26] These questions require some inner contemplative work—a movement into silence and solitude that allows self-examination and listening to the Holy Spirit. The implicit question Jesus asks us is what we most love: for the thing we long for will consume our energy and allegiance. "The desire of our happiness is inseparably [bound] to our nature, and is the spring which sets all our faculties a-moving."[27] What we love determines where and how we lead. Yet the desires are formed by the practices of reflection. Silence moves us into the relational experience of prayer where we can receive guidance in centering prayer, the Jesus Prayer, and practicing the presence of God. Deepening habits of prayer might lead us next into approaching Scripture prayerfully through *lectio divina*.[28] The "one great office of prayer," urged Wesley, "is to produce such a disposition in us; to exercise our dependence on God; to increase our desire of the things we ask for; to make us so sensible of our wants, that we may never cease wrestling till we have prevailed for the blessing."[29]

Spiritual Development

Wesleyan formation for the first half of life naturally begins with shaping the emerging adult's desires and affections as he or she wrestles prayerfully with issues of identity, ultimate meaning, theology, worldview, vocation, sexuality, relationships, economic lifestyle, and more—all in connection with the broader ecclesial community. Ultimately we are directed at this stage toward love of God and neighbor. As Brother Lawrence suggested, "[O]ur sanctification [does] not depend on changing our works, but in doing that for God's sake which we commonly do for our own."[30] It is our heart that changes. That is, our motivation shifts from self-centeredness to putting on the mind of Christ[31] as we approach life-building issues such as our longing for a soul mate or our desire to contribute meaningfully to the kingdom of God through our life's work as a leader. The broad shape of foundational formation thus moves from inner contemplative love of God, through prayerful communion, to outward compassionate love of neighbor in active biblical social justice.

What often happens in the formational process, however, is that in identifying our heart's deepest longings we bump into the core of our human condition—both as broken and as loved by God.[32] Our deepest human longings are represented in Christ's Three Temptations: the desire for comfort or indulgence ("Turn these stones to bread"), the desire for community or intimacy ("Dive off the temple and the crowd will respect if not revere you"), and the desire for control or influence ("All the kingdoms of the world can be yours").[33] Each of these desires allows legitimate human expressions. Nothing is wrong with meeting basic physical needs, with building committed love relationships, or with wanting to live with meaning beyond our finite selves. But behind each desire also lurks a shadow that of which developing leaders must beware: pleasure-seeking indulgence, self-idolizing narcissism, and manipulative power over others. Notice in Matthew 4:1-11, that Satan is tempting Jesus to become a "great" leader—to take control of his destiny. A good leader must always struggle with personal motive and insecurity. Notice, further, that opposite each desire we

"inspire young leaders with the confidence necessary to build a rich life hidden in Christ, to invest in life, to risk, and to set out on their journey boldly with faith"

bump into our greatest human fears: pain, abandonment, and utter powerlessness—perhaps the fear of failing as a leader.

As the course of spiritual development unfolds within emerging adults, the universal experience of human fear raises the important point of brokenness in today's youth. As the Desert Fathers teach us, to move into a posture of stillness—especially for the passionately restless among us—means facing personal demons.[34] And the emerging generation carries deep wounds.[35] If wounds are not addressed, by developing leaders then they will always lead out of those wounds.[36] What we have to take seriously, then, is the inner healing work necessary for real transformation—healing work that sometimes requiring professional counselors. We cannot expect therapeutic grace, however, to be mediated apart from the church. Thus, the question remains: How might the shape of formation unfold as a communal and ecclesial endeavor within our Wesleyan institutions to better prepare us for spiritual growth continuing into the second half of our lives?

Spiritual formation at the foundational stage requires us to tame our affections as we wrestle with the devil, but it also calls us to build a life. The young adult does well to attend not to the parable of the vineyard laborers, where latecomers receive the same pay as those who have worked all day, but to the parable of the talents where employees are encouraged to be busy with what they have received (Matt. 25:14-30). Nemeck and Coombs describe for us what healthy foundational formation should look like: "In the normal course of human events, we must first increase so that Christ can increase. We develop our talents. We take advantage of the opportunities that come our way. We build up as rich a personhood and as productive a life as circumstances permit."[37] We hope to inspire young leaders with the confidence necessary to build a rich life hidden in Christ, to invest in life, to risk, and to set out on their journey boldly with faith. Steward your gifts. Learn to lead.

More and more emerging adults struggle, however, to create a stable life for themselves. Thus, Nemeck and Coombs go on to describe what it looks like when a young adult's development falters, resulting in an emotional, self-centered "drifting" that avoids responsibility toward others and God.[38] How can we, therefore, better connect wounded young leaders with the therapeutic means of grace that offer healing in Christ? For how can anyone lead another without first being able to lead themselves? And, as the Early Christian Church and the Wesleyan movement illustrate so clearly, we learn to lead through the formation of others, those who have gone further along the path than we have.

In our Wesleyan contexts, it seems natural for us to draw young people deeper into the formational work of rightly ordering their loves so that they anchor decisions about worldview, vocation, and relationships, firmly in their love for God. This ordering of loves constitutes a key aspect of inner Wesleyan piety throughout life. But emerging adults face drastic cultural changes today, making the role of the church even more important than ever, precisely at the time many people are dropping out.

Cultural Challenges Facing Wesleyan Formation

Consider some of the significant social shifts emerging adults face: marriage is being delayed considerably, occupational stability is increasingly rare, and education is being prolonged as parents continue to invest financially in their children well after graduation from college. This produces an extended period of experimentation with identity, values, and religious commitments—among what Robert Wuthnow has termed a generation of religious "tinkerers."[39] Sociologists have reflected on the effects of American individualism. As early as 1985, Robert Bellah and his colleagues warned us of the privatization of religion now known as "Sheilaism," and, in 2000, Robert Putnam demonstrated how North Americans are becoming a culture of non-joiners.[40]

These challenges have practical implications for Christian leaders. Setran and Kiesling conclude, "[L]ife disruptions tend to correlate negatively with strong religious commitment." Further, many argue that Christian leaders should not bother attempting to help young people form strong religious patterns at our institutions until later, more stable, stages of life.[41] While Wesleyan ecclesial leaders inherit these problems from the culture, they need not concede so easily to forces of individualism within the culture that lure young people from our churches.

Challenges and Possibilities of Wesley's Ecclesiology

Challenges for Wesleyan leaders may be internal, as well. It may be argued that part of the problem lies within Wesley's thin theological ecclesiology. In contrast to our current individualistic consumer-spirituality, Wesley's commitment to the life of the Anglican Church was simply part of the cultural air that he breathed. But because he took the substance of Anglicanism for granted, he had no need to develop an ecclesiology. He consistently viewed Methodism as a renewal movement within the Church of England.[42] So, does Wesleyan theology itself as "practical divinity" actually encourage ecclesial ambiguity, if not an ecclesial anemia that naturally devolves into individualism? Since Albert Outler posed the question in 1962, Wesleyan scholars have wondered aloud whether indeed "Methodists have a doctrine of the Church" at all.[43] Gwang Seok Oh's recent study, *John Wesley's Ecclesiology*, depicts a legion of ecclesial children who claim Wesley as their theological father.[44] One can argue that Oh's research legitimates almost any kind of ecclesiology—from Anglo-Catholicism to Mennonite Low Church—as falling within Wesleyan boundaries.

For his own ecclesiology, Wesley relied on the position laid out in the Anglican Articles of Religion while at the same time adapting innovative means to promote the renewal movements in Britain and America as they developed. As Ted Campbell observes, "Methodists originated as a religious movement that presupposed existing Church structures, and only later added elements necessary to configuring themselves as 'churches,'" contributing to what he calls a "bipolar" understanding of the church.[45]

In contrast to Campbell's gloomy assessment, however, it can be argued that Wesley offers us just the right balance theologically for the development of a renewed understanding of the church and of participation in ecclesial forms of life. Wesley held a high view of community.[46] And he held a high view of Eucharist.[47] In distinctive ways, William Abraham and James Pedlar both turn what Campbell considers ecclesial ambiguity into a positive dynamic by suggesting a synthesis between Spirit and Eucharist, between charismatic freedom and institutional structure. Think of liturgical "high church" worship paired with a Mennonite communal life akin to Bonhoeffer's Finkenwalde experiment, all driven by Spirit-infused communion with God.[48] We could generate a spiritual formation more like what Wesley's followers experienced in the Bands.

This kind of practiced spirituality is about ordering loves and forming lovers. James Smith joins spiritual formation in the first half of life (the proper ordering of our loves) and the practiced ritual, communal patterns necessary for faith in the second half of life (forming of lovers), so that crises of loss and detachment will be faced within an ecclesial community. He goes on to describe how secular "liturgies" mis-form us spiritually whereas Christian practices, rituals, and liturgies can shape us toward wholeness.[49] Again, what we love governs how we will lead.

A boundless longing for something deeper stirs in the hearts of our younger generation: a longing for more mystery, for more authentic community, for greater spiritual power, for a more complete and more fully integrated human life. We want a substantive faith that can endure life's storms of hardship and doubt. What we long to be taught is how to live the mystery—to know at least partially even as we have been fully known; to recognize that theology is not merely perception of God, but "response to the mystery of God in Christ," a participation in the divine life.[50] Of course, a full-bodied ecclesial spirituality like this is precisely what flowed through the veins of the early Wesleyan movement. Wesley understood "means of grace" sacramentally and charismatically—as spiritually transforming medicines for the sin sick soul.[51] If we do not expose ourselves more thoroughly to the means of grace practiced communally, especially while we're young, not only will we find it harder to reconnect to the church later in life but our spirituality also will likely remain shallow. Thin faith will not serve us when we face subsequent crises of loss and letting go. Thin theology and practice cannot provide a basis for sound leadership.

Spirituality for the Second Half of Life

How shall we describe the spirituality experienced during the second half of life? Most often some crisis (a dark night) promotes the shift: the loss of a loved one, a broken relationship, personal illness, or vocational setbacks.[52] Ronald Rolheiser calls it "mature discipleship" and Hageberg and Guelich use the term "the productive life"—both authors indicating a shift within the individual from sucking energy out of the world to pouring life back into others. We move off center stage and begin to put others first. It's time to hand over the company. Richard Rohr speaks of "the great turnaround" where our focus flips outward in love toward God.[53] Spirituality during this second stage means facing ourselves—our limits and our finitude: "[W]e can no longer hide from our true selves," declare Nemeck and Coombs. We begin to realize that our God has been too small and we start to recognize everywhere he is not. As we die to our unrealistic expectations, "we learn to mistrust what we never should have trusted in the first place." Our previous ways of encountering God prove unsatisfying and we find ourselves thirsting for more, for something deeper. "God removes even the possibility of our clinging to anything or anyone other than himself. Apparently abandoned by all others, we are thus disposed to abandon ourselves more deeply in faith to God himself." God wakens us to our insatiable longing for union in love with him while at the same time we realize everything in life is provisional and that nothing less than God will satisfy us.[54] At this time we need the depth of the church's sacramental life and rituals of order to face life's deeper sufferings and mystery.

However, in contrast to Wesleyanism's rich resources of mediated grace as sacramental, demystification within the contemporary evangelical church continues to squander our heritage. Let me illustrate what I mean by demystification, by citing an example from a practical ministry class I taught for undergraduate religion majors. Sacraments represent one of the main themes in the course as well as certain pastoral practices we might consider sacramental—like marrying and burying. The majority of the students have grown up in Low Church evangelical settings. Theology differs very little between Free Methodist, Wesleyan, Nazarene, or mainline students, and generic non-denominational (often with Baptist leanings). One of the first topics we wrestle with is baptism and it is not surprising to discover that most students hold a relatively low view of this primary sacrament. That is, baptism for them basically signifies a declaration of public faith, without much divine activity or mystery involved, and while it may stand as a "sign," it does not matter much who performs the baptism, where, or how. What counts is the experience of the believer, the sincerity of his or her heart. Baptism, then, as a contractual, communal, but almost civic rite, has become almost totally de-mystified.

How fascinating, therefore, to notice a further domino effect, where Holy Communion and other sacred rituals such as ordination or marriage take on rather ordinary and commonplace significance. The class actually noticed that anything seems allowable today when it comes to getting married. The couple, not the church, decides. Any time, any place, will do, with any old words created for the occasion, by almost anyone, under almost any conditions. But then the lurking fear creeps in that somehow not taking the ceremony seriously may be contributing to our not taking the vows very sacredly.[55]

Let's extend the conversation to death and dying. Thomas Lynch, speaking from almost forty years of experience in the funeral business, describes a massive shift in recent trends, where suddenly "Bridge Over Troubled Waters" has replaced "How Great Thou Art." He suggests the way we deal with death has devolved into something "increasingly absurd," into a "kind of funeral karaoke...a triumph of accessories over essentials, stuff over substance, theme over theology." Consider the young people in our culture longing for the church to offer something deeper, something more nourishing, something more eternally substantive—something that will last through life's hard knocks. Lynch continues: "The loosened ties of faith and family, of religious and ethnic identity, have left [Americans] ritually adrift, bereft of custom, symbol, metaphor, and meaningful liturgy of language." Here we see a description of many of us: "spiritual tourists without home places or core beliefs to return to."[56] More often our young people end up as ecclesial orphans or the spiritually homeless later in life.

When we cease to allow ourselves to be formed spiritually by custom, symbol, metaphor, and meaningful liturgy, there is "a gradual erosion of the ability to engage these ways of knowing, the use of paradox, symbol, and gesture that have come down to us from earliest days."[57] It is precisely this deeper language of mystery we need in the second half of life. It is as if we are losing one of our senses—the sense of the liturgical—a spiritual way of knowing that lay at the heart of religious experience in the biblical world, in the Early Church, and in the practiced, enacted Christianity of the Wesleyan movement.

On one level, this is only one aspect of a deteriorating Protestantism in our culture fighting for survival through efforts at greater relevancy. Maggie Ross, in her essay "Liturgy in Truth," laments: "[T]hese churches seem to have forgotten that worship is precisely about being liberated from the prison of our own experience. Instead, their 'worship experiences' present us with something we can *grasp*, that we can consume by reflecting on whether we enjoy them or not."[58]

It is tempting for churches to adopt leadership models to stay current, but in so doing, to sell their sacramental birthright. Howard Snyder sums up the journey of the Free Methodist Church over the last fifty years that could represent many evangelical traditions:

> As a denomination, Free Methodism cast about for definitions of success to replace its historic sense of mission. Options partially embraced from time to time included Church Growth, charismatic leadership and styles, business models such as Management By Objective, megachurch models, Vineyard approaches, Seeker Sensitivity, and the Purpose-Driven Church.[59]

Nor are mainline denominations exempt from critique. W. Paul Jones offers an accurate assessment: institutions "once called 'mainline' churches, are in survival mode, alarmed by an aging membership and decline in vocations, forcing leadership into the posture of CEOs generating marketing plans to reverse decline in clients and receipts."[60]

American churches continue to trade the supernatural for contemporary, replacing mystery with marketing. It was over twenty years ago that Eugene Peterson brought this indictment:

> American pastors are abandoning their posts.... They have gone whoring after other gods. What they do with their time under the guise of pastoral ministry hasn't the remotest connection with what the church's pastors have done for most of twenty centuries.... The pastors of America have metamorphosed into a company of shopkeepers, and the shops they keep are the churches. They are preoccupied with shopkeeper's concerns.[61]

Marketing tends to mitigate against mystery, depth, and substance in the church.[62] Week-by-week, Americans invest millions of dollars to re-invent worship.[63] Never mind the lectionary, or the Christian calendar, or collects employed for centuries; we barely include the Scriptures in our services and normally treat Eucharist as an add-on. What we long for is Spirit-empowered means of grace for the purpose of healing our souls toward the wholeness of holiness. Legitimate spiritual formation always moves toward the end of freeing us to become our best selves, our Christ-like selves.

Yet without a vigorous sacramental life (the divine presence in Word and Eucharist, the divine power through Spirit and holy living), Wesleyans have precious little to bring to the table that is unique. What, in fact, do most churches give people today not offered by community groups like the Lions Club or the League of Women's Voters? What do Christian colleges provide spiritually that young people have not gotten already at summer camp? What do we offer in our educational institutions and churches for people who are desperately hungry for God? If we lack sacramental depth and mystery—those "things into which angels long to look" (1 Peter 1:12)—if there is not much that is supernaturally distinctive about the church, no wonder folks do not care much for our advice.

Could it be that God is calling us to reconstitute the sacred and sacramental life in our churches and schools—to learn once again how to apply what Wesley called the means of grace?[64] William Abraham describes the purpose of the means of grace, as employed by the Church in the patristic period, as working to "reconnect human agents with their divine source and origin. They are akin to medicine," explains Abraham, "designed to heal and restore human flourishing; they are akin to various exercises appointed to reorient the whole of human existence to its proper goal."[65]

As we move into the second half of life, "letting go" is not an option. It's something that happens to us. For those in leadership, this spirituality of detachment may be much more difficult to embrace than for the ordinary believer. In that place—where we are called to trust in the desert, called to trust in God's presence in the midst of absence—the communal, ecclesial medicines of grace come to our souls like fresh water and cool breezes.

Conclusion

Wesleyan tradition and theology provides valuable resources for the current challenges facing disciples, especially those gifted for leadership. Whether we find ourselves in the first or second half of life, the Wesleyan way can challenge our skewed desires by forming spiritual disciplines in us that can speak to our deeper longings. Through sacramental practices rooted in the ecclesial community, Wesleyan leadership can take cues from its tradition and theology for the future.

Robert Moore-Jumonville, PhD, is Professor of Christian Spirituality at Spring Arbor University, Spring Arbor, Michigan, and pastor of Pope United Methodist Church.

Bibliography

Abraham, William J. *Crossing the Threshold of Divine Revelation.* Grand Rapids: Eerdmans, 2006.

—. *The Logic of Renewal.* Grand Rapids: Eerdmans, 2003.

—. *Canon and Criterion in Christian Theology.* Clarendon: Oxford 1998.

Allen, Diogenes. *Spiritual Theology.* Boston: Cowley, 1997.

Arnett, Jeffery. *Emerging Adulthood: The Winding Road from the Late Teens through the Twenties.* New York: Oxford UP, 2004.

Athanasius. *The Life of Anthony and Letter to Marcellinus.* New York: Paulist, 1980.

Augustine, *On Christian Doctrine.* Indianapolis: Bobbs-Merrill, 1958.

Bellah, Robert. *Habits of the Heart: Individualism and Commitment in American Life.* Berkeley: University of California P, 1985.

Brother Lawrence. *The Practice of the Presence of God.* Grand Rapids: Spire, 1967.

Burton, Vicki Tolar. *Spiritual Literacy in John Wesley's Methodism.* Baylor University Press, 2008.

Campbell, Ted. "Methodist Ecclesiologies and Methodist Sacred Space" in S. T. Kimbrough, ed., *Orthodox and Wesleyan Ecclesiology.* Crestwood, NY: St. Vladamir's Seminary Press, 2007.

Carlson, Kent, and Mike Lueken, *Renovation of the Church: What Happens When a Seeker Church Discovers Spiritual Formation.* Downers: IVP, 2011.

Chilcote, Paul Wesley. *Recapturing the Wesley's Vision.* Downers Grove: IVP, 2004.

Clark, Chap. *Hurt: Inside the World of Today's Teenagers.* Grand Rapids: Baker Academic, 2004.

Clement, Oliver. *The Roots of Christian Mysticism.* New York: New City P, 1993.

Fleming, David, ed. *Draw Me Into Your Friendship: The Spiritual Exercises.* St. Louis: Institute of Jesuit Sources, 1996.

Fleming, David. *What is Ignatian Spirituality?* Chicago: Loyola, 2008

Foster, Richard J. *Streams of Living Water.* New York: Harper San Francisco, 1998.

Guigo II. *The Ladder of Monks and Twelve Meditations.* Kalamazoo: Cistercian, 1979.

Hagberg, Janet O., and Robert A. Guelich. *The Critical Journey: Stages in the Life of Faith,* 2nd ed. Salem: Sheffield, 2005.

Heinzenrater, Richard P. "Wesleyan Ecclesiology: Methodism as a Means of Grace" in S. T. Kimbrough, Jr., ed. *Orthodox and Wesleyan Ecclesiology.* Crestwood, NY: St Vladimir's Seminary Press, 2007.

Jones, W. Paul. *Toward a Post-Christian Spirituality,* Weavings XXIV, no. 1 (Jan 2009).

Kavanaugh, Kieran, ed. *John of the Cross: Selected Writings.* New York: Paulist, 1987.

Kazantzakis, Nikos. *Report to Greco.* New York: Bantam, 1965.

Keating, Thomas. *The Human Condition: Contemplation and Transformation.* New York: Paulist, 1999.

Kelly, Thomas. *A Testament of Devotion.* San Francisco: Harper Collins, 1992.

Kidd, Sue Monk. *When the Heart Waits.* San Francisco: Harper Collins, 1990.

Langford, Thomas. *Practical Divinity.* Nashville: Abingdon, 1983.

Laubach, Frank. *Letters by a Modern Mystic.* Colorado Springs: Purposeful Design, 2007.

Lennox, Steven. "A Sanctifying Context." Paper presented at the Doctrinal Symposium, The Wesleyan Church, 2014.

Louth, Andrew. *Discerning the Mystery*. Oxford: Clerendon, 1983

Lynch, Thomas. "Our Neath-Death Experiences," from New York Times, in *The Best American Spiritual Writing* 2006, ed. Philip Zaleski, Boston: Houghton Mifflin, 2006.

Maddox, Randy. *Responsible Grace*. Nashville: Kingswood, 1994.

May, Gerald. *The Dark Night of the Soul*. New York: HarperCollins, 2005;

Metz, Johannes Baptist. *Poverty of Spirit*. New York: Paulist, 1968.

Mulholland, M. Robert. *Invitation to a Journey*. Downers Grove, IL: InterVarsity, 1993.

Muto, Susan. *John of the Cross for Today: The Dark Night*. Notre Dame, Ave Maria, 1994.

Nemeck, Francis Kelly and Marie Teresa Coombs. T*he Spiritual Journey: Critical Thresholds and Stages of Adult Spiritual Genesis*. Collegeville: Liturgical Press, 1987.

Nouwen, Henri. *In the Name of Jesus*. New York: Crossroad, 1989.

Oh, Gwang Seok. *John Wesley's Ecclesiology: A Study of Its Sources and Development*. Lanham: Scarecrow, 2008.

Outler, Albert C. T*he Works of John Wesley*, vol. 1. Nashville: Abingdon, 1984.

—. *Theology in the Wesleyan Spirit*. Nashville: Discipleship, 1975.

—., ed., *John Wesley*. Oxford: Oxford University Press, 1964.

—. "Do Methodists Have a Doctrine of the Church?" in Dow Kirkpatrick, ed. T*he Doctrine of the Church*. Nashville: Abingdon, 1964.

Owens, Bernie. *More Than You Could Ever Imagine*. Collegeville: Liturgical Press, 2015.

Pedlar, James E. "Ecclesial Institutions as Means of Grace: A Wesleyan View of the Holy Spirit and the Holy Church." *Wesleyan Theological Journal*, 49, no. 1, 2014.

Peterson, Eugene. *Working the Angles: The Shape of Pastoral Integrity*. Grand Rapids: Eerdmans, 1987.

Piatt, Christian, and Amy Piatt. *My Space to Sacred Space: God for a New Generation*. St. Louis: Chalice, 2007.

Putnam, Robert D. *Bowling Alone: The Collapse and Revival of American Community*. New York: Simon and Schuster, 2000.

Rohr, Richard. *Falling Upward: A Spirituality for the Two Halves of Life*. San Francisco: Jossey-Bass, 201.

Rohr, Richard. *On the Threshold of Transformation*. Chicago: Loyola, 2010.

Rolheiser, Ronald. *Sacred Fire: A Vision for a Deeper Humanity and Christian Maturity*. New York: Image, 2014.

—. *The Holy Longing*. New York: Doubleday, 1999.

Ross, Maggie. *Liturgy in Truth: Transfiguring the Mind and the Heart*, Weavings XXI, no. 3 (May 2006).

Setran, David P., and Chris A Kiesling. *Spiritual Formation in Emerging Adulthood: A Practical Theology for College and Young Adult Ministry*. Grand Rapids: Baker, 2013.

Smith, Christian. *Souls in Transition*. New York: Oxford UP, 2009.

Smith, James K. A. *Desiring the Kingdom: Worship, Worldview, and Cultural Formation*. Grand Rapids: Baker Academic, 2009.

Snyder, Howard. *Seven Keys to Free Methodist Renewal, Soul Searching the Church: Free Methodism at 150 Years.* Indianapolis: Marston Memorial Historical Center 2007.

St. John of the Cross, *The Dark Night*, in *The Collected Works of St. John of the Cross*, trans. Kieran Kavanaugh and Otilio Rodriguez. Washington, DC: Institute of Carmelite Studies, 1979.

Tillich, Paul. *The Shaking of the Foundations.* New York: Scribner's, 1948.

Tuttle, Jr., Robert G. *Mysticism in the Wesleyan Tradition.* Grand Rapids: Zondervan 1989.

Ward, Benedicta, ed. *The Sayings of the Desert Fathers.* Kalamazoo: Cistercian, 1975.

Watson, Kevin M. *Pursuing Social Holiness: The Band Meeting in Wesley's Thought and Popular Methodist Practice.* New York: Oxford, 2014.

Wesley, John. *The Works of John Wesley*, ed. Thomas Jackson. London: Wesleyan Methodist Book Room, 1872; Reprint by Baker Book House, 1978.

Whaling, Frank, ed. *John and Charles Wesley: Selected Writings and Hymns, The Classics of Western Spirituality.* Mahwah: Paulist, 1981.

Wuthnow, Robert. *After the Baby Boomers: How Twenty-and Thirty-Somethings Are Shaping the Future of American Religion.* Princeton: Princeton Press, 2007.

Chapter 12 Notes

[1] Narrated in a retreat led by Rolheiser, conveyed in a more complete form in *Sacred Fire: A Vision for a Deeper Humanity and Christian Maturity*, 4-5. Loosely cited from Kazantzakis, *Report to Greco*, 211.

[2] St. John of the Cross, *The Dark Night*, in *The Collected Works of St. John of the Cross*, 376-377, 381, 401; Owens, *More Than You Could Ever Imagine*, 99-107; Kelly Nemeck and Coombs, *The Spiritual Journey*, 190, 175; Rolheiser, *Sacred Fire*, 305-308; May, *The Dark Night of the Soul*, 71-74, 172; Muto, *John of the Cross for Today*, 85-102, 144-145.

[3] Spiritual guides tell us that we do not choose this path intentionally; it chooses us. See Rohr, *Falling Upward*, xix, 65; Hagberg and Guelich, *The Critical Journey*, chs. 7, 13; Nemeck and Coombs, *The Spiritual Journey*, 188-190.

[4] For a good introduction to stages of spiritual development, with special emphasis on the two halves of life, see Rolheiser, *Sacred Fire* and Rohr, *Falling Upward*. A classic scholarly account of spiritual stages is given in Nemeck and Coombs, *The Spiritual Journey*. See also Hagberg and Guelich, *The Critical Journey*. Spiritual formation stages are sometimes depicted as the unfolding experiences of purgation, illumination, and union. See Mulholland, *Invitation to a Journey*, ch. 8; Allen, *Spiritual Theology*, 10-11.

[5] John 21:18-19. See also Mark 8:31-38; 9:30-37; 10:32-45 where the disciples repeatedly misunderstand the cross. "Many Eastern traditions did not allow a man to study spirituality until he was in his mid-thirties at the earliest. Carl Jung imposed similar restrictions for students at his Institute in Zurich. In the Catholic Church, a man cannot become a bishop until he is thirty-five. There is a collective masculine wisdom that says if a man sets out on the journey too early, he has probably not loved enough, not failed enough, and not suffered enough to know the terrain in even rudimentary ways. He will more likely use God or religion for his own career or ego advancement, while swearing that he's not" (Rohr, *On the Threshold of Transformation*, 29).

⁶ For instance, one finds this kind of stout articulation of Wesleyan thought throughout Outler, *Theology in the Wesleyan Spirit,* and Maddox, *Responsible Grace,* 68. In his paper, Steven Lennox, "*A Sanctifying Context,*" articulates this notion well through the lens of sanctification as restoration from the effects of the Fall. In light of these sources stressing Wesley's theology as "practiced" divinity, we could argue the primary aim of John Wesley's theology was *spiritual formation.* For instance, Wesleyan theology as formation seems inherent in the following arguments: in Langford's notion of "practical divinity," where the author claims Wesley orchestrated everything "to introduce the [Methodist] participants to saving faith and, through discipline, to bring faith to fruition" (Langford, *Practical Divinity,* 18); in Maddox's notion of "responsible grace" which he argues "avoids the suggestion of merited salvation while upholding the importance of our transformation in Christ-likeness…in a way that actually enhances the place of human responsiveness" (*Responsible Grace,* 255); or in Abraham's emphasis on the church's canonical heritage and Wesleyan means of grace: "Discourse about God within the canonical heritage of the church is concerned to a great degree to bear witness to God's acts of redemption and to draw us into the life of the church. The primary interest is soteriological, that is, to bring about the healing of human agents and restore them to their proper dignity and destiny" (Abraham, *Crossing the Threshold,* 58).

⁷ For instance, Outler makes the case compellingly that in the 1725-38 period Wesley "consistently misplaced 'holiness'…*before* justification, as preparatory to it…[whereas] one of the decisive shifts in his 1738 transformation was the reversal of this order" (*Theology in the Wesleyan Spirit,* 70-71). Whaling stretches the impact of Aldersgate on Wesley's spiritual development further into 1739, after Wesley responded to Whitfield's appeal to preach in Bristol: "The year 1739 represents a watershed in the development of Wesley's spirituality. From now on, although he continued to learn, others would be far more influenced by him" (*John and Charles Wesley,* 22-23). Abraham alters the signification of Aldersgate, but not its importance as a legitimate spiritual shift for Wesley (*The Logic of Renewal,* 22-23).

⁸ Nevertheless, we ought to pay increasing attention to what recent sociologists are labeling as the "emergent adult" population. See, for instance, Arnett, *Emerging Adulthood;* Smith, *Souls in Transition,* 6; Setran and Kiesling, *Spiritual Formation in Emerging Adulthood,* 3-4.

⁹ On the failures of revivalism, see Abraham, *The Logic of Renewal,* 2-3.

¹⁰ Whaling, *John and Charles Wesley,* 8. Outler described what Wesley learned early on from reading Taylor, a Kempis, and Law: "that the Christian life is *devotio,* the consecration of the whole man in love to God and neighbor in the full round of life and death" (Outler, *John Wesley,* 7). From Lennox, *A Sanctifying Context,* we might be tempted to suggest that "sanctifying" and "spiritually formational" stand as synonyms when presenting Wesley's theology. Notice along these lines all that Wesley learned and appropriated from the mystics—from Brother Lawrence, Fenelon, Madame Guyon, and others (Frank Whaling, *Introduction,* 9-12; Tuttle, *Mysticism in the Wesleyan Tradition,* 143-183).

¹¹ In fact, more and more people are saying "yes" to spirituality while saying "no" to the church. As Rolheiser puts it: "Typical today is the person who wants faith but not the church, the questions but not the answers, the religious but not the ecclesial, and the truth but not obedience. More and more typical too is the person who understands himself or herself as a 'recovering Christian'" (*The Holy Longing,* 35). The authors of My Space to Sacred Space agree: "The institution of church as it is historically understood holds less value for American young adults, while spiritual curiosity remains surprisingly strong" (Piatt and Piatt, *My Space to Sacred Space,* 19).

Martin Marty, the Dean of American Church Historians, expresses a similar notion: "'I don't like religion at all,' people complain, 'However, I'm very spiritual.'" Marty describes this disembodied spirituality as "a kind of vapor: thin, particled, almost invisible, shapeless, hard to grasp"

(Foster, *Streams of Living Water*, preface). If the divorce of spirituality and ecclesiology offers good news for some, signaling emancipation from heavy-handed legalism, others are left with a dizzying emptiness. See also Robert Wuthnow, where he suggests young adults today "behave as spiritual tinkerers" (*After the Baby Boomers*, 114). Also, Setran and Kiesling, *Spiritual Formation in Emerging Adulthood*, 1-10, 81-110. Recently, a student handed me a napkin after class with the words scrawled in pen: "Sometimes it doesn't seem like the church is really moving anywhere—like it has lost its purpose—consequently life has lost its purpose." What a cry for something deeper!

[12] Rolheiser, *Sacred Fire* 16.

[13] Wesley, "The Almost Christian" in *The Works of John Wesley*, 1:131-141; "Awake Thou That Sleepest," in *Works*, 1:142-158; Maddox, *Responsible Grace*; Outler, *Theology*, chapter 2.

[14] Lennox, "*A Sanctifying Context*". See also Burton, *Spiritual Literacy*.

[15] Wesley urged Methodists "not to form any new sect; but to reform the nation, particularly the Church; and to spread scriptural holiness over the land" ("Minutes of Several Conversations," Jackson, *The Works of John Wesley*, 299. See also "The Nature Design and General Rules of the United Societies," where Wesley lays out the trajectory of a Methodist to do no harm, to do good, and to attend to all the ordinances of God (*Works* IX: 69-79).

[16] For instance: Wesley, "Scriptural Christianity" *Works* I:163; "The Way to the Kingdom" *Works* I:231, "The Marks of the New Birth" *Works* I:428; "Sermon on the Mount, I" *Works* I:481.

[17] Wesley, "The Means of Grace" *Works* I: 378-397.

[18] Rolheiser, The Holy Longing.

[19] Christian Smith, *Souls*, 73 Setran and Kiesling, *Spiritual Formation*, 5.

[20] Wesley, "Sermon on the Mount, IV" Works I:533. See Watson, *Pursuing Social Holiness*.

[21] Wesley, "The Way to the Kingdom" Works I:220-224.

[22] See Outler's discussion of the Gospel of "moral rectitude" common among Anglicans during Wesley's day (*Theology* 35-40). Regarding Wesley's habits of self-examination, see his diaries: "the material within the diaries provided a record by which Wesley could measure his spiritual growth" (Ward and Heinzenrater, ed. *Works* XVIII:302).

[23] Did Wesley practice solitude? Reading through his journals and diaries, we might more accurately compare this introspective side of his spirituality to the regimented self-examination of Ignatius of Loyola or to the rigorous form of practicing God's presence we see in Frank Laubach (Fleming, *Draw Me Into Your Friendship*; Laubach, *Letters by a Modern Mystic*.

[24] John Wesley, "The Way to the Kingdom," *Works*, I:225. David Fleming suggests: "our vision largely controls our perception," and right vision lies at the heart of our relationship with God" (*What is Ignatian Spirituality*, 1). "Your eye is the lamp of your body," insists Luke; "If your eye is healthy, your whole body is full of light, but if it is not healthy, your body is full of darkness" (Luke 11:34).

[25] Augustine, *On Christian Doctrine*, 23.

[26] John 1:38, Luke 18:41; John 5:6.

[27] Wesley, "Death and Deliverance" *Works* IV:209.

[28] See Guigo II, *The Ladder of Monks and Twelve Meditations*, 67-86; Mulholland, *Invitation to a Journey*, 12-115.

[29] "*Explanatory Notes on the New Testament*, Jackson ed., Vol. I, Matthew 6:8.

[30] Brother Lawrence, *The Practice of the Presence*, 26. Cf. Kelly, *A Testament of Devotion*, 8.

[31] Abraham, *Logic of Renewal*, 165.

[32] Human beings are mere scraps of life, here only for an instant" (Clement, *The Roots of Christian Mysticism*, 15). See also Tillich, *The Shaking of the Foundations*, 153-163; Johannes Baptist Metz, *Poverty of Spirit*, 3-6, 19-34; Keating, *The Human Condition: Contemplation and Transformation*.

[33] Nouwen, *In the Name of Jesus*. Nouwen frames the three temptations of Christ variously in different books. My rendition of them only partly matches his. See also Margaret Funk, *Thoughts Matter* (New York: Continuum, 1998).

[34] Athanasius, *The Life of Anthony*; Ward, *The Sayings of the Desert Fathers*.

[35] See Chap Clark, *Hurt;* Smith, *Souls,* 34-43; Wuthnow, *After the Baby Boomers,* 20-50.

[36] As a friend of mine suggested.

[37] Nemeck and Coombs, *The Spiritual Journey*, 46.

[38] Ibid, 46-71.

[39] Wuthnow, *Baby Boomers*, 13-16; Smith, *Souls,* 34.

[40] Bellah, *Habits of the Heart;* Putnam, *Bowling Alone*

[41] Setran and Kiesling, *Spiritual Formation*, 20; see also Smith, *Soul,s* 143-165.

[42] Wesley, "Reasons Against a Separation from the Church of England," *Works* IX: 334-349; Wesley, "A Short History of Methodism," *Works* IX: 367-72; Wesley, "Ought We To Seek Separation from the Church of England" *Works* IX: 567-580; Wesley, "Prophets and Priests" *Works* IV: 75-84.

[43] Outler, "Do Methodists Have a Doctrine of the Church?",11. "The question remains whether Methodism as a church itself has a clearly understood separate ecclesiological identity" (Heinzenrater, "Wesleyan Ecclesiology," 119).

[44] Oh, *John Wesley's Ecclesiology*, 249-250.

[45] Campbell "Methodist Ecclesiologies and Methodist Sacred Space," 215-225.

[46] Chilcote, *Recapturing the Wesley's Vision*, 43-65; Burton, *Spiritual Literacy*; Watson, *Pursuing Social Holiness*; Wesley, "The Nature, Design, and General Rules of the United Societies," *Works* IX: 67-76; "Rules of the Band Societies" IX: 77-79.

[47] Wesley, "The Duty of Constant Communion," *Works* III: 427-439.

[48] Abraham, *Logic*, 153-172; Pedlar, "Ecclesial Institutions as Means of Grace," 107-121. The fusion of Spirit and liturgy implied by these authors seems to be taken for granted by Wesley: see "The Means of Grace" *Works* I: 377-397. Dietrich Bonhoeffer, *Life Together* (San Francisco: Harper, 1954). Compare also *The Rule of Saint Benedict*, ed. Timothy Fry (New York: Vintage, 1981); and Stephen A. Macchia, *Crafting A Rule of Life* (Downers: IVP 2012). Many New Monastic communities live by some rule of life. For our purposes, something as simple as small groups and Morning Prayers, or Evening Prayers (even as options to commit to) could have a profound impact on the communal spiritual atmosphere of Wesleyans.

[49] Smith, Desiring the Kingdom, 80; 80-88.

[50] Louth, *Discerning the Mystery*, xiii-xiv. See William Abraham's depiction of knowing as loving: "The final goal of all believing and knowledge is beyond all belief and knowledge; the final goal of faith is simply the deepening of love for God and the neighbor" (*Crossing the Threshold of Divine Revelation*, 188).

[51] Pedlar, "Ecclesial Institutions as Means of Grace;" Abraham, *Canon and Criterion in Christian Theology*, 1, 27, 52, 477; Maddox, *Responsible Grace*, 192-229.

[52] Kavanaugh, *John of the Cross*; May, *The Dark Night of the Soul*; Kidd, *When the Heart Waits*; Muto, *John of the Cross for Today*.

[53] Rolheiser, *Sacred Fire,* 61-282; Hageberg and Guelich, *The Critical Journey,* 71-90; Rohr, *Falling Upward*, 60.

[54] Nemeck and Coombs, *The Spiritual Journey*, 175, 182-83.

[55] Smith, *Desiring*, 75-88.

[56] Lynch, "Our Neath-Death Experiences," 169-172.

[57] Ross, *Liturgy in Truth*, 39.

[58] Ibid, 36.

[59] Snyder, *Seven Keys to Free Methodist Renewal*, 141.

[60] Jones, *Toward a Post-Christian Spirituality*, 7.

[61] Peterson, *Working the Angles,* 1.

[62] James K. A. Smith, *Desiring the Kingdom.*

[63] Carlson and Lueken, *Renovation of the Church,* 19-29.

[64] Maddox, *Responsible Grace*, 192-229. On the means of grace as spiritual nourishment see also Abraham, *Canon and Criterion,* 467.

[65] Abraham, *Logic,* 1.

PART 3

HISTORICAL PERSPECTIVES

13
John Wesley's Practical Divinity
William Willimon

John Wesley was a practical theologian. A leadership theology that emerges from his tradition will be highly concerned with being effective and fruitful in leadership. Wesleyan leadership is concerned about measurements and results for missional advancement. Wesleyan leaders must not grow lazy, ill-equipped, or unconcerned with results. Instead, they must be truth tellers with conviction and kingdom work ethic and global passion.

LEADERSHIP IS ONLY NECESSARY if a group needs to go somewhere. If a group is content with its status quo, confident that it is faithfully fulfilling the purpose for which the group was convened, then no leadership is required. However, if the group is threatened, exists under some mandate more significant than its own interests, or believes itself to be accountable to some external obligation other than its own internal contentment, then leadership is essential.

More to the point, leadership is never optional if the group is convened by *Jesus Christ*. What Jesus demands of his Body cannot be accomplished without the encouragement, orchestration, motivation, and truth-telling provided by leaders. Jesus never said, "Think about me." He said, "*Follow* me!" And that can't be done without someone being called not only to do discipleship, but also the persistent, unspectacular, organizational work of leadership.

When I interview recent seminary graduates, the most frequently cited shortcoming in their preparation for ministry is leadership. As one new pastor put it, "I learned a lot of good ideas but I got no training in how to put those ideas into practice." Another said, "I was taught how to be reflective but not how to be effective."

This outcome is particularly odd if the seminary presumes to be training Wesleyan pastors who are required by our tradition not only to affirm orthodox Christian theology but also to put that into practice; not only to lead a congregation but also to keep up with Christ's move into the whole world.

Wesleyan Foundations: Practical Divinity

In 1780, John Wesley sent to his American Methodists (his "poor sheep in the wilderness") a hymnbook, full of brother Charles's hymns, a *Collection of Hymns for the Use of the People Called Methodist.*[1] In the preface he praised the hymnal as "a little body of experimental and practical divinity," claiming that these were not just uplifting songs but also practiced theology, beliefs put into action through music. That it was practical was the highest compliment that Wesley paid a belief, a theology, a hymn, or an individual Christian.

Not a speculative, theoretical thinker, John Wesley's test for an idea was its practical force, its incarnational applicability. I have little doubt that there would not be a heritage of Wesleyan theology or anything else if it were not for Wesley's practical leadership: the time, energy, and creativity expended crafting liturgies, devising sermons, and patiently, painstakingly building novel institutions.

In 1744, as the Wesleyan movement gathered momentum, Wesley convened a group to discuss the state of the revival. In the "Large Minutes," Wesley organized the conference around three questions: "What to teach?", "How to teach?" and "What to do?" Note that the purpose of doctrine and teaching was to move toward practice. Methodist preachers thought and argued, conferenced and prayed in order to be deployed for the practical purpose "to spread scriptural holiness over these lands."[2]

Leadership *remains* a pressing issue for Wesleyans because Wesley demanded not only that Christians be sincere, pious, thoughtful, and scriptural, but that we also be *fruitful,* which is to say *practical.*[3] When Wesley gave instruction on how to read Scripture, Wesley taught (in the "Large Minutes") that Scripture is a means of grace when we search the Scriptures by "reading: Constantly...carefully...seriously...fruitfully, immediately practicing what you learn there."[4] Wesleyan grace is no mushy pat on the head that says, "I love you just the way you are. Promise me you'll never change." Wesleyan grace is efficacious, the power of God to lead a sanctified, transformed life, the divine empowerment required to perform the faith.

Methodism didn't begin as a church with a mission, but as a mission within a church. As Methodists, we *are* a mission, living under the mandates of the *missio Dei.* In the 1798 *Discipline,* Bishops Francis Asbury and Thomas Coke claimed that Methodism's episcopacy—emphasizing the episcopacy as practical instrument of mission—was a revolt from the adulterated Anglican monarchial episcopacy and recovered the apostolic pattern. According to Asbury, that apostolic pattern revolved around the pragmatic necessity for leadership of mission. Asbury bolstered his invention of a Wesleyan episcopacy (in spite of Wesley's vehement objections to the idea of Methodist bishops) first and foremost on the basis of missional practicality, not merely with claims of apostolic succession. First the task assigned by Christ, then the hard but necessary work of organization and structure cobbled together in order to be faithful to Christ's commission. I know that not all Methodists believe in bishops, but I am bold to believe that bishops are leadership in line with Wesley's "practical divinity" at its pragmatic best.

Leroy Long, comparing United Methodist bishops with other episcopal polities, called United Methodists a "managerial episcopacy" as opposed to the "monarchial episcopacy" (Roman Catholic) or "pastoral episcopacy" (Episcopal Church). A managerial episcopacy, said Long, "is concerned primarily with making the church function effectively. It views the office of bishop in functional terms, as involving

"Faithful discipleship is that which performs the functions that Christ demands. The work must be managed in order to be fruitful"

managerial skills, rather than giving it theological dimensions or sacerdotal significance."[5] With respect to Mr. Long, in Wesleyan practical Christianity, words like "functional," "managerial," and "effective" very much *are* theological and sacerdotal. Faithful discipleship is that which performs the functions that Christ demands. The work must be managed in order to be fruitful. A reliable indicator of our fidelity is our effectiveness.

Because I'm a Wesleyan, I believe that all church leadership, bishops or otherwise, is best rationalized on utility rather than by puffed up theological warrant. Like Martin Luther, I prefer a pragmatic rather than an ontological definition of pastors; claim too much theological *charism* for the ordained *cleros* and next thing you know you have damaged the baptismally bestowed ministry of the *laos*. Pastors are needed only in order to enable the laity to be full participants in the *missio Dei*. As is stated in the United Methodist *Discipline:*

> Our theological task is essentially practical. It informs the individual's daily decisions and serves the Church's life and work. While highly theoretical constructions of Christian thought make important contributions to theological understanding, we finally measure the truth of such statements in relation to their practical significance.[6]

This strong defense of practicality has sometimes made Wesleyans seem anti-intellectual. This is an odd charge against a tradition that has roots on the campus of Oxford University, a people whose father was no less an intellectual than John Wesley and whose churches have been so committed to higher education. Sometimes the anti-intellectual charge is a sign of the critic's too limited definition of "intellectual" or "theological." Wesleyans like to think that we practice a responsible, wider, peculiarly Christian rationality whereby our theological ideas are tied to practical commitments and worldly embodiment.

Practical Divinity Contested

Surprisingly, some resist embracing practical divinity as an appropriate aim of contemporary church leadership. For instance, thousands of pastors have found Eugene Peterson to be the most helpful contemporary writer on ministry. Peterson provides a wonderfully nitty-gritty view of church and ministry. Pastors dearly love his candid, realistic portrayals of North American church life and recognize themselves in his accounts of his founding and 30 years of pastoral work at Christ Our King Presbyterian.

Peterson was a church-planter before we coined the word and early on saw the dangers of church expansion mimicking the consumer driven practices of the secular world. In Peterson's later writing, *consumerism* and *church growth* are used with equal vitriol.[7] Peterson advocates a theologically authorized church that is free from the world's allures, a church devoid of snazzy mass media tricks or church growth tips; that is, a church untethered to the world's standards of success. He advocates and embodies a ministry that is local, personal, prayerful, and eloquent. Peterson displays a warm, positive, generous spirit toward the church and its leaders—with one notable exception—his scorn for the institutional framework for ministry.[8]

For Peterson, the institutional church doesn't extend far beyond the local congregation. "The visible lines of pastoral work are preaching, teaching, and administration," he writes.[9] As a young pastor, he was disillusioned that "[t]he people who ordained me and took responsibility for my work were interested in financial reports, attendance graphs, program planning. But they were not interested in *me*. They were interested in my job: they cared little for my vocation."[10] Peterson aspired to the sort of ministry "that can't be measured or counted, and often isn't even noticed."[11] Above all, he fears being "a bureaucrat in the time-management business for God."[12]

For Peterson, the recovery of a proper pastoral model is vital. He scorns the way pastors have allowed leadership models to

> "[s]eep into our awareness from the culture—politicians, businessmen, advertisers, publicists, celebrities, and athletes. But while being a pastor certainly has some of these components, the pervasive element in our two-thousand year old pastoral tradition is not someone who 'gets things done,' but rather the person placed in the community to pay attention and call attention to 'what is going on right now' between men and women, with one another and with God."[13]

As a result, Peterson stands in fierce opposition to much that passes for pastoral leadership these days. He shows (almost) a disciplined *in*attention to results. People over programs. Dignity over function. Don't ask *how?* ask *what?* Leisurely spiritual direction over ministerial busyness. The quietly balanced spiritual leader versus the showy cheerleader who is jerked about by events.[14]

But is it really true that pastoral leaders throughout church history have historically had little interest in "getting things done"? John Wesley? Gregory the Great? Augustine? Perhaps I'm part of the problem that Peterson is trying to solve. Yet I wonder if now pastors need to be warned, if Methodism is to have a future, not to shun the allures of becoming sanctified business managers, but rather of the danger of fleeing the hands-on, not-so-glamorous, *practical* work that needs doing . As Bonhoeffer said, we must never dream a church that imagines a corporate identity that has never existed.[15] We must resist the tendency to make the Christian life something primarily inward and spiritual rather than visible and historical.[16]

Recently, my colleague Sam Wells chided church leaders for getting caught up in potentially condescending attempts to help people. Wells says it's better for those of us who are powerful and privileged simply to "be with" or to "be for" people rather than to be engage in patronizing and even delusional endeavors to "fix" people.[17] Wells advocates humble, simple listening and "being with" those in need.

But can Wells be sure that his "being with" is not also a function of class and privilege? Are people in need supposed to be pleased that a highly educated, powerful pastor is taking time simply to sit with them and listen to them? How might our willingness to do nothing but empathize with those in need be an evasion of responsibility for their need? Is this somewhat detached, inactive stance a form of Docetism—the avoidance of active contact with bodies in need? Might Wesley call it *Quietism*, an effortless waiting on God rather than effective pastoral ministry?

Is this yet another spiritualizing or intellectualizing of the ministry that we Wesleyans believe is meant to be active, responsive; that is, *practical*? Even as Karl Barth excoriated the smug, boring, culturally accommodated contentedness of much of the church and its ministry, he also warned that we must never, "overlook the visibility of the church, explaining away its earthly and historical form as something indifferent, or angrily negating it, or treating it only as a necessary evil, in order to magnify an invisible fellowship of the Spirit and of spirits." We cannot flee the real church into "a kind of wonderland."[18]

This is a prejudiced Wesleyan statement, but the Methodist in me must remind Wells and Peterson that Jesus' last words to us, before ascending and taking charge (Matt. 28:20), were not "stay put," just "be with people," and "pray," but rather, "Go! Make! Teach! Baptize!" The Body of Christ is a body in motion. Methodism practices a "sent ministry," not only in our deployment of pastors but in the witness of all our people. All ministry is a *demonstration* of the Incarnation. The Trinity refuses to be relegated to the abstract and the detached. Instead, the Triune God who revealed himself as "Word became flesh" locates, incarnates *and* calls us forth in service to the ever-spreading boundaries of Kingdom of God.

Leading and Managing in the Practice of Ministry

Thirty years ago, I wrote that the United Methodist Church is "over managed and under led."[19] We need more visionary leaders and fewer bean-counting managers.

Since then, there has been a chorus of lament over the paucity of good leaders. However, I modified some of my views after being bishop and after reading Harvard professor John Kotter's seminal book, *Leading Change*.[20] Kotter warns that strong leadership without good management gets an organization nowhere, contending that leadership and management are two "distinctive and complementary systems of action."[21]

Both leadership and management are thus necessary and complementary functions for any church that aspires to practice "practical divinity." Leadership is about vision, overall direction, goals and ends. Leadership is necessary for organizational transformation. However, management is required for effective operation and execution. Kotter defines *management* as "coping with complexity."[22] The twentieth century saw the emergence of highly complex, differentiated organizations that easily became chaotic to the point of self-destruction. Many different sorts of United Methodist churches only somewhat interconnected and in many different places served by a diversity of pastors make careful, comprehensive, coherent management essential. The trouble is, however, that at the 1972 General Conference, United Methodists allowed the practice of management to squelch the practice of leadership when we created a form of church where even the lowest levels of the organization were required to duplicate the complexity of the highest. A complex, bureaucratic process of decision-making and governance consumed huge energy. Every congregation, even the weakest, was required to ape the organization of the church-at-large. The greatest good produced by management, said Kotter, is organizational "order and consistency,"[23] which, for the 1972 General Conference, became more important than practicality and productivity. Leadership [in the United Methodist Church (UMC), for example, the bishop], unlike management (in the UMC, for example, the district superintendent), is not primarily about order and consistency. Leadership is more about achieving change than consistency.

North American churches find themselves in a competitive, conflicted environment where mainline Protestantism has lost its monopoly on the practice of Protestant Christianity.[24] Loss of monopoly means that no church can be church as it was even a decade ago. A living God gives churches two choices: grow (change) or die (cease changing). Change must be more than managed; it must be led. Thus, we need *leaders*.

However, an organization moves forward through more than high visions and good intentions; at some point someone must manage the complexity of the organization. Good management increases an organization's capacity to move forward through organization, staffing, developing necessary structures, evaluating and planning events and processes, holding people accountable, rewarding people who contribute, and exiting people who detract from an institution's forward movement.

Both leadership and management are necessary for an institution to thrive. Leadership helps people to move in the same general direction by talking—motivating and inspiring. Management does the face-to-face, nitty gritty work required for an inspiring vision to become a present reality. Managers push people through mechanisms of oversight and control. Leaders inspire people by energetically playing to people's basic need for achievement, a sense of belonging, recognition by others, and the power to live up to their highest ideals. Management values control and devalues risk; leadership requires energy and, therefore, inspiration (literally "filled with spirit"). No grand vision is achieved, says Kotter, without "a burst of energy."[25] Thus good leaders tend to be inspiring motivators; they know how to assess people's highest values and enhance those values. They invite others into decisions and give them a sense that they have some control over their destiny. Leadership is a task, a function of an organization that knows it needs help if it is to thrive.

Practical Divinity Leadership Today

Because of his commitment to practical divinity, John Wesley was determined not only to preach, think, and write, but also to lead. The Methodist revival was driven not only by the surprising outpourings of the Holy Spirit but also by Wesley's determination "not to strike the hammer down in any one place where I could not follow up on the blow."[26] Wesley was not above the unspectacular, often tedious tasks of institution-building. Consequently, he formed "societies" (larger groups of people), "classes" (ten to twenty believers), and "bands" (intimate groups of four to six), thus creating the organizational structure required for the intense accountability and encouragement, the confession and forgiveness necessary to live the perfection in love that Wesley preached.

Wesley's genius was organizational. He invented and embedded practices and forms that enabled the Wesleyan movement to sweep across the globe. In the Methodism of our day, particularly in my branch of the Wesleyan family (United Methodist) our leadership tasks will more likely be those of renewal, renovation, and reclamation than invention. Yet both may still be possible. From my knowledge of Methodist history and my own experience of serving as a pastor and a bishop in United Methodism, this is my list of practical leadership implications for contemporary Wesleyans. Whether invention or renewal, the following are necessary:

Courageous Truth-telling

A courageous willingness to dispose of unproductive (impractical) practices and structures. Most of the resources of contemporary Methodism are expended administering and funding yesterday's good ideas. Much of our leadership is held hostage to expensive, dysfunctional organizational structures that may have served a purpose long ago but are no longer necessary to the church's mission. We have a system that expends large resources subsidizing and propping up congregations whose mission has passed long ago.

For instance, the General Conference of the UMC was once a time for Methodist traveling preachers to gather, to sing and to pray, to report on the fruitfulness of their work, and to receive courage for the demanding tasks that God had given. Now it has become a bloated, unmanageable, unproductive, boringly slow legislative body that is unable to equip the church to move into God's future.

Leaders in the church are for the advancement of the mission of the church. How sad that although the United Methodist *Discipline* begins with wonderful sections on theology, history, and doctrine, that most of our energy in the last decades has been expended to tinker with and augment sections on structure and process. A bishop could now declare (as at least one has) that the Resurrection is hooey and suffer less censure than if he questioned the wisdom of forming the membership of every committee by quotas for gender, ethnic, geographical, and clerical/lay representation. Rather than streamline our church we added more rules and mandates that privileged representation over productivity. The *Book of Discipline* doubled in size in the 1960s and 1970s as we attempted to solve with rules and procedures that which can only be corrected through prayer, a shove by the Holy Spirit, and sensible pragmatism.

When the *Discipline* discusses clergy, it expends most of its effort defining who can and cannot be clergy and mandates a byzantine process for approving or removing clergy but shows little interest in defining what clergy are for. What are reasonable expectations for the performance of clergy? What do effective clergy produce? We have long lists describing the qualities of clergy with little clarity on what sort of fruitfulness we ought to expect at this time and place in our movement. How very un-Wesleyan.

Church renovation begins with truth-telling. Wesley could never have led a revival of "scriptural holiness" without telling some tough truths about the sad state of his beloved ism. In fact, in telling the truth, Wesley was embodying the best of his Anglican tradition. The truth-telling that is a mark of faithful preaching ought to characterize faithful Wesleyan leadership. An effective, Wesleyan leader is one who finds a way to confront a church with painful truth that it has been avoiding (expending some of its best resources in that avoidance), in the conviction that God has given the church the resources needed not only to hear but also to practice the truth. Few of us pastors enjoy putting people in pain. Yet all of us pastors are also preachers. The truth-telling we attempt in the pulpit is wonderful training for the truthfulness required for transformative Wesleyan leadership.

Conviction of Purpose

A conviction that God still has a purpose for Wesleyan Christianity. While Wesleyan Christianity evaporates in the land of its nativity, and while Methodism diminishes in North America, Wesleyans and the South and East may lead us to a recovery of the vitality of Spirit-driven practical divinity. When one considers the decline of marriage and family in the United States, the moral chaos in which many live, the racism, and the plight of the poor and other social challenges it may be that the time at last has come for an outburst of Wesleyan *sanctificationist* spirituality. In the 18th Century, Wesley seems to have believed that it was possible to turn even ordinary English people—especially those who were denied access to educational systems and economic mobility—into saints if you created the right sort of structures.

"The connection," as early American Methodists lovingly termed their far flung consortium of fledgling congregations, proved to be uniquely suited for mobilizing the church for the challenges presented by the American frontier. It can be a resource today, but only if it is led. When Hurricane Katrina devastated the Gulf Coast, the United Methodist Conferences in Alabama and Mississippi quickly moved relief into the hard-hit areas. Less connected, congregationalist denominations sought help from the Methodist Church in mobilizing their churches. In that instance, we learned anew the power of "the connection."

When I served Duke University Chapel as Dean, during a weekly meeting of Chapel ministers and musicians I bemoaned that we attracted too few Duke students to our Sunday services. I announced an initiative in the fraternities and sororities as well as my plans to hang out at a campus bar on Friday nights in attempt to interface with student life in the evenings. Our choir director (a Lutheran) responded with, "You are such a Methodist." When I asked him what he meant, he responded, "You are never satisfied with who is here; you are more worried about who isn't here. You will not rest until you have gotten in the face of every single student."

True, I'm guilty of practicing Wesleyan Christianity! The world, and our churches, need a strong dose of "practical divinity," of Wesleyan Christianity, and Wesleyan leadership, now, more than ever.

Hard Kingdom Work

A willingness to pray for, expect, and do the painful work required be an active part of the growth of the Kingdom of God. Nan Keohane defines leadership as "providing solutions to common problems or offering ideas about how to accomplish collective purposes, and mobilizing the energies of others to follow those courses of action."[27] This is as good a global definition of leadership as I know except for one missing element: *God.* Wesleyans aspire to live our lives in such a way that our lives and actions would make no sense if God is not the crucified and risen Christ, the living, active Father, Son, and Holy Spirit. That means that a peculiarly Wesleyan leader allows God the Father to define our common problems, asking Jesus Christ for the grace to find solutions that are compatible with the Christian view of reality, and then prays for the Holy Spirit to mobilize the energies of fellow disciples to do the work.

In my early days as bishop, I received criticism for reading so many secular business management books and excitedly sharing what I had learned with my clergy. I engaged in a crash course in management and leadership, not only because I was convinced that my church was in an execcutorial crisis but also because I believed in practical divinity.

I also secured the help of a retired business executive whom I called my "leadership coach." Bill Hamer had an office next to mine. He would attend and then help me evaluate meetings. He taught me how to do the administrative and management tasks for which my extensive theological education gave me no training. Our noble ecclesiastical platitudes, grand slogans and bold dreams can never be realized unless someone, in service to the mission needs of the church, submits to the rigorous demands of truly practical divinity.

I'll admit that a danger of practical divinity, particularly in the North American context, is to degenerate into the functionalist, utilitarian "what works is what's right." Secular pragmatist William James has probably influenced American thought more than the theologically driven John Wesley. All Christian leadership is under obligation to keep our leadership theological rather than lapse into leadership a-theism—attempting to lead as if God were not.

Wesleyans believe that the work we do in the name of Christ ought to make a difference, ought to touch the lives of real people living now in this world, because of our strong belief in the Incarnation. We believe that it's not enough to have good intentions; we must actually be with people. And it's not enough simply to be present with people; we must be actively engaged for them and with them. We do this because God did this in Jesus Christ and does this right now in the power of the Holy Spirit. God is not only love, as Wesley periodically reminded us, but is actively love *pro nobis*, love in action for us. We are active, speaking and enacting the gospel in the world, because that's what an incarnate God does. Our practical divinity is what you expect from those who really believe, "God was in Christ reconciling the world to himself." (2 Cor 5:19)

This past year I served a United Methodist congregation. In order to lead, I asked a church consultant for help. He spent a couple of days urging us to be honest about our huge challenges, trials shared by every mainline, aging church in an urban setting. Chief among our struggles is our relationship to our neighborhood and to a new generation of Christians. The consultant convinced us that getting out of our sanctuary and into mission, teaching church staff to lead toward the future rather than simply to care for the aging, expending less resources on internal maintenance and more on external witness were life and death matters.

On his way out of the building, I walked the consultant through our sanctuary with its century old, odd, rather garish stained glass windows. He stopped before our huge window that faces out toward the busy street, the window that we see as we exit church each Sunday. The window depicts a scene from Methodist lore:

John Wesley preaching on his father's tombstone. Wesley was refused permission to preach in the Anglican parish that day, so he had climbed atop his father's tomb in the churchyard and preached. The window shows Wesley outside the church, the closed church doors behind him, haranguing a group of eighteenth-century English people.

"Forget my report," said the awestruck consultant. "Gather your people every Sunday, at the close of the service, and make them stare at that. Everything required of this congregation is shown there. Maybe if they gawk at it long enough they will get the point and enact what that window preaches."

Christ died for the world—the whole world—not just for the church. We can't be the Body of Christ without being a body in motion, sent, moving out into the world that Christ means to have as his own.

Global Passion

A passion for serving God not only in the church but through the church in the world. After my eight years as a United Methodist bishop, I would say that the greatest temptation in ordained leadership is to allow our ministry to degenerate so as merely to provide congregational care rather than, in Wesley's words, "to spread scriptural holiness over these lands."[28]

When I entered ministry in the early 1970s, returning to South Carolina from seminary in Connecticut, my mind was clear that I was entering a war. The test for my ministry would be not only how well I was received by a congregation but also by how well I was able to mobilize that congregation to be a beacon, a light, a sign and signal of something that the world was not.

By the time I became bishop, it seemed to me that pastors had allowed pastoral care and congregational caregiving to trump all other pastoral concerns. Congregations had turned inward, expending most of their resources on internal maintenance. Over half of the congregations under my care had not made a new Wesleyan Christian in the past three years. From a study of a hundred of my congregations, half of them in rapid decline, half experiencing modest growth, I concluded that this inward/outward dynamic was the most important factor in congregational vitality.

The Director of the Baptist House of Studies at Duke disallows his Baptist seminarians from using the term "parish pastor." "Baptists don't have geographic parishes; we believe that Jesus wants it all," he explained to me. And we all know who famously refused to be excluded from preaching the gospel by mere geography, saying, "All the world is my parish."[29]

It's fine for a Methodist congregation to call their leader "pastor," but it's never appropriate for that congregation to think that the pastor's sole responsibility and focus is to that congregation. I find it sad that in my denomination today "evangelical" is too often used to indicate a conservative, even politically right-wing point of view rather than the passionate resolve to do what's necessary to get out of the church and into the world in the name of Jesus Christ who is a sign of God's determination to get back what rightly belongs to God.

Conclusion

Pastors limit their leadership to congregational caregiving simply because that's what we are most comfortable doing. It's easier to care for the saints given to us by the hard work of pastors in previous generations than to reach out to the unchurched who have yet to get the news that Jesus Christ is Lord, that his grace is for all, and that neither Caesar, the Pentagon, nor Wall Street is their Savior.

As some of us bishops pondered the scandal of a church where the median age is now sixty (where did we obtain biblical justification for limiting the church to the spiritual needs of one generation?), one of the bishops said, "Our seminaries are graduating pastors who have more skills for serving people over sixty and too few skills for relating to people under sixty. They do what they know how to do, refusing to grow in their ministerial competence." Or as I put it, "Many of us are making ministry more vague and less interesting than Jesus intends it to be."

Practical divinity compels us to keep the gospel something that is enacted rather than merely pondered. It is arrogant for someone to say, "Oh, I'm more of a pastor than a leader," refusing to acquire the skills necessary to lead people into the practice of the faith. It is not only arrogant; it's certainly not even Wesleyan.

Thanks be to God, John Wesley gave us a faith for the hands as well as the heart, a vision of the People of God in motion, participating in Christ's work in the world. Thanks be to God for Wesleyan practical divinity.

William H. Willimon, STD, is Professor of the Practice of Christian Ministry, Duke Divinity School, Durham, NC, and a retired United Methodist Bishop.

Bibliography

Barth, Karl. *Church Dogmatics* Vol. IV, 2. G.W Bromiley and T.F. Torrance, editors. Edinburgh: T. & T. Clark, 1988.

Bonhoeffer, Dietrich. *Life Together.* New York: Harper and Bros., 1954.

Dawn, Marva, and Eugene Peterson. *The Unnecessary Pastor: Rediscovering the Call.* Grand Rapids: Eerdmans, 2000.

Long, Jr., E. Leroy. *Patterns of Polity.* Cleveland: Pilgrim, 2001.

The Book of Discipline of the United Methodist Church. Nashville: The United Methodist Publishing House, 2012.

Keohane, Nannerl O. *Thinking about Leadership.* Princeton: Princeton University Press, 2010.

Kotter, John. *Leading Change.* Cambridge: Harvard Business School Press, 1996.

Minutes ["Large Minutes"] of Serial Conversations Between the Revered John Wesley, A.M., and Preachers in Connection with Him Containing the Form of Discipleship Established Among the Preachers and People in the Methodist Societies. London: James Nichols, 1797. https://ia902606.us.archive.org/34/items/minutesofseveral00wesliala/minutesofseveral00wesliala.pdf.

Newbigin, Lesslie. *The Household of God: Lectures on the Nature of the Church.* London: SCM Press, 1952.

Peterson, Eugene. *The Pastor: A Memoir.* New York: Harper One, 2011.

_. *Working the Angles: The Shape of Pastoral Integrity.* Grand Rapids: Eerdmans, 1987.

_. *Under the Unpredictable Plant: An Exploration in Vocational Holiness.* Grand Rapids: Eerdmans, 1994.

Richey, Russell, Kenneth E. Rowe, and Jean Miller Schmidt. *The Methodist Experience in America: A History.* Nashville: Abingdon, 2010.

Wells, Sam. "The Power of Being With." *The Christian Century,* June 19, 2015.

Wesley, John. *Journal of John Wesley,* vol. 4, ch. 3, June 11, 1739. CCEL.org. *Christian Classics Ethereal Library.* Available from http://www.ccel.org/ccel/wesley/journal.vi.iii.v.html

Willimon, William H. "Peterson and Institutions." In *Pastoral Work: Engagement with the Thought of Eugene Peterson,* edited by Jason Byasee and Roger Owens. Eugene, Oregon: Cascade, 2014.

_. *Bishop: The Art of Questioning Authority by an Authority in Question.* Nashville: Abingdon, 2012.

_. *We Believe: The Core of Wesleyan Faith and Practice.* Nashville: Abingdon, 2010.

_. *United Methodist Beliefs: A Brief Introduction.* Louisville: Westminster John Knox Press, 2007.

Wilson, Robert and William H. Willimon. *Rekindling the Flame: Strategies for a Vital United Methodism.* Nashville: Abingdon Press, 1987.

Chapter 13 Notes

[1] The following account is abstracted from my history of Methodist practical divinity in Willimon, *United Methodist Beliefs*, 59-66.

[2] Ibid.

[3] I discuss fruitfulness as a key Wesleyan test for leadership in Willimon, *This We Believe*.

[4] *Minutes* ["Large Minutes"], 15.

[5] Long, Jr., *Patterns of Polity*, 29.

[6] The Book of Discipline of the United Methodist Church.

[7] For examples, see Dawn and Peterson, *The Unnecessary Pastor*, ch. 1-2.

[8] See Willimon, "Peterson and Institutions"

[9] Peterson, *Working the Angles*, 3.

[10] Peterson, *Under the Unpredictable Plant*, 80.

[11] Peterson, *The Pastor*, 5.

[12] Ibid, 8

[13] Ibid, 5.

[14] I presume that Peterson's Reformed theology makes him suspicious of human effort and leads to his view of the church as an almost exclusively divinely wrought miracle. Perhaps my critique of Peterson on institutions is attributable to my Methodism. John Wesley had the highest regard for the pietistic Moravians, but broke with them fiercely over their (according to Wesley) "Quietism." The Moravians taught that human effort in pursuing the divine life was dangerous; one ought to quietly and effortlessly await the advent of God into life. Wesley's synergistic view of the human life, his stress that God's grace not only works for us but energetically works in us, led him to castigate Moravian "Quietism" as a rejection of the active, transforming, synergistic grace of God that enlists us in divine activity.

[15] Bonhoeffer, *Life Together*, 97-98.

[16] Lesslie Newbigin stresses the historicity and visibility of the church. Newbigin criticizes the Reformers' conception of the church as having, "no real place for the continuing life of the church as one fellowship binding the generations together in Christ. It makes the church practically a series of totally disconnected events in which, at each moment and place at which the word and sacraments of the Gospel are set forth, the church is there and then called into being by God's creative power." In short, for a failure to practice practical divinity. Newbigin, *The Household of God*, 48.

[17] Wells, "The Power of Being With."

[18] Barth, *Church Dogmatics*, 653-54.

[19] Wilson and Willimon, *Rekindling the Flame*.

[20] Kotter, *Leading Change*.

[21] Ibid, 27.

[22] Ibid, 128-29.

[23] Ibid.

[24] For my thoughts on United Methodist leadership challenges, see Willimon, *Bishop*.

[25] Kotter, *Leading Change*, 135.

[26] Cited in Willimon, *Bishop*, 24.

[27] Keohane, *Thinking about Leadership*, 19.

[28] Richey, Rowe, and Schmidt, *The Methodist Experience in America*, ch. 5.

[29] Wesley, *Journal*, Vol. 4, ch. 3, June 11, 1739.

14
The Leadership of John Wesley

Daniel L. Burnett

While John Wesley did not pen a treatise on leadership, strong leadership principles can be seen in his life. It is better not to see these as original to Wesley, but timeless principles that Wesley employed in his leadership. These principles are missional clarity, situational adaptability, operational diversity, structural connectivity, mutual accountability, and personal integrity. This chapter examines each of these principles in Wesley's life and discusses contemporary applications.

THERE CAN BE LITTLE DOUBT that John Wesley was a man with outstanding leadership qualities. His background, environment, passions, and experiences all contributed to making him the historic figure he came to be. By the end his life he was a nationally celebrated figure His long years of determined leadership in both church and society culminated in a status of elder statesmen. It was a status earned through decades of preaching, publishing, organizing, fundraising, traveling, inspiring, struggling, and mentoring—sometimes failing, usually succeeding—but always persevering. Places that had once opposed him with great vigor now welcomed him with open arms. Places like Falmouth, Cornwall. Early in his Methodist ministry he was met by a boisterous mob of Falmouth antagonists, but forty years later after riding once again into the coastal town he commented, "How the tide is turned! High and low now lined the street, from one end of the town to the other, out of stark love and kindness, gaping and staring as if the King were going by."[1]

Unfortunately for our purposes, Wesley did not leave a systematized treatise of his leadership theory and practice. What he did leave, however, was an extensive record of his life and work. From these records of journals, sermons, letters, and essays, as well as additional writings of those who knew him, it is not difficult to identify a handful of core elements of Wesley's leadership. The purpose of this chapter is not raise those principles as the definitive embodiment of Wesleyan leadership, but rather to illustrate from Wesley's leadership practices how those principles found expression in his own ministry.

Through this examination we see Wesley's practice of leadership not merely as an historical curiosity from a by-gone era, but as a demonstration of enduring leadership principles that transcend the particularities of time and culture. In other words, an analysis of Wesley's leadership is not really about Britain in the 18th century, it is about Christian leadership here and now—whenever and wherever our particular here and now may be. In the following six principles from Wesley's ministry we see that he was not a great leader who invented wise leadership principles; rather, he was a wise leader who deployed great leadership principles. It is that distinction that makes him still relevant today.

Wesley's Leadership Principles

Missional Clarity

John Wesley possessed a clear view of purpose in his ministry. Arguably, he was destined for such missional clarity simply by virtue of a family heritage that thrived on strong commitments to clearly defined causes. His paternal great-grandfather, Rev. Bartholomew Westley (1596-1680), studied medicine and theology at Oxford University. When Puritan rectors were ejected by Charles II after the English Restoration of 1660, he lost his parish but continued to preach as a Nonconformist and practiced medicine. Wesley's paternal grandfather, Rev. John Westley (1636-1678), studied theology at Oxford and preached as an evangelist before serving as a vicar. His Puritan sympathies led to loss of his church and two different imprisonments. Wesley's father, Rev. Samuel Wesley (1662-1735), left his family's Puritan Non-Conformist tradition as a young man and studied for ministry in the Church of England at Oxford. It was also Samuel who changed the spelling of the family name by dropping the "t" from Westley when he signed for his Oxford degree.

The Wesley family tradition of dissent and independent thinking was also evident on the maternal side of Wesley's heritage. His maternal grandfather, Dr. Samuel Annesley (1620-96), was one of the most renowned Non-Conformist preachers of his generation. Wesley's mother, Susanna Annesley Wesley (1669-1742), like his father, also exerted her independent spirit by leaving the Dissenting tradition of her parents and joining the Church of England. Susanna's well known regiment of family order and discipline has earned her the unofficial title Mother of Methodism.

John Wesley's mission was that of an evangelist, and that strong sense of calling was always first and foremost in his mind. Every aspect of his ministry was ultimately focused on bringing people to saving faith in Christ and a subsequent life of holiness. It was a mission that led him, famously, to regard the whole world as his parish. All people regardless of station in life or geographic location were to be reached—from the high and mighty to the convicted and condemned; from aristocrats to coalminers; from bishops to orphans. For Wesley, the mission was clear.

For this reason, Wesley's whole approach to both theology and ministry was thoroughly pragmatic. The reason he regarded theological understanding as an indispensable prerequisite to ministry was not merely for the sake of doctrinal purity, but because he saw it as a practical tool in the work of saving souls. That is why he taught theology through the practical means of sermons, letters, hymns, pamphlets, study aides, and private conversations rather than scholarly publications.

Wesley was intensely practical in the pursuit of his mission. He doggedly researched real life experiences of faith through personal interviews in order to determine if his doctrinal understandings actually passed the test of daily life. He furthermore analyzed and evaluated concepts of ministry practice on the basis of whether or not they actually worked in producing results. For example, after hearing numerous preachers while traveling through Scotland, Wesley summed up his assessment: "I heard many excellent truths…but as there was no application, it was likely to do as much good as the singing of a lark…no sinners are convinced of sin, none converted to God, by this way of preaching."[2] Wesley was a man of practical theology because he was driven by missional clarity.

But one of the important lessons learned from Wesley is that mission clarity is not the same as tunnel vision. Wesley realized that a focus on evangelism, and its subsequent discipleship, did not narrow his ministry options, but rather, greatly expanded those options. He saw that the work of evangelism had to be adaptable.

Situational Adaptability

Although John Wesley was clearly the leader of the Methodist revival movement, George Whitefield was its popular voice. The fame of the dynamic young preacher, eleven years Wesley's junior, was growing not only through the British Isles, but also in the American colonies, through his bold use of outdoor (or "field") preaching. Though Whitefield did not invent the practice, he was the first to popularize it on such a large scale.

While preaching outdoors to huge crowds of miners near Bristol, Whitefield wrote to Wesley pleading for his assistance. The opportunities afforded by field preaching were far greater than Whitefield could meet on his own. Wesley was thoroughly resistant to the idea. Though Whitefield's theatrical style of preaching was meeting with great success in the open air, Wesley was unconvinced of its appropriateness. Finally, at Whitefield's continued insistence, Wesley traveled to Bristol to witness the practice firsthand. Still he expressed his misgivings: "I could scarce reconcile myself at first to this strange way of preaching in the fields…having been all my life (till very lately) so tenacious of every point relating to decency and order, that I should have thought the saving of souls almost a sin, if it had not been done in church."[3]

However, in spite of his apprehensions, the next day, he took Whitefield's place and "submitted to be more vile, and proclaimed in the highways the glad tidings of salvation, speaking from a little eminence in a ground adjoining to the city, to about three thousand people."[4]

That event was monumental for Wesley's future ministry and leadership. He recognized that he could preach the gospel to more people in a single sermon out-doors than he could through multiple sermons in multiple churches indoors. On that day prejudices and presumptions gave way to missional clarity. He suddenly saw his ministry in a whole new light and, much to his own surprise, discovered an amazingly effective avenue of evangelism. The world had indeed become his parish. He would preach wherever the people were—whether open field or town square, hill top or coalmine, pub or pulpit.

For Wesley the issue of field preaching was not a question of whether or not he liked it, but whether or not it worked. But he never could have adapted to field preaching if he had not earlier adapted to a new understanding of the nature of saving grace itself. Shortly before his famous Aldersgate conversion experience in 1735, Wesley became acquainted with the Moravian leader Peter Bohler. It was Bohler who first convinced Wesley of the biblical teaching that salvation comes through faith alone, and that it comes instantly to the one who believes.

Though finally convinced of the biblical foundation of the doctrine, Wesley could not be fully convinced of its practical reality without experiential evidence. In spite of his belief that so-called "deathbed" conversions were invalid because any expression of repentance would be motivated by fear rather than genuine belief, Wesley decided to present the new doctrine of salvation to a condemned prisoner in Oxford. Much to his surprise the man

> kneeled down in much heaviness and confusion, having no rest in his bones, by reason of his sins. After a space he rose up, and eagerly said, 'I am now ready to die. I know that Christ has taken away my sins; and there is no more condemnation for me.' The same composed cheerfulness he showed, when he was carried to execution: And in his last moments he was the same, enjoying a perfect peace, in the confidence that he was accepted in the Beloved.[5]

With this evidence before him, Wesley conceded that he could not refute the reality of such conversions. He accepted that doctrinal assumptions and practical experience did not always agree.

After field preaching, the next most telling evidence of Wesley's adaptability was in his use of lay preachers. Again, such innovation did not come easily. As the revival movement grew throughout the country, Wesley traveled extensively, preaching, organizing Methodist societies, and supervising schools, clinics, and orphanages. Knowing that he could not possibly give local attention to such a far flung enterprise he employed the use lay preachers. Some of these were circuit riding preachers working directly under Wesley's supervision in an assigned geographic region. In addition to the circuit riding preachers, Wesley also appointed a resident local lay preacher to each society for the purpose of providing daily pastoral care.

There is some dispute as to the identity of the first Methodist lay preacher, but Thomas Maxfield was clearly among the first, if not the first. An early biographer of Wesley states that while Wesley was away from his London base known as the Foundry, Maxfield began preaching to the Methodist society there. Some were offended at the uncommon practice and sent word to Wesley. Wesley, too, was disturbed and rushed back to London to put a stop to Maxfield's preaching. Upon arrival at the Foundry he met his mother, Susanna. She saw that he was upset and asked what was troubling him. "'Thomas Maxfield,' he said abruptly, 'has turned preacher I find.' She looked attentively at him and replied, 'John, you know what my sentiments have been. You cannot suspect me of favoring readily anything of his kind. But take care what you do with respect to that young man, for he is as surely called of God to preach as you are. Examine what have been the fruits of his preaching, and hear him also yourself.' He did so. His prejudice bowed before the force of truth and he could only say, '*It is the Lord: Let Him do what seemeth him good.*'"[6]

A further significant step for Wesley was in the use of women as local preachers. Once again his first inclination was opposition to this innovation. However, at the practical level he was continually faced with the need for more preachers. But that alone was not enough to persuade him to appoint women preachers. That persuasion did not come until he was convinced of the biblical evidence that women could be called by God. Methodist societies offered a whole new kind of social as well as spiritual haven for women in eighteenth century Britain. Therefore, although the number of female local preachers was relatively small, their impact was very significant—in part because of their particular ability to minister to the substantial number of women who made up the early Methodist membership.

Clearly, Wesley's most controversial display of adaptability came with his decision to ordain Methodist ministers for service in America. Wesley had long resisted pressure from his lay preachers to ordain them as fully recognized clergymen. He knew that to do so would be tantamount to declaring Methodism a new church denomination. Wesley was always adamant that Methodism was a renewal movement within the Church of England, not a new church. As a loyal Anglican he supported the Church of England position that the authority to ordain resided solely with the office of bishop. For years he searched for an Anglican bishop who would ordain his preachers, but with no success.

As with earlier adaptations, his decision to ordain his preachers was the result of both pragmatic necessity and biblical study. But it was a difficult and trying decision for Wesley. The final straw of pragmatic necessity came from the newly independent America. Methodism had already taken root in the colonies prior to the American Revolution, where Wesley still viewed it as a movement within the Church of England. After American independence, however, the Church of England technically no longer existed in America, thus leaving the American Methodists in ecclesiastical isolation. American Methodism had no choice but to become its own denomination if its members were to receive proper pastoral care and instruction. So over the objections of even some of his closest friends and colleagues, including his brother Charles, Wesley ordained Methodist ministers for America.

Operational Diversity

The idea that ministry could and should involve more than just preaching was certainly nothing new to Wesley or anyone else in eighteenth century England. Compassionate endeavors on behalf of the poor, the sick, widows, orphans, and the incarcerated were common activities among clergymen. Wesley, too, from his earliest days of ministry while still a student at Oxford University, participated in such ministries. But there was a paramount distinction between Wesley's pre-Aldersgate ministry and his post-Aldersgate ministry. Prior to Aldersgate, he readily admitted that his motives were more about trying to save his own soul than the souls of others. After Aldersgate, as his sense of salvation assurance and mission clarity began to coalesce and mature, his ministry efforts clearly became focused on evangelizing others through all possible means. In this Wesley developed a masterful ability to hold to missional clarity while pursuing an impressive range of ministry operations.

The England in which Wesley lived knew an abundance of social ills: violence, poverty, disease, illiteracy, alcoholism, crime, and labor abuses. Although the young Wesley had spent his childhood in the relatively remote region of Epworth, he had not led a sheltered life. Even there he was exposed to the harsh realities of illiteracy, social injustice, addictions, and poverty. His own father suffered the humiliation of imprisonment at Lincoln Castle for several months due to an unpaid debt. Wesley himself endured bullying and hunger after being sent to London's Charterhouse School at the age of ten.

These, and many other personal experiences, certainly helped to instill in Wesley the concern for the welfare of the poor and exploited that later became evident in his ministry. He always carried a strong identity with the common people, but he strategically utilized his status as a Church of England clergyman and Fellow of Lincoln College to mingle with and raise funds from members of high society. These funds built orphanages and schools, purchased houses for leasing to widows, operated medical clinics, and created businesses to provide jobs for the unemployed.

Education was a particularly important priority for Wesley. He founded schools in London, Bristol, and New Castle in order to provide education for poor students. But his attention to education extended far beyond the formal classroom. He was an avid reader and writer in a variety of subjects, even making use of his extensive travel time for that purpose. He stated that "[h]istory, poetry, and philosophy I commonly read on horseback, having other employment at other times."[7]

Wesley's passion for learning was not merely for his own enjoyment, but was tied to an equal passion for educating others. Perhaps his most effective innovation for fulfilling that passion was through publishing. He established a publishing house that ultimately produced more than four hundred thousand pieces. These publications included not only works on Bible, theology, and ministry, but also science, medicine, education, poetry, and language. His goal was to produce large numbers of inexpensive books that were easy to read, convenient to carry, and cheap to buy. In other words, books for the common people.

The education of early Methodist preachers was a particular concern for Wesley. Even though most of his preachers were lay men and women without formal theological training, he still insisted that they endeavor to attain a comparable level of education held by any university trained clergyman. They were expected to read as avidly and widely as Wesley himself. To guide them in their theological development he provided them with the *Christian Library*—fifty volumes of edited writings that Wesley considered most essential for all preachers.

Wesley's broad and diverse approach to the work of evangelism produced a revival movement unlike anything previously seen in his time. For Wesley understood that salvation was not only about eternal life in the hereafter, but also about transformed living here and now. A resulting impact of such transformation was often a marked improvement in the overall quality of life. Many who came under the influence of the Methodist movement found their standard of living rising as they gained employment, practiced financial and family responsibility, abandoned gin and gambling, and pursued generally healthier lifestyles and relationships. Rather ironically, Wesley's success in these regards also caused him concern. His fear was that such prosperity would itself lead to new addictions—that is, addictions to money, possessions, and the pursuit of affluence. This concern was just one of the contributing factors to Wesley's commitment to a system of structured connectivity that would provide ongoing discipleship as well as organizational cohesion.

Structural Connectivity

One of the distinguishing features that separated Wesley's evangelism from Whitefield's was Wesley's insistence that evangelism involved more than just an initial experience of conversion. Christian holiness was the true objective. And the life of holiness that Wesley sought was essentially relational. Holiness was never to be seen as a matter of private piety, but of genuine love for God and neighbor that bore expression in daily living. In order for this holiness to be nurtured and realized, Wesley developed his ingenious system of small groups. In reality, Wesley's system of structured discipleship not only provided a means for the spiritual growth of the

Methodist movement, but actually became the organizational glue that held the movement together. Whitefield himself recognized in hindsight the importance of Wesley's system and reportedly observed that "[m]y Brother Wesley acted wisely. The souls that were awakened under his ministry he joined in class, and thus preserved the fruits of his labors. This I neglected, and my people are a rope of sand."[8]

The structure of the interlocking groups is well known: society, class, band, penitent band, and select society. A society was the largest and most public group. Comprised of at least fifty people, it was essentially a congregation of Methodist members. Societies met regularly for hymn singing, prayer, Bible reading, and preaching. Those holding official membership in a society were required to belong to a class. Classes typically had 10-12 members comprised of a cross representation of the community that blended people of differing age, gender, and social standing. The meeting was characterized by personal testimonies and discussions of spiritual topics. One of Wesley's astute innovations was to issue membership tickets to class members. This simple gesture gave the often illiterate members a sense of status and dignity that strengthened their commitment.

Bands were smaller voluntary groups designed for those who desired deeper spiritual growth and were willing to validate that desire by agreeing to greater commitments of spiritual discipline. The group was structured according to similarities in age, gender, marital status, and social standing. Penitent bands existed for those who had fallen away from the Christian life but wanted to return. Those suffering severe spiritual or behavioral problems could seek counsel and support by joining a penitent band. These bands have been compared to today's Alcoholics Anonymous.[9] Select societies were few in number and consisted of exemplary men and women personally chosen by Wesley both for leadership development and council to Wesley. A key component of the Wesley's class system, as well as his supervision of preachers, was that of mutual accountability.

Mutual Accountability

Mutual accountability was a hallmark of the Methodist movement from the earliest days of the Holy Club in Oxford. Members held each other accountable for such things as the use of their time, participation in worship and communion, good deeds for the needy, and generosity toward the poor. Later, during his time under the influence of Moravian leaders August Spangenberg, Peter Bohler, and Count von Zinzendorf, Wesley subjected himself to their probing, inquiring, and instructing mentorship. In Wesley's later structural development of the rapidly growing movement, the role and significant of mutual accountability became paramount.

This accountability began formally at the band level. Those volunteering for the rigors of band membership agreed to live by a stricter set of rules than other Methodists, including abstinence from (1) all uses of alcohol and tobacco unless prescribed by a physician, (2) ornamental jewelry, lace, or ruffles, (3) buying or selling on Sundays, (4) pawning of any goods, and (5) speaking of the faults of anyone behind their back. Furthermore, band members pledged to attend church services and band meetings weekly, give freely to the poor, pray and read the Bible daily.[10]

While these rules for living were an important feature of the bands, the real heart of the groups was found in its emphasis on accountability. In order to gain admission to a band, prospective members were not only required to give clear testimony of their conversion and present spiritual state, but they also affirmed a sincere desire and willingness to be told of all their faults and shortcomings bluntly and directly by other band members whenever necessary. Each weekly meeting includ-

> *"His leadership did not flourish because he followed a set of leadership principles; it flourished because he followed the dynamic repercussions of Aldersgate"*

ed the following four questions to which each member verbally replied: (1) What known sins have you committed since our last meeting? (2) What temptations have you met with? (3) How were you delivered? (4) What have you thought, said, or done, of which you doubt whether it be sin or not?"[11]

It is important to note that accountability in the Wesleyan system included the leadership itself. This was a major purpose for the select society. Future leadership was developed within this elite group, but present leadership was also held accountable in the group. The group had no designated leader and no prescribed agenda. The meetings could include freewheeling discussions, debates, prayers, confrontations, encouragements, and challenges. Even when Wesley himself was present, he held no position of leadership and was subject to the same level of accountability as all others.

Personal Integrity

Perhaps the greatest testament to Wesley's leadership came at the time of his death. During his long life of ministry and public service John Wesley raised vast amounts of money through direct appeals and sales from his publications. Many of his contemporaries naturally assumed that a large portion of this wealth found its way into Wesley's personal pockets. In fact, as the public records revealed after his death, he owned virtually nothing. The so-called Wesley House in London where he lived in the later years of his life was not his. It was a Methodist-owned property that he used and shared with his traveling preachers. He was well cared for and lived comfortably, but he gave away vast sums of what could have been personal wealth. In other words, perhaps the greatest leadership lesson he left was the lesson of personal integrity.

Wesley led with integrity and by example. He asked nothing of others that he had not already done himself. Even at the age of eighty-one, he spent five days on the streets of London begging for money to buy clothes for the poor. He reported, "I walked through the town, and begged two hundred pounds, in order to clothe them that needed it most. But it was hard work, as most of the streets were filled with melting snow, which often lay ankle deep: so that my feet were steeped in snow water nearly from morning till evening."[12] After the fifth day he became ill and was unable to carry on.

Conclusion

Successful service under Wesley's leadership required total dedication and rigorous activity. He expected much and he gave much. Many of his precise practices would be badly out of place in modern contexts, but the leadership principles he modeled continue with universal applicability. This is leadership in the footsteps of John Wesley. Not a wooden replication of his system, but an embracing of the basic leadership principles that resulted in a worldwide impact far exceeding anything he ever imagined.

Throughout his years of preaching and teaching Wesley was always adamant that he was saying nothing new about the gospel or the Christian life. In fact, he recoiled from the very notion of doctrinal novelty. His purpose was not to create a new theology, but to find new ways to bring people back to the historic orthodox teachings of the church as found in the Bible.

In the same way, there is little, if any, originality in the basic components of Wesley's leadership model. What made his leadership unique for his time was simply the fact that he put his passion into action. His leadership did not flourish because he followed a set of leadership principles; it flourished because he followed the dynamic repercussions of Aldersgate. Those same repercussions are still seeking expression through leaders who possess (1) a clear awareness of their mission, (2) the ability to navigate changing situations without losing sight of that mission, (3) the creativity to employ a diverse range of effective methodologies, (4) the foresight to devise and implement a cohesive and purposeful structure, (5) the wisdom to value full accountability, and (6) the integrity to live and act with holiness of heart and life.

Daniel L. Burnett, DMin, is pastor of Olde Towne Community Church in Ridgeland, Mississippi, and author of In the Shadow of Aldersgate.

Chapter 14 Notes

[1] John Wesley, *The Works of John Wesley*, vol. 4, edited by Thomas Jackson (London: Wesleyan Methodist Book Room, 1872; reprint, Kansas City: Beacon Hill Press, 1979), 468

[2] Wesley, *Works*, 4:155.

[3] Wesley, *Works*, 1:185.

[4] Ibid.

[5] Wesley, *Works* 1: 90.

[6] Henry Moore, *Life of John Wesley* (London, 1824), 505-506. Italics in the original.

[7] Wesley, *Works*, 3:393.

[8] J.B. Wakeley, *The Prince of Public Orators: A Portraiture of Rev. George Whitefield, M.A.* (New York: Carlton and Lanahan, 1871), 219-220.

[9] Michael Henderson, *John Wesley's Class Meeting: A Model for Making Disciples* (Nappanee: Evangel, 1997), 126.

[10] Wesley, *Works*, 8:273-274

[11] Ibid, 273.

[12] Wesley, *Works*, 4:295.

15
The Leadership of Francis Asbury

Bryan R. Easley

Methodist Bishop Francis Asbury was the most influential religious figure in the early American Republic. In the midst of the clash between monarchy and democratism straining church and society alikee, Asbury led American Methodism to become the nation's largest religious movement, one that would permanently change the shape of American thought and life. He did it in an organizational structure that wedded the populism among the laity with the centralized authority of a bishop. Francis Asbury's practice of leadership can be best described using a mimetic model: the imitation of Christ by embracing a life of sacrifice, suffering, humility, submission, and servanthood.

FRANCIS ASBURY WAS THE FOUNDING BISHOP of American Methodism. From its inception, American Methodism rested on a centralized, episcopal form of governance. As bishop, Francis Asbury wielded a significant degree of exclusive power and privilege. At the same time, however, early American Methodism rapidly grew to become the most influential and significant religious movement in the early American Republic, an influence it would wield through the remainder of the 19th century. So how did this uniquely American religious organization that was anything but democratic in its most central leadership role produce and sustain a populist lay-led movement that changed American society?

This chapter explores Asbury's leadership in terms of a model of Christian leadership rooted in the imitation of Christ. It also briefly delves into the relationships that formed Asbury's leadership context from a theological and historical perspective. Analyzing his leadership in these terms provides us with valuable insight into the relationships between a leader's moral character, use of power, and theological and biblical framework. Studying Asbury also can provide new insights for dealing with the tensions between individual freedom and centralized control inherent in most western organizations and church bodies.

A Builder of the Nation

Two miles north of the White House in the nation's capital, a bronze statue of a cloak-clad figure on horseback gazes out down the busy thoroughfare toward 16th Street and Columbia Road. An inscription at the statue's base reads, "If you seek for the results of his labor, you will find them in our Christian civilization." The figure, obscured by the shadows of modern religious history and leadership, and unknown to most passers-by, is Francis Asbury, first bishop of the Methodist Episcopal Church in America. The statue was commissioned in 1916 on the 100th anniversary of Asbury's death. The memorial plan proposing the $50,000 dollar statue declared Asbury had a place among "those who had served their country as warriors, statesmen, and pioneers, inasmuch as his labors helped mightily in laying religious, moral, and social foundations for an enduring republic."[1]

President Calvin Coolidge, giving the keynote address at the statue's dedication, stressed the vital role that Methodism had played in establishing the moral foundation of America's successful self-government. He contended that Methodism under Bishop Francis Asbury was motivated by the same impulses for human freedom as the American Revolution: "the founders of this movement were inspired by the thought that all men were worthy to hear the Word... As our ideal has been to bring all men to freedom, so their ideal was to bring all men to salvation."[2]

Because of Asbury's leadership in the growth of early Methodism, Coolidge believed he was "entitled to rank as one of the builders of our nation."[3] In the 1950s, Asbury's journals were included by the National Historical Publications Commission of the U.S. Government in the list of "sixty-six great Americans whose works [were] recommended for proper editing and publishing, along with Washington, Jefferson, Adams, Lincoln, and the other immortals of the land."[4] Nearly a century earlier, George Peck, an itinerant preacher and contemporary of Asbury, had written that Asbury "occupies the place in the religious history of this country which Washington does in its civil history," calling him "the father of...American evangelism."[5] From his appointment as bishop in 1784 until his death in Spotsylvania County, Virginia, in 1816, Francis Asbury was the undisputed leading figure in early American Methodism.

Asbury was born in Birmingham, England, in 1745, to devout Anglican middle-class parents. As a teenager, he joined a local Methodist class meeting where he had a conversion experience and began sitting under Wesleyan teaching. Asbury began preaching at age 17. By 22, he was a full-time Methodist itinerant preacher. Asbury's journey to America began in 1771, at the annual Conference held in Bristol, England. During that conference, John Wesley called for volunteers who were "willing to go over and help" the brothers in America.[6] Asbury, a veteran Methodist circuit rider at age 26, stepped forward. By September of 1771, he set sail from Bristol headed to Philadelphia. Francis Asbury would never again set foot on his native English soil.

During the 45 years of his ministry in America, Asbury preached 16,425 sermons, presided over 224 annual conferences, ordained more than 4,000 preachers, traveled 270,000 miles (largely on foot or horseback) crossing the Alleghany Mountains 60 times.[7] During his tenure in office, Methodism grew from a handful of small, struggling Methodist societies to the largest Christian movement of the 19th century. Under his leadership, Methodism would take the form that allowed it to shape the social and cultural fabric and history of the entire nation.[8]

As an organization, early American Methodism was a paradox. From 1771 until the 1840s, the organization of Methodism essentially consisted of a centralized, hierarchical, and episcopal center driving a fluid, decentralized, and national religious movement; one so effective and powerful that it redefined American religious life in terms of democratic and populist ideals. The linchpin that made it work was Francis Asbury, the epitome of the episcopal bishop and the itinerant missionary.

Methodism in the American Republic

By the mid 1800s, the largest organization in the United States was the Federal Government. The second largest was the Methodist Episcopal Church, by that time fifty percent larger than any other denomination with a membership surpassing one million members, four thousand circuit riding preachers, and twice that many local preachers.[9] By 1850, Methodism was the largest denomination in America with "more than a third of all American church members."[10]

Early Methodism consisted of a unique blend of monarchial order, traveling bands of zealous, largely uneducated, circuit-riding preachers, and the systematic, methodical formation (hence the name "Methodists") of converts into small lay-led groups. It was, in Mark Noll's estimate, one of the "most significant social developments of any kind in American history."[11] At its heart was a theology of optimistic hope rooted in moral transformation. Its preachers emphasized freedom and autonomy through divine grace, social equality, and faith expressed in popular culture. Religious historian Nathan Hatch argues that "Methodism remains the most powerful religious movement in American history, its growth a central feature of the emergence of the United States as a republic."[12]

Methodism was one of the key sparks in the revival movement called the Second Great Awakening. Tapping into the populist, individualistic impulses fueled by the revolutionary birth of the new republic, the Second Great Awakening was a nationalizing force that spread democratic ideals of religious and cultural freedom. What made Methodism so successful in the context of this national revivalist current "was not the intellectual content of their preaching, which was meager, but their ability to do what voluntary societies, state governments, and even political parties would soon do—organize people."[13] The organizational genius of Methodism rested in the paradoxical combination of episcopal itinerancy (bishops and circuit-riders) and small local, largely autonomous societies (groups) of believers practicing spiritual disciplines and accountability."[14]

Democratic Tensions in Post-Revolutionary America

Tumultuous debate over authority, organization, and leadership marked the socio-political landscape in America in the years immediately following the American Revolution. The Revolution grew out of tensions between British monarchy and democratic independence. During the 1700s, the notion of popular sovereignty challenged traditional religious authority, emphasizing "the right of the people to think for themselves."[15] The same fiery rhetoric of independence, individual expression, and the priority of personal conscience that American clergy had used to boost support for the Revolution was now coming back to bite them.[16]

People were suspicious of traditional ecclesial structures, defiant of clergy who claimed the right to spiritual authority, and intolerant of long-established requirements regarding baptism and church membership. They increasingly insisted that religion be shaped to popular opinion rather than the other way around.[17] People were quick to "question any source of authority that did not begin with an act of individual choice."[18] Consequently, the years surrounding the American Revolution was "a bewildering world of clashing opinion" in American culture.[19]

The looming problem facing the Revolutionary generation (including Asbury and the Methodists) was that the very arguments which justified independence from the British empire—the priority of the individual conscience—worked against the subsequent challenge of unifying this new, fledging nation. The rhetoric of individual sovereignty and autonomy worked well for fanning the flames of revolution. But those who had experienced a taste of that kind of freedom were not as prone to give it up for political leaders just because they were closer to home. People were loathe to trade a king abroad for one in their own backyard. Geographical, ideological, philosophical, and cultural tensions among thirteen sovereign states made the concept of a union seem a distant possibility.[20] Winning the war was enough of a challenge. Forging a new unified nation would prove to be even greater.

Methodism was subject to these same tensions between individual freedom and corporate unity. The anti-authority arguments of post-Revolution America took the form of anti-episcopacy rhetoric in the church.[21] The language of political conflict—of kings and bishops and popes—permeated Methodism's quest for stability and maturity. Methodists, in "a decade riven with class, ethnic, and ideological enmities, now read their differences in the language of the people versus the aristocrats, democracy versus federalism."[22] Even prior to war with England, the movement struggled with dividing lines such Irish versus English origins, grass roots libertarians versus the Methodist hierarchy, and American versus British control.

The tensions were between the whole of the movement and its parts. In the political landscape, the debate between libertarianism and federalism was really a question of which national aspect was of greater consequence: the 'United' or the 'States'? Methodism struggled with whether the sovereignty of annual conferences or a strong, centralized executive government was of greater consequence in accomplishing Methodism's vision of reforming the continent and spreading Scriptural holiness. Events would show that for nation and church alike, the answer was both. In fact, there was no homogenous interpretation for what either this new American republic or the new Methodist Episcopal Church was supposed to look like.[23] In all these tension, Methodism was a microcosm of the American experiment. The challenge Asbury and the other Methodist leaders confronted was how to hold together a vast, disparate, and sometimes-contrary group of sovereign bodies in such a way that both unity and freedom were upheld.

Power as Bishop

The cauldron of the post-Revolutionary era was the setting for Asbury's role as the leader of American Methodism. At the Baltimore Christmas Conference of 1784, the preachers voted to adopt an episcopal structure. However, an episcopal structure headed by a bishop was still very much an English system. As evidence of this, John Wesley sent Thomas Coke with instructions to ordain Asbury as Coke's co-bishop of the new work in America. American sentiments were not kind regarding this form of ecclesial government, such that "the mere suggestion of introducing a bishop…or even the Episcopal office…called for violent opposition among the people."[24] Although Asbury had played the central role in American Methodism for the previous decade, he wisely declared he would not accept the superintendency of the new church without being elected by the conference. Eventually, the General Conference elected Asbury as bishop and granted him significant personal power.

The vast majority of preachers at the Christmas Conference were very purposeful in their decision to appoint Asbury as bishop, but it was a decision with which they were never quite comfortable. So much power concentrated in the hands of one man was a source of perpetual unease, even, at times, to Asbury's closest allies. The conferences recognized the crucial need for the bishop to have centralized control, but they were always keenly aware of the potential danger were somebody other than Asbury to sit in the seat. More than , they took action to limit that power or prevent those they did not trust from holding the office.[25]

The Paradox of Methodism

From its inception, Methodism was episcopal in its organizational structure with bishops overseeing conferences and appointing preachers to circuits and churches.

Yet, organizationally, American Methodism was a "curious paradox"[26] existing in the tension of British monarchism and American democratization. Its history—and present—is the story of the collision between monarchial and democratic conceptions of leadership and organizational autonomy.[27]

Methodism had two natures: a hierarchical centralized authority and an expanding network of voluntary preachers, lay societies, and autonomous conferences. The episcopal hierarchy occupied the center. The dynamic and complex system of semi-autonomous itinerant preachers and societies with local lay leaders occupied the constantly expanding periphery. The movement was simultaneously fixed and fluid, stable and changing, predictable and spontaneous. It ushered in a system built around the power of a bishop, the order of The Discipline, and autonomous annual conferences, yet burst onto the American frontier, embedded itself in America's urban centers, transformed the emerging middle class, became synonymous with American populism,[28] and found itself at the heart of the explosive revivalism of the Second Great Awakening.[29]

The authority of the bishop was ironclad in establishing conferences, opening up circuits, appointing preachers, and enforcing doctrine and discipline. Local preachers had little governing authority; itinerant preachers went where they were told, albeit sometimes grudgingly. On the other hand, although the preachers were expected to work where they were appointed, they had a great deal of autonomy

> *"Asbury sought to operate from a Scriptural paradigm.*
> *He was determined to execute his role as bishop in the*
> *same manner as the first apostles"*

in how they went about that work. They were free to set the pattern and frequency of preaching within the assigned circuit. This autonomy within the circuit allowed each preacher to focus his efforts where he felt showed the most promise and avoid places where there was little interest.

Early Methodism was decidedly not democratic. Yet it is more closely equated with the forces of freedom, expansion, and individual populism of the times than any of its counterparts.[30] The great irony of Methodism's paradoxical nature is that "the very church that most adamantly refused to share ecclesiastical authority with the laity actually came to have the greatest influence among them."[31] The essence of the paradox is that such singular power in the hands of Asbury brought forth the fullest expression of spiritual freedom for the people under his leadership.[32]

Explaining Asbury

So what are we to make of Asbury's leadership? Most modern scholarship has tended to perpetuate the image of Asbury as an iron-fisted autocrat and pious though ambitious power monger. Yet, the evidence suggests quite the opposite.

In the republican climate of early Methodism, no power-hungry leader fueled by lordly ambition would have long endured.[33]

What allowed Asbury's power to flow from the "center to the circumference,"[34] as he described it, in such a way that the centralized power of the bishop resulted in individual religious freedom of the masses? Asbury's outlook was essentially apostolic. He had carefully studied forms of church government, read widely on the episcopacy, and was as informed as any of his day. He was convinced early Methodism's structure was as "primitive," or as close to that of the apostles, as any could be. For all of his flaws and personality shortcomings, Asbury sought to operate from a Scriptural paradigm. He was determined to execute his role as bishop in the same manner as the first apostles. Francis Asbury understood his leadership in spiritual and theological, rather than political, terms.[35] In contrast to the political climate of the day, theology played the *primary* role in Asbury's conception of organizational and social life.

A Mimetic Christological Model

Dr. Jenn Strawbridge of Keble College, Oxford, calls for the reclamation of a theology of leadership grounded in Scripture and a proper understanding of power.[36] Asbury's life offers one powerful source for such a task. One possible theological explanation for understanding Asbury's leadership effectiveness in early Methodism is a mimetic Christological model drawn from Philippians 2:5-11 and rooted in Paul's call to imitate Christ.[37]

The mimetic Christological model beckons leaders to imitate Christ through an intentional and deliberate process of status reversal. The model is built simply around the five qualities or actions of Christ listed in the "kenosis hymn" of Philippians 2:5-7: kenosis (emptying), servant posturing, humility, embracing humanity, and obedience. Leadership begins in place of privilege and status. The five active values demonstrated by Christ's life and death invert the social values of status, honor, and power of the place of privilege. The inversion of these values from their worldly utilization leads to an ethical and truly Christian community in which each member is valued and truly loved.

Francis Asbury's leadership closely corresponds to this mimetic model. As a result, this alternative view of leadership offers an integrated theological framework for interpreting Asbury's role in early American Methodism and helps us better understand how he was able to have the success he did at such a critical and paradoxical time in the church's life.

Kenosis

The kenosis of Christ is a voluntary abandonment of the privileges of his divine office in order to overcome the separation between God and man (Philippians 2:7-

6). Christian leaders who imitate Christ voluntarily pour themselves out in sacrifice to the ones they are called to lead. Few contemporary leaders embody a posture of self-sacrifice and self-emptying better than Francis Asbury. "My soul thirsteth for holiness in myself and others," Asbury's journal records. "[I]f my whole body... could labor and suffer, they should freely be given up for God and for souls."[38]

Asbury lived his entire life in monastic fashion, never taking more than a modest annual salary. Aside from what was needed for his frugal expenses, he gave away most of what he received. He never had a regular home and owned only what little he could carry in saddlebags. "I will live and die a poor man," he wrote in 1800. At his death, he had saved $2000, all of which he left to the church. Asbury held a dim view of preachers who sought to "show the effects [of wealth] by lording it over their poorer neighbors and by securing to themselves all the offices of profit or honor" (1:577). Asbury recounted one episode when a group of preachers at a conference in Tennessee "were in want and could not suit themselves; so I parted with my watch, my coat, and my shirt."[39] Such behavior was a constant habit.

Within weeks of his arrival in America, Asbury concluded that "my brethren seem unwilling to leave the cities, but I think I will show them the way."[40] In a time when most clergy and their superiors confined themselves to the comforts of city life, Asbury did just the opposite, pursuing both the unreached and embracing the uncomfortable. Across forty-five years of ministry, he rode on average 6,000 miles a year across rugged terrain crossing the Appalachian Mountains over sixty times on poor roads and through all kinds of weather.[41] He quickly earned the trust of the preachers because they were never asked by him to go to places or endure hardship in going that he himself was not experiencing. He truly did show them the way.

Asbury viewed leadership in terms of suffering and sacrifice. He suffered from chronic health problems like asthma and rheumatism, as well as the effects of poor diet, lack of sleep, emotional distress, extreme physical exposure, and ill-informed medical treatments. As a result, Asbury was frequently violently ill or in great pain. But he saw suffering as a necessary part of the calling, so he doggedly pressed on, noting in his journal that "it is only on condition that we suffer with him, that we shall also reign with him."[42] Asbury literally sacrificed his physical health for the sake of his calling and office.

Because of this self-sacrificing posture and the willingness to give himself so fully to the work no matter the cost, his contemporaries revered Asbury as the ultimate example of the Methodist itinerant.

Servanthood

Servant leaders lay aside any personal advantage and place themselves wholly at the disposal of others for their good (Phil. 2:7). The primary motif in servant posturing is "a resolute identification with the lowest members in the social ladder within the community."[43] Asbury infused the office of bishop with the posture of a servant.

The vast majority of the preachers entrusted him with the authority and power of the office. Such deep trust was the result of his attitude and posture of service to those in his charge. In a public defense of Asbury, Nicholas Snethen wrote, "[I]n him we see an example of daily labor, suffering, and self-denial worthy the emulation of the young preacher."[44]

Methodism struggled to meet its financial obligations to its many preachers. Asbury established a system to collect a dollar from as many individuals as would give to help care for poor preachers. For all the heavy demands put on traveling preachers, he worked tirelessly to find ways to care for their financial, material, and spiritual needs. Strickland, one of Asbury's earliest biographers, wrote "Wesley himself never devised and carried into execution so many plans of benevolence in connection with his societies as Asbury did" for the Methodist Episcopal Church.[45]

Asbury felt the greatest threat to Methodism's survival was the allure of respectability. "Too often men of gifts and learning," Asbury wrote, "intend to set themselves for sale."[46] With their wealth and the comforts of life, urban churches could "settle themselves to purchase ministers." Thus, the better-trained, dynamic preachers would remain in the cities where the pay was greater; the rural circuits and churches ended up with poorly trained preachers. Left unchecked, this economic temptation would inevitably result in two classes of preachers. It was a constant source of spiritual anguish for Asbury and was a significant factor in his refusal to allow preachers to appeal their appointments.

In his view, a calling to the preaching ministry was first and foremost a call to humble service. Preachers were expected to go willingly wherever needed, among whoever needed them, no matter how poor, rugged, or difficult. Whether Asbury expected too much at this point is a matter of debate, but his paradigm was that of the preacher as servant to all.

Embracing Humanity

The incarnational principle of embracing humanity means the full identification with and participation in the life of those in the leader's care (Phil. 2:7-8). Incarnational leaders adopt what Henri Nouwen calls the posture of downward mobility,[47] choosing to live among the people, showing love, and taking them seriously. Embracing humanity means being vulnerable in relationships, finding appropriate ways to connect and relate to the others, and learning from their perspective.

Asbury's life exemplified his belief that "our spiritual children should be in our hearts, to live and die with them…willing to suffer affliction with them."[48] He had cast his lot with the Americans by refusing to return to England with all the other preachers during the War. In a clear break from Wesley's rule, Asbury declined his appointment as General Superintendent unless elected by the preachers because he knew they would ultimately follow whomever they chose.

By 1778, after war between Britain and America had commenced, all the

English preachers had been recalled by Wesley and returned to England. Asbury refused to go. He wrote, "I can by no means agree to leave such a field for gathering souls to Christ as we have in America. Therefore, I am determined by the grace of God not to leave them, let the consequence be what it may." [49] He had cast his lot with the Americans.

Asbury traveled throughout the conferences and circuits more than any other political or religious leader of his day. Asbury had stayed in more people's homes than any other American before the Civil War. A letter publicly addressed to him simply as "Bishop Asbury, America," would soon end up in his hands. [50] In all likelihood, more people in post-Revolutionary America had seen him face-to-face than Washington, Jefferson, or Adams. Because of his constant travel, Asbury had his finger on the pulse of American culture like few other leaders in the country. He had an intimate understanding of the needs and lives of the people, and his "dogged determinism of blood, sweat, and perseverance was truly American anti-aristocracy, long before Lincoln split rails." [51] Bishop Joshua Soule thought Asbury might be "ranked among the most accurate observer[s] of human nature." [52]

Ordinary Methodists approached him as their spiritual father, and he reciprocated. Everywhere he went people would seek him out for counsel. Often fatigued from difficult travel or illness, he would patiently listen, even late into the night. Darius Salter has noted how "Asbury modeled pastoral care via camaraderie to the extent that few have ever practiced it. Asbury ate and slept with his flock, a commune that covered all of the United States." [53] He exuded deep affection, gentle intimacy, and a sweet disposition in his relationships with others, even his critics. He had a grasp on the needs of each congregation where he preached and was the consummate lifelong student of his flock.

Asbury encouraged popular expressions of worship. He championed the use of exhortation, extemporaneous prayer, and the participation of the laity. Although he initially wore the vestments and followed the liturgy of British Methodism, he soon reverted to the simple and modest dress and worship more suitable to an egalitarian, populist American setting, a act which endeared him all the more to the people.

In the revolutionary climate of post-Revolutionary America, thousands of local and traveling preachers and lay members refused to submit to the leadership of John Wesley, a man whom they had never seen. This fact was unmistakably affirmed in the refusal of the conferences to ordain Richard Whatcoat as bishop or to extend to Thomas Coke the same powers of stationing preachers that they did to Asbury. Whatcoat and Coke were both Englishmen sent by Wesley to assist in the work, Coke having been appointed by Wesley as a bishop to co-lead with Asbury. In contrast to Asbury, Coke and the other English preachers spent a great deal of their time in the large cities of the eastern American seaboard or traveling back to England. Asbury, on the other hand, was constantly seen among the churches and never once returned to England.

If Asbury wielded authority as a king, as some of his fiercer critics charged, he did not do so from above or beyond the people, but from within and among them. Methodists trusted Asbury because of his personal example, his sacrifice on their behalf, his unparalleled knowledge of the people and the nation, and his judgment in difficult circumstances. Asbury, they believed, simply "understood the church as a whole better than anyone."[54]

Humility

Humility is the voluntary abandonment of ego, self-agenda, and the claim to power, rights, or privilege (Phil. 2:8). Asbury had his critics and his flaws, but he was never accused of strutting, something difficult to do "when one lives almost entirely outside of all normal parameters for comfort and prosperity."[55] Asbury viewed the privilege of his office in ironic terms, saying, "I am a bishop and a beggar."[56] Like Wesley, Asbury's critics also compared him the pope. In response, Asbury answered,

> For myself, I pity those who cannot distinguish between a pope of Rome and an old, worn man of about sixty years, who has the *power given him* of riding five thousand miles a year, at a salary of eighty dollars, through summer's heat and winter's cold, traveling in all weather, preaching in all places; his best covering from rain often but a blanket; the surest sharpener of his wit, hunger – from fasts, voluntary and involuntary; his best fare, for six months of the twelve, course kindness; and his reward, suspicion, envy, and murmuring all the year round.[57]

Asbury lamented in a letter that the "love of shining in dress and talents appears to be too prevalent. O my dear child, keep humble, watchful, simple, and walk with God, that you may live as well as preach the very spirit and practice of the Gospel."[58] Notably, Asbury has little positive to say about the personal status of the office of bishop. There is a noticeable lack of preoccupation in his writings with title, position, or a desire for power. He frequently laments the loneliness and turmoil the office inherently involved. Asbury saw himself as anything but a privileged pontiff:

> I have only to say I sit on a joyless height, a pinacle [sic] of power, too high to sit secure and unenvied, too high to sit secure without divine aid. My bodily and mental powers fail. I have a charge too great for many men with minds like mine.[59]

Six years earlier, despondent over criticism and illness, he resolved to resign. "I am about to come down from a joyless height," he wrote, "and stand upon the floor with my brethren."[60] The General Conference convinced Asbury to continue.

His humility emerges in stark relief when compared to Thomas Coke, his original colleague in the episcopacy. The American church had refused to grant Coke any real measure of episcopal authority, due in part to his frequent and extended absences from the continent. In one of three letters to the Conferences in which he expressed disappointment at not being allowed the power of a bishop, Coke complained that "to spend my life in America for nothing but to merely preach, would be to sacrifice so much of my usefulness, that it could not be agreeable to the will of God" (3:338). The conference responded to Coke that in the event of Asbury's death, they would not invest another man with the same power. Asbury, they wrote,

> had been with us from the beginning; he is the proper father under God of us, his spiritual children, and in every instance he has conducted himself as such in adversity and prosperity – in fullness and want; he knew us when we were scarcely a people, and he has traveled on with us through all our difficulties and dangers without ever flinching.[61]

James Lee describes Asbury as "free from jealousy, bent on making the most of his own capacities and those of his associates and subordinates[62]...the purity and sincerity of his piety were evident to all; he carried about him the weighty influence of perfect consecration."[63] Coke demanded his rights as a prelude to his service, whereas Asbury had earned his authority because of his service.[64] With Asbury as their model, Methodists had little tolerance for pretention, pride, and self-posturing, however well intentioned the motive.

Obedience

Obedience is the final posture of imitating Christ, who "became obedient to death—even death on a cross " (Phil. 2:8). Leaders who embrace obedience place themselves readily at the disposal of another in order to accomplish the other's will. In Asbury's mind, sanctification meant a complete yielding out of love to the call of God and a full, willing obedience to go where God led, no matter how hard the circumstance. Sanctification meant active spiritual engagement.

Asbury saw the Wesleyan system of "the disciplined life of devotion, study, and service" as an essential means of grace for living the sanctified and Spirit-filled life.[65] Prayer, in particular, was a daily habit. "My desire is that prayer should mix with every thought, with every wish, with every word, and with every action," Asbury wrote, "that all might ascend as a holy, acceptable sacrifice to God."[66] Nicholas Snethan, a traveling companion of Asbury, said, "It is difficult to conceive how any man could more measure up to that precept 'pray without ceasing.'"[67]

For Asbury, the Christian life meant having "the mind which was in Christ Jesus, in a victory over sin, and a conformity to the will of God; in love, joy, peace, long-suffering, gentleness, goodness, faith, meekness, and temperance; in all the amiable virtues which centre [sic] in the moral character of Christ."[68] In his commitment to the Methodist discipline, Asbury molded his life around a whole-hearted pursuit of obedience in holiness and sanctification. This was his ultimate goal for himself, for his preachers, and for the Methodist movement.[69]

Holy Leaders for a Holy Church

No other model in contemporary leadership more accurately describes Francis Asbury's view and practice of leadership than the mimetic model. Leaders who imitate Christ embrace a life of sacrifice, suffering, humility, submission, and servanthood so that others may be redeemed and transformed. The temptation of all leaders is to emulate the world's value system of seeking honor, privilege, rights, or glory for oneself. In contrast, the imitation of Christ was the defining paradigm for Asbury's leadership.

Asbury's understanding of scriptural holiness and purity of heart was the center of his leadership. He was thoroughly Wesleyan in his optimistic conviction that Spirit-filled life was really possible. By the grace of God, he truly *could* imitate Christ as an apostolic leader. This conviction formed Asbury's character, guided his thinking, inspired his actions, and allowed him to be a selfless vessel of significant personal power at a crucial time in American and religious history.

David McKenna has called for renewed vigor in Wesleyan leadership in the 21st Century where a new awakening is on the horizon, one in which Wesleyans will again have the opportunity to play a significant role.[70] As Wesleyans, our convictions, heritage, and theology bring something vital to the task of contemporary leadership. The challenge to reclaim biblical holiness as the "pervasive principle"[71] of leadership, and the Spirit-filled life as the chief qualification for leaders offers a resounding optimistic solution to the leadership crises caused by self-interest and a lack of character. Francis Asbury is a model of such a leader.

Reflecting on church leadership, Asbury once commented, "[I]f the modern bishops were all as the ancient ones, all would be right."[72] Less than nine decades after President Coolidge's recognition of Francis Asbury, religious historian John Wigger saw in the bronze statue there in Washington, DC, a scathing rebuke:

> Despite their praise for Asbury on that perfect October day [in 1924], none of the monument builders [meaning Methodist leaders] wanted to live as he did. Consequently, they chose to preserve only a shadow of Asbury's life. By the 1920s, the leadership of mainstream Methodism had crossed a great chasm, leaving Asbury, frozen in bronze, on the other side.[73]

Today, the Church is in great need of leaders who exemplify with their heart, mind, soul, and strength a kenotic, Christ-centered model of biblical, holy leadership. Where will we look to find our models? Who will be our examples? Maybe we can reach back across the chasm of culture and time and once again look to Francis Asbury.

Bryan R. Easley, PhD, is the Dean of Online Education at Oklahoma Wesleyan University, an adjunct professor for Oklahoma Wesleyan and Nazarene Bible College, and an ordained elder in the Church of the Nazarene.

Bibliography

Andrews, Dee. *The Methodists and Revolutionary America, 1760-1800*. Princeton: Princeton University Press, 2000.

Asbury, Francis. *The Journal and Letters of Francis Asbury*. E. Clark, J. Potts, and J. Payton, eds. Nashville: Abingdon Press, 1958.

Bangs, Nathan. *About a History of the Methodist Episcopal Church*. 1839.

Bekker, Corné, and Bruce Winston. "Empty to lead: Towards a model of mimetic Christological leadership." In I*ntegrating Spirituality and Organizational Leadership*, edited by Sengupta, S. Singh. New Delhi, India: MacMillian Advanced Research Series, 2009.

British Methodism. *Minutes of the Methodist conferences, From the first, held in London, by the late Reverend John Wesley A.M. in the year 1744*. London, England: John Mason, 1862.

Carroll, Henry K. *The Francis Asbury Centenary Volume: The Makers and Making of American Methodism*. New York: The Methodist Book Concern, 1916.

Duewel, Wesley. *Heroes of the Holy Life: Biographies of Fully Devoted Followers of Christ*. Grand Rapids: Zondervan, 2002.

Elliot, Emory. "The dove and serpent: The clergy in the American Revolution," *American Quarterly*, 31 (1979).

Ellis, J. *Founding Brothers*. New York: Random House, 2000.

Fink, Roger, and Rodney Stark. "How the upstarts won America: 1776-1850." *Journal for the Scientific Study of Religion*, 28, no. 1 (1989): 31.

Gossett, Rosemart. *Francis Asbury: Portrait of the Man in His Journal*. Thesis, University of Texas Arlington, 1987.

Hatch, Nathan. *The Democratization of American Christianity*. New Haven, CT: Yale, 1989.

Hatch, Nathan. "The Christian Movement and the Demand for a Theology of the People," *The Journal of American History*, 67, no. 3 (1980): 546.

Hatch, Nathan, and Wigger, John. *Methodism and the Shaping of American Culture*. Nashville: Kingswood Books, 2001.

Lee, James, N. Luccock, and J. Dixon. *The Illustrated History of Methodism*. New York: The Methodist Magazine Publishing Co, 1900), p. 197.

Mathews, D. "The Second Great Awakening as an organizing process, 1780-1830." *American Quarterly*, 21, no. 1 (1969): 23-43.

McKenna, David. *Wesleyan Leadership in Troubled Times*. Kansas City: Beacon Hill Press, 2002.

Morrill, M. T. A *History of the Christian Denomination in America: 1794-1911*. Dayton: Christian Publishing Association, 1912.

Neely, Thomas. *The Evolution of Episcopacy and Organic Methodism*. New York: Philips and Hunt, 1888.

Noll, Mark. "Methodism Unbound." *Reviews in American History*, 29 (2001): 192-197.

_. *America's God: From Jonathan Edwards to Abraham Lincoln*. Oxford: Oxford University, 2002.

Nouwen, Henri. *In the Name of Jesus: Reflections on Christian Leadership*. New York:

Crossroads Publishing, 1989.

Peck, George. *Sketches and Incidents; or, A Budget from the Saddlebags of a Superannuated Itinerant.* Salem, OH: Schmul, 1988.

Snethen, Nicholas. *A Discourse on the Death of the Rev. Francis Asbury, Late Bishop of the Methodist Episcopal Church.* Baltimore: B. Edes, 1816. Available digitally at https://goo.gl/5uS6hV

Strawbridge, Jennifer. "The Word of the Cross: Mission, Power, and the Theology of Leadership," *Anglican Theological Review,* 91, no. 1 (2009).

Strickland, William. *The Pioneer Bishop: The Life and Times of Francis Asbury.* New York: Carlton & Porter, 1858.

Sweet, William W. *Methodism in American History.* Nashville: Abingdon, 1961.

Wigger, John. *Taking Heaven by Storm.* Chicago: University of Illinois Press, 2001.

_. *American Saint.* Oxford, England: Oxford University, 2009.

_. *Francis Asbury and American Methodism.* In W. Abraham and J. Kirby, eds., *The Oxford Handbook of Methodist Studies* (pp. 51-66). Oxford: Oxford University Press, 2009.

Chapter 15 Notes

[1] Carroll, *The Francis Asbury Centenary*

[2] C. Coolidge, "Address at the Unveiling of the Equestrian Statue of Bishop Francis Asbury, Washington, DC." The American Presidency Project document archives, 1916. Accessed Oct. 2010. http://www.presidency.ucsb.edu/ws/index.php?pid=24170.

[3] Ibid.

[4] Gossett, *Francis Asbury*; Duewel, *Heroes of the Holy Life.*

[5] Peck, *Sketches and Incidents,* 36.

[6] British Methodism

[7] Bangs, *About a History*; Carroll, *The Francis Asbury Centenary Volume*; Peck, *Sketches and Incidents.*

[8] Sweet, *Methodism in American History*; Mathews, "The Second Great Awakening"; Hatch, *The Democratization of American Christianity*; Noll, "Methodism Unbound"; Hatch and Wigger, *Methodism and the Shaping,* 26

[9] Hatch and Wigger, *Methodism and the Shaping*; Noll, *America's God.*

[10] Fink and Stark, "How the upstarts won America".

[11] Ibid; Noll contends "the dramatic rise of the Methodists under his leadership was not only the most remarkable instance of religious expansion but also one of the most significant social developments of any kind in American history."

[12] Hatch and Wigger, *Methodism,* 26.

[13] Mathews, "The Second Great Awakening," 36.

[14] Ibid, 43.

[15] Hatch, *Democratization,* 81; Wigger, *Taking Heaven by Storm.*

[16] Elliot, "The dove and serpent"

[17] Hatch, *Democratization*; Hatch and Wigger, *Methodism*; Eliot, "The dove and serpent"

[18] Nathan Hatch, "The Christian Movement"

[19] Hatch, *Democratization,* 81.

[20] Ellis, *Founding Brothers,* 7; Extreme Jeffersonian Republicans of the late 1700s saw the Congress and the Constitution as threats to the libertarian independence for which the revo-

lution had been fought. Staunchly opposed to the notion of a strong federal government, they railed against any sort of centralized, authoritative structure. Consequently, democratic republicanism in America was hardly the fixed, static, and self-evident it appears to be from a modern perspective. For civic and ecclesial structures alike, democracy was still very much an experiment in its infancy

[21] Andrews, *The Methodists*.

[22] Ibid, 195.

[23] Lee, *A Short History of the Methodists in the United States of America*; Bangs, *About a History*; Richey, *Early American Methodism*; Norwood, *The Story of American Methodism*; Sweet, *Methodism in American History*; Wigger, *American Saint*; Salter, *America's Bishop*.

[24] Neely, *The Evolution of Episcopacy and Organic Methodism*.

[25] Wigger, *American Saint*; Bangs, *About a History*; Salter, *America's Bishop*; Francis Asbury, *Journals and Letters*.

[26] Hatch, *Democratization*, 11.

[27] Hatch, "The Christian Movement"; Hatch, *Democratization*; Noll, *America's God*.

[28] Nathan Hatch wrote that early Methodism was "white-hot with enthusiasm, confrontational and unrefined in its style, and readily dismissed much of…[John] Wesley's liturgical formality."

[29] Andrews, *The Methodists*; Hatch, *Democratization*; Mathews, "The Second Great Awakening"

[30] The paradox of Methodism is that it was a democratic organization built around and sustained by a highly autocratic leader at its center. Early American Methodism was built on essentially democratic principles and perpetuated by the individual experience of freedom; but all the while willingly submitted itself to a central leadership structure that was anything but democratic. Morrill is correct in noting "it is a little singular that the government was not made more democratic, seeing that the popular civil government had recently been established in America" (*A History*, 88).

[31] Hatch, *Democratization*, 82.

[32] The inability of those early groups that broke away from Methodism to gain any traction beyond their localized region of the country suggests as much. For example, the Republican Methodists led out in 1792 by James O'Kelly, never managed to expand much beyond Virginia, and never did come to have the kind of national impact of the Methodist Episcopal Church.

[33] James Ellis wrote that in the American republic, "character mattered because the fate of the American experience with republican government still required virtuous leaders to survive" (*Founding Brothers*, 47). In spite of our contemporary fascination with leadership practice and principles, we all too often forget that a leader's theological framework and dogma significantly shapes the practice and understanding of leadership.

[34] Asbury, *Journals and Letters*, 3:164; Sept. 12, 1797; letter to Jesse Lee

[35] Andrews, *The Methodists*.

[36] Strawbridge, "The Word of the Cross"

[37] Bekker and Winston, "Empty to lead"; Their mimetic Christological model is based on an interpretation of the hymn as an "alternative and exemplary model of ethical leadership" (p. 3).

[38] Asbury, *Journals and Letters*, 1:456.

[39] Ibid, 2:517.

[40] Asbury, *Journals and Letters*, 1:10, November 21, 1771

[41] Asbury's view of the itinerant system stemmed from a commitment to Methodism's mission of proclaiming Scriptural holiness throughout the land. But it was also significantly shaped by his own experiences as a young circuit rider in England under Wesley.

[42] Ibid, 1:181.

[43] Bekker and Winston, "Empty to lead," 11.

[44] Salter, *America's Bishop*, 263.

[45] Strickland, *The Pioneer Bishop*, 216-17.

[46] Asbury, *Journals and Letters*, 3:475.

[47] Nouwen, *In the Name of Jesus*.

[48] Asbury, *Journals and Letters*, Mar. 27, 1777; 3:475.

[49] Ibid 1:161; Aug. 7, 1775

[50] Yet Asbury's forty years of constant itineration doubtless made him the early American who met (and came back to meet again) more individual citizens than any other figure of his generation (Noll, *Methodism Unbound*, 195).

[51] Ibid, 262.

[52] Soule, *Sermon on the Death of Francis Asbury*

[53] Salter, *America's Bishop*, 168.

[54] Wigger, *American Saint*, 280.

[55] Salter, *America's Bishop*, 98.

[56] Asbury, *Journals and Letters*, 3:62.

[57] Ibid, 2:417.

[58] Strickland, *Pioneer Bishop*, 244

[59] Asbury, *Journals and Letters*, 3:356.

[60] Ibid, 3:182.

[61] Salter, *America's Bishop*, 241.

[62] Asbury was not threatened by other leaders around him. He was not as good a preacher as many others, but he constantly had better preachers traveling with him and sharing the spotlight with him (Wigger, *Saint*, 285). Asbury had a "tolerance for strong-willed colleagues" Lee, McKendree, and Coke.

[63] Lee, Luccock, and Dixon, *The Illustrated History of Methodism*, 197.

[64] Wigger, *American Saint*, 342.

[65] Salter, *America's Bishop*, 153.

[66] Asbury, *Journals and Letters*, 1:290; September 30, 1778

[67] Snethen, *Discourse*, 14.

[68] Asbury, *Journals and Letters*, 3:571.

[69] Understanding Asbury's life and leadership begins "with an appreciation for his lasting commitment to the Wesleyan standards of piety and discipline" (Wigger, 37). More importantly, Asbury was committed not just to the Methodist discipline but to the theology behind it (Salter). Asbury believed that in carrying out the office of bishop the way he did, he was being faithful to the primitive vision of the apostolic office and to his own calling to serve in America.

[70] McKenna, *Wesleyan Leadership in Troubled Times*.

[71] Ibid, 12.

[72] Strickland, *Pioneer Bishop*, 478.

[73] Wigger, *American Saint*, 414.

16
Wesleyan Pragmatism in Leadership

Thomas Tumblin

Wesley learned leadership models from his predecessors and contemporaries. The evidence he saw of transformed lives which enabled people to love God and others formed the foundation of his leadership. Wesley's leadership genius was found in the discipline of spiritual and corporate life, especially as it was lived out through various structures. However, Wesleyan leadership was far more driven by immediate pragmatic concerns of pastoral life than any fundamental commitment to a particular model. So, too, today, a good dose of Wesleyan pragmatism enables leaders to be innovative and adaptive to current events and needs of the community.

JOHN WESLEY BEGINS his published journal: "It was in pursuance of an advice given by Bishop Taylor, in his *Rules for Holy Living and Dying*, that about fifteen years ago I began to take a more exact account."[1] This entrée into Wesley's ministry log encapsulates a common motif in his life. He mastered the art of drawing from both classical and contemporary wisdom to develop models for his leadership. The Holy Club, for example, emulated the religious societies of that era, e.g. Anthony Horneck's gathering which began around 1676. There were also clear influences from the Moravians as the Oxford group worked out their salvation individually and corporately.

Wesley emulated wisdom from a variety of spheres as he multiplied bands, classes and societies across England and beyond.[2] In doing so, he applied their principles to fit the particular challenges of each context. The writings of Jeremy Taylor, William Law and Thomas à Kempis became formational for Methodist leaders just as they had shaped Wesley. Methodist preachers were expected to ground themselves in Wesley's *Explanatory Notes on the Old and New Testament*, along with his *Standard Sermons*. They were to grow in holiness via the means of grace while claiming souls "from the wrath to come," all the while expanding their learning. Wesley held for himself, and for those who joined him, a high expectation that leaders be grounded in the wisdom of their spiritual predecessors. While Scripture was primary, he advocated for engagement with classical philosophers, scientists and cultural critics. He makes clear that broad study deepens clergy effectiveness.

Qualities of a Wesleyan Leader

Reading and study were intended to sharpen critical traits in the awakened soul. The regenerative work of the Spirit at the new birth initiated a chain reaction of holiness. That work of grace sparked renewal of the imago Dei personally and enlivened the love of neighbor corporately. The very character of the Methodist believer transformed. The qualities of righteousness were nurtured in the communal incubators of the class meeting and bands, allowing leaders of the movement to emerge. Steve Harper helpfully summarizes the basic traits of a Methodist in his *Five Marks of a Methodist*. This distillation of Wesley's "The Character of a Methodist" identifies the qualities of loving God, rejoicing in God, being thankful, praying constantly and loving others.[3] For Wesley, they are character traits common to all Christ followers. Methodists embrace those traits as part of the Church Universal. They were to be faithful Christians first.

As we consider what Wesleyan leadership is, based on Wesley's own writings, we start at spiritual character. Wesley never deviated from the full salvation of every true Methodist. The experience and expectations of the Christian faith are applied to Methodists as part of the larger Christian tradition. To be in Christ and growing in that faith by grace yields the dispositions of loving God and neighbor. There is a deepening joy in the gift of God's sanctifying work in the believer that results in overflowing gratitude and intimate communion. Wesley's "way of salvation" pictures an interplay of grace upon grace that woos, convicts, redeems and transforms the individual toward entire sanctification.[4]

To lead as a Wesleyan assumes ongoing formation by God's grace. Christian character is being worked out in the leader as she or he is maturing by grace. Devotion, gratitude, joy, prayer and service mark the one who seeks to embody Wesley's model. If the leader is not being continuously formed by grace, attentive to God's Spirit at work in and through the person, the leader is simply not a Wesleyan leader.

In his 1756 "An Address to the Clergy," Wesley identifies other essential qualities. Pastoral leaders needed to be naturally gifted with "sound judgment", "readiness of thought", and "good memory." To those natural abilities would be added acquired knowledge of the stewardship entrusted to them as they study the Scriptures, original biblical languages, history, sciences, logic, early Church Fathers, the world, common sense and good behavior.[5]

A commitment to spiritual formation was not enough for Wesley. He expected those leading the movement to have significant natural abilities and education. As "shepherds of souls," their learning plan was to include a deep understanding of Scripture, Christian tradition, arts, sciences, culture and decorum. One could argue that training in the Bible and the Christian traditions is critical for all Christian leaders. At the very least the Wesleyan Christian leader systematically studies and

> *"If the leader is not being continuously formed by grace,*
> *attentive to God's Spirit at work in and through the person,*
> *the leader is simply not a Wesleyan leader"*

applies the Word daily. She or he certainly grasps the seriousness of what has been entrusted, the people and mission with whom the leader relates. He or she also understands that learning is lifelong. Whether degreed or not, the leader is educated. That education includes being wise to the world and culture as well as to the arts and sciences. There is relational intelligence as well as "book learning."

Discipline of a Wesleyan Leader

The overarching guidelines for a disciplined life were Wesley's General Rules: do no harm, go good, and attend to the ordinances of God.[6] The bands, classes and societies were vehicles for forming this dispostion in every Methodist. Kenneth Collins notes that in 1743 Wesley removed several from the Societies because "they flouted the rules of the United Societies by habitual Sabbath-breaking, drunkenness, spouse abuse, habitual lying, speaking evil, and the like."[7] As believers showed leadership gifts in the Society, the leader would mentor them into the new role. For example, persons called to preach were apprenticed by the assistant. They often spent considerable time together on the preaching circuit as the elder would critique and encourage the novice. This was a normal part of the examination of preachers.

Any Methodist clergy person today will recall the moment of responding to "Wesley's Historical Questions" as part of the ordination process. For some, this entailed standing before a crowd of thousands as the bishop read the questions and the ordination class answered. Those questions took the form of statements and first appear in the Minutes for the June 1744 Conference held at the Foundry. Rather than qualities per se, these statements were more about discipline. The twelve "Rules of an Assistant" admonished:

> Never be triflingly employed. Be serious. Touch no woman. Believe evil of no one. Speak evil of no one. Tell everyone what you think wrong in him. Do nothing *as a gentleman* [as one privileged vs. as a servant of all]. Be ashamed of nothing but sin. Take no money of anyone. Contract no debt without my knowledge. Be punctual; do everything exactly at the time. Act in all things, not according to your own will, but 'as a son in the gospel.'[8]

For the United Methodists, the historical questions to pastors in full connection focus on growing perfect in the love of Christ and being fully committed to the denomination's rules, doctrine and polity. Caring for the children, visiting house-to-house and modeling fasting and abstinence are the pastoral admonitions. Avoiding moonlighting, embarrassing debt and wasting time round out the expectations.[9]

The very design of Wesley's societies, with their classes and bands, was to bring accountability in the form of holy conferencing. Each soul was to be examined on a weekly basis. As these societies multiplied, Wesley knew another layer of accountability would be required. The ministers, assistants, stewards and leaders of the various groups would need direction and a common understanding of their life together. As an example, to the twelve rules for assistants listed above, the Disciplinary Minutes of 1749 adds, "Take no step toward marriage without first acquainting us."[10] Evidently, to be under Methodist authority included seeking endorsement of one's change in marital status.[11]

Given the daily routine expected of assistants and helpers, the Large Minutes of 1753-63 summarize the measure of individual effectiveness. They were to have their personal devotions 4:00-5:00 a.m. and 5:00-6:00 p.m. Their mornings were to be spent reading and studying selections from the Christian Library.[12] The inquiry about their formational practice, "Do you use all the means of grace yourself, and enforce the use of them on all persons?", is followed by three and a half pages of how to do so. Lest other segments of their day be wasted, the Large Minutes suggest that no more than one hour should be spent in conversation with anyone. [13]

"A desire to flee from the wrath to come, to be saved from their sins,"[14] was the sole motivation required to become a Methodist. One's giftedness and education required the focus of discipline. On the individual level, daily routines of formation, study and time management were indicators of one's seriousness. Whether a coal miner or a lay preacher, the general rules mandated spiritual attentiveness. There was also an expectation on how one stewards one's assets.

In his sermon "The Use of Money," Wesley teaches Methodists to "gain all you can," "save all you can," and "give all you can."[15] Wesley saw the predictable impact of preaching the gospel to the marginalized. For those who embraced it, and the accountability by which he contextualized it, the common pattern was to rise out of poverty into the middle class. One of his greatest fears was the spiritual wandering of people who depended on their new economic wellbeing (relatively) more than their faith in God. To help avoid that temptation, Methodists were encouraged to support the poor in their weekly class meetings. The more committed would hold each other accountable on how they spent their money. Wesley modeled frugality himself, living on about 30 pounds sterling annually. Charles Edward White notes that one year Wesley made 1400 pounds but gave all but thirty of it away.[16] Many believe Wesley earned over $1 million in today's value while maintaining a modest, disciplined lifestyle that allowed him to be exceptionally generous.

Organizing Like a Wesleyan

We have acknowledged that Wesley borrowed from the wisdom of his day to renew the Church of England. From the Holy Club forward, he sought to evangelize and disciple believers in scriptural holiness. His brother Charles, while in Oxford, initiated the first gathering when he asked John for advice. John came to campus to meet with John and a few men personally. Soon, their group multiplied in various colleges. This campus ministry began to gain momentum and Oxford Methodism was born. Their pattern was similar to the Society for Promoting Christian Knowledge, of which John and his father Samuel were members.[17]

When the movement extended beyond Oxford and into the fields, the revival necessitated more complex structures. Using the precedents of Oxford Methodism and Moravian practices, Wesley established bands for those wanting to go deeper in holiness and for those who were struggling with the faith. Classes were formed with lay leaders calling participants to salvation and growth in grace. Stewards were appointed to care for fiscal concerns while group leaders cared for spiritual concerns. Trustees were appointed to care for the preaching houses. When there were not enough Anglican clergy to do the soul care, Lay Preachers were accepted as necessary stand-ins. The multiplying of societies, collections of classes, required the creation of "circuits" or "rounds." From 1744 onward, conferences were held, quarterly at first, to coordinate the doctrinal and disciplinary life of the Methodists.[18]

As Methodism spread to Ireland, the American colonies and beyond, Wesley pressed for loyalty to the Church of England. He died an Anglican and resisted efforts by some of his preachers to create a separate denomination. He acquiesced in the case of America, in part due to the tensions of "The Rebellion," to ordain Coke, Whatcoat and Vasey and to send them to oversee the American Methodists with Asbury's help.[19]

Each level of complexity that Wesley faced caused him, in consultation with other Methodists, to adapt to the circumstances. The proliferation of Oxford groups led him to adapt the society models. The rapid growth resulting from the Methodist revival outstripped the number of Anglican clergy willing to shepherd the flock, so Wesley (reluctantly, at first) embraced lay preachers. The need for preaching houses, and how to pay for them, gave rise to classes, stewards and trustees. The spread of the societies required conferences for gathering leaders for doctrinal and disciplinary alignment. The virility of Methodism in America forced him to adapt once again in the ordination of elders and superintendents. At each turn, Wesley sought to borrow from best practices and to adjust them for the new challenges.[20]

Always at the heart of these organizational shifts was Wesley's passion for evangelism and scriptural holiness. He writes in 1781, about ten years before his death, "We all aim at one point...to spread true religion through London, Dublin, Edinburgh, and, as we are able, through the three Kingdoms; that truly rational religion…namely, the love of God and our neighbor.…"[21] The movement became an enterprise built on the same mission: holiness of heart and life.

What Makes a Leader Wesleyan?

How does John Wesley translate into the twenty-first century? At the very least, a leader is Wesleyan in attending to the qualities and disciplines entrusted to him or her. There is a progressively rich journey in the means of grace that opens the leader to the Spirit's handiwork. Individually and corporately, the leader practices the institutional (established by Christ; i.e., baptism and Eucharist) and prudential (works of mercy) means of grace. The Wesleyan leader positions formatively by practicing prayer; reading, studying and meditating on Scripture; regularly celebrating Eucharist; fasting and Christian conferencing—encouraging and holding one another accountable for growth in inward and outward holiness.[22] The Wesleyan leader will also be prudent in living out the General Rules mentioned above, also known as the prudential means of grace. The leader will seek to stand against social and systemic harms and to do well in the lives of his or her family, the marginalized and other believers. Wesley called Methodists to care for the sick[23] and imprisoned, confront social injustices, and provide for the flourishing of all segments of culture. The Foundry in London, a preaching house that became a sort of headquarters for Wesley "included a school for girls, a home for widows, a food bank, a clothing store, and a literacy program as well as the full complement of preaching, worship, and small-group expressions."[24] Fulfilling General Rule #3 meant that Methodists complete the circle of grace by practicing the ordinances of God, i.e. works of piety, otherwise known as the instituted means of grace.

The Wesleyan leader will advocate for systems and structures that encourage and hold accountable those within his or her sphere of influence. While Methodists were placed in bands, classes and societies for spiritual formation, today's Wesleyan leader will seek ways not only to foster growth in faith, but maturation as a person as well. If God's grace is at work in every human being, then one is entrusted with the stewardship of each person's gifts and abilities. The Wesleyan leader creates opportunity for learning and service. Persons are given space for developing relationally and culturally in ways that shape character.

The Wesleyan leader also stewards his or her time, relationships and assets. There may not be a one-hour limit on conversations, but there will be an avoidance of frivolous behavior. Relationships will be means of grace as well as emotional and functional in nature. Income and property will be "held in trust"—in submission to God and a few accountability partners rather than hoarded as the leader practices generosity. One's life will be marked as a journey in holiness, both inward and outward, both individual and communal. Our neighbors and fellow citizens will be able to recognize the difference our faith is making in the world.

Given the vision of renewing a lapsing Church of England, Wesley's "little church within the larger church" (*ecclesiola* in *ecclesia*) strategy sought to bring scriptural holiness alive in England and beyond.[25] He believed an institution could be transformed from within as the Methodists returned to first century Christian practices. The Church could become redemptive again, awakened from its spiritual slumber. This re-commitment to basic practices was a key catalyst for the Great Awakening in England during the Eighteenth Century. In the same way, Wesleyan leaders today can be forces of renewal via a return to the basics of an institution's original mission, often in catalytic groups within the institution.

Modeling

First, organizations can become "redemptive" again as courageous leaders speak into dysfunction and model the original intent of the institution. As often happens, there may need to be momentum from outside of the system to assist in the transformation. Nonetheless, enterprises can be rejuvenated from within as shrewd coalitions model the way.[26] The Wesleyan leader understands organizing as a means toward the end of the flow of God's grace in the lives of the enterprise. The goal is the "saving of souls," not beautiful organizational charts. In parachurch and marketplace contexts, the end may be less obvious, but it is the goal nonetheless. How do we align structures that facilitate the permeation of God's grace throughout organizations? How does that grace foster growth in holiness, or at least, in the case of a non-religious context, moral courage and right practices?

Adaptability

Second, Wesley mastered the art of collective pragmatism. While he was respected early on for his insights, as demonstrated with the Oxford Methodists, he regularly called together peers and subordinates to work through doctrinal and disciplinary issues. From 1744 onward, initially on a quarterly basis, the Methodist leaders would wrestle with optimum approaches to spreading scriptural holiness.

The prime example of this pragmatic and adaptive approach to mission is Wesley's field preaching. He writes in his journal, "What marvel the devil does not love field preaching? Neither do I. I love a commodious room, a soft cushion, a handsome pulpit. But where is my zeal if I do not trample all these under foot in order to save one more soul?"[27] Challenged to adapt from his dependence on access to Anglican pulpits by his colleague George Whitefield, Wesley took to the fields to preach the Gospel. That uncomfortable shift, while shunned by his Anglican colleagues, helped catalyze the spiritual awakening in England.

Commitment beyond the Institution

Third, Wesley understood the need to call for commitment beyond the institutional norm. There were many believers in the Church of England who never joined

Wesley's renewal movement. For those who did sense the need to return to early Christianity, Methodism offered a pathway for going deeper. The Wesleyan structures were spiritual vestibules established in the Anglican house where Church of England members could go deeper while living out that deeper walk in society. Wesley structured opportunities for the believer to mature.

That same system developed pools of leaders for the real challenges of stewarding a burgeoning movement. Lay preachers, stewards, class leaders, area superintendents and, eventually, bishops were nurtured through the system. The rigors of accountability and study produced the army of leaders who carried the movement forward. From the open air preaching as entry point to highest level of responsibility in the Methodist system, Wesley always provided a "next step" for his followers.

Understand and Use the Times

Fourth, as Albert Outler famously popularized the phrase, Wesley modeled the art of being grounded in the Bible while "plundering the Egyptians."[28] Wesley was both *homo unius libri* (man of one book) and voracious student of philosophy, science, literature, history and contemporary events. "Wesley, like most Christian thinkers before him (back to St. Paul), had to grapple with the problem of...how are the treasures of human culture to be related to and appropriated by a credible Christian theology that appreciates godly wisdom wherever found—without forfeiting its own integrity."[29] More recent authors compare this mindset to imitating the tribe of Issachar who understood the times in which they were living and were prepared to meet the challenges. (See 1 Chronicles 12:32.)

Wesley knew that God's wisdom can be mined from any number of sources as long as Scripture serves as the final arbiter. His "Christian Library" was a collection of writers from various generations of saints. Outler notes that Wesley often would quote Greek philosophers as well as noted authors of his day. He certainly tapped the insights of medical wisdom in his "Primitive Physick." The leader who serves in a Wesleyan spirit will be just as attentive to amplifying God's voice using the language that can be quickly appropriated by her listeners as long as those sources align with biblical integrity.

As this volume illustrates, there are multiple perspectives on what makes leadership Wesleyan. Over the years there have been countless Wesleyan personas. Each era has its own generation of those who have emulated and adapted Wesley for the realities they faced. For this generation, may Wesley's commitment to growth in grace, godly pragmatism, pathways for next steps and a willingness to seek holy treasures from any source inspire greater faithfulness.

Thomas F. Tumblin, PhD, is Associate Vice President for Global Initiatives and Professor of Leadership at Asbury Theological Seminary in Wilmore, KY.

Bibliography

Collins, Kenneth. *A Real Christian: The Life of John Wesley.* Nashville: Abingdon Press, 1999.

Collins, Kenneth, and Jason Vickers, editors. *The Sermons of John Wesley: A Collection for the Christian Journey.* Nashville: Abingdon Press, 2013.

Dreyer, Frederick. "A 'Religious Society under Heaven': John Wesley and the Identity of Methodism." *Journal of British Studies* 25, no. 1 (1986): 62-83

Harper, Steve. *Devotional Life in the Wesleyan Tradition.* Nashville: Upper Room Books, 1983.

Maddox, Randy. *Responsible Grace: John Wesley's Practical Theology.* Nashville: Kingswood Books, 1994.

Meyerson, Debra. "Radical Change, The Quiet Way." *Harvard Business Review* (October 200):92.

Outler, Albert. *Theology in the Wesleyan Spirit.* Nashville: Discipleship Resources-Tidings, 1975.

Ritchey, Russell, Kenneth Rowe, and Jean Miller Schmidt. *The Methodist Experience in America: A History.* Nashville: Abingdon Press, 2010.

Tumblin, Thomas. "Wesley's Methods: An Organizational Analysis." *The Asbury Theological Journal* 59, no. 1 (2004): 181-189.

Wesley, John. *The Works of John Wesley,* vol. 18, edited by W. Reginald Ward and Richard P. Heitzenrater. Nashville: Abingdon Press, 1988.

Chapter 16 Notes

[1] Preface to volume one of Wesley's Journal from *The Works of John Wesley*, 121. All citations from Wesley in this chapter are found in this edition of Wesley's *Works* unless otherwise noted.

[2] See Rupert Davies' introduction to *The Works of John Wesley*, vol. 9, The Methodist Societies: History, Nature and Design for more details on the precursors to the Methodist Societies.

[3] In paragraphs 10—16 of "The Character of a Methodist," which Harper positions as subtext to loving others, Wesley delineates a pure heart, doing God's will, keeping God's commandments, etc.

[4] For a discussion of the way (vs. order) of salvation, see the chapter "The Way of Salvation---Grace Upon Grace" in Randy Maddox, *Responsible Grace.*

[5] "An Address to the Clergy," written from London in February 6, 1756, as recorded in Jackson's 1872 edition of Wesley's *Works*, accessed 7/2/15 at http://wesley.nnu.edu/john-wesley/an-address-to-the-clergy/.

[6] *Works*, vol. 9, 70-73.

[7] Collins, *A Real Christian*, 81.

[8] *Works*, vol. 10, 140-41.

[9] The Book of Discipline of the United Methodist Church, 2012, 336.

[10] *Works*, vol. 10, 809.

[11] This particular rule does not appear in the Large Minutes 1753-63.

[12] This collection of devotional classics curated by Wesley and first published in 50 volumes in 1750 can be found at http://wesley.nnu.edu/john-wesley/a-christian-library/.

[13] *Works*, vol. 10, 854-58.

[14] Ibid, vol. 9, 70.

[15] Ibid, vol. 2, 263ff.

[16] Charles Edward White. "About Money - John Wesley" saintluther.blogspot.com, May 29, 2007. Accessed July 3, 2015. http://bit.ly/1TR0Hsi

[17] *Works*, vol. 10, 3.

[18] Ibid, 5-7.

[19] For an intriguing account of the machinations between Wesley and the American Colonies, see Ritchey, Rowe, and Schmidt, especially their chapter "Making Church: 1777-84."

[20] For an organizational behavior perspective on early Methodism, see Tumblin, "Wesley's Methods".

[21] "A Short History of the People Called Methodists," *Works*, vol. 9, 502.

[22] A strong resource for understanding the means of grace is Harper, *Devotional Life in the Wesleyan Tradition*. To understand how Wesley preached the "way of salvation," see Collins and Vickers, *The Sermons of John Wesley*.

[23] Wesley opened a dispensary for the poor in 1746. He also is well known for his *Primitive Physick, or an easy and natural method of curing most diseases* that was published anonymously at first in 1747. See also Christian History Institute. "John Wesley and the 18th Century World." Accessed July 2015. http://bit.ly/1XHfZ47

[24] Harper, Devotional Life, 148.

[25] For a discussion of this identifying mark of Methodism, see Dreyer, "A 'Religious Society under Heaven'. D. Martin Lloyd Jones argues that Martin Luther was the first reformer to use the model. See "Ecclesiola Ecclesia," www.reformedperspectives.org. Accessed July 2015. http://bit.ly/25uzeEi (

[26] For a contemporary example, see Meyerson, "Radical Change, The Quiet Way".

[27] Wesley's Journal, 6/23/1759.

[28] See Outler, Theology in the Wesleyan Spirit, ch. 1.

[29] Ibid, p. 4.

17
A Wesleyan Critique of Political Leadership

Charles Gutenson

While John Wesley was not a politician, he cared deeply about the public life and worked to raise the standard of life for the poor through preaching, education, and organization. Further, Wesley's commitment to Scripture, skepticism toward reason, and skepticism toward democracy can provide critique, even in contemporary political life and expression for those committed to the Christian faith in his company.

WHAT WOULD POLITICAL LEADERSHIP LOOK LIKE if conducted in a way consistent with a Wesleyan perspective? It is an interesting question, given that Wesley was not a "politician," at least not in the common sense of the term.[1] Some have suggested that Wesley avoided being overtly political because he did not want political differences to become an obstacle to his ministry. Wesley admitted of no expertise in politics, once writing: "I am no politician; politics lie quite out of my province. Neither have I any acquaintance, at least no intimacy, with any that bear that character."[2] Nevertheless, Wesley's movement had significant effects on the culture of his day. Since politics rightly understood is about how we live together as social persons, his movement has profound political implications. Given Wesley's reticence to take on the issue directly, our approach will need to be more oblique and inferential than direct and evidential. Therefore, our primary question is what can be gleaned from Wesley's body of work which will help us to draw inferences about the principles and guidelines he would have used in making decisions of a political nature?

A careful perusal of Wesley's work will yield at least four different themes that have to address as we reflect on political leadership from a Wesleyan perspective:

1. The importance of the biblical narratives in helping us to understand human nature as well as to understand the way of living together that pleases God.

2. An affirmation of the doctrine of original sin and a clear sense of the implications it has for human behavior and the human ability to make right judgments.

3. The recognition of the fallen nature of all human faculties, including human reason. Therefore, we have to advance our thinking on Wesleyan political leadership with a healthy degree of skepticism about the ability of human reason to discern the life that pleases God, unless it is aided by God's revelation in Scripture.

4. An understanding of Wesley's skepticism toward democracy. No doubt part of this is connected to his own context and embrace of the British monarchy.[3] While many of us may disagree with Wesley on this point, this should not deny hearing his reasons for being skeptical that democracy will lead us to right judgments about the life that pleases God.

The reader will notice the recurrence of the term "skepticism" in the four themes. At the heart of this skepticism, however, is the juxtaposition of Wesley's understanding of humanity's sin nature with the corresponding antidote found in Scripture. Thus, the narrative of Scripture – especially related to both the consequences of original sin and the potential of redeeming grace in social systems such as politics – is foundational to any leadership than can be even marginally considered Wesleyan. Our skepticism here is rooted, of course, in the ease with which the pursuit of our own self-interest can become the motivating force behind so much of what we do, politically and otherwise. Jacques Ellul captures this well when he writes:

> Christianity imbibes cultures like a sponge. Dominated by Greco-Roman culture, it became territorial and feudal…It then became bourgeois, urban, and argentiferous with the capitalist system. It is now becoming socialist with the diffusion of socialism. It helped to spread Western culture throughout the world when the West was conquering and subjugating the world. Today it is letting itself be permeated by the values of African, Oriental, and American Indian cultures. Always quick to justify itself, it claims to be on the side of the weak. Tomorrow we might have adjustment to Islam as today we have adjustment to Marxism. We now have a rationalist or liberal Christianity as we used to have an Aristotelian or Platonic Christianity in a mockery of being "all things to all men."[4]

Wesley's skepticism is rooted in his understanding of the depravity of fallen human faculties and their consequential inability to make right judgments. He learns this lesson from Scripture, and, as Ellul frames it, from the historical evidence of the ease with which Christianity is subverted. With these reflections as a beginning point, let us explore the implications of the four themes we have identified.

The Importance of Scripture

The first step in developing a Wesleyan perspective on political leadership *is not* to make sure it is right, acceptable, or even useful. The first step is to make sure it is genuinely *Wesleyan*. We must begin with our best attempt to allow Wesley to be Wesley and to hear him on his own terms. Only after we first hear what Wesley has to say can we then make a determination about what of his thoughts we can appropriate for today and what might not apply. If we say there is a *sense* in which political leadership must be Scriptural in order to be Wesleyan, it will have to be full-throated and robust; a sense that seeks to learn rather than to co-opt, one that is guided by Scripture more than it seeks to bend Scripture to *a priori* commitments. In short, while we allow there will be disagreements, a public theology of political leadership must take Scripture seriously if it is to be Wesleyan.

Wesley was wholly committed was the Bible. He unabashedly considered himself *homo unius libri* (a man of one book), an expression he used to affirm the primacy of Scripture for his life. Wesley's application of the phrase ought not be taken as overly narrow, for as my theology professor Laurence Wood likes to say, "Wesley surely read a lot of other books in order to understand that one." Wesley was not the sort of "man of one book" that Aquinas was said to fear: one who blindly and unreflectively followed the words of a particular text. The wide breadth of Wesley's reading makes this clear.

Nor ought we to take Wesley's commitment to being "a man of one book" to mean that he favored a facile application of Scripture to our lives. For example, it is hard to imagine he would look at the Years of Jubilee in the Old Testament and argue that we should follow that practice in our own modern context, simply on the basis of God's commanding Israel to observe such years of debt relief in their own setting. On the other hand, it is going too far in the other direction to suggest we learn nothing from God's command for gracious debt relief of the sort we find in Scripture. Good political leadership that takes Scripture seriously asks *why* God commanded such actions. What underlying social harm was God trying to avoid? What good was God trying to promote? That we might come to different answers to these questions does not negate the importance of asking them.

Wesley's work was immersed in Scripture because he believed that Scripture is important revelation from God. Scripture is God's communication to us about how to restore right relationship with God and about how to live in right relationship with those around us. Political leadership in general and a theology of political leadership in particular are most fundamentally about the nature of relationships that should exist between the members of a given society. A theology of political leadership concerns how we humans are to live out our shared, common life in light of God and God's work. Because Scripture paints pictures of what the life that pleases God looks like, any attempt to provide leadership in the political arena, at least on

Wesleyan terms, should be grounded firmly in what those biblical pictures show.[5] This is not the ending point, but it is the starting point.

The Doctrine of Original Sin

There can be no doubt but that Wesley took the doctrine of original sin to be critically important to understanding both Christianity and human nature.[6] He was clear that he understood original sin *not merely* to be an affirmation that humans have some failings, but rather as a strong statement about the total depravity of human nature. Left to ourselves, our imaginations will conceive only evil, our pride will blind us to our depravity, and that depravity will work its way into every human faculty. In fact, Wesley observes that he comes quite close to Calvin himself in affirming that natural humanity commits only sin and only God does good.[7] In contrast to Calvin, however, it is Wesley's appeal to prevenient grace (the idea that God gives to all grace enough to free their wills to respond to God's active seeking) that allows him to be able to affirm free will and avoid the conclusion that all must be predestined by God.

As in Wesley's day, even now we do not look favorably on those who push us to realize the consequences of our own sinfulness, particularly when the subject is original sin. We much prefer to say that humans are essentially good. We make mistakes, of course, but we are basically good and this leads us to an optimistic view of human nature and its collective work. However, if we follow Wesley's lead and consider humanity as fundamentally fallen and sinful, we end up with a much more pessimistic view of human nature. That pessimism leads us to conclude that, left to their own devices, humans will come to self-serving and flawed conclusions about how we ought to order our shared life together. Rather than developing a view of public and political leadership that trusts our fundamental human intuitions, the doctrine of original sin leads us to be skeptical of those faculties and their deliverances. Wesley will have no part in claims that try to smooth over the depravity of human nature, and he consistently resists attempts to make the fallen nature of humanity seem less severe.

Looking back at the importance of Scripture, it is the fallen nature of humanity and our inherent tendency to be led astray by our sinful natures that contributes to Wesley's strong commitment to Scripture. Human depravity extends to and influences all human faculties. It is this understanding that fuels a healthy skepticism in human reason and in the ability of humans, even when they come together in a democratic fashion, to make right judgments about the way in which shared human life ought to be structured. If sin pervades all of human life, then skepticism regarding the conclusions we draw on our own is the only appropriate response. For example, we do not naturally elevate the interest of others over our own interests, we do not "turn the other cheek," nor do we naturally see the power of the Cross.[8] The way of God's kingdom subverts and often turns upside down our normal power paradigms. And this is why human reason must be supplemented by Scripture if we are to provide political leadership that guides us to the sort of human flourishing God intends for all.

Skepticism Regarding Human Reason

In his sermon *The Case of Human Reason Impartially Considered*, Wesley hews a path between those whom he sees as overvaluing human reason and those whom he sees as undervaluing human reason. I do not suggest that Wesley was an opponent of human reason. In fact, he required his preachers to be familiar with philosophy and showed his own familiarity.[9] What he meant was that the tools of the philosopher, such as the laws of logic, serve as invaluable aids to the apologetic enterprise in that they help us to find the flaws in the arguments of the critics of Christian faith. So, we cannot count Wesley among those who simply decry human reason as untrustworthy or as not useful.

At the same time, though, Wesley readily recognizes the limits of human reason. In the first half of his sermon on reason, Wesley talks about those places wherein human reason can rightly be trusted. In the second half, he shifts his attention to what he thinks reason cannot do. First, reason cannot produce faith. Second, reason

"Wesleyan political leadership must guide people to live together in the way consistent with God's having created us for relationship"

cannot produce hope in humans, particularly hope "in the glory of God" and our participation in it. Third, reason cannot produce the love of God. Finally, reason cannot produce the love of neighbor in us.

So, what have these to do with being skeptical of reason as regards political leadership? For political leadership to be Wesleyan, it must lead us toward a common good, toward a shared life that is consistent with the divine intent. Wesleyan political leadership must guide people to live together in the way consistent with God's having created us for relationship. To human reason, protection of ourselves and our own "kind"[10] is of primary importance, but God intends us to love and to bless even our enemies. To human reason, it makes complete sense to watch out for our own interests, but God intends us to elevate the interest of others over our own interests. In short, the divine picture of what should characterize the life of a society runs counter to the normal power paradigms that human reason affirms. As Wesley reminds us, reason cannot lead us to love God or our neighbors rightly. Yet, love of God and neighbor is the very reason for which God has created us, so a Wesleyan view of political leadership must have these at the very center. Wesley rightly would remain skeptical that the deliverances of human reason, apart from God's revelation, will provide the type of political leadership that could, in any sense, be called

Wesleyan. Wesley summarizes at the end of his sermon: "Let reason do all that reason can: Employ it as far as it will go. But, at the same time, acknowledge it is utterly incapable of giving either faith, or hope, or love; and, consequently, of producing either real virtue, or substantial happiness."[11]

Some might say that we aim too high, expect too much of politics, that it might produce in "real virtue or substantial happiness." Perhaps. But why settle for some watered down version of human life together, some standard lower than God intends for us? As John Howard Yoder writes:

> The calling of the people of God is thus no different from the calling of all humanity. The difference between the human community as a whole and the faith community is a matter of awareness or knowledge or commitment or celebration, but not of ultimate destiny. What believers are called to is no different from what all humanity is called to. That Jesus Christ is Lord is a statement not about my inner piety or my intellect or ideas about the cosmos. Thus the fact that the rest of the world does not yet see or know or acknowledge that destiny to which it is called is not a reason for us to broker some wider or thinner version, some lower common denominator or halfway meeting point, in order to make the world's destination more acceptable or more accessible.[12]

Wesleyan political leadership ought to be focused on the realization of God's intentions for human life together, but we will not "reason those out" apart from our reason being aided by God's revelation.

Skepticism toward Democracy

In light of his view of the fallen nature of human faculties, Wesley saw no reason to think that creating societies in which the majority ruled would overcome our tendency to err in our determination of how we ought to live together. Consider his response to Richard Price's "Observations on the Nature of Civil Liberty," written, interestingly enough, in 1776: "The great share the people have in the government, the less liberty, either civil or religious, does the nation enjoy. Accordingly, there is most liberty of all, civil and religious, under a limited monarchy, there is usually less under aristocracy, and least of all under democracy."[13] He goes on to respond to Price's claim that self-determination is the centerpiece of freedom by observing that "this is the very quintessence of republicanism; but it is a little too barefaced; for, if this is true, how free are all the devils in hell, seeing they are guided by their own will! And what slaves are the angels in heaven, seeing they are guided by the will of another."[14]

Now, let me be clear: I am not suggesting, in offering these quotes, that we ought to embrace his assessment of the relative merits of democracy and monarchy, Wesley was, after all, a citizen of the monarchy and believed this form of human governance was the best imitation of the divine model. However, we should not too quickly dismiss what Wesley is bringing to our attention.

Regarding the nature of human freedom, Wolfhart Pannenberg commented that while he affirmed the reality of the human ability to choose, we should not overlook the fact that, though free, the addict inevitably chooses to return to his drugs.[15] The formal ability to choose is of little value to the person whose choices are ultimately self-destructive and destructive of those around them. In an age where individual liberty and democracy are frequently viewed as the *summum bonum* of political life, this lesson is difficult and conceptually challenging. Pannenberg and Wesley remind us of a critically important point: on our own, fallen humans inevitably use our freedom in ways that run counter to God's intentions for us, and, by implication, in ways that are destructive. For a Wesleyan form of political leadership, the highest value is to love God with our whole beings and to love our neighbors as ourselves. The communal life that God intends for us is not rooted in personal liberty in the sense of being free to do as we please, but rather in the reality of being freed from our fallen human natures so that we can truly love God and neighbor.

Conclusion

We have been created by God to flourish through living together in a particular way that is characterized by loving God wholly and loving our neighbors (and enemies!) as we love ourselves. I have argued, however, that fallen human faculties, driven as they are by self-preservation and self-interest, will not discern the life that pleases God unless aided by the biblical narratives. Consequently, a Christian or Wesleyan form of political leadership will look askance at approaches that require an over-confidence in fallen human faculties, but will always seek to have those faculties aided by careful attention to the biblical narratives, particularly with regard to the ways in which Scripture challenges us to different values—such as other-interest rather than self-interest and the resistance to rather than embrace of violence as a tool.

While space does not allow a rebuttal of every anticipated criticism, there is one in particular that I wish to address. It goes something like this: "Gutenson may or may not be off his rocker in theory, but surely what he proposes could never be made to work in a pluralistic culture like 21st century America." To the extent this criticism means to suggest that one cannot march into the public marketplace of ideas, quote some particular biblical passages, and expect everyone to acquiesce, I agree. While we, as faithful followers of Jesus, must have our political theology formed by God's revelation in Scripture, I readily admit that we cannot expect non-Christians simply to go along. We will have to do our own hard work of examining history and researching a whole host of questions in order to make our case. But, here's the thing—we either believe that the way God instructs us to live together in community is ultimately what best leads to human flourishing, or we do not. If the former, then we can advance our arguments in the public square, nuanced and carefully crafted, with the full confidence that the better we can empower the way of living together communicated to us through Scripture, the better humans will flourish, Christian or not. Of course we must expect opposition, for when it comes to building a case, historical and other data can be read in a variety of ways. We cannot control the others with whom we do life in the public square. So, the question becomes: Will we read the available data through the lens of God's revelation, in the confidence that in so doing, the narratives of Scripture will aid us in making better decisions? Or will we justify setting the narratives aside, choosing rather to read the data through the lens of "common sense," "statecraft," or some other creation of the human imagination? If the political leadership we wish to offer is to have any kinship with Wesley, the answer could not be clearer.

Charles (Chuck) Gutenson, PhD, is a church consultant and former Chief Operating Officer at Sojourners. He previously served for 10 years at Asbury Theological Seminary in Wilmore, KY, most recently as professor of theology and philosophy. He recently partnered with a local church to launch a program aimed to combat some of the most difficult aspects of homelessness.

Chapter 17 Notes

[1] If space allowed, I would argue that this common understanding of the term politician is both inadequate and degenerate, but that will have to await another time.

[2] John Wesley, Free Thoughts on The Present State of Public Affairs, in a letter to a friend dated 1768.

[3] One might consider, for example, Graham Maddox in *Political Writings of John Wesley* (Thoemmes Press), 1998, p. 10. See a similar discussion about the tensions between democracy and monarchy in American Methodism in Bryan Easley, *The Leadership of Francis Asbury*, chapter 15 in this anthology.

[4] Jacques Ellul, *The Subversion of Christianity* (Grand Rapids: Eerdmans), 1986, p. 17-18.

[5] For more detail, see Charles Gutenson, *Christians and the Common Good*, Brazos Press, 2011.

[6] This comes through in more succinct form in Wesley's sermon *On Original Sin* and in more detail in his book *The Doctrine of Original Sin*.

[7] Letter to John Newton, 14 May, 1765.

[8] One thinks of I Corinthians 1:18-25.

[9] John Wesley, "An Address to the Clergy," delivered February 6, 1756. Reprinted in *The Works of John Wesley*, 3d ed., 7 vols. (Grand Rapids, Mich.: Baker, 1996), 6:217-31; cited in Craig and Moreland, 4.

[10] With the term "kind" often being taken very, very narrowly.

[11] Concluding paragraph, see: http://wesley.nnu.edu/john-wesley/the-sermons-of-john-wesley-1872-edition/sermon-70-the-case-of-reason-impartially-considered/

[12] Yoder, John H., "Firstfruits: The Paradigmatic Role of God's People" in *For the Nations*, William B Eerdmans, 1997, 24.

[13] *The Works of the Rev. John Wesley*, vol. 11, p. 105

[14] Ibid.

[15] personal correspondence

18

Institutional Thinking and Living in the Wesleyan Tradition

L. Gregory Jones and Laceye C. Warner

While institutions seem to be falling out of favor in contemporary society, the Wesleyan tradition has long recognized their wisdom and importance. Wesleyan institutions provided means of transformation, organizational longevity, and missional effectiveness through such things as small groups, bands, and societies. This value for institutions is also exemplified in universities and hospitals. Wesleyans must recover and reinforce the value of institutions to reclaim long term missional effectiveness. This calling is not simply for established leaders, but as vision for emerging leaders.

WESLEYAN CHRISTIANS HAVE LONG RECOGNIZED the importance of thinking and living institutionally. In his sermon, "On the Inefficacies of Christianity," John Wesley recognizes the needs of Christians, the Church, and the broader culture of his time and emphasizes the importance of doctrine, discipline, and self-control.[1] However, what sets Wesley apart from other critics was his ability to think and lead institutionally. Wesley wrote tracts, compiled resources, and preached—not a unique formula for leadership—but alongside these more 'typical' practices he also facilitated the establishment of key institutional networks that tended deeply to the practices that he believed communities needed to nurture.

Among these institutional networks – whose mission was "to spread scriptural holiness"[2]—were class and band meetings, the Foundry Society in London, and the Kingswood School. While the networks were established in the early days of the Wesleyan movement, they continued to be vital for Wesleyan Christians in the nineteenth, twentieth and twentieth-first centuries, not only in England but also in the United States and around the world. When examined more closely, healthy and outward looking institutions are key contributors to meaningful and impactful movements within church and society. Today, while institutional skepticism might be all too common, especially among North Americans who have become cynical as a result of institutional failures and bureaucratic inertia, a Wesleyan approach can and should continue to speak to the challenges faced by our institutions.

We begin by outlining a distinction between thinking *about* institutions and *thinking institutionally*. Then, in the central section of the chapter, we use that framework to unpack Wesley's own practices and experiences with thinking institutionally. In our final two sections, we briefly explore how those practices have been carried forth by Wesleyan Christians around the world over the last two centuries, concluding with some reflections for Wesleyan renewal through a revitalization of institutional thinking for the twenty-first century.

Thinking and Living Institutionally

In twenty-first century United States, we love to hate the institutions we need. We grumble about them, malign them as lifeless bureaucracies, and create comic strips and TV shows about their dysfunction. Even if we recognize institutions are necessary—some would say necessary evils—we would rather ignore them than engage them or serve them. We despise institutional leaders as self-serving careerists or as interchangeable bureaucrats.

Yet, we cannot escape institutions, nor should we try. The institutions within which we already live serve as the backgrounds of our lives, giving shape and form to who we are. Political scientist Hugh Heclo argues that institutions enable us to be "mindful in certain ways, exercising a particular form of attentiveness to meaning in the world."[3] Vibrant institutions are crucial to sustaining meaning and purpose in our lives and in the world.

What do we need to overcome this negative perception of institutions? Heclo suggests that the headlines about corruption—clergy sexual abuse, corporate financial misconduct, military torture and the list goes on—give us "performance-based" reasons for wariness.[4] Some institutions are indeed of the worst sort. Some institutional leaders have been careerist bureaucrats who have betrayed the public trust and damaged our common life.

Even more damaging, though, is what Heclo calls our "culture-based" distrust of institutions, observing that "in the modern mental landscape, institutional distrust goes with the territory."[5] This deep distrust of institutions is a "modern impasse." Our romanticized search for personal meaning places institutions in the way of our quests. We become increasingly bitter when we learn that institutions are so powerful we cannot escape them.

One would think Christians, especially Wesleyan Christians, might offer a way beyond the impasse. Christian wisdom illustrates our need for institutions to shape and form us—as well as the vulnerability of institutions and their leaders to corruption. The reality and persistence of sin, including the ability for self-deception, must make us wary of the romantic quest for personal meaning through individualistic personal fulfillment. And our persistent capacity for sin points us back to the significance of institutions, revealing our need for the church to teach and train us, through faithful practices and holy friendships, to unlearn sin and learn holiness.

Unfortunately, many North American Christians have drunk too deeply from the well of romantic individualism and have eaten persistently at the trough of anti-institutionalism. Karl Menninger's question "What Ever Became of Sin?" is as

"we cannot afford any longer to be cynical about or hate institutions. It is time to develop a robust Christian theological imagination for and understanding of them"

relevant today as it was a generation ago.[6] Not that sin has disappeared and we have become virtuous. Rather, we Christians have lost our own vocabulary and become seduced into thinking we can discover our best selves through introspection and self-help manuals. We have pretended that authentic Christianity can occur solely between an individual and God, or, for evangelicals, between the individual and Jesus. Even those Christians who want to overcome individualism turn to community devoid of institutionalization as an alternative. Yet communities and their practices cannot exist for long without institutional form, so those romantic quests are caught in the same impasse.

Perhaps, as Heclo suggests, we suffer from a neglect of "institutional thinking" and fail to appreciate just how and why institutions are crucial to flourishing human lives and thriving communities. Institutional thinking requires an interpretive standpoint of affirmation and trust rather than thinking "about" institutions as an observer or critic. Institutional thinking still requires critical attention to the failures of institutions, but with "respect in depth."[7] Institutions are not only "houses" for faithful practices; caring for institutions—and so thinking and living institutionally—is itself a practice.

Heclo situates this practice in an appropriately longer and larger horizon. He notes, "[I]nstitutional thinking has to do with living committed to the ends for which organization occurs rather than to an organization as such."[8] And Christians should have a clear sense of the end for which we live and move and have our being. We are well-equipped to narrate the vices and virtues that are intrinsic to thinking institutionally.

In this time of cultural turmoil, when economic challenges are troubling even strong institutions, we cannot afford any longer to be cynical about or hate institutions. It is time to develop a robust Christian theological imagination for and understanding of them. Indeed, we need to learn, by God, to understand and love the institutions we need.

Participants in the Wesleyan tradition have wonderfully rich resources on which to draw—resources that go back to John Wesley's own practice and the work of "the people called Methodists" in the eighteenth century.

Methodism as Institution

Institutions are essential to Christian formation. It is not accidental that successful Christian renewal movements attend carefully to the creation and renovation of institutions that enable that formation. Unfortunately, we often discover belatedly just how impoverished Christian life is without vibrant institutions.

The Methodist renewal movement began modestly early in 1739 in Bristol with the inauguration of field preaching by George Whitefield among the coal miners of Kingswood, followed soon thereafter by smaller clusters of people in "class meetings."[9] The field preaching was characteristic of revivalist preachers, but the attentiveness to the need for organizing Christians into class meetings displays Wesley's savvy appreciation of and commitment to institutional thinking.

Although John and Charles Wesley were initially reluctant to follow Whitefield into field preaching, they did so relatively quickly. Open air preaching, often called field preaching (though not necessarily limited to fields), was not illegal, but it was highly irregular, especially among respectable Anglican clergy. Nevertheless, John claimed he had been "so tenacious of every point relating to decency and order that [he] should have thought the saving souls almost a sin if it had not been done in a church."[10]

However, Jesus' Sermon on the Mount—John's text for April 1—provided a persuasive precedent alongside his witnessing Whitefield preach to approximately 30,000 persons.[11] The following afternoon, John "submitted 'to be more vile'" and preached in the open air to 3,000–4,000, by his estimate.[12] During his first month in Bristol, Wesley estimated a total attendance of 47,500 persons at his field preaching, an average of 3,000 per event.[13] Charles was skeptical of the practice, and particularly of the excessive numbers reported by Whitefield and his brother,[14] but his skepticism waned following his reluctant preaching at Moorfields in June of 1739 to a crowd he calculated at 10,000. The large crowd convinced him it was a work of God's will.[15] John, Charles, and Whitefield continued to preach in the open air attracting tremendous crowds, with Whitefield usually attracting the largest. In addition to the "fields," these itinerant preachers and their cohorts addressed crowds in a variety of contexts such as prisons, gallows, graveyards, market squares, mines, as well as an occasional advantageous acoustical spot under a tree.[16]

Despite the staggering numbers reported at such gatherings, in 1744, John cautioned against excessive field preaching as his leadership turned to consolidating the movement and creating a foundation of doctrine and discipline.[17] The aim of John's leadership of the early Methodist renewal movement to "spread scriptural holiness" was not to create a "wildfire," but rather to manage an intentional and steady pace of growth.[18]

John, with Charles, oversaw the organization of the early Methodist movement with intentional connectedness, not merely to one another for mutual support and accountability, but also to the movement's aim to form believers in holiness of heart and life. John consistently urged that authentic spiritual formation could not take place "without society, without living and conversing with [others]."[19]

Class and Band Meetings

John's pamphlet "A Plain Account of the People Called Methodists" addresses questions about the organization and practices of the movement, particularly small group gatherings for spiritual nurture. In response to pleas for guidance and prayer, John facilitated regular gatherings of interested persons. Only one condition was required of those requesting admission: "a desire to flee from the wrath to come, to be saved from their sins."[20] These gatherings resembled religious societies common among the Church of England as well as Pietists and grew into networks of Methodist circuits across Britain.[21] These United Societies, specifically class meetings alongside penitent, select and other bands, provided opportunities for early Methodist lay persons, including women, to assume leadership roles such as class and band leaders, lay assistants, stewards, and sick visitors.[22] More importantly, such small groups provided a context in which most early Methodists experienced spiritual conversions facilitated by consistent practices of piety and mercy. This program of spiritual formation permeated the ecology of early Methodism and provided a frame as it grew into an institution.

The General Rules for the United Societies describe the gatherings as "a company of men [and women] having the form and seeking the power of godliness, united in order to pray together, receive words of exhortation, and to watch over one another in love, that they may help each other to work out their salvation."[23] The one condition for admission remained "a desire to flee from the wrath to come, to be saved from their sins." Continuance in the societies then required a bearing of fruits to that effect facilitated by the following three general rules: (1) by doing no harm, and avoiding evil of every kind; (2) by doing good; and (3) by attending upon the ordinances of God.[24]

While John, Charles, and Whitefield attracted substantial crowds with their field preaching, these venues were less often occasions for spiritual experiences, though they sometimes contributed to an individual's awakening to an ongoing process of conversion.[25] According to Thomas Albin's illuminating study, lay people were more influential than clergy in facilitating key spiritual experiences such as conviction or awakening, new birth, and sanctification.[26] The social environment of the new birth was significantly different from that of the awakenings, with the most frequent social context for early Methodist conversion occurring in solitude, followed by small groups.[27] In Albin's study, most individuals began participating in Methodist societies prior to their experience of the new birth. While more than half received a spiritual experience within the first year, one individual in the study received such an experience after 48 years, creating an average time of two years and four months between initially participating in a society and subsequently receiving a spiritual experience.[28] The institution of the society helped move the participant to spiritual experience.

The institution of societies not only facilitated spiritual experience, but spiritual nurture. Beginning in the earliest decades of the movement, preaching accompanied the creation of religious societies or occurred in areas where religious societies such as bands and class meetings existed. In 1745, the Methodist Conference under John's leadership decided to experiment with preaching wherever opportunities arose without forming societies, or regardless of the presence of societies, to nurture those responding.[29] The results were unequivocal: Christian formation provided by the Methodist small groups organized by John Wesley allowed a significant number of those moved by the revival's preaching to be nurtured and maintained in the faith.[30] When these groups were not accessible, those moved by the preaching were often lost. The experiment ceased in 1748, and the Conference turned its focus to the formation of societies.[31] As these historical examples illumine, institutions matter for Christian formation.

The Foundry Society

The Foundry Society in London was organized in April 1740, demonstrated by agreement upon its rules.[32] The Foundry was a site for deliberations for early Methodists about their governance; it was also known as a site for innovative Christian outreach in the midst of complex systems of poverty in London. Previously an armory, the facilities were relatively expansive providing seating for 1500 as well as rooms for teaching, ministry, and accommodations. While an active Methodist site from 1739–1785, most of the activities were eventually moved to a larger and more fitting facility, City Road Chapel, later in the century.

Wesley facilitated several experiments in outreach from the Foundry including: a lending stock, poorhouses, and a medical dispensary. These demonstrated Wesley's pastoral wisdom and innovation to treat both symptoms and systems of poverty, empowering many Methodists not merely to survive, but to live sustainably and even flourish. In the early decades of the Methodist renewal movement many of those attracted to the classes and band meetings, mostly women and youth/young adults, were considerably impoverished. In the later decades of the eighteenth century following the movement's consolidation, those active in the movement represented in greater numbers the middle classes, possibly demonstrating a long-term effectiveness of such programs and the support of new institutional contexts.

Wesley had hoped that the Methodist movement would eventually "have all things common."[33] This proved difficult to coordinate and was increasingly complicated as the movement grew. In 1746, Wesley experimented with a different economic program of assistance: the lending stock, a sort of micro-loan program funded by a collection among Wesley's more affluent friends in London. Two stewards were appointed from the society to hold the fifty pounds collected for disbursement in no or low interest loans up to 20 shillings (one British pound) at the Foundry each Tuesday morning. The micro-loans could be used for financial relief, but they could also be used to assist small business owners/managers. The loans were disbursed to members of Methodist societies who had to pledge their repayment within three months. In the first year, the lending stock assisted 250 people.[34]

Wesley also implemented services for those in need of charity and relief such as "feeble, aged widows" through the establishment of a poorhouse. The poorhouse, consisting of two small houses near the Foundry, housed approximately twelve people, initially including a blind woman and two poor children, with whom Wesley and the preachers occasionally visited and ate.[35]

John Wesley pursued a lifelong interest in medicine demonstrated in part by his publication, *Primitive Physick* or *An Easy and Natural Method of Curing Most Diseases*. He published the text anonymously in 1747, eventually putting his name to it as author in 1760. Skeptical of the effectiveness of physicians, and most likely moved by those too poor to gain access to medical care, he began stocking a number of the preaching houses with medicines. Consulting with those trained in the field, he engaged a surgeon and an apothecary to help him late in 1746 to implement a regular system of dispensing medicine at the Foundry each Friday. Thus, in December 1746, the Foundry became a medical dispensary in accord with Wesley's intention of "giving physic to the poor,"[36] and treating those with chronic rather than acute illnesses. Following Wesley's announcement, the Foundry's medical dispensary soon grew to a steady monthly clientele of approximately 100 visitors at an annual cost of less than 120 pounds. When treatments were effective in relieving some ailments, Wesley was quick to refer to God's work in all things. Unlike the lending stock, medical dispensary services were not limited to members of the Foundry Society. Similar medical dispensaries were also generally provided at the preaching houses in Bristol and Newcastle.[37]

Kingswood School and Christian Library

Beginning in 1739, Wesley carried out the plan Whitefield had initially conceived of building a school for the coal mining families of Kingswood, holding together knowledge and vital piety in the early Methodist renewal movement. The school included a large preaching hall and facilities for school administrators near Bristol. Scholars of all ages were welcome. In 1748 a new Kingswood school was opened closer to Bath, still near Bristol. The Conference deliberated on the details of the rules as well as the curriculum, which instructed children on topics from the alphabet to preparation for ministry. Subjects included reading, writing, arithmetic, French, Latin, Greek, Hebrew, rhetoric, geography, chronology, history, logic, ethics, physics, geometry, algebra, and music. Wesley wrote grammars for the English and other language courses and claimed that upon completing the Kingswood curriculum a student would be a better scholar than ninety percent of those completing degrees at Oxford and Cambridge.[38]

Alongside his contributions to the Kingswood School's curriculum, Wesley also compiled the Christian Library for the education of Methodists and its preachers. Begun in 1749, he completed the extensive publishing project in 1755, largely at his own expense. The Christian Library made accessible "extracts from, and abridgements of, the choicest pieces of practical divinity which have been published in the English tongue."[39] Consisting of fifty volumes arranged chronologically from the Early Church, the project was meant to give readers access to the most eminent authors and works of Christian tradition.[40]

Throughout Wesley's life, he was attentive *both* to the powerful importance of preaching and revivals to awaken people to the "new birth" of the Holy Spirit *and* to the formative power of institutions in shaping Christian discipleship, engaging in outreach, and in educating people in Christian faith. The Wesleyan renewal movement's impact in England in the eighteenth century is found both in its Spirit-infused passion and its organizing brilliance. Both dimensions are critical to the movement's success. We sometimes have been tempted to pit "movement" against "institution," liking the former and disliking the latter. That contrast, though, has been rooted more in a fantasy about what is needed to sustain a movement and in fears that any institutional forms will necessarily degenerate into bureaucracy. Movements require and utilize institutions and institutions can be vibrant, keeping movements enthused and moving forward beyond their initial force.

Rather than creating a false dichotomy, we need to recognize that living as Wesleyans consistently requires *both* Spirit-infused passion *and* thinking and living institutionally. Indeed, when the Wesleyan movement has been at its best since the eighteenth century, both elements have typically been present.

Wesleyan DNA & Innovation

Since the first days of the revivals in the 1700s, Wesleyans have typically exhibited Spirit-infused passion and institutional thinking and living. We have practiced "traditioned innovation" as a means of deepening and extending the commitments of our Wesleyan forebears, just as they did so with their predecessors. Traditioned innovation is a commitment to drawing on the best living faith of those who have gone before us, receiving it with gratitude, and then discovering innovative ways to carry on that living faith into the future.[41] Such "traditioned innovation" also depends on giving up "traditionalism," what Jaroslav Pelikan calls "the dead faith of the living," as opposed to tradition's "living faith of the dead."[42] The Wesleyan movement at its best has continually drawn on the living faith of our forebears throughout the Christian tradition in order to address new challenges and opportunities.

Discipleship

Indeed, Wesley's own practice of the class meetings and bands was an innovative approach that drew on the resources of the early church. Wesley writes in "A Plain Account of the People Called Methodists ":

> Upon reflection I could not but observe, this [i.e., societal organization] is the very thing which was from the beginning of Christianity. In the earliest times those whom God had sent forth 'preached the gospel to every creature.' And the *hoi akroatai*, the body of hearers, were mostly either Jews or heathens. But as soon as any of these were so convinced of the truth as to forsake sin and seek the gospel salvation, they immediately joined them together, took an account of their names, advised them to watch over each other, and met these *katechoumenoi* (catechumens, as they were then called) apart from the great congregation, that they might instruct, rebuke, exhort, and pray with them and for them, according to their several necessities.[43]

At our best, Wesleyans have practiced *traditioned innovation* with the class meetings as we have sought to cultivate practices of accountable discipleship to nurture deep and rich Christian formation. African-American Methodists, especially in the American Methodist Episcopal Church (AME) and American Methodist Episcopal Zion (AMEZ) traditions, have continued to innovate out of the class meeting tradition. Anglo Methodists in the nineteenth century tended to innovate through the development of Sunday Schools. Alas, however, as Wesleyans of all stripes have become more established in the United States, it is all too tempting to settle for traditionalism on the one hand or to abandon all elements of tradition, on the other—and our focus on forming accountable disciples for faithful, transformative witness in the world has suffered.

The Poor

Wesleyans have also practiced *traditioned innovation* in extending the Foundry's commitment to health care, especially for the poor. Consider the remarkable history of the Methodist Hospital in Indianapolis (now Indiana University Health Methodist Hospital). At the time of the hospital's centennial anniversary in 1999, it had achieved more than your run-of-the-mill hospital. It was the site of the largest neuro-critical care unit in the country. It was the hospital where the first heart transplant in a private hospital in the world was conducted. It was one of only two Level 1 trauma centers in the area. Today, as Indiana University Health Methodist Hospital, it is the largest health care provider in the state of Indiana. *And it was founded by Methodist teenagers.*

In July 1899, the Methodist Church's Epworth League, the era's equivalent of youth ministry, held a convention in Indianapolis. At the time, Indianapolis had three other hospitals, yet with persistent diseases that still lacked vaccines, the hospitals were forced to turn away one out of every two patients. Almost all were poor. Inspired by the need, the Epworth League challenged the Methodist Church to start a hospital. The youth raised $8,000—a very significant sum at the time—to prove their seriousness.

They were convinced, as Wesley was, that bearing Christian witness in the world involves caring for the sick. And just as Wesley's practices in the Foundry drew on a longer tradition of Christian care for the sick, so Methodist Hospital carried forth a deeply Wesleyan practice. Unfortunately, as the Wesleyan movement as a whole has become more established in the United States, it has become easier to allow our commitments to hospitals, clinics, hospices, and other forms of care to become increasingly indistinguishable from secular forms of medicine—and our witness in the field of health care has suffered.

Education

Wesleyans have practiced *traditioned innovation* in the field of education, especially higher education. Many of the United States' strongest colleges and universities—Boston University, Syracuse, Drew, Duke, Emory, Vanderbilt, Northwestern, the University of Denver, Southern Methodist University, the University of Southern California—were founded by Methodists. Or take Valparaiso University, founded in 1859 by Methodists. Who would have wanted to start a new institution in 1859, with the nation on the brink of civil war and the economy in shambles? Wesleyans who recognized that Christian witness in the world requires engagement with ideas.

In so doing, Wesleyans have been practicing *traditioned innovation*, extending, deepening, and building on Wesley's commitments in the Kingswood School and the Christian Library. As Wesleyans of all stripes have become more established in the United States, we have typically allowed those educational institutions to suffer either from a reified mission or mission drift. We have tended either to preserve a strong Christian identity in traditionalist ways, suffering from a lack of innovation and excellence, or to allow those institutions to become accommodated to the culture such that they are barely identifiable as having any Christian ethos. And our witness has suffered as a result.

Our examples have thus far focused on the United States, because this is the context where *traditioned innovation* in the Wesleyan tradition took its strongest and most life-giving forms in the late-eighteenth and nineteenth centuries. Our Wesleyan forebears in the United States often embodied in powerful ways the connections between Spirit-infused passion and thinking and living institutionally.

Recapturing Our DNA

Yet we argue that contemporary Wesleyans have regularly failed to continue to embody these connections, often allowing their institutional enterprises to degenerate into passionless bureaucracy. Indeed, even our discussions about renewal tend to reflect polarizations between naïve calls for rejecting institutions for the sake of passion, or restructuring our organizations without any attention to passion.

In order to recapture our Wesleyan DNA, we need to learn how to think, live, and feel as people who combine Spirit-infused passion and organizational brilliance. Re-learning the wisdom, texture, and vitality of our Wesleyan histories, and the ways those Wesleyan histories bear witness to the larger Christian tradition, will be critically important. And we will also need to be attentive to our brokenness and failures in living and thinking institutionally.

At the same time, we can also learn from living laboratories in the majority world where Wesleyans are practicing *traditioned innovation* in beautiful, faithful ways. For example, we can learn practices of "cell groups" that focus on Christian formation from Wesleyans in Korea; microfinance and health care practices from Wesleyans in Cote d'Ivoire; and the importance of new patterns of education from Wesleyans in Zimbabwe and the Democratic Republic of Congo. They understand the significance of thinking and living institutionally, especially because they are acutely aware of how impoverished life is without those institutions.

These suggestions are not meant to romanticize these developments and experiments in the majority world, as if what we have in the United States is all bad and what our brothers and sisters in the majority world are doing is all good. We are, however, suggesting that exploring what Wesleyans sometimes do when they are not preoccupied with maintaining an "established" context might offer instructive examples for helping us re-discover the challenges and opportunities of Christian renewal in our own context.

Conclusion

We do not believe we need to start from scratch in order to think and live institutionally and cultivate faithful Christian witness. There is much that we can draw on and learn from as we begin ever afresh to cultivate vibrant institutions. To be sure, many of our historic institutions may have moved too far away from their Wesleyan roots to be renewable. There is a need to create new forms of Wesleyan institutions, both to meet new challenges in the twenty-first century and to offer faithful Christian witness in contexts where Christianity is beginning to flower in fresh ways.

Yet there are also wonderful Wesleyan institutions across diverse sectors, in the United States and around the world, to which we ought to remain committed, and which can be deepened, extended, and enriched as Wesleyan institutions. An institution such as Methodist LeBonheur Healthcare in Memphis has re-discovered its Wesleyan identity in recent years, especially by connecting more deeply to Christian congregations through its "congregational health network" and its commitment to innovative Christian practices of health care. These commitments have offered significant renewal for the organization, for the church, and for the health care that people receive in Memphis and its surrounding region.

What will thinking and living institutionally as Wesleyans look like in the twenty-first century? We will need as much faith in the creative power of God through the redeeming power of Christ, and the transforming power of the Holy Spirit, as we see in the Wesley's and in our Wesleyan forefathers. We will need to recognize that Spirit-infused passion and organizing brilliance are not opposed, but rather integral features of faithful Christian living that must be held together in tension. And we will need to repent of our anti-institutionalism (or even a-institutionalism) to re-discover the power, and life-giving and life-transforming character, of practicing traditional innovation and institutional thinking and living.

L. Gregory Jones, PhD, is Williams Professor of Theology and Christian Ministry at Duke Divinity School. He is also Executive Director of A Foundation for Theological Education. Laceye C. Warner, PhD, is Associate Professor of the Practice of Evangelism and Methodist Studies at Duke Divinity School.

Bibliography

"A Plain Account of the People Called Methodists (1749)." In *The Works of John Wesley*, Volume 9: *The Methodist Societies: History, Nature and Design*, edited by Rupert E. Davies. Nashville: Abingdon, 1989.

Abraham, William J. *The Logic of Evangelism.* Grand Rapids: Eerdmans, 1989.

Albin, Thomas R. "An Empirical Study of Early Methodist Spirituality." In *Wesleyan Theology Today: A Bicentennial Theological Consultation*, edited by Theodore Runyon. Nashville: Kingswood Books, 1985.

Church, Leslie F. "Charles Wesley—The Man." *The London Quarterly and Holborn Review* 182 (1957): 247–253.

Doughty, W. L. "Charles Wesley, Preacher." *The London Quarterly and Holborn Review* 182 (1957): 263–267.

Heclo, Hugh. *On Thinking Institutionally.* New York: Oxford University Press, 2008.

Heitzenrater, Richard P. *Wesley and the People Called Methodists* (Nashville: Abingdon, 1995), 97

Maddox, Randy. "Wesley's Prescription for 'Making Disciples of Jesus Christ': Insights for the Twenty-First-Century Church," *Quarterly Review* 23, no. 1 (2003). https://divinity.duke.edu/sites/divinity.duke.edu/files/documents/faculty-maddox/21_Wesleys_Prescription.pdf

Menninger, Karl. *Whatever Became of Sin?* New York: Hawthorn, 1973.

Pelikan, Jaroslav. *The Vindication of Tradition*. New Haven: Yale, 1984.

Runyon, Theodore. *The New Creation: John Wesley's Theology Today*. Nashville: Abingdon, 1998.

Tyson, John R. *Charles Wesley: A Reader*. Oxford: Oxford University Press, 1989.

Chapter 18 Notes

[1] Maddox, "Wesley's Prescription for 'Making Disciples of Jesus Christ'," 15–28.

[2] In the "Large" *Minutes*, John Wesley summarized his understanding of Methodism's purpose: "What may we reasonably believe to be God's design in raising up the Preachers called Methodists? A. To reform the nation and, in particular, the Church; to spread scriptural holiness over the land."

[3] Heclo, *On Thinking Institutionally*, 97.

[4] Ibid, 17.

[5] Ibid, 37.

[6] See Menninger, *Whatever Became of Sin?*

[7] Heclo, *On Institutional Thinking*, 4.

[8] Ibid, 90.

[9] Richard P. Heitzenrater, *Wesley and the People Called Methodists* (Nashville: Abingdon, 1995), 97. As Heitzenrater explains, Bristol was a growing industrial center and port of nearly 50,000 (about one-tenth the population of London) (98–99).

[10] Ibid, 99.

[11] Ibid.

[12] Ibid, 100.

[13] Ibid. Presumably, these field preachers felt some need to justify their irregular practice, leading to the emphasis upon such staggering numbers.

[14] Ibid.

[15] Ibid. CWJ 1:155. For another account of Charles' initial move into field preaching, see Doughty, "Charles Wesley, Preacher," 264. For references to Charles and preaching, see also Tyson, *Charles Wesley*, 137, 155, 159, 240, 246. For twenty years Charles was a traveling evangelist, while continuing as a priest and pastor. See Church, "Charles Wesley—The Man," 251.

[16] Heitzenrater, *Wesley and the People Called Methodists*, 99–100.

[17] Ibid, 99–100. According to Heitzenrater, John suggested, "To avoid giving needless offense, we never preach *without* doors when we can with any conveniency preach *within*." The expansion was to be gradual, to "go a little and a little" from the society meetings "so a little leaven would spread with more effect and less noise, and help would always be at hand" (Minutes, 23).

[18] Ibid, 149.

[19] Sermon 24, "Sermon on the Mount IV," I.1, *Works* 1:533–34, referred to in Randy L. Maddox, "Formation for Christian Leadership: Wesleyan Reflections," *Summary of Proceedings of the American Theological Library Association* 57 (2003): 124.

[20] "A Plain Account of the People Called Methodists," I.8, *Works,* 9: 257 and see "Rules of the United Societies," *Works,* 8: 269–71.

[21] Heitzenrater, *Wesley and the People Called Methodists,* 21. The Society for Promoting Christian Knowledge has its roots in the religious societies founded by Anthony Horneck in the 1670s, the English counterparts to the *collegia pietatis* organized by Jacob Spener.

[22] "A Plain Account of the People Called Methodists," II. 5, IX. 2, X. 2, XI. 4, *Works,* 9: 254–80.

[23] See also "Rules of the United Societies," *Works,* 8: 269–71.

[24] The General Rules were meant for mutual support, but were also enforced, serving as a guide for accountability specifically in the Newcastle societies of 1743. The General Rules are protected as formal doctrine within the UMC tradition and appear in the UMC Discipline. General Rules of United Societies, *United Methodist Book of Discipline* (2004), 72–74.

[25] Albin, "An Empirical Study of Early Methodist Spirituality".

[26] Ibid, 277. In relation to awakening and conviction, lay people are mentioned three times more frequently than clergy, twice as often in relation to the new birth, and four times more often in relation to sanctification. Interestingly, in many accounts there is no human catalyst identified (278).

[27] Ibid, 278.

[28] Ibid.

[29] Abraham, *The Logic of Evangelism,* 54–55. The experiment started in Wales and Cornwall and then moved to the north.

[30] Runyon, *The New Creation,* 115. Runyon argues that despite George Whitefield's larger crowds and greater public attention, John Wesley and his religious societies most likely preserved more fruits from the eighteenth century revival preaching as a result of their Christian nurture and discipleship.

[31] Heitzenrater, *Wesley and the People Called Methodists,* 165. John noted in the Minutes: "Almost all the seed has fallen by the wayside; there is scarce any fruit of it remaining." According to Heitzenrater, quoting John, "The preacher had little opportunity for instructions, the awakened souls could not 'watch over one another in love,' and the believers could not 'build up one another and bear one another's burdens.'"

[32] Ibid, 110.

[33] Ibid, 166.

[34] Ibid.

[35] Ibid, 167.

[36] Ibid, 166.

[37] Ibid 167.

[38] Ibid, 168–69.

[39] Ibid, 178.

[40] Ibid, 167–79.

[41] For further discussion of "traditioned innovation," see L. Gregory Jones, "Traditioned Innovation," *Faith & Leadership* (www.faithandleadership.com), January 19, 2009; and C. Kavin Rowe, "Traditioned Innovation as a Biblical Way of Thinking," *Faith & Leadership* (www.faithandleadership.com), March 16, 2009.

[42] Pelikan, *The Vindication of Tradition,* 65.

[43] "A Plain Account," 258, sec. I, para. 10.

PART 4

LEADERSHIP THEORY AND PRINCIPLES

19
Authentic & Ethical Leadership

Tim Beuthin

While Christians often resonate with the command to be innocent as doves, they can also neglect Jesus' advice to be wise as serpents. Both shrewdness of mind and purity of heart are necessary for leaders, especially as lived out authentically and ethically. This chapter presents the importance of these theories and how they may be applied for such issues as self-awareness, transparency, ethical thinking, and the cardinal virtues. Leaders need not sacrifice either a kind of worldly wisdom or heavenly innocence to be effective and faithful.

IN MATTHEW 10, JESUS PREPARES his newly minted disciples to engage in the work of his Kingdom. He commissions them to proclaim the Good News, heal the sick, raise the dead, cleanse the lepers, and drive out demons. They were not to accept compensation for their labors but rely solely upon the hospitality of those who would welcome the message. Though vested with Kingdom authority, they would not be insulated from resistance, rejection, hatred, and arrest. At times, the way would be unclear, the personal risk great, and the long-term outcomes uncertain.

The disciples would be sheep in the midst of wolves; the virtuous would serve in the midst of the vicious. The metaphor was intended to communicate clearly and convincingly the reality of the situation. A failure to differentiate between sheep and wolves would be catastrophic for the messenger as well as the message. How were the disciples to behave in the face of such reality? Jesus introduced a second paradox; they must be as shrewd as serpents and as innocent as doves. Though it may seem to be a strange juxtaposition of metaphors to the contemporary reader, some scholars contend that Jesus was drawing upon a familiar Jewish proverb:

"With me the Israelites are simple as doves, but against the heathen cunning as serpents."[1]

A Shrewd Mind

The serpent was the embodiment of shrewdness and cunning. These characteristics were first observed in the Garden, where the Serpent showcased an uncanny ability to identify a strategic course of action in order to accomplish goals. Though these goals were guided by evil intent, shrewdness when properly directed was a commendable attribute in Scripture. For example, the men of Issachar understood their times and what needed to be done during a period of great social upheaval in Israel (1 Chron. 12:32). Shrewdness was often associated with being discerning, astute, clever, savvy, perceptive, and effective.

Jesus employed several parables to illustrate the nature of shrewdness. In Luke 12:42, the wise manager did what was best in order to satisfy the master. The wise virgin was commended for her readiness (Matt. 25:4). The wise man built his house upon the rock to secure his foundation (Matt. 7:24). The parable of the dishonest manager seems to come closest to the meaning of shrewd. The manager was not commended for his character but rather for his ability to discern what was required and to resolve the problem strategically and expeditiously. One wonders if Jesus wished some measure of this characteristic upon his followers when he opined, "For the people of this world are more shrewd in dealing with their own kind than are the people of light" (Luke 16:8).

A Pure Heart

Jesus, understanding a shrewd mind must be supervised by a pure heart, employed another striking metaphor to illustrate the kind of characterrface required of his disciples. The dove, which was the form the Holy Spirit took at the baptism of Jesus, was characterized as simple, unblemished, innocent, harmless, and pure. The disciples were to conduct themselves so as to be free from fault and censure from others. They were to be street smart in their competence and unalloyed in their character; prudent yet simple, discerning yet guileless; savvy yet sincere. In sum, their dispositions, attitudes, affections, and actions were to be guided by a pure heart.

Paul's use of the terms *wise* and *innocent* comes close to Jesus' admonition. In Romans 16:19, he warned the faithful against those in the church who, driven by their own appetites, deceived the minds of naïve people. He both affirmed and admonished them by saying, "Everyone has heard about your obedience, so I rejoice because of you; but I want you to be wise about what is good, and innocent about what is evil." In essence, he was calling them to emulate Jesus' first disciples by discerning what was good while remaining unmixed with the evil around them. In Philippians 2:5-16, Paul described the mindset of Christ Jesus, who emptied himself of his own interests and took on the nature of a servant to do the will of His Father. Then, he follows with the application to his audience, "Do everything without grumbling or arguing, so that you may become blameless and pure, children of God without fault in a warped and crooked generation. Then you will shine among them like stars in the sky as you hold firmly to the word of life." They were to be without blame in their conduct and without alloy in their character.

Over the past two decades, ethical scandals in every sector of public life have created a palpable sense of urgency for ethical and authentic leaders. Some of the best and brightest leaders have acted without a moral compass while others have been brought down by unbridled hubris or foolishness. Best-selling books have acted as a bellwether. Topics related to ethics, integrity, values, and authenticity emerged during the first decade of the millennium. The Academy also responded with a spate of research and theoretical frameworks, such as transformational leadership, ethical leadership, authentic leadership, responsible leadership,, spiritual leadership, and servant leadership, which included competency and character components. Research findings continue to offer a window into the shadow side of leaders while calling for leaders whose behaviors are consistent with their values.

The purpose of this chapter is to assist Christian leaders in seeing clearly, thinking differently, and acting nobly. They must be shrewd in their understanding of themselves and the world yet pure in their values, dispositions, motives, desires, and conduct. To that end, a brief overview of research on authentic leadership, ethical leadership, behavioral integrity, and moral imagination will be discussed. Finally, implications for enhancing moral excellence in leadership will be considered.

Authentic Leadership

For hundreds of years, the attribute of authenticity was the domain of philosophers and theologians. The inscription over the oracle of Delphi to "know thyself" echoed in the exhortations of the Greek philosophers "to thine own self be true."[2] Over the past twenty years, there has been a renewed interest in authenticity. Authentic leaders understand themselves and their purposes, are passionate about their missions, act to do the right thing guided by strong values, develop trusting relationships, and demonstrate strong self-discipline.[3] William Gardner, Bruce Avolio, and others stated that authenticity involved "both owning one's personal experiences (values, thoughts, emotions and beliefs) and acting in accordance with one's true self (expressing what you really think and believe and behaving accordingly)."[4] Though theoretical work is still in the formative stages, several critical components of authentic leadership have emerged, such as self-awareness, relational transparency, balanced processing, and internalized moral perspective.

Self-Awareness

The first component of authentic leadership involves *self-awareness*. Leaders with high levels of self-awareness understand the complex nature of the self, especially as it relates to their own strengths and weaknesses, core values, emotions, and motives. Greater clarity of self enables them to discern how to monitor and regulate the impact of their conduct on those who look to them for direction. Jesus demonstrated a high degree of self-awareness as he prepared to wash his disciples' feet on the eve of his crucifixion.

> The evening meal was in progress, and the devil had already prompted Judas, the son of Simon Iscariot, to betray Jesus. Jesus knew that the Father had put all things under his power, and that he had come from God and was returning to God; so he got up from the meal, took off his outer clothing, and wrapped a towel around his waist. After that, he poured water into a basin and began to wash his disciples' feet, drying them with the towel that was wrapped around him. (John 13:2-5)

Jesus emptied himself of any self-interest. He knew who he was, where he had come from, and where he was going. He was fully aware of what was going on around him and the impact his conduct would have on his followers.

Relational Transparency

A second component of authentic leadership involves relational transparency. This is the ability to present one's true self to others through open, truthful, and consistent expressions of thoughts and feelings with the goal of developing close relationships between leaders and followers.[5] The leader's modeling of transparency and vulnerability over time will encourage followers to become more authentic.

Balanced Processing

A third component of authentic leadership involves balanced processing. This refers to a leader's capacity to seek out and analyze information from a divergent range of perspectives before a decision is made. He or she practices self-critical introspection and invites dissenting input in order to develop an accurate sense of self and the quality of work relationships.

Internalized Moral Perspective

Finally, the fourth component of authentic leadership involves internalized moral perspective. This refers to a leader's ability to act according to internal beliefs and moral values. It serves as a moral compass[6] keeping the leader from being unduly influenced by external pressures. Leaders whose words and deeds are guided by a moral compass build trust and respect with followers.

It is important to note that the four components are mutually interdependent. A deep understanding and acceptance of internal beliefs is critical to self-awareness and self-clarity. How the leader expresses that self is moderated by a careful understanding of the situation informed by input from various perspectives.

Authentic leaders possess the psychological attributes of confidence, hope, optimism, and resilience.[7] They are more persistent and successful in the face of challenges; expect goals to be accomplished, anticipate positive outcomes in the future; and are able to recover from setbacks with greater resourcefulness. These attributes enable them to come through critical life events with greater personal clarity and a deeper sense of purpose. Authentic Christian leaders understand the times and what needs to be done in the midst of chaos and uncertainty. They are able to set direction, create alignment, and maintain commitment among flawed human beings because they remain aware of their own strengths and weaknesses and sensitive to the strengths and weaknesses of others. They possess a humility and vulnerability that frees them to receive input from followers. As they strive to be true to themselves, permission is extended to others in the organization to do the same. Their commitment to a surrendered life in Christ positions them to realize the requisite attributes of an authentic leader: confidence, hope, optimism, and resiliency.

The Shadow Side of Self-Knowledge

Early research on authentic leadership focused on the positive aspects of self-awareness. However, as the concept matured, scholars began to turn their attention toward the shadows and limitations of knowing oneself. A heightened sense of self-knowing could lead beyond pride in one's work to hubris, or pride in oneself, another issue first raised by Greek philosophers. The literature is very clear that leaders who are overconfident or arrogant are susceptible to a host of ethical problems. Furthermore, the goal of complete self-knowledge is at best aspirational because leaders don't know what they don't know; nor do they want to know. Leaders are often woefully unaware of gaps in their self-knowledge. They cannot know the extent to which they commit errors of omission.[8]

Given this gap in self-knowledge, Diddams and Chang recommended that epistemic humility be included in self-knowledge. Epistemic humility is the ability to admit that one does not know everything or that their perspective is not always correct. For them, it would be presumptuous, even hubris, to believe so. Because they are aware of their own limitations and biases in processing information, they are quick to seek out additional feedback and flexible in making decisions in ambiguous situations. Socrates illustrated this kind of humility when he conceded to the Athenian jury of his peers "that he was indeed wiser than other wise men since he was willing to acknowledge that he did not know what he did not know about himself."[9]

Authentic leaders should be more aware of their vulnerability to self-deception and the limits of self-knowledge.[10] A preoccupation with obtaining self-knowledge can lead to the illusion of arrival. In other words, leaders who believe they have attained high levels of self-understanding and self-efficacy are prone to rationalize away inappropriate moral conduct or disregard negative or dissenting information about themselves or the situation.[11] Furthermore, they show a greater tendency to distort situations in order to enhance their social and psychological capital with followers. Since authenticity is validated by followers, leaders may knowingly, or unknowingly, manage or spin their self-presentation to their advantage. Leaders who consider themselves morally superior are also prone to a variety of cognitive errors, especially in new, ambiguous, or stress-filled situations. They tend to be either overly optimistic about or undervalue the collective outcomes of a course of action. Furthermore, they are more likely to ignore outcomes perceived to be less likely to occur or to miscalculate the scope of the risks. Finally, leaders prone to hubris are less likely to acknowledge flaws, solicit feedback from others, or initiate accountability relationships.

A balanced, humble view of self-knowledge can serve as an antidote to creeping hubris. Humility in the literature is not considered an exercise in self-abasement or a descent into lower self-esteem, but a realistic self-evaluation of one's limitations, negative characteristics, and positive attributes. Such leaders remain open to gaps in their self-knowledge. They learn to restrain those self-protective mechanisms that block difficult but useful developmental or organizational feedback. This restraint allows the leader to become more effective in balanced processing, a requisite skill for an effective authentic leader. Research findings are consistent with an ancient admonition from the writer of Proverbs, "Pride goes before destruction, a haughty spirit before a fall" (16:18). Paul also warned, "Do not think of yourself more highly than you ought, but rather think of yourself with sober judgment, in accordance with the faith God has distributed to each of you" (Romans 12:3). And he continues, "If anyone thinks they are something when they are not, they deceive themselves" (Galatians 6:3). Hubris is a slippery slope.

Ethical Leadership

The spate of moral failures among leaders over the past 15 years has served as a catalyst for the development of ethical leadership theories focusing on character, as well as competency. Building on the premise that individuals develop behavior patterns by emulating role models, Brown, Trevino, and Harrison defined ethical leadership as "as the demonstration of normatively appropriate conduct through personal actions and interpersonal relationships, and the promotion of such conduct to followers through two-way communication, reinforcement, and decision-making."[12] For them, leaders are the moral managers of the organization with an explicit agenda to develop structures, systems, and processes that support critical moral values.

In addition, they serve as the custodians of the culture by communicating, modeling, and defending the core beliefs, values, and assumptions that shape the organization's moral purpose and identity.

Moses, an early example of a moral manager, offered a strategy for creating and sustaining a moral culture. In Deuteronomy 6:6-9 he wrote:

> These commandments that I give you today are to be on your hearts. Impress them on your children. Talk about them when you sit at home and when you walk along the road, when you lie down and when you get up. Tie them as symbols on your hands and bind them on your foreheads. Write them on the doorframes of your houses and on your gates.

These commandments, or core values, were to inform and transform the thoughts, desires, attitudes, motivations, and actions of every leader and follower through the natural rhythms of conversation and daily activity. In addition, these core values were to be displayed publically through various symbols and rituals to remind them of their identity, values, and priorities and to guide their daily activities.

While many leaders accept the mantle of articulating and defending core moral values, it is often the lack of management, or mismanagement, of organizational structures, systems, and processes that diminishes their moral integrity, their credibility, and ultimately their followers' perceptions of competence and character.

The Role of Virtue in Ethical Leadership

Leader competencies such as skills, training, knowledge, and experience will be compromised by character flaws like self-indulgence, immorality, hubris, and poor habits.[13] Many leaders highly skilled in casting vision, building momentum, establishing alliances, and marshalling follower commitment have fallen because of a character flaw. A leader's effectiveness will be diminished unless these flaws are addressed. While a relativistic culture may disagree about right and wrong actions, a virtue-based ethical leadership theory should still be effective.[14] An ethical leader's character and behavior must align with and be guided by the four cardinal virtues of prudence, fortitude, temperance, and justice.

Prudence

Prudence, a practical wisdom or insight developed through experience, reflection, and subsequent learning, balances doing too little or too much in a given situation. Aristotle believed that prudence moderated the other three virtues by keeping courage from becoming foolishness, temperance from becoming fanaticism, and justice from becoming cowardice.[15]

Fortitude

Fortitude, or courage, is the ability to persevere through fear and adversity in pursuit of a noble cause or end. It requires prudence, conviction, and resolve. There is no need for courage without the presence of fear. Whereas fear can dissuade an individual from taking action, courage can embolden the individual to work through fear to achieve a noble end at any cost.

Temperance

Temperance is the capacity to control one's desires and emotions. Aquinas believed that humility was an important part of this virtue because a balanced understanding and acceptance of one's self and one's situation would moderate against intemperance.[16]

Justice

Finally, justice is described as acting fairly toward others and demonstrating a consistent commitment to give them what is deserved. In summary, the virtuous leader is to be discerning, courageous, self-regulated, humble, and just.

The Value of Virtue

Through the cultivation of virtues, leaders can learn to balance between doing too little or too much in any given situation. Prudent decisions can be made by carefully considering the multiple perspectives of others, correctly determining the proper course of action, and then efficiently directing resources to arrive at the proper action. Prudent decisions and actions are more likely when leaders practice restraint over their personal interests, desires, and emotions. Because temperate individuals are not easily preoccupied with their personal concerns, preferences or agendas, they are better equipped to suspend those impulses that might preclude a

> *"Intelligent leaders do foolish things because they do not believe they are capable of such foolishness"*

better way. Fortitude will enable them to stand immovable in the presence of personal fears and adversity. Prudence will direct; temperance will control, and fortitude will carry leaders through to the desired end.

King Saul's leadership failure in 1 Samuel 13 offers an excellent example of leadership without prudence, temperance, or fortitude. Like a swarm of angry bees, the Philistines marshaled their imposing war machine to the front lines of Saul's distressed army that was fleeing to the hills. Saul could not go into battle until Samuel, who was seven days late, offered the sacrifice. Israel's nemesis was preparing to crush what was left of Saul's decimated army. Beset with a scarcity of time, competing considerations, potentially dire consequences, and imperfect options, Saul offered the sacrifice. Samuel arrived soon after the sacrifice and rebuked him for his foolishness. Had Saul acted prudently, temperately, and with fortitude, the Lord would have established his kingdom forever. Instead, it was taken from him. Like Saul, the trajectory of many leaders' legacies has changed in a moment because they did not act prudently, temperately, and with courage.

Foolish Thinking and Ethical Failure

Some of the best educated and most intelligent leaders had been involved in some of the most egregious ethical failures.[17] Intelligent leaders do foolish things because they do not believe they are capable of such foolishness. Robert Sternberg said the primary difference between a wise and foolish decision rested upon the degree of balance between intrapersonal (self), interpersonal (relationships), extra-personal (greater good) interests, and short and long term outcomes. He argued there are six fallacies of thinking that could create such an imbalance.

1. Leaders believe they can accomplish whatever they desire (fallacy of unrealistic optimism). They reason there is no point in worrying about the outcomes because everything will come out all right in the end.
2. Leaders think they are the only ones that matter and not the people who rely upon them (fallacy of egocentrism). As a result, they ignore responsibilities to other people and the institutions they serve.
3. Leaders believe they know everything (fallacy of omniscience). Over time, they lose sight of the limitations of their own knowledge by assuming that what they know or have access to is all that can be known.
4. Leaders believe they are all-powerful and capable of doing whatever they wanted to do (fallacy of omnipotence). This fallacy is often associated with hubris. They overreach or abuse power believing they can wield whatever level of influence they deem necessary.
5. Leaders believe they can get away with anything, because they were too clever to be caught (fallacy of invulnerability). If caught, they expect to get away because of who they imagine themselves to be. They live in the illusion of complete protection.
6. Leaders believe that ethics applies to others, but not to themselves (fallacy of ethical disengagement).

David's behavior with Bathsheba in 2 Samuel 11 suggests he may have succumbed to one or more of these fallacies. Ludwig and Longenecker developed the "Bathsheba syndrome" because their findings so closely paralleled the story of David and Bathsheba.[18] They discovered that leaders can become complacent and lose their focus when attention is diverted toward pursuits outside the scope and mission of the organization. In David's case, he should have been on the field of battle, not on the roof of the palace. Furthermore, success and advantage can lead to privileged access to information, people, and objects. As king, David used his information channels to discover more about individuals and situations than anyone else in his kingdom. His unrestrained control of kingdom resources was driven by the belief he could manipulate all the consequences of his decisions.

Leaders should focus on what is in the best interest of their organizations making sure they are in the right place and doing what is expected of them by their followers.[19] Temptations often accompany privilege and power. Inattentive, unprepared, or self-focused leaders could be vulnerable to compromising situations. Leaders may continue to perpetuate unethical acts as long as personal gratification is more important than the needs of the organization. It is very likely a personal act will affect other followers or stakeholders. Cover-ups will have dire consequences for the organization. Innocent individuals will be hurt and reputations damaged. Power will be abused, trust will be breached, and scarce organizational resources will be compromised. Finally, leaders who escape consequences will be more likely to develop a veil of invulnerability that could set them up for future ethical failures.

Seeing Clearly, Thinking Differently, Acting Nobly

The capacity to see oneself and the situation clearly is confounded by many self-protective and self-deceptive tendencies. Many times, moral failures are the result of a lack of moral imagination.[20] Leaders with high levels of moral imagination demonstrate the ability to see the context clearly, are mindful of their patterns of thinking as well as the patterns of others, and are sensitive to the potential for moral conflict. These leaders imagine different possibilities by reframing situations from different perspectives and revising their entrenched ways of thinking. Finally, they are able to create morally sound alternatives that make sense to others.

Mental Models

There are many challenges to seeing a situation for what it really is. In his classic, *The Fifth Discipline,* Peter Senge asserted that leaders process experiences through mental models, which are based upon past experiences, personality structures, socialization patterns, cultural values, and self-identity.[21] They serve as filters for organizing and making sense of an otherwise overwhelming barrage of sensory data. Unfortunately, this efficient selective mechanism can block or distort data. That is one reason why two individuals can interpret the same experience very differently. Organizational cultures also operate on mental models capable of creating boundaries and traps that mask toxic ethical practices. The authentic leader with high levels of balanced processing will break out of a restrictive mental model by considering multiple perspectives and seeking to create acceptable moral alternatives for the organization.

Pattern Recognition

Leaders are also susceptible to *pattern recognition,* a term borrowed from neuroscience to describe a leader's tendency to make assumptions based upon past experiences and decisions.[22] Whereas mental models exclude information, pattern recognition behaviors assume that new situations are familiar to old ones. As a result, leaders believe they recognize situations clearly and ascribe to them all the characteristics of past experiences. Any unusual characteristics are ignored. Consequently, leaders can make critical decisions based upon outdated or incomplete input.

Leaders are also prone to focusing on failures while attempting to process all the information in a given situation.[23] They focus on those items that capture their attention or appear to be relevant to the situation at hand. In the process, this state of bounded awareness can cause the leader to ignore or overlook relevant and accessible information while focusing on equally accessible and irrelevant information. This condition is complicated by blind spots or unconscious patterns of thinking, feeling, and behaving that can negatively influence how they perceive a situation. Unexamined mental models can mask inappropriate levels of self-interest and cloud judgment.[24]

If leaders lead out of who they are, then it is essential for leaders to understand who they are. This understanding is affected by what is going on within and around them at any given time. Educational and cognitive psychologists have observed, and Scripture has affirmed, that individuals are a complex mixture of beliefs, emotions, attitudes, values, motives, and desires that serve as a filter through which they see and respond to a situation. Given the dynamic, and at times, morally ambiguous world in which they serve, leaders encounter conflicting opinions, competing duties, multiple considerations, and imperfect options as they seek to lead with clarity, consistency, and courage.

Self-Knowing

George Bernard Shaw stated, "Better keep yourself clean and bright; you are the window through which you must see the world."[25] As poet Anais Nin recognized nearly a century ago, "We don't see things as they are, we see them as we are."[26] In 1 Corinthians 13:12, Paul acknowledged the limits of what we can really know when he stated, "For now we see only a reflection as in a mirror; then we shall see face to face. Now I know in part; then I shall know fully, even as I am fully known." That reality should not keep leaders from deeper levels of self-understanding, but it should serve as a constant reminder that clearly knowing self, others, and situations could be an illusion.

Conclusion

Authentic leaders seek to know themselves. They humbly acknowledge they do not know what they do not know about themselves. The very cognitive structures that help them organize chaos also limit what they see. Furthermore, they understand that "the heart is deceitful above all things and beyond cure. Who can understand it?" (Jeremiah 17:9). But, they also realize the better they understand themselves, the better they will understand those who look to them for leadership. And, a strong alignment between who they know themselves to be and how they conduct themselves will have a positive impact upon follower trust and commitment.

Authentic leaders have a realistic assessment of their limitations and negative characteristics as well as their positive attributes. They remain open to input regarding imperfections, blind spots, and gaps in self-knowledge and solicit valid feedback from a variety of perspectives. They identify personal issues, such as hot buttons, baggage, weaknesses, and the factors that trigger them. Leaders must identify the middle space where their skill sets and strengths intersect with negative personal and interpersonal limitations and patterns.[27] The identification and resolution of these issues must be resolved if they are to flourish.

Christian leaders are under the biblical mandate to lead with street smarts (competence) and pure hearts (character). As has been argued, unexamined and unaddressed beliefs and behaviors can have dire consequences for the leader and the organization. On the other hand, high levels of leader competence and character will have a positive effect on follower outcomes, such as job satisfaction, organizational commitment, extra effort, as well as perceptions of organizational culture and climate, psychological safety, trust, and team effectiveness.[28] We have the resources to lead effectively in a world yearning for authentic and ethical leaders.

Tim Beuthin, PhD, is a Professor in the Department of Leadership Studies at Indiana Wesleyan University.

Bibliography

Brown, Michael E. and Marie S. Mitchell. "Ethical and unethical leadership: Exploring new avenues for future research." *Business Ethics Quarterly* 20, no. 4 (2010): 583-616

Brown, Michael E., Linda K. Treviño, and David A. Harrison. "Ethical leadership: A social learning perspective for construct development and testing." *Organizational Behavior and Human Decision Processes* 97, no. 2 (2005): 117-134.

Campbell, Andrew, Jo Whitehead, and Sydney Finkelstein. "Why good leaders make bad decisions." *Harvard Business Review* 87, no. 2 (2009): 60-66.

Chang, Glenna and Margaret Diddams. *"Hubris or humility: Cautions surrounding the construct and self-definition of authentic leadership."* In Academy of Management Proceedings, 2009, no. 1 (2009): 1-6.

Chugh, Dolly, and Max H. Bazerman. "Bounded awareness: What you fail to see can hurt you." *Mind & Society* 6, no. 1 (2007): 1-18.

Cloud, Henry. Integrity: The Courage to Meet the Demands of Reality. New York: Harper Collins, 2006.

Diddams, Margaret and Glenna C. Chang. "Only human: Exploring the nature of weakness in authentic leadership." *The Leadership Quarterly* 23, no. 3 (2012): 593-603.

Gardner, William L., Bruce J. Avolio, Fred Luthans, Douglas R. May, and Fred Walumbwa. "'Can you see the real me?' A self-based model of authentic leader and follower development." *The Leadership Quarterly* 16, no. 3 (2005): 343-372.

George Bill and Peter Sims. *True North: Discover your Authentic Leadership.* San Francisco: Jossey Bass, 2007.

Kernis, Michael H. "Toward a conceptualization of optimal self-esteem." *Psychological Inquiry* 14, no. 1 (2003): 1-26.

Klenke, Karen. "The internal theatre of the authentic leader: Integrating cognitive, affective, cognative, and spiritual facets of authentic leadership." In *Authentic Leadership Theory and Practice: Origins, Effects, and Development,* edited by W. L. Gardner, B.J. Avolio, F. O. Walumbwa, 43-81. Amsterdam: Elsevier, 2005.

Ludwig, Dean C. and Clinton O. Longenecker. "The Bathsheba syndrome: The ethical failure of successful leaders." *Journal of Business Ethics* 12, no. 4 (1993): 265-273.

Luthans, Fred and Bruce J. Avolio, "Authentic leadership development". In *Positive Organizational Scholarship,* edited by K.S. Cameron, J.E. Dutton, and R.E. Quinn, 241-258. San Francisco: Berrett-Koehler, 2003.

Nin, Anais, *Seduction of the Minotaur* Sky. Blue Press, 2014.

Regan, Richard J. *The Cardinal Virtues: Prudence, Justice, Fortitude, and Temperance.* Hackett Publishing, 2005.

Reynolds, Scott J. and Tara L. Ceranic. "The effects of moral judgment and moral identity on moral behavior: an empirical examination of the moral individual." *Journal of Applied Psychology* 92, no. 6 (2007): 1610-1624.

Riggio, Ronald E., Weichun Zhu, Christopher Reina, and James A. Maroosis. "Virtue-based measurement of ethical leadership: The Leadership Virtues Questionnaire." *Consulting Psychology Journal: Practice and Research* 62, no. 4 (2010): 235.

Ross, W. D., trans. "Aristotle, Nicomachean Ethics." In *The Basic Works of Aristotle.* Random House. 1941.

Senge, Peter M. *The Fifth Discipline Fieldbook: The Art and Practice of the Learning Organization*. New York: Doubleday, 1994.

Sternberg, Robert J. "Why smart people can be so foolish." *European Psychologist* 9, no. 3 (2004): 145-150.

Werhane, Patricia H., Laura P. Hartman, Dennis Moberg, Elaine Englehardt, Michael Pritchard, and Bidhan Parmar. "Social constructivism, mental models, and problems of obedience." *Journal of Business Ethics* 100, no. 1 (2011): 103-118.

Werhane, Patricia H. *Moral Imagination and Management Decision-making*. Oxford University Press, USA, 1999.

Chapter 19 Notes

[1] See Adam Clarke's commentary on Matthew 10:16. Adam Clarke, *Commentary on the Bible* (1831), available at http://www.sacred-texts.com/bib/cmt/clarke/mat010.htm.

[2] Klenke, "The internal theatre of the authentic leader," 43-81.

[3] George and Sims, *True North*.

[4] Gardner, Avolio, Luthans, May, Walumbwa, "Can you see the real me?" 343-372.

[5] Kernis, "Toward a conceptualization of optimal self-esteem," 1-26.

[6] George and Sims, *True North*.

[7] Luthans and Avolio, "Authentic leadership development," 241-258.

[8] Diddams and Chang, "Only human," 593-603.

[9] Ibid, 596

[10] Chang and Diddams, "Hubris or humility".

[11] Reynolds and Ceranic, "The effects of moral judgment and moral identity on moral behavior," 1610-1624.

[12] Brown, Treviño, and Harrison, "Ethical leadership," 120.

[13] Cloud, *Integrity*

[14] Riggio, Zhu, Reina, and Maroosis, "Virtue-based measurement of ethical leadership," 235.

[15] Ross, "Aristotle, Nicomachean Ethics".

[16] Regan, *The Cardinal Virtues*.

[17] Sternberg, "Why smart people can be so foolish," 145-150.

[18] Ludwig & Longenecker, "The Bathsheba syndrome," 265-273.

[19] Ibid.

[20] Werhane, *Moral Imagination and Management Decision-making*.

[21] Senge, T*he Fifth Discipline Fieldbook*.

[22] Campbell, Whitehead, and Finkelstein, "Why good leaders," 60-66.

[23] Chugh and Bazerman, "Bounded awareness," 1-18.

[24] Werhane, Hartman, Moberg, Englehardt, Pritchard, and Parmar, "Social constructivism, mental models, and problems of obedience," 103-118.

[25] Shaw, Man and Superman.

[26] Nin, *Seduction of the Minotaur Sky*.

[27] Cloud, *Integrity*.

[28] Brown and Mitchell. "Ethical and unethical leadership," 583-616.

20

Transformational Leadership

Priscilla Hammond

Transformational leadership, while more recently developed, has its roots even in Scripture. More recently, the theory attempts to explain leadership that is effective through four qualities: Inspirational motivation, intellectual stimulation, individual consideration, and idealized influence. This chapter unpacks how these four elements are found in Scripture or Christian example and how this leadership style is faithful to the leader working among people of faith.

SCRIPTURE CONTAINS EXAMPLES OF ancient leadership, some of which point to two classic, yet contrasting leadership styles. On the one hand, Scripture has stories in which a landowner (the principal) expects a tenant farmer (the agent) to work the owner's land and return the profit to the owner. Numerous leadership concepts such as *agency theory* and *transactional leadership theory* have arisen from this ancient model. These leadership theories assume employees are motivated by the desire for compensation (wages, salary, etc.) in exchange for producing a profit for the owner. In this type of organizational structure, the owner's profit is the primary goal and under-productive employees may be at greater at risk of being replaced by those able to produce greater profits. This profit-driven goal creates a competitive atmosphere in organizations, where the principal and agent look out for their own agendas and are each motivated by personal gain. *Transactional leadership theory* describes a relationship between a principal (owner/manager) and an agent (employee) in which both parties are motivated by personal gain.[1]

On the other hand, in contrast to transactional leadership, is *transformational leadership*, the second classic leadership style, which leads people to transcend their own self-interest and collaborate through mutual, unselfish processes that raise the morality and motivation of everyone involved. The collaborative, unselfish, and process-driven ideals of transformational leadership can be found in Scripture, and can serve to improve leadership in the church leading to harmony, unity, sympathy, peace, and mutual surrender. Whereas transactional leadership may be effective in developing contractual employment agreements for the harvesting of crops, transformational leadership is required in order to plant and reap covenantal relationships for the harvesting of souls.

There are 4 instances of the word *transformation* (Gr. metamorphóō / μεταμορφόω) in the New Testament. Matthew and Mark use the term to describe Jesus' transfiguration (Matt. 17:1-8; Mark 9:2-8). Paul admonishes believers to be transformed by the renewing of their minds (Rom. 12:2) and writes of all believers being transformed into God's image (2 Cor. 3:18). The Christian understanding of transformational leadership is drawn from these verses: as the leader is transformed by Christ, they may then call followers to transformation and purpose beyond themselves, so that the organization can better advance the kingdom.

This vision of leadership is very much the opposite of a highly competitive mentality of some transactional leadership practices. Whereas transactional leadership may be effective in developing contractual employment agreements for the exchange of goods, transformational leadership is required in order to develop and sustain healthy, biblical relationships. To better understand how to develop as a transformational leader, this chapter explores the four factors of transformational leadership and offer examples of the application of each transformational leadership factor to the practice of ministry.

Transformational Leadership Theory

Leadership theory has been evolving since it was first studied as an academic discipline in the early 1900s. In the 20th century, leadership moved from being defined as a power position demanding command and control, to being defined, first, by the traits of leaders, then by the behaviors of leaders, and eventually within the leader-follower relationship.[2] James MacGregor Burns' conceptualization of what he initially termed *transforming leadership* began with a philosophy of leadership as a process rather than a set of traits or behaviors.[3] This philosophy moved leadership away from leadership definitions focused on traits and behaviors to create a new definition:

> Leadership is the reciprocal process of mobilizing by persons with certain motives and values, various economic, political, and other resources, in a context of competition and conflict, in order to realize goals independently or mutually held by both leaders and followers.[4]

Burns' new definition brought several things to the forefront of leadership studies. Leadership as a process, not a position, is driven by values and goals, fraught with change and challenges, and externally focused. What sets transformational leadership apart is the way in which these larger, external goals are accomplished through the interaction of the leader and followers. Transformational leaders may lead out of their natural charisma, learned skill, or developed overall competence. Their influence may arise from their positional title or from their personal temperament.

However, though transformational leaders may have certain traits and behaviors that must be present in order to behave in transforming ways, the theory of transformational leadership focuses not on these traits and behaviors, but on the

"as the leader is transformed by Christ, they may then call followers to transformation and purpose beyond themselves, so that the organization can better advance the kingdom"

ultimate goals of the organization. Transformational leadership is a process by which leaders focus on understanding follower needs and motivations, inspiring both themselves and their followers to lift their motivations to a higher moral level, to make moral decisions, and to take moral action to accomplish goals greater than they thought possible.

Leaders may be more or less transformational in various situations and at different times in their leadership journey. Bernard Bass added to Burns' work on transformational leadership theory by creating a continuum with *transformational leadership* at one end, *transactional leadership* in the middle, and *laissez-faire leadership* at the other end.[5] No leader is entirely transformational, transactional, or laissez-faire in every situation. Instead, transformational leaders are continually developing into role models who make moral decisions and take moral action toward higher goals. Transformational leaders do this through *idealized influence, inspirational motivation, intellectual stimulation,* and *individualized consideration.*[6] In order to understand each of these factors better, the following sections will describe each through a pastoral leadership perspective. As you develop as a transformational leader, you too can develop followers to their highest capacity.[7]

Idealized Influence

Idealized influence, the first factor in transformational leadership, is the ability to connect with followers emotionally. Often, this factor is called charisma, but charisma could be seen as a personality trait that is inborn or bestowed spiritually on certain individuals. Though some leaders may be more naturally charismatic than others, idealized influence is more about the leader's *actual* behavior rather than the leader's personality. Idealized influence is achieved as followers identify with the leader, the leader's aspirations, subsequently desire to emulate the leader.

Imagine a leader whom you admire and that is a strong role model. Does this person have high moral standards and exhibit ethical conduct? Can you imagine this person ever making a conscious decision to sin? Have they earned the trust of their followers? Most likely this leader was not simply born with an innate ability to draw followers and rally people to a mission greater than they could accomplish on their own, but that instead they developed an authentic, practical faith that garnered the respect of followers while they developed skills that enhanced natural leadership gifts. Transformational leaders earn idealized influence over time, through practical, ethical living.

Abraham is a biblical example of a transformational leader with idealized influence. Abraham's response to the capture of one of his relatives demonstrates his idealized influence: "When Abram heard [about Lot's capture]…he called out the 318 trained men born in his household and went in pursuit as far as Dan" (Gen. 14:14). Abraham attracted followers to himself, as is demonstrated by hundreds of people joining him to confront four powerful military forces. Follower loyalty is an outcome of idealized influence, and Abraham's followers remained loyal to him throughout his lifetime (and hundreds continue to visit his burial site daily, thousands of years later). Abraham influenced even pagan kings such as King Abimelek, who told Abraham, "God is with you in everything you do" (Gen. 21:22). Abraham's moral conduct earned him the respect of this pagan king, who joined in covenant with Abraham, which indicated his expectation that Abraham would be faithful to a mutually beneficial relationship. Idealized influence should inspire leaders, especially leaders in faith contexts, to be of high character and reputation so that the kingdom is advanced outside the walls of the local church—in the community and even into the hearts of pagan "kings."

Inspirational Motivation

The second factor in the transformational leadership model is *inspirational motivation*. Transformational leaders need to be able to communicate their high expectations for each follower to aspire to a greater vision. It is not enough for leaders to have an *individual* vision that others admire; they must have a vision that resonates with followers *personally*. Transformational leaders inspire the follower's commitment to this shared vision because they tap into the personal, possibly latent motivations of followers and inspire greater motivation.

The role of the leader is to understand followers' motivation and tap into followers' potential.[8] That has been the lifelong approach of Kazuo Inamori, who founded two successful Japanese companies and established the Center for Ethics and Excellence at Case Western Reserve University. To tap into followers' motivation, Inamori believed that he was responsible for not just the material wellbeing of his employees, but their spiritual welfare, too.[9] Thus, the corporate motto of Kyocera, the Japanese consumer and industrial electronics manufacturer he founded in

1959, is "Respect the Divine and Love People."[10] Inamori motivated employees with this philosophy not just at Kyocera, but when he founded telecommunications giant KDDI, and in his later leadership at Japan Airlines (JAL). The first thing he communicated to JAL was the philosophy that had resulted in years of business success at Kyocera and KDDI: "Management's goal is to pursue the happiness of all employees, both physically and mentally" (Maxwell, 2012). This is not just a slogan; it has been Inamori's characteristic of inspirational motivation throughout his career. Inamori believes that empowered, motivated followers will carry the organization to success.

It was through the same inspirational motivation that church leaders exhibit that connects the great commandment to Jesus followers' daily lives. Transformational leaders use inspirational motivation to communicate high expectations, which will translate into organizational goal attainment. Peter is a biblical example of a transformational leader. He effectively used emotional appeals, which are a key characteristic of inspirational motivation.

In Acts 2, Peter has an audience with "God-fearing Jews from every nation under heaven" (2:5) in Jerusalem. He reminds them of their own history and the prophecies concerning the church and Jesus, calls them to repentance, baptism, and sanctification, and inspires them to accept the promise made to them and all whom the Lord calls. Peter's call and appeal worked, as "about three thousand were added to their number that day" (2:41). Beyond just moving forward for an altar call, however, these new believers "devoted themselves to the apostles' teaching and to fellowship, to the breaking of bread and to prayer" (2:42), saw miracles, shared everything, sold material possessions and gave to the needy, met together daily, were unified and praised God, and "the Lord added to their number daily those who were being saved" (2:47).

Inspirational motivation is not manipulation. Transformational leaders do not manufacture a need and push others to achieve it. Inspirational motivation is sharing the truth about what people already know about themselves and others and introducing them to a higher goal. Peter helped people to know that their desire to worship, for community, and for a Savior was God-given and attainable by God's grace. Once they had received it they were inspired to share it with everyone in their circles of influence. Transformational leaders tap into the motivations of followers and inspire even greater motivation for higher goals outside of themselves.

Intellectual Stimulation

Transformational leadership is characterized by a third factor: *intellectual stimulation*. Intellectual stimulation is the encouragement of out-of-the-box thinking, problem solving, and innovation. Intellectual stimulation is about developing practical wisdom. Transformational leaders encourage followers to think deeply, ask questions, and meet challenges in better ways than the leader may have considered on their own.[11] Transformational leaders engage intellectual stimulation as they encourage followers to be creative rather than indoctrinating them into the leaders' ways of thinking.

Perhaps we can see Peter engaged in this kind of leadership. For example, in the Acts account, Peter did not tell new believers how to "do" church. He did not stand before them and give them a step-by-step plan for church planting or a pamphlet on winning the lost. He reminded them of their history and painted a picture of their future. He inspired them to connect their motivation to the achievement of that goal, not just for themselves, but for the entire community. The result was a collective desire to meet together. In these meetings, imagine them discussing the problem and possible solutions. As the church grew geographically, there was not a formula for every new context; churches had to form in pagan societies where the influence of Roman or Hellenistic society was greater than that of the Jewish synagogue. The followers had to be innovative. They had to revisit past beliefs about thing such as Judaism (for Jewish converts), emperor worships, or any of the number of mystical pagan cults that were prevalent throughout culture. As leaders, the apostles – and eventually pastors in the subsequent generations of the church – guided converts in examining their beliefs in light of the truth and discerning the best way to deal with organizational issues while remaining focused on the primary objective: the living out of the gospel. For example, at the Council at Jerusalem (Acts 15), questions were brought to the apostles and elders regarding the law and its application to Gentile believers. There was agreement among them that there were a few rules that must be adhered to, but that they should not be burdened with anything beyond those requirements (Acts 15:23). Beyond these explicit instructions from the leaders, followers were encouraged to solve problems creatively in their unique context.

A contemporary example of intellectual stimulation is Wendy Kopp, who founded the non-profit Teach for America (TFA) in 1989 as a 22-year-old graduate of Princeton. Kopp was concerned about the lack of education equity in urban schools because of their inability to recruit teachers. Building on her senior thesis, Kopp created a teacher job corps that recruits and places quality graduates in these underserved low-income schools and provides training and development for the two years that the teachers are engaged in those schools. When graduates apply, they cannot be guaranteed where they will be placed or what salary they will receive, yet 40,000 people will apply this year.

Being a part of the TFA corps has become a prestigious addition to a teacher's resume.[12] In 2007, due to the success of TFA, "Kopp was approached by social entrepreneurs from India, Chile and Lebanon."[13] This led to the development of Teach for All, which was in 35 countries by 2015. Though she developed the Teach for America model for U.S. schools, it translated well into other countries' goals of improved education; however, the different contexts of each country required collaborative, innovative thinking. Intellectual stimulation is a characteristic of transformational leaders that encourages dialogue among teams. Kopp wisely collaborates with leaders of different contexts to challenge assumptions and solve the problem of inequity in education throughout the world.

Intellectual stimulation requires the creation of innovative ways for people to work out their own issues. In Exodus, prior to Jethro suggesting a new organizational structure, Moses represented the antithesis to intellectual stimulation. He did not empower creative thinking among his followers, but served as the intellectual authority for all situations requiring judgment: "Moses took his seat to serve as judge for the people, and they stood around him from morning till evening" (Exod. 18:13). When his father-in-law asked what he was doing, Moses said he was telling the people God's will, and solving all of their problems. Jethro replied, "What you are doing is not good" (Exod. 18:17) and encouraged Moses to delegate this decision-making to other capable leaders. Imagine the story of the nation of Israel if Jethro had not taken Moses aside that day and taught him his first management lesson. If their leader took his seat every day to solve disputes, then no forward movement would occur. For example, the next thing that happens in Scripture is that Moses goes up to meet with God on Mount Sinai. Leaders cannot be in two places at the same time; Moses could not have gone up the mountain if he remained in the seat of judgment. Transformational leaders choose to delegate and encourage intellectual stimulation among their followers so that everyone can focus on what they can do best. Moses was the spiritual leader, but had Jethro not challenged the status quo, he would have missed a meeting with God in exchange for a complaint committee meeting.

Transformation is not necessarily right or good. Thus, intellectual stimulation must include critical thinking and wisdom. Transformational leaders "are more likely to pursue any of a number of options that defy conventional paradigms, such as redirection and re-initiation. They are crowd-defiers."[14] However, defiance is not necessarily *wisdom*. As Sternberg pointed out, just because a leader is transformational does not mean that the leader is wise. Organizations, including churches, can engage in change that is risky and creative, but fails. Applying new techniques in unwise ways is transformational, but does not result in beneficial transformations.

Transformational leaders, as a result, must make a habit of being with God. James 1:5 says, "If any of you lacks wisdom, you should ask God, who gives generously to all without finding fault, and it will be given to you." Proverbs tells us that wisdom is the most important characteristic we should hope to attain: "The beginning of wisdom is this: Get wisdom. Though it cost all you have, get understanding" (Prov. 4:7). As may have happened with Moses had he not learned to empower the people for their own critical judgment and creative thinking, the transformational leader cannot miss missional meetings with God, for God is the source of wisdom and promise of ongoing transformational leadership.

Individualized Consideration

Followers are motivated in personal and various ways. Individualized consideration is the capacity to view followers as individuals, listening carefully to their needs and helping them to grow. Individual consideration may happen through delegation or by coaching. By assigning meaningful work to help the followers to grow as believers or by providing feedback and action plans, transformational leaders see followers as individuals and treat them accordingly. Transformational leadership places great emphasis on analyzing the morality of leaders, actions, and values since transformational leaders inspire followers to attain "higher levels of morality and motivation."[15]

Effective leaders are concerned with the individual. In a study of transformational leadership factors and pastoral leader effectiveness, transformational leadership was significantly correlated to pastoral leader effectiveness; specifically, individual consideration was the one dimension that was a significant predictor of pastoral leadership effectiveness.[16] Of course, one pastor may not be able to meet with and challenge each individual to personal growth. However, they must be available and interested in people. There may be organizational solutions to individualized consideration. For example, the transformational pastor will not teach every Sunday school class, but will emphasize the importance of spiritual formation from the pulpit, and must encourage everyone to participate. The transformational pastor models evangelistic zeal in the community and incorporates testimonies into worship services.

Individualized consideration does not need to remain with individual persons, but can extend to unique cultures and communities. Transformational pastors, therefore, keep the Bible in one hand and the newspaper in the other—they engage current reality with biblical truth and wisdom. They listen to the culture in order to better understand the reality people are acting within when they leave the walls of the church. Transformational leaders consider the culture when writing sermons, designing outreach, and planning programs. The mission of the church will fall on deaf ears if the leadership is deaf to the reality of the culture. Since the goal of transformational leadership is effective followers which are developed to their full potential, the method of coaching (or individualized consideration) of each follower or group of followers may be different; however, the timeless gospel message remains the same.

Conclusion

Transformational leadership is but one of a multitude of leadership theories. It takes a broad view of leadership, viewing leadership not as something or a set of traits possessed by leaders but as a process. Transformational leadership does not go as far as servant leadership to make the development of the follower *the* goal of leadership, but it does require a focus on followers' needs and values in the process of achieving organizational goals.

Paul's idealized influence drew people such as Onesimus to him as he modeled a way to reconciliation and forgiveness. His inspirational motivation matured the faith of young believers such as Timothy, whom he encouraged to grow from a timid believer to a faithful church leader and martyr. Paul demonstrated intellectual stimulation as he encouraged the Romans to *renew their minds* for transformation (Rom. 12:2), the Philippians to *think* about what is true, noble, right, pure, lovely, admirable, excellent, and praiseworthy (Phil. 4:8), and the Corinthians to *judge* his words for themselves (1 Cor. 10:15). And finally, Paul's relationship with Aquila and Priscilla emphasizes individual consideration. Because they were tentmakers by trade, Paul had an immediate occupational connection and he built on this opportunity to work and live together with them for one and a half years. They travelled together on mission trips. Paul encouraged them when they eventually separated and began their own ministry. Paul's individual consideration factor allowed him to see the motivation of each individual, tap into their story and potential, and help them to pursue their personal call to ministry. Through the Apostle Paul's transformational relationships with followers, the message of Jesus moved from a small sect in Jerusalem to Judea, Samaria, and beyond.

Paul said to follow his example, as he followed the example of Christ: "Remember your leaders, who spoke the word of God to you. Consider the outcome of their way of life and imitate their faith" (Heb. 13:7). His followers imitated his faith. For thousands of years, people have considered the outcomes of their leaders and learned from them. Followers have imitated leaders and become leaders themselves. This cycle of followership and leadership continues today, and transformational leaders engage in this process with idealized influence, inspirational motivation, intellectual stimulation, and individual consideration.

Priscilla Hammond, PhD, is adjunct professor of business at Southern Wesleyan University and Oklahoma Wesleyan University, and teaches ministerial preparation courses as an ordained minister of The Wesleyan Church.

Bibliography

Bass, Bernard. *Leadership and Performance Beyond Expectations.* New York: Free Press, 1985.

Bass, Bernard, and Bruce Avolio. *Improving Organizational Effectiveness Through Transformational Leadership.* Thousand Oaks: Sage Publications, 1994.

Bass, Bernard, and Bruce Avolio. "The implications of transactional and transformational leadership for individual, team, and organizational development." *Research in Organizational Change and Development,* 4 (1990): 231-272.

Bass, Bernard & R. Bass. *The Bass Handbook of Leadership: Theory, Research, & Managerial Applications.* New York: Free Press, 2008.

Burns, James. *Leadership.* New York: Harper & Row, 1978.

Carter, J. Transformational leadership and pastoral leader effectiveness. *Pastoral Psychology,* 58, no. 3 (2009): 261-271.

Christian Broadcasting Network. (n.d.) Karol Wojtyla (Pope John Paul II) Timeline. Retrieved from http://bit.ly/25nVpbL.

Garton Ash, Timothy. "The first world leader." *The Guardian.* April 3, 2005. Retrieved from http://bit.ly/1Ub6ViA.

Seifert, Kevin. "Tony Dungy: The most memorable emergency QB of all time." ESPN: NFL Nation [Blog]. Nov. 24, 2015. Retrieved from http://es.pn/1P7DC3p.

Galvin, Patrick. "Teach for America Applications Hold Steady." The Harvard Crimson. March 1, 2011. Retrieved from http://bit.ly/1sTHXib.

Goethals, G. R., and G.J. Sorenson. *The Quest for General Theory of Leadership.* Cheltenham, UK: Edward Elgar, 2006.

Inamori, Kazuo. "The perfect company: Goal for productivity." [Speech]. Cleveland, OH: Case Western University, June 5, 1985.

Kyocera. (n.d.). Corporate Motto/Management Rationale. Retrieved from http://global.kyocera.com/company/philosophy

Kopp, Wendy. World Affairs Council, "Taking Teaching for America International," April 223, 2014, para. 5. Retrieved from http://bit.ly/1TO8ffl.

Maxwell, Kenneth. "'Mikoshi' Management: How Kazuo Inamori lifted Japan Airlines." *Wall Street Journal.* July 30, 2012. Retrieved from http://on.wsj.com/1WReu4k.

Northouse, P. G. *Leadership: Theory and Practice* (6th ed.). Thousand Oaks, CA: Sage Publications, 2013.

Sternberg, R. "A model of educational leadership: Wisdom, intelligence, and creativity, synthesized." *International Journal of Leadership in Education,* 8 no. 4 (2005): 347-364.

Chapter 20 Notes

1 Burns, *Leadership*.

2 Goethals and Sorenson. *The Quest*; Northouse, *Leadership*.

3 Burns, *Leadership*.

4 Ibid, 425

5 Bass, Leadership and Performance.

6 Bass, Leadership and Performance; Bass and Bass, The Bass Handbook of Leadership.

7 Bass and Avolio, "The implications of transactional".

8 Kyocera. (n.d.). Corporate Motto/Management Rationale.

9 Inamori, "The perfect company".

10 Ibid, para. 1

11 Bass and Avolio. Improving Organizational Effectiveness.

12 For example, according to *The Harvard Crimson*, 18 percent of the Harvard class of 2011 applied for TFA (Galvin, 2011).

13 Kopp, World Affairs Council, Taking Teaching for America International, para. 5.

14 Sternberg, "A model of educational leadership," 360.

15 Burns, *Leadership*, 20

16 Carter, "Transformational leadership and pastoral leader effectiveness".

21
Contingency Theory

Aaron Perry

Different contexts call for different leadership styles. Leaders are tasked with discerning reality and responding accordingly. Contingency theory argues that leadership is not a one-style-fits-all contexts, but that leadership can be modified to achieve desired outcomes. Various cultural contingencies and leadership styles to match are offered to propel leaders into using contingency theory to their advantage in their current context.

THINK ABOUT THE THREE BEST LEADERS you have encountered. How were they similar? How were they different? Were their leadership contexts alike or unalike? Did they lead through inspiration? Brilliant strategy? Charisma? Which leader was better at empowering followers rather than at holding the standard of accountability high? Did they prefer to work in teams or by themselves? Given these differences, what do you think made the leader successful in their context? Do you think if one leader switched settings with another that they would have been just as successful?

I expect that the leaders you selected were at least somewhat different in leadership personality, style, and practice. If they weren't, then just expand the amount of quality leaders under consideration to five or seven and ask the same questions. We expect to find differences in people. No two people are exactly alike. However, we sometimes expect organizations to be alike. We expect principles of leadership to transfer from one context to another. However, many times they do not. Organizations, like people, have different histories, practices, expectations, key relationships, resources, and memories. Organizations are situated in the context of communities at given times with given problems. All of this means that organizations are different—not just from each other across cultures, but from themselves over time. Because organizations are different, to think that there is one best way to lead is a mistake. There is no "Rosetta Stone of leadership."[1]

Organizations are different because organizations face *contingencies*. A contingency is a condition. This is not a condition like my wife and I required the seller to meet before we bought our first home. Rather, it is something already true but that doesn't *need* to be true. A contingency is something real and true that a leader must account for in order to lead an organization but that might not be real and true to another organization—even a very similar one. Contingencies will even change for the same organization over time. Some conditions that are *currently* true for organizations will not *always* be true.

To say that every organization faces different contingencies means that every organization faces different *realities*. Leaders must understand the reality they are facing and shift to address it. Max DePree famously said that the first job of leadership is to define reality.[2] Leaders who do not get in touch with reality do not lead appropriately.[3] You cannot lead well if you are fighting reality. Leaders can *change* reality but they cannot *beat* reality. For example, you cannot beat gravity by sheer personal power, but you can change the conditions in which you are trying to work with it through levers, pulleys, aerodynamics, and well-constructed steps. Contingencies exist and must be acknowledged and understood or they cannot be used, modified, or overcome.

This understanding of contingent reality is both simple and devilishly difficult. It can be especially difficult for leaders who consider themselves highly principled. A leader with strong personality and will can feel uncomfortable modifying leadership styles, believing they are not being true to themselves. A leader with highly structured, rule-based ethics can be committed to the cross-cultural truth of principles that lie beyond a given reality. Finally, a leader with a track record of success can be convinced of the ubiquitous effectiveness of their leadership style and practices. But contingency theory does not deny *all* principles, nor does it undermine ethics, and it recognizes the appropriate leadership style in some contexts.

Successful leaders learn to operate within reality—regardless of their personality or preferred leadership style. Contingency theory seeks to explain and predict the success of certain leaders in certain situations. There are various understandings and presentations of contingency theory, but they all point to the varied realities that organizations face. Some realities might be intangible: Is the role of the leader highly empowered? What are the relationships like among the leadership team or between levels of hierarchy? Other realities might be tangible and internal: Does the organization have a well defined structure? Is the internal system of communications working? Other realities might be more mundane: Does the organization have a competitive dis/advantage with regard to suppliers? What advantages or disadvantages are posed by its geographic location? Other realities might involve employees: Are its employees motivated to achieve when they are satisfied or are they less likely to be results oriented when satisfied?

Given different contingencies that organizations must face, contingency theory affirms that there is no best leadership type or style. While this might tempt the leader to think that leadership is pointless, in fact it makes leadership *more* important. Leadership is more important when dealing with differing realities rather than applying a one-size-fits-all technique. That there is no one best leadership style to motivate employees, align organizations, or clarify roles, for example, does not mean that there are *no* effective leadership approaches. Perhaps we could say it like this: Contingency theory affirms that there is no one best leadership style, only that there are best leadership *styles*.

Malcolm Gladwell illustrates this point in a 2004 TED Talk by telling the story of Dr. Howard Moscowitz.[4] Howard was approached by Pepsi to analyze people's taste in Diet Pepsi and come up with the perfect Pepsi. But Howard soon found a problem. There is no perfect Pepsi. It doesn't exist. The discrepancies—the contingencies!—of taste varied enough that there was no strong consensus on the best flavor for Diet Pepsi. While Pepsi didn't believe Howard, Gladwell points out that Campbell's Soup, maker of Prego tomato sauce, *did*. Howard analyzed the taste of

> *"Maybe one particular, single strategy, product, style, or approach won't be effective in your context, but contingency theory argues for the possibility that another will"*

tomato sauce and found that some people like a thick(er) sauce, while others like a zesty sauce, while others prefer a chunky sauce, and that some like spicy sauce. There is no perfect sauce; there are only perfect *sauces*. Likewise in leadership: Different situations require different styles of leadership. There is no perfect style; there are only perfect *styles*.

People inherently know the truth of contingency theory. They know that contexts change practical requirements. For example, it would surprise no one that I do not parent my daughter the same way at age four as I did at age two; I do not lead volunteers the same way I lead junior colleagues; I did not lead my Bible college softball team the same way I tried (note the not-so-subtle indication of failure!) to lead my community based slow-pitch team. However, while people know the there is no one perfect leadership style but rather multiple leadership styles, people can also use contexts as an excuse. It sounds like this: "That might work somewhere else, but it won't work here." The resulting discouragement and cynicism sometimes means leadership is left unattempted. Maybe one particular, single strategy, product, style, or approach won't be effective in your context, but contingency theory argues for the possibility that *another* will. That since there isn't *a* perfect leadership style does not mean that there is *no* effective leadership style. So, take hope! A difference can be made in your context. And you can make it.

Much more could be said about contingency theory. This brief introduction and illustration of contingency theory is not meant to be exhaustive and interested readers can follow up elsewhere.[5] This foundation should, however, provide a context to see (1) different leadership realities that might go unnoticed and (2) frequent tensions in leadership, before (3) introducing possible styles of leadership that may be developed and deployed for effective leadership.

Realities of Leadership

A reality of leadership is simply a context and a context is simply a set of contingencies—things that are true for a situation or place, but that need not be true at all times in all places. Thus, while contexts change and are necessarily unique, there are some common circumstances that every leader must consider in their situation. Specifically, I want to highlight leadership relationships, in terms of power-distance and follower development.

To discern leadership relationships, the leader should, first, discern whether or not there is a pre-existing leadership structure. This leadership structure can be formal (a clear organizational chart) or informal (where the organizational chart is clear in someone's head, but not on paper). When leadership is summed up as influence, then it is clear that many people have opportunity to lead. You can lead regardless of your context because you can influence. You can influence people above, below, and beside you. However, this multi-directional leadership is neither always welcome nor appropriate. Some contexts have expectations for leadership relationships that must be navigated.

In certain contexts, leadership is not simply influence, but an expected role. Pre-existent leadership structures require your attention regardless of whether your official position is leader or follower. Where there is a pre-existent leadership structure, the unwelcome imposition of a follower or the lackadaisical approach of the leader are easily felt. No doubt if you have worked in a highly structured environment you have experienced the awkwardness when an employee disagrees with the boss about a crucial issue. On the other hand, you may have seen leadership vacuums get filled because the structure of leadership was not readily understood by the official leader. They were expected to be in charge, but when they deployed more collegial leadership their actions created a vacuum.

Power dynamics on a team are described as a power distance index.[6] Some cultures (and contexts) have a high respect for authority and high expectation of hierarchical structure between leader and follower. (Think Captain Von Trapp and his children from *The Sound of Music*. When the Captain blew the whistle, the children were expected to gather. At once!) Other cultures (and contexts) expect the "distance" between leader and follower to be minimal. (Think how Maria interacts with

Captain Von Trapp in her initial meeting. She is disarming and without expectation or guile.) There are advantages and disadvantages to leader and follower regardless of power distance index, although it is typically thought to be more advantageous as leader in high power-distance settings and more advantageous for followers in low power-distance contexts. However, what is essential is for the leader (and follower) to recognize what context already exists and to work within the framework. Leaders discern reality and function accordingly.

Secondly, when discerning leadership relationships, leaders must discover where the follower (or team) is in development. Followers come in varying degrees of preparation, skill, and giftedness. As a Christian, I believe that every person is gifted and can learn specific and valuable skills that can be used in God's Kingdom. These gifts can include creativity, emotional strength and empathy, giving, leadership, mercy, and others, while skills can include anything from arithmetic, to building, to counseling. While not everyone is equal in giftedness or potential, every person can grow in skill, develop gifts, and gain confidence to contribute to meaningful projects with eternal consequences.

The question is not, "How intelligent are you?" but "How are you intelligent?"[7] Sir Ken Robinson's turn of phrase reveals the deeply rooted optimism that a leader must hold. This optimism is not to be confused with a kind of naiveté. A leader must properly analyze and assess followers, which will include times when followers have a lack of desire, skill, or fittedness for different roles. Followers can be well-trained and confident, untrained (or poorly trained) and confident, well-trained and unconfident, or untrained (or poorly trained) and unconfident. To trained, confident agents, leaders must delegate. With untrained, confident agents, leaders should participate through encouragement and problem-solving. When the follower is untrained and lacks confidence, the leader may invest in the follower. This will involve explaining realities, persuading to the leader's point of view, and exercising patience. With the trained but unconfident follower, the leader must provide direct guidance and clear instruction to empower the follower.[8]

Different contexts have different expectations and requirements for leadership relationships. While I have noted two—pre-existent structures and expectations for leadership and follower development—others could be noted that would contribute to the various condition(s) facing leaders.

Tensions in Leadership

Leaders must hold certain items in tension. That is, leaders must know that one demeanor will not be right all the time and neither will its opposite be wrong all the time. Or, to use the language above, there are contingencies that are managed only by leaning one way at one time, and another way at a different time. Contingency theory recognizes that various approaches will be necessary at various times and with various followers.

Professor Tal Ben-Shahar teaches leadership by sharing about Janus.[9] Janus, from whom we get the name of the month January, was the Roman god of beginnings, endings, and transitions. Janus was portrayed as a bearded fellow with two faces. One faces the future, the other faces the past. Janus could look, seemingly, in opposite directions. Professor Ben-Shahar argues that leaders must develop "Janusian" thinking, which means being able to look in two different directions at once—or to hold opposites in tension. Frequent opposites that leaders must hold in tension include being democratic/authoritarian, dogmatic/relativistic, and severity/pleasantness. Let's explore these common tensions in leadership.

Should a leader be democratic or authoritarian? *Yes*. Or, it depends. At times, democratic leadership is needed while at others, authoritarian leadership is needed. One of the joys of parenting is watching a child grow from always needing specific direction to being able to contribute to making a decision. When there is time, a thorough thought process is often very beneficial not just for my children, but for various teams I lead. When followers are listened to, they feel valued, respected, and important. And, in truth, they are! Democratic leadership can uncover helpful feedback that would otherwise be lost in the memories of silent followers or recent hires. Yet, democratic leadership can also waste time and lead to poor decisions. Rorke Denver, former military commander for the United States Seals, shows the risk involved in democratic leadership: The leader's demeanor is contagious. For Rorke, this is why exuding *calmness* is so important: "Calm is contagious."[10] If the leader distributes power to the group, however, the group can become the source of its own dynamics. Calm is not the only thing that is contagious; so is stupidity. A group that has been invested with power that is unable to handle its responsibility may have stupidity spread faster than a common cold! Democratic leadership can lead to worse decision making and wasted time. So, does that mean that authoritarian leadership is better? Of course not. Consider the contingencies of time, power structures (and power-distance), and layers of information. Each of these contingencies may call for times of authoritarian leadership. For example, when discussing theology with members of my church, I can be authoritarian because it is not up for debate about whether or not Jesus is God Incarnate. However, that does not mean that I should make a simple declaration of this theological truth. Even when there is no room for debate, there can be room for questioning, opining, and reflecting. The conditions of the group leave room for the best form of leadership.

Should a leader be dogmatic or relativistic? *Yes!* These terms are not being used in an axiomatic sense. Core values, theological dogma, and certain other truths require are not for the leader to deploy and reconsider at their discretion. Rather dogma and relativism are used in terms of the leader's *attitude*, even about important things. Have you ever developed a vision for a preferred future? Perhaps the vision was for your dream home. You could picture it in your mind's eye. Or perhaps it was for an event. When you closed your eyes, you could picture the event clearly. If that vision ever came to be, it likely didn't come to be simply by your own efforts. The most challenging and worthwhile visions take *leadership*—which includes working with others. In cases where experts are involved in the building of your dream home, there are times when you cannot be dogmatic about your vision. Perhaps, the proper design might simply preclude a second bathroom just where you wanted it. Leaders must learn when to be dogmatic and when to be relativistic.

Let me offer an example. Six years ago, I had a vision for *Leadercast* to come to my city. *Leadercast* is a leadership-development conference that brings together various scholars and practitioners of leadership to teach to a wide variety of people in various locales around the world via satellite. I had played a small part in *Leadercast* in another city and I knew that it would work well in my current city. After its initial year, I knew that increasing my overall steering committee was necessary. Because of the initial momentum, obtaining high quality recruits for the team was not difficult. What was difficult, however, was understanding when I needed to be dogmatic and when I could be relativistic. To see the vision go forward, I needed to entrust parts of it to other people—even if they wanted something slightly—or greatly—different than I did. My vision needed to be *relative* to the desires of other teammates. However, there were also parts about which I needed to be maintaining an unwavering conviction and dogmatism. One of those values was to keep its individual price point affordable for it to present as little a barrier to attending the event as possible. But now the conditions have changed and I am faced with asking whether the price for the day will remain something about which I am dogmatic or whether it will become relative to the emerging vision. To lead the steering committee well, I need to be willing to be dogmatic *and* relative—and to know which is required when.

Styles of Leadership

I grew up in a hockey town in rural Quebec, Canada. As a Christian, I sometimes thought the town would be heaven on earth if people were as devoted to God as they were to hockey! The game often provided after school fun, Friday night entertainment, and plenty of exercise on cold winter Saturdays. Hockey has also provided several leadership lessons, one of which came via my Dad. Speaking with my father, the coach of a nearby professional hockey team said, "Ellard, the biggest challenge in coaching is knowing when they need a pat on the back and when they need a kick in the rear." While the quote has modified one word from its original phrase, the basic principle exemplifies contingency theory in a sports context. The style of leadership one needs to be a successful coach *depends*.

Emotional intelligence and leadership expert Daniel Goleman has created a very helpful summary of six leadership styles.[11] Goleman argues that each style has a context where it is appropriate—even *necessary*—and, while some styles are better in more contexts with greater frequency, that each style can be misused and misplaced. While the root of each style is faithful to Goleman's understanding, I will also expand and utilize the previous discussion on leadership relationships and leadership tensions to help offer insight for your own current leadership context.

Commanding

This leadership style is driven to achieve through personal initiative and high levels of self control. The leader senses that s/he is endowed with authority and uses it with the expectation the leader will be followed. Cultures and contexts with high-power index or untrained, unconfident teams will benefit from this style, although it will keep a team from developing and cohering well over time.

Visionary

This self-confident leadership style is focused not on the self, but on the picture of reality worth attaining. The visionary picture painted achieves the desired results. Leaders must be willing to balance dedication to the vision with the inclusion of followers for their greater investment. Visions only become reality with modification and dealing with conditions as they arise, so leaders must exercise wisdom to know when to involve followers in key decisions.

Affiliative

This leadership style builds relationships and creates a wonderful team-oriented environment. The affiliative leader is empathetic to followers. This leadership style can only be exercised in low power-distance contexts and cultures. When introduced in a context expecting strong leadership, the leader will appear as weak and abdicating leadership responsibility. Leaders must believe and have accurately assessed that the most heavily endowed followers are capable of making the right decision or correcting mistakes.

Democratic

The democratic leader values team input, communication, and shared leadership. The style emphasizes the equality of people on teams and believes that one has something of value to offer in some capacity. A leader can exercise democratic leadership on various points in the power index continuum, so long as there is clarity about where power ultimately resides. Democratic leadership works well in a context where teams have high trust and high commitment to a vision or goal rather than to the individual.

Pace Setting

The pace-setting leader is driven to succeed and accomplish, often through personal initiative. This leader subsequently models effective and valued behavior for employees. Pace-setting leaders may or may not be concerned with followers. Thus, team climate can decrease over time as individual drive, focus, and responsibility is rewarded and reinforced. Pace-setting leadership is beneficial in contexts where followers are highly trained, highly confident and possess individual responsibility. Over time, however, the style is detrimental to teamwork and cohesion.

Coaching

Leaders who take this approach are accepting a lesser present for the sake of a better future. They are focused on developing their followers' skills, mindset, attitudes, etc. while they develop empathy for and in other people. Different power-distances may allow this style. In a highly structured environment, the leader can be choosing of their volition to invest in a follower. In a more collegial environment, the leader can display the value of followers through personal investment. Either way, the leader must balance dedication to the vision/task with dedication to the follower. Not all players will be vital for success and not all aspects of a vision are worth the loss of a teammate. Coaching leaders need to assess followers and emerging future consistently and accurately.

Conclusion

Let me return to the softball team vs. slow-pitch team story above. The softball team was made of students who were (generally) younger and more personally disciplined than the slow-pitch team. The softball team had stricter limitations on personal freedoms (like a curfew and alcohol restrictions) and more opportunity for camaraderie between games. The slow-pitch team, on the other hand, was comprised of older players with no restrictions on personal freedom. Slow-pitch (and its post-game wallows!) *was* the time for camaraderie and team building. The college team was comprised of many players without overwhelming skill but commitment to the team, while the slow-pitch team had a higher amount of skill with lesser commitment to each other. For one team, I was vocal, passionate, determined; for the other, I was humble, encouraging, and relaxed. For one team, I exhibited moments of visionary and pace-setting leadership; for the other, I was much more affiliative and democratic.

The point is not to argue that these were the appropriate approaches; that could only be determined with an examination of results—which I'm sure would not interest many readers. The point is that it was *obvious* to me that the different contingencies required different leadership approaches. Think about a time you failed at leading. Perhaps you didn't recognize a team dynamic or banked too hard to the wrong side of a tension. Perhaps you were overly focused on being liked rather than developing followers. Think about another time where you succeeded. Chances are that some of the practices or approaches you took in the context where you failed you replicated in the context where you succeeded. What made you successful in one context and unsuccessful in another at least partially depended on the context.

Regardless of the failure or success, I have news for you—actually, several pieces of news. First, the neutral news: You got (at least partially) lucky when you won and (at least partially) unlucky when you lost. Better news: You can modify your leadership to make winning a greater possibility because you can grow to be more aware of your context. Challenging news: Contingency theory says you have to stay alert in your leadership. You can never take your approach for granted.

Think back to the start of this chapter. What three or five leaders came to mind who influenced you? Whether they intended to or not, they worked within the reality they were given. They operated within their contingencies. So can you! And as you do, you can become an influential leader to someone else, as well.

Aaron Perry, PhD, is Assistant Professor of Pastoral Care at Wesley Seminary at Indiana Wesleyan University in Marion, Indiana. He recently served as Associate Pastor at Centennial Road Church in Ontario, Canada.

Chapter 21 Notes

[1] J.B. Ciulla, "Leadership Ethics: Expanding the Territory," in J.B. Ciulla (Ed.), *Ethics: The Heart of Leadership*, 3rd ed. (Santa Barbara, CA: Praeger), p. 8

[2] Max DePree, *Leadership is an Art* (New York: Doubleday, 1989), p. 1.

[3] Henry Cloud, *Necessary Endings* (New York: Harper-Collins, 2010), p. 4-76.

[4] Malcolm Gladwell, "Choice, Happiness, and Spaghetti Sauce," TEDTalks.com. Accessed November 30, 2015. http://bit.ly/22tjQml

[5] For a fuller introduction and subsequent deeper readings, see Gary Yukl, *Leadership in Organizations*, 8th ed. (Upper Saddle River, NJ: Prentice Hall, 2012); John M. Ivancevich, Robert Konopaske, and Michael T. Matteson (eds.), *Organizational Behavior and Management*, 8th ed. (New York: McGraw-Hill, 2008).

[6] Power distance index is one of the intercultural factors discovered by Gert Hofstede. For the most recent exploration of power-distance and other factors, see Geert Hofstede, Geert Jan Hofstede, & Michael Minkov, *Cultures and Organizations: Software of the Mind*, (McGraw-Hill, 2010).

[7] Ken Robinson and L. Aronica, *The Element: How Finding Your Passion Changes Everything* (New York, NY: Viking, 2009), p. 42.

[8] Paul Hersey, Kenneth H. Blanchard, & Walter E. Natemeyer, "Situational leadership, Perception, and the Impact of Power." *Group & Organization Management* 4, no. 4 (1979): 418-428.

[9] Tal D. Ben-Shahar, "Harvard - Psychology of Leadership - 1. Introduction," YouTube video, 38:53, posted by Brain Candy, posted on April 27, 2014, accessed on December 2, 2015, http://bit.ly/1TGVobf; Tal D. Ben-Shahar, "Harvard - Psychology of Leadership - 2. Janusian Thinking," YouTube video, 48:45, posted by Brain Candy, posted on April 10, 2014, accessed on December 2, 2015, http://bit.ly/1sG7Ilj

[10] Rorke Denver, "Calm is Contagious," Leadercast.com. Accessed December 2, 2015. https://www.leadercast.com/now/decision-making/calm-is-contagious/.

[11] Daniel Goleman, "Leadership that Gets Results," *Harvard Business Review*, April-March 2000.

22
Shared Leadership and Expert Followers

Bryan R. Easley

Independent followers are competent, well-qualified, and highly self-directed members of an organization. Senior leaders sometimes fail to fully understand how to allow such followers to flourish and be successful, often resulting in those with great talents and expertise to leave for greener pastures. Shared leadership encourages leaders to invite such followers into the leadership process itself through mutual visioning, taking the time to listen, and showing vulnerability and trust. Such an approach allows for greater levels of synergy, innovation, commitment, and productivity,

LEADING PEOPLE WHO ARE INDEPENDENTLY-MINDED and have significant expertise or experience is sometimes like herding cats, says noted leadership writers Warren Bennis and Jeff Ballard.[1] Adam Hartung, writing for Forbes.com, observed the frequency with which senior leaders fail to adequately coach and relate to such highly talented staff, remarking that such people are sometimes "misunderstood and the organization pushes them out rather than figuring out how to get the most out of them."[2]

These are *independent followers*, or, as Robert Kelley calls them, "effective" followers: "well-balanced and responsible adults who can succeed without strong leadership "; believe they can contribute as significantly to the organization as the leader does; and they are able to "think for themselves and carry out their duties and assignments with energy and assertiveness."[3] Independent, effective followers tend to be competent and well-qualified, led by internal principles, passionate about their field, and highly committed to the ideals or purpose of organization. They are good self-managers, tending to do best in roles requiring self-initiative, independent thinking, and a measure of autonomous authority. Within the organization, they often take a personal interest in shaping the organizational vision or mission and prefer to view their supervisors or those in executive authority as colleagues who function primarily in administrative capacities rather than as superiors.[4] As such, they are are more prone to express disagreement or offer suggestions about organizational direction and process.

How do organizational leaders gain the commitment and maximize the potential of such highly skilled and independently minded followers? Harnessing the diverse skills, ideas, passions, schedules, and expectations of a team of "effective followers" is a unique but potentially rewarding challenge. Leading this kind of an organization requires a different approach than traditional leadership theory has tended to emphasize.

Leadership Approaches

A traditional top-down approach to leadership usually views the leader as the source of knowledge and power. The followers, consequently, help to enact or fulfill the leader's vision. Two common theories of leadership – charismatic leadership and transformational leadership – have influenced much of contemporary leadership thinking. Both have their strengths but are insufficient approaches for the effective leadership of independent followers. The predominant model of leadership as something that flows one way, from the leader down to followers, is inadequate.[5] From a Christian leadership perspective, it also fails to account fully for the biblical understanding of persons as bearers of the image of God.

Charismatic Leadership

Charismatic leadership, popularized by German sociologist Max Weber, emphasizes the importance of the leader as a magnetizing, inspirational force. The charismatic leader exhibits certain personality skills, demeanor, motivational communication, and inspirational action. Followers personally identify with the leader and leader approval is a primary source of their motivation.[6] Charismatic leadership can be effective in a situation where the followers are uncertain, tentative, unassertive or unskilled in critical tasks. People who tend to respond well to dominant personalities and gain confidence through the assertiveness of others often find charismatic leadership appealing.

On the other hand, charisma in leadership has little tolerance for competition. Charismatic leadership tends to produce solo artists. Followers who have their own ideas, are internally self-motivated, are confident and capable of moving ahead on their own often view charismatic leaders as egotistical and arrogant with little concern for other's thoughts. These followers will either fall into outright conflict with the charismatic leader or abandon the organizational effort (either literally or emotionally) for their own pursuits.

Moreover, as Scripture and experience make abundantly clear, charismatic influence is not necessarily synonymous with truth or wisdom. One can be extremely inspirational, influential, and motivational and be leading people in the wrong direction. Independent followers, driven by their own moral compasses, are less likely to be swayed or guided by charismatic leadership that they perceive as superficially brilliant but substantively deficient. In the long run, charismatic leadership can fall prey to becoming a "resounding gong or a clanging cymbal," as so poetically described in 1 Corinthians 13. Charisma tends to attract people to the leader, but if a charismatic leader will direct that energy, attention, and enthusiasm toward others, they make space for independent followers to flourish and be satisfied. In short, charismatic leaders who learn to use their strong personalities to show love for their followers are much more likely to create a healthy, collaborative, and synergistic team environment.

Transformational Leadership

In transformational leadership theory, the leader builds group participation by helping followers rise above self-interest and focus on achieving group goals.[7] The leader appeals to the follower's need for meaning and significance in work, encourages the follower to surpass their own expectations, and affirms the value of reaching the organizational goals. Transformational leadership's emphasis upon individualized attention and intellectual stimulation can have positive benefits for the work environment and organizational effectiveness.

However, the primary strength of transformational leadership—transcending self-interest—can also be its Achilles' heel. The assumption that followers are self-interested and in need of transformation is not necessarily valid. Who is to say that followers are not intrinsically driven by interests other than their own self actualization? Transformational leadership rests on the implicit assumption that followers will drift into self-interest without the guidance of a leader. Even more problematically, it assumes that leaders themselves are not motivated by self-interest. Even a simple perusal of news stories across the last decades quickly proves this false. At its heart, the logical paradigm of transformational leadership is that leaders inherently are not self-interested whereas followers are. As a result, the latter need the former in order for the whole organization to focus on something greater than itself.

A second critique is the assumption that self-interest is inherently a bad thing or in conflict with the purposes of the organization. In transformational leadership theory, little consideration is given to this belief. In fact, effective independent followers are quite proficient at balancing personal and corporate goals[8] and seeing them as mutually compatible rather then in competition. These followers are more likely to see their own personal calling inextricably linked with the vision of the organization. The opportunity to live out this calling is often a primary for joining the organization in the first place. Put another way, for these kinds of followers, the mission of the organization is a part of their own positive self-interest. The interests of the organization significantly conform to their own self-interests.

When leading independent followers, the objectives of transformational leadership are often moot. Levels of commitment to the vision do not need elevating. Self-interest on the part of the followers often works in favor of and not against the organization; in fact, it can often be an asset to wise leaders willing to let followers have autonomy and freedom. Independent followers are self-learners and routinely pursue intellectual stimulation. In general terms, independent followers tend to operate at a level well beyond where transformational leadership theory typically assumes they are capable or willing.

When it comes to independent followers, both charismatic and transformational leadership suffer from one major shortcoming: they assume a particular dependency of the follower upon the leader. This assumption leads to misaligned expectations on the part of both leader and follower and problems ensue:

> Followers actively evaluate their leaders and find most of them wanting. Followers are insulted by the suggestion that they need empowering or transformation. They are not enslaved, waiting to be freed by benevolent masters. The major constraint upon their best performance is the stereotypes inside the leader's head.[9]

In reality, independent followers are often as capable and qualified to lead as the leaders themselves. The distinction between leading and following is one of role and responsibility; not competency, skill or ability. Leadership that assumes distinctions along the lines of the latter inevitably will become mired in conflict (active or passive), turmoil, or apathetic maintenance of the status quo. In contrast, a shared view of leadership between a strong leader and strong followers coupled with a biblical view of community produces a mutual, shared, and interdependent process, even while allowing distinct positional roles and authority between leaders and followers.

Sharing the Wheel: Rethinking Leadership

Shared leadership offers an alternative that can enhance the value of independent followers while making the most of corporate effort in pursuit of organizational and personal mission. Shared leadership can be defined in a variety of ways depending on whether one wants to emphasize formal authority, work-team structures, or interpersonal relationships. In its essence, though, shared leadership is the sharing of power and responsibility in moving towards a shared goal.[10]

The principle of shared leadership is a departure from a more traditional view of leadership as a set of individual traits or behaviors. Instead, leadership is seen as broader set of processes within the larger group; it is a role that is bigger than any one person. Shared leadership is less concerned with who is in charge and more with how to work together to achieve goals, solve problems, and make decisions. Shared leadership operates on several crucial assumptions.

First, leadership is a system, not an individual function. Viewing the organization through the lens of system thinking reinforces notions such as the power of shared vision, paying more attention to the interrelationships among people rather than formal structures, thinking in terms of processes rather than snapshots, and the significance of team learning.[11] These are characteristics of successful learning organization. How much greater the need in a setting of expert, independent fol-

> *"Shared leadership requires the balance of power, shared goals and responsibility, personal respect, and working together in complex, real-life circumstances"*

lowers. Shared leadership requires a systems view. There is a distinction between "leadership" within the whole organization and individual leaders. Leadership in its fullest sense is bigger than what any one single formal leader does at any point in time. Multiple individuals can fill the role either in sequence or in tandem and the configurations can be temporary or long-term.[12] Shared leadership can be formal as seen in traditional role structures and titles. Shared leadership can also be informal as a designated leader recognizes the capacity and skill of others to participate in the work of leadership and intentionally seeks to tap that potential in leading the organization. Whether formal or informal, leadership involves the shared contributions of all those having leadership roles. Leadership itself does not fully rest in any one individual.[13]

Second, *leading* and *following* are equal but different roles in an organization. This contrasts with the traditional hierarchical positioning of leaders above followers. The current trend of servant leadership is an example of a theoretical model that inverts the relationship between leader and follower. However, followership is not the antithesis of leadership but a collaborative partner in the work of the organization.[14] Leadership is guiding "the development of the system" and followership is the pursuit of "the common cause."[15] Successful organizations require both leaders and followers in collaborative partnership towards the common purpose.

Third, the increased complexity and demands of the contemporary marketplace often require more than a single leader can provide. In defining leadership as "doing things through the efforts of others," organizational consultants O'Toole, Galbraith, and Lawler question if a single leader can even "affect company performance...other than trying to 'look good' to investors."[16] In contrast, shared leadership potentially allows the organization to expand problem-solving capacity, draw from a deeper creative pool, allow for more insightful decision making, and streamline the exchange of crucial information. Shared leadership allows individual strengths and weaknesses to balance one another and permits leaders focus on what they are best at doing.

From a biblical perspective of the community of God at work, no single leader or role bears the burden for the entire work. Even in roles we tend to identify as executive, the leadership need and process extends well beyond the confines of that one person. The biblical theme of spiritual gifts is an example. While the doctrine of spiritual giftedness within the body has a specific theological context, it nonetheless points to a broader underlying truth: people in God's image were made to be productive and work best in community. The body as a whole is synergistic, exceeding the sum of its parts. At the heart of this synergy are different roles and different kinds of people with different abilities working in unity and harmony. The New Testament offers us a vision for what organizations of all stripes can be like when this optimistic view of the human person and what they mean to the whole is taken.

Fourth, the organizational context must be suitable for shared leadership. Not every context is ideal for the sharing of leadership responsibility. Start-up organizations such as entrepreneurial endeavors or organizations in crisis are two instances where circumstances prohibit the kind of investment and culture that shared leadership requires.[17] In these situations, the top-down focus of a single leader may be necessary to originate or maintain the life of the organization. It is unwise for any leader to assume a one-size-fits-all approach to leadership for all situations. Leaders are certainly called to be wise and exercise prudence in leading those for whom they have responsibility. To give leadership away too early or to share leadership with those who are unprepared can lead to chaos or dysfunction, thus putting the organization at risk.

Leadership Behaviors

Themes such as collaboration, training, communication, and reevaluation of leadership philosophy are common throughout much of the current research on shared leadership. Lambert identifies at least five crucial features required for effective shared leadership: skillful participation, vision, inquiry, collaboration, and reflection.[18] Organizations can maximize exemplary followership through redefining leader and follower roles, training for leader and follower skills, offering performance feedback, and obtaining collaboration on organization structure.[19] Shared leadership requires the balance of power, shared goals and responsibility, personal respect, and working together in complex, real-life circumstances.[20] While these are all valuable and legitimate components of effective shared leadership, most of these various elements can be identified in one of four foundational behaviors.

Giving Away the Vision

The leader must share ownership of their vision with others and invite them to help sharpen it, grow it, and bring it to life. In this context, however, sharing means more than just simply communicating it. To share ownership of vision means allowing a part in determining what that full vision ultimately will be. This does not mean that the leader takes a democratic approach or seeks to build a vision by consensus or vote. But it might mean allowing others to offer critique, to challenge assumptions, to add new ideas, or to suggest improvements. In the case of an established organizational mission, this might mean inviting others to aid in the articulation and strategic pursuit of that mission.

Shared leadership recognizes that independent followers are motivated by being co-creators of vision, not merely consumers of it. If a leader values proprietary possession of an idea or a vision and is unable to relinquish full control over that vision, shared leadership will be very difficult. On the other hand, allowing others to participate in leadership at the point of having a voice about the direction and vision of the group creates rich possibilities for enthusiasm, creativity, productivity and long-term participation. Independent followers who are allowed to help lead through contributing to vision and direction are much more likely to remain engaged and connected to the core of organization. More to the point, as Kelley wrote, they "want to forge the vision together to increase the probability of success."[21] Such an environment becomes self-reproducing by attracting other like-minded independent followers who also have a strong sense of personal direction and the desire for shared vision.

Taking the Time

The leader must intentionally structure time with those sharing the leadership. Leadership depends upon information, problem-solving, strategic planning and interpersonal relationships. When these elements are being executed by a team, regular opportunities for dialogue, brainstorming, relationship development and trust-building are essential. Formal, agenda-driven meetings once a month are no substitute for frequent, informal gatherings over lunch, coffee or the office water cooler or even outside of working hours. These ordinary moments allow maximum possibility for the formation of the kind of trust and shared values that make shared leadership desirable and worthwhile.

Such a value of time-based leadership development mirrors a Christian and Trinitarian view of community. As Wesleyans, the historical emphasis on the Tri-une life in both pulpit and pew offers us a powerful vision of how the shared life of fellowship, mutual encouragement, and authentic vulnerability can lead to healthy and vibrant organizations, regardless of size. We are made to thrive in relationships. A Wesleyan trinitarian theology affirms the power of this in all dimensions of life.

Showing Vulnerability

The leader must be willing to share their own perspectives and thoughts about the various issues facing the group. This required a certain level of vulnerability and openness on the part of the leader. Dialogue in shared leadership is often the art of "thinking out loud" together. To be effective and valuable, dialogue requires a strong sense of security and safety between group members. Leaders who intentionally invite and demonstrate this kind of environment and dialogue are more likely to see it come about. Such vulnerable sharing transcends planning and involves the exchange of spontaneous ideas, sometimes foolish or unrealistic, insights, future dreams, present concerns, past lessons learned, or fears about direction or decisions. Smith wrote:

> Top leaders who hope to set the energies and performance of people on fire through rich, promising visions must know when to follow their people's interpretation of those visions in order to truly benefit from the creativity and meaning that any vision-driven enterprise requires.[22]

Leaders willing to take the risk of vulnerability in sharing in dialogue significantly increase the creative power and potential of the group.

Trust with Responsibility

The leader must be willing to abdicate some primary responsibility and decision-making power to others. This is a particular threat to leaders because in many instances the designated leader is singularly accountable for group performance to some external group such as shareholders, presidents or trustee boards. In these cases, the decision for shared leadership is an internal one and the primary leader alone carries the public weight of leadership.

Nonetheless, shared leadership is not truly shared unless the leader shares responsibility and power. This power involves relatively high degrees of autonomy and freedom in areas such as problem solving, use of resources, decision-making, goal-setting, and evaluation. Responsibility in shared leadership goes two directions as the co-leaders are accountable to one another and the primary (or facilitating) leader.

Jumping In

So what can organizations or leaders do to begin cultivating an environment of shared leadership that maximizes the passion, calling, and value of independent, effective followers?

Commit to sharing leadership. The organization's primary leadership commits to facilitating leadership in others. This means an intentional shift in the perception and practice of leadership. This may well mean learning a new set of rules, a new vocabulary, and undergoing an uncomfortable process of letting go of some power and responsibility. Leaders willing to make this commitment must be willing to see leadership as a role in which different members of the organization can function in various ways. This in turn means being willing to see colleagues as potential partners in leadership rather than people in need of being led along the journey. Effective leadership in this mode recognizes the possibilities when skilled, passionate individuals are able to harmonize their efforts and achieve something far greater together than they ever could on their own.

Encourage dialogue and collaboration. Adopting shared leadership in an existing organization likely means a redefining of roles and the organization's understanding of leadership and followership. Primary leadership intentionally creates space for this dialogue to take place and gives followers opportunities to talk about their past roles and future possibilities. This dialogue may also include various kinds of training on topics such as communication, brainstorming, working with constructive criticism, and feedback exchange and general leadership skills.

Invite and reward feedback. There are strategic place in which primary leadership can create this dialogue is through the solicitation of follower feedback about their own leadership performance. In most leadership structures, the evaluation of performance moves from the top down: the leader evaluates the follower. Inverting this approach can be a powerful way to begin to build shared leadership. When followers are invited to evaluate the leader's performance it can help create a sense of equality, trust, and mutuality essential to shared leadership.

Initially, leader-oriented feedback may not be high due to a fear of potential retaliation.[23] Followers are frequently unused to such requests and may be suspicious or unwilling to be honest and candid for fear of jeopardizing their job or hurting the supervisor's feelings. Here the leader must patiently affirm the intent and demonstrate their willingness to reward even the most difficult and painful criticism. Inviting this kind of feedback can be painful to a leader's ego and requires the leader to develop a sense of humility and self-confidence that honors the perspectives and input of others without threatening their own leadership.

Reward "positive disruption." An organization wanting to maximize shared leadership encourages unsolicited ideas and feedback, encourages creative, spontaneous outside-the-box thinking, is not threatened by the constructive criticism of its outspoken employees, and actively rewards those who passionately share their perspectives and opinions. An organization wanting to maintain top-down leadership, on the other hand, is threatened by unsolicited feedback that is critical (even when it is valid), insists on dictating the terms and place of follower dialogue, and is more likely to reward those who comply rather than those who identify places for improvement.

The psychology of positive reinforcement shows us that we tend to get what we reward. Positive reinforcement produces much greater fruit than consequential discipline. Seek out and reward shared leadership efforts in others. Post a comments box, invite employees or followers to share their candid suggestions, and then find ways to act on or implement these suggestions. Affirm those who contribute such ideas, even anonymously. Most importantly, leaders need to learn to appreciate the difference between negative criticism and legitimate critiques aimed at making the organization better. Be a good listener and look beyond the surface to the motive. The employee who sees things differently and willingly speaks their mind without invitation is easily swept aside and labeled as a troublemaker. Do not ignore or avoid the "positive disruptor" who is willing to share their thoughts or ideas, especially when they contain critiques or suggestions for improvement. Many organizations do not value or reward such behavior; yet, shared leadership recognizes the potential value in these voices.

Summing it up

Effective shared leadership requires a great deal of willingness on the part of the facilitating leader and trust between the leader and the others involved. Shared leadership is not the primary leader spending lots of time talking about his ideas. It is not seeking input without offering power, nor is it the using the language of sharing for the purpose of gaining followers. Shared leadership recognizes that the vision or purpose of the organization transcends both leaders and followers and requires the collaborative effort of each. The leader that can maximize and organization of independent followers in this context acknowledges the leadership potential in others, invites others to participate in the task of leadership, recognizes the complementary roles of leadership and followership, and engages in foundational behavior that exemplifies the true nature of shared leadership..

Bryan R. Easley, PhD, is the Dean of Online Education at Oklahoma Wesleyan University, an adjunct professor for Oklahoma Wesleyan and Nazarene Bible College, and an ordained elder in the Church of the Nazarene.

Bibliography

Bass, Bernard. "Leadership: Good, better, best." *Organizational Dynamics*, 13, no. 3 (1985).

Bennis, Warren. *Managing People is Like Herding Cats*. Covey Leadership Center, 1997.

Deiss, K. J., and M. Sullivan, M. "The shared leadership principle: Creating leaders throughout the organization." *Leading Ideas*, no. 2 (1998).

Hartung, Adam. "Herding Cats – 4 Leadership Lessons from Top Publicist Jeff Ballard." Forbes.com. June 5, 2014. Accessed November 2015. http://onforb.es/1TRbPp1

Janov, J. *The Inventive Organization: Hope and Daring at Work*. San Francisco: Jossey-Bass, 1994.

Kelley, Robert "In Praise of Followers." *Harvard Business Review*, Nov-Dec (1998): 142-148. Accessed March 2016. https://hbr.org/1988/11/in-praise-of-followers

Kelley, Robert "Leadership Secrets from Exemplary Followers." In *Leading Organizations*, edited by G. R. Hickman, 193-201. Thousand Oaks: SAGE Publications, 1998.

Lambert, L. "A Framework for Shared Leadership." *Beyond Instructional Leadership*, 59. no. 8 (2002): 37-40.

MacNeil, A., and A. McClanahan. "NCPEA: Shared leadership." Cnx.org. 2005. Accessed February 2016. http://cnx.org/contents/CuSQhCun@2/Shared-Leadership

Moxley, R. *Leadership and Spirit*. San Francisco: Jossey-Bass, 2000.

O'Toole, J., Galbraith, J., and Lawler, I. E. "When two (or more) heads are better than one: The promise and pitfalls of shared leadership." Leadership Teleconference. 2002. Center for Effective Organizations.

Pearce, C. L., and Charles Manze. "The new silver bullets of leadership." *Organizational Dynamics*, 34, no. 2 (2005): 130-140.

Powell, S. R. "Employee growth and development: A shared leadership model for changing organizations and people." *NJ Psychologist*. Spring (2002).

Senge, Peter. *The Fifth Discipline*. New York: Doubleday, 2006.

Smith, D. K. "The following part of leading." Edited by Frances Hesselbein, Marshall Goldsmith, and Richard Beckhard. The Leader of the Future: New Visions, Strategies, and Practices for the Next Era, 199-207. San Francisco: Jossey-Bass, 1997.

Yukl, Gary. *Leadership in Organizations* (5th ed.). Upper Saddle River: Prentice-Hall, 2002.

Chapter 22 Notes

[1] Bennis, Managing People is Like Herding Cats; Hartung, "Herding Cats"

[2] Hartung, "Herding Cats"

[3] Kelley, "In Praise of Followers," 144.

[4] And for good reason. In many contexts, independent, effective followers often possess the same or greater qualifications, credentials, or even experience than those in higher leadership roles.

[5] Pearce and Manze, "The new silver bullets of leadership"

[6] Yukl, Leadership in Organizations, 243

[7] Bass, "Leadership: Good, better, best," 26.

[8] Kelley, "In Praise," 147.

[9] Ibid, 193.

[10] Moxley, *Leadership and Spirit.*

[11] Senge, *The Fifth Discipline*

[12] The long-term formal sharing of leadership using such constructs has been uysed in major corporations like Microsoft, Disney, Dell, and Hewlett-Packard. See O'Toole et al, "When two (or more) heads are better than one"

[13] Lambert, "A Framework for Shared Leadership," 37-40.

[14] Kelley, "In Praise"

[15] Janov, *The inventive Organization,* 224.

[16] O'Toole et al, "Promise and pitfall of shared leadership"

[17] Pearce and Manze, "Silver bullets"

[18] Lambert, "A Framework"

[19] Deiss and Sullivan, "The shared leadership principle"

[20] MacNeil and McClanahan, "Shared leadership"

[21] Kelley, "In Praise," 196.

[22] Smith, "The following part of leading"

[23] Kelley, "Leadership Secrets"

23
Leading Well Under Pressure

Rob McKenna and Amy Nagley

Leaders, especially in ministry, can be tempted to take on the desires, worries, and pressures of others. In this chapter, leadership differentiation is offered as a healthy alternative to taking on these elements from other selves. Yet leaders must be concerned with the other not appear to be cold or disconnected. Thus, purpose can be the leader's best friend in maintaining a healthy sense of self while being accessible to others. The chapter concludes with helpful tips and strategies to connecting with others from the position of leadership responsibility.

JOHN WESLEY HAD A SINCERE CONNECTION to the moments when "the eyes of your understanding are opened"[1] to God's presence in our lives. His emphasis on these important moments provides relevance not only to our experience of God, but also to our self-understanding. Leaders are no strangers to these moments. Because of the daily pressures leaders face to manage multiple stakeholders and their own convictions, moments of potential insight and learning are plentiful. John Wesley's position on the power and potential impact of these moments was clearly grounded in the idea that insight was freely provided to those who were humbly looking for it.

While definitions of leadership vary greatly, the fundamental truth about leaders is that leaders go first. As children, we never struggled with defining a leader. In fact, we played a game called "Follow the Leader" that required no explanation of the rules, at all. The fundamental rule was that the leader goes first. The leader stepped out and said or did something, and the other children followed. We understand this principle today as adults. Leaders are the people who have the courage to step out, often alone, and go first in doing or being something that others who might follow have not done first. When we think about leadership this way, it is important to note that leadership, in ministry or in any other context, is a neutral term. It isn't until we attach a certain type of leadership to the term that we start to see the kind of leader that we would want to follow. Sacrificial, servant, charismatic, or transformational leaders are all types of leaders who have a certain value attached to the way in which we expect them to go first.

What is a Leader?

The challenge for would-be leaders in a ministry context is that potential followers have their own perceptions about what it means to be a leader and the type of leader they want to follow. The more followers a leader has, the more opinions that leader will face about his or her leadership and about every decision she or he makes. The most effective leaders that we have worked with are those who not only have the courage to go first, but also the courage and sacrificial character that urges them to pay attention to what is happening inside and around them, and to the needs of their followers. In keeping with a Wesleyan view of the optimistic potential of grace, these are the people who do not feel immediately worthy of God's favor, but are continually working hard at humbly becoming better versions of themselves. They are people who are working hard at being better listeners, more purposeful, and asking questions that open up a realm of potential (instead of filling every meeting with their voice). They are leaders who are willing to change their behavior, while maintaining their identity and their own voice in different decisions and situations. These types of leaders begin their day in prayer, asking God to enable them to better listen, see what is around them, and discern God's will in their leadership.

Over the last two decades, many of the leaders we have helped to develop – whether they were seminary students, pastors, or lay leaders in the church or in a parachurch ministry – had two things in common: They felt called to serve where they were leading, and they had little idea of how much pressure they would face as a leader. Many of them had received great theological training or had been taught how to preach, but they hadn't been prepared for what it would feel like when they stepped out alone as the leader. These years of participating in a such wide range of leadership development has provided opportunity to study the journey of thousands of ministry leaders and the impact of pressure on their ability to lead well. If there is a reality they all faced, it went something like this: "The potential rewards will be big, but the pressure is coming, and I need to be ready—for the sake of my followers, my ministry, and myself." James 1:2-4 offers some challenging words about the pressure leaders face:

> Consider it pure joy, my brothers, whenever you face trials of many kinds, because you know that the testing of your faith develops perseverance. Perseverance must finish its work so that you may be mature and complete, not lacking anything.

Each one of us should not only be thankful for the adverse situations we face, but also recognize the necessity of adversity for taking us to the next level. James goes on to advise his hearers to "be quick to hear, slow to speak, slow to anger, for the anger of man does not produce the righteousness that God requires" (1:19-20). Is it a coincidence that James speaks of listening, regulating what we say, and warning against our inflated egos in the context of trials and testing? Or was he highlighting some basic tendencies we have as human beings and as leaders when we face these moments where the stakes are highest?

Leading during times of personal and organizational pressure is hard work. When the stakes are high and you are the one who must decide the course of action, communicate the plan, and then build up your employees to journey ahead, it is inevitable that things will not always go perfectly and smoothly. However, it is in these times that a leader has the greatest opportunity for growth and strides in self-awareness. The leader's strengths and weaknesses come to light, as the situation presents the leader with the continuous challenge of maintaining a sense of self and voice, while at the same time listening to those around him/her and ensuring

"a primary factor that will help individuals to sustain their leadership over the long haul is something called leadership differentiation"

a humble, yet solid stance. In these times, the leader can be tempted to lean on his/her competence, and in response, lose their willingness or ability to empathize, to connect to others, and to care for the very real needs and wants of those they lead. On the other hand, they might feel an overwhelming need to maintain their relationship with stakeholders, even if it means sacrificing their own convictions. This is why leading in adversity is really hard work.

There are three basic truths about leading under pressure: 1) high pressure situations will happen often; 2) those situations will challenge leaders emotionally, physically, and spiritually; and 3) there are strategies that can enable leaders to navigate the high pressure moments more effectively. The capacity of a leader to manage him- or herself well when under pressure can make the difference between sustaining a meaningful career as an influential leader in ministry and burning out or fading away. While being a competent leader, having the right theological training, being a good speaker or pastor, or even having the "right" personality will have some impact, a primary factor that will help individuals to sustain their leadership over the long haul is something called *leadership differentiation*.

Leadership Differentiation

The concept of leadership differentiation was born out of *family systems theory*, put forth by Dr. Murray Bowen. Through the lens of family systems theory, individuals are part of an inter-connected emotional system, where the experiences of every person are constantly affecting those of the larger system for better or worse. During times of high stress, the anxiety of one family member can spread throughout the emotional system and put the entire family in a downward spiral. For the overall wellbeing of the family, however, Bowen advocated for *differentiation of self*, which is the extent to which individuals are able to stay calm and clear headed enough to think through their own plan of best action without being swayed toward the negativity that permeates the emotional system. A colleague of Bowen, Edwin Friedman stated that if you want to help a family toward well being, target the person with the most differentiated self, because he/she has the potential to spread something new throughout the system (rather than falling into old family habits).

While Bowen remained in the family systems realm, Friedman was interested in how the theory of self-differentiation played out with leaders. Building on his life of work, Friedman's family published a book entitled, *A Failure of Nerve: Leadership in the Age of the Quick Fix.* To Friedman, some leaders are anxious people pleasers that are more concerned with consensus than progress. But what happens if the consensus is not the healthiest for the group? He advocated for leaders to be emotionally connected to the system around him/her, but simultaneously maintain a clear sense of vision, purpose, and one's own principles in the midst of what is happening within the group. Crucial for this type of emotional differentiation is the leader's ability to understand his/her own tendencies under stress, and to effectively control his/her own emotions. A well-differentiated leader is one who can stand in the middle of an emotional storm and be clear-headed enough to come up with an effective plan that will move the system toward healthy outcomes.

Leadership Differentiation in Context

If you are a leader in ministry, you understand the fundamental tension we all face in staying true to ourselves while staying connected to the needs of those around us. If you don't understand that tension, it is highly likely that you have failed to stay connected to the needs of your followers or that you have lost yourself along the way. Leadership differentiation is about maintaining your capacity to manage two seemingly contradictory things at one time; you lead from your convictions *and* from your connections with others. If you have ever been to see a family systems therapist, you likely understand this concept, as many family systems therapists have been trained to build up personal convictions, self-efficacy, and identity in family members, while at the same time helping them to see others convictions, thoughts, emotions, and desires. Therapists working with families understood this principle long before those of us in the business of developing leaders.

A key challenge in this fundamental tension is that we all have habits that emerge under pressure. Some ministry leaders focus most of their attention on the feelings of others, while others naturally express their own thoughts and feelings without as much concern for others. For that reason, the place to start is to understand your emotional habit under pressure—your tendency either to lead too strongly or to care too much about what others think. The point is not to deny the value of either, but to embrace the fact that becoming a more differentiated leader is to manage the pressure of doing one but not at the expense of the other; providing strong direction and vision while still caring for the perspective and thoughts of others.

Attending to Yourself

For many of us who lead in ministry contexts, it often feels self-serving to know what we want with clarity and conviction; like it's not okay to be clear about what we want, the direction of our church or organization, or even the next steps we will take as our teams move forward together. Openly and clearly expressing ideas and goals with conviction is not only something that we shy away from, but also something that is sometimes shunned by our church communities.

For leaders who have never given themselves permission to express their wants or desires, or to lead out more strongly, the initial attempts can feel heavy handed. This is especially true for leaders who care deeply about the thoughts and feelings of others. However, we do a disservice to those we lead when we fail to offer them clarity about the direction the ministry is taking. When working with leaders who need to pay more attention to God and to their own mission, the conversation can be narrowed down to one simple question: "What do you want and when will your followers know?"

Attention to Others

For other leaders, the problem looks very different. The problem isn't that they spend too much time being managed by the thoughts or feelings of others, but that they are forthright about their own convictions, potentially causing them to miss what other people need. Working with ministry and business leaders over the years has taught us much about this group. These are leaders who often describe themselves as Type A or as non-emotional. They know they are strong as leaders, and they will tell you very quickly that they aren't as touchy-feely as the people they lead. They will know there is something to fix, but the reality is that deep down they may also feel that other people are weak, or that expressing emotion or a desire for relational connection somehow lacks strength. These leaders describe themselves as strong and no-nonsense, and as someone who gets straight to the point. Just like the first group, they care deeply about what other people think of them, but less about what they think of themselves.

For ministry leaders like this, the advice is equally simple but doesn't come in the form of a question. Ministry leaders with a high attention to self don't need questions. They want answers. The answer is this: *Shut up.*[2] If you are this kind of leader, the key to becoming more differentiated is to stop talking long enough to give others the space to bring their own answers and ideas. You will feel the pressure to start talking again, but the objective is to let them speak. The answers will get better as you let others contribute their ideas.

Well-differentiated leaders provide strong, personal leadership, care for the thoughts and feelings of others, and regulate their emotions in controlling how they respond emotionally and behaviorally in different situations. They lead out of clear convictions while simultaneously remaining connected to others. The challenge many leaders face is not about how to maintain conviction *or* connection, but how to do *both* of these things at the same time.

Differentiation Strategies Profile

There are certain strategies that are more powerful than others when it comes to a ministry leader's ability to be differentiated under pressure and to self-regulate emotionally when the pressure is highest. The following tool we have provided can help you regulate emotions and be more differentiated under pressure.[3]

Think of a high-pressure situation you are currently facing. Using the Differentiation Strategies Profile provided at the end of this chapter, rate yourself on each of the dimensions, noting the areas where you are strong and the ones being underutilized. Purposefully rate yourself high on 3 dimensions, medium on 4 dimensions, and low on 3 dimensions. Then, invite someone on your ministry team or from your family to rate you as well. Use this conversation as an opportunity to understand your strengths under pressure, and what others need from you when the pressure is on.

The Power of Purpose: Why Do You Lead?

Of all the differentiation strategies, leaders who have a sense of purpose and stay connected to it during high-pressure situations are better able to regulate their own behavior and emotions, and therefore be more effective within the larger system in which they lead. Why have you chosen to be in a position of accountability for others? This responsibility is the reality of leadership. It is only a matter of time before the position will provide pressure, anxiety, opportunity, and challenge. If God has gifted you to lead, you have a tremendous opportunity and daily challenge.

One of the most powerful contributors to a ministry leader's ability to handle the pressure is the extent to which they have clearly defined their purpose for being in the situation in the first place. The challenge for each of us is to be clear about why we are doing what we are doing; the more specific the purpose, the better the clarity and the stronger the commitment. For example, "Because God called me to do it" is very different from "God called me to rally our church to reach the two dozen single moms with children who live within two miles of our church." Specificity provides stability and direction on how to move toward fulfilling that purpose. To become more in tune with your purpose you need to know who God has made you to be and what Christlike passions drive you. We often speak in broad generalizations such as, "I am meant to serve in God's kingdom." While true, these generalities do not provide specific direction for followers. Delving deeper into the specifics of who you really are and what you want is crucial for moving toward fulfillment, keeping in mind that it is not of the self but from God.

Know Who You Are & What You Want

Quite possibly, you got into your current position because someone you knew had confidence that you knew your ministry well enough to do the job. That person probably also knew you had the courage necessary to make tough decisions, and the wisdom to get feedback from your key stakeholders before acting. However, as the responsibilities of the job increase, like many leaders, you may find yourself becoming so busy that you lose track of the meaning in your work. You may forget about the bigger picture, and even forget to listen for God's voice in your work. Without taking time for prayer and reflection, emotional pressure from others can cause you to react to the moment, drifting away from strategic goals and what is best for the organization. Being reflective and deliberate as a leader provides a context to every situation, conversation, and decision. Many ministry leaders struggle with reflection and deliberation. Where does my will begin and end in relationship to God's will for my life? If Christ is at the center of your purpose, your purpose is made clearer, but you still have to do the work of defining your position during difficult leadership times.

If you abandon any part of your conviction and identity for the sake of group consensus, then the outcome can be a lack of respect from your followers and even a lack of self-respect. The people in your organization may not always like the decisions you make, but they will respect you more if they know you have the courage to follow through. One way to make sure you are maintaining internal conviction and identity in any high pressure situation is to ask yourself some tough questions that will open you up to some of your most deeply rooted, subconscious thoughts. We encourage you to get out a journal or notebook for writing, and set aside some time to answer these questions. After you write down your responses, share them with someone you trust and allow yourself to go into deep discussion.

What do you want? The book of Nehemiah begins with a straightforward question from the King to Nehemiah. "What do you want?" When was the last time you gave yourself permission to ask yourself that question? While Nehemiah starts off his journey with a prayer of confession before his God, he finishes by answering that question before the king: "I want to build the wall." What is it that you want for your ministry, and when will your followers know?

What would you do in this situation if you weren't afraid? Even when you are not fully aware of your fears and insecurities, they will impact what goals and tasks you take on. You may want to start by thinking about the things you tend to avoid. This reflection may shed light on your fears, and from there you can begin identifying what those fears are inhibiting you from doing that may bring satisfaction, engagement, and joy to your life.

What do you need to do in this situation to look yourself in the mirror next week? Leadership will come with a cost, often a relational one. Rarely is the leader able to get everyone to agree, but getting as much input as possible being courageous enough to take a risk—even relational ones, may lead to a consensus of satisfaction with the outcome, and moving people beyond the edge of their comfort zones.

Considering all the stakeholders involved, what are the tough decisions you'll need to make? This is easy to say and tough to do. If you lead others in times of adversity, it's unlikely they'll all agree with you. Nevertheless, you must make tough decisions, and continue considering the impact on others along the way.

What support do you need? Let's face it, we can't do it all. There are times when we need to call on others to help us with tasks, talk to us about our experience, or just let us know that they care. What do you need in order to best navigate this situation?

Paying Attention

Maintaining personal conviction and identity is not the entirety of leadership in high-pressure situations. For ministry leaders who value high performance, celebrate and reward the tough-minded, and increasingly rely on achievement as a means of satisfaction, what does it take to stay connected to key stakeholders? As successes add up, ministry grows, and there is greater pressure to produce, our ability and willingness to hear others may become limited. Others know immediately when you no longer value their input. In fact, you might think and say that you value the input of others, but the pressure to do more and to do it better can completely mute your ability to stay in touch. What should a leader do in this situation?

Realize that your ability to stay connected, to slow down, and to hear the voices of your stakeholders is key to your ability to lead well. Second, realize that pressure and adversity may hinder your ability to listen. In the New Testament, James knew this: "My dear brothers, take note of this: Everyone should be quick to listen, slow to speak, and slow to become angry" (James 1:19).

Reflective Questions

Here are some questions to ask yourself to help you feel more confident that you're paying attention to the voices around you. Get out your journal and take some time to respond thoughtfully.

Who are the key stakeholders in the situation and what's at stake for each of them? Take the time to make a list of those who will be affected by or have a stake in the outcome. Hopefully you understand the adversity you are facing, but do you understand what others are feeling and why? For many of leaders, this means being deliberate about checking in with even the most challenging individuals, whether peers, bosses, subordinates, volunteers, family members or the community. The trick, however, is not to ask simple closed questions, but instead to focus questions on the potential of the situation. For example, "Given your perspective of our department, what do you think needs to happen to accomplish this goal?" When you ask open-ended, solutions-focused questions, you receive answers that are more closely aligned with the potentially effective action steps (rather than more talk about the problems).

Do you tend to fill the silence with your own voice? Leaders often become uncomfortable with silence when they feel personal pressure. They feel an expectation to have answers, to be right, and to produce results. Speaking into silence for the sake of filling the silence is an anxious response. Find a trusted colleague who can watch you under pressure in the presence of others, and ask them to tell you if you need to listen more and talk less.

How can you create an environment where people will come to you with good and bad feedback? If you are a strong leader, even though you may be good, those you lead may not communicate with you enough. Followers may dismiss the value of their contribution, think you're too busy for them, or feel intimidated. Remember, you are more than likely in a position of authority. Encourage feedback from others and allow them to fill the silence with their voice. Leaders who dominate the conversation unwittingly train those they lead to remain silent and not offer feedback or counsel.

When you're confident you finally understand other people's perspective, how will you know you're correct? Be careful of silent agreement. We often ask leaders if they know what others are thinking in the midst of organization or personal adversity. Many leaders say, "Yes, I know what they're thinking." When challenged *how* they know, leaders often respond, "I asked around the office and I brought up the issue at our last board meeting and no one had any objections, so they're on board." If you do not have much feedback, or have not been deliberate about processing the different opinions of your stakeholders, chances are you do not yet know their perspective.

Summing it all Up

If you have been called to be a leader, this means that your followers are waiting for you to go first. Throughout your leadership journey there will be times of ease and joy, and times of challenge. Adversity and pressure can provide a crucible in which your leadership can mature. And as your ability to leader well under pressure grows, the temptation to be reactive, to make decisions unilaterally, or to be paralyzed in the pursuit of consensus will diminish, allowing leadership to flow more freely and effectively. The advice of the leaders we have worked with is clear: take the time necessary to step back and see the big picture. If you take time in silence to listen to God, ask potential-focused questions of your followers and really listen to them, and be clear-headed enough to create and communicate a vision, you will be more effective on many fronts.

As you come up against stress and pressure and are pulled in many directions (or are too hard-headed to see what is around you), learn to regulate your emotions and behavior in real time so you can get the necessary perspective to manage the anxiety others are feeling. In other words, know your hot buttons and foster an outside perspective, so you can pay the necessary attention to what you know needs to be done and to the needs and wants of the other key stakeholders, even those bringing you the most heat. Maintain a focus on the possibilities in the midst of challenges, and differentiate yourself by refusing to react one way or the other when others push you. Regulating your reactivity will help others know you're a leader who's in touch with their reality, and that you have the courage to maintain conviction and identity, even in the most challenging times. While others are experiencing the stress, you as the leader can bring a sense of calm and grounding to the rest of the system.

Rob McKenna, PhD, is Chair of the Department of Industrial-Organizational Psychology at Seattle Pacific University and Executive Director of the Center for Leadership Research & Development.

Amy Nagley is completing her PhD in Industrial-Organizational Psychology at Seattle Pacific University with research, teaching, and consulting experience in holistic well-being and engagement.

Chapter 23 Notes

[1] Ephesians 1:8

[2] These words have been so important to leaders I coach that I wrote an entire chapter entitled "Shut Up," found in by book, *Dying to Lead: Sacrificial Leadership in a Self-Centered World*

[3] Discussed in our article entitled, "The Differentiated Leader: Specific Strategies for Handling Today's Adverse Situations."

Appendix: Differentiation Strategies Profile

CONVICTION				
Dimensions	**L**	**M**	**H**	**Coaching Questions**
Sense of Purpose: The ability to think about the current situation in the context of a larger mission, purpose, and/or set of values that the leader holds to in his or her life.				• What would you do if you weren't afraid? • To what extent are the people in this situation challenging your sense of identity and purpose? • How can you keep your eyes on your greater purpose?
Perceptions of Control: The ability to focus more attention on the things that can be controlled or influenced by the leader instead of wasting effort on things that can't be controlled.				• What are the battles worth fighting? • Where do you have some leverage? • What are some of the things you can influence? • What do you need to let go?
PERSPECTIVE				
Dimensions	**L**	**M**	**H**	**Coaching Questions**
Seeing the Big Picture: Recognizing that the larger organization and system is often causing people to act the way they are; considering the impact of one's actions and decisions on the other systems that will be affected.				• What will be the ripple effects of the actions you are considering in this situation? • If you were to step onto the balcony above all the fray, what would you see? • What in the organization's history might explain the way people are acting?
Focusing on Potential not Problems: Focusing on the possibilities and potential within the system instead of focusing on the problems and deficits; problems aren't ignored, but are talked about in the context of the potential that can be achieved on the other side when the obstacles are overcome.				• For every obstacle that you have identified, what is the potential you are trying to achieve? • In what areas have you engaged in "either/or" thinking instead of both/and thinking? • What unsolicited voices or unexpected opportunities are presenting themselves to you that you may have missed?
RELATIONSHIPS				
Dimensions	**L**	**M**	**H**	**Coaching Questions**
Taking Others' Perspective: Taking the perspective of the other key stakeholders in the system, even the ones who are causing the most anxiety; talking about the goals of other people from their perspectives instead of only discussing them in the context of the leader's goals.				• Assume each of the stakeholders are acting the way they are for very good reasons. What is motivating them to make the decisions they are in this situation? How will you know? • How can you create an environment that will allow people to come to you with negative and positive feedback?

Empathy: Understanding and discussing how other people in the system feel; identifying with the people who will be negatively affected by the leader's decisions.				• What would allow you to have the courage to make the difficult decisions and not lose your empathy for the people who are negatively affected? • How can you create the time and space necessary for other people to tell you what matters the most to them?
It Isn't Personal: The ability to identify other contributors, constraints, and stakeholders in the system that could be causing people to react the way they are; recognizing that anger and negative emotions are often motivated by other factors, not personal attacks.				• Assume that other people aren't acting against you out of spite, but out of their own convictions, or out of fear. If true, why are they are acting the way they are? • To what extent are your actions primarily a reaction against other people in the system? • What can you do to make sure you are taking actions that are about you and not about them?

SELF-UNDERSTANDING

Dimensions	L	M	H	Coaching Questions
Self-Awareness: Ability to see and talk openly about one's strengths and personal weaknesses; awareness of how one's actions are being perceived by others.				• What triggers the strongest reactions in you in these situations? How do you respond, good or bad, in these situations? • What would your "older and wiser self" tell you to do in this situation? • What can you put in place to ensure that you see yourself the way that other people see you?
Self-Regulation: Ability to see the tactics and actions that are available and modify/ adapt one's behavior as the situation emerges.				• What is the smallest step you could take today that would have the greatest impact in moving you closer to your goals? • Recognizing that there probably isn't a perfect solution, what are the advantages and disadvantages of the best actions you could take in this situation? • What about you allows you to stay centered when you are the target of blame and sabotage?

© Real Time Development Strategies

24
Gender and Organizational Leadership

Aaron Perry

While not often considered together, gender theory and organizational theory can be linked through the story of the Ethiopian eunuch in Acts 8. In this story, the eunuch's identity is radically altered through his encounter with Philip who interprets the text of Isaiah for him in light of Christ. Yet in this alteration, the eunuch's gender identity is maintained. This chapter suggests that gender always provides a certain insight and a certain obliqueness and as such must both be affirmed and critiqued in order to obtain the best leadership practices from every leader.

THE CBS REALITY SHOW *Undercover Boss* recently told the story of Breckin, a transgender employee at Sky Zone.[1] The premise of *Undercover Boss* is that the company's owner or another high ranking supervisor is disguised to go undercover and examine how employees are doing at other levels of the organization. The boss found Breckin to be a model employee—conscientious, diligent, and honest. According to the show's custom, when the undercover boss is revealed, this kind of worker is significantly rewarded in a personal way. For Breckin, the reward included gender modification surgery beyond the hormone treatment he currently received. Unfortunately, *Undercover Boss* left untold Breckin's self-perceived impact of gender on performance. How did Breckin's gender experience contribute or detract from workplace benefit?

Regardless of one's opinion of transgender process, the question would have been unique for Breckin to answer. The question has almost become taboo for either male or female—how being male impacts leadership and how being female impacts leadership. Yet gender remains an important aspect of being human, intersecting with human activities like leadership, followership, and performance within an organization. So, we ask the question, how might one's gender impact and influence one's ability to express and succeed in one's role within an organization?

This is an important question for the purpose of organizational leadership. This chapter attempts to explore part of the relationship of gender and leadership and organizational role through the Ethiopian eunuch in Acts 8:26-40. To do this, I will, first, show that the fields of gender studies and organizational leadership overlap and that an organization may become, strange as it sounds, *gendered*. Second, I will examine Acts 8:26-40 to give insight into the challenges facing organizations in light of gender. This will include considering eunuch as a third gender and how being a eunuch is a defining characteristic of the Ethiopian in Acts 8. Here, we use gender to mean a set of practices, roles, and images that are relatively fixed, and distinct from, though often linked to, biological sex.[2] The Ethiopian eunuch provides an example of a separate gender and offers an example of how gender has both advantages and disadvantages in situations that are crucial to leadership and organizational behavior. The Ascension of Jesus offers a key hermeneutical event for understanding the eunuch in Acts 8:26-40 and the practice of baptism shows value in the eunuch's gender for ongoing mission. I will conclude with several observations and suggestions for leadership practice.

Gender Studies and Organizational Leadership

Engaging the fields of gender studies and organizations has opened new possibilities in thinking about systems and structures in organizations. These are not two fields of study that people often place together. Some scholars worry that considering them together may threaten the integrity of either field.[3] However, perhaps we can test the connection and see if the mutual insights are helpful in addressing leadership questions by exploring what it means to be a gendered organization.

An organization may be gendered in systematic and structural ways.[4] First, there may be an unnecessary segregation of work roles between men and women. Are men believed more suited to certain roles simply by being men? This can become more formal as an organization succumbs to a belief in the "ideal manager." This faulty belief develops when a managerial or leadership job that requires no specific biological sex skews to certain roles, images, and practices that are often connected to a specific gender. For example, the ideal manager may be expected to be available for long and inconvenient hours, to lead rationally and with force, and to be unbridled by other responsibilities. While no biological sex is named, this ideal manager most naturally fits with a male and masculine gender.[5] Thus, the position has become an example of a gendered position. The expectations to be unencumbered are more prevalently associated with a man, whether married or not, as women are more often considered nurturers. Such expectations propagate the gender of a position.

Second, there may be a differentiation between paid and unpaid labor between men and women.[6] This happens when an organization, perhaps unknowingly, assumes that one gender is more suitable for volunteering while another is more suitable for employment.

Third, hiring and firing processes may enforce and reinforce gender differentiation. This may include differentiation in pay, job descriptions, and ideal images for employees that have developed through the organization's history. This may also include informal practices that form how decision-making bodies are gathered, who is given supervisory power, and even the physical design of work environments. For example, organizations can facilitate through history and tradition the consistent interaction between powerful people of the same gender. Do extra- or inter-organizational networks reveal mainly men with men and women with women?

Fourth, an organization may uncritically present or accept cultural images of gender. This may include narratives in the organization's history that capture its identity, or narratives used to explain its current reality.[7] For example, who are the heroes of an organization? Is there a pattern according to gender when assessing failures and successes of the organization? Conversely, rather than accepting images from culture, the organization may consistently apply certain metaphors for roles according to gender. For example, a woman prison officer may think of herself as a 'mother' or 'babysitter.'[8]

Fifth, an organization may be gendered if the organization becomes a collection of individuals with certain approaches to gender.[9] The effects of gender in the organization are not official or established in an organization's history, but as a chance collection of people make up a group, taskforce, or department within the organization.

These considerations of gender and organization may be corrected from the biblical narrative and smaller narratives within Scripture. While it is not always the best practice to read Scripture with pre-established lenses, we are encouraged to seek the wisdom of Scripture for our lives and then to engage its understanding by the whole of Scripture. This book aims to present different questions against Scripture, so while I do so cautiously, I also do so hopefully that Scripture can be read for organizational leadership insights. Because the Bible addresses gender at different times, then, we can also examine narratives with gender in mind to explore their implications for organizations and organizational leadership.[10]

Gender and Acts

In what follows, the narrative of Acts 8:26-40 is explored to help us answer the question about how a gender can contribute to organizational leadership in light of the uncritical gender formation organizations can take. This passage will offer insights that can form a foundation for considering gender and organizational leadership.

Acts begins with the ascended Jesus, now King of the Universe, giving the Holy Spirit who empowers Jesus' disciples for witnessing (Acts 1:1-8).[11] Let's focus on the ascension for a moment. Not only is the ascension the enthronement of Jesus as an event, but Luke-Acts uses the event as a hinge both to culminate the Gospel of Luke and to initiate the book of Acts. This means that it is both event that recounts the story of Jesus (Luke) and a tool that helps us to understand the stories that follow it (Acts).[12] Do not miss how important it is that the ascension closes the gospel and initiates Acts. Jesus is King, has not ceased to be King, and will be seen to be King![13] The book of Acts, then, is committed both to the historicity of the ascension and its theological implications for the ongoing mission of the church. These implications include expected signs and wonders, fruitful ministry, and faithfulness in light of persecution as Acts is a continuation of all that Jesus began to do and teach (Acts 1:1). The Ascension grounds the disciples' ministry as Jesus' ongoing activity, if mediated by the Holy Spirit whose coming is foretold and expected.[14]

Examining the Text

Take a moment and read Acts 8:26-40. Let's lay some foundation before engaging the story for organizational leadership. First, we encounter Philip. The Philip in this story is Philip the Evangelist, or Philip of the Seven (Acts 21:8-9), who was set aside by the Twelve to help care for the Grecian widows in order that the Twelve may continue their ministry of prayer and the word. After the apostles are scattered from Jerusalem (8:1), Philip began preaching through Samaria (8:5) and the result is conversion and baptism. This spiritual outbreak prompts the apostles in Jerusalem to send Peter and John to pray for the Samaritans to receive the Holy Spirit (8:15). But notice that God uses *Philip* to accomplish these ends, even though Philip had been set aside for service other than the ministry of the word. Also, notice that Acts sets Philip's story alongside Stephen, another unexpected leader. Stephen was another set aside for service to the Grecian widows, but God ordained him to minister in other ways. Placed alongside each other, the book of Acts lets us know that we should be ready to be surprised in this story.

Second, notice the mediated action of Jesus and the consistent activity of the Holy Spirit. First, the angel of the Lord gives Philip specific travelling instructions (8:26). Philip is to travel by a certain route between Jerusalem and Gaza. The Spirit then tells Philip to go and stand near the chariot of an Ethiopian eunuch (8:29). The Spirit directs Philip (by an angel) to the right road (8:26), to the right proximity of the chariot (8:29), and takes Philip to a new area of mission (8:39). The activity of the Spirit, however, should not surprise us: Acts 1:8 records that the Spirit will facilitate witnessing by coming on the disciples. In Philip's case, the Spirit's communication facilitates the mission of Jesus by bringing Philip to the eunuch for witnessing. Philip's encounter with the eunuch begins with his question, "Do you understand what you are reading?" (8:30) and then Philip finishes with explicit witness of Jesus (8:35). The story finishes with Philip baptizing the Ethiopian eunuch and then being transported by the Spirit of the Lord (Acts 8:39) to continue his witnessing ministry.

The role of the Spirit in this story fits with Acts' ascension theology. Jesus is certainly central in the narrative, but his activity is always mediated: an angel of the Lord speaks to Philip; the Spirit gives further instructions to Philip and transports Philip to a new location (8:39). Jesus is absent physically, yet his mission progresses and expands.

Third, look at the structure of the passage where the ascension of Jesus and the identity of the eunuch are seen to be connected. The passage reveals a chiasm that draws the identities of Jesus and the eunuch together:

    A. Philip goes south at the direction of the angel of the Lord (v. 26)

        B. Philip meets the eunuch (v. 27)

            C. The eunuch is in the chariot; Philip approaches chariot (vv. 28-29)

                D. Philip asks the eunuch a question (v. 30)

                    E. Eunuch cannot understand Scripture (vv. 31-32)

                        F. Passage of Scripture from Isaiah (vv. 32-33)

                    E.' Eunuch asks for Philip's interpretation (v. 34)

                D.' Philip answers the eunuch's question (v. 35)

            C.' eunuch stops chariot; Philip and eunuch descend for baptism (v. 38)

        B.' Philip departs and is no longer seen by the eunuch (v. 39)

    A.' Philip appears in Azotus (v. 40)

Ethiopian Eunuch

With these foundational pieces in place—the surprising characters, the Spirit's presence, the ascended Jesus—we can now take a deeper look at the Ethiopian eunuch. First, text makes explicit that the characters meet on the road (8:26) a place of travel and change. Second, we understand the eunuch has come from Jerusalem where he has been worshiping (8:27). Third, the text explicitly mentions several factors in quick succession: the character is a eunuch, Ethiopian, an important official, works with the treasury, and serves the queen of the Ethiopians (8:27). As would be expected, but made explicit, the character is able to read—even read aloud (8:30). To summarize: the individual is a traveler, a foreigner, powerful, and racially distinct.[15]

Readers should look for multiple identifying characteristics of complex characters. Gender studies often consider race and class as typically interconnected with gender.[16] In the passage of Acts 8:26-40, there have been considerations of race (Ethiopian), gender (eunuch), and office (works for Queen). We know more about this character than we otherwise might expect. Here we can see a phenomenon called "intersectionality," which suggests that "various categories work together and mutually construct each other"[17] when it comes to a person's identity. In other words, nobody is completely defined by one characteristic—even a very important one. Specifically, in the text of the Ethiopian eunuch, the character cannot be understood simply as Ethiopian, for example, but as an Ethiopian-eunuch-official-worshiper.

So, while we should not oversimplify the eunuch as a character, neither should we miss important unique characteristics, such as the character being a eunuch. What might catch the attention of a first century Jewish reader is that eunuchs are excluded from Israel's covenant, yet here the fellow is reading from the Jewish Scriptures and has been worshiping in Jerusalem. It could be that the character being a eunuch is the most important, though not solely important, thing about him. Being a eunuch, in coordination with all other descriptions, can be a master-status, which is a status that "overshadows all other labels and most poignantly defines his identity." [18] Certainly the character being a eunuch is very important. First, the term eunuch appears as an identifying characteristic four times (vv. 34, 36, 38, 39) after the initial description in v. 27. Second, while some argue that eunuch may simply indicate holding a kind of office—being an official—in this passage, this understanding would be redundant in v. 27 where both *eunouchos* and *dunastes* are used. Eunuch adds nothing to the description of the person if it only means official. Finally, the centrality of Isaiah 53 (see the chiasm above) and its important notation that the suffering servant is without descendants (Is. 53:8), just like a eunuch, suggests that the character in Acts 8 is a eunuch, beyond simply an official. The identity of the eunuch and the centrality of the suffering servant should that each character would identify with each other.

Let's take this one step further. Is eunuch really that important as a gender category? *Eunuch* is a third gender, beyond the genders connected with the male and female sexes. Strictly speaking, part of the physical anatomy that makes one male and the subsequent physiological make up that results from the removed physical anatomy, has been removed from the eunuch, though at one time the eunuch may have been male. Would we not expect this to alter one's sense of self, roles, and other social constructs that make up gender? One contemporary study helps to illustrate this consideration. Males who have undergone androgen deprivation therapy ("chemical castration") report not feeling *manly*. Neither, naturally, do they experience themselves as women.[19] Without a specific gender with which to identify, there is psychological and social trauma. Are these people left without a gender? Strictly speaking, their biological sex has been altered; could their gender be altered, as well? With these biological, psychological, and social challenges, it can be suggested that eunuch itself be considered a gender. This suggestion, for our purposes, is not ideologically naïve—as though the manner in which males are made eunuchs in the 21st century is necessarily the same as it was in the 1st century, where eunuchs were often made so through violence and without consideration of one's will. Yet the complexity of gender role for eunuchs in the 1st century shows a similarity to the complexity of gender identification with 21st eunuchs. Eunuchs were often politically powerful, guarded women as property of men (because they were not thought to be sexual threats), "orchestrated palace intrigues and coups," formed and informed secret police, and led military operations.[20] With this affirmation of eunuch as a third gender and as an identifying characteristic of the character, let us continue to explore the character.

Eunuch as Gender Empowered

The identity of the eunuch is an identity of power in this text. As noted earlier, eunuchs were set aside for the purpose of service in government administration.[21] By virtue of the office associated with gender, the eunuch's gender in this case is imbued with power inasmuch as it is ideal for political rule. The Acts 8 text affirms elements of the eunuch's power. First, the eunuch can read. Second, the eunuch is on the road, riding in a chariot, so the eunuch is mobile when many others were typically not. Further, the eunuch is mobile for the eunuch's own purpose: the eunuch has travelled to Jerusalem to worship. Third, the eunuch is an official for the queen. Presumably, the eunuch has obtained permission to be released temporarily from the queen's service to be in Jerusalem to worship. Thus, the eunuch, in connection with this gender, is given multiple privileges. The gender of eunuch has helped to provide the context where the eunuch obtained and exercised these privileges.

Eunuch as Gender Excluded

Yet the eunuch is also a gender with disadvantages. Leviticus 20:21 excludes eunuchs from the priesthood. Deuteronomy 23:1 excludes eunuchs from the assembly of God. For the purposes of the Acts 8 passage, Clarice Martin notes the intertexture of the Acts passage with Isaiah.[22] Observe that Isaiah 56:3-7 notes the typical exclusion of foreigners and eunuchs from the covenant but begins to reverse this phenomenon. While Martin emphasizes the exclusion of the eunuch as a foreigner, the typical exclusion and so the anticipated inclusion of the eunuch as a eunuch is at least as important.

Ascension and Gender Reconsideration

Because the passage is understood in light of the ascension as the mission of Jesus is mediated by his Spirit and his people, in light of this consideration of gender, the text of Acts challenges both gender advantage and gender disadvantage. Reconsider the centrality of Isaiah 53:7-8, which the eunuch is reading. The passage presents the suffering of a leader as the means of sacrificial cleansing for a people. Philip's interpretation of this passage as prophetic of Jesus reveals an interpretation of the death of Jesus. Jesus' death is a sacrificial death for the benefit of the people of Israel. However, the context of Isaiah 53 must also be considered. Isaiah 56:3-7 reveals that those previously expelled from the covenant community, specifically the eunuch and the foreigner, will be welcome because of this vicarious suffering. The text of Acts, using this passage, now reveals an initial form of this inclusion as the eunuch has come from Jerusalem where the eunuch has been worshiping, yet now the interpretation of the Isaiah 53 passage by Philip reveals a deeper theological text: the death of *Jesus* has been the means of securing the eunuch's entry into the new covenant. The event becomes a fulfillment of Old Testament prophecy where foreigners to Israel come to worship Israel's God (Ps. 68:31).

The chiasm included earlier now becomes important to think about the eunuch. By connecting Acts 8 with its intertexture in Isaiah 56:3-7, the mutual passages are not simply important for understanding Jesus, but, *through* Jesus, help us to understand the eunuch. Jesus' identification as the sacrificial sheep who ultimately achieves covenantal entrance for the eunuch provides a comparison with the eunuch: the lamb who was slaughtered achieves covenantal belonging for the one who was physically emasculated. Notice the reconfiguration of Isaiah 53:7-8. Whereas Isaiah 53:8 says, "For he was cut off from the land of the living," Acts 8:33 says, "For his life was taken from the earth." Critical to understanding this reconfiguration is that Acts 8:33 uses the same root word as the ascension narrative in Acts 1:9: *airo*. Thus, in Acts 8:33c, the line, "For his life was taken up from the earth" does not continue the theme of injustice as in Isaiah, but now reconfigures the text to be about *victory*. The ascension, which is the God-given victory of Jesus through the death of Jesus, does not continue the defeat, but signals victory. The cross has been the victory of Jesus and the means of his enthronement. With this in mind, the immediately preceding line, "Who can speak of his descendants?" (Acts 8:33b) does not indicate *lack* of descendants for Jesus, as it does in Isaiah. Rather, the ascension motif reveals *multiple* descendants. Jesus is now the King with multiple descendants in his kingdom, *most notably the eunuch who is present.* The eunuch finds not just a counterpart to his own story, but a hopeful reversal of his own story. Perhaps this is why the eunuch is perplexed by the Isaiah passage![23] The gender of the eunuch, previously instrumental in setting the eunuch outside the covenant, is brought into the community of Jesus through the death of the now ascended of Jesus. This is an important part of the Good News that Philip brings to the eunuch. This is not to denigrate the other ways in which the eunuch is brought in—as a foreigner—but to tie together the master status of the eunuch.

As the text unfolds, the power of the eunuch is also reconsidered. The eunuch is described as traveling from Jerusalem where he had gone to worship. The eunuch's means of transportation, the chariot, is mentioned four times (vv. 28, 29, 30, 38). This is contrasted with Philip's means of transportation—his feet (Philip *runs* to the chariot in v. 30) and the Spirit (v. 39). However, the chariot is not mentioned after the baptism, when the eunuch ordered the chariot *stopped* (v. 38). This movement ceases multiple aspects of the eunuch's story: the eunuch is no longer traveling; the display of wealth is ceased as the eunuch dismounts the chariot; the service being rendered the eunuch in honor of the eunuch's position of authority is (at least temporarily) discontinued; the eunuch is no longer returning to the eunuch's home nation; the eunuch is no longer returning to service of the Queen in that moment. By coming under the authority of the ascended Jesus in baptism, the eunuch has set aside the privilege afforded by the socially constructed role, image, and responsibilities given through eunuch's gender.

Yet, while the ascension has reworked the privilege of gender (power) and the disadvantage of gender (covenantal exclusion), in the context of baptism, the gender of the character as a eunuch is reaffirmed twice (8:38, 39). Post-baptism, the chariot is no longer mentioned, yet the eunuch is said to 'go on his way rejoicing' (8:39). Here the inner texture of Acts begins to uncover an important insight. Eleven times after this instance in Acts the word 'way' is used in accordance with the work of God, salvation, the mission of the church and/or Jesus. Specifically, 'way' is used as a description of followers of Jesus six times (9:2; 19:9, 23; 22:4; 24:14, 22). The inner texture of Acts with the progressive-repetitive use of 'way' reveals the journey of the eunuch as a key aspect in the work of Jesus, too. The reaffirmed gender of the eunuch who is on the way shows that gender of the eunuch will be used as part of the eunuch's faithfulness in the ongoing mission of Jesus.

In this light, and with the ongoing identity of the eunuch throughout the story, what has been a symbol of shame for the eunuch is now connected with the eunuch's descent from Jesus, thus becomeing a symbol of God's power. The baptism of the eunuch, as it records the eunuch coming "up out of the water" (Acts 8:39), becomes literal and spiritual fulfillment of the *Magnificat* where Mary proclaims that God "lifts up the humble" (Luke 1:52a).[24] In Jesus, God has lifted up the eunuch and given him a place with the honored in Christ. The disadvantages of exclusion with the eunuch gender are overcome in the work of God to establish the eunuch's place in the church. Yet it is also an affirmation of God bringing down the exalted (Luke 1:52a). Baptism is a ritual where God "brings down" the advantages of the eunuch in that privileges are not mentioned, but where God also "lifts up" the eunuch by including the eunuch in the community and giving the eunuch a role in mission.

Baptism and Gender Identity

We might wonder why gender is reaffirmed post-baptism while elsewhere the New Testament various identifying points, including gender, nationality, and social position are no longer distinguishing features given one's *baptism* in Christ (e.g., Galatians 3:27-29). Anglican theologian Oliver O'Donovan notes that some of the categories eliminated in Christ's baptism are bad (e.g., slavery) and some are good (e.g., men and women; Jew and Gentile). However, these markers are not to be barriers. The communication, the sharing, that makes community in the church is not stopped by any barriers.[25] So, the eunuch's gender is no longer a barrier to fellowship with Christ nor to others, but it may give insight into the lives of others, just as it did the suffering servants of Isaiah 53.

The eunuch's experience and inclusion in the community of Jesus might remove blind spots that others will have toward Jesus as the slaughtered lamb. In suffering physical violence at the hands of others for their purposes through the violence of castration, the eunuch may understand the lamb who was led silently to the slaughter and suffered humiliation. The eunuch's baptism may be seen to have relativized the eunuch's identifying markers of nationality, role, and social power, but to have left in place the eunuch's gender for mission purposes. Perhaps the eunuch's gender is reemphasized for the sake of the community in Christ and those whom he will serve in mission. Likewise, baptism is a practice for Christians that removes identifying markers that may bring division, while raising up those elements of one's story which bring further insight to the story of Jesus for reflection and proper witness, including gender.

Conclusion: Gender and Leadership

This chapter ends with a large, "So what?!" The issue of gender is one of the most pressing of our day and the leadership task in its red-hot context is not always clear. Is strong leadership needed? Is empathy? Is a willingness to hold various truths in tension vital? If so, what truths? How can the leader exhibit empathy in the midst of ambiguity and tension? Leadership is necessarily connected with gender as part of a complex identity. Leaders are persons, after all; not genders. However, gender plays a role in shaping the leader, thereby giving them advantages, disadvantages, insights, shortcomings, strengths, and weaknesses.

> *"Leaders are not simply interchangeable regardless of gender, but may require resources, support, affirmation, challenge, or critique in light of their gender"*

In applying these insights in organizational leadership, leaders should consider rites and rituals that will both affirm and challenge gender privilege *and* disadvantage while maintaining gender as an integral portion to a person's identity. Just as the eunuch moves from being a God-fearer to being a part of the community,[26] so can other rites serve to promote unity and identification with a new community. Organizations may utilize rituals, as well, that affirm gender while removing privilege. This may include being intentional about the narratives that capture its identity or which heroes are lifted up as models of certain positions. These narratives and model employees can emphasize gender by naming individuals or including their gender. This avoids the ideal manager trap by mentioning gender and not simply being abstract.

Second, organizations may develop exercises that help employees develop eyes to see their own experiences, roles, and images as gender with both advantages and disadvantages. When obtaining feedback on recent organizational practices of financial management, I listened to women reflect on their narratives as people with the role and responsibility of listening to the feedback of clients in their experience to the financial practices of the organization. Part of their gendered vantage point was because they were seen as approachable women rather than authoritative men. On the other hand, men in the organization used different language of 'driving' and 'results' when discussing their own experiences.

Clearly there is room for more specific practices, examples, and concrete expressions of dealing with gender. The narrative of the eunuch provides a foundation that organizations ought to find ways to affirm certain aspects of gender, while being aware of other aspects, all the while understanding that gender may provide specific insight. Different genders bring different strengths to leadership. Leaders are not simply interchangeable regardless of gender, but may require resources, support, affirmation, challenge, or critique in light of their gender.

Aaron Perry, PhD, is Assistant Professor of Pastoral Care at Wesley Seminary at Indiana Wesleyan University in Marion, Indiana. He recently served as Associate Pastor at Centennial Road Church in Ontario, Canada.

Bibliography

Acker, Joan. "Gendered Organizations and Intersectionality: Problems and Possibilities." *Equality, Diversity, and Inclusion: An International Journal,* 31, no. 3 (2012): 214-224.

Ashcraft, K. "Gender, Discourse, and Organization: Framing a Shifting Relationship." In *The Sage Handbook of Organizational Discourse,* edited by D. Grant, C. Hardy, C. Oswick, and L. Putnam, 275-291. London: Sage, 2004.

Britton, Dana, and Logan, Laura. "Gendered Organizations: Progress and Prospects." *Sociology Compass,* 2, no. 1 (2008): 107-121.

Browning, Larry D. "Organisational Narratives and Organisational Structure." *Journal of Organizational Change Management,* 4, no. 3 (1991): 59-67.

Butler, J. *Gender Trouble: Feminism and the Subversion of Identity.* New York & London: Routledge, 1999.

Collins, Jim. *Good to Great.* San Francisco, CA: Harper Business, 2001.

Eisenberg, E.M., Goodall, Jr., H.L., & Trethewey, A. *Organizational Communication,* 5th ed. Boston, MA: Bedford, St Martin's, 2007.

Farrow, Douglas. *Ascension and Ecclesia.* Grand Rapids, MI: Eerdmans, 1999.

Fitzmeyer, Joseph A. *The Acts of the Apostles.* New York, NY: Doubleday, 1998.

Fletcher, J.K. "The Paradox of Postheroic Leadership: An Essay on Gender, Power, and Transformational Change." *The Leadership Quarterly,* 15 (2004): 647-661.

Green, J.B. *Luke.* NINCT. Grand Rapids, MI: Eerdmans, 1997.

Kartzow, M.B. and Moxnes, H. "Complex Identities: Ethnicity, Gender and Religion in the Story of the Ethiopian Eunuch (Acts 8:26–40)." *Religion and Theology,* 17 (2010): 184-204.

Manville, J.C. (1997). "The Gendered Organization of an Australian Anglican Parish." *Sociology of Religion,* 58, no. 1 (1997): 25-38.

Martin, Clarice J. "A Chamberlain's journey and the challenge of interpretation for liberation." *Semeia,* 47 (1989): 105-135.

Martin, Patricia, and Collinson, David. "'Over the Pond and Across the Water': Developing the Field of 'Gendered Organizations.'" *Gender, Work, and Organization,* 9, no. 3 (2002): 244-265.

Mumby, Dennis K. and Ashcraft, Karen L. "Organizational Communication Studies and Gendered Organization: A Response to Martin and Collinson." *Gender, Work, and Organization,* 13, no. 1 (2006): 68-90.

O'Donovan, Oliver. "What Kind of Community is the Church?" *Ecclesiology* 3, no. 2 (2007): 184.

Rasmussen, B. "Between Endless Needs and Limited Resources: The Gendered Construction of a Greedy Organization." *Gender, Work, and Organization,* 11, no. 5 (2004): 506-525.

Retief, F. P., Cilliers, J. F. G., & Riekert, S. P. J. K. "Eunuchs in the Bible." *Acta Theologica,* 26, no. 2 (2006): 247-258.

Robbins, Vernon K. *The Tapestry of Early Christian Discourse.* London: Routledge, 1996.

Spencer, F. Scott. "The Ethiopian Eunuch and His Bible: A Social-Science Analysis." *Biblical Theology Bulletin: A Journal of Bible and Theology*, 22, no. 4 (1992): 155-165.

Stalp, M.C. and Winders, B. "Power in the Margins: Gendered Organizational Effects on Religious Activism." *Review of Religious Research*, 42, no. 1 (2000): 41-60.

Wall, Robert W. (2002). "The Acts of the Apostles: Introduction, Commentary, and Reflections." In *The New Interpreter's Bible: Acts, Introduction to the Epistolary Literature, Romans, 1 Corinthians*, vol. X. Nashville, TN: Abingdon Press, 2002.

Wassersug, Richard J., Emma McKenna, and Tucker Lieberman. "Eunuch as a Gender Identity After Castration." *Journal of Gender Studies*, 21, no. 3 (2012): 253-270.

Chapter 24 Notes

[1] *Undercover Boss*. CBS Television. Video clip provided by xfinitytv.com. Accessed February 2016. http://bit.ly/1Pa0Dnj

[2] Ashcraft, "Gender, Discourse, and Organization," 276.

[3] Martin and Collinson, "Over the Pont and Across the Water," 68-90.

[4] Acker, "Gendered Organizations and Intersectionality," 214-224.

[5] Britton and Logan, "Gendered Organizations," 108.

[6] I am using men and women in this case because biological sex is linked to gender, though it is not the sum total. Thus, there could be a female in a role that might be better shaped for a gender role that is typically masculine.

[7] Browning, "Organisational Narratives and Organisational Structure."

[8] Britton and Logan, "Gendered Organizations," 110.

[9] Mumby and Ashcraft, "Organizational Communication Studies," 78-79.

[10] Ibid, 68.

[11] Farrow, *Ascension and Ecclesia*.

[12] Ibid, 17.

[13] Fitzmeyer, *The Acts of the Apostles*.

[14] Wall, *The Acts of the Apostles*.

[15] Martin, "A Chamberlain's Journey," 122.

[16] See Acker, "Gendered Organizations and Intersectionality."

[17] Kartzow and Moxnes, "Complex Identities," 194

[18] Spencer, "The Ethiopian Eunuch and His Bible," 155. What follows is owed to Spencer.

[19] Wassersug, McKenna, and Lieberman, "Eunuch as a Gender Identity," 253-270.

[20] Ibid, 264.

[21] Martin, "A Chamberlain's Journey," 105-106.

[22] Ibid, 109-110.

[23] Spencer, "The Ethiopian Eunuch and His Bible," 158.

[24] Ibid.

[25] O'Donovan, "What Kind of Community is the Church," 184.

[26] Spencer, "The Ethiopian Eunuch and His Bible," 161.

25
Adaptive Wesleyan Spiritual Leadership

Bryan Sims

Wesleyan leadership can be formed for the coming future by analyzing and appropriating adaptive spiritual leadership. Adaptive spiritual leadership involves learning with each other as values, assumptions, and practices are challenged and critiqued with the help of the Holy Spirit to be formed in Christlikeness. Such leadership can be effectively deployed to build teams and systems that can handle fast changing cultures and contexts.

THE WORLD HAS CHANGED. For those of us serving the Church, whether lay or clergy, it is common to feel ill-equipped to lead effectively in this changed and changing context. We are working from scripts that once served us well, but do so no longer. The loneliness, isolation, and frustration of leadership leaves us wondering how, and even whether, to continue.

In his chapter in this volume, *Wesleyan Leadership in a Postmodern Context,* Rob Muthiah reminds us that in the midst of widespread cultural changes we can take encouragement from a historical Wesleyan ethos of adaptability. He argues that modernity assumed human reason promotes progress, while postmodernity often exhibits a dystopian worldview that illumines a loss of control resulting in hopelessness and despair. Within this postmodern worldview, there is a resurgent rational atheism alongside a syncretism of multiple religious and spiritual traditions mixed together. Muthiah describes what he refers to as both a monetized culture and a therapeutic culture where people are valued based on their efficiency and earning power and where the goal of life is personal fulfillment. These new realities dehumanize, while promoting rampant self-focus.

In the midst of these radical cultural changes that oppose a biblical worldview of *imago Dei* (the image of God) and *missio Dei* (the mission of God) in self-sacrificial love, leaders within the Church must offer and embody a vision of hope that promotes a true Christian solution like that of the early Wesleyans. Is there a new answer, a new solution, that we can find from looking back? What patterns and practices could move us to fruitful ministry and leadership? By retrieving things lost from Scripture and the early Wesleyan revival, we can shed light on a pathway into the future that is resonant with recent developments in social science and leadership theory. Carder and Warner highlight the potential of such developments if considered through a biblical worldview:

> When seen and evaluated through Christian theological lenses, leadership principles espoused by such thinkers as Ron Heifetz and Jim Collins have the potential to deepen our theological foundations and enhance the church's effectiveness in fulfilling its mission. However, without a firm grounding in the church's doctrine and mission, those insights and principles become improved means to unimproved ends; and they become a form of 'works righteousness,' which adds to the burdens of pastors and church leaders as something else to learn and master in order to be 'a good leader.'[1]

In order to move into a conversation about the future of Wesleyan leadership, it is necessary to contrast typical patterns and practices of leadership with a different way of being and leading. So, let us begin by redefining leadership.

Leadership Redefined

Leadership studies have often been too simplistic in their approach, assuming that the actions and attitudes of leaders bring the rise or fall of organizations. Much of the current leadership research has simply focused on leaders themselves, specifically their actions, roles, attitudes, and characteristics.[2] While leader actions and attitudes are important, a more realistic view of the world must see that what occurs within organizations and beyond is much too complex to make such simple judgments. While certain research has sought to look at the context or situations in which leadership happens,[3] and still other research has looked at the dynamics occurring in the relationship of leaders and followers,[4] there remains a gap in understanding the actual process of leadership within organizations that takes the complex realities of twenty-first century organizational leadership into account.

Many organizations are facing today what leadership theorist Ronald Heifetz referred to as *adaptive challenges*.[5] These are challenges that require new learning because applying current know-how is no longer effective. In the midst of such challenges, it is the natural response of many organizational leaders to lead based on former experience or simply to "fake it" when technical competence or previous experience no longer produce results. Such natural response of leaders in the midst of such adaptive challenges is often due to the expectations of others associated with the organization or the expectations of the leaders themselves. Heifetz insisted that learning new ways of doing things requires adaptive work on the part of not only those with leadership roles but all involved in facing a challenge or problem. Adaptive work requires creating an environment where values and assumptions can be challenged and revised and where learning is welcomed.

In view of this, there must be a distinction drawn between *leaders* (including their most important roles) and the actual *process of leadership*; they are two different things. Leadership is most often defined as a process whereby one person influences a group toward achieving a common goal.[6] By contrast, a complexity perspective sees leadership as a complex dynamic process that emerges in the interactions of people and ideas.[7] Leadership, then, shifts the primary focus away from the individual as a leader, but still recognizes the importance of leadership within organizations. Thus, leadership is fundamentally a system phenomenon.[8] Within that system, leaders enable the conditions within which the process of adaptive leadership occurs. But the leaders themselves are not the direct source of change.

Although researchers have recently been developing the field of complexity theory in leadership and the field of spirituality in the workplace, no published work previous to that of Eric Dent has seriously endeavored to relate complexity theory with workplace spirituality.[9] One notable insight from Dent's work is the absence of consideration of spiritual dimensions or wisdom traditions within research on organizational complexity. Dent argues that although most researchers do not see God's hand in the data, many complexity theory philosophies and evidence strengthen the case for the existence of a supreme being.

These observations by Dent relating complexity perspectives to Christian spirituality are not unique. Hirsch studied the two most explosive Jesus movements in history—the early church and the Chinese underground church in the latter half of the twentieth century—and identified six key themes that were resident in both movements that are consistent with complexity.[10] Hirsch begins by saying:

> We find ourselves lost in a perplexing global jungle where our well-used cultural and theological maps don't seem to work anymore…. The truth is that the twenty-first century is turning out to be a highly complex phenomenon where terrorism, paradigmatic technological innovation, an unsustainable environment, rampant consumerism, discontinuous change, and perilous ideologies confront us at every point. In the face of this, even the most confident among us would have to admit, in our more honest moments, that the church as we know it faces a very significant adaptive challenge. The overwhelming majority of church leaders today report that they feel it is getting much harder for their communities to negotiate the increasing complexities in which they find themselves. As a result, the church is on a massive, long-trended decline in the West.[11]

Hirsch goes on to say that the inherited formulas, tools, and techniques will not likely work anymore and that a new paradigm is necessary to face the adaptive challenge that is the globalized 21st Century. Additionally, when glimpses of an answer come they are so radical and disturbing in nature that it often leads to retreat to the safety of the familiar and the controllable. Hirsch insists that "we are now living in a time when only a solution that goes to the very roots of what it means to be Jesus's [sic] people will do."[12]

By studying several of the greatest Jesus movements in history, Hirsch discovered the makeup of what he refers to as missional DNA (mDNA). As he puts it, "Einstein said that when the solution is simple, God is speaking.... There are six simple but interrelating elements of mDNA forming a complex and living structure."[13] These elements represent the simple rules or principles that form the fractal-like pattern of any authentic, missional Jesus movement. Simply put, these elements are present at every level within a living system: at the macro level (the overall movement), the group level, and the micro level (the individual). In fact, Hirsch says that this mDNA is present in every true follower of Jesus and every group of Jesus followers, although it may be latent or dormant. These six elements of mDNA are: (a) Jesus is Lord; (b) disciple-making; (c) missional-incarnational impulse; (d) apostolic environment; (e) organic systems; and (f) *communitas*, not community.[14]

Spiritual Leaders Are Disciples First

If the church today is indeed facing adaptive challenges, how does leadership through a Wesleyan lens shape how those challenges are addressed so as to embody the mDNA that Hirsch describes? *The answer begins with a different kind of leader.* Jesus said, "Abide in me as I abide in you. Just as the branch cannot bear fruit by itself unless it abides in the vine, neither can you unless you abide in me. I am the vine, you are the branches. Those who abide in me and I in them bear much fruit, because apart from me you can do nothing." (John 15:4-5, NRSV). Christian leaders, no matter their title or experience, never cease from being disciples who are called to abide in Jesus. The intentional connection with Jesus is crucial because "leadership formation apart from Christian discipleship risks fostering qualities and values counter to Christian character and community."[15]

John Wesley and the other leaders of the early Wesleyan movement embodied authentic, accountable discipleship and developed systems that invited others to do the same. These systems were built on the assumption that only by grace can

> *"modeling Christlikeness and creating the conditions for discerning the Spirit's leadership in a process of dynamic, interactive learning together"*

individuals be conformed into the image of Christ. In other words, it is the Holy Spirit's presence and power that moves us to be true disciples of Jesus that bring God glory. Discipleship and Christlike leadership is rooted in and sustained by the Triune God, who is restoring in us the divine image and transforming us to embody that Triune life in perfect love.

This authentic discipleship practiced by the early Wesleyans was centered in Jesus and mirrors Hirsch's mDNA. Such DNA, however, is all but missing in many churches, as well as in the lives of many Christian leaders today. In discussing the Wesleyan movement specifically, Dr. Michael Henderson notes, "[A]s the Church continued to develop through the centuries, outside influences began to dilute and diminish its initial impetus. The tight focus on 'making disciples' was lost, and many other activities gained priority."[16] Thus, the top priority for the future of Wesleyan leadership must be returning to this most basic pattern of discipleship in Triune grace. After all, Christ is our leader and by the Holy Spirit we are, at most, "lead *followers.*" In grace, true spiritual leaders imitate Christ in step with the Holy Spirit.

Adaptive Spiritual Leadership

Based on this description, how do these authentic spiritual leaders effectively lead others in the midst of adaptive challenges? It requires a fundamental choice where a person no longer lives a divided life but is surrendered to a cause that leads to deep change.[17] This deep change begins within and transforms a person into becoming inner-driven and other-focused. Such a changed leader then becomes a living symbol for others.[18] In Philippians 2, the Apostle Paul invites deep change where disciples of Jesus are challenged to live the same way as Jesus himself; where they surrender willingly and follow wherever God leads, even to the point of death. In Philippians 2 and 3, Paul invites others to imitate his own example along with that of Timothy and Epaphroditus since they had each become living symbols of a Christlike life for others to follow. In the 18th Century, the Wesleys did not want the movement to be about them, but they were transformed by grace into authentic disciples themselves and were also the living example for others to emulate.

Adaptive spiritual leadership is modeling Christlikeness and creating the conditions for discerning the Spirit's leadership in a process of dynamic, interactive learning together. Modeling grace that enables Christlikeness has already been described and remains the single most important criteria for a Christian leader. It is critical for such leaders, however, not only to be in step with the Holy Spirit (as described in Galatians 5), but also to create the environment where the people of God discern the Spirit's direction together—an environment that can lead to creative, world-changing activity.[19] Roxburgh and Romanuk write, "Cultivating environments requires processes that create the space for people to develop the ability to listen to one another and ask questions."[20] While many leaders might not consider the importance of the environment, the creation and cultivation of the right kind of environment is one of the most critical elements that leads to transformation. Before digging into environment more deeply, it is important to clarify some assumptions within this definition.

Inherent in this definition of adaptive spiritual leadership is the assumption that the leader is not the source of change. As Quinn points out, "Formal leaders normally do not have the power necessary to transform a system."[21] Taken from a biblical perspective, only the Holy Spirit can transform us (2 Corinthians 3) and bring forth Christlike fruit (Galatians 5), which is why John Wesley centered his theology and practice entirely in grace.[22] It is only in this grace that our relationships can exist and only by this grace that disciples can be made and spiritual leaders can be developed. It is also only in this grace that a group of broken people can discern God's will together.

Thus, adaptive spiritual leadership is not only centered in modeling Christlikeness but is also focused on discerning the Spirit's leadership together. This brings out yet another assumption in this definition: namely, that spiritual leadership must be done together with God and one another. The Apostles demonstrated this in the first recorded church conflict in Acts 6, which involved cultural differences and neglect. Rather than stepping in to solve the problem, the Apostles listened and then challenged the community as a whole to raise up a new set of leaders to address the challenge. It was not the work of one person to follow God's will and tell others where to go. It was the work of the whole people of God. The Council of Jerusalem in Acts 15 also illustrates this practice as the early church leaders were discerning perhaps the most difficult decision in church history. At the end of their prayers, listening, and conversation, James stood up and said, "For it has seemed good to the Holy Spirit and to us."[23] They discerned *together* the Spirit's leadership and by grace followed it.

Leaders must give adaptive challenges back to the people with the problem and create the environment among those people that will allow effective solutions to emerge. This is adaptive leadership. Heifetz states,

> In a crisis we tend to look for the wrong king of leadership. We call for someone with answers, decision, strength, and a map of the future, someone who knows where we ought to be going—in short, someone who can make hard problems simple…. Instead of looking for saviors, we should be calling for leadership that will challenge us to face problems for which there are no simple, painless solutions—problems that require us to learn in new ways.[24]

As spiritual leaders, we must indeed give adaptive challenges back to those we lead and cultivate the environment for the Spirit's leadership to emerge. This requires dependence on God and the humility to trust the Holy Spirit to work through people rather than controlling or manipulating situations as the leader.

The final piece of this definition of adaptive spiritual leadership suggests that modeling Christlikeness and discerning the Spirit's leadership occurs within a process of dynamic, interactive learning together. Notice the importance of *process*. Much of our church practice assumes that new programs can bring about new DNA in a congregation or organization. While programs can be valuable for accomplishing a specific strategy, they do not take the complex realities of each church's context into account. Developing new programs can and often have diverted us from our primary calling to be and make disciples by reducing the Christian life simply to transmitting information, often accompanied by low accountability for participants.[25] Rather than building programs that tend to be prescriptive, an effective process allows us to truly learn and discern together as we move toward God's vision.

The Wesleys were intentional about these types of effective processes that resulted in noticeable fruit. For instance, rather than simply gathering a crowd or getting people to show up to groups or events, everyone involved in the early movement participated in class meetings where they regularly gave account of their spiritual life. This resulted in countless transformed lives. They established effective processes for spiritual growth, leadership development, and financing the movement. In general, processes become effective if they bridge the gap between the current reality and the vision in a clear, actionable, and fruitful way. In other words, effective processes become the "how" of getting to the vision as empowered by the Holy Spirit. As such, practical processes are critical if adaptive challenges are to be addressed.

If the solutions to our adaptive challenges are already known, adaptive leadership is unnecessary. However, if we are unclear on how to address those challenges, it is critical to engage in a process that is both dynamic and interactive in order for those facing the challenge to adopt new ways of being and acting. It is dynamic in that the conversation and learning is alive and changing. It is interactive because only through rich dialogue in a highly committed, trust filled environment led by the Holy Spirit can solutions emerge in complex situations.

Built on this definition and discussion of adaptive spiritual leadership, our discussion now turns to practical implications of how this Christ-centered, Spirit-led type of leadership can be operationalized. After all, if this is the type of leadership exhibited in the early Wesleyan movement, it is critical for us to understand how to embody it in the times in which we live. The focus will first be on how to create environments that foster transformation and then will shift to generative systems that bear Kingdom fruit.

Creating Environments that Foster Transformation

Have you ever recognized that certain environments seem to be ripe for change, while others actually deter change? What environments are best suited for mDNA transformation? What conditions allow the Holy Spirit to really lead in order to facilitate such transformation? After modeling authentic discipleship, creating a transformative environment is one of the key roles of an adaptive spiritual leader.

The environment in which leadership happens is not typically the first thing on the minds of most leaders. It is more common to think about vision or decision-making as high priorities for leaders. While these things are important, the church of the future must be moving courageously into unknown territory and addressing the massive adaptive challenges facing the 21ˢᵗ Century Church. No single leader will ever have the capacities necessary to address these challenges, but they are able to increase the adaptive capacity of those around them such that together challenges can be addressed. The leadership environment is critical to bringing about that increased capacity.

Wesley's Structures

If the future of the Wesleyan movement is going to in any way mirror its origins, the first priority is being grace-empowered disciples who embody holy love. John Wesley insisted that there is no holiness but social holiness. Holiness, in other words, is not an individual pursuit but instead the work of grace in us in the context of covenant community. In speaking about the necessity of living in accountable relationships, Wesley said:

> I was more convinced than ever that the preaching like an apostle without joining together those that are awakened and training them up in the ways of God, is only begetting children for the murderer. How much preaching there has been for these twenty years all over Pembrookshire. But no regular societies, no discipline, no order or connection, and the consequence is that nine in ten of the once awakened are now faster asleep than ever.[26]

The early Wesleyan class meetings and other small group structures "provided an environment in which people could trust and be trusted, love and be loved, and be vulnerable in a way that is needed for true growth in grace and love of God, neighbor, and self to occur."[27] The class meetings were characterized by a climate of acceptance, high commitment, trust, understanding, friendship, and intimacy.[28] People were authentic and transforming grace was experienced.

According to Henderson, Wesley himself saw these class meetings as a return to first-century Christianity in practice. Amazingly, one hundred percent of those participating in the societies were involved in accountable relationships in class meetings. Participation was part of the culture they created, which meant that true accountability to those high commitments was practiced. It is not an understatement to say that the environment itself was critical to the fruit born out of this movement.

Building Your Team

This is not a call for leaders to go out and start implementing mandatory class meetings in existing churches. The goal is not to replicate the particular form and structure of Wesleyan class meeting. Those were adaptive for Wesley's day and context, not necessarily our own. On the other hand, the *goal* remains the same: creating environments appropriate to our modern social context that provide these same commitments and accountability.

Adaptive spiritual leaders must have the priority and courage to create these environments. This can begin simply by inviting a few key leaders into a process of growth and learning together. Invite them with a vision of true disciple-making and allow that group of people to shape what their covenant commitments should be. If the leader dictates that covenant, others will resist. If, however, the leader invites others into the process of developing deep, covenant commitment together, the outcome can bring about deep trust and high commitment just like the early Wesleyans experienced.

One of the ways this highly committed covenant group can be framed is by contrasting current reality with a preferred future. In the Lay Mobilization Institute (LMI) within the Beeson Center at Asbury Seminary, we commonly describe two primary mind shifts. First, a move from a culture of membership to discipleship. This moves us away from existing for ourselves or simply surviving, to becoming a Christ-centered and Spirit-mobilized Church. Second, a shift from solo to team leadership. This moves us from pastor or staff driven models of leadership to one where leadership is shared and spiritual leaders are multiplied. These shifts occur as a new team is gathered around a pastor or leader to practice Wesleyan spiritual formation and discern together how to most effectively be and make disciples in their context.[29] This is an environment where Christ-likeness is pursued together within a team that is discerning the Spirit's direction in a dynamic, interactive learning process.

With true covenant relationships, these teams can embody a Wesleyan vision and overcome the typical team dysfunctions described by Patrick Lencioni.[30] Trust is primary for teams and insists that vulnerability among leaders brings trust. Built on this foundation of trust, teams only become highly effective when they can have healthy conflict, high commitment, true accountability, and are focused on their intended results. Covenantal relationships in a team environment become the backbone for effective adaptive leadership.

Only in this type of trusting and committed environment can discernment and learning occur that leads to true team leadership. Trust is essential because entering into the unknown of our adaptive challenges brings fear and great tension. Tension in organizational contexts is often avoided and leaders are often thought to be effective if they can eliminate tension and bring about equilibrium.

On the contrary, adaptive spiritual leaders must see tension as an ally and make sure the environment is healthy enough to handle such tension. Heifetz describes this as a holding environment where the leader keeps the pot boiling but never lets it boil over.[31] Tension is the key to moving forward into a new reality, but the environment must be able to handle the tension as an opportunity and learn together to discover new pathways forward. This requires transcending our own fears, identifying and embracing our potential, surrendering the self to the larger purpose or mission, and engaging together in risk.[32]

Generative Systems that Bear Kingdom Fruit

With a healthy environment in place, what processes and systems bring about fruit fit for the Kingdom of God? The early Wesleyans were known for their commitment to a system of interlocking groups.[33] These groups were particular environments each with their own purpose. The overarching vision of these groups was to move people through what is described as the Way of Salvation: prevenient grace, justifying grace, and sanctifying grace. This Way of Salvation is itself a system of transformation that acknowledges the necessity of divine action in grace and assumes our participation in, with, and through grace to be a world changing Church. It also assumes that persons made in the image of God can indeed grow together into Christlikeness and be led by the Holy Spirit to embody holy love.

If the early Wesleyan movement was characterized by such a system, could the future of Wesleyan leadership attain something similar? The early Wesleyan systems were built on those we see in the early Church of the New Testament where everything was centered around Jesus and disciple-making was intentional.[34] The relational pattern of intentional discipleship led to the multiplication of spiritual leaders who lived and acted as Jesus did. This is what Ogden referred to as internalization and multiplication as Jesus focused his ministry on a few who were so transformed in relationship to Jesus that they became transforming.[35]

The team environment described earlier is where intentional discipleship best occurs and where the values of Jesus are internalized and multiplied. The priority in this environment is not only on being disciples but on discerning how to make disciples effectively in a specific context. The early Wesleyans were compelled by seeing people become true disciples in the grace of God and took great risks to see that occur. If this remains the Church's priority, how are such disciples made?

Spiritual Leadership, Inc. (SLI) is a Christ-centered coaching ministry that invites people into these environments and into a process of discerning how to make disciples.[36] They refer to this as developing a disciple-making system. A system is a group of interrelated parts that bring about a result greater than the sum of the parts. A generative system reproduces itself over and over again as life gives birth to more life. Rather than having a myriad of programs that have no sense of sequence, churches are encouraged to think through three to five simple, repeatable steps that will effectively make disciples in their context. These steps take the Way of Salvation seriously and identify the stages in the journey to becoming a disciple-making disciple. The steps may be articulated in terms like engage, relate, equip, and send *or* know, grow, and go. Churches are then coached to develop simple strategies in each stage of their system that can intentionally move people to the next stage of the system. The natural consequence of a system like this working is that disciples are made and spiritual leaders are multiplied as the system is repeated again and again. Often, leaders on a team that develop a disciple-making system then develop their own teams to multiply the work of disciple-making in a church and community.

Inherent within the process of developing a disciple-making system is what Heifetz, Grashow, and Linsky describe as the two core processes of adaptive leadership: diagnosis and action.[37] According to these authors, "The single most important skill and most undervalued capacity for exercising adaptive leadership is diagnosis."[38] Diagnosis requires a team of people to get "on the balcony" to gain perspective on the reality. This means living with the tension and disequilibrium associated with the adaptive challenges and asking tough questions. They remind leaders to never lead alone and to resist the urge to leap into action too quickly. From the balcony view, deep reflection can occur on the existing systems within the organization. The next step is to diagnose the adaptive challenge. They outline four adaptive challenge archetypes in organizations, including churches: a) the gap between espoused values and behavior; b) competing commitments; c) speaking the unspeakable; and d) work avoidance. Diagnosing a church's primary adaptive challenge highlights priorities for action.

If the first core process of adaptive leadership is diagnosing the system, the second is mobilizing the system.[39] Quick technical fixes will not work to address adaptive challenges, so mobilizing for action first requires slowing down to ask more questions from the balcony and identifying issues as systemic and not merely personal. These questions and identification of systemic issues provide new ways of seeing the problem and help generate creative solutions as those problems are owned by a team of people rather than just a leader. As creative solutions emerge, accountability must be in place to move into experimentation and action. Such action is done in tandem with continual learning. SLI refers to this accountable discernment process as *reflect-adjust-do* where each action or strategy is reflected upon in prayer and conversation, continually adjusted, and accountability is applied to ensure another action. Over time, this action-learning accumulates to bring about a new reality.

It is important to note that diagnosis and action must be done in the context of Spirit-led discernment if this is to be adaptive spiritual leadership. Assuming this, Heifetz *et al* provide many practical tools and tactics throughout their book that assist in both diagnosing and mobilizing a system.[40] It is critical that adaptive challenges are named and addressed in systems that develop disciples and multiply spiritual leaders.

Conclusion

The genius of the early Wesleyan movement was the intentional environments and systems they created that fostered grace-empowered transformation of disciples and the world. The future of Wesleyan leadership requires similar focus that takes seriously the complex realities of our current context. Muthiah reminded us of the Wesleyan ethos of adaptability,[41] which is greatly needed in the midst of the adaptive challenges facing the church today. What is needed now is *adaptive spiritual leadership* defined as modeling Christlikeness and creating the conditions for discerning the Spirit's leadership in a process of dynamic, interactive learning together. Such leadership mirrors this early Wesleyan ethos.

There are several key implications of this type of Wesleyan\ leadership. First and foremost, leaders must be disciples. Only then can they be spiritual leaders. Second, tension is critical for movement to occur, so adaptive spiritual leadership capitalizes on tension and creates an environment that fosters growth and learning together. Third, leadership is shared in a team that lives within highly committed, accountable covenant relationships with God and one another. This accountability is both for the purpose of formation and mission. Fourth, simple patterns of disciple-making can be multiplied through intentional, repeatable systems that bring generative fruit. Finally, all of this only occurs in grace, and, as a result, God alone receives glory. If adaptive spiritual leadership can be embodied in critical segments of the Church, such segments can connect to form true movement again. This will bring renewal of the mDNA present in both the early Church[42] as well as the early Wesleyan revival. Such renewal will mean a bright future in Wesleyan leadership. .

Bryan Sims, PhD, is Associate Professor of Leadership and Lay Equipping, Director of Center for Lay Mobilization & Lifelong Learning at Asbury Theological Seminary, and Leadership & Organizational Change Coach at Spiritual Leadership, Inc.

Bibliography

Carder, K. L., and L. C. Warner. *Grace to Lead: Practicing Leadership in the Wesleyan Tradition.* Nashville, TN: Board of Higher Education and Ministry, 2010.

Dent, E. B. "Reconciling Complexity Theory in Organizations and Christian Spirituality," *Emergence* 5, no. 4 (2003): 124-140.

Fiedler, F.E. *A Theory of Leadership Effectiveness.* New York: McGraw-Hill, 1967.

Graen, G. B., and M. Uhl-Bien. "Relationship-Based Approach to Leadership: Development of Leader-Member Exchange (LMX) Theory of Leadership over 25 Years: Applying a Multi-Level Multi-Domain Perspective." *Leadership Quarterly* 6, no. 2 (1995): 219-247.

Henderson, D. Michael. *A Model for Making Disciples: John Wesley's Class Meeting.* Nappanee, IN: Francis Asbury Press, 1997.

Heifetz, Ronald. *Leadership Without Easy Answers.* Cambridge, MA: Harvard University Press, 1994.

Heifetz, Ronald, Alexander Grashow, and Martin Linsky. *The Practice of Adaptive Leadership: Tools and Tactics for Changing Your Organization and the World.* Boston, MA:

Harvard Business Press, 2009.

Hersey, Paul, and Kenneth Blanchard. "Life Cycle Theory of Leadership." *Training and Development Journal* 23 (1969): 26-34.

Hirsch, A. The Forgotten Ways: Reactivating the Missional Church. Grand Rapids, MI: Brazos Press, 2006.

Lencioni, Patrick. *The Five Dysfunctions of a Team*. San Francisco, CA: Jossey-Bass, 2002.

Lichtenstein, B. B., M. Uhl-Bien, R. Marion, A. Seers, J. D. Orton, and C. Schreiber. "Complexity Leadership Theory: An Interactive Perspective on Leading in Complex Adaptive Systems." *E:co* 8, no. 4 (2006): 1-13.

Manskar, Steven W. *Accountable Discipleship: Living in God's Household*. Nashville, TN: Discipleship Resources, 2000.

Marion, R., and M. Uhl-Bien. "Leadership in Complex Organizations." *Leadership Quarterly* 12, no. 4 (2001): 389-418.

¾. "Complexity Theory and Al-Qaeda." *Emergence* 5 (2003): 56-78.

Northouse, Peter. *Leadership Theory and Practice,* 3rd ed. Thousand Oaks, CA: Sage Publications, Inc., 2004.

Ogden, Greg. Transforming Discipleship: Making Disciples a Few at a Time. Downers Grove, IL: IVP Press, 2003.

Quinn, Robert E. Change the World: How Ordinary People Can Accomplish Extraordinary Results. San Francisco, CA; Jossey-Bass

Roxburgh, Alan J. Missional Map-Making: Skills for Leading in Times of Transition. San Francisco, CA: Jossey-Bass, 2010.

Roxburgh, Alan J., and Fred Romanuk. *The Missional Leader*. San Francisco, CA: Jossey-Bass, 2006: 76.

Uhl-Bien, M., R. Marion, and B. McKelvey. "Complexity Leadership Theory: Shifting Leadership from the Industrial Age to the Knowledge Era." *Leadership Quarterly* 18, no. (2007): 298-318.

Wesley, John. *The Works of John Wesley*, 3rd ed., edited by Thomas Jackson. Kansas City: Beacon Hill, 1979.

Yukl, Gary. *Leadership in Organizations*. Upper Saddle River, NJ: Pearson Prentice Hall, 2006.

Chapter 25 Notes

[1] Carder and Warner, *Grace to Lead,* 20.

[2] Yukl, *Leadership in Organizations.*

[3] Fiedler, *A Theory of Leadership Effectiveness*; Hersey and Blanchard, "Life Cycle Theory of Leadership."

[4] Graen and Uhl-Bien, "Relationship-Based Approach to Leadership."

[5] Heifetz, *Leadership Without Easy Answers.*

[6] Northouse, *Leadership Theory and Practice.*

[7] Lichtenstein et al, "Complexity Leadership Theory."

[8] Marion and Uhl-Bien, "Leadership"; Marion and Uhl-Bien, "Complexity Theory and Al-Qaeda"; Uhl-Bien et al, "Complexity Leadership Theory."

9 Dent, "Reconciling Complexity Theory in Organizations and Christian Spirituality."

10 Hirsch, *The Forgotten Ways*

11 Ibid, 16.

12 Ibid, 17.

13 Ibid, 24.

14 Hirsch describes *communitas* by saying the "most vigorous forms of community are those that come together in the context of a shared ordeal or those that define themselves as a group with a mission that lies beyond themselves – thus initiating a risky journey" (Hirsch, *The Forgotten Ways*, 25).

15 Carder and Warner, *Grace to Lead*, 14.

16 Henderson, *A Model for Making Disciples*, 14.

17 Quinn, *Change the World*.

18 Ibid.

19 Roxburgh, *Missional Map-Making*.

20 Roxburgh and Romanuk, *The Missional Leader*, 76.

21 Quinn, *Change the World*, 204.

22 Carder and Warner, *Grace to Lead*.

23 Acts 15:28, NRSV.

24 Heifetz, *Leadership Without Easy Answers*, 2.

25 Ogden, *Transforming Discipleship*, see Chapter 2.

26 Wesley, *The Works of John Wesley*, 144.

27 Manskar, *Accountable Discipleship*, 93.

28 Henderson, *A Model for Making Disciples*.

29 See http://laymobilization.seedbed.com/lmi-overview/

30 Lencioni, *The Five Dysfunctions of a Team*.

31 Heifetz, *Leadership Without Easy Answers*, see Chapter 5.

32 Quinn, *Change the World*, see Chapter 5.

33 Henderson, *A Model for Making Disciples*.

34 Hirsch, *The Forgotten Ways*.

35 Ogden, *Transforming Discipleship*, see Chapter 3.

36 See www.spiritual-leadership.org

37 Heifetz, Grashow, and Linsky, *The Practice of Adaptive Leadership*, 6.

38 Ibid, 7.

39 Ibid, see Part 3.

40 Ibid.

41 Muthiah, *Wesleyan Leadership*.

42 Hirsch, *The Forgotten Ways*.

PART 5

LEADERSHIP IN MINISTRY

26
Rethinking Servant Leadership

Kevin Mannoia

While Christian leadership is servant leadership, exactly who and what is being served? Why is the leader serving? Answering these questions may not be as straightforward as expected. Servant leadership is an approach to leadership grounded in serving God—not people, not the church, and not the self. It is not an approach to leadership that is taken because it is effective. Instead, the leader, as servant of God, can become a deep model for others that surpasses simple performance based leadership to provide a counter-cultural, healthy identity for the leader.

THE FIRST QUESTION I ASKED the class on Servant Leadership was, "Why are you here?" In one form or another, most of the students answered the question as one young lady did, "I want to learn to do servant leadership because I heard it really works!" At face value, that response is more than a professor could want. These students were ready to learn and already had a positive attitude toward the class. Yet it gave me pause. I wondered: "Do they really know what they're in for? Where have they gotten the preconceived ideas they bring to the class?" As the class progressed, it became evident that they were like so many others who are caught in a pragmatic trap that filters everything through the grid of results. If it works, it's good. If it doesn't, then it's not good.

There is a growing interest in servant leadership in the secular arena and among religious organizations. Leaders hear the ideas and are naturally drawn to the apparent selflessness of the paradigm that puts others first. This interest gets reinforced by the results servant leadership yields in real life situations. Too many experiences of positive outcomes exist to deny that it has merit as a serious and increasingly attractive pattern of leadership.

In the face of these results, the natural tendency is to approach servant leadership as a model or style of leadership. Embarking on a journey to learn servant leadership, a person presumes he or she will be gaining skills in behaviors that will make them a servant leader. This in turn will help others become fulfilled and thereby the desires of the organization will be achieved. The result is that the servant leader will be effective. And isn't that the desire of every leader?

But the genius of servant leadership is really not in its observable behaviors or in its outcomes. Anyone can adapt their activities to conform with prescribed behaviors in order to achieve results. The result of learning servant leadership is not merely changed behavior. It is a fundamentally different way of looking at oneself and the responsibility of influence. Servant leadership is not so much a style of leadership as it is a condition of the leader. Its uniqueness is not in its outcomes but in its genesis. It is not a series of activities to be mimicked or skills to be acquired. Rather, it is a mindset, a life, an identity to be forged. Admittedly, there are behaviors that are descriptive of servant leaders, but they occur as a result of what the person has become. Anything less cheapens the depth and significance of servant leadership, which is a call first to be a servant. Because we always behave out of who we are, it is natural that a servant will exhibit servant leadership skills.

Certainly you can approach the subject as if it is a set of skills to be learned. And perhaps that will provide help in leadership. There is merit in recognizing that learned behavior, when repeated often, can become habitual. These habits can become second nature and begin to transform the character of a leader. This personal transformation happens from the outside in. But the true power of servant leadership is ultimately found in the inner being of the leader. It begins with identity questions that provide a solid foundation out of which skills will naturally flow with integrity and ultimate effectiveness through a variety of styles of leadership. Therein lies the true genius of servant leadership.

The Model of a Leader

Identity gives rise to behavior. Who we are will always have an effect on what we do. Like opposite sides of a coin, these two dimensions of leadership are inseparable. Better yet, it is like an iceberg. One tenth of the mass of an iceberg is found above the waterline. Nine-tenths lies beneath the waterline where no one can see it. The top of the iceberg is in the visible realm; the bottom is unseen. There is one iceberg but two dimensions. The top of the iceberg represents the leadership activities that we perform and which others may see and evaluate—vision casting, management, budgets, decision-making, strategic planning, counseling, directing. The bottom of the iceberg represents the identity of the leader. It is much less measurable and often goes unobserved by others. It answers the question "Who am I?" while the top of the iceberg answers the question, "What am I here to do?" The top speaks to activity, performance, achievement, and competence. The bottom deals with the person's nature, formation, personhood, and character. Both are essential elements for a leader. But you can quickly see that one cannot exist without the other. The top is *doing*, and the bottom is *being*. The top of the iceberg is able to keep balance and stability only to the extent that the bottom is well-formed and deep.

A leadership style simply describes the activities at the top of the iceberg and their effect on the surrounding context. Effectiveness in this pattern of thinking is defined by the results that come in measurable outcomes. The pursuit of good leadership is merely the mastery of skills and activities to be applied with increasing competence in response to particular needs or situations. If we think about leadership only as a style, we are assuming that outcomes or results are the priority and primary reference point for leadership. Effective leadership is reduced to being much more about the mastery of prescribed skills rather than an intrinsic quality that is formed. The adaptive nature of leadership becomes limited to the repertoire of skills in a particular leader. The capacity of the leader to discern the critical circumstances around them is reduced to observing the effect of the selected behavior.

In reality, wholeness and long-term effectiveness come from building integrity between who we are and what we do; between the bottom and the top of the iceberg. To relegate servant leadership only to the category of a leadership style limits it to the top of the iceberg which is only a fraction of who the leader really is. Furthermore, seeing it as just another style makes it entirely dependent upon the results of "doing" leadership. When servant leadership is seen first as the condition of the leader, then the priority is identity formation, which will give rise to activity that is consistent with its nature. The bottom of the iceberg always provides a foundation and nature out of which activities in the top of the iceberg are performed. Servant leadership is much more than merely a style of leadership. It is a description of the leader him/herself.

Identity of a Servant

Putting the "servant" back in "servant leadership" means more than doing greater acts of service for others in fulfilling our leadership responsibility. It means shaping the character of the leader with identity questions that will transform the leader into a servant in their very nature. The resulting activities of leadership, irrespective of the style they reflect, will be servant motivated. Clearly there are some activities that by nature are inconsistent with a servant identity. However, servant leadership may manifest itself in a diversity of behaviors that cross the standard lines of established leadership styles. The foundation of servant leadership is the "bottom of the iceberg" identity of the leader which, when extended into "top of the iceberg" activities, shapes the behavior. This integrative pattern provides a level of discrimination that eliminates inconsistent actions and, at the same time, multiplies the effects of activities that are consistent with its nature.

The Self

In reality, we all serve someone or something. The question is what or who. It may be that upon careful examination, we find we are serving our own agenda. Self is probably the most prevalent master in the lives of leaders today. In this paradigm, we strive to fulfill our own agendas. Self becomes the central point of reference for all activities. Personal betterment becomes the test against which all decisions are evaluated for effectiveness. The measure of good leadership, then, is whether we are in better shape and obtain greater power, prestige, or influence personally; or in the view of others if we have achieved self-fulfillment and a greater reach.

Others

Another strong contender for center stage in a leader's life is others. At first the thought of serving other people sounds noble if not downright righteous. When it comes to the conversation around servant leadership, this is most often the focus. The presumption is that servant leadership is all about serving others. Yet under closer examination it becomes apparent that making leadership all about serving others can be a pitfall for burnout and frustrated vocation. Consider all the differing agendas of people in the organization. Trying to fulfill all of those while still maintaining some level of growth in the organization and personal balance is a formula for overload. This is particularly true in volunteer organizations like the church and is perhaps the greatest source of frustration and attrition for pastors. Their constant attempt to please people and serve them creates inner stresses that can quickly come to a breaking point in tough situations. At the same time, the visionary element necessary for these situations becomes hidden in the cloud of serving others' agendas.

Performance

A third possibility as the primary objective in a leader's work is organizational performance. Outcomes overshadow all other agendas or interests. Leaders with this "master" may very quickly slide into a pattern of leadership that is controlling, manipulative, and potentially abusive to people unless there are careful check points. They may be so intent upon seeing results that potential collateral damage in staff members is inconsequential.

Perhaps the most important feature of understanding servant leadership is to describe what one may call the "servant/master construct." Inherent in the very word servant is the implication that there is a master. Each gives the other meaning. Of course the concept of servant not only implies a master, but it also involves free choice. Servants voluntarily choose to submit themselves to the influence of a master thereby being formed into the nature of their master and realigned by the priorities of their master. The deepest desire is to become like the principal reference point they have chosen and to fulfill the agendas of that same master. The choice of that primary reference point we may call a "master" occurs either by intention or it becomes evident through patterns of behavior important to a person. The description in the Bible of the kenosis or emptying (Phil. 2:5-11) is perhaps the most obvious example of the volitional choice required in becoming a servant. It evidences a release of rights and personal priorities as well as a humbling of the will in adopting the nature and priorities of another.

The healthiest, and perhaps only "master" of a true servant leader, is God. While it may sound so general as to be irrelevant, in reality it is the most relevant and healthiest point of reference for a leader to have. Clearly there are many assumptions attached to such a declaration, but when understood well, the idea that servant leaders are servants of God first helps a leader to find meaning, balance, fulfillment, and motivation in exercising their leadership activities in any context. Before you discard the idea as spiritual jargon, consider the reality that the uncontested greatest leader of all time was Jesus. In order to understand his effectiveness, we have to take a look behind the scene and get a glimpse of his identity. He did not come to set up an organization or to manipulate people into performance under his control.

> *"If the one we serve is good and righteous, then we will become like-minded. The character of the leader will take on the nature of the one they serve"*

The best descriptor we have is that of a servant. But it's important to note that even though he was meeting the needs of people, he was not their servant. He came as a servant of God, and it was God's agenda that directed his activities. His service to people was to help them discover wholeness in response to their greatest need as they too came into an understanding of God's greatest desire for them. In short, Christ came as a servant of God and a minister to people. There is a vast difference in the concept of service or ministry and servanthood.

As a manifestation of his ultimate choice to serve God, Jesus surrendered his own agenda to fulfill the principal agenda of the one he served. That agenda was to restore people to wholeness through reconciliation with God. In fulfilling the agenda of his master, he ministered to people. Servant leaders do well to begin their journey of formation here.

The bottom of the iceberg, our identity, is the place where no one else sees. It is the ballast that gives our lives stability and meaning. Out of the overflow of that identity, our activities are motivated and focused not only in a manner consistent with the inner DNA of our being, but in a way that fulfills God's vocation and calling for us.

Making the willful choice to serve God means that first our nature is transformed. Our nature is affected by our submission to the one we serve. If the one we serve is self, we will by nature become selfish. If the ones we serve are others, we will become manipulative and insecure in the many different demands placed on us by others. If the one we serve is good and righteous, then we will become like-minded. The character of the leader will take on the nature of the one they serve.

In addition to our nature being affected, our priorities are also affected based upon whom we serve. If we serve self, our priority is to preserve and exalt self at all cost. In serving God, however, we find that his priorities become ours. What is important to God becomes important to us. His greatest priority since creation has been for people to be reconciled to God's own self in becoming whole and healed of the brokenness resulting from the great fall. Hence, in serving God, our priority becomes like his: meeting the needs of people thereby maximizing their sense of fulfillment and effectiveness. The difference is that we do so not out of a manipulative motivation to achieve good results, but out of a deep desire to please the one we serve. So the most important question every leader must consider is: "Who's your master?"

Serving God simply means trying to fulfill what God has in mind for us. That is the basis of vocation which at its root is a calling, a destiny, a deep passion and motivation that transcends the mere implementation of leadership activities. When a leader discovers this fountainhead, suddenly all of the activities in the top of the iceberg begin to make sense. They flow out of a natural wellspring of identity and are focused with consistency as the nature of that identity finds expression in actions. Who we are always gives rise to what we do. Our nature as a servant first will affect our actions as a leader.

The error that many students of leadership make is to assume that servant leadership is merely a style of leadership complete with formulas, behaviors and patterns which, when learned well, will result in positive outcomes. Servant leadership is not merely a style. It is a condition of the leader. As such, a servant leader may employ a variety of leadership styles. What makes them a servant is the fact that they are acting out of servanthood to God, compelled by a God-given vocation in fulfilling a God-given destiny. It is most evident in the condition of the leader. Therefore, while we may perform service for people, we are not their servants. A servant leader is servant to One.

Conclusion

In a day when efficiency and outcomes are the center of attention for leaders and leadership studies, calling people to servanthood is countercultural. It goes against the grain of a 21st century entrepreneurial, success-oriented culture. From school days to work situations, we are imprinted with the importance of performance and results. The bottom line is the most influential element in promotions, hires, and bonuses. The expectation is that not much else is important as long as the results are good. Even the character of a person is minimized if performance is strong. And so we create a culture that is built upon results, performance, and outcomes. While at first glance this appears to be effective, owing to the net improvement of organizations and their ability to service communities, it is a trap that can become destructive.

The shallow nature of performance-based identity leaves a leader dependent upon outcomes to determine personal value. If the outcomes of leadership activities are good, then the leader assumes she is a good person. Conversely, if performance is poor, the leader begins to think they are a bad person and begins to seek other, perhaps inappropriate, sources of personal validation. Burnout, moral failure, misbehavior are all potential consequences of an identity that is based merely upon performance that fails. Arrogance, abuse, self-centered corruption can become the consequences of performance-based identity that is successful. In either case, the value of a person is reduced to the ability to perform and they become a commodity to be used or an asset to be leveraged.

Although the servant leadership model is best exemplified by the person of Jesus, it is a principle that applies universally to all people. It is not a style to be learned as much as it is a condition to be embraced by the leader. For a leader the starting point is to ask the question, "Who am I?" As this leads to basic identity formation, the activities that follow in engaging the work situation will be shaped and adjusted into consistency. In that consistency, otherwise known as integrity, there is power and effectiveness that is healthy, productive and selfless.

Kevin Mannoia, PhD, is Chaplain and Professor of Ministry at Azusa Pacific University, as well as Founder and Chair of the Wesleyan Holiness Consortium.

Further Readings

Greenleaf, Robert. *Servant Leadership*. Paulist Press, 1977.
Heifetz, Ronald. *Leadership without Easy Answers*. Harvard University Press, 1994.
Mannoia, Kevin W. *The Integrity Factor*. Regent College Publishing, 2006.
Spears, Larry, ed. *Insights on Leadership*. John Wiley & Sons, 1998.

27

Leading in an Urban Context

Richard L. Gray

The world is urbanizing. While the church, and its educational institutions, have often neglected the city, Christians can do so no longer. Christian leaders, then, must engage the city to lead in this global era. This engagement involves developing a theology of the city, including understanding God's love for cities, and developing an ecclesiology for cities that facilitates churches thriving in whatever their identity and mission.

UNTIL RECENTLY, SOME CHRISTIANS VIEWED MINISTRY to the city with a certain degree of trepidation. Because of the nature of the city, ministry there was considered a task best left to the specialist, to the professionals. It was easy therefore to focus leadership ministry efforts in other directions and neglect ministry to an urban context. Roger Greenway writes,

> Cities, seminaries, and Christian colleges have been living apart for too long, and it's a broken relationship that urgently needs to be repaired.... Our schools produce thousands of graduates each year who know little or nothing about cities. They've spent their lives and received all their education in the cushioned middle class world of antiseptic isolation from harsh urban realities. As a consequence, they are unprepared to minister in cities. They are bewildered by them and avoid them. The world on the one hand has been urbanizing, but we've gone the opposite direction. Now we're faced with the dilemma that the world to which Christ sends us to be ambassadors, servants, and transformers lies mainly in the cities, and we're outside.[1]

Today, however, a change is taking place. The world is urbanizing and Christians are now looking at our cities as a modern day mission field.

The Cultural Mandate

Genesis 1:28 contains the Cultural Mandate in which God admonishes humanity to "be fruitful and increase in number; fill the earth and subdue it." The Cultural Mandate is an exercise in delegated sovereignty. In this passage, God empowers humanity to take control of his world. Humanity has been given divine authority over every living thing that exists. On the basis of this authority, humanity has tried to mold and shape the world so as to make life more comfortable for himself. Elliston writes,

> The content of this mandate includes the distribution of wealth, the balance of nature, marriage and the family, human government, keeping the peace, cultural integrity, and liberation of the oppressed. These and other global responsibilities rightly fall within the Cultural Mandate.[2]

Cities can be viewed as a direct result of humanity's delegated sovereignty over the earth because cities showcase humanity's greatest attempts to actualize the Cultural Mandate. Within the cities of our world, humanity has controlled nature as much as he is able and he has established systems designed to give structure and order to his life. The current explosion of people inhabiting the earth and the great increase in the number of cities in which they congregate and live is a testimony to humanity's ability to carry out God's commands.

The Population Explosions

It took from the time human beings first walked the earth until around AD 1800 for the world's population to reach one billion.[3] But it doubled just a little over a hundred years later in the early 1900s. By the 1980s, it passed four billion; in 2012, seven billion, and today is approaching eight billion. The global population currently increases at a rate of 1.8 percent per year. This means that the world adds approximately 84 million people per year.

The world has not always been in this situation. For centuries, the world grew just under one percent annually,[4] doubling in population around every 70 to 80 years. With a relatively small population, such growth was not especially consequential. But as time and population growth passed, inescapable difficulties developed for human kind. These difficulties can be illustrated by using a chessboard and rice. By beginning with a single grain of rice on the first square, doubling it to two grains on the second square, four grains on the third square and so on, by the time the eighth square is reached it would require 128 grains of rice. The twelfth square would require more than a pound. By the time we reach the final square of the board, it would require more than 200 billion tons of rice.[5]

Two factors have come together to help create the present situation.

1. *The world's natural tendency to grow exponentially.* In recent years there has been a decline in the growth rate from 2 percent per year to the present 1.8 percent. However, there are so many people on the earth that the effects of the decline are all but negated.

2. *Advances in science.* We can produce more food and we have developed medicines that help us stay alive longer. This has had the effect of causing mortality rates in developing countries to plunge.

Given that the physical dimensions of the globe on which we reside are static, it is inevitable that a time would come when serious attention would need to be given to the implications for such tremendous population increases. By the year 2040, the population could increase to over nine billion people. But how many people can our world accommodate before its resources are used up? No one knows for sure, but best estimates suggest that the population will stabilize at about 9-10 billion people.[6] What is known is that today 92% of the world's growth is occurring in "developing" or Third World countries. By contrast, the more developed nations have seen a steady decline in their rate of growth.[7]

The Urbanization of the World

Throughout the early history of the world, the vast majority of people lived in rural areas. Men and women were hunters, gatherers, and, later, farmers. Over time, as civilization advanced, villages, town, and cities emerged for trade, government, and security. But even as late as 1800, the dominant means of livelihood for the world was agriculture. Just over two percent of the population of Europe, the most urbanized continent, lived in cities.[8]

As a natural result of the world's population explosion, there has been a massive growth in the development of cities since the 1800s. In recent years, the world has spawned cities larger than any that have ever existed. Ray Bakke observes that at its peak, ancient Nineveh (in modern Iraq) was home to approximately 120,000 people. And, in the 1st century AD at the time of the Apostle Paul, ancient Rome housed about a million people. However, these cities were not typical. As late as 1850, only 94 cities in the world had a population of 100,000. Fifty years later, that number had nearly tripled. By the middle of the 20th century, there were 760 such cities with a total combined population of 241 million people. IN 1950, only about ten percent of the world's population would have been considered urban.[9]

The most urbanized parts of the world during the mid twentieth century were Australia, northwest Europe, North America, northeast Asia, and the southern portions of Latin America. In those areas, 52% of the population was living in cities of 100,000 or more. Africa was the least urbanized with only 9% of the continent living in cities of 20,000 or more.

Until the mid-twentieth century, there were only two cities (New York and

London) with populations over 10 million people. However, with the majority of the population explosion happening in urban areas, the rise of cities accelerated rapidly:

1. By 1980: ten world cities have populations of at least 10 million people.
2. By 2000: sixty cities around the world have populations over five million people; twenty-five cities over ten million; and five cities with populations of over twenty million people.

The cities of the world are growing at a rate twice that of the population.[10] In 2000, the population of our planet living in cities equaled the total population of the world in 1965. Just over half of the world today lives in urban areas and this figure is only expected to increase. Undoubtedly, for those engaged in building the Kingdom in a globalized, highly populated 21st century world, understanding the *city* as a primary context for Christian leadership is critical.

A Theology of the City

Bakke describes theology as God in dialogue with his people.[11] This dialogue occurs regardless of the environment in which they find themselves. As people of God, however, we need to realize that the world's trajectory is towards global urbanization. Our theology needs to include that reality. Cities continue to grow and develop. As God's ministers on earth, our effectiveness is enhanced as we understand the relationship between the cities of our world and the living God we serve.

Cities are a human invention. They were originally intended as places of safety, sustenance, and community. Unfortunately, also from their inception, cities were seen in opposition to the Holy God. This negative view of the city was reinforced by the work of Jacques Ellul in his famous book, *The Meaning of the City*. This book is seen as bold attempt to develop a biblical theology of the city. According to Ellul, the Bible views the city as the concentration of humanity's sin and the center of rebellion against God. Because the city is the product of humanity's technology, it is humanity's substitution for God's creation. This is perhaps the reality alluded to in the story of Tower of Babel in Genesis 11. The city is humanity's attempt to live without God.[12]

Genesis 4:17 informs us that Cain was the builder of the first city which he named after his son Enoch. Cain was condemned by God to wander. However, still in rebellion against God, Cain defied God by taking roots in the new city. This city he intended to be a new beginning for himself and a substitute for Eden. Cain perpetuated his own name in the self-sustaining security of his city. Because of Cain's actions, in defiance of God's explicit instruction, Ellul argues that all cities from that time forward are founded and built in opposition to God and his plan.[13]

The church and its leadership is God's chosen vessel for the redemption of the city. This redemption can only occur to the degree that we as Christians develop an effective theology with a vision for the city.

A Growing Urban Reality

With the advent of factories and new technology during the Industrial Revolution, people migrated to the cities in great numbers in search of jobs and a better way of life. In Western Europe and the Unites States, factories replaced the farm as the focal point of community and people began to find it more convenient to live clustered together. Factories meant a steady stream of raw materials coming and manufactured goods going out. As such, they required a larger and more complex social infrastructure. First, workers became more specialized and their entire working day was spent in the factory. Factory workers simply no longer had the time and even the knowledge to be self-reliant in producing their own food and goods for living. As such, the presence of factories and their large work force required a whole supporting cast of butchers, bakers, tanners and tailors, blacksmiths, carters, carpenters, and, yes, farmers.

Second, it was a matter of convenience and affordability for factory workers to live as close to the factories as possible, soon giving rise to the phenomenon of factory towns. Factories would be built often near rivers or railroads. Workers would settle and build housing in close quarters within easy travel distance of the factories. Secondary industries necessary to support the factory's supply chains and workforce then moved in, adding further social and economic structure. The availability of existing workers and supply chains would then attract more factories, and the cycle would begin. Thus, the Industrial Revolution helped trigger a change in residence patterns, and, as a result, in the way in which people interacted with each other.[14]

As a result of this revolution, by 1900 more than half of the population of Great Britain lived in cities. Today, like Europe and the United States, most industrialized nations tend to be highly urbanized. This supports the belief in a strong correlation between economic development and urbanization. Factories, government agencies and distribution centers tend to be located in the cities. In contrast, places where development is diminished, the rate of urbanization is similarly affected.[15]

The Classic View of the City

Ferdinand Tonnes described the development of the urban society as a shift from a community based on kinship ties to a society based on common practical interests. The famous French sociologist Emile Durkheim suggested that a distinction be made between what he termed "mechanical solidarity" (ties based on shared ideas and common experiences) and "organic solidarity" (ties based on mutual dependence between people engaged in specialized tasks). George Simmel added to the development of the Classical View by offering that urban life fundamentally affected the psychology of individuals. Louis Wirth of the Chicago School of Sociology would later take these strands of theory and weave them into a cogent, comprehensive statement about "Urbanism as a Way of Life." Wirth's statement is revered as the most important synthesis of the Classical View in sociology in the United States.[16]

Central to the perspective of all of these thinkers was the notion that industrialization and urbanization were very disruptive forces. They saw the emergence of urban society as a process in which a stable society of rural communities was shattered. As a result, they observed that at the level of the individual social life, there was a major change in the nature of social relationships. The consequences of the urbanization process were seen to create social disorganization, psychological stress, anomie and alienation.

Social disorganization occurred when primary ties provided by the extended kinship system decayed. This meant that the emotional support, intimacy, and security, which these ties provided, were lacking in most social relationships. Subsequent relationships were transitory, calculating and impersonal. Rapidly changing and frequently conflicting values resulted in a loss of clear, consistent guidelines for behavior.

Psychological stress resulted from the constantly changing social environment, the tremendous diversity of social experiences and the large number of superficial, transitory social relationships. As a response, urban dwellers simply learned to be emotionally unresponsive to a large number of stimuli in the urban environment.

Anomie is a feeling of "normlessness." Individuals feel that there are no clear rules and values by which to evaluate his or her behavior.

Alienation is described as feelings of: (1) powerlessness, (2) meaninglessness, and (3) social isolation. Individuals feel that they have no control over their lives or a particular social environment. Power is seen to be in the hands of distant and unknown people and impersonal forces.

The end result of these various consequences to urbanization the classical theorist saw as chronic depression, increased likelihood of committing suicide, increased risk of mental illness, cynicism and distrust in personal relationships, apathy and withdrawal, alcoholism, drug addiction, aggression and criminality.

The Heavenly City

There is a common belief that although God created men and women and placed them in a garden, humanity's final reality will be a heavenly city that God will establish. Current trends, signs and indicators all suggest that the world is rushing towards this ultimate urban reality. During his earthly ministry, Jesus hinted at his knowledge of this truth. Luke's gospel tells us that even though much of his work occurred in other places, Jesus' face was "set towards Jerusalem" (Luke 9:53). After arriving at the city, the gospel writers inform us that Jesus cried over it. This was one of only two occasions where the scriptures say that the Lord cried. We are not told what his eyes saw as he gazed at the city, but we know that it touched him deeply.

Throughout the scriptures, urban settings figured prominently in the narratives. It is not surprising, therefore, that our present day cities should be the site of our ministry endeavors. Nor should it be surprising that Christians should occupy a significant leadership role in how our cities are shaped and function. DuBrin offers that leadership is "*interpersonal influence directed through communication, toward goal attainment.*"[17] This definition hints at the fact that God has designed his church in such a way that it becomes ideally suited for the task of leading in an urban context. Elliston and Kauffman relate the task in the following way:

> Ministry refers to any leadership status and role in the church that aims to contribute to the life and purpose of the church.... Ministry is intended to be holistic in which three key relationships come into focus: 1) one's relationship with God through Jesus Christ, 2) one's relationship with one's neighbors, and 3) one's relationship to the local context.[18]

In order for ministry to be effective, these three relationships need to be integrally connected. Imagine three overlapping, interconnected circles. For the purposes of this chapter, relationship with the context, the third of the three relationships, is the crucial relationship with which we will be most concerned. This is necessary because the city provides a unique context within which ministry is to be done.

Often confusion arises when one talks of an urban context over and against what constitutes a "city." This confusion comes about because the two terms are often used interchangeably. However, there is a difference that comes into sharper focus when one looks at the original meanings of the words.

"Christians should occupy a significant leadership role in how our cities are shaped and function"

City incorporates the idea of administration and government. It is Latin in its derivation (*civitas*) and carries with it the sense of citizenship with all of its attendant rights and privileges. We associate cities with large buildings and dense populations. In a phrase, *city* is a place.

Urban is used as an adjective and carries with it the notion of a densely populated place but speaks more to the lifestyles of those who inhabit that place. Like *city*, *urban* is also Latin in its derivation (*urbs*) and is associated with the palisades that were once used to surround and protect a settled place from intruders. From earliest times, those who lived in settled protected places developed a characteristic way of life that was non-agricultural and non-nomadic in its expression. Our English word *urbane* came into use around the sixteenth century and was associated with a sense of a quality of life and thought that have been traditionally linked with lives lived in an urban setting.[19]

Elliston and Kauffman find the task of urban ministry resting on two different but complementary imperatives. These imperatives are (1) making disciples of all nations and (2) loving one's neighbors. Both imperatives are best accomplished through leadership that promotes an attitude of service and servanthood.

Therefore, to minister in an urban context, one must minister to more than just the place. Urban Ministry is unique because its focus must be on the *attitude* that is intertwined with the place. The forces that mold and shape the cities of our world also affect the people that inhabit those cities and in our rapidly urbanizing world, almost every human being is impacted. Remember, what began in a garden called Eden, will one day end in a grand and glorious city. A city not made with human hands.[20] Our planet and its inhabitants are being prepared for that eventuality.

The Urban Church and Ministry

Urban ministry encompasses both the urban church and ministry[21] and cannot be properly understood apart from the work of the church. The church is God's unique instrument through which the inhabitants of a city are to be affected for the Kingdom of God. Urban ministry should be understood as those ministry endeavors and initiatives that are facilitated through the church and uniquely suited for people *urbane* in their living and thinking processes. What then is the church and why is it so important to the task of urban ministry?

What is the Church?

The urban church is "a community, usually organized formally, of God's people in the city."[22] Ministry is carried on both within to the members of the urban church and without to the inhabitants of the city. This explanation of the church's mission has given rise to separate ways of viewing the church's reason for being.

For the theologian, the church finds its reason for being and identity in the God-human relationships of grace and salvation based on the work of Jesus Christ, experienced through the Holy Spirit, and displayed in worship and witness by the obedient response of God's people. The social scientist, on the other hand, looks at the church from the viewpoint of what processes are taking place in the fellowship of believers and the community at large.

Understanding the church as the bride of Christ or as the Lord's "wife", it is helpful to think of the work of the urban church in six facets. They are:

1. *Worship* — the adoration of God;
2. *Instruction* — the work of developing mature followers of Christ;
3. *Fellowship* — the care and intimacy among the members;
4. *Evangelism* — reaching those on the outside with the gospel;
5. *Stewardship* — responsible earthly citizenship aimed a advancing justice and improving the quality of life in a neighborhood;
6. *Service* — addressing the social, physical, mental and spiritual needs of those within the membership and those without.

Types of Churches

Not every urban church possesses all of these facets, but is instead likely to focus on one or two to the exclusion of the others. In some instances, an urban church will have all six facets but will stress them in different proportions. It is in this way that a church develops a distinctive identity. We can identify three categories of churches, depending on which facets an urban church focuses: the experiential church, the relational church, and the task church.[23] Of these categories, the relational church is the most numerous. However, because of the changing nature of our society and world, the task church is fast gaining popularity. This is occurring because these churches are distinguished by their focus related to instruction and evangelism (experiential), worship and fellowship (relational), or stewardship and service (task). Each type of church plays an important role in offering ministry leadership to an urban environment in that each type of church speaks to a particular type of community experience for a city dweller.

The *Experiential Church* highlights instruction and evangelism. These churches appeal to individuals who desire to build community around expanding their own spiritual knowledge base. They seek out a church that teaches them those things they feel necessary for their growth and edification within the body of Christ and then seek to take what they have learned and enhance the kingdom of God through evangelism efforts.

The *Relational Church* emphasizes worship and fellowship, appealing to those individuals who build their community around a common sharing of experiences and sense of intimacy.[24] This is the most popular and numerous type of church in our Western society. People are able to build their community around a common approach to express their love for God and around their ability to gather together with individuals they have come to know over a period of time.

The *Task Church* focus on stewardship and service and appeals to those individuals who desire to share their faith walk with others in the form of outreach initiatives.[25]

Three Rs of Urban Ministry

As the world has become more and more urban, the need has grown for greater attention to be given to the church's responsibility for providing programs of service and stewardship. To that end, the urban church has become very adept at designing its programs around the 3R's of urban ministry: relief, reconciliation and reform.

1. *Relief.* These are programs that are intended to provide temporary solutions to the problems that vex urban dwellers. They include: food pantries, clothing thrift shops, emergency funds, etc.
2. *Reconciliation.* These are initiatives that seek to heal the rift that tends to

exist between various peoples and groups.
3. *Reform.* These are efforts aimed at providing a more permanent solution to problems that vex urban dwellers by addressing those systems and structures that have the greatest potential of helping to alleviate the problem. These efforts should be the focus of our leadership.[26]

When studying the interconnected systems that make up our cities, the acronym PREFER is helpful: Political, Religious, Economic, Family, Educational, Recreational. PREFER reminds us to consider these systems as an interrelated and interconnected whole if we hope to design successful programs that will have a more lasting impact on our cities and its inhabitants.

Urban Specialization of the Church

Given the great diversity within the urban context, there is ample room and need for all three types of churches with their varied programs. In order to be effective, the urban church has to have a clear idea of its aims. These aims should be focused upon the particular people to be reached and the specific methods to reach them. The urban church is best served as it teaches people about the diversity of churches within the city. In many cases, the urban church has learned the need to specialize. The specialized churches which can be found in the city include the authoritarian church, the charismatic church, the relationship church, and the structure church.

The Authoritarian Church

This style of church is usually attractive to blue-collar workers and some minorities. They are attracted by an authoritarian pulpit figure that does not falter or shy away from spiritually confronting the people.

The Charismatic Church

This style of church is usually attractive to those who are event-oriented people. They search the church page to see where God will be on Sunday. They seek celebration in the city and will often travel great distances to sit anonymously among strangers to sing and clap hands. These people will praise God and hug people that they do not know.

The Relationship Church

This style of church is usually attractive to those whose lives have somehow been fragmented by the city. They do not care for the anonymous charismatic celebration but seek to have their needs met through involvement in small groups that usually meet in a home. These types of churches do not grow but their numbers grow.

The Structure Church

This style of church is attractive to active people who like churches with extensive programs and which demand high commitment. Within this type of church, a distinction can be made between those individuals who want *to be* and those individuals who want *to do*. Both kinds of people are essential for the effective functioning of this style of church.[27]

Come and Go Churches

Churches can be roughly categorized under two models: the "come-all-ye" church and the "go" church.[28] The "come-all-ye" church functions in such a way that people must be brought into the church programs in order to be evangelized. Once this occurs, they are discipled into church fellowship and incorporated into the lifestyle of the covenant group. Growth occurs from the center and is seen as the goal of discipleship. The come-all-ye model fits the more traditional church structure within our society and is often busy and well organized. With a strong, charismatic, authoritarian pastor, this kind of church provides security and structure for people.[29]

The "go" church sees its members as ministers to their own worlds of relationships. This church equips and empowers its members to identify a mission within their own sphere of influence. For example, a banker would set up a Bible study within the bank with colleagues. This particular model lends itself more readily to the Relationship style of church and has other added advantages for a present day urban context. Bakke sees those advantages as (1) legitimizing the call of the lay person to mission; (2) reaching a much wider portion of the an urban population; (3) following the urban twenty-four hour clock more easily than a structured program; (4) fulfilling the need of specialized urban people to affirm their personal vocations as their ministry.[30]

While these church models are very different, it is possible that one or more of the church styles discussed earlier can be found within either. Like Bakke, I have a marked preference for the "go" church model in an urban context. However, church leadership and traditional church society will have to undergo significant change before this particular model will come into widespread use. Such an occurrence is possible, for the church has frequently been modified by its contemporary society.

Conclusion

It is a basic truism of urban ministry that *what began in a garden will one-day end in a grand and glorious city*. This city will not be made with human hands but will be delivered by God out of the heavens. As we have entered the 21st century, the truth of that statement appears more and more realistic. The world is urbanizing and the consequences of those urbanization processes are effecting how people interact, relate to one another and function in this rapidly changing environment. Changing, too, is the way that urban ministry and leadership must be approached.

Because of the uncertainty that accompanies rapid change, people today are looking for leadership that is not afraid to live their lives in a more transparent fashion; leadership that is not afraid to "live inside out" and who lead with integrity. This is the challenge to which Wesleyan leadership must rise. It is not enough today to just minister to a place. We must shape our service to minister to the people as they are being affected by the forces that impact their lives as they make their homes within a given place: a place that is becoming more urban every day.

Richard L. Gray, PhD, is Professor of Leadership and Christian Ministries at Asbury Theological Seminar and the author of Beneath the Lode of the Cross, The PSDA [Personal Spiritual Development Analysis (How-To)] Guide, and a series of children's books featuring Evangel the Smallest Angel.

Bibliography

Bakke, Ray. *The Urban Christian.* Downers Grove, IL: InterVarsity Press, 1987

Claerbaut, David. *Urban Ministry.* Grand Rapids: Zondervan, 1983

DeVito, J. A., "Relational Principles for Effective Church Leadership." *Journal of Leadership Education.* (Spring 2014).

DuBrin, Andrew J., *The Complete Idiot's Guide to Leadership.* New York: Penguin Putnam, 2000

Elliston, Edgar J. and J. Timothy Kauffman. *Developing Leaders for Urban Ministry.* New York: Peter Lang, 1993.

Ellul, Jacques. *The Meaning of the City.* Grand Rapids, MI: William B. Eerdmans, 1970.

Greenway, Roger S. "Cities, Seminaries and Christian Colleges." *Urban Missions* 3, no. 1 (September 1985).

Herson, Lawrence J. R. and John M. Bolland. *The Urban Web: Politics, Policy and Theory.* Chicago, IL: Nelson-Hall Publishers, 1991.

Rose, Larry, and C. Kirk Hadaway. *An Urban World.* Nashville, TN: Broadman Press, 1984.

Shannon, Thomas R., Nancy Kleniewski, and William Cross. *Urban Problems in Sociological Perspective.* Prospect Heights, IL: Waveland Press, 1991.

Tonna, Benjamin. *Gospel for the Cities.* Maryknoll, NY: Orbis Books, 1985.

Wagner, C. Peter. "A Missiological View of Relief and Development." In *Christian Relief and Development: Training Workers for Effective Ministry,* edited by Edgar J. Elliston. Dallas: Word Books, 1989.

Chapter 27 Notes

[1] Greenway, "Cities, Seminaries and Christian Colleges"

[2] Elliston and Kauffman, *Developing Leaders for Urban Ministries*, p. 70. See also Wagner, "A Missiological View of Relief and Development," 119-120.

[3] Rose and Hadaway, *An Urban World*, 13-18

[4] Ibid, 15.

[5] Ibid.

[6] Hans Rosling, "Religions and babies," TED Talks lecture (April 2012).

[7] Rose and Hadaway. *An Urban World*, 16-17.

[8] Ibid, 22.

[9] Bakke, *The Urban Christian*, 28-30.

[10] Rose and Hadaway. *An Urban World*, 21

[11] Bakke, *The Urban Christian*, 62.

[12] Jacques Ellul, *The Meaning of the City*, (Grand Rapids, MI: William B. Eerdmans, 1970), 48-52.

[13] Ibid.

[14] Rose and Hadaway. *An Urban World*, 22.

[15] Ibid.

[16] Shannon, Kleniewski, and Cross, *Urban Problems*, 64-65.

[17] DuBrin, *The Complete Idiot's Guide to Leadership*, 4.

[18] Elliston and Kauffman, *Developing Leaders for Urban Ministries*, 5.

[19] Herson and Bolland, *The Urban Web*, 5

[20] See Hebrews 11:10.

[21] Claerbaut, *Urban Ministry*, p.13.

[22] Ibid.

[23] Ibid.

[24] DeVito offers that people seek relationships in order to satisfy a sense of belonging, decrease feelings of loneliness, find opportunities for intellectual and physical stimulation, and achieve personal empowerment as well as to enhance self-esteem. As reported by Dr. Willis M. Watt, "Relational Principles for Effective Church Leadership" in the *Journal of Leadership Education*, Spring 2014.

[25] These facets and categories were modified from the work of Claerbaut, *Urban Ministry*, 13.

[26] Claerbaut, *Urban Ministry*, 25-26.

[27] Bakke, *The Urban Christian*, 127-128.

[28] Ibid.

[29] Ibid, 131- 132.

[30] Ibid.

28
Leading Ministry Teams and Small Groups

Daryl Smith

Leadership involves teams. This chapter builds a foundation for community in leadership and from there presents helpful tips for group leadership in light of team dynamics, including creating a welcoming atmosphere, balancing different spiritual activities, and accessing biblical narratives for group discussion.

WE ARE EACH PURSUING a dream-packed quest to release the image of God planted deep within. Often that dream is trapped for fear that exposure would bring scorn. Most times we have forgotten how to hear the call of that dream without a company of others—those who can see in us things we cannot see in ourselves. As leaders, we have the challenging privilege of guiding small communities who join together as co-adventurers to call forth that creation-self in one another. So whether we call them small groups or ministry teams, our primary mission as leaders is discipleship—assisting people "in the process of being conformed to the image of Jesus for the sake of others."[1]

Leaders always lead groups (or teams), which includes serving the team, equipping the team's members and, as possible, sending team members for greater accomplishment. Yet teams present unique challenges to leadership. One such challenge is that leading a team may initially require more time to produce the desired results. This is a challenge because we are often in just too big a hurry. Our "hurry-up" syndrome can make leading through teams seem more cumbersome than going at it alone, but this slower pace must not be used this as an excuse. Teams can keep us on track, hold us accountable, give us advice, and say "No" when we charge off in an idolatrous moment. Leading healthy groups effectively leads to richer and longer lasting rewards as the Kingdom of God becomes visible as more people are equipped to serve and have secure foundations in a team.

Put into Christian language, groups/teams also provide the very best opportunity for discipling/mentoring others into the image of Jesus. The heart of discipleship is connecting three stories: God's Story, Your Story, My Story. Recall Jesus' words in Matthew 18:20, describing the life transformation that happens when two or three persons gather in his name. Disciple-making leaders help connect those three stories within the context of the group because they understand that the Kingdom of God is always *communal* when it is functioning in God's creation plan.

God's Communal Design

Individualism runs deep in Western civilization. But this is not God's original design for humans. From the beginning, God's plan included human beings created for deep, healthy relationships. Like the relationship between a man and woman described in Genesis 1-2, we are called to live in partnership with one another.[2] But the creation dream was short-lived. In Genesis 3, the dream is destroyed as the woman and man—seduced by the serpent and willfully defiant—decide to go their own direction, breaking relationship with God and with each other.

The final act of sabotage comes in Genesis 3:20. In a statement of dominion over the woman, the man announced himself as *Adam*—stealing the name given to both woman and man together, and names the woman Eve, or childbearer.[3] Every Jewish reader would recognize that when the human named the animals in Genesis 2, the human was taking lordship over the animals. When the man named

"they don't begin to burst with the potential for life without work. It takes intentional, specific steps in partnership with God's Holy Spirit to facilitate the process"

the woman, he declared lordship over the woman. Instead of co-stewardship, the man took the authority for himself and demoted the woman to the status of other created beings and instead of an exalted name, he gave her functionary value. From that point forward her value would come as the incubator of humanity: one who births and nurses. From that point forward, most relationships became a struggle for power. Community was lost.

Yet, in our brokenness and struggle for independence, God's call to community never wavered. The reality of community as God's created purpose brackets the story of the fall, sin, and redemption that spans Genesis to Revelation. At the beginning of God's revealed story, God fashions humanity his own Trinitarian image, establishing the first woman and man as a model of how community is to live and grow within the bounds of time. At the other end of the biblical narrative, God's eternal community culminates in a reversal of Adam and Eve's fall: a great wedding party of Jesus as groom and his bride, the Church. Just like in a marriage, this is a relationship to grow through the ups and downs of life, bound together by a common mission.

Going "Green"

Imagine *green* for a moment. What flavor do you taste? What picture pops before your eyes? What sounds do you hear? *Green* often means life. To apply this metaphor to our study of community, *green* is what happens when a group becomes a community of people seeking healthy, vibrant relationships with one another, with God, and with the world. Now, imagine the group you lead, whether an administrative board, a sports-bar Bible study, or a music team. Imagine it as *green*—a healthy, growing place. What images flood your mind about what this group might become? This can sometimes be a challenge for leaders who often want to start new groups. But before beginning a new group, focus your attention on *greening* a current group. Groups don't just turn *green* with wishful thinking; they don't begin to burst with the potential for life without work. It takes intentional, specific steps in partnership with God's Holy Spirit to facilitate the process.

From Small Groups to Village Groups

So far, I've used the terms *small group, community,* and *teams* interchangeably. I'll now switch to *Village Group.*[4] Village groups expand the best of small groups. An ancient proverb says, "It takes a village to raise a child." It also takes a village to grow a disciple of Jesus. Whether we're talking about a Board of Administration, a home Bible study, a worship team, or an usher team, the term *Village Group* fits. Like a village, Village Groups are ideally places where everyone belongs, everyone is equipped for ministry, each one is cared for, and there is a common mission. The leader of the group may have responsibilities to move through an agenda, lead a congregation in worship, or help guests find seats, but the primary attention is on ministry to the Village Group's people and their discipleship, rather than strictly on the group's function.

Getting Perspective

Before we move forward to specific steps for bringing *greenness* to our teams, let's take an historical perspective to provide a broader vantage point. First, there is nothing new about the idea of Village Groups. When Jesus traveled the earth, he never did it alone. He surrounded himself with a small group of three, a larger group of twelve, and others who supported him throughout his three years of public ministry. His Village Group (and the generations of Village Groups to follow) was the central theme of his prayer in John 15-17. He prayed that all who followed would live in unity—would know the community that he and his Father knew.

Church history has many examples of small communities that carried on God's small group design. From Acts 2:42 (where early believers met in home groups), slipping through the final pages of the New Testament and into the multiple generations that followed, small communities gathered to affirm, support, and launch into ministry. Wherever and whenever the Church has been vitally alive, there has always been a form of Village Groups at the core.

As patriarch, John Wesley may be the most important historical guide within the Wesleyan tradition. The heart of the Methodist movement was the use of different groups to meet specific needs. *Class meetings* connected believers who met to grow as Jesus followers. *Bands* were groups where high accountability and deep honesty were demanded. *Select Societies* were groups where ministry leaders were trained. *Penitent Bands* were groups where people found opportunity for restoration from addictions.

Yet there are more recent examples and champions for small group ministry. The last 100 years has seen a profound resurgence of the small group movement. Sam Shoemaker, an Anglican priest in New York City and Pittsburgh who was grounded in the Oxford Movement in England, founded the *Faith at Work* ministry. Bill Wilson attended Sam Shoemaker's Oxford Group, searching for ways to meet the needs of alcoholics and founded Alcoholics Anonymous. Lyman Coleman, from the shoulders of Sam and Bill, founded Serendipity House that became *the* undisputed center for small group studies, training seminars, and the Serendipity Bible, a true example for discipleship and discipling ministries for the last fifty years. Finally, Roberta Hestenes has pioneered as a scholar and mentor in the small group movement for more than 40 years. Her *Using the Bible in Groups* is a seminal classic. In addition, from her leadership as a college president and pastor, her voice has resonated across the small-group landscape.

Better than Devotions

Village Groups take seriously the spiritual life of the group. What would happen if the trustees, administrative board, or ushering team became more like a Village Group? Would there be the kind of infighting often prevalent in many teams? Would the agenda change if people were living deeply into one another's lives?

Most groups have specific and good purposes, or at least they started that way. Patrick Lencioni recognized that at the heart of organizations there once was something grand and aspirational.[5] But each group falls short if we exclude the broader aspects of what's working at the heart of a Village Group. Village Groups include intentional relationship building, relational Bible study, and a common mission outside the group.

The Three-Legged Green Group

If we fail to include the intentional relationship building in a team, the group will never grow people who become more like Jesus. They'll never learn to apply what they're absorbing into their minds since they'll have no place to "practice" in community. And head-knowledge is never sufficient. If leaders fail to include service or mission beyond the group agenda, groups quickly become stagnant and never reach their full potential. Yet, for the transformative process to begin leaders must apply the theological and historical lessons.

Groups function like three-legged stools. To stay upright, all three legs must be on the ground. Earlier I asked you to dream about a team you lead. I encouraged you to think about how it could begin teeming with life—how it could become green. Here I will provide three "legs" for your stool to stay grounded. As each is presented in detail, imagine how the teams that you lead can become green by being shaped into the model of a Village Group.

Leg One: Build Relationships

The first leg of the stool is building healthy relationships between group members. Let me offer some foundational and practical tips.

1. *Be intentional.* Healthy groups never happen accidentally. They are the result of intentionally sharing joys and needs, of praying together, and maybe most importantly, affirming one another.

2. *Gently gather the group.* Begin with a question that gathers the group together. This question can be indirectly related to your group's meeting purposes—a study, a meeting, a planning session, etc. It's important, particularly for introverts, to create a simple connection among the group. A beverage or light snack works well. Often standing around a coffee pot or tea kettle will help to warm up the group.

3. *Connect new people.* As the group leader, *you* are the best one to *open* the group to new people. Think about it this way. If you've been around young teens, you noticed that they stand in circles facing one another. They don't mean to be cliquish, but the posture makes it difficult for new teens to break into the established circle. An effective leader will "pry open" a space in the circle for the new teen to step into. The leader's actions say, "This is a safe person. You can trust them in your group." The same is true for adults. The group leader will introduce new people to the team, making sure they get fully connected.

4. *Subdivide.* While it may seem strange to think about sub-dividing a ministry team when you gather to work, it provides several advantages. When a group gets larger than about seven people, the group needs to subdivide for at least part of the Village Group time. Have you ever noticed in a larger

group that about half of the group joins in discussion while the other half observes? Subdividing the group can provide more opportunities for relationships to deepen.

As the leader, you will need to decide what works best for your people. Consider this meeting agenda to get you started in *greening up* your ministry team.

1. Convene the entire team for the *Gathering* question, a drink, and some food in a casual setting.

2. Move into a time of *Finding our Stories in the Story,*[6] by dividing your group into groups of four so everyone can participate in a relaxed way. Send each subgroup to separate table areas.

3. You may want to stay in groups of four for a time of *Accountability and Caring.*

4. If your Village Group is a ministry team, they will reconvene for their business, rehearsal, or other work.

5. Save time at the end of your meeting for The *Mission* commitments that can be declared back in the subgroups or with the *entire team.*

6. Bring everyone back together for prayer, so the whole group can be aware of issues that everyone should be know about. Leave plenty of time for these last two sections of your agenda, so mission and prayer remain important.

If you plan carefully, the Gathering, Finding our Stories in the Story, and Accountability and Caring can be worked through in about 30 minutes. Leave at least 15 minutes after the meeting business or rehearsal for *The Mission* and *Prayer.*

Leg Two: Relational Bible Study

Whenever a group meets together, assume that there are people with little or no biblical knowledge and limited church background. How wonderful! Now they have a chance to grow by being part of your Village Group. By making this assumption, you are helping to ensure that everyone has a chance to belong—that all team members are equals. This can be done in a few simple ways.

Connect Through Story

As described earlier, the *three stories* must connect. The first story is God's story (primarily told through the Bible). That story shows God's design for humans, documents our walking away and separating from God's plan, and explains God's offering us a way home. The second story is another person's life story, with all its "stuff." The third story is my story, with all of *my* "stuff." We tell our stories, primarily, as we answer questions related to the Bible study.

Use Biblical Narratives

It's easiest for people to connect their story to God's story if the Bible passage they are studying is actually a story rather than a more involved section from one of Paul's letters. It is possible to use a non-narrative section of the Bible as a compliment to the narrative but let stories from both the Old and New Testaments be your focus. You can never go wrong if you hang out primarily in the Gospels with Jesus.

Use the Right Questions

The right *kinds* of questions and the *order* of questions are vitally important. Questions must be open-ended (not yes-or-no), never fill-in-the-blank with a *correct* answer. Writing great questions is hard work so gather a few people who can edit and re-edit questions until you get the best ones.[7] No one should need previous biblical knowledge to answer any question that comes up. Everyone is respected for their response even if it seems strange. This does not mean that Bible study should become sharing ignorance but allow the Holy Spirit to give insights as a group works together. If you do get into a really troublesome scripture passage, you may need to get help from a resource person. However, this is the exception, not the place to begin.

A Relational Bible-Study Group Model

With those simple guidelines in place, here's what a Relational Bible Study might look like for your team.

Gathering. The Gathering question(s) is to get the group thinking about the biblical topic in a non-threatening way, often producing laughter, and reducing barriers to the deeper questions that follow.

Finding Our Stories in the Story. Each subgroup of four will read through the Bible passage together, preferably out loud. Use caution when calling on a person to read aloud since they may have difficulty reading in front of others. This is especially true when reading the Bible which has difficult-to-pronounce names or complicated language structures.

The two or three discussions questions right after the Bible reading will help people put themselves into the scripture passage. This is the best of inductive Bible study. Two or three more questions should help the group *dig out some of the content.* However, avoid the trap of sliding into *deeper study*, limiting the study to cognitive functions and information rather than letting the Bible touch whole lives.

Finally, a set of *personal application* questions will encourage a response to the scripture. These responses may become really profound and life transforming. As a leader, carefully affirm all responses as the group members' answers become more and more transparent.

Accountability and Caring. If team members never help one another take their next steps in response to the Bible study, the team will not become a Village Group. *Accountability* should never be a negative word. Instead group members commit to stand together, to support each person's next step, and work toward the deeper health of the group. As group members share life joys and concerns, you as leader will have the opportunity to guide the group in *pastoring* one another.

The Mission. Each session should include opportunity for group members to declare a commitment to serve (go on mission) in their community. At the next team meeting, each group member will report the results of their mission.

Prayer. After sharing joys, concerns, and plans for a mission, the group will join together to pray for one another. You may need to guide the group in simple ways of praying out loud until they are comfortable. Remind them that there are no magic "prayer words." Brief, conversational sentences are great prayers.

From this model you can create a pattern that fits your Village Group, your ministry team, within your time constraints and your context.

Leg Three: Finding a Mission

Alan Hirsch reminds us, "The church doesn't have a mission. God's mission has a church."[8] In other words, God's plan is to fulfill God's work through us. Jesus came on God's mission and Jesus' followers (God's Church) are called to that same mission/ministry.

First, each ministry team (except elected groups) should plan, from their very beginning, to birth new groups out of the original group. This is part of the group's collective mission. Imagine the number of people you would have equipped and serving in ministry, if every ministry team saw duplicating themselves as part of their mission! Individually, each team member should be serving in some capacity each week. Mature discipleship is marked by understanding that we are all in ministry, all the time, all our lives. This is when team members realize that their ministry extends beyond performing in worship, teaching a church class, or sitting in a board meeting. Ministry is a lifestyle of concrete, specific, ongoing actions. The mission may be something as simple as introducing oneself to the grocery cashier. The key is staying alert to serve the invisible people they pass every day.

Collectively, the Village Group should serve together outside the church at least every two months. Simply serving outside the church will stretch people who see their ministry only inside a church building. However, if the mission of serving outside the church becomes part of the team's purpose, it becomes transformational. Consider something as simple as calling your board meetings in a restaurant to "serve" the servers and mangers with great tips, learning their names, and getting to know their needs. Or challenge a music team to learn a secular repertoire and perform as a community service in the local mall. Debriefing these experiences can strengthen the group's collective memory and connect a certain activity with the wider mission of the Village Group.

Wrapping It Up

Amid all the details, I trust that the most important point is resonating deep inside you: leadership means leading healthy groups. It's the way we are created; it's the way ministry gets done; it's our protection from arrogance as leaders; it's the context of discipleship; it's the best guarantee that God's Kingdom values stay in focus, calling forth that creation-self in one another. So, lead a group! While there are many logistical questions remaining, those answers are best discovered on the job—while *greening* your teams into Village Groups.

Daryl Smith, EdD, is team leader of The Orlando Fellowship, an incarnational, missional community, and Associate Professor of Mentored Ministry and Christian Leadership, Asbury Theological Seminary-Florida Dunnam campus.

Chapter 28 Notes

Much of the content for this chapter comes from my new book, *The End of Small Groups: Leading Incarnational Villages*. However, this chapter presents new and specific interpretation for the challenges leaders face with a team model.

[1] M. Robert Mullholland Jr., *Invitation to a Journey* (Downers Grove, IL: InterVarsity, 1993).

[2] Until Genesis 3:20, the Hebrew word *adam* is the term for both the "first woman" (Hebrew, *ishsha*) and "first man" (Hebrew, *ish*)—together.

[3] For further reading, check out Joseph E. Coleson, *Ezar Cenegdo: A Power Like Him, Facing Him as Equal* (Grantham, PA: Wesleyan/Holiness Women Clergy Second Edition, 1996; http://www.whwomenclergy.org/booklets/power_like_him.php) and Daryl L. Smith, *More Than a Great Wedding, 2nd Edition*. DonQDox.org, 2015.

[4] *Small groups* stimulate varied responses—many of them negative.

[5] Patrick Lencioni, *The Advantage: Why Organizational Health Trumps Everything Else in Business* (San Francisco, CA: Jossey-Bass, 2012), 82.

[6] Again, these are group-meeting terms that will be described in the next section of this chapter.

[7] For examples to get you started, check out the books we've listed on DonQDox.org. After working for a while with materials we've written, you may want to write your own.

8 Alan taught a public session at VERGE\13, Austin, TX, March 27-28, 2013. Also he has written on this subject in several books.

29
Leadership through Preaching

Lenny Luchetti

Leaders preach and many leadership responsibilities depend on communication. In this chapter, Aristotle's ancient wisdom for speakers, to engage logos, ethos, and pathos, is appropriated for the 21st century. John Wesley's foundation of perfection in love presents the optimism the author holds for biblical, theological preaching to achieve true life change.

A LEADER'S ABILITY TO LEAD is directly related to the leader's capacity for communication. This is especially true for the pastoral leader who is called to preach. Internationally known leadership expert, John Maxwell, has said, "All great leaders are effective communicators."[1] Communication happens when a sender conveys a message to a receiver. In his seminal work, *Rhetoric*, Aristotle explored and emphasized the logos of the message, pathos toward the receiver, and ethos of the speaker.[2] Though logos, pathos, and ethos are communication concepts conceived by Aristotle, they were baptized for the Church by Augustine, and embodied by Wesley and the early Wesleyan-Methodist preachers.

In this chapter, we will consider how to apply basic communication theory to Christian preaching through the grid of Wesleyan theology and history. Going back to our historical and theological roots can expose the treasure trove of practical benefits available to help preachers proclaim the Gospel with power today.

While vacationing with my wife in San Francisco over Easter Sunday, we decided to attend a nationally known church in the Methodist tradition. We stood in line behind hundreds of people to get a seat at one of their worship services. I couldn't help but notice that all around us were people still intoxicated from their Saturday night adventures. The sights and smells made this obvious. I wasn't disgusted but excited. I remember thinking, "On Easter Sunday I'm going to see broken people raised from death to life in Jesus' name!"

My hopes were dashed as the name of Jesus was barely mentioned during the entire service, including the sermon. There was no mention of the resurrection of Jesus at all. The choir sang, the people prayed, and the pastor preached, but there was no Gospel, no kerygmatic proclamation that Jesus is risen indeed. This church is probably a rare exception, since most sermons preached in the Wesleyan Methodist tradition mention Jesus Christ and his resurrection—especially on Easter! But I have heard and even preached sermons that would be more appropriately shelved in the self-help than the Gospel section of a bookstore.

Logos: Content about God

Grounded in Theology

The preacher's value system and sermonic content must be grounded in Christian theology, not pop-psychology, if preaching is going to be a faithful witness to God. When the core content of preaching is designed to help the listener "be happy and to feel good about oneself,"[3] the preacher is not proclaiming the Christian gospel but Moral Therapeutic Deism. Moral Therapeutic Deism focuses on "inculcating a moralistic approach to life. It teaches that central to living a good and happy life is being a good, moral person. That means being nice, kind, pleasant, respectful, responsible, at work on self-improvement, taking care of one's health, and doing one's best to be successful."[4] It is not difficult to find the do good, be good, and feel good message of Moral Therapeutic Deism declared in sermons today. However, if congregants need counseling, they can get it from a therapist. From the preacher, they must get Christ in all his fullness and glory.

The content, or logos, of the sermon preached in the Wesleyan Tradition will say something of substance about God, the Father, Son or Spirit. It is difficult, perhaps impossible, to find a sermon preached by John Wesley that does not focus on God, his nature and/or his work.[5] Making known the Trinitarian God in Christ as the centerpiece of sermonic content facilitates the work of God in the hearer.

Emphasize the Work of God

Most of the preaching and preachers in Wesley's day, regardless of the Protestant stream from which they flowed, emphasized the work of God in salvation. Like Wesley, they called people to "flee from the wrath to come."[6] More than a few of Wesley's sermons focused on God's mission to save souls. What makes Wesley distinct from many of his contemporaries, however, is that he not only stressed the wedding day of salvation but the sanctification that comes through the marriage of the human soul to God. Wesley preached salvation, to "flee from the wrath to come," *and* sanctification, to become an "altogether Christian."[7] For Wesley, salvation is restoring a person's relationship with God while sanctification is restoring the image of God in that person.

To preach in the Wesleyan tradition is to proclaim the nature of the Trinitarian God made known in Christ and his saving and sanctifying work. Since only God can save and sanctify humanity in his quest to redeem and restore what was lost in the fall, he must be the focus of the sermon's content. Wesley did not merely mention God in his sermons. What he said about God was substantive. Wesley did not utilize theological language to offer moral therapeutic advice to humanity; he employed theological language to make strong statements about God that would lead to the saving and sanctifying of human beings.

Communication that is Truly Christian

Communication that occurs in the context of Christian worship ought to be Christian. John Wesley ministered to the poor masses of English society who were losing their jobs to machines during the Industrial Revolution. Many of them tried to drown out the noise of their impoverishment with alcohol. Good advice about finances and psychological self-help was not going to save them. Entertaining eloquence would not cut the proverbial mustard either. Wesley knew that if the people were to have any hope at all, the force of Christian preaching must usher them toward the saving and sanctifying Trinitarian God who dwelt among us in Christ. The people in Wesley's preaching context, and our own, needed theology and not therapy.

The Christian sermon that refuses to be hijacked by anything less than a proclamation of who God is (nature) and what God does (work), will incarnate Christ in the moment the sermonic words are released so that he saves and sanctifies the listener. Or, put another way, the Wesleyan-saturated sermon will say something of substance about who God is (Trinity and Christology) so that God uses the sermon to do what God does (salvation and sanctification).

How can the preacher ensure that her sermonic content contains the best of what the Wesleyan preaching tradition offers? The preacher who prayerfully reflects on and takes seriously the following questions throughout the process of developing and delivering sermons will be in a good position to proclaim substantive logos.

1. What does the sermon say about the nature of God as Trinity?
2. What does the sermon say about the nature of God in Christ?
3. What does the sermon do to proclaim and partner with God in his work of salvation?
4. What does the sermon do to proclaim and partner with God in his work of sanctification?

Every sermon preached will probably not find points of contact with all four questions, though that is an ideal worthy of pursuit. But every Christian sermon preached in the Wesleyan tradition will have at its core a faithful response to at least one of the four inquiries.

Pathos: Connection to Listeners

Aristotle taught that *pathos* is the manner in which a speaker evokes the emotions of the listener to compel them to embrace the message. Pathos is the listener's emotional connection to the message and/or the messenger. Redeemed for Wesleyan preaching, pathos is not only the emotional appeal of the message to the listener but the emotional concern *of the messenger* for the listener. The speaker who connects at an emotional, even spiritual, level with listeners exhibits empathy in a culture of apathy. Preachers who are able to put themselves in the situational shoes of the people to whom they preach are most likely to cultivate a shared emotional connection with listeners.

I was once called to pastor a congregation that had seen five pastors in ten years and was in desperate need of a turnaround. I spent the first two years of my ministry there focused on listening to and loving the people. Preaching flowed out of this empathetic listening and loving. The church grew, in part because of the emotional bond between the preacher in the pulpit and the people in the pews. As the church grew, I allowed busyness to prevent me from spending time with the diverse cross-section of people who attended the church. I spent less time with people and more time with paper, working on administrative details. The administration needed to be done by someone, but it stifled the pathos in my preaching. I took my finger off the pulse of the congregational heartbeat when I abandoned the space necessary for empathetic listening. The *logos* I preached was true, but it lacked *pathos*.

Contextualizing the Audience

The truly Wesleyan preacher refuses to be cloistered off in study, inaccessible to congregants. John Wesley was driven beyond the walls of the Anglican Church and into the fields among the poor and disenfranchised. Like Christ, Wesley dwelt among the people to whom he preached. Wesley's preaching connected with the poor, drunk masses of English society who had been forsaken by the Anglican Church of the day, because he spent enough time with them to hear their hopes and hurts. He adjusted his content and style according to the needs of listeners. One of his rules for preaching was, "[A]lways suit your subject to your audience."[8] Wesley wanted his preaching to be accessible to the particular people who heard him in the fields. "I design plain truth for plain people," he wrote.[9] "Because we are to instruct people of the lowest understanding…[w]e should use the most common, little, easy word (so they are pure and proper) which our language affords."[10] John Hampson, Wesley's first biographer, noted Wesley's aptitude for contextualizing his preaching to the needs of the listeners: "Wesley's manner was graceful and easy…his style neat, simple, perspicuous, and admirably adapted to the capacity of his hearers."[11] Empathetic love that drives the preacher into the realities of the listener through the sermon is a hallmark of preaching in the Wesleyan tradition.

There are two *pathos* errors to avoid. First, angry preaching can be a temptation. Some preachers preach as if the listener is Satan himself. Preaching as though the listener is an enemy to shame rather than a soul to save and sanctify has no place in Wesleyan circles. Second, apathy is another plague having its way in preaching today. Some preach as if there's little at stake. Multi-level marketers can be more passionate about scents, oils, and nutrition than some preachers can be about the redemption of all things! Preaching with a flippant "take it or leave it" posture betrays a Wesleyan homiletic.

Perfected in Love

There are two ways that Wesleyan theology and history confront anger and apathy to cultivate empathy in the preacher. First, as we yield ourselves to the fullness of God's grace in Christ, he makes us "perfect in love" (1 John 4:18b). Christian perfection, as Wesley defined it, is not absolute perfection but the perfection of love. The Christian is sanctified, Wesley taught, when "perfect love drives out fear" (1 John 4:18).[12] The why, what, and how questions of Wesleyan preaching are addressed by love, not just for God but for the listeners who participate in the preaching event. In fact, the two loves are virtually one in the same. The more the preacher loves God the more the preacher will love people made in God's image. Preachers perfected in love will perfectly love the objects of God's love. This "perfect love" drives out the fear in the preacher, leaving no room for anger and/or apathy.

Optimism of Grace

Along with Wesley's view of Christian perfection, his optimism of grace heightens pathos. Unlike the majority of Reformed preachers in his day, Wesley was convinced that God's grace can overcome human depravity.[13] If the preacher didn't believe this, Wesley concluded, why preach at all? The preacher's perception of the listener impacts how the preacher preaches. If the preacher is convinced that the listener is fallen beyond the point of restoration, deemed incorrigible, and ultimately unable to live up to the call from God to "be holy because I am holy" (1 Pet. 1:16), the preacher will become angry, apathetic, or both.

Wesleyans believe that although humanity is fallen, Jesus came to swing the pendulum back in the direction of pre-fall existence, to restore what was lost in Eden. The restoration of the *imago dei* in humanity does not start in the afterlife but in this life. The capacity of God's grace to turn sinners into saints is not merely a "then and there" but a "here and now" reality. A preacher who is rightly optimistic about the ability of God's grace to redeem and sanctify humanity will preach with an optimism of grace that elicits passionate pathos in the preacher for the people and in the people for the message.

The preacher with an optimistic theology possesses an optimistic homiletic, a hopeful conviction that God can and does convey holy content to hungry people through preaching in a way that saves and sanctifies the soul. In a world in which some wonder if preaching has run its course, Wesleyans keep preaching with optimism about what God can make of the human race.

At the root of the Wesleyan preaching movement is a willingness to believe the best about humanity, not because of what is in humanity, but because of what is in God. One of Wesley's rules for preachers was, "Believe evil of no one, unless fully proved; take heed how you credit it. Put the best construction you can on everything. You know the judge is always supposed to be on the prisoner's side."[14] Wesley knew that a pessimistic view of people would diminish the power and purpose of Christian preaching.

Nurturing Pathos

There are ways for the Wesleyan preacher to engage the homiletic process so that pathos is cultivated, and anger and apathy annihilated. Wesleyan preaching involves not just communicating true theological content (*logos*), but communicating it in a manner that is faithful to the people being addressed (*pathos*). In other words, true content must be put in a contextual cup from which a particular group of people can drink. When Wesley preached in the fields, his *logos* didn't change but his pathos did. As noted, he preached in "plain language" that would connect with the poor and uneducated people of early Methodism. This was *contextualization* not *conde-*

> *"At the root of the Wesleyan preaching movement is a willingness to believe the best about humanity, not because of what is in humanity, but because of what is in God"*

scension. Like the Apostle Paul before him who adjusted his sermonic language as necessary to fit the context,[15] Wesley resisted the temptation to impose his preaching style across contexts. Instead, he allowed the particular needs of the people to whom he preached to trump some of his homiletic preferences. Wesleyan communication, then, involves knowing the listeners intimately enough to convey true *logos* with passionate, empathetic *pathos*. Here are several practices for the nurturing of *pathos* in the preacher.

Listen with empathy

The best preachers are not the best talkers but the best listeners. There are endless ways for the preacher to listen with empathy to congregants. Consider scheduling a visit with one congregant each workday. Make sure that the people you visit represent the variety of people who attend your church in terms of age, ethnicity, education, socio-economics, and spiritual maturity. Let the congregant do most of the talking. Ask questions that will help you to discern the deepest hopes and hurts, dreams and disappointments of the people in your congregation. Try to hope and hurt with the people. As your pathos toward your people increases, the pathos in the preaching event will come through as loud as words.

Contemplate the contexts

As the weekly sermon idea comes into focus, prayerfully discern how the biblical reality intersects with people in the church, community, nation and world. How does the sermon offer a biblical response to the local, national, and global issues with which people are struggling? How might the sermon's "word from the Lord" find footing in the home, workplace, neighborhood, school, or other settings? When *logos* connects to context, it drips with *pathos*. Prayerful reflection during sermon preparation on the various contexts that impact listeners will significantly enhance preaching.

Pray the directory

One of the ways to increase *pathos* in the preaching event is to pray through the church directory. Once you know the direction of the sermon, pray for specific people in the church in light of the sermon focus. This helps to ensure that the sermon will be grounded in the real lives of the real people who listen to the sermon. For example, the preacher preparing to proclaim a message about God's healing power might pray empathetically for specific people in the congregation who need spiritual, physical, and emotional healing. The hope is that a homiletic exercise like praying the sermon focus through the congregational directory will produce deep love in the preacher for the people, and that the people will sense and appreciate this love in the moment of delivery. Such is the important fruit of pathos.

Ethos: Character of the Preacher

When I began to preach on a weekly basis at a local church, I was twenty-three years old. My inexperience and lack of skill drove me to dependence upon God. I knew that if I strayed from intimacy with God, I would be in trouble during the preaching event. As a result, in the early days, preaching was more of a spiritual discipline than a rhetorical task. I engaged preaching as a devotional journey to get

Christ, not merely as a rhetorical chore to get a talk. Abiding in Christ throughout the process of developing and delivering sermons was ethos-enhancing. *Ethos* is the character of the speaker that compels trust in the listener for the message.

Over time, I learned how to preach. I allowed my experience and skill, unfortunately, to diminish my dependence on God. Corner-cutting in sermon preparation became my *modus operandi*. And the corners I cut were not rhetorical, but devotional. I spent more time seeking illustrations than I did seeking God. I succumbed to ulterior motives for preaching that were more consumed with building my reputation than God's kingdom. My ethos decreased. Even if no one sensed it, I certainly did. More than a few preachers experience seasons like the one just described. There is, though, a way forward for the Wesleyan preacher.

Character Matters

The first, and most obvious step forward, is for the preacher to recognize that their personal character matters. When the character, or ethos, of the messenger is perceived by listeners, the latter are more receptive to the logos of the message. Words like authenticity, credibility, and integrity are synonymous with ethos. Wesleyan preachers call this holiness. Holiness can and should be cultivated in the preacher through the practice of preaching. That is, the consistent, sustained practice of preaching can make the preacher holier. In order for preachers to harness the formative potential of preaching, they must engage the task as a spiritual discipline. This means that the homiletic process allows consistent space for engagement with God. If the ten to fifteen hours it takes most pastors to prepare a sermon is engaged devotionally and not just rhetorically, then those hours will not just produce good sermons but godly preachers. When the preacher engages preaching as a loving act of worship, the ethos of the preacher is intensified.

John Wesley was known more for his ethos than his eloquence in preaching. Professor J. H. Liden, after hearing Wesley preach, noted, "He has not great oratorical gifts, no outward appearance but he speaks clear and pleasant…, he is the personification of piety, and he seems to me as a living representative of the loving Apostle John."[16] Wesley's ethos enhanced his preaching, perhaps making it seem better than it was.

Model holiness

Wesley taught preachers in the Methodist movement to model holiness. He admonished in his rules, "Let your motto be, 'Holiness to the Lord.'"[17] In his *Address to the Clergy,* Wesley challenged ministers to acquire the skills necessary for preaching and leading the flock. He wanted preachers in the movement to have philosophical, rhetorical, mathematical, exegetical, and etiquette skills. About halfway through the message, Wesley shifted the focus of his address from skill acquisition to the character development of clergy with the following statement: "And yet there is a higher consideration than that of gifts; higher than any or all of these joined together; a consideration in view of which all external and all intellectual endowments vanish into nothing." One sentence later, Wesley continues his emphasis on the ethos of the preacher, "What was my intention in taking upon me this office and ministry? What was it, in taking charge of this parish, either as Minister or Curate? Was it always, and is it now, wholly and solely to glorify God, and save souls? Has my eye been singly fixed on this, from the beginning hitherto? Had I never, have I not now, any mixture in my intention?" Wesley did not denigrate the importance of the preacher's skill building for ministry. In fact, he seemed to believe that holiness, perfect love, would lead the preacher to seek the necessary abilities to rightly divide the word of God for the people of God. But clearly Wesley refused to put the cart of rhetorical ability before the horse of the preacher's spirituality. Each has their proper place in Christian preaching. Rhetoric travels behind devotion.

Spiritual disciplines

Wesley did not separate what he believed God joined together. Sermon preparation and spiritual disciplines were wedded together in his preaching ministry, a ministry marked more by ethos than eloquence. Wesley engaged God throughout the homiletic process and calls those of us who preach in the Wesleyan Methodist tradition to do the same. Building devotional exercises into the process is vital. Let's explore a few that can be sprinkled at different points in the sermon's progression.

The starting line

Before jumping into the text or topic for the impending sermon, pray a small portion of Psalm 119 slowly and reflectively. Ask God for revelation and insight into his word. Quiet your soul by sitting before the Lord and allowing him to remind you of his love for you and the important calling he has placed upon your life to preach Christ. Ask God to purify your preaching motives and to spiritually form you through the homiletic process to be the "fragrance of Christ."

During the race

Read the main preaching text devotionally. You may want to practice a form of ancient Christian meditation called *lectio divina*, or some other method for engaging the Bible devotionally. This is your chance to connect with God. As you do, consider the personal implications of the text for your own life. Consider what God is saying to you through the text. How does the text apply to your relationships with Christ and others? How does the text confirm, challenge, comfort, or convict you? What does it reveal about who Christ is and who you are? This exercise prevents the preacher from unleashing the Bible on others before the "two-edged sword " cuts to the preacher's heart. The sermons preached with the most power are the ones in which the preacher devotionally wrestles with the angel of the text. That's when the preacher comes away resembling Jacob, limping under the weight of a word from the Lord.

Nearing the finish line

Spend time in prayer as close to the sermon's delivery as possible. Preferably, pray in the worship space where the sermon will be delivered. Pray for personal purity, love, humility, and the ability to communicate and incarnate the sermon through your own life. Invite God to search your heart to root out any impure preaching motives. Express your desire to love and glorify him through the act of preaching.

Conclusion: Love Binds Them Together

When Aristotle's rhetorical categories are given a Wesleyan holiness twist, *logos*, *pathos* and *ethos* are driven and connected by love. For the Wesleyan preacher, the necessity of love is a core conviction: Love "binds them all together."[18] Love for the nature and work of God revealed in Scripture (*logos*), compels the preacher's love for people (*pathos*) and love for God (*ethos*). Preaching and leading with love is a hallmark of Wesleyan pastoral ministry.

———————

Lenny Luchetti, DMin, is Associate Professor of Proclamation and Christian Ministries at Wesley Seminary in Marion, IN.

Bibliography

Duduit, Michael. "Preaching and Leadership: A 25th Anniversary Retrospective." *Preaching Magazine*. December 7, 2009. http://www.preaching.com/resources/articles/11623288/.

Hampson, John. *Memoirs of the Late Rev. John Wesley, A.M.* Sunderland, 1791.

Minutes of the Methodist Conferences. London: John Mason, 1862.

Outler, Albert C., ed. "Sermons." In *The Works of John Wesley*, vols. 1-4. Nashville: Abingdon Press, 1984.

Proceedings of the Wesleyan Historical Society. 1929.

Smith, Christian with Melinda Lundquist Denton. *Soul Searching: The Religious and Spiritual Lives of American Teenagers.* New York: Oxford University Press, 2005.

Telford, John, ed. *The Letters of John Wesley*, 8 vols. London: Epworth Press, 1931.

Wesley, John. *The Works of John Wesley*, 14 vols. 3rd Edition. Edited by Frank Baker. Grand Rapids: Baker Books, 1996.

Chapter 29 Notes

1 Duduit, "Preaching and Leadership"

2 Aristotle. *Rhetoric*. 4th Century.

3 Smith, *Soul Searching*, 163.

4 Ibid.

5 http://bit.ly/27Yt6mi. I analyzed two of John Wesley's sermons per decade of his ministry from the 1720s thru 1790s. I selected sermons that were the earliest and latest in each decade, according to agreement by Timothy Smith and Albert Outler. I read the following chronology of numbered sermons: 135, 136, 140, 128, 134, 29, 129 (This sermon may have been written by Charles Wesley but was adopted and preached by John.), 44, 41 (Much space in this sermon is devoted to how one loves God but still focuses primarily on how God empowers the Christian to live a faithful and fruitful life.), 11, 53 (Even though this sermon, *On the Death of George White-field*, focused on the character and works of the deceased, the God who made Whitefield was the hero of the sermon.), 131, 70, 117, 119, and 122. The will, way, and work of God figure prominently in these sermons that span the ministry of John Wesley.

6 This was a common theme in Wesley's preaching and structuring of the Methodist movement.

7 John Wesley's used "altogether Christian" to depict sanctification in his sermon, "The Almost Christian."

8 *Minutes of the Methodist Conferences*, 1:38, 527.

9 Outler, *Sermons I*, (Works, 1:104).

10 Telford, *The Letters of John Wesley*, 4:258 (July 16, 1764).

11 Hampson, Memoirs of the Late Rev. John Wesley, 3:158.

12 Wesley made this case in his *A Plain Account of Christian Perfection*.

13 Wesley's sermon, *Free Grace*, is his way of combating Reformed theologians and preachers who, from his perspective, had a pessimistic view of grace stemming from their convictions about limited atonement and a total depravity that cannot be overcome in this life. Wesley preached out of the conviction that God's free grace was available to all, and not just for the forgiveness of sin but the cleansing from sin. The idea of optimistic grace permeates Wesley's preaching.

14 This is the fifth of Wesley's Twelve Rules for the Helper/Preacher.

15 The Apostle Paul allowed the preaching context to shape what and how he preached. His kerygma did not change but how he communicated it did based upon the particular needs of listeners in various contexts. Paul preached differently to Greeks in Athens than he did to Jews in the synagogue. He appealed to philosophy and poetry when preaching to Athenian Greeks and to the Old Testament when among Diaspora Jews. Paul's pathos, his empathic concern for the people to whom he preached, came through in his ability to preach contextually without theological compromise.

16 Proceedings of the Wesleyan Historical Society, 17:2.

17 This is rule number two in Wesley's Twelve Rules for Helpers/Preachers.

18 Paul used this phrase in Colossians 3:14. He was declaring how love binds together the virtues he mentioned in Colossians 3:12. I am borrowing the phrase from Paul to declare that the Wesleyan preacher's logos, pathos and ethos are developed, motivated and connected via love.

30
Ethical Leadership and Gifts

Aaron Perry and Eric R. Hallett

Leaders must always find value. Gifts appear to maximize values because there is no associated monetary cost. But the true costs of such gifts that may be paid in other ways. From the foundation of ethical leadership which focuses on the other, this chapter provides lines of questioning for leaders accepting gifts to consider the other.

SINCE THE FOURTH CENTURY, we have been told not to look a gift horse in the mouth. Sure, the language of origin was Latin and its current form has come through a couple of English modifications, but the principle is the same. Actually, the principle likely extends back much beyond the fourth century. The principle? Don't criticize a gift. As horses age, their gums recede, leaving the appearance of longer and longer teeth. (This is also where we get the phrase "Long in the tooth.") If someone was giving you a horse, you might be tempted to see just what kind of horse you were getting—a young horse, with nice, short teeth, or an old horse well on its way to eternal pasture; equine inspection was not to be encouraged. A gift is a gift. Take the horse and do not look in its mouth.

We think this is bad advice—especially for leaders of non-profit organizations and churches. Forget what you've heard. Look that horse right in the mouth. This must be done cautiously and with care because every true gift matters to the giver, but, with subtlety, we think you should figure out if the horse has been using Crest or Colgate.

How counterintuitive! Leadership concerns value. Leaders determine what is and is not of value, and act accordingly. Why found a school and not a manufacturing plant? Why raise funds rather than establish services? Why go here rather than there? Why sacrifice production for fair trade? Why emphasize living wages rather than profit margins? The movement, achievement, or goal of leadership is always a determination of value. In non-profit worlds, leaders quickly learn to see value where no one else does. This is not simply the skill of due diligence, but the character of grace, mercy, and hope.

And along comes the gift. Gifts seem to be the value jackpot. After all, the nature of the gift is free, right? Wouldn't something of no cost be all value? Not only does seeing the flossing condition of the horse seem potentially rude, but unnecessary. A gift is a gift is a gift...value, value, value! But ethical leadership, a formulated way of intentional leadership, has helped us think otherwise.

Ethical Leadership

Ethical leadership is still about value, but has significantly shifted the specifics. Ethical leadership is a style of leadership concerned with demonstrating appropriate conduct by developing meaningful relationships, modeling right behavior, and reinforcing this leadership through communication and decision-making.[1] Trustworthiness, honesty, care, and fairness are deep, driving concerns not only for leaders, but for their followers, too. Leadership, both in personal character and action, gives dignity and worth to followers and works to ensure dignity and worth is communicated systematically.

No longer is the generating question of leadership, "What do we need to get done?" No longer leadership's determinative question for justifying an act be, "Will what's done be worth it?" Instead, while the significance of value is still present, ethical leadership shifts the focus to that of people and, for their sake, process. What is of value is not the bottom line, but those at the bottom rung of the organizational

Leadership, both in personal character and action,
gives dignity and worth to followers

chart. What is of value is not simply the destination, but the journey. Along the way, are people treated as beings of dignity by their leaders? How do established processes protect and communicate worth—the value of people—all along the way? Another way this can be said is that ethical leadership is concerned with the Other.[2]

Which brings us back to equine dental inspection. Ethical leadership provides a reminder for leaders that there is more to receiving gifts than getting something for nothing. Gifts impact the Other. Gifts impact those whom we lead in ways that we must consider. Gifts also impact the giver. Gifts cannot simply be considered in terms of something for nothing, all value-no cost. Gifts are fun and gifts are serious. With that in mind, here are four questions ethical leadership asks of gifts.

Question 1: Whose horse will this be, anyway? Translation: How does this gift create a ripple effect personally for people other than you as the leader? Ethical leadership is reminded of its responsibility to the Other. This includes one's followers. Gifts create expectations that extend not only to the leader, but to the follower, as well. For example, a high quality volunteer recently offered services on a task team. The person was qualified, talented, and they volunteered! However, as leaders, we are responsible not just for the gift, but for its ripple effect. In this case, the task team, which was previously comprised of people familiar with each other and their professional dynamics, now faced change. The team was, in some ways, back to square one. We had not fully considered the ripple effect in receiving this valuable gift. Was it wrong to accept it? No. And it certainly was not wrong for it to be offered. But we had not considered who would actually receive the gift. We had neglected the ripple effect and our full responsibility to the Other.

Question 2: How does this horse fit in the stable? Translation: How does this gift create a ripple effect organizationally? A gift's ripple effect is not just personal, but organizational. Ethical leadership is responsible not just for the Other as an individual, but for the narratives, memories, and symbols of organizations. Gifts are powerful: they can change narratives, make memories, and make new symbols. Gifts can shape futures. Some horses don't just alter a stall, but an entire stable. In our circles, a multi-million-dollar gift is such a stable altering horse. In this case, it literally changed the landscape of the organization. The gift provided a beautiful location for the use of an entire community. Yet, the gift had long-term implications for the organization. Was the gift wrong? Not in the least! But the stable must now always consider this horse.

Question 3: Does a horse divided against itself stand? Translation: How does a gift create dynamics of competition and inequality in your team? Ethical leadership not only takes seriously meaningful relationships among leader and follower, but also facilitates meaningful relationships in the team dynamic. Gifts can create relationships, but they can also create inequality and imbalance. Ethical leadership reminds the leader that gifts must be considered for the inequality and imbalance that may arise within the relationships of followers.

We have seen this most keenly in our experience in churches where departments are expected to raise their own budgets through targeted giving to specific segregated funds. For example, the student ministry targets and obtains funds for its activities, while adult ministry targets and obtains funds for its activities, etc. What may happen is that congregants may give to their preferred projects or to the best fund raisers, causing inequality and imbalance to develop between ministry departments. Patrick Lencioni spells this out most clearly as "silos" where teammates are competing for limited goods.[3] He captures this ensuing conflict as a turf war. The fallout is that gifted fundraisers gain more influence in the organization and the ongoing gifts they obtain create organizational imbalance.

Ethical leadership considers the potential inequality created by the gift and seeks to emphasize and maintain meaningful relationships not only in the leader-follower relationship, but in the relationships of the organization.

Question 4: Sometimes the horse dies. Can you bury it? Translation: Every gift comes with a risk. Can you afford it—literally and figuratively—if it goes wrong? In the previous examples, we have discussed gifts that came with risks. The truth is that every gift comes with a risk. Every horse comes with teeth. Sometimes the risk is immediately known; sometimes it only becomes clear in time. My (Eric's) experience brings this to light. A contractor made a generous donation of materials and labor on a certain project only to go bankrupt halfway through the project, leaving the organization with the task of raising necessary funds to complete the work. While even more diligence may or may not have picked up on the precarious nature of the donor's company, ethical leadership takes seriously the risks involved in the gift and how it may be taken to completion should it not come to full fruition.

While this direction in receiving gifts may not be unique to ethical leadership, it is in its consideration to the gift giver. Gifts half given can easily result in bitterness, frustration, and shame. Ethical leadership considers affording the potential half-given gift for the sake of the giver. In the case where the horse dies, a proper burial can also put to rest the fallout. Ethical leadership works to ensure the initial giver is valued and honored.

Conclusion

In all of this, it should be clear that it is the horse under inspection, not the giver. When there is a horse who doesn't fit the stable, it is not a judgment on the giver. As a result, when employing ethical leadership in the realm of gift giving, we urge the following mindset: Everyone's got a healthy pony. (Everybody has some gift to give that is dignifying.) Not everyone can give a fully grown, healthy, short-toothed horse. Not everyone has such a gift to give. However, ethical leadership sees value in the Other and, as a result, recognizes that every person has something of value to give. There is dignity in gift giving. Ethical leadership in gift giving sees the value laden in each potential giver; not for what they give, but for who they are. Even in the cases where the gift is not accepted, the dignity of the giver can be recognized, affirmed, and blessed. So, look that gift horse in the mouth. Get him to open wide and say "ahh." Consider running some x-rays. It's your responsibility as leader. It's the right thing to do.

Aaron Perry, PhD, is Assistant Professor of Pastoral Care at Wesley Seminary at Indiana Wesleyan University in Marion, Indiana. He recently served as Associate Pastor at Centennial Road Church in Ontario, Canada. Eric R. Hallett, DMin, is Lead Pastor of Centennial Road Church in Brockville, Ontario. He serves as part of the ministry training faculty of The Wesleyan Church's FLAME program.

Chapter 30 Notes

1 Brown, M. E., Trevino, L. K., and Harrison, D. A, "Ethical leadership: A social learning perspective for construct development and testing," *Organizational Behavior and Human Decision Processes* 97 (2005): 117–134.

2 Knights, D., and O'Leary, M., "Leadership, ethics, and responsibility to the Other," *Journal of Business Ethics* 67 (2005): 125-137.

3 Lencioni, Patrick. *Silos, Politics and Turf Wars: A Leadership Fable About Destroying the Barriers That Turn Colleagues into Competitors.* San Francisco, CA: Jossey-Bass, 2006.

31
Clergywomen and Ministry Leadership

Beth K. Armstrong

Women may be accepted in leadership officially in the Wesleyan tradition, but there are still challenges to be overcome. These challenges are connected with assumptions and mindsets that must be corrected and altered. There are practical steps that established leaders, often men, may take to help validate and promote women leaders for a stronger overall body of leadership in the Wesleyan tradition.

DESPITE EQUITY EFFORTS, women remain underrepresented in senior leadership positions across a broad swatch of careers, including ministry.[1] Two primary lines of thought explain this disparity: the Choice Argument and the Barrier Argument. According to the Choice Argument, glass ceilings do not exist, the days of gender discrimination have passed, and any income and attainment differences between men and women result from *choices* women have made.[2] Proponents claim that women's maternal instincts guide them to earn college degrees in family-friendly fields that offer greater flexibility in exchange for less pay, such as education and nursing.[3] Once in the workforce, women make work decisions based on their children's needs: they opt-out of time- or travel-intensive senior leadership track positions and voluntarily accept lateral or downward moves on the career ladder.[4] Men's decisions, on the other hand, allow them to develop more impressive resumes. Therefore, when senior leadership positions become available, qualified male candidates far outnumber females.

On the other hand, the Barrier Argument contends that women face societal and structural obstacles, including deeply embedded attitudes, biases, and assumptions that prevent them from attaining leadership parity.[5] Even when women make all the "right" choices, studies show that they still lag behind: Despite earning the same degrees, being mentored, working long hours, and securing high job performance ratings, women do not earn salaries or attain senior-leadership status at a level comparable to men.[6]

Choice Argument proponents push back by citing examples of women who have attained elite leadership positions, like corporate CEOs and elected officials. If a "glass ceiling" truly exists, how did these women make it to the top? Barrier Argument adherents respond by suggesting that the image of a labyrinth more accurately describes the obstacles and greater complexity women face in the workplace.[7] Only a small handful of elite women successfully master this complex senior-leadership maze and reach the upper echelons of organizational leadership; many other highly capable women get lost in the process.[8]

Second-Generation Gender Discrimination

Before the Feminist Revolution of the 1960's, organizations could blatantly discriminate against female job applicants and employees. While legislation has overturned much of this overt anti-woman bias, Barrier Argument supporters contend that it has merely morphed into covert forms. Deemed "second-generation gender discrimination," these subtle yet potent obstacles to women in leadership, particularly senior leadership, show up in cultural assumptions about gender as well as organizational systems, structures, interactional dynamics, and practices that benefit men while marginalizing women. Second-generation gender discrimination manifests in myriad ways, such as:

1. school advisors disproportionately directing women toward less prestigious academic paths and vocational counselors and family members discouraging them from seeking management positions;[9]
2. equally qualified mothers hired less frequently, promoted less often, and paid less money than childless women or men;[10]
3. managers overlooking women for challenging assignments or directing them to what they consider less stressful jobs based on their assumptions about female workers' family needs;[11]
4. women continuing to bear a disproportionate load of domestic responsibilities in households;[12] and,
5. social, legal, and political climates that subtly penalize workers who request affordable high-quality childcare, adequate parental leave policies, and flexible working hours.[13]

The subtlety of this discrimination makes it difficult to recognize, leading Ibarra, Ely, and Kolb to assert: "Second-generation bias…creates a context—akin to 'something in the water'—in which women fail to thrive or reach their full potential."[14] The assumption that all women possess an innate proclivity to nurture undergirds second-generation gender discrimination.[15] Within organizations, these presuppositions fuel the opt-out narrative, which is the conviction that young women's career commitment "vanishes into thin air the moment children arrive."[16] Throughout the work world, the opt-out narrative has become the default to explain why women quit high-intensity jobs, despite workplace retention studies showing men and women leaving for the same reasons.[17] The claim that women prioritize motherhood over work inaccurately oversimplifies a much more complex reality.

In addition to false perceptions about their career aspirations, women also struggle against a presumed lack of competence, meaning that they need to demonstrate more potential than men to be given a chance and need to continue to prove themselves as leaders more than men.[18] If they succeed, "they are viewed as having

"they fight overt resistance grounded in a complementarian theology that claims it is God's will for men to lead and women to follow"

some special stroke of good fortune—a wonderful mentor, a lucky break, being at the right place at the right time. Their success is treated as a happenstance, an outcome over which they had no particular control."[19] If they fail, however, it is because they are defective. This failure extends not only to them as individuals, but also to all women.[20] The increased scrutiny and high stakes that come from being a visible woman in leadership can produce risk-aversion, a tendency to micromanage, and vocational paralysis, all of which negatively impact career development and stunt leadership identity formation.[21]

Constraints on Clergywomen

Clergywomen face a two-headed beast that constrains their leadership. On the one side, they fight overt resistance grounded in a complementarian theology that claims it is God's will for men to lead and women to follow. Top-down organizational mandates that ban women from certain leadership positions mirror the type of first-generation gender discrimination largely overturned by legislation in secular workplaces.[22] Even in denominations that espouse an egalitarian theology, a rising fundamentalist influence in the pew threatens the acceptance of women clergy.[23] This bottom-up resistance has grown in recent years as complementarian voices have dominated evangelical Christian radio, publishing, and other media.[24] On the other side, clergywomen also experience covert, second-generation gender discrimination, including questions about their qualifications and assumptions about their ambitions. Like their counterparts in the secular marketplace, they face the opt-out narrative, perceptual double-binds, and differential access to mentors and networks because of their gender.

Evangelical History and Culture

These challenges become more complex as they play out against the history and culture of the Evangelical movement. In the late 1800s, opponents of women's ordination claimed gender equity efforts would weaken the family and destroy the home; this rhetoric resurfaced when the feminist movement in Evangelicalism grew in the 1970s and 1980s. Fundamentalists questioned Christian feminists' commitment to biblical authority and alleged that they had sold out to accommodate worldly standards. This sell-out mindset persists among many evangelicals, including those within denominations that ordain women.[25] These congregants react strongly to anything associated with feminism, viewing it as the slippery slope to being pro-choice and pro-gay-rights, both anathemas to conservatives.[26]

Clergywomen who work in these anti-feminist churches need to go out of their way to calm fears about what they might represent. Being married with children helps in that it demonstrates a commitment to the traditional family and is "an indication that the person is 'safe' and does not represent a threat to the moral order of the community."[27] Women who are unmarried or childless, whether by choice or not, face a more challenging road because others perceive them as dangerous.

Perceptual Barriers of Gendered Leadership.

Clergywomen face additional perceptual barriers associated with gender and leadership. In the United States, qualities traditionally associated with leadership include assertiveness, independence, decisiveness, self-confidence, and authoritativeness; traits that align more closely with perceived masculine qualities. Women, on the other hand, have typically been viewed as selfless, caring, friendly, and kind.[28] Particularly within the Evangelical world, women who display traditionally masculine attributes face disapproval. For example, an ambitious female runs the risk of being labelled as prideful.[29]

At the core of these views is "the unspoken but firmly held belief that there is a natural order in which males are innately and uniquely endowed to take charge, whereas females are innately and uniquely endowed to take care."[30] These preconceived notions about gender and leadership set in motion a

> vicious cycle [where] people see men as better fit for leadership roles partly because the paths to such roles were designed with men in mind; the belief that men are a better fit propels more men into leadership roles, which in turn reinforces the perceptions that men are a better fit, leaving gendered practices intact.[31]

The incongruity between leadership qualities and women's traits and the alignment between these attributes and the perception of men has led to the assumption that men make better leaders and contributed to hiring and promotion practices based on the false premise that women are less effective.[32]

Minister Equals *Man*?

The pastoral functions of leadership within the church can be subdivided into three categories: sacramental, organizational, and subordinate. Sacramental functions include preaching, baptizing, and conducting funerals. Organizational functions involve coordinating staff, addressing personal problems, and planning budgets. Subordinate functions revolve around Christian education and music ministry. Studies of congregational biases suggest more people tend to prefer that men perform the organizational functions, those day-to-day duties associated with running the church. However, when it came to sacramental duties, those preferences were predominately gender-neutral. A key conclusion from this discovery was that congregants' preference for men as pastors was not rooted in theology; if it were, the sacramental arm would have been as strongly male-inclined. Since most laypeople agreed that women could capably fulfill the responsibilities of a pastor, and most didn't mind whether a man or a woman performed the sacramental functions of a pastor, there was something about the title *pastor* that was associated with the masculine for the majority of the subjects.[33] As one writer asserted, "One need not claim to be called by God to enter the fields of accounting or carpentry. The concept of ministry, however, is cloaked in layer upon layer of Scripture, interpretation, tradition and church law."[34]

Another factor was more practical: congregants' concern for the future of their churches. The role of clergywomen is still controversial enough for many that the desire to avoid such disruption in the life of the congregation may also contribute to some latent bias. Rather than potentially divide their church, congregants will follow the least controversial path, even if that means discriminating against a qualified female candidate.

The Maintenance Motif and "Divisive" Clergywomen

One particularly powerful barrier clergywomen face in attaining senior leadership positions is the fear that a woman in this role will harm the church. Some of those who are resistant claim that having a woman pastor will make men less likely to engage in church life. In a study conducted by Henderson, one subject put it this way: "When women lead, it demotivates men from becoming what they are supposed to be. God has given a man certain qualities. He is the one God has equipped for leadership. Putting a woman in leadership over him is almost like whipping him."[35] Demoralized men may stop coming to church altogether, taking their money and their families with them.[36] Church hiring boards may be hesitant to support a "divisive" woman in leadership as this decision could derail growth.

This concern could also be extended to male clergy who turn a blind eye to gender discrimination for fear that advocating for female colleagues might lead to a congregational split or uprising.[37] Higher up the organizational chain, if numeric growth is a top priority for denominational leaders, they may be hesitant to enforce policies to promote equity, particularly if putting these into effect might alienate those unsupportive male clergy who are bringing in the money and the members.

Organizational Barriers

Some argue that research on clergy gender equity suggests that congregational and denominational systems unconsciously interfere with or diminish the ministry roles of women.[38] Some possible factors for this unconscious bias could be male ministers' ambivalence about having women as pastoral peers, congregations socialized to the default assumption of male senior leadership, a lack of appropriate mentors, or structural issues within denominations related to identifying, training, and deploying leaders.[39]

Career Development Norms

Traditional understandings of ministry career development have been based on rational-choice assumptions: a "normal" ministry career follows a steady upward trajectory from entry-level assignments to those with increasing autonomy and influence, typically in churches with larger budgets and higher membership numbers or in positions of denominational leadership.[40] Women's clergy careers do not develop along these clear lines: they have a much higher likelihood than males of forced, lateral, or even downward job mobility and encounter gender-rooted barriers to attaining full-time, full-pay jobs. Nonetheless, because they don't follow this normative career development template, organizational gatekeepers label them as lacking ambition or possessing sub-standard ministry leadership skills.[41]

Mentoring

For clergywomen, particularly younger ones, mentors and sponsors play a critical role: "Young women who perceive a call on their lives from God and then face conflicting messages about its legitimacy often find that the single most important factor determining whether they pursue that call is the availability of supportive mentors."[42] Because of organizational barriers, women need benevolent male advocates in positions of authority to open doors for them.[43] Even in denominations with seemingly objective computerized candidate-position matching programs, the recommendation of a key insider, like an influential clergyperson or denominational official, opens placement doors.[44]

Women's mentors tended to have less clout in organizations than men's.[45] Highly influential men may not invest in a female apprentice because of a lack of identification or hesitancy over how colleagues might view the cross-gender relationship.[46] As a reaction to this fear of perceived impropriety, some organizations—including many churches—have instituted strict policies that limit if and how men can mentor women.[47] These rules create tension for would-be apprentices as they are forced to seek mentoring from a more-senior woman. Given the paucity of these leaders in some fields, junior women encounter severely constrained options.[48] The few senior women who are in an organization may be in high demand, such as when senior clergywomen end up serving as the token female on multiple denominational boards and committees.[49] This busyness impacts their availability to invest in protégés.

Deployment and the Hope of a Better Job

The hope of securing a better job can keep women engaged in ministry when discouragement tempts them to throw in the towel.[50] Unfortunately, women tend to fall short in the eyes of hiring committees and appointment boards when it comes time to deploy for open positions. Married men, particularly first-career married men, top the hiring desirability list, a dynamic consistent with queue theory.[51] Particularly in cases where they have children, gatekeepers assume clergymen will be more committed to doing a good job because of the responsibility they carry to support their families.[52] Access to a pastor's wife, considered a "utilitarian asset value in terms of potential labor contribution within the congregation,"[53] further increases the desirability of male candidates. Throughout their careers, men receive higher-prestige posts than women, with cohort-based regression models showing that male gender is the only consistent predictor of this higher level attainment.[54]

Clergywomen are underpaid and underemployed relative to men and are continually tracked into less powerful and influential positions. While clergymen dominate the primary job market—full-time, good pay, promotion-friendly opportunities to develop skills and gain access to better jobs—women are segregated into the secondary job market. These jobs are part-time, less secure, offer less pay, and provide fewer opportunities for growth and advancement because they are isolated from the primary job market.[55]

Clergywomen are significantly more likely than clergymen to be working outside the traditional, brick-and-mortar-church pastorate. While both male and female respondents state that they choose these non-parish positions for a variety of reasons, women are significantly more likely to say that they are working outside of the parish because they can't get a parish position in their area and they are not able to relocate.[56]

When given the opportunity to lead a church, clergywomen typically serve under-resourced, struggling congregations in small communities, rural areas, or racially transitional neighborhoods of larger cities with attendance that has plateaued or is declining.[57] For men, accepting a call to one of these marginal churches is "but a temporary stage in career development"[58] while for women, it represents a vocational black hole often resulting a greater number of women clergy leaving the pastorate altogether as a result.[59] Settings like these may be called glass cliff environments: high-risk turnarounds where failure seems highly probable.[60]

The expectation that workers must relocate in order to secure a first pastorate or to advance to a higher level post creates additional obstacles for women. Men have an advantage in this area, as research has consistently shown wives are more likely to uproot their careers in deference to their husbands than husbands are for the sake of their wives.[61] A married clergywoman's career relocation decisions tend to default to her husband, particularly when his income is primary for the household. This inability to move for the sake of a ministry job may impede progress toward senior leadership as frequent job mobility correlates with clergy occupational attainment for both men and women.[62]

Lack of Support from Male Clergy

There may also be significant ambivalence toward women clergy among the male pastors, which can include both men serving as local church pastors and those in organizational roles like seminary professors and regional leaders. Though less apt than laypeople to carry stereotypes and prejudices against clergywomen, a significant number of male pastors and organizational leaders, especially older men, showed a preference for men in senior or sole pastor positions. To the extent these older males set policy and played gatekeeping roles within denominations, they can set the tenor for an entire generation of clergy.[63]

But researchers have also found that clergywomen report high levels of tangible and moral support from male colleagues as long as they are paid less and have less experience than the men.[64] Once their experience and pay surpasses clergymen's, the support drops off, suggesting perhaps that men began to view their female colleagues as competitors for more desirable positions. To the extent that these attitudes persist, clergywomen continue to face an uphill battle to attain equity.

Henderson offered an intriguing frame through which to view the discussion of organizational obstacles to clergy gender equity within evangelical denominations. He observed, "Evangelicals are passionate about personal sin—swearing, adultery, gossip, drunkenness, lust, anger, and so on. They have significantly less interest in systemic sin—racism, greed, selfishness, and repression of women."[65] Given this emphasis on personal decisions, perhaps the Choice Argument becomes a natural way for the organizational system to displace responsibility for inequity.

Now what?

In 1987, Nancy Nason-Clark identified five obstacles clergywomen face: formal barring from ministry by denominations, difficulties receiving a placement, resistance from congregations, resistance from fellow clergy, and traditional symbolism and liturgy in the church that has a male bias. A decade later, Nesbitt[66] predicted a backlash to the influx of women clergy that would include overt attacks on the legitimacy of women's ordination as well as covert assaults like the devaluation of women's educational credentials, the growth of gender-related job segregation, the use of tokenism as a means to grant ideological concessions to supporters of gender equality while isolating tokens in a manner so as to limit their opportunity to make substantive change, and the strategic deployment of women with traditionalist views to counter those with progressive commitments to feminist ideological and social change.

Almost 20 years have passed since Nesbitt's forecast and many of her predictions appear to be coming to pass. Rather than acknowledging this backlash, some claim clergywomen face no systemic obstacles to attaining senior leadership in those denominations that have formally endorsed it. They assert women who aspire to these positions need only get an education, work hard, have a mentor, build their networks, do an effective job, and say "Yes" as the opportunities to climb the organizational ladder appear. Such assertions oversimplify a much more intricate phenomenon. While clergywomen's choices may have some impact on how their careers unfold, a multifaceted web of subtle barriers complicate the process for them. These barriers, consistent with second-generation gender discrimination, add complexity to an already perplexing leadership labyrinth, perpetuating women's underrepresentation in senior leadership positions.

So what can be done? I offer the following six ideas for denominations, churches, pastors, and lay leaders to consider.

Examine the Church's Openness to Women in Leadership

The first step to reduce or eliminate second-generation gender discrimination is to identify it. One place it often appears is in organizational norms and practices that create an unfriendly climate toward clergywomen. Consider how a church or denomination might respond to these questions: What are the unspoken norms for leadership, especially senior leadership? Have women ever served in these positions? What does it mean to be a "good" pastor? Does it mean working 60+ hours a week? What does the church's rhetoric communicate about gender and leadership? Do women serve in leadership roles other than in children's and women's ministries? Are women on staff called "directors" while men are "pastors"? Do those in leadership gatekeeping positions consider both men and women for any available positions, or are some roles gender-specific? To what extent are current pastors identifying, equipping, and deploying capable women in ministry leadership? Responses to these questions can help identify areas that need to be addressed within the organization before movement toward clergy gender equity will be possible.

Amplify Female Voices

Many Christians have never seen a clergywoman in action. One way to remove perceptual barriers erected against women pastors is through exposure. Equity-minded individuals can recommend gifted female preachers to speak at local, regional, or national church events. They can nominate capable clergywomen for influential boards, committees, and task forces within their churches or denominations. At their local churches, they can encourage hiring boards to consider qualified female candidates for open positions that transcend the traditional jobs in children's or women's ministry.

Encourage Innovation

Churches may need to create and fund positions that capitalize on the skill sets that highly capable women offer. Some churches do this by adopting alternative leadership structures, like strengths-based team leadership. In contrast to traditional hierarchical models that revolve around a single senior pastor who develops vision, communicates it, and oversees a staff who implements it, strengths-based team leadership models redistribute the ministry workload, allowing people to operate from their giftedness and releasing any one person from laboring under a 60-hour work week. Another option is for an existing church to plant a new church led by a clergywoman. Such new works lack the entrenched male-biased mindsets found in many established churches. From the outset, the DNA of the new church can be egalitarian.

Implement Gender-Inclusive Leadership Development Programs

Many churches meld leadership development with personal discipleship: The senior pastor has a group of guys he meets with to mentor them as men and leaders. Due to the intimate discussions that unfold within the accountability aspect of their gatherings, many pastors prefer to keep these groups male-only. By separating personal and professional development, churches can then offer appropriate mixed-gender leadership training. To meet many women's developmental needs, such a program would need to focus not only on increasing competence but also on helping to develop courage and confidence, as these are areas with which many women struggle. In addition, it can encourage honest conversation around issues like second-generation gender discrimination, congregational resistance to women in ministry, complementarian theologies, leadership structures designed from a masculine bias, and working with colleagues of the opposite sex.

Educate about Egalitarianism

Much resistance to women in ministry leadership resides within the pews. As was stated earlier, complementarian voices dominate Christian media, leaving many church members ignorant about the theological basis for women in ministry leadership. Churches can educate their members by presenting the biblical case for egalitarianism using sermons, classes, and written materials.

Leverage Benevolent Male Advocacy

Egalitarian men with power in churches hold the key to progress, in large part because women cannot self-advocate for fear of being labeled aggressive or prideful. Male pastors and denominational leaders can use their clout to help advance women in ministry leadership. They can demonstrate appropriate collegial relationships by both mentoring and being mentored by women. They can cite female authors in their sermons, do a pulpit-swap or team-preach with a clergywoman from another church, and ask capable women to serve on and lead church boards and committees. Perhaps the most impactful way to promote clergy gender equity is for a man in a position of power to prepare a female successor and then voluntarily leave his post. This succession model allows for smoother leadership transitions. During the emerging female leader's training period, the Benevolent Male Advocate acts as a buffer between her and those who may be resistant toward her.

Some Final Thoughts

Clergy gender equity will not happen on its own. Many of the recommendations previously offered rely on men to spearhead them; however, women can be a part of the process as well. They can seek out Benevolent Male Advocates to serve as mentors and guides through the leadership labyrinth. They can develop networks with other women in ministry leadership, recognizing that the covert nature of second-generation gender discrimination isolates individuals impacted by it. They can do the hard work of developing courage and confidence. They can refine the skill sets associated with high-level ministry leadership, like speaking in public, writing, leading teams, and casting compelling vision. Perhaps most importantly, they can pray: for eyes that will see the injustice of gender bias, for hearts that will burn to reverse it, and for hands that will do the hard work necessary to help the Church become more whole.

Beth K. Armstrong, PhD, is a leadership development consultant and adjunct faculty member at Central Christian College of Kansas.

Bibliography

Anderson, Melissa J. "Are We Wearing Work-Family Blinders?" *The Glass Hammer*, June 5, 2013. http://bit.ly/27YVJQh

_. "The Glass Ceiling is Real—Why Are Leaders Taking So Long to Get Rid of It?" *The Glass Hammer*, June 20, 2013. http://bit.ly/24gDelQ

_. "Why Do We Need Male Mentors and Sponsors?" *The Glass Hammer*, May 23, 2013. Accessed February 2016. http://bit.ly/1TObPrU

Aujla, Harjinder. "Helping Women Break through the Glass Ceiling." *Nursing Management* 15, no. 10 (2009):13.

Barnett, Rosalind Chait. "Women, Leadership, and the Natural Order." In *Women and Leadership*, edited by Barbara Kellerman and Deborah L. Rhode, 149-173. San Francisco: Jossey-Bass, 2007.

Belkin, Lisa. "The RetroWife Opts Out: What Has Changed, and What Still Needs To." *HuffPost Parents*. March 19, 2013. Accessed February 22, 2016. http://huff.to/22u3w4y

Berthoud, Diane A. Forbes. "Education for Global Leadership: A Leadership Agenda for Women. In *Communicative Understandings of Women's Leadership Development: From Glass Ceilings to Labyrinth Path*, edited by Elisha L. Ruminksi and Annette M. Holba. Plymouth: Lexington Books, 2012:

Bessey, Sarah. *Jesus Feminist*. New York: Howard, 2013.

Bosak, Janine, and Sabine Sczesny. "Exploring the Dynamics of Incongruent Beliefs about Women and Leaders." *British Journal of Management* 22 (2011):254-269. doi: 10.1111/j.1467-8551.2010.00731.x

Bousquet, Marc. "Lady Academe and Labor-Market Segmentation: The Narrative of Women's Success via Higher Education Rests on a House of Cards." *The Chronicle of Higher Education*. October 29, 2012. Accessed February 2016. http://chronicle.com/article/Lady-AcademeLabor-Market/135284/

Carli, Linda and Alice H. Eagly. "Overcoming Resistance to Women Leaders: The Importance of Leadership Style." In *Women and Leadership*, edited by Barbara Kellerman and Deborah L. Rhode, 127-148. San Francisco: Jossey-Bass, 2007.

Carnes, Molly, Claudia Morrissey, and Stacie E. Geller. "Women's Health and Women's Leadership in Academic Medicine: Hitting the Same Glass Ceiling?" *Journal of Women's Health* 17, no. 9 (2008):1453-1462.

Chaffins, S., M. Forbes, H. E. Fuqua, Jr., and J. P. Cangemi. "The glass ceiling: Are women where they should be?" *Education* 115, no. 3, (1995): 380-386.

Chang, Patricia M. Y., and Viviana Bompadre. "Crowded Pulpits: Observations and Explanations of the Clergy Oversupply in the Protestant Churches, 1950-1993." *Journal for the Scientific Study of Religion* 38, no. 3 (1999):398-410.

Chang, Patricia M.Y., and Paul Perl. "Enforcing Family Values? The Effects of Marital Status on Clergy Earnings." *Sociology of Religion* 60, no. 4 (1999):403-417.

Chaves, Mark. Ordaining Women: Culture and Conflict in Religious Organizations. Cambridge: Harvard University Press, 1997.

Cramer, David C. "Is Egalitarianism on a Slippery Slope?" *Christians for Biblical Equality's Arise E-Newsletter*, May 16, 2013. Accessed February 2016. http://www.cbeinternational.org/resources/egalitarianism-slippery-slope

Demaiter, Erin I., and Tracey L. Adams. "'I really didn't have any problems with the male-female thing until...': Successful Women's Experiences in IT Organizations." *Canadian Journal of Sociology* 34, no. 1 (2009):31-53.

DeMuth, Mary. "I'm Sick of Hearing about Your Smoking Hot Wife." *Christianity Today*, April 19, 2013. Accessed February 2016. http://bit.ly/1UdUUJ7

Dickins, Thomas E. "A 'Considered' Evolutionary Perspective on the 'Glass Ceiling.'" *Psychology, Evolution & Gender* 2, no. 2 (2000):161-166;

Eagly, Alice H. Foreword to *Communicative Understandings of Women's Leadership Development: From Glass Ceilings to Labyrinth Paths,* edited by Elisha L. Ruminksi and Annette M. Holba, ix-xii. Plymouth: Lexington Books, 2012.

Eagly, Alice H., and Linda L. Carli. "Women and Men as Leaders." In *The Nature of Leadership,* edited by John Antonakis, Anna T. Cianciolo, and Robert J. Sternbery, 279-301. Thousand Oaks: Sage, 2004.

Ely, Robin J., Herminia Ibarra, and Deborah M. Kolb. "Taking Gender into Account: Theory and Design for Women's Leadership Development Programs." *Academy of Management Learning & Education* 10, no. 3 (2011):474-493.

Federal Glass Ceiling Commission. "Good for Business: Making Full Use of the Nation's Human Capital." U.S. Department of Labor (1995). http://www.dol.gov/oasam/programs/ history/reich/reports/ceiling.pdf

Hendelman, Michelle. "Want More Women at the Top? It's Time to Fix the Leaky Talent Pipeline." *The Glass Hammer*, July 30, 2013. Accessed February 2016. http://bit.ly/1RFfX5T

Henderson, Jim. *The Resignation of Eve: What if Adam's Rib Is No Longer Willing To Be the Church's Backbone?* Carol Stream: BarnaBooks. 2012.

Huber, Randy, and John E. Stanley. "Reclaiming the Wesleyan/Holiness Heritage of Women Clergy: Sermons, a Case Study and Resources " WHwomenclergy.org Grantham, PA: Wesleyan/Holiness Clergy, Inc. 1999. Accessed February 2016. http://www.whwomenclergy.org/booklets/reclaiming.php

Ibarra, Herminia, Robin Ely, & Deborah Kolb, "Women Rising: The Unseen Barriers," *Harvard Business Review* (2013). Accessed February 2016. http://bit.ly/1BuvMJR

Ingersoll, Julie. *Evangelical Christian Women: War Stories in the Gender Battles.* New York: New York University Press, 2013.

Kantor, Jodi. "A Titan's How-To on Breaking the Glass Ceiling." *The New York Times.* February 21, 2013. Accessed February 2016. http://nyti.ms/1U7vxZS

Kaufman, Gayle, and Peter Uhlenberg. "The Influence of Parenthood on the Work Effort of Married Men and Women." *Social Forces* 78 (2000):931-949.

Kay, Katty, and Claire Shipman. "The Confidence Gap." *The Atlantic,* April 14, 2014. Accessed February 2016. http://theatln.tc/1m7if0Q

Knowledge Center. *Women CEOs of the S&P 500.* Catalyst.org. February 3, 2016. Accessed February 2016. http://www.catalyst.org/knowledge/women-ceos-sp-500;

Lehman, Edward C., Jr. *Women Clergy: Breaking through Gender Barriers*. New Brunswick: Transaction Books, 1985.

_. *Women in Ministry: Receptivity and Resistance*. Melbourne: The Joint Board of Christian Education, 1994.

Lennon, Tiffani, Dorey Lindemann Spotts, and Marissa Mitchell, *Benchmarking Women's Leadership in the United States*. Denver: University of Denver—Colorado Women's College, 2013.

Lynch, Michael, and Katherine Post. "What Glass Ceiling?" *The Public Interest,* Summer (1996): 27-36

Madell, Robin. "Is There Really a Choice between Work and Family?" *The Glass Hammer*, April 10, 2013. Accessed February 2016. http://bit.ly/1smJ4X7

McDuff, Elaine M., and Charles W. Mueller. "Social Support and Compensating Differentials in the Ministry: Gender Differences in Two Protestant Denominations." *Review of Religious Research* 40, no. 4 (1999):307-330.

Naff, Katherine C., and Sue Thomas. "The Glass Ceiling Revisited: Determinants of Federal Job Advancement." *Policy Studies Review* 1, no. 3/4 (1994):249-269.

Nesbitt, Paula D. "Clergy Feminization: Controlled Labor or Transformative Change?" *Journal for the Scientific Study of Religion* 36, no. 4 (1997):585-598.

_. "Dual Ordination Tracks: Differential Benefits and Costs for Men and Women Clergy." *Sociology of Religion* 54, no. 1 (1993):13-30.

_. *Feminization of the Clergy in America*. New York: Oxford University Press, 1997.

_. "Gender, Tokenism, and the Construction of Elite Clergy Careers." *Review of Religious Research* 38, no. 3 (1997):193-210.

_. "Marriage, Parenthood, and the Ministry: Differential Effects of Marriage and Family on Male and Female Clergy Careers." *Sociology of Religion* 56, no. 4 (1995):397-415.

Perl, Paul. "Gender and Mainline Protestant Pastors' Allocation of Time to Work Tasks." *Journal for the Scientific Study of Religion* 41, no. 1 (2002):169-178.

Reed, Josephine, Regina Anderson, and Vashti McKenzie. "Bishop Vashti McKenzie." In *Breaking through the Stained Glass Ceiling*, edited by Maureen E. Fiedler, 12-15. New York: Seabury Books, 2010. Original interview conducted in 2004.

Rhode, Deborah L. *The Difference "Difference" Makes*. Stanford: Stanford Law and Politics, 2003.

Rhode, Deborah L., and Barbara Kellerman. "Women and Leadership: The State of Play." In *Women and Leadership,* edited by Barbara Kellerman and Deborah L. Rhode, 1-62. San Francisco: Jossey-Bass, 2007.

Slaughter, Anne-Marie. "Why Women Still Can't Have It All." *The Atlantic,* July/August (2012). Accessed February 2016. http://theatln.tc/190nlr1.

Smith, Christine A. *Beyond the Stained Glass Ceiling: Equipping and Encouraging Female Pastors*. Valley Forge: Judson Press, 2013.

Sools, Anneke M., Marloes L. Van Engen, and Chris Baerveldt. "Gendered Career-Making Practices: On 'Doing Ambition' or How Managers Discursively Position Themselves in a Multinational Corporation." *Journal of Occupational and Organizational Psychology* 80 (2007):413-435.

Spar, Debora L. "Shedding the Superwoman Myth." *The Chronicle of Higher Education*, September 2, 2013. Accessed February 2-16. http://bit.ly/1UosYoK

Tomlinson, Jennifer. Review of *Breaking through the Glass Ceiling*, by Linda Wirth. *Gender, Work and Organization* 13, no. 5 (2006).

Weedon, Chris. *Feminist Practice and Poststructuralist Theory* (2nd ed.). Malden: Blackwell, 1997.

Witherington, Ben. "John Piper on Men in Ministry, and the Masculinity of Christianity." *Patheos*, February 12, 2012. Accessed February 2016. http://bit.ly/20QnR2w.

Woodiwiss, Catherine. "In the Image of God: Sex, Power, and 'Masculine Christianity'." *Sojourners*, May 15, 2013. Accessed February 2016. http://bit.ly/1XIW6to

Zikmund, Barbara B., Adair T. Lummis, and Patricia M. Y. Chang. *Clergy Women: An Uphill Calling*. Louisville: Westminster John Knox Press, 1998.

Chapter 31 Notes

[1] Knowledge Center, *Women CEOs*; Kantor, "A Titan's How-To on Breaking the Glass Ceiling"; Lennon, Spotts, and Mitchell, *Benchmarking Women's Leadership*.

[2] Tomlinson, Review of *Breaking through the Glass Ceiling*, 495-497.

[3] Dickins, "A 'Considered' Evolutionary Perspective," 161-166; Lynch and Post, "What Glass Ceiling," 27-36.

[4] Carnes, Morrissey, and Geller, "Women's Health and Women's Leadership in Academic Medicine"; Slaughter, "Why Women Still Can't Have It All"

[5] Carli and Eagly, "Overcoming Resistance to Women Leaders"; Federal Glass Ceiling Commission, "Good for Business: Making Full Use of the Nation's Human Capital"

[6] Ibarra, Ely, and Kolb, "Women Rising"; Lennon et al, "Benchmarking."

[7] Eagly, Foreword to *Communicative Understandings*.

[8] Berthoud, "Education for Global Leadership," 57-71.

[9] Chaffins, Forbes, Fuqua, and Cangemi, "The glass ceiling"

[10] Belkin, "The RetroWife"; Kaufman and Uhlenberg, "The Influence of Parenthood"; Rhode and Kellerman, "Women and Leadership"; Lennon, Spotts, and Mitchell, *Benchmarking*; Naff and Thomas, "The Glass Ceiling Revisited"

[11] Naff and Thomas, "The Glass Ceiling Revisited"

[12] Eagly and Carli, "Women and Men as Leaders"; Madel, "Is There Really a Choice between Work and Family?"; Rhode and Kellerman, "Women and Leadership"

[13] Aujl, "Helping Women Break through the Glass Ceiling"; Bousque, "Lady Academe and Labor-Market Segmentation"; Demaiter and Adams, "'I really didn't have any problems with the male-female thing until...'; Naff and Thomas, "The Glass Ceiling Revisited"; Rhode and Kellerman, "Women and Leadership"

[14] Ibarra et al, "Women Rising", 64

[15] Weedon, *Feminist Practice and Poststructuralist*.

[16] Sools, Van Engen, and Baerveldt, "Gendered Career-Making Practices", 427

[17] Anderson, "Are We Wearing Work-Family Blinders?"; Lennon et al, *Benchmarking*

[18] Anderson, "The Glass Ceiling is Real", Carli and Eagly, "Overcoming Resistance to Women Leaders"; Lehman, *Women Clergy*; Rhode, *The Difference*.

[19] Barnett, "Women, Leadership, and the Natural Order", 157

[20] Demaiter and Adams, "'I really didn't have any problems'; Rhode, *The Difference;* Spar, "Shedding the Superwoman Myth"; Barnett, "Women, Leadership, and the Natural Order"; Reed, Anderson, and McKenzi, "Bishop Vashti McKenzie"; Nesbitt, *Feminization of the Clergy in America*; Rhode and Kellerman, "Women and Leadership"

[21] Ely et al, "Taking Gender into Account"; Ibarra et al, "Women Rising"; Kay and Shipman, "The Confidence Gap"

[22] Chaves, *Ordaining Women.*

[23] Huber and Stanley, "Reclaiming the Wesleyan/Holiness Heritage of Women Clergy"

[24] Bessey, *Jesus Feminist;* Chaves, *Ordaining Women;* DeMuth, "I'm Sick of Hearing about Your Smoking Hot Wife"; Witherington, "John Piper on Men in Ministry, and the Masculinity of Christianity"; Woodiwiss, "In the Image of God"

[25] Chaves, *Ordaining Women*; Ingersoll, *Evangelical Christian Women*

[26] Bessey, *Jesus Feminist;* Chaves, *Ordaining Women;* Cramer, "Is Egalitarianism on a Slippery Slope?"; Ingersoll, *Evangelical Christian Women.*

[27] Ingersoll, *Evangelical Christian Women,* 41.

[28] Eagly and Carli, "Women and Men as Leaders"; Ely et al, "Taking Gender into Account"; Ibarra et al, "Women Rising",

[29] Ingersoll, *Evangelical Christian Women*

[30] Barnett, "Women, Leadership, and the Natural Order", 151.

[31] Ely et al, "Taking Gender into Account", 478.

[32] Bosak and Sczesny, "Exploring the Dynamics of Incongruent Beliefs"; Carli and Eagly, "Overcoming Resistance"; Chaffins et al, "The glass ceiling"; Eagly and Carli, "Women and Men as Leaders"; Rhode and Kellerman, "Women and Leadership"

[33] Studies explored and reported in Lehman, *Women Clergy* and *Women in Ministry.*

[34] Lehman, *Women Clergy,* 229

[35] Henderson, *The Resignation of Eve,* 45

[36] Lehman *Women Clergy;* Nesbitt, "Clergy Feminization"

[37] Smith, *Beyond the Stained Glass Ceiling*

[38] Zikmund, Lummis, and Chan, *Clergy Women,* 7

[39] Nesbitt, "Dual Ordination Tracks"

[40] Nesbitt, *Feminization of the Clergy in America*

[41] Ibid.

[42] Ingersoll, *Evangelical Christian Women,* 87

[43] Ingersoll, *Evangelical Christian Women*; Smith, *Beyond the Stained Glass Ceiling*

[44] Nesbitt, *Feminization of the Clergy in America*

[45] Hendelman, "Want More Women at the Top?"

[46] Anderson, "Why Do We Need Male Mentors and Sponsors?"; Chaffins et al, "The Glass Ceiling"; Rhode, *The Difference*; Rhode and Kellerman, "Women and Leadership"

[47] Ingersoll, *Evangelical Christian Women*

[48] Hendelman, "Want More Women at the Top?

[49] Perl, "Gender and Mainline Protestant Pastors' Allocation of Time to Work Tasks"

[50] Zikmund et al, *Clergy Women*

[51] Chang and Bompadre, "Crowded Pulpits"; Nesbit, "Marriage, Parenthood, and the Ministry"; Nesbitt, "Clergy Feminization"; Nesbitt, *Feminization of the Clergy in America*

[52] Chang and Perl, "Enforcing Family Values"

[53] Nesbit, "Marriage, Parenthood, and the Ministry," 412

[54] Nesbit, *Feminization of the Clergy in America*

[55] Zikmund et al, *Clergy Women*

[56] Chang and Bompadre, "Crowded Pulpits"; Zikmund et al, *Clergy Women*

[57] Lehman, Women Clergy; Smith, *Beyond the Stained Glass Ceiling*

[58] Lehman, *Women Clergy*, 241

[59] Ibid.

[60] Ely et al, "Taking Gender into Account"

[61] Ibarra et al, "Women Rising"; Zikmund et al, *Clergy Women*

[62] Nesbitt, "Gender, Tokenism, and the Construction of Elite Clergy Careers"

[63] Lehman, *Women Clergy*

[64] McDuff and Mueller, "Social Support and Compensating Differentials"

[65] Henderson, *The Resignation of Eve*, 21

[66] Nesbitt, *Feminization of the Clergy in America*

32
Challenge of Board Leadership

Brian S. Simmons

Boards need certain kinds of leaders. Boards are meant to steward what is entrusted to their care. This chapter provides values and encouragements for appropriate board leadership including stewardship, governance, and personal transformation. Boards must not over-exert themselves, but should also provide ongoing accountability to senior leaders who have been hired, selected, or supported by the board. The chapter also provides helpful tips for accomplishing these values and avoiding distractions.

I HAVE SERVED in numerous leadership capacities involving some aspect of board leadership over the past 33 years. I have served as Superintendent of two private Christian schools, board member of a Christian college, senior leader of two Christian universities, church elder, board member of several nonprofit organizations and President of two Christian non-profit organizations. From these experiences, I can readily say that effective board leadership is a challenge.

A board is a team that oversees an organization in order that it fulfills its mission, accomplishes its vision, and operates in a manner consistent with its core values. Easy enough, right? In truth, most boards are not as effective as they could or should be, and many are dysfunctional. There are numerous reasons for this dysfunction, including lack of training about best practice, self-serving behavior and hubris, lack of clearly defined roles for board members and senior leaders, poor organizational structures, and lack of understanding and/or commitment to biblical principles guiding effective board leadership. At the heart of the problem is the fact that all boards are led by fallible human beings.

Why is a discussion of board leadership important? Because people working together as a team can accomplish results that individuals working alone could never even hope to accomplish. This is the principle of *synergy*. Further, trustees exist to fulfill the purposes of the Master for the organizations that ultimately belong to Him. This is the value of *service*. Finally, board leadership is important because of spiritual warfare. In Christian ministries, it should come as no surprise that one of the primary strategies of the Evil One is to attack organizational teams including senior leaders, board members and especially the CEO-board relationship.

In this chapter, I will, first, discuss Christian organizations, including several challenges they face. Second, I will explore the biblical construct of steward leadership explaining how it provides a solid foundation for effective board leadership. Finally, I will suggest what effective boards do. This chapter is written with the prayer that leaders of organizations, including churches, schools and universities will be inspired to follow theoretical and biblical principles defining best practices of board leadership to the glory of God.

Christian Organizations

Conflict occurs when values from divergent belief systems clash. Sometimes conflict is not vocalized, but perceived when actions do not match supposed worldviews. My friend, Dave Jewitt, founder of Your One Degree, recently wrote, "How we work, lead, handle conflict, treat others, and conduct ourselves impacts how people view the gospel and Christianity."[1] For those who lead "Christian" organizations, then, it is important for leadership actions and values to match the Christian worldview.

An organization is "a social invention that accomplishes goals through group effort."[2] Effective organizations meet their aims through various means and thus may provide insight when studying organizational culture and climate, organizational change, leadership, decision-making, conflict, and motivation.[3] This chapter uses the metaphor of stewardship to explore human behavior in board leadership, specifically human behavior that is faithfully Christian. From a biblical perspective, all believers are to be faithful stewards, entrusted with creation's care—including organizations—in fulfilling the purposes of the Master.

Numerous obstacles hinder this kind of stewardship. First, the reality is that all believers live in a fallen world, and may struggle with selfish, sinful behavior. Christian leaders are tempted to make decisions based on pride, selfish motives, anger, or fear. Second, Christian organizations do not always know how to handle conflict, even though it is inevitable. While we must encourage and embrace constructive conflict—open and honest debate about ideas and ideology[4]—we must never cross the line into destructive conflict where discussion of ideas is replaced by personal attacks. This type of conflict is always harmful. Third, while many organizations are in desperate need of innovation, they are resistant to change. Christian ministries can struggle with negative climate including ineffective structure, negative milieu, and secular culture, where God, and godly principles, including ethos, historical purpose, power distribution, healthy motivation, are ignored. Christian leaders can become practical atheists.

The Bible establishes a very high bar for church elders which can be applied to board leadership, too. Overseers are to be above reproach, humble, tempered, peaceful, and not greedy (Titus 1:7). Many Christian organizations seek board members who live up to these high standards for organizational leadership. With the previous obstacles in mind, then, let's accept that most Christian organizations with board leadership are led by competent, godly, Christian men and women who love the Lord and desire to lead well. What principles are beneficial for these high-character, well-intentioned leaders to thrive so that the organizations they lead can thrive as Christian organizations?

Biblical Steward Leadership

Let's accept for a moment another hypothesis: The primary reason Christian leaders of Christian organizations sometimes act "un-Christianly" is a lack of a theoretical and biblical understanding of and consistent commitment to principles of effective leadership. For some answers to this specific problem, we turn our attention to the biblical construct of steward leadership.

It was July of 2009 and my family was preparing to move to Colorado Springs from Indianapolis, Indiana. My daughter, Aubrey, was out late in the downtown area our last Friday night. Bonnie and I had just slipped into bed. It was a few minutes after midnight when the phone by my bedside rang. It was Aubrey. She said, "Hi Dad. We are finished down here and I am on my way home. Do I go east or

"Biblical stewardship is an all-of-life paradigm. Every decision in life is ultimately a stewardship decision"

west on I70…" Just then there was a loud crash and the phone went dead. I scrambled out of bed pulling on my pants and a shirt when the phone rang a second time. It was Aubrey. "Dad," she said, "I am OK, but your Durango is another story." Relieved, I drove from our home in Fortville to her location downtown. As I drove I thought "That's OK. We can buy another Durango. The SUV is God's anyway, and if he wants us to use his money to buy a new one that's OK with me." But then, another thought came to my mind, "Not only is the Durango God's, so is Aubrey!"

When we think of biblical stewardship, we often think only of money. Sometimes we may even expand our paradigm to include time and talent. But the Bible teaches very clearly that *everything* in the universe belongs to the Creator. Dutch theologian and politician Abraham Kuyper (1837-1920) often said to this point, "There is not one square inch of the entire creation about which Jesus Christ does not cry out, 'This is mine! This belongs to me!'"[5] Or consider David's prayer in 1 Chronicles 29:10-13:

> Praise be to you, Lord, the God of our Father Israel from everlasting to everlasting. Yours, Lord, is the greatness and the power and the glory and the majesty and the splendor. For everything in heaven and in earth is yours. Yours, Lord, is the kingdom; you are exalted as head over all. Wealth and honor come from you; you are the ruler of all things. In your hands are strength and power to exalt and give strength to all. Now, our God we give you thanks and praise your glorious name.

The biblical concept of a steward is explicitly described by Jesus in the parable of the talents (bags of gold) in Matthew 25. All of "our stuff," including the organizations we serve, really belongs to God and has been entrusted to our care for only a short time. But what about people? In Psalm 24:1, the Bible tells us, "The earth is the Lord's and everything in it. The world and all its people belong to him." The steward leader, according to Scripture, is responsible for everything the Master has entrusted to his or her care. Certainly, this responsibility includes time, treasure and talent, but this biblical paradigm of leadership goes beyond these three limited areas of life and ministry to include everything including relationships with the people entrusted to our care, such as employees, spouses, children, grandchildren, and neighbors. Biblical stewardship is an all-of-life paradigm. Every decision in life is ultimately a stewardship decision.[6]

Principles Guiding Exemplary Leadership

Theories help to explain behavior.[7] Good theories are well-tested, based on real observation, and provide evidence that can guide appropriate action.[8] For our interests, steward leadership theory "views the primary identity and role of the leader as one who is a steward managing the resources of another that are entrusted into his or her care."[9] These resources may include tangible goods or resources such as power and its distribution.[10]

Personal Transformation

A mission-based steward consistently leads the organization by managing its resources, including personnel, to maximize mission effectiveness. The life of a mission-based steward is characterized by virtues such as balance, humility, accountability, and integrity.[11] In this setting, good stewardship and self-interest are antithetical. Because stewards are given a level of trust that many are not used to holding, there is often a necessary personal transformation in three areas: (1) Rooting the leader's self in the image of God; (2) Experiencing the radical freedom and joy that comes as a result of obedience to God; and, (3) Emphasizing being over doing as the foundation of healthy stewardship that reflects an inward transformation.[12]

Thus, one principle that should form proper leadership is that stewardship involves a deep commitment to something greater than and outside of one's self. In Block's words, choosing "service over self-interest" means that we are willing to be deeply accountable without choosing to control the world around us.[13]

Gaps between theory, biblical truth, and practice expose problems many stewards experience as they serve the Master in Christian organizations. The gaps become clear when the leader's actions do not line up with best practices or Christian principles. One strategy to move toward more effective practice is to fill in these gaps through training that can provide self-awareness. For example, a former board member of a Christian organization recently emailed me about the board's dismissal of the CEO. He wrote that the board had voted unanimously to dismiss this Christian brother because of some particular behavior. However, the board member exhibited a gap between good leadership principles and actual practice (especially Christian practice) by failing to understand the cultural and political influences that led to the board's decision. As an outsider, it was obvious to me that part of the context for the dismissal was the board structure. The structure had become factional and dominant, causing relationships between the CEO and board members to be "constrained because of incessant conflict and competing demands for loyalty."[14] Beyond this relational dysfunction, power and benefit was unequal and disproportionate between the CEO and the board.[15] This resulted in unhealthy politics where community elites exerted their power to influence important board decisions.

Biblical Unity

The dismissal of the CEO revealed the gaps between Christian principles and best practices, but provides valuable opportunity for reflection and growth. For example, just because a decision is unanimous does not mean it is good or right. It may be the result of groupthink, which happens when the desire for harmony and concurrence in the group becomes so dominant that it causes group members to ignore legitimate concerns, avoid potential problems, or fail to seek out alternative directions.[16] Where there is groupthink, pressure may be applied, even unwittingly, by dominant board members for others in the group to go along with decisions.

It is essential that board members and leaders learn the crucial difference between true, biblical unity and uniformity or unanimity. Using the metaphor of the church (organization) as a body, the Apostle Paul affirms in 1 Corinthians 12 that the whole body needs different parts, different functions, and even different perspectives in order to be mature and whole. For Paul, biblical unity was not uniformity of function and appearance but of harmony and oneness in purpose!

A board can improve its ability to evaluate its CEO properly and effectively by engaging in careful, considered, and objective reflection. Historically, the boards of Christian secondary schools have tended to lack effective evaluation of superintendents,[17] often failing to engage in effective dialog about performance as much as they should (although this problem exists in plenty of other Christian organizations as well). By avoiding the pitfalls of groupthink and cultivating a healthy understanding of biblical unity, boards such as the one in my example above can learn to implement effective accountability structures and practices.

Ethical Wisdom

Steward leadership also involves holding potentially opposing values or issues in tension. For example, the tension between what is good for individual employees and what is best for the organization. As a steward leader, one of the most important things to keep in mind is that the organization *and* its employees belong to God. As we manage this tension, we need to seek the will of the Master continually as we prayerfully make important decisions which have far-ranging impact and the potential to affect many lives. Leaders are charged by the Master to make these important decisions while staying faithful to him as expressed in continued fulfillment of the mission and vision of the organization guided by the organization's statement of faith and core values.

Finally, steward leaders must be prepared and willing to deal with difficult ethical situations if they are committed to fulfilling the will of the Master for the organizations entrusted to their care. Steward leaders exercise wisdom in this regard because we live in a litigious society. What is difficult, however, is that in dealing with such complicated matters, steward leaders must deal wisely with the fear associated with threats of lawsuits and critical opinions of other staff, board members and stakeholders.

Characteristics of Effective Boards

Boards made up of leaders often struggle to define how they will lead. The first and most important task of all boards is to hire an effective leader as the CEO of the organization. Once this person is in place, boards must grapple with the question of who does what in the organization. If the CEO is hired to lead, then what does the board do? It is of paramount importance that boards and CEOs work together to accomplish the purposes of the organization. One primary reason for this dysfunction is confusion of roles. Simply put, boards need to do board stuff and CEOs need to do CEO stuff. So, which is which? This question can be answered by focusing on the characteristics of effective boards.

Avoid Dysfunction

First, effective boards recognize and refuse destructive practices. Let me give two examples. First, great harm occurs when organizational stakeholders are permitted to go around the CEO to register complaints directly with board members. This violation is exacerbated when the topic of these discussions somehow makes its way to the board room. And the worst violation of all occurs when board members discuss such issues in closed sessions without the CEO or in parking lot meetings before or after board meetings. As dysfunctional as these practices are, they occur on a regular basis with the trustees of nonprofit organizations. This type of activity destroys trust and can do great harm to people and organizations.

A second example of destructive practices is micromanaging. A common error is the board whose committees mirror staff functions. As a result, board meeting time that could be spent leading through strategic and generative discussion is instead spent micromanaging. One example of micromanaging is reading staff reports, which are properly the domain of the CEO. When this happens, boards are engaged in management, not governance and leadership. This error increases the likelihood that board members will, however unintentionally, usurp the power they have delegated to the CEO of the organization.

It is especially tempting for board members to micromanage in areas where they have high levels of training and experience outside of the organization they are governing. The worst board members bring these frames of reference into the board room and become involved in staff work. I once worked with a board member who was an executive Vice President for Human Resources at a large corporation. Where did this board member micromanage? In the day-to-day decisions about hiring and firing of staff by asserting his influence through informal breakfast meetings with the CEO. Clearly, personnel matters are the purview of the CEO and senior leadership team. Micromanagement destroys effective governance. Board members only function as a board member when the board is in session. Outside of these meetings, views and opinions of board members are only advice and not directives backed by the power of the board.

Focus on Governance

Second, effective boards focus on governance rather than on managing. My colleague, Phil Graybeal, who has worked with boards for many years defines governance as "the coming together of a group of elected or appointed individuals to act as one for the purpose of guiding the organization of which they hold trusteeship toward the accomplishment of its ends while establishing appropriate boundaries for accountability."[18]

Effective governance begins with ensuring that the structure of the organization is sound. Structure defines the ways labor is divided and how information flows between people and groups. Structure influences the feelings, attitudes and emotions of individuals and ultimately the behavior of people and groups within every organization. While there is no guarantee that an organization with clear and appropriate structure will be effective, if the structure is wrong, then effectiveness will be difficult if not impossible.[19]

A Christian school with which I am familiar provides an example of a broken structure. The school was founded with an "A" board and a "B" board. The superintendent of the school met monthly with the "B" board that appeared to be the governing board of the school. But the founder and two other board members served on the "A" board which met annually and made the "important decisions" for the school. The founder established himself as the chairman of the "A" board and had five votes, while the second member had three votes and the third member had one vote. You do the math! This school was led for 30 years by these three men, and years after the death of this founder and the dissolution of this autocratic, ineffective board structure, the school still struggles with a negative climate. This scenario often plays out in organizations with large boards and Executive Committees because the Executive Committees are tempted to wield the power of the organization and make decisions without involving the larger board. An obvious solution in this scenario is to reduce the size of the board so that all board members can participate equally in the governance of the organization.

Term Limited

Third, effective boards establish and maintain term limits. Numerous organizations are led by board members who have "served" for decades in this manner. This prevalent, ineffective structure leaves one to wonder about the motivation of those in power who lead these organizations. In some of these organizations, self-preservation replaces effective leadership. This is the epitome of hubris.

It is the responsibility of the board to develop policies that guide staff behavior which keep the organization grounded in its mission, striving toward the accomplishment of its vision all the while living out its core values.

Generative Leadership

Thus, fourth, effective boards lead generatively. This means that boards as they fulfill their responsibility to bring a sense of direction to the organization as they define for the CEO, senior leaders and staff what they ought, and ought not to do as they lead the organization forward. In common vernacular, the best board members take some of the heat! The primary function of effective boards in providing generative leadership is the ratification of policies that address tensions in core values (care of employees versus care for the organization as an example), define expectations (what should be done), and identify constraints (what cannot be done).[20]

Exercise Authority

Fifth, effective boards exercise fiduciary and strategic authority.[21] This involves the establishment of policies and practices for regular and on-going accountability for results including formal and informal evaluation of their CEO, regular and open dialogue about important issues, and self-evaluation of their practice as a board. While boards have the ultimate fiduciary responsibility for the organizations entrusted to them by God, it is the day-to-day work of the CEO, senior leaders and staff to create and monitor the budget and accompanying financial and development plans for the organization. Boards approve budgets and are responsible to ensure that the organization is spending its resources appropriately as board members and staff work together to bring into reality the vision of the organization.

Once broad strategic direction is in place, the CEO should be empowered and supported by the board to serve as their only employee tasked by the board with the responsibility to carry out the mission of the organization. The CEO, in turn, hires senior staff leaders who provide leadership, guided by board policy, to the various departments of the organization. Ideally, the CEO and staff of the organization will create and maintain a strategic plan for the organization. They are best suited to this work because they understand the inner working of the organization better than board members. The role of board is to review, approve, and identify the resources and policies of that plan. Finally, in their generative role, board members need to provide thoughtful judgment about what the organization they lead ought and ought not do. Their primary means in accomplishing this generative responsibility is the authoring of organizational policies.

The Bible provides valuable principles that can help board members fulfill their responsibility as stewards and function as a unified, effective board. As such, Christian leaders often exercise a pastoral role. In this role, as shepherds, they are to provide for the needs of the sheep under their care. This role is especially difficult at times because there is sometimes a tension between what is best for the organization (for example a necessary downsizing) and the needs of the employees (for example to keep their jobs). It is also difficult in board leadership, but as stewards, boards must care for the organization's leadership in addition to the organization. Christian leaders should strive to be good examples for others to follow. The common axiom says that your walk talks and your talk talks, but your walk talks louder than your talk. Subordinates hate inconsistency and hypocrisy.

Christian leaders should be like steel wool. They need the moral fortitude to make difficult decisions, yet they need to be loving, empathetic and kind at all times in their dealings with others. Decades from now, most followers will forget the details of the decisions leaders made, but they will long remember how they were treated by those in positions of authority over them! Board members need to apply these principles in their dealings with the organization's CEO, and the CEO needs to apply these principles in his dealings with the organization's employees.

The last decade provided a number of ideal opportunities for this principle to be exemplified. Many organizations were affected and some are still struggling financially from the economic downturn of 2008. Often when budgets have been reduced due to decreasing revenue, the only way for many Christian leaders to balance the budget was to lay off staff. *How* we do this is of utmost importance to the Master as we lovingly manage relationships with the people entrusted to our care.

As a leader, ask yourself, "How would I want the board and CEO to treat me if the roles were reversed?" I once led an organization in decline through several years of necessary downsizing. In hindsight, I would have been more involved in the process than I was and more focused on expressing love and concern for the individuals who suffered.

To complicate matters, as we lead our organizations we all realize that the world is changing. We now live in a globalized, highly connected economy. In what James White has called "the rise of the nones,"[22] citizens of the United States are increasingly embracing a secular worldview or abandoning any form of religious worldview whatsoever. We experience opportunities and threats from the convergence of technological, financial and demographic factors. Change requires innovation and innovation is aided by shifting resources during times of limited or declining revenue. These changes often involve people and how we lead through times of change is of utmost importance to the Master. These are not problems to be solved, but rather tensions we need wisdom to manage.

Conclusion

We have important work to do. We are to lead. As stewards, we must keep in mind that it is God who has given us the ability and responsibility to lead. We need to rely on the empowerment of the Holy Spirit to accomplish God's purposes for the organizations we lead. The result will be that God ultimately receives all of the glory for the good deeds accomplished through the work of the organizations we are called to faithfully lead. Let me conclude with some final applications of biblical steward leadership to effective board leadership.

First, a steward leadership approach to board leadership is not about rights but responsibilities. We are responsible to be faithful stewards of all the Master has chosen to entrust to our care. When we operate in the realm of rights, we can replace the Master as the final judge of our actions. This relates directly to effective board leadership because God owns the organization he has given board members the responsibility to lead. With this in mind, what board members do and how they do what they do matters to God.

Second, a steward remembers that how much the Master chooses to entrust to the steward's care is God's prerogative! As owner, God alone maintains the right to distribute that which belongs to him however he chooses. It is encouraging to note that the steward to whom was given two talents and the one to whom was given five were both faithful and received identical commendations (Matt. 24:14-30). The unfaithful steward was the only servant that received a condemnation because his motivation and resulting action was grounded in a mistrust of the Master. This relates directly to effective board leadership because a faithful steward will trust his Master and seek simply to be faithful. The measure of effectiveness in God's eyes is not size of the ministry or monetary value of facilities. Bigger is not better. Better is better. The Master values and rewards faithful service.

Third, steward leaders understand the weight of authority. Leaders who have been entrusted with relationships involving teaching others have a greater responsibility. An example is the warning in Scripture to stewards who have been entrusted with the responsibility to care for God's precious children. "But whoever causes one of these little ones who believe in me to sin, it would be better for him to have a great millstone hung around his neck and to be drowned in the depth of the sea" (Matt. 18:6). And again a specific warning to steward teachers, "Not many of you should become teachers, my brothers, for you know that we who teach will be judged with greater strictness" (Jas 3:1). All board members teach and influence others.

Fourth, steward leaders steward themselves. Consider the promise of a future day of reckoning: "Here is the end of the matter; all has been heard. Fear God and keep His commandments for this is the whole duty of man. For God will bring every deed into judgment, with every secret thing whether good or evil" (Eccl. 12:13-14). Hebrews 4:13 affirms that "no creature is hidden from his sight, but all are naked and exposed to the eyes of him to whom we must give account." Realize that one day we will all give an answer to the Supreme Judge of the World for what we did with everything he entrusted to our care, so it is wise to give thought to the answer before we are asked the question! There is an eternal reward for effective service as a faithful board member. Effective board members do not serve for themselves. They serve for the sake of others, and this selfless service over self interest brings glory to God. Stewards understand the self as a resource that must be enriched, empowered, and deployed in the mission of God.

Try this activity: Take out a sheet of paper and list your various roles in life—leader, husband, father, and so on. Beside each role give yourself a score from 1-10, rating your faithfulness to the Master in fulfilling his purposes through you in each of these areas of your life. How are you doing? Are you happy with your scores? If so, great. Continue to serve the Master as a faithful steward in each of these areas of your life. But if there is some room for improvement in an area or two, the really good news is that there is still time to change and do better. While the challenge of board leadership is great, the opportunities are even greater! Steward yourself not for the sake of yourself, but for those under your care, whom you serve through leadership.

Finally, "it is required of stewards that we be found faithful" (1 Cor. 4:2). As Christian leaders of Christian organizations, let's decide today to lead as faithful biblical stewards, so that one day we may hear the Master say to us, "Well done, good and faithful steward. Come, let's celebrate!"

Brian S. Simmons, EdD, is Associate Provost of Online Studies at Columbia International University.

Bibliography

Block, Peter. *Stewardship*. San Francisco, CA: Berrett and Koehler, 1996.

Bowen, William G. *The Board Book, an Insider's Guide for Directors and Trustees*. New York: Norton, 2008.

Bridges, Jerry. *Pursuit of Holiness*. Colorado Springs: Navpress, 2006.

Brinckerhoff, Peter C. *Nonprofit Stewardship, a Better Way to Lead Your Mission-based Organization*. Saint Paul, MN: Fieldstone Alliance, 2004.

Chait, Richard, Ryan William, and Barbara Taylor. *Governance as Leadership*. Hoboken: Boardsource, 2005.

Janis, Irving J. "Groupthink." *Psychology Today*, November, 1971.

Kowalski, Theodore. *The School Superintendent, 3rd edition*. Thousand Oaks: Sage, 2013.

Kuyper, Abraham. "Sphere Sovereignty." In *Abraham Kuyper: A Centennial Reader*, edited by James D. Bratt. Grand Rapids: Wm. B. Eerdmans Publishing Co., 1998.

Lencioni, Patrick. *Five Dysfunctions of a Team: A Leadership Fable*. San Francisco, Jossey-Bass, 2002.

Owens, Robert G., and Thomas Valesky. *Organizational Behavior in Organizations*, 10th edition. Upper Saddle River: Pearson, 2011.

Rodin, Scott. *The Steward Leader*. Downers Grove: Intervarsity Press Academic, 2010.

Simmons, Brian S. "An Analysis of Procedures Used to Evaluate Administrators in Larger Member Schools of the Association of Christian Schools International". Doctoral dissertation. Ball State University, 1996.

Westbrook, Kay. *Enter into the Joy of Living as God's Steward*. Boston: Pauline Books and Media, 1996.

White, James E. *The Rise of the Nones: Understanding and Reaching the Religiously Unaffiliated*. Baker Books, 2014.

Wilson, Kent R. "Steward Leadership: Characteristics of the Steward Leader in Christian Nonprofit Organizations". Doctoral dissertation. The University of Aberdeen, 2010.

Chapter 32 Notes

1 personal correspondence, March 25, 2014.

2 Kowalski, *The School Superintendent*, 79.

3 Owens and Valesky, *Organizational Behavior in Organizations*.

4 See Lencioni, *The Five Dysfunctions of a Team*.

5 Kuyper, "Sphere Sovereignty," 488.

6 Westbrook, *Enter into the Joy of Living as God's Steward*.

7 Kowalski, *School Superintendent*, 80.

8 Ibid, 81.

9 Wilson, *Steward Leadership*, 76.

10 Block, *Stewardship*, 41.

11 Brinckerhoff, *Nonprofit Stewardship*, 4.

12 Rodin, *The Steward Leader*, 30.

13 Block, *Stewardship*, 41.

14 Kowalski, *School Superintendent*, 140.

15 Ibid, 138.

16 Janis, "Groupthink".

17 Simmons, "An Analysis of Procedures Used to Evaluate Administrators".

18 Personal Correspondence, July, 2014.

19 Bowen, *The Board Book*, 149.

20 Kowalski, *School Superintendent*, 162.

21 Chait, William, and Taylor, *Governance as Leadership*, 6.

22 White, *The Rise of the Nones*.

About the Editors

Aaron Perry (PhD, Regent University) is Assistant Professor of Pastoral Care at Wesley Seminary at Indiana Wesleyan University. Previously he served at Centennial Road Church in Brockville, Ontario, and at Calvary Community Church in Johnson City, NY. Aaron is the editor of *Developing Ears to Hear: Listening in Pastoral Ministry, The Spiritual Life, and Theology* (Emeth Press) and co-author (with Tim Perry) of *He Ascended into Heaven* (Paraclete Press). He and his wife, Heather, have three children.

Bryan Easley (PhD, Regent University) is Dean of Online Education and member of the faculty at Oklahoma Wesleyan University. Previously he served as Rector of Emmaus Biblical Seminary (Haiti) and on staff at Wesley Biblical Seminary in Jackson, MS. He is ordained in the Church of the Nazarene and an adjunct instructor for Nazarene Bible College. Bryan serves as a small group pastor and Bible teacher at Rejoice Church. He and his wife, Leslie, have five children.

Index

A

academic
  discipline 57
  theology 143
  training of leaders 102
accountability 184–187, 210–213,
    322–328, 404–409, 409
  and pastors 392
  and temptation 78
  for others 296
  for sanctification 169
  high standard 267
  in bands 22, 184, 210, 358
  in discipleship 62
  in early American Methodism
    192
  in groups 361
  in leaders 246
  in Methodist movement 229
  in relationship 328
  low levels of 323
  mutual 184
  of a steward 404
  of John Wesley 185
  of overseers 88
  partners in 212
  relationships of 65
  to Christ 89
  to high commitments 324
adaptability 41, 317–327
  of Wesley's methods 180–181
  Wesleyan 30
adaptive 23, 213
  challenge(s) 317–328
  work 319
administration 75, 347
  church 368
  pastoral 166
African Methodist Episcopal
    Church 233

Aldersgate 142, 180–185
alignment 211
  leaders create 245
  of leaders and followers 252
American Revolution 22, 191–195
  and command 256
Anglican Church 22, 148
  Articles of Religion 148
  clergy 211
  episcopacy 164
  inherited from tradition 63
  John Wesley as 18, 181, 211
  number of clergy 211
  preaching in parish 173
  pulpits and Wesley 213
  respectable clergy 228
  tradition 170
  Wesley beyond 368
apostles 85–89, 122, 195, 259–260
  and leading community 84
apostolic pattern 164
Arminianism 22
Asbury, Francis 31, 58, 164,
    189–201, 201
  power 194, 195
atheism 35, 317
atonement 59
authenticity
  and ethos 372
  definition of 243
authentic leadership 243–246
  and confidence 245
  and holy power 109–112
authority 19, 77, 96, 107–119
  autonomous 280
  commitment to biblical 386
  cultural respect for 270
  ecclesiastical 194
  endowed with 274
  executive 280

formal 282
in Methodism 210
intellectual 261
men in 388
of an office 86
of bishop 181, 194
of boards 408
of God 133
of humanity 342
of husband 127
of Israel's leaders 133
of Joseph 74
of Kingdom 241
of leaders 282
patterns of 47
position of 102, 311, 409
religious 200
spiritual 192
taking 356
weight of 411
women in OT 129
autonomy 280
organizational 194

B

baptism
as means of grace 150, 212
by John 101–103
called to 259
institutional requirement 192
of eunuch 311–312
of Jesus 100–102, 242
requirements of 192
bishop
as leader 165
as servant 196
authority to ordain 181
epitome of 191
Francis Asbury 31–39, 164–172,
193–201
head of system 193
Methodist 163–174, 214
modern 201
power of 170, 194–199

United Methodist 165
Wesley's objection 165
office
of bishop 165, 181, 195, 196
board(s) 401
boards, members of 401–411
boundaries
and ethics 250
lack of 21
of the Kingdom 167
budgets 334, 387, 409
bureaucracy 73, 226, 232
burnout 336–339
business
creating innovative 58
creation of 182
lack of Wesleyan view 48
leadership and Holy Spirit 102
managers 167
philosophy and success 53, 259

C

Caesar 99, 103, 174
Calvinism 22
Christian Reformed Church 45
Dutch 46
theology 101
Calvin, John 71, 220
Catholic Church
becoming bishop 155
monarchial episcopacy 165
ordination 22
CEO 384
and board 406
model of leadership 151
change
and gifts 379
and innovation 30
and organizations 261, 268
and reality 268
and uncertainity 352
best environment 323
cultural 23
generational 45

leaders, leadership 168, 257, 292,
  319–322, 351, 410
  of urbanization 341
  organizational 402
  resistant to 403
  theological ground for 29
character
  and building trust 372
  of Christ 200
  of a Christian 208, 320
  developing in clergy 373
  flaws of leader 247
  godly and holiness 108
  holy, of Messiah 107
  and idealized influence 258
  imitating Christ 201
  lack of 201
  life-transforming 236
  of a Methodist 208
  of a person 339
  of leader 61–65, 189, 243, 246,
    247, 338
  of manager in parable 242
  of preacher 372
  and pure hearts 252
  required of disciples 242
  sacrificial of leader 292
  shaping, transforming of leader
    334–335
  spiritual 208
charisma
  in leadership 280
  personality trait 257
  and transformational leader 257
charismatic
  authoritarian pastor 351
  church 350
  freedom in community 148
  influence 281
  Joshua as leader 75
  leaders 257
  leadership 151, 282
  leader's personality 280
  view of leaders 280
charity 24, 231

Christ. *See* Jesus Christ
Christ, Body of
  38, 89, 163–173, 284, 349, 405
Christendom 23, 79
church
  in Acts 260
  and adaptive challenges 320
  African-American 41
  and anti-episcopal rhetoric 192
  and orthodox teaching 186
  body as metaphor 405
  as Bride of Christ 348
  challenges facing 328
  community in 311
  conflict in 322
  confronting 170
  contemporary 166
  contentedness of 167
  context (changing) of 31, 39
  depth of 151
  direction of 295
  disciple-making in 326
  distinctiveness 152
  division in 387
  early 71, 121–124, 233, 319–322
    real context of 323
    Timothy as leader of 263
  early American 189–206
  effectiveness 165
  elder 401
  employees 48
  engaging world 115
  evangelical 99, 150
  examples in 125
  family imagery 48
  form of 168
  for the poor 31
  functions in 168, 387
  generations of 260
  government 195
  and grace, means of grace
    142–147
  high 148
  history 322
  institutional 166

interest in 31
Kingdom of God in 80
Korean-American 39, 41
law 387
leaders 28, 53, 58, 78, 167–170, 259
leadership 120–130
life & discipline 31
liturgy in 390
local 258
location of 31
longing for 150
membership requirements 192
men in 387, 390
Mexican-American 40
mission of 170, 262, 306, 311
model for leading 89
models 351
movements 226
New Testament
    in Antioch 85
    in Corinth 126
    in Judea 85
    in Philippi 121
North American 166
of the future 323
optimistic grace 59
organization of 168
participation in 62
pastors in history 166
people in/out 38, 371
practice 322
prophecies about 259
purpose/reason 39, 348
reconnecting to 149
regarding women 128
role in spirituality 143
role of 147
role of Scripture in 38
roles in 120
rural 41
sacraments 150
sphere beyond the 48
streamlining of 170
structure 40, 169, 351

style
    authoritarian 350
    charismatic 350
    relationship 350, 351
tensions in 193
type
    experiential 349
    relational 349
    structure 350
    task 349
underground 319
understanding of 48, 148
universal 31
view of 166
visibility of 167
within a church 212
women leading/speaking in 124, 126, 393
work of 348
churches
    and adaptive challenges 327
    and budgeting 379
    and disciple-making 326
    and egalitarianism 393
    and mainline environment 168
    and staying current 151
    anti-feminist 386
    call to marginal 389
    concern for future 387
    focus on spiritual needs 28
    Holiness and upward mobility 52
    mainline 151
    Paul addressing 126
    preachers appointed to 193
    three types of 349
    trends in American 151
    urban 41, 197, 348–354
church growth 166, 368
church planting 40, 166, 392
circuit rider 29, 191
city 144, 196–198, 344–347, 389
    urban ministry 352
clergy
    and education 31
    Anglican 211, 228

corruption of 226
development of 373
ecclesial leadership 48
effectivenss and study 208
gender discrimination 387
gender equity 391–393
in American Methodism 58
influence on spiritual life 229
Methodist 209
Methodist Discipline 170
staying in cities 196
theological authority 165
view of in American Revolution
192
women as 385–393
leaving pastorate 389
nominating 392
resistance to 390
role of 387
senior leaders 389
underpaid 389
coaching 53
and leadership style 273–275
followers 262
of leaders 275
coercion 107–116
Coke, Thomas 58, 164, 193–199
collaboration
and org structure 284
and team environment 281
and transformational leadership
256–261
college(s)
Christian 152, 401
cultivating religious life 31
faculty 47
founded by Methodists 234
Holy Club / Oxford 165, 211
purpose of 37
seminary 136, 173–174, 341, 390
universities 144
commitment
and board leadership 401
and leadership work 17
leaders maintain 245

of followers 247, 252
of Wesley to Scripture 219, 220
organizational 252
religious 147
to basic practices 213
to bigger things 38, 213
to covenant 325
to discipline 200
to family 386
to God 49
to life of church 148
to mission or vision 23, 280–288
to team 275, 325
to woman's career 385
Wesley to formation 209–214
communicating
core beliefs 247
theology 370
vision 285
communication
two-way 246
communion 19, 208
with God 32, 148
with Holy Spirit 28
community
African-American 39
and cities 344
biblical view of 282–284
building in small groups 355–364
Christian 48, 227
church 39
church in city 348
covenant 310, 324
desire for 146–160, 259
ecclesial 145–149
and eunuch 310
experience of 20
of faith 222
God's call 356
high view 148
Holiness 52
human 47
leadership formed in 22
living in 223
role in spirituality 143

and Trinity 285
zeal for evangelism 262
compassion 146, 182
competence
and board members 403
and power 112
growth in 174, 335, 392
lack of 78, 318
leader effect on followers 252
leading with 252
of followers 279
of leader 243–247, 257, 293
relying on 293
conference
Christmas 193
General 168, 209
holy 210
Methodism 164
confidence
and authentic leadership 245
developing 393
follower lack of 271
in fallen human faculties 223
inspire in young leaders 147
in women leaders 392
conflict
and organization 281, 402
between husband and wife 124
between Jesus and disciples 100
cultural 22
female prophets in early church
124
healthy 325
in church 322
moral 250
over limited resources 379
political 192
strategic 22
with leader 280
Congregational Church 30
congregations 171
connection
and spiritual development 145
Methodist 171, 210
power of 171, 235

context
21st century 41
African-American 39
and leadership styles 273
ecclesial 143
high trust teams 274
hostile to Christian faith 50
immediate historical 123
in ministry 292
Korean-American 39
leadership effectiveness in 269
Mexican-American 40
national revival 191
non-religious 213
of church in North America 31
of conflict 22
of covenant 324
of ecclesial life 48
of leadership 189
of Spirit-led discernment 327
of success 276
of urban ministry 341
of Wesley 218
of worship 367
postmodern 35
transfer of leadership principles
267
urban 347, 351
work in existing 271
contingency leadership theory 18,
267–285
control
and management 169
and social environment 346
centralized in organization
190–193
desire for 146
giving up 285
in public arena 224
lack of in life 35
of desire and emotion 248
of spiritual disiplines 142
over world 342
own household 87
tension over 193

unrestrained 250
conversion
  as pardon 144
  in bands 185
  moral image 61–65
  of Wesley 180
  power model 95
  process of 229
corporations
  attacks on 35
cosmos
  created by God 51
  king of 112
courage
  and conflict 20
  and prudence 247
  creating accountability 325
  developing 393
  and ethical leadership 248–251
  moral 213
  of leaders 291
covenant
  Abraham & Abimalek 258
  and eunuch 310
  commitments of disciples 325
  community 310
  groups in church 351
  in Old Testament 76–79, 108–113
  ministers of new 85
  new 79
  people of 110
  relationship 328
  relationships 325
  with God 137
creation
  and city 344
  and innovation 261
  and reconciliation 338
  care for 49
  environment of transformation
    321
  God's design 47–51
  in Genesis 78
  leadership in 65
  "new" 58–65

of Caesar 95
of institutions 228
owned by Christ 403
theology of 48
creative 23, 77, 260–261, 321
  creativity 285
  generating solutions 327
  leadership and social good 23
  thinking 261
creativity 23, 164
  of methodologies 186
cross 97–106, 111–113
  and obedience 113
  at center of Kingdom 96
  of Jesus 100
crucifixion 95–98, 244
culture
  18th century Britian 217
  21st century 338
  accommodating to 234
  ancient 123
  ancient Israel 98, 132
  and pagan cults 260
  apathy 368
  church engaging 40
  Confucian 39
  definition of 23
  Hellenistic/Greek/Roman 84, 95,
    218
  individualistic, materialistic 143
  leaders as custodians 247
  live wisely in 80
  Methodist 45
  Mexican-American 40
  monetized 36
  moral 247
  North American 143
  of Evangelicalism 386
  of non-joiners 147
  of shared leadership 284
  of Wesley's time 225
  organizational 250, 252, 402
  pluralistic in America 223
  popular 191
  relativistic 247

religious U.S. 36
secular 403
theology of 47
therapeutic 38, 39
understanding of 209
utopian view 34
Value system 103
Western 142
world 128

D

David (King) 76–80, 111–113,
   132–138
and Bathsheba 249
anointed as king 132
as shepherd 88
family of 137
kingdom of 96
prayer of 404
and Spirit of the Lord 120
throne of 98, 100
deacon (New Testament) 85–87,
   122
decision-making
aided by Scripture 224
and boards 402–406
and prudence 248
bureaucracy in United Methodism
   168
cultural roles 39
difficult 409
and ethical leadership 246–251,
   378
flexibility 245
forming in orgs 305
give up 286
leader priorities 323
leader activities 334
moral 257
Moses delegating 261
of board 408
of David 250
of men 383
of women 383

purpose of leading 297–299
relying on academic training 102
and shared leadership
   283–286
decisions
budget 38
faulty 94
followers in 274
of a board 405
of women 390
personal, of clergy 390
poor 272
delegation 262
democracy
and federalism 192
danger of 78
democratizing 75
freedom under 222
skepticism of 218
democratic
early Methodism 194
leadership 194
democratization
and early Methodism 194
and power 78
impulse in Old Testament 78
denominations
congregationalists 171
evangelical 390
mainline survival mode 151
Wesleyan heritage 29
women as clergy 390–391
discernment 335
disciples
and Wesleyan leadership 171
character of 242
current 152
emulating 242
focus on making 321
leaders as 328
mission to make 323
obedience 99
of Jesus 84, 95–99, 103, 241,
   321–322
process of making 326. *See*

also discipleship
  spiritual leaders as 320
  washing feet 89
  in Wesleyan groups 22
discipleship
  accountability in 62
  authentic 323
  Christian 94
  early Wesleyan 321
  goal of 351
  and groups 356
  and holiness 53
  and leadership 19, 392
  leadership as 355
  leadership formation without 320
  mature 149
  means of 16
  methodical approach 19
  Wesleyan 19–22
disruption
  early Wesleyans as disruptors 29
  innovation (disruptive) 29
  speech in worship 125
  urbanization as 346
doctrine
  and bishop's role 194
  and Conference 211
  and love of God 28
  and theological understanding
    179–186
  effects of change on 45
  of church, Methodist 148
  of original sin 220
  of salvation 58–65
  pastoral commitment to 210
  purpose/importance of 164,
    225–229

E

ecclesial
  ambiguity 148
  community 145
  formation 143
  form of goverment 193
  forms of life 148
  leadership focus 49
  life, view of 48
  orphans or homeless 150
  spirituality 149
  structure 192
  theology and spirituality 143
  Wesleyan leaders 148
  Wesleyan life 48
ecclesiology
  of Wesley 148
  theological 148
  Wesleyan 48
education
  acces of women 128
  access to 52
  and discipline 210
  and Wesley's writings 23
  churches providing 393
  for poor 182
  goals for improving 260
  higher 58, 165, 234
  increase in 23
  lack of equity 260
  leader expectations 209
  leadership trait theory 18
  low-quality 40
  of leaders 58
  of preachers 183, 232
  purpose of 37
  theological 46, 172
  values by community 18
  variety in church 371
effectiveness
  and communication 365
  and education 183, 208
  and fidelity 165
  being effective 163
  board leadership 401–416
  of decisions 336
  definition of 335
  engaging culture 33–41
  of God (Yahweh) 110
  God's measure of 410
  individual 210, 281

in leading groups 355–364
and integrity 335
of Jesus 337
of leader 103, 167, 195, 208, 247, 292–302, 317
and leadership style 242, 256, 268–270
leadership 28, 107–118, 195
  and paradox 107
and management 165–174
men vs women 386
of mission 404
and obedience 113
of followers 279–290
of Wesley 183–186
of organization 191, 281
of programs 231
and purpose 296, 350
role of episcopacy 165, 191
and servant leadership 334–338
team 252
and transformational leadership 262
and vision 323–327, 350–354
efficiency
  and value of people 317
  in health care 37
  and servanthood 338
emotional intelligence 273
  in idealized influence 257
emperor worship 260
employees
  and board leadership 401–416
  of church 48
  future pool and education 37
  happiness of 259
  and transformational leadership 255–266
  treatment by CEO 409
  under-productive 255
empowering
  creative thinking (Moses) 261
  followers 267
  for integrity 61
  for new communities 61–65

empowerment
  divine 164
  and employee success 259
  of the Holy Spirit 65, 152, 306, 323, 410
  and human flourishing 223
  in community 223
  means of Wesley 23, 230
  of CEO 409
  of followers 261, 282
  of Jesus through prayer 103
  and sanctification 24
  task of leader 271
  to flourish 230
  to serve neighbor 61
episcopacy
  Anglican 164
  managerial 165
  Methodist 164
  monarchial 165
  pastoral 165
Episcopal Church 165
eschatological
  event 98
  key event 102
  theme of leadership 88
  view of Wesley 61–64
  vision 64
ethics
  and leadership 380
  of Kingdom 108–118
  rule-based 268
  scandals 243
  subject of study by pastors 232
Eucharist / Communion 61, 184, 212
  high view 148–152
evangelical
  church 99
  denominations or traditions 151, 390
  faith experience 101
  movement 50
  point of view 173
evangelism

father of 190
exaltation 112
  and servant 113
  of Christ 63
  of Jesus 65

F

failing 177
failure
  ethical 249–250
  fear of 146
  focused on 251
  moral 339
  moral 246–250
  of institution 226
  of institutions 227
  supporting slavery 40
faithfulness 38, 214, 311
  of God 132
fear 145–150, 402
  and courage 248
  dealing with 406
  incentive 116
  of failing 146
  of prosperity 183
  of uprising in community 387
feedback 246, 272
  and follower growth 262
  follower about leader 287, 299
  organizational 246
  performance 284
  seeking out 245
  soliciting 252
finances
  contributions 85
  factors 410
  gifts 85
  loans for relief 231
  misconduct 226
  obligations to preachers 197
  reports 166
  resources 86
  responsibility 183
firing 305, 407

followers 19, 103, 144, 242–246,
    256–263, 271–275, 409
  development of 275, 276
  empowerment of 267
  expectations 250
  focus on needs 263
  followership 19, 263
  independent 285
  interaction with leaders 257
  love of Christ in 116
  mature 348
  motivating 262
  motivation of 259
  next step for 214
  of Jesus Christ 96–104, 208, 223,
      244, 311
  of Moses 261
  of Spirit 321
  of Wesley 148
  perception of leader 247
  perception of leadership 292
  relationship with leaders 244, 318
  respect of 244
  specific direction for 297
  wrong incentive 116
followership 16, 283–288, 304
follow God 131
Follow me 163
forgiveness
  declared by priest 101
formation 24, 61, 146, 191, 212,
    229. *See* sanctification
  and cell groups 235
  by grace 208
  Christian 228, 230
  foundational 143
  leadership 61, 320
  nurture of Christian 233
  of a leader 337
  of character 37
  of congregation 38
  of leaders 62
  of others 147
  personal 65
  spiritual 38, 142, 143, 144, 145,

146, 148, 152, 209, 262, 325
spiritual, of leaders 144
spiritual program 229
Wesleyan 145
freedom 88, 190–191, 404
  charismatic 148
  impulses of human 190
  of being shepherded 134
  of followers 116
  religious 195
  under democracy and monarchy
    222
Free Methodist Church 150–151
future 108, 172, 260, 328
  concern for 387
  messianic 96
  of churches 31
  of Methodism 167
  of Wesleyan leadership 318
  outcomes 245
  predicting 74
  priority of 321
  shaping 24

G

gender 384–400
  and job segregation 391
  and leadership 312, 386
  and performance 303
  differences in 121
  discrimination 383–385
  male and job attainment 389
  specific roles 304
  studies 304
gender differentiation 305
General Conference 170
Gentile 260, 311
gifts 124, 212
  leadership 209
  of Holy Spirit 62
  of leaders 58–65
  of Spirit 89
  oratorical 372
  spiritual 53, 284

Gnosticism 63
goals 17–18, 37, 47, 142, 168, 245,
    402
  concern of leadership 19
  of group 281
  of leadership 65
  organizational 259–263
  shared 282–284
gospel 38–40, 172–173
  hope of 35
  how people view it 402
  and Jesus as Leader 79
  John 3:!6 51
  and Paul's work 122
  and preaching 30, 210
  proclamation of 90, 366
  propserity 38
  pseudo 100
  Wesley preaching 180
Gospels 19
  of Mark 96–106
government 58, 190, 347
  attack on 35
grace 58–59, 191
  ability to renew 60
  divine 61–65
  divine redeeming 62
  justifying grace 59, 326
  optimistic view of 292
  overcoming depravity 369
  prevenient 59, 220
  prevenient grace 59
  sanctifying 59–60
  saving 144, 180
  Wesleyan view of 164
greatness
  and servanthood 108
  redefining 86–90

H

Hellenism 84–88, 260
heritage
  family 178
  historical 30

squandering 150
of Wesleyan theology 164, 201
hiring
CEO and boards 407–410
and gender differentiation 305
practices of men and women
386–389
holiness
a life of 88
attribute of God 108
as objective of conversion 183
cultivating 53
Francis Asbury 196–201
growth in 22, 208, 212, 213
leader life of 86
and leadership 116
leadership perspectives 48
life of 90, 179
modeled by leaders 372
and moral image 60
movement 50–52
multi-sphere framework 50
need to learn 227
and obedience 200
of God 108
of heart and life 186, 212, 229
and ontology 109
personal growth in 19
and preaching 374
priestly 75
reclaim 201
scriptural 170, 173, 211
and shepherds 88–90
social 324
and Spirit 208
and spiritual formation 142–152
spread of 164, 193, 213, 225, 229
synonyms of 372
and vocation 53
Wesley's bands 211–212
holy 109, 201, 214, 369, 370
and power 116
conferencing 210
friendship 227
living 131, 152

love 61, 62, 65, 324, 326
love and power 61
nation 75, 108
paradox of power 111
people 52
priest 79
vocation 144
Holy Spirit
baptism 102. See also baptism, of
Jesus
descent on Jesus 102
and empowerment 323, 410
gifts 89
gives insight 361
and grace 59
in leaders 115
leaders filled with 85
and leadership 65
leadership gift 58
leadership of 323
leaders in step with 28, 321
led by 326
listening to 145
partnership with 357
and Pentecost 120
power of 46, 152, 172, 320
role 307
sanctifying work 39
transformation 60, 101, 322
working through people 322
work of 306
home
leadership in 120
homiletics 369–373
homo unius libri 214, 219
hospitality 241
toward Jesus 84
hospitals 23, 58, 234
hubris 243–247, 401, 408
and omnipotence 249
human interaction 47–53
human reason 35, 218–221, 317
human resources 102
humiliation 90, 312
of Christ 87

humility 322, 404
  and self-control 248
  Christian leaders 245
  and elders 87–90
  epistemic 245
  imitating Christ 195–201. *See also* Asbury, Francis
  in leadership 62
  life of 90
  of Jesus 103
  of leader 287
  personal 374
  and power 107–114

I

identity 143–144, 150, 247
  and group consensus 297
  ethnic 45
  experimentation with 147
  of church 348
  of leader 335
  of organization 247
  of the church 349
  performance based 339
  preserving Christian 234
  with common people 182
imagination 250
  human 224
  moral 243
    of leader 250
  theological 228
imago dei 60–65, 280, 318, 404
  male and female 74
  renewal of 65
imitation of Christ 189, 201
Incarnation 167–172
individual consideration 263
individualism 142–148
  expressive 38
  romanticization of 227
influence 24, 95, 184, 189, 212, 257, 347–351
  and faith tradition 18
  and innocence 107, 108

  as leadership 18
  bishop and laity 194
  circles of 259
  desire for 146
  idealized 258
  idealized 263
  idealized 257, 263
  leadership more than 270
  negative 251
  of atheism 36
  of consecration 200
  of culture 38
  of leader and trust 116
  of Methodism 183
  therapeutic 38
  wielding 249
initiative 274
innovation 29, 148
  changes for evangelism 29
  disruptive 29
  disruptive in churches 29
  innovative 230
  sustaining in churches 29
  traditioned 234
innovative 23
  business and Wesleyan 58
  practices in health care 236
  strategies of Holy Spirit 102
  thinking 261
  Wesley and bands 233
  work 261
insecurity 146
institutions 225–238
integrity 46, 136–139, 186, 214, 243, 352, 372, 404
  and effectiveness 335
  behavioral 243
  biblical 214
  empowered for 61
  lesson of personal 185
  moral 247
  of heart 131, 132
  personal 52
intellectual stimulation 259, 259–263

itinerancy 192–196

J

Jesus Christ 83–89
  ascension of 304, 307
  as Good Shepherd 136
  as greatest leader 337
  as King 98
  as Lord 174, 222
  baptism of 100
  birth of 89, 110
  blood of 126
  call of 99–103
  came to save 51
  confess as Messiah 71
  conformed to the image of 355
  death of 98, 309
  exaltation of 63, 65
  faith in 59
  following 95
  having the mind of 200
  in wilderness 102
  life of 83
  mind of 242
  mission of 94
  model as leader 108
  model of 96
  movements (in history) 319–320
  obedience of 102
  people of 320
  personal relationship with 61
  prophecies about 259
  reveals God's love 28
  self-awareness 244
  share in suffering 90
  Spirit of 128
  story of 100
  temptation of 146
  title for 96
  transfiguration of 256
  values of 326
  voice of 105
  words of 104
job satisfaction 252

Judaism 260
  converts to 102
judge(s) 75–76, 263
  Moses as 261
justice 49, 58, 75, 80, 132, 247, 348
  and prudence 247
  and virtue 248
  causes for 144
  social 146

K

kenosis 195, 337
king
  holy rule 108
  slave as 111
kingdom 87, 256–258
  ancient 133
  ethics of 116
  lost by Rehoboam 138
  of Christ 51
  of David 79, 96, 250
  of priests 75
  of Saul 135, 249
  of Solomon 76
  of the world 146
  revelation of 104
Kingdom of God 18, 58–65, 79,
    94–99, 107, 112, 135, 145,
    167–171, 220, 297, 326,
    348–349, 356, 372
  mystery of 100
  subordination of women 128
king(s) 76–77, 111
  authority like 199
  David 250
  none in Israel 76
know thyself 243

L

laity 29
  theological authority 165
lamb 312
leader(s)
  adaptive spiritual 323

as bishop 86
as deacon 84
as shepherd 139
authentic 243–252
bad 131
Christian 252
church
  Timothy 263
ethical 252
relationship with followers 244
skills of 335
suffering 309
transformational 263
leadership
activities of 334
adaptive (spiritual) 319–335
alternative structures 392
and groups 163
as (spiritual) gift(s) 258
authentic 18, 109, 243–244
biblical 114, 201
of board 401–402
of Caesar 94
calling 46
CEO model 151
charismatic 151, 280
Christian 47–53, 57–65, 94, 100,
    144, 172, 178, 189, 280
Christlike 320
church 40, 165, 201, 351
college administrative 47
complexity theory in 319
as congregational caregiving 174
congregational, in society 35
contemporary church 166
contemporary models 200
context of the city 344
contingency theory 267–276
decisions 94
define reality 268
definition of 16, 171, 256, 291,
    347
democratic 272–274
denominational 388
development 21, 142

development by Wesley 184
differentiation 300
and discipleship 392
effective 28, 107, 269–270, 280,
    335
effective board 401
effective style of 270
ethical 243–247, 380
  definition 246
evaluating 284
exemplary 83
failures of 132
formation 61
forms of 71
formula for 225
and gender 312
as (spiritual) gift(s) 58–65
Great Man theory 18
health of 138
of Holy Spirit 322
holy (holiness) 108–110, 116, 201
implications for 101
in early Methodism 190
in New Testament 90
in Old Testament 80, 132
in Wesleyan system 185
isolation of 317
of Jesus Christ 96
laissez-faire 257
male as norm 123, 387
and management 168
and Messiah 107–118
mimetic 195
of mission 164
model(s) 107–115, 151, 166, 207
  new 96
  of Wesley 186
multi-cultural 20
multi-sphere 49
norms of 391
obstacles to women 125, 384
of board 411
organizational 306–312
pace-setting 275
paradigm 112, 201

paradox 78, 107–111, 241
pastoral 166
pastoral functions 387
patterns of 47–53
perspectives on 48
pleasing to God 134
political 46
practical, of Wesley 164
practice of 178
preparation for ministry 163
principles from business 102
process of 319
of prophets 74
public 46–53
purpose of 65
qualities and women 386
qualities of 177, 195–206
respect for 39
responsibility of 17
responsible 243
rises and falls on 131
role in creation 64
role of 24
of Saul (King) 248
Scriptural examples 255
senior positions and women 387
servant 18, 243, 262, 283, 339
  as style 338
shared 274, 282–290, 328
spiritual 18, 78, 243, 322
steward theory 404
style 269–274, 334–335
success of Wesley 186
and suffering 196
sustaining 293
as a system 283
team 325
temptations in 173
theology of 49, 59, 195
theory 177, 280, 318
top down approach 280
transactional 255–257
transformation. See transforma-
    tional leadership
and urban environment 349

vision of 49
warped by Fall 78
of Wesley 185, 228
Wesleyan 16, 20, 22, 24, 57, 58,
    77, 90, 109, 119, 170, 171,
    201, 208, 214, 320, 328
  future 326
  future of 318
  without management 168
  women attaining parity 383
  women in 123, 124, 128
lead(ing)
  from below 87, 89
  institutions 236
  learning to 147
learning
  lifelong 209
listening 17
liturgical 148–151
liturgy 151, 164
lordship 19
love
  and influence 116
  and leader's perception 24
  and power 107, 116
  and sanctification 24
  and service to another 84
  and taking risks 24
  empatheti 369
  for followers 281
  for God 32, 99
  for God's work 374
  God's for world 51
  governs leadership 149
  holiness 183
  holy 61, 62, 324, 326
  Holy 62
  leadership rooted in 20
  of Christ 116, 210
  of enemies 221
  of God 28, 30, 149, 221, 403
  of God and neighbor 60, 65, 142,
      144, 145, 212, 221, 223
  of God for you 373
  of God, neighbor 144

of institutions 228
of mother 48
of neighbor 61, 208
of possessions 199
of the world 51
perfect 321, 369, 373
personal 374
self-giving 115
Self-sacrificial 318
showing to people 197
yielding in 200
love for God 349
love of God 113

M

male
    priesthood limited to 74
management 168, 261, 334
    and leadership 168
    business 172
    lack of 247
    of growth 229
    pastoral 166
    role of 168
    time 210
manager 231
    in church 167
    moral 247
    moral, of organization 246
    parable of 242
    the ideal 304
managerial 48
    role 304
marketing 53, 151
    and mystery in churches 151
marriage 38
    in 1 Timothy 127
    ritual of 150
means of grace 61–65, 143–152,
        164, 200, 208–212
    and healing 142
men of Issachar 242
mental illness 346
messiah 71, 95–97, 142

Jesus as 110, 113
power of 116
Methodism / Methodist(s) 45–48,
        148, 167–172, 177, 189–190,
        211–214, 229
    African-American 233
    American Revolution 192
    as microcosm of America 193
    becoming 210
    bishops 165
    Conference 190
    congregation calling pastor 173
    culture 45
    discipline 200
    early American 164, 171, 190–194
    early movement 29
    episcopal organization 193
    growth under Asbury 191
    in colonial America 182, 211
    largest denomination 191
    organization of movement 229
    origins 148
    people called 228
    preachers 164
    renewal movement 228–230
    revival 169
    system 214
    traits 208
    United Methodist 171
Methodist Church 48
Methodist Episcopal Church
        190–206
ministry 41, 85, 121, 166, 173,
        177–178, 263, 307, 347–351,
        362, 410
    and leadership 94
    approach to 166
    campus 211
    career development 388
    of Christ 99
    church 134
    of clergy 373
    effective pastoral 167
    husband and wife in 124
    initiatives of service 36

of Jesus 102, 346
of laity 165
practical 150
of preaching 197, 373
preparation for 163, 232
roles 120–122
sent 167
sharing workload 392
traditional jobs for women 392
urban 341–348
of Wesley 180, 217
Wesley's approach 179
women in 119–128, 392
youth 234
missio Dei 164–165, 318
mission 38, 99, 151, 172, 209,
        212–213, 263, 351, 401
Christian 122
of church 169–170, 311, 348, 362
cities as mission fields 341
clarity of 179
commitment to 23
of God 113, 318, 366
of Jesus 100–104
of organization 249, 280, 285
pay attention to 295
of serving 362
to serve 23
of Wesley's network 225
missions 58
modeling 321–323
and spiritual leadership 322
core beliefs 247
leadership and Christlikeness 328
leadership of Spirit 322
of transparency 244
models 19, 108–109, 211
business 151
leadership 166
mental 250–251
of leadership 207, 325
Old Testament 72
regression 389
traditional hierarchical 392
models of church 351

monarchy 73–76, 107
and early Methodism 194
British 218
British tensions 192
freedom under 222
moral 60–62, 74–79, 131, 366
chaos 171
character of leader 189
conduct 246
conscience 59
failure 136
failures 246–250
fortitude 409
foundation 190
image of God 60–65
imagination 243, 250
order of community 386
paradigm 61
renewal 61
transformation 191
values 247
morality
internalized 244
lack of 243
Moral Therapeutic Deism 366
Moses 74–79, 88, 132, 247, 261
and law 74
motivation 257, 258, 262
inspirational 258, 263
inspirational 259
of followers 259
of leaders 247
motives 251
of disciples 99
of leader 146
of leaders 200

N

networks 225

O

obedience 61, 76, 112, 195
and effectiveness 108
and holiness 109, 200

of Christ 200
of disciples 99
of Jesus 114
response 136
response of people 348
to God 60, 404
occupation 144
of shepherd 133
office
of clergy 373
of deacon 84–85
of king 109
loneliness of 199
New Testament leadership 77
privilege of 199
of shepherd 89
optimism 35, 58, 245, 370
and grace 59
in technology 34
needed by leaders 271
of grace 60, 369
unrealistic 249
organizational 319, 390
and episcopacy 193
barriers to women 388
behavior 304
chart 270
climbing the ladder 391
cohesion 183
consistency 168
direction 280
feedback 246
functions 387
gatekeepers 388
genius of Methodism 192
genius of Wesley 169
goals 259, 263
imbalance 379
issues 260
leaders 402
leadership 304, 312, 384, 403
of Wesley 24
leadership categories 387
leadership insights 305
life 195

mission 285
networks 305
norms 391
people in 378
performance objectives 336
policies 409
poor structures 401
pressure 293
resources 250
role 304
shifts 211
solutions 262
stakeholders and CEO 406
structure 169, 247, 255, 261
systems 384
teams 402
tension 325
top-down mandates 385
transformation 168
organizations 29, 252, 256, 268–
269, 384, 401–402
adaptive archetypes 327
challenges and gender 304
Christian 402
collaborative partnerships 283
divine grace in 213
early Methodism 189
follower contribution 279
and innovation 402
interests of 250
mentors in 388
mission of 249
non-profit 377, 401
startups 284
outcomes and leadership 336–338

P

Palestine 94
paradigm 19, 61, 404
leadership 112, 201
of personal fulfillment 38
paradox 151, 191–192
Methodism as 194
of leadership 111

of leadership in Old Testament 78
of power and holiness 110–116
of servant 111
serpents and doves 241
strength and weakness 107
parish
and church 30
cosmic 53
leadership of 373
pastor 173
world. *See* world as parish
pastor(s) 36, 38, 48, 53, 166, 168,
    173, 174, 390, 391
African-American 40
definition of 165
Mexican-American 40
transformational 262
Wesleyan 41, 164
pattern recognition 251
Paul 85–89, 114, 121–128, 214,
    242–251, 256–263, 321, 343,
    361, 370, 405, 412
1 Timothy 127
imitating Christ 195
pay attention 38, 103, 292–300
pay (compensation)
differentiation in 305
full-time jobs 388
lower 383
of clergywomen 390
perfection in love 32
personality 250, 268
of leader 195
of leaders 267
trait theory 257
planning 166–168
policies
and boards 408
men mentoring women 388
political leadership
    46, 192, 217–219
politics / political
alliances 112
and Christendom 79
conflict 192

decision 217
image 60–63
in early America 192
influences and boards 405
and leadership 62
parties 192
renewal of image 61
socio-political activism 47–50
sphere 59
sum of life 223
theocracy 79
poor 23, 64, 182, 196, 370
and health care 233
as unifying 30
education for 182
generosity towards 184
in England 367
in Wesleyan movement 30
ministry to 368
social challenges 171
supporting 210
populism 194
power 19–24, 58, 77–79, 87–89,
    95–96, 132, 194–201, 268,
    280, 291, 322, 371
abuse of 76, 249, 250
alienation and cities 346
balance of 284
biblical concept 116
of bishop 189, 193, 194, 199
and boards 408
of Christian preaching 370
in churches 393
concentrated 193
continuum 274
creative 286
of the Cross 220
decision-making 286
definition of 115
distribution of 272, 403
divine 152
and doctrine 28
free from sin 24
of God 24, 108, 111, 114, 164,
    236, 311

of God in world 59
of godliness 229
of Gospel 62
to govern 60
of grace 63
high power index 274
holy 110, 116
of Holy Spirit 46, 172, 320
human 97, 107, 112
of instutitions 232
of Israel's leaders 133
of king and servant 111
leadership defined as 256
loss of spiritual 28
lost by church 30
low power index 274
model of conversion 95
over others 146
paradigms of 221
personal desire for 199
in preaching 365
preventing absolute 78
redefining 108
of relationships 285
releasing to others 287
of Rome 97
of a servant 334
sharing of / shared 282–286
as social value 195
social 312
in society 35
spiritual 149
supervisory 305
and temptation 250
usurping CEO 407
wage earning 37
and weakness 112, 116
of Wesleyan tradition 31
power-distance 270–275
practical divinity 164–176, 232
and Wesley 169
Wesleyan theology 148
pragmatic/pragmatism 46, 164–
165, 179–181, 213, 333
prayer

and strategic solutions 327
answer to 132
contemplative 144
of Jesus 51
means of grace 61, 212
relational experience 145
start of day 292
time spent in 374
Wesley's model 208
Wesley's small groups 229
preachers
Anglican ordaining Wesley's 181
appointed by bishop 198
bishops appointing 193
commissioning of lay 78
demands on 197
early American Methodism 200
early Methodist education 183
electing bishop 197
examination of 209
gathering at Conference 170
itinerant 194
lay 180, 194, 211, 214
listening to congregation 371
local 194
Methodist 164
ordained by Asbury 191
as pastors 170
preparing sermon 372
Reformed 369
requirements of 221
revivalist 228
taught to model holiness 372
theological development and
books 183
urban and poor 197
in Wesley's time 366
Wesley's charge to 28
women as 181
preaching
on the circuit 194
communication in 365
field (and Methodism) 29–30,
179–180, 214, 228–229
of gospel 85

grounded in theology 366
and holiness 372
impact of 210
importance of 232, 367
and mentoring 209
ministry 197, 373
motives for 372
of Paul 85
pastoral work 166–173, 387
pathos in 368–371
of Philip in Samaria 306
and religious societies 230
as act of serving 84
skills for 372
Spirit-filled 85
temptation in 369
the gospel 173
of Wesley 177, 368
Wesleyan 370–371
Wesley's ethos 372
predestination 220
priesthood 73–78
heriditary 76
priests 75–80, 108
kingdom of 75
privilege 199–201, 312
of bishop 189
and leadership 195
of roles 311
and temptation 250
problem solving 260
process
choosing leadership roles 85
decision-making 168
of developing sermon 367
of experience 250
of formation 146
goal of leadership 17–18
growth 325
homiletic 370–372
of homiletics 373
interdependent 282
of leadership 319
leadership as 256
learning 321–325, 328

of ordination 209
organizational 280
organizational leadership 318
of spiritual formation 144, 145
profit 255
prophet 71–77, 107, 132–135
par excellence 74
Samuel 135
purity 75, 200
of doctrine 179
of heart 115, 201
personal 374
and sin 108

R

rationalistic atheism 35–36
reading Scripture 164, 185
reconciliation 62, 337, 349
of creation and society 63
work of in humanity 64
redemption 58, 107–108
and obedience 112
biblical story of 356
of city 344
of created order 65
of political image 62
Wesleyan theology of / understanding 59
relationship(s)
of accountability 65, 246
covenant 256, 325–328
cultivating 144–147
disposition in 198
family 47–48
goal of leadership 17–18
goals 19
and grace 322
healthy 138, 183, 256, 356
interpersonal 246–249, 285
and kingdom of God 63
and leader vulnerability 197
of leaders and followers 244
leadership 268–274
shared 282

leadership and Old Testament 138
monetizing 38
politics and society 219
small groups 362
social and cities 346
social media 34
stewarding 212
transformational 263
trust in 243
and urban ministry 347–351
repentance 38, 99, 136, 144, 180, 259
resilience 245
of spirit 28
resources 48–49, 57, 143, 152, 172, 252, 343
of church 170
collection of 85
distribution of 84
of grace 150
intellectual 143
of kingdom 102, 250
maintaining church 173
managing, of organization 404
organiational 250
spiritual 46
theological 143
responsibility 390, 411
abdicating by leader 274
avoiding 147
of board 408
building in others 103
of counseling 38
difference between leading and following 282
evading 167
family 183
for mission 409
giving up 286–287
group handling of 272
highest level of 214
and injustice 40
of leader 17
and leadership 296

listening to feedback 313
to others 379
of pastor 173
personal 144
priest and king 74
rewarding 275
sharing of (leadership) 282–286
of shepherd 136
and stewardship 404
and supporting families 389
resurrection 63–65, 95, 104, 122, 142
revelation
general 59, 97, 111, 218–224
new 105
of kingdom 104
risk 241, 255, 286, 380
aversion to 385
in democratic leadership 272
and management 169
rituals. See also sacraments, sacred
role models
leaders as 16
role(s)
of Aaron 75
of accountability 184
and privilege 311
as king 137
of bishop 189
of church 143, 147
of clergywomen 387
of leader 258, 283
leadership 347
of leadership 24
of Methodism 190
ministry 120–122
models 246
priestly 77
of Spirit 307
spiritual leadership 78
of women 123
women 73
Roman 77, 95–98, 272
culture 218
ruler 132

S

sacraments / sacramental 150–152, 387
  life 152
  mediated grace 150
  practices 152
  view of baptism 150
sacred
  life 152
  rituals 150
sacrificial 292
  sheep 310
salvation 50, 58–61, 142, 180, 207–211, 229, 367
  beginning of 97
  doctrine of 58
  full 208
  through faith 180
  work of God 366
sanctification 60–65, 142–145, 200, 208, 229, 259, 366–367
  and love 24
  and obedience 200
  perfection 24, 61, 136, 169, 369
  sanctifying grace 59–60, 326
sanctified
  life 164
Saul 134
school(s) 143–152, 181, 232, 341, 402–405
  building funds 182
  Christian 401
  founded by Wesley 182
  purpose of 37
  urban and equity 260
  Wesleyans established 23
Scripture
  Wesley's approach 119
Second Great Awakening 191
self-awareness 244–245, 293, 405
self-centered 147, 339
  formation 143
self-confidence 274, 287, 386
self-control 225, 274, 294

self-discipline 243
self-efficacy 246, 294
self-emptying 244
self-esteem 246
  low 38
self-identity 250
self-initiative 280
self-interest 111, 144, 201, 218–223, 244–251, 256, 281, 404–405
self-knowledge 245–246, 252
self-managers 280
self-reference 336
self-regulating 296
self-sacrifice 38, 83–89, 196, 318
self-serving 220
  institutional leaders 226
self-will 79
seminary
  graduates and preparation 163
sense-making 18
sermons 164
servant 84, 111, 132, 195–196
  call to be 334
  leadership 262
  Messiah as 116
  nature as 338
  posture of 86
  power of 112
  preacher as 197
  suffering 308
  the nature of 243
  and Yahweh 113
servanthood 79, 111, 201, 348
  and greatness 108
servant leadership 339
serve/serving
  in Acts 85–89
  called to 292
  desire to 96
  followers 83
  God 78, 79, 173
  as a group 362
  institutions 226
  Jesus' role 89
  leader behaviors 18

leadership and desire 19
a meal 84
as mediators 73
as pastor 169
people 336
people being equipped 356
as priests 77
tables 84
the common good 37
underserved groups 29–32
widows and orphans 90
service
attitude of 348
business as 53
a call to 197
and Christian character 208–212
to God 19, 411
of Jesus 337
leader's posture 197
in New Testament 84–88
to our people 352
public 185
value of 402
in Wesleyan system 200
shadow
side of leadership 243
shame 98, 311
in Kingdom 96
of cross 97
of Eve's gullibility 128
social 96
sheep 89
care for 89
disciples as 241
sacrificial 310
shepherd 21, 72, 84, 87, 211
as leader 139
Chief 88
Good Shepherd 89, 90, 134, 136
leader as 88
like David 89
shepherding 72, 86, 89, 90
metaphor 88
sin 38, 51, 60, 61, 64, 149, 227, 390
human 108

human nature 218
in Wesleyan theology 62
leaders in Bible 134
of David 135
of Eve 126
original 77, 218, 220
pervades all life 220
purity from 108
removed stain of 128
victory over 200
skills
mastery of 335
slavery 22
social
disorganization 346
entrepreneurship 23
injustice/justice 50, 144, 182
status 37
Son of God 95–99
Caesar 96
soteriology 58–59
Wesleyan 63
Spirit-filled life 200
spiritual development 146
spiritual disciplines 65, 142–152,
192, 373
formed by 65
spirituality
consumer 148
ecclesial 149
generic 28
and means of grace 143
personal 46, 48, 49
practice of 148
sanctificationist 171
two halves of 142–152
of Wesleyan preacher 373
Wesleyan 49, 143
workplace 319
spiritual maturity 143
staff
church 172
Stephen (Acts) 84–88, 306
stewardship 60, 208–212, 348–349,
402–404

Adam and Eve 356
and board leaders 411
of creation 58, 64
strategic 391
pursuit of mission 285
strategic planning 285, 334
submission 107, 113, 212
of Jesus to cross 103
to the Law 126
successor
David of Saul 135
suffering 64, 96, 145, 197–200, 234, 312
empathize with 87
and Jesus 87
in Kingdom 96
and leadership 196
of leader 309
of Messiah 96–100
Sunday School 29
symbol 150–151, 151
leader as 321
synagogue 260
system 78, 214, 268, 322, 390
capitalism 218
class 184
cultural value 103
diagnosing 327
disciplined life 200
of education 37
franchises 37
of itinerancy 194
kinship 346
new value 98
of small groups 183
social power 35
structured connectivity 183
of unbelief 35
value 201, 366
Wesleyan accountability 185

T

talents
parable of 147

teachers 89
false 127
teaching
purpose of 164
team(s)
and democratic leadership 274
dysfunction 325
of followers 280
temptation
of Jesus 146
Testament, New 77, 85–88, 110–113, 119–129, 138, 256, 284, 298, 311, 326, 358
model of leadership 83
Testament, Old 71–79, 99, 120–129, 131–138, 219, 310
leadership in 132
theological 28, 48, 57, 76, 148, 172
assumptions 123
claim for clergy 165
communicating 370
conflict 22
dogma 272
ecclesiology 148
education 46
heirs of Wesley 63
heritage of Wesley 30
ideas of Wesleyanism 165
imagination 228
language 367
leadership 195
basis for women in 393
framework for 195
perspective on 189
principle 45
promised of liberalism 101
themes in Isaiah 108
training
and preachers 292
lack of formal 183
worldview 142, 144
theology
and Asbury's leadership 195
and Wesleyan preaching 365–370
biblical 101, 119

of city 348
complementarian and gender 385
of creation 48
and culture 214
definition of 344
ecclesial 143
egalitarian and gender 385
formulating biblical 127
of hope 191
and leadership 19, 57–62, 71, 94,
    195
  political 219–223
of leadership 57–58
of culture 47
 of personal spirituality 49
of redemption 59
of the Spirit 102
orthodox Christian 164
and politics. *See* political leader-
    ship
practical 164, 179
preaching grounded in 366
preference for men as pastors 387
Reformed 59
related to women 126
sacramental 149–150
Wesleyan 62–65, 143–152, 164,
    369
Wesleyan and relationships 285
Wesley's approach 179
theory
  agency 255
  communication 365
  complexity 319
  contingency 18, 276
  ethical leadership 247
  family systems 293
  leadership 96, 177, 255–256
  purpose of 404
  queue 389
  self-differentiation 294
  transformational leadership 22,
      257
  urban life 345
  women in ministry 122

tradition 145, 369
  Anglican 170
  Christian 208–209
  class meeting 233
  family of Wesley 178
  Methodist 165
  Non-Conformist 178
  of learning 20
  of "warmed heart" 28
  of wisdom 72
  peacemaking 50
  religious 36
  Wesleyan 38–41, 50, 57, 120,
      143–152, 164, 228
training
  Biblical 209
transfiguration of Jesus Christ 104
transformation 256, 261, 321–326,
    334, 362, 404
transformational leadership 22,
    243, 256–263, 280–281
Trinity 167, 285, 320–321, 366–367
trust 64, 152, 212, 252, 325, 372,
    410
  affirmation of 227
  betrayal of 226, 250
  build 285
  building 244
  creating 287
  destroying 407
  earning 196
  earning of followers 258
  environment of 323
  following people 116
  in God 110, 113, 131
  in Holy Spirit 322
  importance of 325
  and influence 116
  and office of leader 193
  of followers 252
  placed in God 87

U

United Methodist Church 167, 168,

171, 172
Discipline 165
United Methodist Discipline 170
urban 341–354
    church(es) 41, 197
    context 341
    development of society 345
    nations 345
    setting 172
    settings in the Bible 347
    urbanized 343
    world 344, 349
urban centers 194
urban ministry 348–349, 349

V

values 243, 251
    challenging 319
    of Christian leaders 243
    of Christ's life 195
    clash of 402
    core 244, 247, 272, 401
    counter-Christian 320
    critical 246
    cultural 36, 250
    of early Methodism 30
    guided by 243
    moral 247
    of other cultures 218
    of Scripture 51, 223
    in tension 406, 408
virtue
    cultivation of 248
vision 48–49, 75, 168, 274–275,
        280, 318, 393, 401
    of Bible 77
    casting 334
    casting of 247
    of Christian leadership 65
    of church 174
    for city 344
    co-creators of 285
    commitment to 274, 282
    and direction 138

disciple-making 325
    eschatalogical 64
    for future 272
    of God's reign 28
    of groups 326
    of Isaiah 107, 109
    of leadership 49
    loss of 138
    of Methodism 28
    of organization 280
    of renewal 212
    of society 63, 65
    for public leadership 46
    sharing ownership 285
vocation 108, 143–147, 166, 336
    and calling 338
    and holiness 53
    discovering 142
    holy 109–112, 144

W

weakness 87, 107, 110, 112, 113,
        139
    and poiwer 116
    and power 108, 116
    and strength 107
    physical 111
Wesley
    Charles 19, 58, 164, 182, 211, 228
    John
        advancing Kingdom 58
        among the poor 367
        and image of God 63
        approach to evangelism 183
        and Calvinism 22, 71
        and contemplation 144
        as a disruptor 29
        embody discipleship 320
        engaging culture 40
        fear for Methodism 30
        field preaching 30, 173
        and holiness 170
        and image of God 60
        interpretive method 119

leading like 186
leading revival 169
and medicine 231
objection to bishops 165
organizational genius 169
organizing small groups 230
passion for humanity 28
as politician 217
and the Puritans 20
raising money 185
social holiness 324
spiritual sensitivity 291
and theology of grace 322
Wesleyan
accountability 185
activism 50
as anti-intellectual 165
bands 23, 38, 148, 169, 184–185,
191, 212, 233, 358
challenges for leaders 148
churches and schools 143
class meetings 21–22, 324
conviction 201
early movement 225, 320
ecclesial leaders 148
formation 145
future of movement 324
genius of movement 327
growth of movement 29
homiletics 370
institutions 146
leader 208–213
behaviors 171
leadership 20–24, 28, 77, 83, 170,
201, 208, 214, 217, 352
and holiness 109
and politics 219–221, 222
principles of 178
theology of 62
movement 30, 147, 164–169
new forms of instutitons 235
pastors 41, 164
perspective on leadership 19, 61
perspective on women 127
practical Christianity 165

practical implications 169
preaching 367
renewal movement 232
soteriology 63
spirit 214
spirit of creativity 23
spiritual formation 142
spirituality 49, 143
structure 214
system 200
theological heritage 30
theology 64, 65, 143, 369
theology of spirituality 49
tradition 38–40, 50, 58, 120, 152,
228
understanding of creation 64
understanding of life 48
wisdom 24, 65, 72–79, 121, 186,
207–208, 227, 259–261, 274,
281, 319
in conflict 410
contemporary 207
culture and theology 214
of the day 211
divine 77
exercising 406
given by God 74
godly sources 214
nurting in education 37
pastoral 230
practical 247
pursuit by leaders 102
sages 73
of Scripture 305
of the Spirit 103
women
access to education 128
barrier to as pastors 392
as clergy 391
differences from men 304
and disruptive innovation 29
face obtacles 383
full equality of 128
in 1 Timothy 127
in creation 346

as independent agents 127
in leadership 123, 124, 128, 229
in ministry 119, 120
in Paul's writings 122
males identifying as 308
obstacles for advancement 390
obstacles to leadership 384
opponents of ordination 386
perceived lack of confidence 385
as preachers 181, 183
as priests 73
prohibition on leadership 124
roles of 388
and self-advocacy 393
skill sets 392
subordination of 123
teaching 126
theological basis for leadership
        393
underrepresented in leadership
        383
wise 76
work roles 304
world as parish 24, 30–31, 50, 52,
        173, 179–180
worldview 142–147, 402, 410
  biblical 318
  non-biblical 108
  postmodern 317
  theological 144
worship 73–76, 131, 151, 212
  desire for 259
  disruption of 125
  high church 148
  of power 78
  popular forms and Methodism
        198
  problems in public 124